REGULATING BLOCKCHAIN

Regulating Blockchain

Techno-Social and Legal Challenges

Edited by

PHILIPP HACKER
IOANNIS LIANOS
GEORGIOS DIMITROPOULOS
and
STEFAN EICH

OXFORD
UNIVERSITY PRESS

OXFORD

UNIVERSITY PRESS

Great Clarendon Street, Oxford, OX2 6DP,
United Kingdom

Oxford University Press is a department of the University of Oxford.
It furthers the University's objective of excellence in research, scholarship,
and education by publishing worldwide. Oxford is a registered trade mark of
Oxford University Press in the UK and in certain other countries

Published in the United States of America by Oxford University Press
198 Madison Avenue, New York, NY 10016, United States of America

British Library Cataloguing in Publication Data
Data available

Library of Congress Control Number: 2019936267

ISBN 978-0-19-884218-7

Printed and bound by
CPI Group (UK) Ltd, Croydon, CR0 4YY

Preface

This book arose out of a joint research initiative of the editors at the Centre for Law, Economics and Society at University College London. After an exploratory conference on digital currencies in Athens in the summer of 2016, the Centre hosted a number of conferences and workshops dedicated to research at the intersection of technology and the law throughout the following two years.

During these gatherings, a truly global and interdisciplinary discourse developed on the role of decentralized technology for money, markets, and competition, in particular in their relation to the legal order. This book is the result of this ongoing conversation. It is divided into five parts which move from 'Technological and Business Challenges of Blockchain Technology' (Part I) to 'Blockchain and the Future of Money' (Part II), 'Blockchain and the Future of Banking, Finance, Insurance and Securities Regulation' (Part III), 'Beyond Finance: Blockchain as a Legal and Regulatory Challenge' (Part IV), and ends with a general reflection on 'Connecting the Dots: Competitive Advantage and Regulation in the Era of Blockchain' (Part V). An introduction highlights the most important points of interaction and friction between decentralized technology and the law and provides a thorough outline of the chapters included in the book. At a moment at which several cryptocurrencies and blockchain-based projects have fallen into crisis mode, it is more timely than ever to reflect on the broader social and legal challenges of the underlying technology. Our book is in this sense an enquiry into the broader impact of decentralized technology in various financial, economic, and legal domains beyond the hype that peaked at the end of 2017.

We are very grateful that our initiative was generously supported along its way by a number of institutions through conference and research grants, such as the Fritz Thyssen Foundation, the Modern Law Review, and the UCL Public Engagement Fund. Professor Lianos would also like to acknowledge the financial support of the Leverhulme Trust. We furthermore want to thank our editorial assistant, Megan Cochrane, for her excellent work in the preparation of the chapters of the book. Finally, we are indebted to the editorial team at Oxford University Press for their steadfast support of the project and for bringing it to a timely completion.

We would like to dedicate this book to the memory of Jonathan Rohr, a distinguished scholar and contributor to this volume, who passed away, much too young, before its publication.

Philipp Hacker
Berlin, Germany

Ioannis Lianos
London, UK

Georgios Dimitropoulos
Doha, Qatar

Stefan Eich
Princeton, USA

December 2018

Contents

PART III. BLOCKCHAIN AND THE FUTURE OF BANKING,
FINANCE, INSURANCE, AND SECURITIES REGULATION

PART IV. BEYOND FINANCE: BLOCKCHAIN AS A LEGAL
AND REGULATORY CHALLENGE

List of Contributors

Michael Abramowicz, Carville Dickinson Benson Research Professor of Law, George Washington University

Roger Brownsword, Professor of Law and Founding Director of TELOS, Dickson Poon School of Law, King's College London; Professor of Law, Bournemouth University

Georgios Dimitropoulos, Associate Professor of Law, HBKU College of Law; Associate Member, Centre for Law, Economics and Society, University College London; Research Fellow, Centre for Blockchain Technologies, University College London

Stefan Eich, Assistant Professor of Government, Georgetown University

Jonathan Greenacre, Hitachi Center Faculty Fellow, Hitachi Center for Technology and International Affairs, The Fletcher School, Tufts University

Rohan Grey, President and Founder, Modern Money Network; J.S.D. Candidate, Cornell Law School

Philipp Hacker, Postdoctoral Fellow, Humboldt University of Berlin; Associate Member, Centre for Law, Economics and Society, University College London; Research Fellow, Centre for Blockchain Technologies, University College London

Agnieszka Janczuk-Gorywoda, Assistant Professor, Utrecht University School of Law

Ioannis Lianos, Professor of Global Competition Law and Public Policy, Faculty of Laws, University College London; Director, Centre for Law, Economics and Society (CLES), Faculty of Laws, University College London; Research Fellow at the Centre for Blockchain Technologies, University College London; Vincent Wright Chair at the Faculty of Law at the Paris Institute of Political Sciences (Sciences Po); Academic Director, BRICS Competition Law and Policy Centre, HSE, National Research University, Moscow

Florian Möslein, Professor of Law and Director of the Institute for Law and Regulation of Digitalisation, Philipps-University Marburg

Pietro Ortolani, Assistant Professor of Law, Radboud University

Riccardo Piselli, Research Assistant, Centre for Blockchain Technologies, University College London

Jonathan Rohr,[†] Assistant Professor of Law, University of Tennessee, Knoxville

Alexandros L. Seretakis, Assistant Professor in Law, School of Law, Trinity College Dublin

Houman B. Shadab, Professor of Law and Co-Director, Center for Business and Financial Law, New York Law School

Paolo Tasca, Founder and Executive Director, Centre for Blockchain Technologies (UCL CBT), University College London

Chris Thomale, Lecturer, University of Bremen / University of Heidelberg

Angela Walch, Professor of Law, St. Mary's University School of Law; Research Fellow, Centre for Blockchain Technologies, University College London

Aaron Wright, Associate Clinical Professor of Law, Cardozo Law School; Founder and Director, Cardozo Blockchain Project

Claus D. Zimmermann, Senior Associate, Sidley Austin LLP, Brussels

Regulating Blockchain

Techno-Social and Legal Challenges—An Introduction

Philipp Hacker, Ioannis Lianos, Georgios Dimitropoulos, and Stefan Eich

I. Introduction

In July 2017, a start-up called Tezos, almost unknown outside the world of blockchain, completed a fundraising in the form of an initial coin offering ('ICO') that netted it the equivalent of around $230 million. Investors paid to receive digital Tezos tokens (or 'coins') that they hoped would rise in value. The amount raised was then the largest ICO and it was accompanied by high-flying rhetoric that promised to reshape social interaction through technology. Tezos pledged to use the funds it had raised to develop a software platform that would overcome the governance issues that plague existing blockchain-based networks, such as Bitcoin or Ethereum. Despite their open source roots, most of these platforms are based on a take-it-or-leave-it approach, akin to the ubiquitous and non-negotiable online 'terms and conditions' that provide a kind of constitution in which users have little or no say. Tezos instead promised that its own software would empower users to democratically shape the future of the platform they were interacting on. In its own language, Tezos aimed to create a 'digital commonwealth'.

Only shortly after its record-breaking fundraising, clouds began to gather over Tezos's technological utopia. Feuds and disagreements mounted. By the end of 2017, investors hit the company with several US class-action lawsuits based on its perceived failure to deliver on its extraordinary claims. Not for the first time and certainly not for the last, a technology that promised to liberate exchanges from the shackles of centralizing authority, ended in a US court. Having bought into the vision of a 'digital commonwealth' with its own cryptocurrency beyond the state, the plaintiffs now turned to the US legal system to recover their investments as well as any possible compensation in dollars.

The mismatch between technological promise and legal reality is not unique to Tezos but a constituent feature of the new world of blockchain. If anything, Tezos pales in comparison to the size and brazenness of more recent ICOs. In the first six months of 2018 alone, around $16 billion were raised through ICOs, more than thrice the amount raised in the whole of 2017; EOS alone cashed in approximately $4 billion in 2017/18.[1] But Tezos, with its disappointed vision of a democratic self-governing platform, neatly illustrates the simultaneous inadequacy and indispensability of governance and law. While blockchain technology proliferates rapidly in a seemingly legal vacuum, it is clearly not beyond legal norms, even where these norms struggle with the technology's implications. Many governments have for a long time taken a reactive role to these developments—often consciously creating spaces of experimentation through non-intervention. However, nowadays, blockchain applications are increasingly coming under regulatory and court scrutiny.

This book takes a distinct techno-social perspective in understanding the legal implications of blockchain technology as a possible new general-purpose technology ('GPT') (see

---

[1] CoinSchedule, 'Cryptocurrency ICO Stats 2018' (2018) https://www.coinschedule.com/stats.html.

Chapter 18 by Lianos in this volume). From a technological and business perspective, there is still considerable uncertainty as to the possible direction(s) that blockchain technology could take and the industries in which it could attain a prominent role. The risks and opportunities that it offers are widely discussed in the literature, but, for the most part, these discussions remain prospective and constitute, at best, an educated guess about technological developments and not-yet-realized business potential. At the same time, there is a clear anxiety among scholars and government officials as to the need for the legal system to be pro-active and to experiment with and develop the establishment of a legal framework capable of adequately responding to the social and economic challenges raised by blockchain technology. These discussions should not be limited to a simple analysis of the technological possibilities offered by blockchain technology. They need to engage with the broader social context in which the various applications of this technology are inevitably embedded (see, e.g., Chapter 4 by Eich, Chapter 6 by Dimitropoulos, Chapter 16 by Ortolani, Chapter 17 by Brownsword, and Chapter 18 by Lianos). Technological development and the direction of innovation are not only dependent on technological capabilities but also profoundly rely on the social forces that promote their use. Every significant technological revolution is accompanied by a narrative of broader change of the social, economic, and legal processes that govern value generation. Therefore, it is important to consider that technological change operates on multiple socio-economic dimensions while recognizing that, at this initial stage of the development of the blockchain technology, it is too early to predict its evolution and the new socio-economic structures to which it will give rise. Hence, our distinct approach in this book does not take a deterministic view on the development of the new technology of blockchain by seeking to predict future changes. Rather, we emphasize the social, legal, and political factors that will affect the direction of the 'disruptive' innovation promised.

Law profoundly influences the process of technological change and its diffusion at numerous levels. First, law can be used as a weapon in the initial 'framing struggles', by the proponents or the opponents of a new technology, in order to establish regulatory barriers to curtail the spread of the new technology or, on the contrary, to eliminate existing strategic barriers put in place by the incumbents (see Chapter 18 by Lianos in this volume). Second, legal change can be actively promoted in order to facilitate the development of the new technology and its rapid diffusion into various other fields of economic and social activity. The logic here is to encourage innovation by providing the main actors of technological change with the legal capabilities for organizing new processes of new value-generation. Some even go as far as suggesting discounts to the application of existing regulatory norms and of 'outdated' values that had so far animated risk regulation, as these may jeopardize the expected rents from the application of the new GPT, and, thus, affect the pace of its diffusion. At this initial period of the development of the technology, this generates struggles over whether there should be more regulation or less. It also leads to the more frequent intervention of regulatory authorities, in diverse forms. It is not only limited to the classic command-and-control or risk-based approaches to regulation and the application of 'hard' law; it may also consist in a broader communicative effort aiming to steer the activity of the various communities of experts, nudging the development of the technology towards an approach that is more compatible with existing regulatory values (i.e. 'regulation by design').

Following the imbrication of blockchain technology with various forms of state action, inherent tensions between enabling and constraining modes of law, and between libertarian and regulatory political narratives, have become ever more apparent. As all the chapters in this volume stress, the legal system consequently plays a significant role in the blockchain enterprise. The interaction of blockchain technology with the legal system raises key questions concerning governance and government, private order and state authority, and the relationship between different 'calculative' spaces for assessing, monetizing, and allocating value. These questions not only have a long pedigree, but they are also acutely relevant to our immediate future.

II. Background: The Emergence of Blockchain Technology

To the extent that the first domain of systematic application of blockchain has been the financial sector, the evolution of the regulation of this sector may provide important insights as to the way the technology interacts with the legal system and the various possibilities offered. Less than a decade after the Financial Crisis, we are witnessing the fast emergence of a new financial order driven by three different, yet interconnected, dynamics: first, the rapid application of technology—such as machine learning and distributed computing—to banking, lending, and investing, in particular, with the emergence of virtual currencies[2] and digital finance; second, a disintermediation fuelled by the rise of peer-to-peer lending platforms, novel forms of crowd investment, and ICOs which challenge the traditional (investment) banking model and may, over time, lead to a transformation of the way both retail and corporate customers bank, invest, and consume; and, third, a tendency of de-bureaucratization under which new platforms and technologies challenge established organizational patterns that regulate finance and manage the money supply.[3] The outcome of these processes remains uncertain. They may eventually lead to greater decentralization, when different (independent) institutions share authority in the financial and informational sphere; to centralized control through a different form, for instance via code, or core developer teams, instead of centralized regulators and central banks; or to hybrid distributions of authority, as in the emergence of central bank-issued digital currencies.[4]

These changes are to a significant degree, but not only, driven by the development of blockchain technology;[5] the centrality of blockchain to the European Commission's 'FinTech Action Plan' testifies to the pivotal role of this technology.[6] Currently, blockchain is referred to as the most important type of a distributed ledger technology ('DLT'),[7] i.e. a decentralized form of record keeping that can store many different kinds of information ranging from monetary transactions to land titles, or even to digital identities. More specifically, a

---

[2] The terms 'virtual currency', 'digital currency', and 'cryptocurrency' are used interchangeably in the field, and also in this volume; while 'cryptocurrency' is often the term of choice in the industry and technology sector nowadays, legal documents tend to speak of 'virtual currency' (which is, technically speaking, the broader term since it does not imply cryptographic processes); see the European 5th Anti-Money Laundering Directive (n 58); New York's BitLicense Regulation, 23 NYCRR Part 200 Virtual Currencies (hereafter 23 NYCRR); Mai Ishikawa, 'Designing Virtual Currency Regulation in Japan: Lessons from the Mt Gox Case' (2017) 3 *Journal of Financial Regulation*, 125; for a definition, see European Central Bank, 'Virtual Currency Schemes—A Further Analysis' (February 2015) 25; more in detail European Central Bank, 'Virtual Currency Schemes' (October 2012) 13–16; Dong He, Karl Habermeier, Ross Leckow, Vikram Haksar, et al., 'Virtual Currencies and Beyond: Initial Considerations' (January 2016) IMF Report; and n 58.

[3] See, for these three dynamics in an earlier transformation, Karl Polanyi, 'Great Transformation' in *The Great Transformation: The Political and Economic Origins of our Time* [1944], edited by Fred Block (Beacon Press 2001).

[4] See John Barrdear and Michael Kumhof, 'The Macroeconomics of Central Bank Issued Digital Currencies' (2016) Bank of England, Staff Working Paper No. 605; Michael D. Bordo and Andrew T. Levin, 'Central Bank Digital Currency and the Future of Monetary Policy' (2017) National Bureau of Economic Research Working Paper No. 23711; Sahil Gupta, Patrick Lauppe, and Shreyas Ravishankar, 'Fedcoin. A Blockchain-Backed Central Bank Cryptocurrency', Yale Law School Working Paper (2017) https://law.yale.edu/system/files/area/center/global/document/411_final_paper_-_fedcoin.pdf; Bank of Thailand, 'Wholesale Central Bank Digital Currency', Announcement of Project Inthanon Collaborative Partnership, 21 August 2018, BOT Press Release No. 54/2018.

[5] See World Government Summit, 'Building the Hyperconnected Future on Blockchains' (2017).

[6] European Commission, 'FinTech Action Plan: For a More Competitive and Innovative European Financial Sector', COM(2018) 109 final.

[7] UK Government Office for Science, 'Distributed Ledger Technology: Beyond Block Chain', Announcement of Project Inthanon Collaborative Partnership, (2016), UK Government Chief Scientific Adviser Report, 10; Michael Mainelli and Mike Smith, 'Sharing Ledgers for Sharing Economies: An Exploration of Mutual Distributed Ledgers (aka Blockchain Technology)' (2015) 3 *The Journal of Financial Perspectives*, 38; for distributed ledger technology beyond the blockchain, see Serguei Popov, 'The Tangle' (2018) White Paper, which introduces the technology behind the IOTA token; Brent Xu, 'Blockchain vs. Distributed Ledger Technologies' (*consensys.net*, 5 April 2018) https://media.consensys.net/blockchain-vs-distributed-ledger-technologies-1e0289a87b16, which discusses Hyperledger Fabric and R3 Corda.

blockchain constitutes a cryptographically secured database distributed on many computers ('nodes') and combines decentralized consensus mechanisms with cryptographic verification.[8] This endows a blockchain with a number of important characteristics. First, it is *resilient*: even if one copy of the blockchain is erased or damaged, there are many other copies on nodes that continue to provide the relevant information.[9] Second, it is highly *tamper-resistant*: going forward in the chain, new information can only be added by specific nodes (so-called 'miners') once they have invested significant time and energy into solving a mathematical puzzle, for which they earn block rewards and transaction fees if the new information is accepted as valid by the other nodes.[10] This sets sufficient incentives and introduces significant mathematical obstacles to prevent cheating on the chain. The content of the information is compressed and timestamped using a hash function,[11] and units of value (e.g. bitcoins) are secured through public–private key cryptography.[12] Going backward in the chain, the blocks of information are mathematically linked to one another so that information already recorded in the chain cannot be unilaterally altered without changing (and recomputing) the entire chain. This is prevented by *decentralized consensus algorithms* that ensure that the authentic state of the chain is always the one backed by the greatest amount of computing power.[13] Therefore, an attacker would, in general, have to amass 51% of the decentralized computing power to unilaterally change transactions in his or her favour.[14] Finally, by virtue of its decentralization, a blockchain is *censorship-resistant*. There is no central authority that could block any information, provided it is validated by miners, from entering the chain.[15] The openness to the recording of any type of information, in conjunction with the decentralized verification of its integrity (transparency, validation, and immutability), make the blockchain a genuine GPT, with potential applications far beyond the realm of finance in which it originated.

More recently, blockchain technology has also been applied to smart contracts and blockchain-based organizations that are funded by ICOs (also called 'token sales'), the so-called 'blockchain 2.0'. Smart contracts are software programs embedded in a blockchain that can receive and send assets as well as information.[16] The distribution of information and assets by smart contracts is entirely predefined in code and triggered by the fulfilment of certain conditions. Companies are increasingly launching smart contracts as prototypes.[17] It should be noted, however, that these smart contracts do not automatically inherit the trustlessness and informational integrity of the blockchain because they often have to rely on off-chain information, provided by specialized intermediaries.[18] These concerns

---

[8] See the foundational document: Satoshi Nakamoto, 'Bitcoin: A Peer-to-Peer Electronic Cash System' (2008) White Paper; overviews in Arvind Narayanan, Joseph Bonneau, Edward Felton, Andrew Miller, and Steven Goldfeder, *Bitcoin and Cryptocurrency Technologies: A Comprehensive Introduction* (Princeton University Press 2016); Andreas M. Antonopoulos, *Mastering Bitcoin: Programming the Open Blockchain* (2nd edn, O'Reilly 2017); non-technical overview in Primavera de Filippi and Aaron Wright, *Blockchain and the Law* (Harvard University Press 2018), Part I.

[9] Antonopoulos (n 8), 277; see also Masashi Sato and Shin'ichiro Matsuo, 'Long-Term Public Blockchain: Resilience against Compromise of Underlying Cryptography' (2017), IEEE European Symposium on Security and Privacy Workshops (EuroS&PW), 42.

[10] This process is known as proof-of-work verification, see Narayanan et al. (n 8), Chapters 8.1–8.3.

[11] Narayanan et al. (n 8), Chapter 1.1. for an elegant introduction.   [12] See Nakamoto (n 8).

[13] Antonopoulos (n 8), 217–39.   [14] Antonopoulos (n 8), 254.

[15] Ittay Eyal, Adem Efe Gencer, Emin Gün Sirer, and Robbert van Renesse, 'Bitcoin-NG: A Scalable Blockchain Protocol' (2016), Proceedings of the 13th USENIX Symposium on Networked Systems Design and Implementation, 50; note that this may be different in private blockchains.

[16] See Narayanan et al. (n 8), Chapter 10.7; Richard Brown, 'A Simple Model for Smart Contracts' (2015) https://gendal.me/2015/02/10/a-simple-model-for-smart-contracts/; Stefan Grundmann and Philipp Hacker, 'Digital Technology as a Challenge to European Contract Law' (2017) 13 *European Review of Contract Law*, 280 et seq.

[17] For example, the insurance giant AXA has rolled out the Fizzy insurance contract that automatically compensates travellers for delayed flights; see AXA, 'AXA Goes Blockchain With Fizzy' (*axa.com*, 13 September 2017) https://www.axa.com/en/newsroom/news/axa-goes-blockchain-with-fizzy.

[18] Elisa Mik, 'Smart Contracts: Terminology, Technical Limitations and Real-World Complexity' (2017) 9 *Law, Innovation and Technology*, 278.

notwithstanding, smart contracts can be combined to create blockchain-based organiza-tions. These smart contracts govern the collection and distribution of funds belonging to the organization on a blockchain, typically on Ethereum.[19] Such organizations automatic-ally execute financial decisions, for example, by sending payments to an investment target and distributing profits. This was, for example, the aim of the most famous and notorious vehicle created by an ICO so far, 'The DAO',[20] which was hacked in 2016, and subsequently investigated by the Securities and Exchange Commission ('SEC').[21] On a more general level, ICOs have morphed into a novel, multi-billion-dollar funding source for tech entre-preneurs.[22] In these entirely online-mediated offerings, start-up entrepreneurs sell tokens registered on a blockchain in exchange for fiat currency or for cryptocoins (typically bitcoins or ethers). These tokens can be understood as cryptographically secured coupons which embody a bundle of rights and obligations that varies widely.[23] Thus, blockchain technology has the potential to be a game changer in various sectors in which economic activity has so far been organized through centralized platforms, by providing a basis for decentralized applications, such as decentralized messenger apps (Status; Telegram);[24] or even a new type of decentralized internet that blockchain token holders may navigate (Blockstack).[25]

Blockchain technology has also been used to develop digital financial marketplaces, particu-larly in conjunction with the Internet of Things ('IoT'), bypassing financial middlemen and al-lowing almost any asset to be digitized and traded over a decentralized computer network (e.g. Bitshares).[26] The domain of application of blockchain technology has also largely expanded in recent years, thus, hinting at new areas of interaction (and tension) with the legal system. It is currently being applied in trade, ranging from 'traditional' online retail (e.g. OpenBazaar)[27] to the trade of commodities,[28] and will certainly expand in other areas, such as supply chain management, private transport and car sharing, cloud storage, government services, health care, the online music industry,[29] electricity management,[30] and so on.[31] Consumer markets

---

[19] Vitalik Buterin, 'Ethereum' (2014) White Paper.

[20] Christopher Jentzsch, 'Decentralized Autonomous Organization to Automate Governance' (2016) https://download.slock.it/public/DAO/WhitePaper.pdf.

[21] Securities and Exchange Commission ('SEC'), 'Investigation Pursuant to Section 21(a) of the Securities Exchange Act of 1934: The DAO' (2017), Report Release No. 81207 (henceforth 'SEC Report').

[22] CoinSchedule (n 1).

[23] See, e.g., the definition in Monetary Authority of Singapore, 'MAS Clarifies Regulatory Position on the Offer of Digital Tokens in Singapore' (*mas.gov*, 1 August 2017) http://www.mas.gov.sg/News-and-Publications/Media-Releases/2017/MAS-clarifies-regulatory-position-on-the-offer-of-digital-tokens-in-Singapore.aspx, para. 2: 'A digital token is a cryptographically-secured representation of a token-holder's rights to receive a benefit or to perform specified functions.'

[24] See Jarred Hope, 'The Status Network' (2017) White Paper; Nikolai Durov and Pavel Durov, 'Telegram Primer' (2017).

[25] Muneeb Ali and Ryan Shea, 'Blockstack: A New Internet for Decentralized Applications' (2017), White Paper.

[26] See Konstantinos Christidis and Michael Devetsikiotis, 'Blockchains and Smart Contracts for the Internet of Things' (2016) 4 *IEEE Acces*, 2295; Alex Mizrahi, 'A Blockchain-Based Property Ownership Recording System' (2015) https://chromaway.com/papers/A-blockchain-based-property-registry.pdf; more generally, de Filippi and Wright (n 8), Chapter 10.

[27] See Nikki Baird, 'Blockchain and Retail: Four Opportunities' (*forbes.com*, 9 August 2017) https://www.forbes.com/sites/nikkibaird/2017/08/09/blockchain-and-retail-four-opportunities/#10f1829a72bf; Accenture Consulting, 'Blockchain Wave Headed Toward CPG and Retail Industries' (2017) https://www.accenture.com/us-en/insight-highlights-cgs-blockchain-cpg-and-retail-industries.

[28] *Financial Times*, 'BP Experiments with Blockchain For Oil And Gas Trading' (*financialtimes.com*) https://www.ft.com/content/100622d0-a680-11e7-93c5-648314d2c72c>.

[29] Although possibly not to the extent initially predicted: see Bobbi Owsinski, 'Despite Predictions, Blockchain Will Not Be the Future of the Music Industry' (*forbes.com*, 18 November 2017) https://www.forbes.com/sites/bobbyowsinski/2017/11/18/blockchain-music-industry/#38a280776a0b.

[30] Mike Orcutt, 'How Blockchain Could Give Us a Smarter Energy Grid' (*MIT Tech Review*, 16 October 2017) https://www.technologyreview.com/s/609077/how-blockchain-could-give-us-a-smarter-energy-grid/.

[31] See World Economic Forum, 'The Future of Financial Infrastructure. An Ambitious Look at How Blockchain Can Reshape Financial Services' (2016), which explores nine 'case deep-dives' from payment systems via insurance

stand to be particularly affected by 'utility tokens' providing access to platform services of any kind.[32]

The aim of this book is to understand the legal challenges faced by blockchain technology and the adjustments made in order to accommodate its technological and economic potential. It will start with a focus on the challenges blockchain technology has so far faced in its first application in the areas of virtual money and finance but will also include those that it will inevitably face (and is partially already facing, as the SEC Investigative Report of June 2017[33] and ongoing SEC securities fraud investigations show)[34] as its domain of application expands in other fields of economic activity.

III. Blockchain, Calculative Spaces, and the State

Over the past decade, in the years following the Financial Crisis, technological innovation has radically reshaped the financialized economy. These developments are widely expected to further accelerate and many will likely be related in one form or another to the application of blockchain technology. If we focus on the domain of finance, clearly much hinges on whether these technological developments end up making banking more accessible or whether they are the latest iteration of what the investor Warren Buffett dubbed in 2002 'financial weapons of mass destruction', carrying dangers that, 'while now latent, are potentially lethal.'[35]

On a basic level, while the banking sector has witnessed both increasing integration and consolidation over the past decade, the rise of coded finance has introduced a novel sort of competition based on access to technology and data science, the quality of algorithms, and the ease of mobile user interfaces. As a result, traditional players are coming under threat from financial technology firms (so-called 'FinTechs') that challenge existing business models. For example, financial intermediaries are currently being challenged by technological platforms that portray themselves as mere matchmakers but that often wield substantial financial and economic power.

These technological changes in the financial system do not occur in a vacuum but are necessarily connected to the global monetary system, which functions as a hierarchical pyramid with one key currency, the US dollar, at its top.[36] Economists have traditionally described money as having three functions: (i) as a medium of exchange; (ii) as a unit of account; and (iii) as a store of value.[37] By providing a calculative space and an order of worth, money becomes in all three senses an essential instrument of social value, as well as the calculative bridge between present and future. Defining what is money becomes of paramount importance for the operation of markets, the latter being perceived as 'calculative collective devices' allowing economic agents to engage in economic exchanges over goods or money itself.[38] These calculative spaces are an essential feature of the need

---

to investment management and market provisioning; Future Thinkers, '19 Industries the Blockchain Will Disrupt' (*futurethinkers.org*, 16 June 2017) http://futurethinkers.org/industries-blockchain-disrupt/.

[32] See Chapter 12 by Hacker and Thomale in this volume; The Brooklyn Project, 'Framework for the Establishment of Consumer Tokens' (2018), Working Paper https://docs.google.com/document/d/1DkAN3p7t0q efUOnvIkKS3PxgU6tCYEmCYxv2wBAeLng/edit.

[33] SEC Report (n 21); ESMA, 'ESMA Alerts Firms Involved in ICOs to the Need to Meet Relevant Regulatory Requirements' (2017), Statement of 13 November; ESMA, 'The Distributed Ledger Technology Applied to Securities Markets' (2017), Report, 2: 'the presence of [blockchain technology] does not liberate users from the need to comply with the existing regulatory framework.'

[34] See, e.g. *SEC v. Recoin Group Foundation, LLC*, Complaint (29 September 2017); *SEC v. AriseBank* et al., Complaint (25 January 2018).

[35] Berkshire Hathaway, *Annual Report* (2002).

[36] Adam Tooze, *Crashed: How a Decade of Financial Crises Changed the World* (Viking 2018).

[37] N. Gregory Mankiw, *Macroeconomics* (9th edn, Worth Publishers 2015), 82; Ben J. Heijdra, *Foundations of Modern Macroeconomics* (2nd edn, Oxford University Press 2009), 319.

[38] Michel Callon and Fabian Muniesa, 'Les Marchés Economiques Comme Dispositifs Collectives de Calcul' (2003) 122(6) *Réseaux*, 189.

for integrating futurity, as the expectation that the adoption of this new technology will generate important future value (in terms of profits or, more broadly benefits) is an essential motivating force in attracting the necessary investment for the diffusion of that technology in various economic sectors. The constitution of such calculative spaces has been a pre-requisite to the expansion of blockchain technology, as is attested to by the explosion of ICOs.

However, even if money is essentially whatever society accepts and uses as such, the state holds a special legitimating authority through its unrivalled powers of taxation and regulation.[39] Money remains linked to the state, both as the sole wielder of fiscal powers and as the sole provider of risk-free assets.[40] Private calculative spaces must, thus, be placed in a hierarchical relation to a pyramid of money, with state fiat currencies at its top.[41] Moreover, with the end of the Bretton Woods system, the value of fiat money is no longer dependent on any kind of convertibility commitment (or enforceable money-back guarantee) on the basis of gold but, instead, derives from the central bank's monetary policy. By setting interest rates and intervening in the financial system, the central bank regulates money and its supply and fulfils its mandates of ensuring price stability as well as establishing the necessary level of trust for the operation of the monetary system.[42] During the 'Great Moderation', many governments turned central banks into formally independent entities, composed of technocratic experts with the express mission to ensure the performance of the economy in a global context, thus, nominally operating independently from the executive and legislative powers and subject to limited democratic accountability.[43] While the state thus holds ultimate sovereignty over the currency, it frequently delegates its authority to govern money to an 'independent' central bank—tasked with a given mandate of guaranteeing price stability and, potentially, employment—while granting private banks the prerogative of credit creation.[44]

As is clear from the preceding discussion of money, financial markets possess a feature that makes them, to some extent, different from other markets: they are intrinsically linked to the sovereign.[45] In principle, the modern state holds the ultimate legal power to create currency and monetize debts. Even where it has granted the privilege of credit creation to private banks or tolerated the development of societal calculative spaces (local currencies, credit networks, or virtual currencies), the state continues to claim and exercise an exclusive legal control over money. Despite the global reach of capital, financial markets are intimately tied to national central banks, whose balance sheets, after all, reflect those of the private banking system. Central banks may be nominally 'independent', but they are political institutions that will assert public power and act as lenders (or dealers) of last resort if necessary.[46]

---

[39] Geoffrey Ingham, *The Nature of Money* (Polity Press 2004).

[40] John Maynard Keynes, 'A Treatise on Money: The Pure Theory of Money' in *The Collected Writings of J.M. Keynes*, edited by Elizabeth Johnson and Donald Moggridge (Volume 5, Cambridge University Press 2012).

[41] Katharina Pistor, 'Money's Legal Hierarchies' in *Just Financial Markets?*, edited by Lisa Herzog (Oxford University Press 2017), 185–204.

[42] Antonio Sáinz de Vicuña, 'An Institutional Theory of Money' in *International Monetary and Financial Law: The Global Crisis*, edited by Mario Giovanoli and Diego Devos (Oxford University Press 2010), 517.

[43] Paul Tucker, *Unelected Power: The Quest for Legitimacy in Central Banking and the Regulatory State* (Princeton University Press 2018).

[44] Ed Balls, James Howat, and Anna Stansbury, 'Central Bank Independence Revisited: After the Financial Crisis, What Should a Model Central Bank Look Like?' (2016) M-RCBG Associate Working Paper Series, No. 67, provides a contemporary account on the independence of central banks.

[45] In addition, the very boundary of what may or may not be subject to financial calculation depends on the decision of the sovereign, as illustrated by debates over financial derivatives as a form of illegal gambling, when they were first introduced in Chicago option markets. Donald MacKenzie and Yuval Millo, 'Constructing a Market, Performing Theory: The Historical Sociology of a Financial Derivatives Exchange' (2003) 109(1) *American Journal of Sociology*, 107.

[46] Perry Mehrling, *The New Lombard Street: How the Fed Became the Dealer of Last Resort* (Princeton University Press 2010).

The emergency measures of the Financial Crisis were a potent reminder of where ultimate authority resided.[47]

Yet, monetary sovereignty has also been altered by the pressures of globalization. Fuelled by comprehensive capital mobility, the proliferation of Eurodollars, and advances in technology, transnational communities of economic actors beyond the state have emerged that form networks of transnational financial integration. If the Financial Crisis challenged this perception of a depoliticized monetary technocracy by highlighting the ongoing centrality of the state for effectively functioning financial markets, technological developments and global financial flows also challenge the current *détente* from the opposite direction. The financialization of the world economy, with its staggering international capital flows, ever new forms of shadow banking, and the development of new forms of electronic and virtual money, have led to a multiplication of actors involved in the creation of money and a further privatization of credit, and, thereby, the supply of money. This does not mean that monetary sovereignty has been rendered mute but that its nature is in a process of transformation that can perhaps be more adequately understood as a shared form of sovereignty affected by the behaviour of private financial intermediaries operating in vast transnational markets.[48] Fiat currencies, while still at the top of the monetary pyramid, are now only one form of money that co-exists alongside electronic and private forms of money in global markets. These developments undoubtedly pose important new challenges to traditional forms of financial regulation and monetary policy.

From this perspective, the development of new fields of economic activity and fundraising, on the basis of blockchain technology—including peer-to-peer lending platforms, cryptocurrencies, and ICOs, challenges not only the traditional banking sector but also existing forms of macroprudential regulation and monetary policy. In threatening traditional financial intermediaries and enabling new transnational calculative spaces to emerge, the new financial technologies create new spaces the control of which by states may be limited. Not coincidentally, offshore tax havens are major players in the world of ICOs. Blockchain technology is likely to deepen this regulatory elusiveness further.[49]

Blockchain technology accordingly carries an alternative vision of the economic system that envisages a shift towards a decentralized international order in which politics may be completely absent. This is, for instance, currently the case for virtual currencies, which, unlike bank account balances, are not linked to government fiat money but, instead, constitute a 'market of competing private irredeemable monies'—reminiscent in some respects of Friedrich August Hayek's proposal to 'denationalize' money forty years ago.[50] Bitcoin constitutes an extreme example of this and it is most fundamentally based on a quantity commitment that fixes the money supply. This imposition of artificial scarcity is not enforced through contract or the authority of an institution such as a central bank, but through the operation of code. The upper limit on the number of possible bitcoin units in the market is programmed into Bitcoin's observable source code and monitored through an algorithmic system of a public ledger, its blockchain, which is shared among all 'miners' involved in Bitcoin transactions. As mentioned,

---

[47] Tooze (n 36), 166–201. Following the Crisis, states have re-affirmed their monetary sovereignty by creating new forms of macro-prudential regulation that seeks to rein in shadow banking and submit private intermediaries once more to public authority. See Kevin Davis, 'Regulatory Reform Post the Global Financial Crisis: An Overview' (8 March 2011) https://kevindavis.com.au/secondpages/Miscellaneous/Regulatory%20Reform%20 Post%20the%20GFC-%20Overview%20Report.pdf.

[48] Claus D. Zimmermann, *A Contemporary Concept of Monetary Sovereignty* (Oxford University Press 2013).

[49] On similar problems to regulate the Internet, see Grundmann and Hacker (n 21), 271 et seq.; Jack Goldsmith and Tim Wu, *Who Controls the Internet? Illusions of a Borderless World* (Oxford University Press 2006), Chapter 9.

[50] See Friedrich A. von Hayek, *The Denationalisation of Money* (Fordham University Press 1978); Lawrence H. White, 'The Market for Cryptocurrencies' (2014) GMU Working Paper in Economics No. 14-45. On the new politics of cryptocurrencies, see Primavera de Filippi and Benjamin Loveluck, 'The Invisible Politics of Bitcoin: Governance Crisis of a Decentralized Infrastructure' (2016) 5 *Internet Policy Review*.

this blockchain operates in the system's global network and is continuously operated and maintained by the miners. The miners update the blockchain and independently verify transactions in exchange for cryptocoins they receive for their work. As a result, the supply of bitcoins is inescapably constrained by an algorithm.[51] Whether this constitutes a celebrated check against over-issuance or an inbuilt deflationary bias lies in the eye of the beholder. In addition, cryptocurrencies, such as Bitcoin, constitute a disruptive payment system, in the sense that they enable payments without relying on banks and other centralized institutions to keep track of payments. Code is expected to deliver the necessary level of trust needed for the system to function. Businesses use bitcoins to transfer money abroad because they presumably lower transaction costs, attract a tech-forward clientele and enable them to make a speculative investment, while seeking to protect consumers' personal information.[52]

These three characteristics—decentralized peer-to-peer exchange, a quantity commitment embedded in the open source code, and the shared public ledger—are widely shared by other cryptocurrencies that have recently been issued.[53]

Such decentralized digital currencies and automated financial markets denote a financial architecture that has been intentionally disembedded from the political sphere and appears disenfranchised from political accountability and, more generally, regulatory control. This holds all the more true for the heated market of ICOs, which is replete not only with innovative and collaborative applications, but also fraught with scams and cryptosecurity issues, generally leaving users with insufficient legal redress.[54] Hence, blockchain constitutes a major challenge for regulators, central bankers, and the banking system itself, which is co-opting the technology for its own purposes.[55] To the extent that blockchain technology, and the automation and decentralization it brings, expands to other economic fields, there is a need for the legal system and the regulatory state as a whole to respond to such rapid changes and eventually to re-conceptualize the philosophy and mechanisms of its intervention in the new markets and societal structures that are emerging.

IV. The Legal Grammar of Blockchain

Starting with cryptocurrencies, over the past three years, regulators and policy-makers have become ever more interested in blockchain technology.[56] The revision of the European

---

[51] It should be noted that this artificial supply limit could be algorithmically changed, and that some cryptocurrencies, such as Ethereum, indeed entirely dispose of it; see Ethereum, 'Ether: FAQ' https://www.ethereum.org/ether.

[52] Nicholas A. Plassaras, 'Regulating Digital Currencies: Bringing Bitcoin within the Reach of the IMF' (2013) 14 *Chinese Journal of International Law*, 377; on re-identification strategies, however, see n 99.

[53] Dong He et al. (n 2).

[54] See, e.g., Jonathan Rohr and Aaron Wright, 'Blockchain-Based Token Sales, Initial Coin Offerings, and the Democratization of Public Capital Markets' (2018) 70 *Hastings Law Journal*.

[55] See Andrew Meola, 'How Banks and Financial Institutions Are Implementing Blockchain Technology' (*businessinsider.de*, 20 September 2017) http://www.businessinsider.de/blockchain-technology-banking-finance-2017-9?r=US&IR=T.

[56] See UK Government Office for Science (n 7); European Commission, 'Consumer Financial Services Action Plan: Better Products, More Choice' COM(2017) 39, final, 12–13, announces, *inter alia*, the creation of a FinTech Task Force at the Commission, and a pilot project to reinforce capacities concerning distributed ledger technology; European Parliament, 'Virtual Currencies', Resolution of 26 May 2016, 2016/2007(INI), notes high volatility, 'absence of traditional forms of regulatory supervision, safeguards and protection', as well as 'legal uncertainty surrounding new applications of DLT'; World Economic Forum (n 31); European Banking Association ('EBA'), 'Crytotechnologies, a Major IT Innovation and Catalyst for Change' (2015) Report, documents cases in trade and finance); European Central Bank, 'Eurosystem's Vision for the Future of Europe's Financial Market Infrastructure' (2016), 6, announces an assessment of the relevance of distributed ledger technology to European financial services and market structures; European Central Bank, 'Virtual Currency Scheme' (n 2); Andrea Pinna and Wiebe Ruttenberg, 'Distributed Ledger Technologies in Securities Post-Trading' (2016) European Central Bank Occasional Paper No 172/2016; European Central Bank, 'Distributed Ledger Technology (2016) 1 *In Focus*; Bank of England, 'FinTech Accelerator Proof of Concept: Distributed Ledger Technology' (2016), documents an experimental transfer of assets using blockchain; Sead Muftic, 'Overview and Analysis of the Concept and

Anti-Money Laundering Directive ('5AMLD') first proposed in 2016, and adopted by the European Parliament in April 2018,[57] not only submits wallet providers and cryptocurrency exchange operators to anti-money laundering ('AML') provisions, but also contains the first legal definition of virtual currencies: ' "virtual currencies" means a digital representation of value that is not issued or guaranteed by a central bank or a public authority, is not necessarily attached to a legally established currency and does not possess a legal status of currency or money, but is accepted by natural or legal persons, as a means of exchange, and which can be transferred, stored and traded electronically'.[58] In the United States, cryptocurrency exchanges and wallets were subjected to AML requirements in 2013, with the state of New York following up with a contentious BitLicense framework, establishing licensing requirements for these and other entities engaging in virtual currency business.[59] In the aftermath, ICOs have increasingly become the focus of regulatory interest, with not only SEC offering its report on the DAO,[60] but also the European Securities and Markets Authority ('ESMA'),[61] the UK Financial Conduct Authority ('FCA'),[62] and regulators from other countries equally issuing warnings or guidelines on ICOs,[63] or even banning them entirely.[64] Despite significant enforcement activity of the SEC,[65] detailed legal guidance and broader analysis is lacking. Except for regulators operating in the field of finance, government agencies ranging from tax authorities[66] to commodities regulators[67] have also dealt with the applications of the blockchain technology. The European Commission has, in its FinTech Action Plan of March 2018, made the monitoring and analysis of ICOs, and blockchain applications more generally, a priority, but has done so without embracing regulatory action on this point or providing specific guidance.[68]

Arguably, the objective of the law would be to facilitate new modes of civic or economic interaction between thus far unrelated actors by establishing rules that spur trust and support fairness, while at the same time guarding against the unilateral appropriation and utilization of power by unregulated platforms and financial entities. Questions of legal frameworks and regulation span from the world of banking and finance via retail and consumer markets all

---

Applications of Virtual Currencies' (2016) JRC Technical Report; d'Artis Kancs, Pavel Ciaian, and Moroslava Rajcaniova, 'The Digital Agenda of Virtual Currencies' (2015) JRC Technical Report.

[57] See Vice-President Timmermans, Vice-President Dombrovskis, and Commissioner Jourovà, 'Statement on the Adoption by the European Parliament of the 5th Anti-Money Laundering Directive' (19 April 2018) http://europa.eu/rapid/press-release_STATEMENT-18-3429_en.htm.

[58] Proposal for a Directive amending Directive (EU) 2015/849 on the Prevention of the Use of the Financial System for the Purposes of Money Laundering or Terrorist Financing and amending Directive 2009/101/EC, COM(2016) 450 final, 30.

[59] See 23 NYCRR (n 2); Stan Higgins, 'New York Lawmakers Open to Revisiting the BitLicense' (*coindesk.com*, 23 February 2018) https://www.coindesk.com/bitcoin-crypto-ny-lawmaker-pledges-make-bitlicense-something-works; de Filippi and Wright (n 8), 179.

[60] SEC Report (n 21).   [61] ESMA (n 33).

[62] Financial Conduct Authority ('FCA'), 'Initial Coin Offerings' (2017).

[63] See, e.g., German Federal Financial Supervisory Authority ('BaFin'), 'Initial Coin Offerings: High Risks for Consumers' (2017); French Autorité des Marchés Financiers ('AMF'), 'Initial Coin Offerings' (26 October 2017) Discussion Paper; Swiss Financial Market Supervisory Authority ('FINMA'), 'Enquiries Regarding the Regulatory Framework for Initial Coin Offerings' (16 February 2018) Guidelines; see Chapter 12 by Hacker and Thomale in this volume.

[64] See the ICO ban in China: ICO ban in China: The People's Bank of China, Central Office of the Ministry of Industry and Information Technology, Banking Regulatory Commission, and China Regulatory Commission, 'Notice on the Prevention of Tokens' (4 September 2017). See ICO ban in South Korea: Rachel O'Leary, 'South Korean Regulator Issues ICO Ban' (*coindesk.com*, 29 September 2017) https://www.coindesk.com/south-korean-regulator-issues-ico-ban/).

[65] See SEC, In the Matter of Munchee Inc., Order (11 December 2017); SEC (n 21).

[66] See Internal Revenue Service ('IRS'), 'Virtual Currency Guidance' (2014) IRS Notice 2014-21; HMRC, 'Bitcoin and Other Similar Cryptocurrencies' (2014) Revenue and Customs Brief, 9.

[67] In *re Coinflip, Inc. d/b/a/Derivabit*, et al. (17 September 2015) Order Instituting Proceedings Pursuant to Sections 6(c) and 6(d) of the Commodity Exchange Act, Making Findings and Imposing Remedial Sanctions ('Derivabit Order'), CFTC Docket No. 15-29.

[68] European Commission, 'FinTech Action Plan' (n 6), 4–7.

the way to the use of blockchain for the provision of government services (as well as other areas where blockchain technology may receive a large-scale application).

With regard to finance and banking, there is something of an ironic mismatch nowadays between, on the one hand, the post-Financial Crisis recovery of the political and constitutional importance of finance, money, and credit, and, on the other hand, a new wave of decentralization, automatization, and depoliticization in the same realm through peer-to-peer lending, blockchain banking, cryptocurrencies, and other similar techniques. The pressing legal and political question in response to these two trends is how they can be reconciled. What would an appropriate regulation and lender-of-last-resort function look like in a system of competing electronic currencies and blockchain banking? How can financial regulators encourage innovation but prevent FinTech from becoming a potentially unregulated, destabilizing shadow on the banking sector? What would appropriate patterns of crisis response look like in a decentralized, tech-driven banking industry that seems increasingly out of reach for traditional central banks?

The distributive consequences of a shift to virtual currencies and digital financial markets must also be taken into account by the new regulatory frameworks that will emerge as a response to the blockchain-driven world. The emergent technocracy of FinTech experts, digital currency promoters, miners, and Big Data aggregators may demand new and imaginative legal tools as they sail the turbulent and still largely undiscovered seas of the digital revolution. Public authorities should also be vigilant in protecting the various stakeholders involved in these new marketplaces (operating as collective calculative devices) from various sorts of externalities and internalities, which—coupled with the considerable network effects one may observe in the digital world—may lead to permanent winners, but also losers of the new system. Similar concerns will undoubtedly influence the way the legal system may regulate, and use, blockchain technology in various areas of law, ranging from securities regulation, insurance law, utilities, and access regulation to competition law and labour law.

As these subchapters of the legal grammar are written, the law and the blockchain space inevitably find themselves in a mutually engaging relationship. On the one hand, to a certain extent, the application of the law will determine industry standards and practice, as we today are observing it with the enforcement practice of the SEC concerning ICOs,[69] and AML rules concerning wallets and exchanges.[70] On the other hand, the performativity of actors, and code in particular, is bound to shape the legal environment itself, not only through contractual design and private ordering, but also through the more informal dynamics of the genesis and expansion of novel, coded arrangements cutting across different geographical and regulatory landscapes. With coders, regulators, and legislators developing (not always cooperatively) the legal grammar of blockchain and DLT, a number of questions will need to be answered that will determine the fate of its legal framework. First and foremost, the relationship between code and law is to be clarified. Second, it must be determined which country's laws may legitimately claim jurisdiction over globally connected, decentralized institutions. Third, within these legal orders, the relevant regulatory regimes for different blockchain and DLT applications must be specified. Fourth, particularly with the recent entry into force of the European General Data Protection Regulation ('GDPR'),[71] cross-cutting privacy issues in blockchains need to be addressed. Fifth, potential addressees of regulation have to be identified in decentralized structures. Finally, we may ask to what extent new legislation, tailored to the blockchain space, is necessary and appropriate. We shall briefly touch upon each of these points in the following sections.

---

[69] See Chapter 12 by Hacker and Thomale and Chapter 13 by Shadab in this volume.

[70] See (30)–(31).

[71] Regulation (EU) 2016/679 of the European Parliament and of the Council of 27 April 2016 on the Protection of Natural Persons with regard to the Processing of Personal Data and on the Free Movement of Such Data, and repealing Directive 95/46/EC ('General Data Protection Regulation'), OJ 2016 L 119/1.

A. Code, law, and narratives

The seminal work of Lawrence Lessig has explored how in cyberspace, code complements or even substitutes law as a normative order.[72] Blockchain potentially reinforces and complicates this tendency as it enables code to run autonomously, with very limited third-party intervention, and to produce real effects in terms of value transfers.[73] In the crypto space, the relationship between code and the law has a factual, legal, and political dimension. On a factual level, it is true that it is difficult for the law (absent a regulatory intervention interface)[74] to directly alter the code of a smart contract, stop its execution, or reverse its effects if they were contrary to the law. This inflexibility not only impedes 'legal overruling', but for the parties it also creates significant costs for filling gaps in incomplete smart contracts.[75] Moreover, it may be difficult for parties to some smart contracts to enforce their legal rights if their counterparty is unknown (due to pseudonymity) or based in a country with a weak judicial system. If, for example, a person in the European Union buys a mobile phone directly from an Asian merchant by means of a smart contract, the payment is executed after GPS-verified delivery, but the phone is not in conformity with the contract, the buyer may—depending on the applicable legal regime—have remedies against the merchant, irrespective of and in fact (partially) reversing the automated payment under the smart contract.[76] However, if the buyer fails to undertake due diligence before contract formation by seeking unambiguous identifying information, it may be *factually* difficult, in practice, to recover the payment or to enforce remedies. To this extent, code, which is specified *ex ante*, may trump the law that only offers remedies *ex post*. However, this merely shifts contractual risks between parties and does not affect the general relationship between code and the law. It bears noting, however, that such risks, as well as the need to import off-chain data (e.g. GPS localization; information on contractual conformity), does reinfuse a necessary and significant element of trust into blockchain transactions initially thought to dispense of it.[77]

Even more importantly, on a legal level, it may be asked to what extent participants to a blockchain-based arrangement may opt out of the legal system, or at least out of specific legal protections. As Rohr and Wright argue in Chapter 2 in this volume, US business law grants far-reaching leeway to private ordering solutions that seek to minimize external legal constraints (see also Chapter 10 by Abramowicz in this volume on private ordering in the insurance sector). This will be different in other legal orders, particularly in the European Union, where large parts of consumer, but sometimes also of company, law are mandatory, and for which opting out is not permitted.[78] It remains a debated question as to what extent such rules can and should be mandatory on the international level, in transactions cutting across legal and geographic borders.[79] While different legal regimes will therefore offer different degrees to which blockchain users can contract around *substantive* legal provisions, a more subtle but potentially even more far-reaching question arises with respect to the *interpretation* of blockchain-based legal arrangements:[80] can the parties opt out of the traditional

---

[72] Lawrence Lessig, *Code and Other Laws of Cyberspace* (Basic Books 1999).

[73] See de Filippi and Wright (n 8), Chapter 12; Karen Yeung, 'Regulation by Blockchain: The Emerging Battle for Supremacy Between the Code *of* Law and Code *as* Law' (forthcoming) *Modern Law Review*.

[74] See de Filippi and Wright (n 8), 181.

[75] See Jeremy Sklaroff, 'Smart Contracts and the Cost of Inflexibility' (2017) 166 *University of Pennsylvania Law Review*, 262; Usha Rodrigues, 'Law and the Blockchain' (2019) 104 *Iowa Law Review*, 47–63; for a seminal treatment of incomplete contracting, see Ian Ayres and Robert Gertner, 'Filling Gaps in Incomplete Contracts: An Economic Theory of Default Rules' (1989) 99 *Yale Law Journal*, 87.

[76] Mik (n 18), 287.

[77] See Benito Arruñada, 'Blockchain's Struggle to Deliver Impersonal Exchange' (2018) 19 *Minnesota Journal of Law, Science & Technology*, 55; Mik (n 18), 277–78 and 296–98.

[78] Oren Bar-Gill and Omri Ben-Shahar, 'Regulatory Techniques in Consumer Protection: A Critique of European Consumer Contract Law' (2013) 50 *Common Market Law Review*, 109.

[79] See James J. Fawcett, 'Evasion of Law and Mandatory Rules in Private International Law' (1990) 49 *Cambridge Law Journal*, 44; Moritz Renner, *Zwingendes transnationales Recht* (Nomos 2010).

[80] See Grundmann and Hacker (n 16), 287; in depth, Mik (n 18), 287–98.

way of interpreting contracts, and more specifically, for example, restrict interpretation to the equivalent of a 'literal approach' to the meaning of the code, devoid of good faith-based or purposive modes of interpretation (see Chapter 17 by Brownsword)? This is crucial whenever specific features of a smart contract are unilaterally exploited by one party or an attacker in ways that may violate the spirit, but not the actual code, of the arrangement. This happened in the famous DAO hack, after which the attacker, having siphoned off the equivalent of $50 million, claimed that he or she had a right to do so because the smart contract provided for this opportunity and threatened to sue anyone aiming to recover the spoils.[81] The answer to this challenge should probably turn on how trustworthy external evaluators (such as judges) can be considered to correctly identify the purpose(s) of the arrangement.[82] In the case of the DAO, it seems fairly straightforward that its purpose was to collect funds for further investment and redistribution of profits to all investors, a purpose that was clearly violated by the unilateral appropriation of funds by the hacker. Other cases may be less clear and, indeed, judges may want to exercise some restraint in overruling coded arrangements if the purpose of that particular clause cannot be easily established and if parties chose to 'integrate' their coded contract by expressly insulating it against external evidence.[83] Ultimately, different blockchains may develop with different community expectations about the relative weight of hard code versus purposive, pragmatic interpretation; this can already be seen in the fork between Ethereum and Ethereum Classic that arose precisely from different approaches to the necessity to reverse the DAO hack.[84]

Ultimately, on a political level, this reflects the divergence between views stressing the self-sufficiency and autonomy (in the literal sense) of the blockchain space,[85] and approaches situating blockchain, just as any other technology, within the broader realm of socio-technological instruments that necessarily communicate with, and are nested within, broader political and legal contexts and claims (see Chapter 4 by Eich, Chapter 16 by Ortolani, and Chapter 18 by Lianos in this volume).[86] These different normative predispositions and conflicts will not be easily resolved, not within code, law, or politics. They can also be found in the variety of approaches inherent in the contributions to this volume that range from a focus on private ordering (see Chapter 2 by Rohr and Wright and Chapter 10 by Abramowicz), decentralized versions of global financial capitalism (see Chapter 11 by Seretakis), to calls to reclaim the political dimension of blockchain and money (see Chapter 4 by Eich and Chapter 6 by Dimitropoulos), and even to the discussion of potential fundamental rights violations by smart contract enforcement (see Chapter 16 by Ortolani).

The blockchain space can be seen as an epitome of such competing political, legal, and social frames: different narratives, which may sometimes formalize in fully fledged ideologies, are promoted by technology evangelists and a community of 'experts' that is progressively formed during the period of the expansion of this new technology. Quite often, in these 'liminal' times, this narrative has to compete with established communities that have come to dominate the value-generation process during previous periods of technological

---

[81] See A. Guest, 'An Open Letter' (*pastebin.com*, 18 June 2016) http://pastebin.com/CcGUBgDG; Chapter 7 by Hacker in this volume; David Siegel, 'Understanding The DAO Attack; (*coindesk.com*, 25 June 2016) http://www.coindesk.com/understanding-dao-hack-journalists/.

[82] Eric Posner, 'The Parol Evidence Rule, the Plain Meaning Rule and the Principles of Contractual Interpretation' (1998) 146 *University of Pennsylvania Law Review*, 547.

[83] See, on integration and the parole evidence rule in US law, Posner (n 82); Peter Linzer, 'The Comfort of Certainty: Plain Meaning and the Parol Evidence Rule' (2002) 71 *Fordham Law Review*, 799.

[84] See Arvicco, 'A Crypto-Decentralist Manifesto' (*ethereumclassic.io*, 11 July 2016) https://ethereumclassic.github.io/blog/2016-07-11-manifesto/; Chapter 7 by Hacker in this volume.

[85] See, e.g., Arvicco (n 84).

[86] See, e.g., Mark Verstraete, 'The Stakes of Smart Contracts' (2018) 50 *Loyola University Chicago Law Journal*; Frank Pasquale, 'A Rule of Persons, Not Machines: The Limits of Legal Automation' (2019) *George Washington Law Review*, 41–47; Max Raskin, 'The Law and Legality of Smart Contracts' (2017) 1 *Georgetown Law Technology Review*, 333–40; de Filippi and Loveluck (n 50), 1.

change. These initial liminal periods are marked by 'framing struggles', where the comparative advantages of the new technology and of its community of experts are put forward and opposed to the *status quo*. This is particularly significant with blockchain and the logic of decentralization that differentiates it from the previous stages of the digital revolution, that of centralized digital platforms, the dominance of which the proponents of blockchain technology promise to end (see Chapter 18 by Lianos in this volume). These claims are usually accepted without critical analysis in an effort to constitute a 'winning' narrative for the new GPT. In view of its application in various domains of economic activity, the rents flowing from the exclusion of competing technologies are significant and operate as a rallying cry for the community of experts supporting the new GPT. In addition to this inter-GPT competition, there is another competition taking place: that between the various groups in the community of technology 'experts' for a higher percentage of rents from the value generated by the application of this new GPT in an increasing number of economic sectors. This intra-GPT competition profoundly influences the direction of the innovation effort, the structure of the value-generating activity, and consequently the allocation of the surplus between the various members of the 'expert' community. Therefore, it seems natural that novel technologies form points of crystallization for these different normative approaches; this means, at a minimum, that the blockchain space will continue to develop as a field of tension, contestation, and political action clad in code.

B. Spaces, types, and addressees of regulation

Independent of one's stance in the code versus law debate, the blockchain space has numerous points of interconnection to the legal order, as the promoters of ICOs that have been hit by SEC enforcement or class-action lawsuits have felt.[87] In fact, one might argue that it exhibits an excess of such points in numerous legal orders. Blockchain, in this way, is replicating the regulatory curse of the internet,[88] the content of which is often ruled by a multitude of intersecting, partially contradicting national and supranational legal orders. Similarly, in the realm of blockchain, initiators of ICOs, for example, arguably have to comply with the legal regimes of each and every country from which tokens can be legitimately bought.[89] This book cannot survey all of these legal orders and their relationship to the blockchain space; it does provide, instead, a focus on US and EU legal regimes, with specific and extended references to Australia, China, France, Germany, the UK, and the United States.[90]

Within these national or supranational legal orders, it remains an unresolved conundrum which regulatory regimes are best suited to tackle the challenges and risks exhibited by cryptocurrencies and other, token-based, coded arrangements. From a regulatory perspective, it makes sense to distinguish between different types of tokens that fall under different regulatory regimes.[91] Currency tokens, primarily designed for payment purposes, would fall under currency and payment services regulation; investment tokens, constructed to provide future cash flows, under securities and investment regulation; and utility tokens,[92] meant to provide access to digital platforms, under consumer and general contract law. While tokens

---

[87] Michael Foster, Mark Olthoff, and Richard Levin, 'Cryptocurrency Class Action Lawsuits: A New Frontier' (*Polsinelli News*, March 2018).

[88] See, e.g., Goldsmith and Wu (n 49); Jacqueline Lipton, 'Law of the Intermediated Information Exchange' (2012) 64 *Florida Law Review*, 1361–67; Dan Svantesson, 'Digital Contracts in Global Surroundings' in *European Contract Law in the Digital Age*, edited by Stefan Grundmann (Intersentia 2018), 49.

[89] Philipp Hacker and Chris Thomale, 'Crypto-Securities Regulation: ICOs, Token Sales and Cryptocurrencies under EU Financial Law' (2018) 15 *European Company and Financial Law Review*, 1645, 694–5.

[90] See Chapter 6 by Dimitropoulos, Chapter 11 by Seretakis, Chapter 12 by Hacker and Thomale, and Chapter 18 by Lianos in this volume.

[91] See Hacker and Thomale (n 89), Part II.C.3.

[92] While 'utility tokens' has become the term of art, it may make more sense, over time, to rebrand them as 'consumer tokens': see The Brooklyn Project (n 32).

clearly do not fit perfectly into the existing structures of these regulatory regimes, a number of chapters in this book elaborate on how these structures can be adapted and understood to accommodate the novel challenges and risks of blockchain space. In a broader perspective, however, one may again ask whether token systems are best conceived of as networks of private exchange, best ordered primarily by private parties through consensual arrangements, or whether they exhibit characteristics of public goods or utilities that come with their own regulatory superstructure. Again, the answer to this question will be heavily dependent on the political stance of the blockchain space, but it will also almost certainly be nuanced by the concrete token ecosystem under scrutiny.

More generally, one may raise questions as to the 'non-regulatability' of blockchain, to the extent that the *lex cryptographia,* the private and mostly technical framework that effectively governs the blockchain, consists in an amorphous and highly decentralized set of socio-technical *agencements* (supporting a range of application protocols) that sit on top of the transportation layer of the internet network (the TCP/IP stack) and cannot be linked to a central node that can be easily identified, and eventually regulated, by a national or international legal framework.[93]

To provide an illustration, we may refer to a regulatory regime that cuts across all of those previously mentioned, and that is gaining increasing attention, also in the blockchain space: privacy and data protection regulation. Particularly with the GDPR,[94] in force since May 2018, the issue has gained prominence not only in the European Union, but also internationally. Blockchain data processing may fall under the scope of the GDPR to the extent that the offering of blockchain-based transaction services outside of the European Union is envisaged to nevertheless address data subjects in the European Union (Article 3(2) GDPR).[95] The GDPR, like most types of data protection regulations, only applies to personal data, i.e. 'any information relating to an identified or identifiable natural person' (Article 4(1) GDPR). According to that provision, identifiability can be direct or indirect. For public blockchains, this raises the question of the extent to which public keys and the addresses identified by them can be understood as personal data.[96] This depends, inter alia, on whether data is just encrypted and anonymized, in which case it may escape the ambit of the GDPR,[97] or if parties can be re-identified, in which case it may fall within the GDPR's scope, even if only authorized parties have access to it: the easier it is for concrete identities to be linked to pseudonymous addresses, the more likely it is that courts will find that blockchains, such as Bitcoin or Ethereum, store personal data. As the Court of Justice of the European Union (CJEU) ruled in *Breyer*, data qualifies as 'personal' if it may be 'likely reasonably' combined with other data, even if held by third parties (think of wallets or exchanges performing 'Know Your Customer' checks ('KYC')), to identify the data subject; this is different only if such combination is illegal or requires a disproportionate effort.[98] Recent studies

---

[93] See de Filippi and Wright (n 8), 48–49 and 144.   [94] See n 71.

[95] On the GDPR's international reach and impact, see Ira Rubinstein and Bilyana Petkova, 'The International Impact of the General Data Protection Regulation' in *Commentary on the General Data Protection Regulation,* edited by Marc Cole and Franziska Boehm (Edward Elgar forthcoming); Bart Sloot and Frederik Zuiderveen Borgesius, 'The EU General Data Protection Regulation: A New Global Standard for Information Privacy' (2018) Working Paper.

[96] See, answering in the affirmative, French Autorité des Marchés Financiers ('AMF'), 'Summary of Replies to the Public Consultation on Initial Coin Offerings ('ICOs')' (2018), 10; Jean Bacon, Johan David Michels, Christopher Millard, and Jatinder Singh, 'Blockchain Demystified' (2017) Queen Mary University of London, Legal Studies Research Paper No. 268/2017, 40; Matthias Berberich and Malgorzata Steiner, 'Blockchain Technology and the GDPR—How to Reconcile Privacy and Distributed Ledgers?' (2016) 3 *European Data Protection Law Review,* 423 et seq.; Garry Gabison, 'Policy Consideration for the Blockchain Technology Public and Private Applications' (2016) 19 *SMU Science and Technology Law Review,* 330–35; Mario Martini and Quirin Weinzierl, 'Die Blockchain-Technologie und das Recht auf Vergessenwerden' (2017) *NVwZ,* 1251.

[97] However, this is quite unlikely as to the extent that blockchain data will arise in blockchain transactions regarding certain services or products, it will be possible to establish easily the link between the pseudonymized data and the data subject.

[98] CJEU, Case C-582/14, *Breyer v. Germany,* EU:C:2016:779, [45]–[46].

demonstrating the identifiability of Bitcoin users from public data sources, for example via transaction graph analysis,[99] suggest that the applicability of data protection regulation is a real and serious threat to the viability of immutable blockchain registers. This is even more the case when blockchains contain directly identifying information, such as land registration titles. At the same time, the threat of data protection violations may be understood as a welcome wake-up call to further develop privacy preservation[100] and pruning solutions that might not only address privacy concerns but also scaling limitations.[101] Greater privacy preservation, however, may violate anti-money laundering provisions which are currently being updated, at the EU level, to include blockchain-based payments.[102]

If the data is personal and within the GDPR ambit, this harbours the potential for further legal battles as users could demand—from the data controller(s) responsible for public blockchains[103]—erasure of certain types of information (Article 17 GDPR)—in direct confrontation with the principle of immutability technically and ideally enshrined in public blockchains. The idea of 'privacy by design' (as enshrined in Article 25 GDPR) may also require the consideration of the privacy implications when designing the specific blockchain (and the decentralized apps), imposing the choice of GDPR-compatible technologies and overall IT architecture.[104]

This is not the only dilemma data protection law faces with respect to blockchains. The difficult question for the relevant data controller or processor in a decentralized ledger system[105] points to the more general regulatory challenge of identifying agents to whom regulation can be meaningfully addressed. Regulation has, for ages, been designed to apply to centralized units (e.g. corporations), in which hierarchies of control and responsibility can be more easily identified. Here, one may establish a distinction between private blockchains in which the data controller may be more easily identified, as, for instance, the entities controlling the joint venture that operates the system, and public blockchains in which practically the blockchain data are simultaneously processed by every node of the system, thus not enabling the identification of the responsible data controller.[106] However, the fact that such structures are missing, prima facie, in such decentralized environments does not per se speak against their regulation. A number of other agents can be identified that could be—and, in fact, already are, as SEC enforcement and AML rules show—the addressees of legal intervention. This includes not only actual users, but more importantly intermediaries (wallets, exchanges, but also internet service providers (ISPs), etc.) and, eventually, core

---

[99] See, e.g., Michael Fleder, Michael Kester, and Sudeep Pillai, 'Bitcoin Transaction Graph Analysis' (February 2015) https://arxiv.org/abs/1502.01657; Husam Al Jawaheri, Mashael Al Sabah, Yazan Boshmaf, and Aiman Erbad, 'When a Small Leak Sinks a Great Ship: Deanonymizing Tor Hidden Service Users through Bitcoin Transactions Analysis' (April 2018) https://arxiv.org/abs/1801.07501.

[100] See, e.g., the monero and zcash tokens; see further Ahmed Kosba, Andrew Miller, Elaine Shi, Zikai Wen. and Charalampos Papamanthou, 'Hawk: The Blockchain Model of Cryptography and Privacy—Preserving Smart Contracts' (2016) IEEE Symposium on Security and Privacy (SP), 839; Dom McCann, 'The Blockchain Dilemma: GDPR + Right to be Forgotten' (*artificiallawyer.com*, 24 May 2018) https://www.artificiallawyer.com/2018/05/24/the-blockchain-dilemma-gdpr-right-to-be-forgotten/; Alyssa Hertig, 'MIT Tests Smart Contract-Powered Bitcoin Lightning Network' (May 2018) https://www.coindesk.com/mit-testing-smart-contract-powered-bitcoin-lightning-network.

[101] Pruning goes back to the original Bitcoin White Paper; see Nakamoto (n 8), 4; Emanuel Palm, 'Implications and Impact of Blockchain Transaction Pruning' (2017) Masters Thesis.

[102] See Proposal for a Directive amending Directive (EU) 2015/849 (n 58), 12–13; Nejc Novak, 'EU Introduces Crypto Anti-Money Laundering Regulation' (*medium.com*, 2 January 2018) https://medium.com/@nejcnovaklaw/eu-introduces-crypto-anti-money-laundering-regulation-d6ab0ddedd3.

[103] Those may be identified with the management organ proposed in Chapter 7 by Hacker in this volume; see also Bacon et al. (n 96), 41.

[104] Berberich and Steiner (n 96), 425.

[105] See, e.g., Paulina Pesch and Christian Sillaber, 'Distributed Ledger, Joint Control?' (2017) *Computer Law Review International*, 169–71.

[106] As this is required by Article 26(1) of the General Data Protection Regulation ('GDPR') 2016/679.

developers and founders of token-based ventures.[107] As financial market regulation shows, intermediaries have often been singled out as a way of policing the on- and off-ramps of more complex systems;[108] we expect a similar development in the blockchain space.

Finally, given the regulatory uncertainty about the proper treatment of cryptocurrencies, tokens, and other blockchain-based ventures under the law, calls have repeatedly been made for novel legislation tailored specifically to the blockchain space.[109] However, it may be more advisable to specify how existing regulation applies to blockchain applications, and to modify it where necessary. First, new pieces of legislation take time, particularly in multi-actor jurisdictions like the European Union; guidelines on how to apply existing regulation can often be issued by regulatory agencies in a more expeditious way.[110] Second, and more importantly, tailoring legislation to novel technologies always harbours the risk of overfitting; the rules might be technologically outdated at the moment they enter into force.[111] Therefore, the foremost challenge for the future legal framework of the blockchain universe will be (i) to precisely specify how different blockchain applications interact with technologically neutral, general provisions of legislation in the major jurisdictions these applications play out in; and (ii) to point to novel forms of legal intervention, from self-regulation to new hard laws, that take the stage where existing regulation fails. This book aims to make a critical contribution to this double endeavour.

V. Outline of the Book

This edited volume is divided into five parts. Part I (Chapters 1–3) deals with the 'Technological and Business Challenges of Blockchain Technology' providing for a positive and normative account of the future structuring of business in the age of blockchain technology. Part II (Chapters 4–7) discusses the issue of 'Blockchain and the Future of Money', focusing on the use of blockchain technology as a means of payment and value storage. The chapters in this Part give a historically and contextually informed account of the reasons and the ways to regulate virtual currencies. Part III (Chapters 8–13) moves beyond the application of the blockchain technology in virtual currencies and presents 'Blockchain and the Future of Banking, Finance, Insurance, and Securities Regulation'. The different contributions discuss the application of various types of legal regimes to blockchain-backed financial products. Part IV (Chapters 14–17) take the reader 'Beyond Finance' and more broadly discusses 'Blockchain as a Legal and Regulatory Challenge'. The aim of this Part of the book is to offer a general account of the overall relationship between blockchain and the law, and even more broadly, new technologies and the law. While it is notoriously difficult to predict the future, it can be stated that at the current stage of development, law and politics have a unique opportunity to shape this relationship both in order to protect the citizens and, at the same time, to promote the public good in promoting innovation. Part V (Chapter 18) provides a dynamic and reflexive approach of this interaction between technology, law and economics, by focusing on how the competitive strategies of economic actors shape the rules of the competitive game, the broader 'industry architectures' that structure competitive interactions, and how this, in turn, may influence regulatory intervention.

---

[107] See Chapter 6 by Dimitropoulos, Chapter 7 by Hacker, and Chapter 18 by Lianos in this volume; de Filippi and Wright (n 8), 175–80.

[108] Kitty Lieverse, 'The Scope of MiFID II' in *Regulation of EU Financial Markets*, edited by Danny Busch and Guido Ferrarini (Oxford University Press 2017), 27; Patrick Leyens, *Informationsintermediäre des Kapitalmarkts* (Mohr Siebeck 2017).

[109] See, most importantly, the initiative by the French AMF, 'Summary of Replies' (n 96), 16–17.

[110] For concrete proposals on such guidelines, see Hacker and Thomale (n 89), Part V.A.

[111] Roger Brownsword, 'So What Does the World Need Now? Reflections on Regulating Technologies' in *Regulating Technologies*, edited by Roger Brownsword and Karen Yeung (Edward Elgar 2008), 26–28.

Part I of the book starts with a Chapter by Paolo Tasca and Riccardo Piselli, who discuss the challenges of blockchain with a focus on the challenges limiting the widespread potential of the distributed ledger technology and categorizing them into business, legal, and technical challenges. The author then presents four alternative use cases and the future potential of the technology. Aaron Wright and Jonathan Rohr, in Chapter 2, present the ways in which blockchain technology revolutionizes the funding, management, and organization of business enterprises. They claim that the age of shareholder empowerment and agency capitalism is upon us and they specifically demonstrate how smart contracts offer a cost-effective and trustworthy mechanism for implementing firm-by-firm private ordering. By contrast, Angela Walch, in Chapter 3, examines the implicit legal relationships within public blockchains in claiming that those actors creating and operating the blockchain, such as core software developers and major miners, function as fiduciaries of those who rely on the blockchain, and proceeds to develop a general theory of blockchain fiduciaries with a focus on software developers.

Introducing Part II of the volume, in Chapter 4 Stefan Eich discusses the politics of cryptocurrencies in a historical perspective. While cryptocurrencies are most often described as a move away from politics, the author's historical account suggests otherwise, and places the historical development of cryptocurrencies in the perspective of the international politics of money and the call for privatization of money since the 1970s. Chapter 5 by Claus Zimmermann looks into several regulatory challenges for monetary policy in the age of virtual currency systems and comes to the conclusion that restrictions on the proliferation of virtual currency products are currently difficult to justify. According to the author, the sustainability of a monetary regime that relies on such systems can be assessed against three criteria: (i) the regime's capacity to control structural 'deflation'; (ii) the regime's flexibility when it comes to responding to temporary shocks to money demand and, thus, to ensuring a smooth business cycle; and (iii) the degree to which the regime is able to effectively function as a lender of last resort. Georgios Dimitropoulos' contribution in Chapter 6 identifies virtual currencies as global currencies that may have a major impact on national jurisdictions given that they may operate in the future as a more efficient version of the international gold standard. This has spurred the development of a paradoxical 'anti-countermovement' that restricts global currencies as currencies and, at the same time, enables their technology in different jurisdictions. The author suggests that the way to mitigate the dangers of 'embedding through enabling' is by regulating the new cryptocurrency intermediaries. Chapter 7, written by Philipp Hacker, aims to develop a framework for stability and decision making in blockchain-based monetary systems. By treating them as 'complex systems', the author argues that complexity-induced uncertainty can be reduced and elements of stability and order strengthened by adapting a corporate governance framework to cryptocurrencies. The identified 'comply-or-explain' approach combines transparency and accountability with the necessary flexibility to allow developers to continue their innovation experimentation.

Moving into Part III, Rohan Grey's Chapter 8 looks into the relationship between banking and monetary system design with the purpose of identifying the elements of banking that remain viable and necessary in a world defined by the creation of digital fiat currency instruments that are fully liquid, interoperable across all payments networks, and can be held as either an account balance or a bearer instrument by both retail and wholesale actors alike. Jonathan Greenacre, in Chapter 9, deals with the regulation of shadow payment systems and the development of FinTech in the African Continent. The chapter explains how the existing institutional environment in different African countries has created a fertile ground for FinTech. It explores the key policy and regulatory insights and issues that arise in relation to 'mobile money' and how these can be applied to cryptocurrencies. Michael Abramowicz claims, in Chapter 10, that smart contracts could serve as a substitute for conventionally conceived insurance companies. Blockchain-based insurance may successfully provide a means of avoiding cost-intensive regulations and could, thus, gain a competitive advantage over conventional insurance, at least in some areas. Abramowicz argues that it could become an important area of private ordering. Chapter 11, by Alexandros Seretakis' tries to disentangle the myths from the realities of the blockchain and discusses how the law may act both as an impediment and a catalyst to the widespread adoption of the technology, with a focus on securities markets and central banking. In Chapter 12, Philipp Hacker and Chris Thomale discuss the definition of tokens as securities in initial coin offerings ('ICOs'). In doing so, they contrast the regulatory regime in the United States and the European Union, placing their focus on the European Union. The chapter further develops an approach that distinguishes between three types of tokens: currency, investment, and utility tokens. It proceeds to analyse the differential implications of each of these types, as well as their hybrid forms, for EU securities regulation. In Chapter 13, Houman Shadab offers an introduction to similar questions with respect to US securities laws. The chapter discusses the application of US securities regulation to blockchain financial products. It argues that traditional approaches to regulation of securities and derivatives markets may be difficult to apply when blockchain enables transactions to take place without regulated intermediaries and enables new types of transactions such as token sales.

Part IV of the book discusses law and technology-related developments beyond finance. In Chapter 14, Agnieszka Janczuk-Gorywoda, while acknowledging the deep changes that may be brought about in the payment systems sector by the use of the blockchain technology, suggests that the change will be less revolutionary than that which the anarchists and libertarians who developed the technology and the system had initially hoped and anticipated. The blockchain will either make possible the rise of new—potentially very powerful—intermediaries, or it will be embraced by the established payment services providers, who will use blockchain to transform their own service provision. Accordingly, decentralized virtual currencies will remain on the margins of the mainstream payments system. In Chapter 15, Florian Möslein discusses to what extent corporate law can be substituted by the blockchain. Möslein claims that law is not, and will never be, entirely redundant. For this reason, it becomes important to identify the boundaries of digital jurisdictions and develop new conflict of laws principles to regulate the relationship between blockchain technology and corporate law. Pietro Ortolani argues in Chapter 16 that the demand for dispute resolution, triggered by the increase in the use of blockchain, is mostly met by internal systems of private adjudication, rather than the traditional means of dispute resolution by courts. The judicialization of blockchain challenges the traditional notions of sovereignty, jurisdiction, and use of force by the state. In Chapter 17, Roger Brownsword presents three perspectives on smart contracts: the transactionalist, the relationalist, and the regulatory-instrumentalist. Each perspective draws on a separate paradigm of transaction obligation that is elaborated in the chapter.

In the last Part of the book, Chapter 18 by Ioannis Lianos takes a dynamic and reflexive perspective on the interaction between technology, law, and economics. Lianos places its focus on the role of competition in shaping the economic, but also regulatory, eco-system in which blockchain technology becomes embedded. There is the promise that the technology and the social space it will foster will give rise to more competitive structures in the organization of economic activity in the digital economy, in comparison to the current paradigm of digital platforms, which is highly centralized. The narrative of disruption has, indeed, been quite important in promoting the greater use of blockchain technology and has also framed the socio-technical 'agencements' that have so far guided regulatory action in this area. By critically engaging with this rhetoric, Lianos's chapter unveils how blockchain can contribute to competitive advantage, and, thus, shape the distribution of surplus value in various industries. It then draws lessons for the work of regulators, in particular, for competition law enforcers.

VI. Bibliography

Accenture Consulting, 'Blockchain Wave Headed Toward CPG and Retail Industries' (2017) https://www.accenture.com/us-en/insight-highlights-cgs-blockchain-cpg-and-retail-industries, accessed on 20 January 2019.

Al Jawaheri Husam, Al Sabah Mashael, Boshmaf Yazan, and Erbad Aiman, 'When A Small Leak Sinks a Great Ship: Deanonymizing for Hidden Service Users through Bitcoin Transactions Analysis' (2018) https://arxiv.org/abs/1801.07501, accessed on 15 February 2019.

Ali Muneeb and Shea Ryan, 'Blockstack: A New Internet for Decentralized Applications' (2017) White Paper, https://blockstack.org/whitepaper.pdf, accessed on 15 February 2019.

Antonopoulos Andreas M., *Mastering Bitcoin: Programming the Open Blockchain* (2nd edn, O'Reilly, 2017).

Arruñada Benito, 'Blockchain's Struggle to Deliver Impersonal Exchange' (2018) 19 *Minnesota Journal of Law, Science & Technology*, 55.

Arvicco, 'A Crypto-Decentralist Manifesto' (*ethereumclassic.io*, 11 July 2016) https://ethereumclassic.github.io/blog/2016-07-11-manifesto/, accessed on 7 January 2019.

AXA, 'AXA Goes Blockchain With Fizzy' (*axa.com*, 13 September 2017) https://www.axa.com/en/newsroom/news/axa-goes-blockchain-with-fizzy, accessed on 7 January 2019.

Ayres Ian and Gertner Robert, 'Filling Gaps in Incomplete Contracts: An Economic Theory of Default Rules (1989) 99 *Yale Law Journal*, 87.

Bacon Jean, Michels Johan David, Millard Christopher, and Singh Jatinder, 'Blockchain Demystified' (2017) Queen Mary University of London, Legal Studies Research Paper No. 268/2017.

Baird Nikki, 'Blockchain and Retail: Four Opportunities' (*forbes.com*, 9 August 2017) https://www.forbes.com/sites/nikkibaird/2017/08/09/blockchain-and-retail-four-opportunities/#10f1829a72bf, accessed on 7 January 2019.

Balls Ed, Howat James, and Stansbury Anna, 'Central Bank Independence Revisited: After the Financial Crisis, What Should a Model Central Bank Look Like?' (2016) M-RCBG Associate Working Paper Series, No. 67.

Bank of England, 'FinTech Accelerator Proof of Concept: Distributed Ledger Technology' (2016) https://bankofengland.co.uk/-/media/boe/files/fintech/pwc, accessed on 15 February 2019.

Bank of Thailand, 'Wholesale Central Bank Digital Currency', Announcement of Project Inthanon Collaborative Partnership, 21 August 2018, BOT Press Release No. 54/2018.

Bar-Gill Oren and Ben-Shahar Omri, 'Regulatory Techniques in Consumer Protection: A Critique of European Consumer Contract Law' (2013) 50 *Common Market Law Review*, 109.

Barrdear John and Kumhof Michael, 'The Macroeconomics of Central Bank Issued Digital Currencies' (2016) Bank of England, Staff Working Paper No. 605.

Berberich Matthias and Steiner Malgorzata, 'Blockchain Technology and the GDPR—How to Reconcile Privacy and Distributed Ledgers?' (2016) 3 *European Data Protection Law Review*, 422.

Berkshire Hathaway, *Annual Report* (2002) (2002).

Bordo Michael D. and Levin Andrew T., 'Central Bank Digital Currency and the Future of Monetary Policy' (2017) National Bureau of Economic Research Working Paper No. 23711.

Brown Richard, 'A Simple Model for Smart Contracts' (2015) https://gendal.me/2015/02/10/a-simple-model-for-smart-contracts/, accessed on 7 January 2019.

Brownsword Roger, 'So What Does the World Need Now? Reflections on Regulating Technologies' in *Regulating Technologies*, edited by Roger Brownsword and Karen Yeung (Edward Elgar, 2008), 23.

Buterin Vitalik, 'Ethereum' (2014) White Paper.

Callon Michel and Muniesa Fabian, 'Les Marchés Economiques Comme Dispositifs Collectives de Calcul' (2003) 122(6) *Réseaux*, 189.

Christidis Konstantinos and Devetsikiotis Michael, 'Blockchains and Smart Contracts for the Internet of Things' (2016) 4 *IEEE Access*, 2292.

CoinSchedule, 'Cryptocurrency ICO Stats 2018' (2018) https://www.coinschedule.com/stats.html, accessed on 7 January 2019.

d'Artis Kancs, Ciaian Pavel, and Rajcaniova Miroslava, 'The Digital Agenda of Virtual Currencies' (2015), JRC Technical Report.

Davis Kevin, 'Regulatory Reform Post the Global Financial Crisis: An Overview' (8 March 2011) https://kevindavis.com.au/secondpages/Miscellaneous/Regulatory%20Reform%20Post%20 the%20GFC-%20Overview%20Report.pdf, accessed on 7 January 2019.

de Filippi Primavera and Loveluck Benjamin, 'The Invisible Politics of Bitcoin: Governance Crisis of a Decentralized Infrastructure' (2016) 5(3) *Internet Policy Review*, 1.

de Filippi Primavera and Wright Aaron, *Blockchain and the Law* (Harvard University Press 2018).

de Vicuña Antonio Sáinz, 'An Institutional Theory of Money' in *International Monetary and Financial Law: The Global Crisis*, edited by Mario Giovanoli and Diego Devos (Oxford University Press 2010), 517.

Durov Nikolai and Durov Pavel, 'Telegram Primer' (2017).

ESMA, 'ESMA Alerts Firms Involved in ICOs to the Need to Meet Relevant Regulatory Requirements' (2017) Statement of 13 November.

ESMA, 'The Distributed Ledger Technology Applied to Securities Markets' (2017) Report.

Ethereum, 'Ether: FAQ', https://www.ethereum.org/ether, accessed on 7 January 2019.

European Banking Association ('EBA'), 'Cryptotechnologies, a Major IT Innovation and Catalyst for Change' (2015) Report.

European Central Bank, 'Virtual Currency Schemes' (2012).

European Central Bank, 'Virtual Currency Schemes—A Further Analysis' (2015).

European Central Bank, 'Distributed Ledger Technology' (2016) 1 *In Focus*, 1.

European Central Bank, 'Eurosystem's Vision for the Future of Europe's Financial Market Infrastructure' (2016).

European Commission, 'Consumer Financial Services Action Plan: Better Products, More Choice' COM(2017)139 final.

European Commission, 'FinTech Action Plan: For a More Competitive and Innovative European Financial Sector' COM(2018) 109 final.

European Parliament, 'Virtual Currencies', Resolution of 26 May 2016, 2016/2007(INI).

Eyal Ittay, Gencer Adem Efe, Sirer Emin Gün, and van Renesse Robbert, 'Bitcoin-NG: A Scalable Blockchain Protocol' (2016), Proceedings of the 13th USENIX Symposium on Networked Systems Design and Implementation.

Fawcett James J., 'Evasion of Law and Mandatory Rules in Private International Law' (1990) 49 *Cambridge Law Journal*, 44.

Financial Conduct Authority ('FCA'), 'Initial Coin Offerings' (2017).

Financial Times, 'BP Experiments with Blockchain For Oil And Gas Trading' (*financialtimes. com*) https://www.ft.com/content/100622d0-a680-11e7-93c5-648314d2c72c, accessed on 7 January 2019.

Fleder Michael, Kester Michael, and Pillai Sudeep, 'Bitcoin Transaction Graph Analysis' (February 2015) https://arxiv.org/abs/1502.01657, accessed on 15 February 2019.

Foster Michael, Olthoff Mark, and Levin Richard, 'Cryptocurrency Class Action Lawsuits: A New Frontier' (*Polsinelli News*, March 2018).

French Autorité des Marchés Financiers ('AMF'), 'Initial Coin Offerings' (26 October 2017) Discussion Paper.

French Autorité des Marchés Financiers ('AMF'), 'Summary of Replies to the Public Consultation on Initial Coin Offerings ('ICOs')' (2018).

Future Thinkers, '19 Industries the Blockchain Will Disrupt' (*futurethinkers.org*, 16 June 2017), http://futurethinkers.org/industries-blockchain-disrupt/, accessed on 7 January 2019.

Gabison Garry, 'Policy Consideration for the Blockchain Technology Public and Private Applications' (2016) 19 *SMU Science and Technology Law Review*, 327.

German Federal Financial Supervisory Authority ('BaFin'), 'Initial Coin Offerings: High Risks for Consumers' (2017).

Goldsmith Jack and Wu Tim, *Who Controls the Internet? Illusions of a Borderless World* (Oxford University Press 2006).

Grundmann Stefan and Hacker Philipp, 'Digital Technology as a Challenge to European Contract Law' (2017) 13 *European Review of Contract Law*, 255.

Guest A., 'An Open Letter' (*pastebin.com*, 18 June 2016) http://pastebin.com/CcGUBgDG, accessed on 7 January 2019.

Gupta Sahil, Lauppe Patrick, and Ravishankar Shreyas, 'Fedcoin. A Blockchain-Backed Central Bank Cryptocurrency', Yale Law School Working Paper (2017), https://law.yale.edu/system/files/area/center/global/document/411_final_paper_-_fedcoin.pdf , accessed on 7 January 2019.

Hacker Philipp and Thomale Chris, 'Crypto-Securities Regulation: ICOs, Token Sales and Cryptocurrencies under EU Financial Law' (2018) 15 *European Company and Financial Law Review*, 645.

He Dong, Habermeier Karl, Leckow Ross, et al., 'Virtual Currencies and Beyond: Initial Considerations' (January 2016) IMF Report.

Heijdra Ben J., *Foundations of Modern Macroeconomics* (2nd edn, Oxford University Press 2009).

Hertig Alyssa, 'MIT Tests Smart Contract-Powered Bitcoin Lightning Network' (May 2018) https://www.coindesk.com/mit-testing-smart-contract-powered-bitcoin-lightning-network, accessed 15 February 2019.

Higgins Stan, 'New York Lawmakers Open to Revisiting the BitLicense' (*coindesk.com*, 23 February 2018) https://www.coindesk.com/bitcoin-crypto-ny-lawmaker-pledges-make-bitlicense-something-works, accessed on 7 January 2019.

HMRC, 'Bitcoin and Other Similar Cryptocurrencies' (2014), Revenue and Customs Brief.

Hope Jarred, 'The Status Network'(2017) White Paper.

Ingham Geoffrey, *The Nature of Money* (Polity Press 2004).

Internal Revenue Service ('IRS'), 'Virtual Currency Guidance' (2014), IRS Notice 2014-21.

Ishikawa Mai, 'Designing Virtual Currency Regulation in Japan: Lessons from the Mt Gox Case' (2017) 3 *Journal of Financial Regulation*, 125.

Jentzsch Christopher, 'Decentralized Autonomous Organization to Automate Governance' (2016) https://download.slock.it/public/DAO/WhitePaper.pdf , accessed on 7 January 2019.

Keynes John Maynard, 'A Treatise on Money: The Pure Theory of Money' in *The Collected Writings of J.M. Keynes* (Volume 5, Cambridge University Press 2012).

Kosba Ahmed, Miller Andrew, Shi Elaine, Wen Zikai, and Papamanthou Charalampos, 'Hawk: The Blockchain Model of Cryptography and Privacy—Preserving Smart Contracts' (2016) IEEE Symposium on Security and Privacy (SP).

Lessig Lawrence, *Code and Other Laws of Cyberspace* (Basic Books 1999).

Leyens Patrick, *Informationsintermediäre des Kapitalmarkts* (Mohr Siebeck 2017).

Lieverse Kitty, 'The Scope of MiFID II' in *Regulation of EU Financial Markets*, edited by Danny Busch and Guido Ferrarini (Oxford University Press, 2017), 27.

Linzer Peter, 'The Comfort of Certainty: Plain Meaning and the Parol Evidence Rule' (2002) 71 *Fordham Law Review*, 799.

Lipton Jacqueline, 'Law of the Intermediated Information Exchange' (2012) 64 *Florida Law Review*, 1337.

MacKenzie Donald and Millo Yuval, 'Constructing a Market, Performing Theory: The iology of a Financial Derivatives Exchange' (2003) 109(1) *American Journal of Sociology*, 107.

Mainelli Michael and Smith Mike, 'Sharing Ledgers for Sharing Economies: An Exploration of Mutual Distributed Ledgers (aka Blockchain Technology)' (2015) 3 *The Journal of Financial Perspectives*, 38.

Mankiw N. Gregory, *Macroeconomics* (9th edn, Worth Publishers 2015).

Martini Mario and Weinzierl Quirin, 'Die Blockchain-Technologie und das Recht auf Vergessenwerden' (2017) *NVwZ*, 1251.

McCann Dom, 'The Blockchain Dilemma: GDPR + Right to be Forgotten' (*artificiallawyer.com*, 24 May 2018), https://www.artificiallawyer.com/2018/05/24/the-blockchain-dilemma-gdpr-right-to-be-forgotten/ , accessed on 7 January 2019.

Mehrling Perry, *The New Lombard Street: How the Fed Became the Dealer of Last Resort* (Princeton University Press 2010).

Meola Andrew, 'How Banks and Financial Institutions are Implementing Blockchain Technology' (*businessinsider.de*, 20 September 2017) http://www.businessinsider.de/blockchain-technology-banking-finance-2017-9?r=US&IR=T, accessed on 7 January 2019.

Mik Elisa, 'Smart Contracts: Terminology, Technical Limitations and Real-World Complexity' (2017) 9 *Law, Innovation and Technology*, 269.

Mizrahi Alex, 'A Blockchain-Based Property Ownership Recording System' (2015) https://chromaway.com/papers/A-blockchain-based-property-registry.pdf, accessed on 7 January 2019.

Monetary Authority of Singapore, 'MAS Clarifies Regulatory Position on the Offer of Digital Tokens in Singapore' (*mas.gov*, 1 August 2017) http://www.mas.gov.sg/News-and-Publications/Media-Releases/2017/MAS-clarifies-regulatory-position-on-the-offer-of-digital-tokens-in-Singapore.aspx , accessed on 7 January 2019.

Muftic Sead, 'Overview and Analysis of the Concept and Applications of Virtual Currencies' (2016) JRC Technical Report.

Nakamoto Satoshi, 'Bitcoin: A Peer-to-Peer Electronic Cash System' (2008) White Paper.

Narayanan Arvind, Bonneau Joseph, Felton Edward, Miller Andrew, and Goldfeder Steven, *Bitcoin and Cryptocurrency Technologies: A Comprehensive Introduction* (Princeton University Press 2016).

Novak Nejc, 'EU Introduces Crypto Anti-Money Laundering Regulation' (*medium.com*, 2 January 2018) https://medium.com/@nejcnovaklaw/eu-introduces-crypto-anti-money-laundering-regulation-d6ab0ddedd3, accessed on 7 January 2019.

O'Leary Rachel, 'South Korean Regulator Issues ICO Ban' (*coindesk.com*, 29 September 2017) https://www.coindesk.com/south-korean-regulator-issues-ico-ban/, accessed on 7 January 2019.

Orcutt Mike, 'How Blockchain Could Give Us a Smarter Energy Grid' (*MIT Tech Review*, 16 October 2017) https://www.technologyreview.com/s/609077/how-blockchain-could-give-us-a-smarter-energy-grid/, accessed on 7 January 2019.

Owsinski Bobbi, 'Despite Predictions, Blockchain Will Not Be the Future of the Music Industry' (*forbes.com*, 18 November 2017) https://www.forbes.com/sites/bobbyowsinski/2017/11/18/blockchain-music-industry/#38a280776a0b, accessed on 7 January 2019.

Palm Emanuel, 'Implications and Impact of Blockchain Transaction Pruning' (2017) Masters Thesis.

Pasquale Frank, 'A Rule of Persons, Not Machines: The Limits of Legal Automation' (2019) 87 *George Washington Law Review*, 1.

Pesch Paulina and Sillaber Christian, 'Distributed Ledger, Joint Control?' (2017) *Computer Law Review International*, 166.

Pinna Andrea and Ruttenberg Wiebe, 'Distributed Ledger Technologies in Securities Post-Trading' (2016) European Central Bank Occasional Paper No 172/2016.

Pistor Katharina, 'Money's Legal Hierarchies' in *Just Financial Markets?*, edited by Lisa Herzog (Oxford University Press 2017), 185.

Plassaras Nicholas A., 'Regulating Digital Currencies: Bringing Bitcoin within the Reach of the IMF' (2013) 14 *Chinese Journal of International Law*, 377.

Polanyi Karl, 'Great Transformation' in *The Great Transformation: The Political and Economic Origins of our Time* [1944], edited by Fred Block (Beacon Press 2001).

Popov Serguei, 'The Tangle (2018) White Paper.

Posner Eric, 'The Parol Evidence Rule, the Plain Meaning Rule and the Principles of Contractual Interpretation' (1998) 146 *University of Pennsylvania Law Review*, 533.

Raskin Max, 'The Law and Legality of Smart Contracts' (2017) 1 *Georgetown Law Technology Review*, 304.

Re Coinflip, Inc., d/b/a/Derivabit, et al., (17 September 2015) Order Instituting Proceedings Pursuant to Sections 6(c) and 6(d) of the Commodity Exchange Act, Making Findings and Imposing Remedial Sanctions ('Derivabit Order'), CFTC Docket No. 15-29.

Renner Moritz, *Zwingendes transnationales Recht* (Nomos 2010).

Rodrigues Usha, 'Law and the Blockchain' (2019) 104 *Iowa Law Review*, 679.

Rohr Jonathan and Wright Aaron, 'Blockchain-Based Token Sales, Initial Coin Offerings, and the Democratization of Public Capital Markets' (forthcoming) 70 *Hastings Law Journal*, https://papers.ssrn.com/sol3/papers.cfm?abstract_id=3048104, accessed on 15 February 2019.

Rubinstein Ira and Petkova Bilyana, 'The International Impact of the General Data Protection Regulation' in *Commentary on the General Data Protection Regulation*, edited by Marc Cole and Franziska Boehm (Edward Elgar, forthcoming).

Sato Masashi and Matsuo Shin'íchiro, 'Long-Term Public Blockchain: Resilience against Compromise of Underlying Cryptography' (2017), IEEE European Symposium on Security and Privacy Workshops (EuroS&PW).

Securities and Exchange Commission ('SEC'), 'Investigation Pursuant to Section 21(a) of the Securities Exchange Act of 1934: The DAO' (2017), Report Release No. 81207 ('SEC Report').

Siegel David, 'Understanding the DAO Attack' (*coindesk.com*, 25 June 2016) http://www.coindesk.com/understanding-dao-hack-journalists/, accessed on 7 January 2019.

Sklaroff Jeremy, 'Smart Contracts and the Cost of Inflexibility' (2017) 166 *University of Pennsylvania Law Review*, 262.

Sloot Bart and Borgesius Frederik Zuiderveen, 'The EU General Data Protection Regulation: A New Global Standard for Information Privacy' (2018) Working Paper.

Svantesson Dan, 'Digital Contracts in Global Surroundings' in *European Contract Law in the Digital Age*, edited by Stefan Grundmann (Intersentia 2018), 49.

Swiss Financial Market Supervisory Authority ('FINMA'), 'Enquiries Regarding the Regulatory Framework for Initial Coin Offerings' (16 February 2018) Guidelines.

The Brooklyn Project, 'Framework for the Establishment of Consumer Tokens' (2018), Working Paper, https://docs.google.com/document/d/1DkAN3p7t0qefUOnvIkKS3PxgU6tCYEmCYxv2wBAeLng/edit, accessed on 7 January 2019.

The People's Bank of China, Central Office of the Ministry of Industry and Information Technology, Banking Regulatory Commission, and China Regulatory Commission, 'Notice on the Prevention of Tokens' (4 September 2017).

Timmermans Vice-President, Dombrovskis Vice-President, and Jourovà Commissioner, 'Statement on the Adoption by the European Parliament of the 5th Anti-Money Laundering Directive' (19 April 2018) http://europa.eu/rapid/press-release_STATEMENT-18-3429_en.htm, accessed on 7 January 2019.

Tooze Adam, *Crashed: How a Decade of Financial Crises Changed the World* (Viking 2018).

Tucker Paul, *Unelected Power: The Quest for Legitimacy in Central Banking and the Regulatory State* (Princeton University Press 2018).

UK Government Office for Science, 'Distributed Ledger Technology: Beyond Block Chain', (2016) UK Government Chief Scientific Adviser Report.

Verstraete Mark, 'The Stakes of Smart Contracts' (forthcoming) 50 *Loyola University Chicago Law Journal*, https://papers.ssrn.com/sol3/papers.cfm?abstract_id=3178393, accessed on 15 February 2019.

von Hayek Friedrich A., *The Denationalisation of Money* (Fordham University Press 1978).

White Lawrence H., 'The Market for Cryptocurrencies' (2014) GMU Working Paper in Economics No. 14-45.

World Economic Forum, 'The Future of Financial Infrastructure. An Ambitious Look at How Blockchain Can Reshape Financial Services' (2016).

World Government Summit, 'Building the Hyperconnected Future on Blockchains' (2017).

Xu Brent, 'Blockchain vs. Distributed Ledger Technologies' (*consensys.net*, 5 April 2018) https://media.consensys.net/blockchain-vs-distributed-ledger-technologies-1e0289a87b16, accessed on 7 January 2019.

Yeung Karen, 'Regulation by Blockchain: The Emerging Battle for Supremacy Between the Code *of* Law and Code *as* Law' (forthcoming) *Modern Law Review*.

Zimmermann Claus D., *A Contemporary Concept of Monetary Sovereignty* (Oxford University Press 2013).

PART I

TECHNOLOGICAL AND BUSINESS CHALLENGES OF BLOCKCHAIN TECHNOLOGY

1

The Blockchain Paradox

Paolo Tasca and Riccardo Piselli

I. Introduction

'Bitcoin anarchy is a feature, not a bug. Sometimes it's good to have no human governance' read the headline of a recent and interesting article in Bloomberg.[1] The *leitmotiv* of the entire debate has been synthesized as follows: 'In blockchains, anarchy is the worst form of governance.'

However, this was not the first time that the now-famous cryptocurrency and the technology upon which its functioning is based, the blockchain, has been coupled with terminology taken from political philosophy, specifically that of 'anarchy'. In a public discussion that took place in February 2018, Thiel, while comparing the blockchain to another now-famous technological innovation, artificial intelligence ('AI'), declared: 'crypto is libertarian, AI is communist'.[2] In spite of their differences, 'libertarianism' and 'anarchy' agree on two points: (i) the full affirmation of individual freedom as a political end; and (ii) the elimination or reduction of the public authorities from the individual's autonomy.

The same values, come to think of it, were even invoked prior to Bitcoin's popularity. Back in 1996, Barlow warned that 'cyberspace does not lie within your borders. Do not think that you can build it, as though it were a public construction project. You cannot. It is an act of nature and it grows through our collective actions.'[3] Whilst the difficulty of regulating cyberspace (i.e. its 'unregulability') by public authorities has been debunked in the literature for some time,[4] the contemporaneous development of distributed ledger technologies has reinvigorated this declaration and caused it to assume renewed substance.

This chapter is organized as follows. Section II introduces Lessig's four modalities of regulation. Section III applies Lessig's framework to distributed ledger technologies in order to illustrate the complexity of the regulatory dynamics involved in the already complex blockchain code. Finally, in section IV, the results of the analysis are applied to a particularly topical problem in this area: the so-called single-ledger dependency due to the absence of interoperability between blockchain systems.

II. Lessig's Four Modalities of Regulation

The relationship between technology and regulation has been the object of study by jurists, science and technology studies, and sociology scholars for many years. No formula has

---

[1] Elaine Ou, 'Bitcoin's Anarchy Is a Feature, Not a Bug' (*Bloomberg*, 14 March 2018) https://www.bloomberg.com/view/articles/2018-03-14/bitcoin-blockchain-demonstrates-the-value-of-anarchy.
[2] Peter Thiel and Reid Hoffman, 'Technology and Politics' (January 2018) Conference speech, Stanford.
[3] John Perry Barlow, 'A Declaration of the Independence of Cyberspace' (Davos, 8 February 1996).
[4] See, Julie Cohen, 'Cyberspace as/and Space' (2007) 107 *Columbia Law Review*, 210; Mireille Hildebrandt, 'Extraterritorial Jurisdiction to Enforce in Cyberspace? Bodin, Schmidt, Grotius in Cyberspace' (2013) 63(2), *The University of Toronto Law Journal*, 196, 203. Goldsmith and Wu summarize the dreams of cyber-utopianism as those of self-governing cyber-communities that would escape geography forever. However, in their history of the (partial) territorialization of cyberspace, they argue that, even if geography no longer rules, national states still manage to pull the strings—or, rather, the wires. Jack Goldsmith and Tim Wu, *Who Controls the Internet? Illusions of a Borderless World* (Oxford University Press 2008).

caused as much stir among jurists as Lawrence Lessig's famous assertion that 'Code is Law',[5] according to which the technology architecture constitutes a 'form of regulation', together with state legislation, market forces, and social norms.

Indeed, the concept of technology capable of regulating is not novel. The example proposed by Winner, according to which the overpasses of the Long Island roadway system were planned by architect Robert Moses with a maximum height that prevented the transit of buses and coaches, known to be used by people of the lower classes, to Manhattan, is emblematic in this regard.[6] Thus, an engineering technology lent itself to the realization of a policy of social exclusion. In the same way, Bruno Latour affirmed the technological artefacts in some examples: speed bumps, or cars which do not start unless the seat belts are buckled, have prescriptive capacities, operating like silent traffic cops.[7] Therefore, whether technology is a complex information technology architecture or a simple functionality, it is capable of modifying and re-orienting the scope of permitted actions and, in so doing, contributes to the regulation of an individual's behaviour.[8]

However, Lessig's contribution does not end here. Rather, the biggest part of the novelty is the observation that the different modes of regulation do not operate in isolation. The interaction between architecture, law, market forces, and social norms is a property of regulation in the physical world just as it is in cyberspace. Each modality, in fact, causes two distinct effects—one direct, the other indirect. 'One is the effect of each modality on the individual being regulated i.e. how does law, for example, directly constrain an individual? How does architecture directly constrain an individual? The other is the effect of a given modality of regulation upon a second modality of regulation, an effect that, in turn, changes the effect of the second modality of individuals.'[9] A regulator acts directly when it uses just one modality; it acts indirectly when it avails itself of a second modality to pursue its own purposes.

Finally, two other points of Lessig's analysis are particularly important for our study. First, the interaction between law and architecture can be adversarial: when architecture promotes a value which conflicts with those espoused by the law, the latter may accept or reject it. Second, the greater the decentralization of the architecture, the less effective the government's power to regulate: regulating open-source software is far more difficult than regulating proprietary software.[10] Thus, the granting of property rights is fundamental to the control of behaviour, particularly in cyberspace.

III. Blockchain Regulation and Its Multiple Facets

The framework offered by Lessig is of the utmost importance in providing a comprehensive framework for distributed ledger technologies.[11] The initial studies on this subject have mainly focused on the effects that the blockchain code has introduced in the law (of contracts) and on models of governance.[12] However, these studies have ignored the action of the

---

[5] Lawrence Lessig, *Code and Other Laws of Cyberspace* (Basic Books 1990), 5.

[6] Langdon Winner, 'Do Artifacts Have Politics?' (1980), *Daedalus*, 121, 124.

[7] Bruno Latour, 'On Technical Mediation—Philosophy, Sociology, Genealogy' (1994) 3(3) *Common Knowledge*, https://philpapers.org/rec/LATOTM.

[8] Julia Black defines regulation as 'intentional attempts to manage risk or alter behavior in order to achieve some pre-specified goal': Julia Black, 'Learning from Regulatory Disasters' (2014) 24 LSE Law, Society and Economy Working Papers, http://eprints.lse.ac.uk/60569/1/WPS2014-24_Black.pdf. See also, Julia Black, 'Critical Reflections on Regulation' (2002) 27 *Australian Journal of Legal Philosophy*, 1–35.

[9] Lawrence Lessig, 'The Law of the Horse: What Cyberlaw Might Teach' (1999) 113 *Harvard Law Review*, 511.

[10] ibid., 534.

[11] Chief Scientific Adviser, 'Distributed Ledger Technology: Beyond Block Chain Report' (Crown 2016) UK Government Report, 17: 'Distributed ledgers are a type of database that is spread across multiple sites, countries or institutions, and is typically public. Records are stored one after the other in a continuous ledger, rather than sorted into blocks, but they can only be added when the participants reach a quorum.'

[12] Primavera De Filippi and Aaron Wright, *Blockchain and the Law* (Harvard University Press 2018).

other modalities, in particular those of market and social forces and their interaction with the code.

This approach result from a failure to correctly frame the nature of blockchain, to adequately account for weaknesses in the law in regulating this sector, and to guide public authorities in their regulatory actions. Blockchain code, like the law, not only modifies individual behaviour directly, but it also does so indirectly; it conditions other modalities, which, in turn, condition it. It is essential to understand the dynamics of above-mentioned interactions in order to be able to soundly regulate blockchain. In the following sections, we will isolate the reciprocal effects of the following modalities: blockchain code and the law; blockchain code and the market; and blockchain code and social norms.

A. Blockchain code and the law

Initially introduced as a technology to support the functioning of a decentralized payments system outside the brokering circuit of central banks, distributed-ledger technologies have evolved from both a quantitative and a qualitative perspective. In addition to the Bitcoin network, many other distinct blockchain systems have been developed and have gone beyond the simple transferring of funds to implementing different and/or supplementary functions.[13] Despite the passage of time, the philosophy upon which the operation of blockchain is based has remained substantially unchanged. It is a distributed database based on two core cryptography technologies seeking to ensure the validity and authenticity of transactions: (i) the public–private key cryptography for storing and spending money; and (ii) the cryptographic validation of transactions.[14] The data of past transactions is ordered in a series of 'blocks', such as in a public register, and cannot be altered except through the consensus of, at least, 50% of the blockchain nodes.[15] Cryptographic technologies can create a 'trustless' infrastructure to enable transactions:[16] the trust is directly guaranteed by the blockchain system.

The application potential of blockchain has increased with the development of modern blockchain codes. The result of the 'datafication'[17] of society is that more and more information has become available in digital format. Consequently, it has become clear that the blockchain code could be used for multiple other applications beyond money circulation.

Modern blockchain technologies make it possible to incorporate instructions into the code, thereby permitting any person to enter into contractual relations with other persons or machines. The contractual agreements are validated in a decentralized manner by the various nodes of the blockchain and are immediately and automatically executed. In practice, these agreements have been labelled 'smart contracts',[18] they simplify the organization and execution of the contract to a mere blockchain transaction. The intricacy of smart contracts can

---

[13] For a complete blockchain taxonomy, see Paolo Tasca and Claudio Tessone, '"Taxonomy of Blockchain Technologies", Principles of Identification and Classification' (31 March 2018) https://ssrn.com/abstract=2977811.

[14] Rainer Böhme, Nicolas Christin, Benjamin Edelman, and Tyler Moore, 'Bitcoin Economics, Technology, and Governance' (2015) 29(2) *Journal of Economics Perspectives*, 213.

[15] Similar characteristics apply to blockless blockchains (e.g. DAG- dependent blockchains). See Tasca and Tessone (n 13).

[16] De Filippi underlines the paradox of a 'trustless' technology, only relying on maths and cryptography, which is precisely what is needed in order to build a new form of distributed trust. Primavera De Filippi and Benjamin Loveluck, 'The Invisible Politics of Bitcoin: Governance Crisis of a Decentralised Infrastructure' (2016) 5(3) *Internet Policy Review*, 5.

[17] Sue Newell and Marco Marabelli, 'Strategic Opportunities (and Challenges) of Algorithmic Decision-Making: A Call for Action on the Long-Term Societal Effects of "Datification"' (2015) 24 *Journal of Strategic Information Systems*, 3.

[18] According to Nick Szabo, smart contracts are 'programs whose correct execution is automatically enforced without relying on a trusted authority': Nick Szabo, 'Formalizing and Securing Relationships on Public Networks' (1997) 2(9) *First Monday*, https://journals.uic.edu/ojs/index.php/fm/article/view/548/469; Melanie Swan, *Blockchain: Blueprint for a New Economy* (O'Reilly Media 2015), 16.

vary depending on the number of parties seeking to interact in complex organizations, as demonstrated by the so-called decentralized autonomous organizations ('DAO').[19]

Nowadays, the broad trend is to incorporate contractual agreements and clauses into the code. This leads to recognition in the blockchain of an authentic 'regulatory technology',[20] in the sense that it orients and modifies the behaviour of the individuals who use it in their personal capacity and in their relations with others.

The majority of legal studies have focused on the effects that blockchain technology entails for contract law.[21] In particular, the literature has noted how, unlike other technological innovations (such as digital rights management systems ('DRMs'), which impact upon legal enforcement by rendering the relevant rule self-executing),[22] the blockchain also effects the creation of the law that stems from the contract. In this respect, a new process according to which 'law is progressively turning into code' has been observed.[23] This process conditions both the modalities of negotiation and stipulation of the contract and the whole system of guarantees prescribed by the (national or international) contract law system. One may think of principles, such as *bona fide*, or institutions, such as force majeure and the hardship clause, or of vitiating factors. However, in smart contracts, because the effects of the contract are indelibly written in the relevant code the parties can easily bypass these traditionally necessary contractual safeguards.

Conversely, the law has yet to regulate the blockchain system. For example, although in the literature questions have been raised regarding the possibility of equating smart contracts with traditional contracts,[24] there have been only a few legislative interventions concerning either their qualification or the penetrating effects of this architecture on contract law. The only legislative interventions to date, with blockchains as their object, have been in relation to some categories of subjects (e.g. the promoters of an Initial Coin Offering) and assets (e.g. token) and their qualification.[25] This raises questions as to whether the law is

---

[19] A decentralized autonomous organization ('DAO') is a computer program, running on a peer-to-peer network, which incorporates governance and decision-making rules programmed to operate autonomously.

[20] The literature has extensively investigated the so-called regulatory technologies. See Jonathan Wiener, 'The Regulation of Technology and the Technology of Regulation' (2004) 26 *Technology in Society*, 483, 500; Karen Yeung, 'Towards an Understanding of Regulation by Design' in *Regulating Technologies*, edited by Roger Brownsword and Karen Yeung (Hart 2008).

[21] De Filippi and Hassan focus on smart contracts by pointing out their rate, efficiency, clarity, and ability to cut trading, monitoring, and execution contractual costs, turning traditional legal obligations into self-executive transactions. Primavera De Filippi and Samer Hassan, 'Blockchain Technology as a Regulatory Technology: From Code is Law to Law is Code' (2016) 21(12) *First Monday*, 5, http://firstmonday.org/ojs/index.php/fm/article/view/7113/5657#author.

[22] Dan L. Burk, 'Legal and Technical Standards in Digital Rights Management' (2005) 74(2) *Fordham Law Review*, 53. Graber states the difference between code and law: in the real space, law is a means of communication resulting from a political process and enacted by a constitutionally competent legislative body. The laws regulating the architecture of technology (of code) are imposed by a private actor, which leads to serious concerns from a constitutional perspective. Furthermore, code is different from law since it is self-executing. Law, instead, needs to be enforced by the state and accepted by its addressers. Christoph B. Graber, 'Internet Creativity, Communicative Freedom and a Constitutional Rights Theory Response to "Code is Law"' in *Transactional Culture in the Internet Age*, edited by Sean A. Pager and Adam Candeub (Edward Elgar 2012), 137.

[23] De Filippi and Hassan (n 21).

[24] Reggie O'Schields, 'Smart Contracts: Legal Agreements for the Blockchain' (2017) 21 *North Carolina Banking Institute*, 177.

[25] The Swiss Federal Supervisory Authority for Financial Markets ('FINMA') published a practical guide explaining how it intends to handle requests to access *initial coin offerings* in accordance with current financial market law. FINMA identifies the minimum information required to process these requests and the applicable principles, thereby rendering the process transparent to the market operators involved: https://www.finma.ch/it/news/2018/02/20180216-mm-ico-wegleitung/. Furthermore, virtual currencies are defined by European Banking Authority ('EBA') as a 'digital representation of value that is neither issued by a central bank or public authority nor necessarily attached to a fiat currency ("FC") but is used by natural or legal persons as a means of exchange and can be transferred, stored or traded electronically'. European Banking Authority, *EBA Opinion on 'virtual currencies'* (EBA/Op/2014/08), 11; Sarah Jane Hughes and Stephen T. Middlebrook, 'Advancing a Framework for Regulating Cryptocurrency Payments Intermediaries' (2015) 32 *Yale Journal*, 495.

capable of reaffirming its primacy over the blockchain system and the values it promotes, or whether it is the particular configuration of the blockchain system that exercises a certain restraint. It is useful to recall Lessig's lesson that as decentralization increases, the possibility of control decreases.

The availability of open-source blockchain software, together with the extreme fragmentation of the single nodes of the network, which is not controlled by a single well-defined entity when it comes to public blockchain, renders it difficult for public authorities to directly regulate the architecture. Even if, hypothetically speaking, public authorities decided to deprive a smart contract of legal validity, thereby removing the guarantee of its enforcement before a court of law, this would not discourage the use of the technology by the individual users. Rather, the enforcement of the contract would be ensured by the very same code by which it was enacted. Once signed, a smart contract seeks to fulfil the terms and conditions it contains because the parties, in their contractual autonomy, have previously decided to forfeit the guarantees supplied by the legal order. In this case, public authorities could seek to impose behavioural obligations on the physical persons behind the terminals but given the obvious enforcement difficulties (e.g. the controlling and sanctioning of a node failure, which could be located anywhere in the world) the blockchain system could decide to refuse them *en bloc*.

Thus, we have reached an important conclusion regarding the relationship between blockchain code and the law. In the blockchain ecosystem, the code makes changes to the law but the reverse process of the law changing the properties of the blockchain code is much more difficult to occur.

B. Blockchain code and market forces

Blockchain constitutes an ecosystem in which one may find different markets. One of the primary markets is that of 'mining' (or better that of transactions' validation): it sustains the entire blockchain code and it can only exist within completely decentralized public blockchain systems.[26] The services offered by miners consist in the resolution of complex mathematical problems required for the creation of a new, valid, and encrypted block. In return for payment, the miners offer a system-verification service.

With the increase in the popularity of Bitcoin and the development of other blockchains, new ancillary markets have subsequently emerged downstream of the mining market.[27] One of these is the market for currency exchanges. It operates like a trading platform for cryptocurrencies.

Other examples include markets for digital wallet services and those for mixing. With the development of smart contracts, yet another new market has opened up: that of decentralized applications, namely software applications that run on a peer-to-peer network of computers.[28] These are distinguished from both centralized systems, which follow a centralized server-client model, and from distributed systems, which are based on a network made up of autonomous computers connected by a middleware of distribution. The potential link to the development of blockchain applications and the opening of these new markets has brought about the emergence of the term 'blockchain as a service' to indicate the possibility

---

[26] On the distinction between public and private blockchain, see further on in this section.

[27] For a market report see, e.g., Paolo Tasca, 'Digital Currencies: Principles, Trends, Opportunities, and Risks' (7 September 2015) https://ssrn.com/abstract=2657598.

[28] Among these, Cunningham mentions Airlock, a 'next generation keyless access protocol for smart property', and Boardroom, a 'blockchain governance suite' that, among its proposed uses, includes arbitration and equity allocation to board members: Alan Cunningham, 'Decentralisation, Distrust and Fear of the Body—The Worrying Rise of Crypto-Law' (2016) 13(3) *SCRIPTed*, 235.

of making a series of applications necessary for the provision of various services, aimed at satisfying the needs of individuals, available to the public.

Even in the great diversity of the ecosystem, it is worth highlighting one distinction: on one side, there is the market, which is instrumental to the operation of the blockchain code; on the other side, there are downstream markets based on the original market. This distinction recalls two other prevalent distinctions found on the internet: (i) the distinction between the physical infrastructure to access audio-visual content and the market for audio-visual content; and (ii) the distinction between the intermediaries involved in content accessibility and the market of downstream applications. The blockchain code suffers from the same problem as that of the physical infrastructure required for access and that of the intermediaries, namely that of the non-interoperability by design. We will discuss this issue in more detail below.

Let us now consider the complex effects between the code and the market. Using Lessig's words, it can be said that the market regulates behaviour in cyberspace and it does so, for example, through prices.[29] The same occurs in blockchain: the price of mining is affected by the price of energy and it affects in turn the behaviour of the blockchain nodes; the transaction fees determine the behaviour of the network members; the elevated costs of verification of a transaction through the proof-of-work mechanism bring the miners together in mining pools; the long validation times, which are indirect costs, cause developers and users to migrate to alternative models of blockchain. In all of these cases, the market regulates the behaviour of individuals. However, Lessig has further stated that the market is only able to modify individuals' behaviour where there exists a framework of social and legal norms and that this framework is capable of influencing individuals' behaviours: reference is made to property and contract law.[30] Similar rules also exist in the blockchain ecosystem, but here they are often informed by the logic underlying the architecture of the code. The infrastructure, which supports the network within completely public blockchain systems, does not belong to anyone: given the free nature of the code, there are no inherent property rights in it. Furthermore, the asset software is freely available online and the contract is written in the language of the code, with all the limits that derive from it. The assets, cryptocurrencies, and tokens, which are stored in the system, are the network members' property but they only have value insofar as the network is capable of connecting these assets to a unique member's ID code. Finally, the contracts for transferring such assets are written in the language of the code, with all the consequences that derive from it. These circumstances have an effect on the configuration of the markets upstream and/or downstream of the ledger. For example, the mining market presents atypical rules, which differentiate it from any other type of market. The system's demand for the service does not affect prices directly; rather, it is the blockchain system that determines the miners' (future) level of retribution as the number of transactions increases. The architecture of the blockchain (i.e. the blockchain code) thus moulds the market, according to the consensus mechanisms embedded in the system. A further example is the block size limit,[31] which is inserted into the blockchain system. It limits the number of transactions that the circuit of a blockchain system can process per second; in other words, it limits the speed at which transactions can be verified and added to the chain. The size of the blocks generated large-scale debate immediately, dividing proponents and opponents on the issue of enlargement of the block size.[32] Proponents of enlargement hold that the limited capacity of the system reduces the scalability and mass adoption of the technology: Bitcoin miners would, thus, have to add additional capacity to the system, instead

---

[29] Lessig, 'The Law of the Horse' (n 9), 507.　　[30] ibid.

[31] The Bitcoin max block size limits the rate at which information is etched into the blockchain. Essentially, it acts to throttle the entire system. Jordan Clifford, 'Understanding the Block Size Debate, The Crux of the Issue' (*Medium*, 27 September 2017) https://medium.com/@jcliff/understanding-the-block-size-debate-351bdbaaa38.

[32] De Filippi and Loveluck (n 16), 7.

of being bound to a certain production quota. Conversely, opponents to enlargement argue that this would cause decentralization which, in turn, would raise the miners' costs of participation in the market, and thereby erect a barrier to entry.

Also, a particular rule of the system which opposes the miners' contractual freedom to offer more efficient services would impact upon markets downstream of the ledger, which are structurally dependent upon the operation of the upstream system. Thus, the code influences individuals' behaviour and the markets' functioning; it redefines proprietary and contractual concepts. However, it is not possible to find any direct effect of the market on the code. The market limits itself to regulating individual behaviour: any change in the code underlying a particular market is mediated through the intervention of social forces external to the code.

C. Blockchain code and social forces

The qualification of blockchain as a complex ecosystem also accounts for the fundamental role played by the social forces involved into the promotion of a project (founders, developers, and users), which eventually decide the internal operational and organizational rules. From the very beginning, these social forces have accompanied, and continue to accompany the development of any single blockchain system.

Generally, each project begins with the study and presentation of a White Paper by their promoters.[33] The White Paper commonly results from a process of creative debate within a community or group of diverse people in a forum or in another circle or physical place. It illustrates the founders' vision regarding the function of the new blockchain and how this specific blockchain could contribute to a particular social purpose. The White Paper also contains technical information regarding the specific protocol, the internal rules that the software follows, specific security measures, its scope, scalability, roadmaps, and other information. In some cases, the White Paper may contain rules concerning community involvement and/or rules concerning the system's internal governance;[34] in other cases, the rules may not be expressly written down but are premised upon informal mechanisms.

However, in each case, it is the overall community that defines the rules of the system by embedding them into the code.

However, what is peculiar is that within each individual blockchain system there exists not one but two types of rules: those that inform the operation of the system (i.e. the rules which structure the consensus network topology, the transaction capabilities, the security and privacy, etc.) and those that define how the first type of rules can be changed. This is reminiscent of the distinction developed by Hart to describe the essence of the law on the distinction between primary and secondary rules.[35]

The identification of these two types of rules helps to understand the reciprocal interactions between the code and social forces. Take as an example of the first kind of rule the principles embedded in the consensus mechanism. These principles shape the operation of the blockchain system: in fact, blockchain verification is managed on the basis of consent between multiple nodes. These rules are entered into the code and impose a certain structure on a specific system. From this structure derives a (actually, more than one) certain obligation upon all the members of the community: for example, this obligation could be to keep copies of the previous transaction blocks in one's own terminal and to permit the verification to only happen in the case where 50% or more of the nodes have consented

---

[33] The most famous is certainly Satoshi Nakamoto, 'Bitcoin: A Peer-to-Peer Electronic Cash System' White Paper.

[34] The concept of corporate governance is defined within the Cadbury Report as 'the system by which companies are directed and controlled'. Committee on the Financial Aspects of Corporate Governance, 'Report of the Committee on the Financial Aspects of Corporate Governance' (1992).

[35] Herbert L. A. Hart, *The Concept of Law* (first published 1961; Oxford University Press, 2002), 87.

to it. In any case, it is the matter of an obligation entered in the code by a programmer or by a company in response to one political end or another: for example, to decentralize or centralize the control. Thus, in relation to the chosen architecture of the distributed consensus mechanism, three different categories of blockchain systems can be distinguished: public (i.e. permission-less), private (i.e. permissioned), and consortium. The public category allows all nodes to participate in the consensus mechanism. Conversely, in the consortium category, access and participation in the consensus mechanism is granted exclusively to specific pre-chosen nodes (partially decentralized structure). In the middle of these two categories lies the private category in which access and participation in the consensus mechanism is only granted to certain nodes from specific organizations that control the network (centralized structure). Acceptance of the obligations by an individual occurs at the moment in which he adheres to the system and its rules and becomes a part of the community.

Upon becoming a member of the community each node is not necessarily confined to a system whose rules were set by others; rather, in certain cases it may contribute to their modification. This governance possibility derives from the existence of a second nucleus of (possibly informal) rules that are either based on consensus or have been written into the code. These so-called governance rules can establish, for example, the process to implement the protocol, the process to upgrade the system, or the process to change the internal coordination of the nodes. In turn, these rules directly affect the interaction dynamics between participants in the network; indirectly, they affect the content of the system's operating rules. Governance models which are more participative will tend to shape operating rules in a way that responds to the interests of a larger range of members.

In general, two alternative models of governance can be contrasted here.[36] On the one hand, there are the so-called informal models of governance (e.g. Bitcoin, Ethereum). On the other hand, more complex systems of governance have emerged, the so-called 'on-chain' models (e.g. EOS, NEO). The first model[37] provides for the participation of a nucleus of developers who formulate the proposals for protocol amendments and to whom the duty of obtaining the stakeholders' consensus (that of the miners, those very same developers and the relevant users) is assigned. Once established, this mechanism effectively acts as a self-reinforcing cycle that concentrates power in the hands of a small group of people, often to the detriment of others, who are sometimes forced to get out of the system by breaking the main blockchain: this is the so-called 'hard fork'. The second governance model differs from the first for two reasons. First, its voting procedures are open to all coin holders thereby rendering the system more democratic. Second, the result of the vote is directly incorporated into and implemented by the system. The system is able to automatically execute the decision made by the majority of votes cast. Without entering into a detailed analysis of the various models, it is necessary to emphasize the following point in relation to the architecture of the blockchain system. On the one side, the architecture of the blockchain system is the result of the interaction of social forces and markets external to the system, both of which serve to shape the operating rules and rules of governance. On the other side, the architecture of the blockchain system affects upstream social forces: the more the code provides models of participative and open governance, the less it is likely that a hard fork will result, even in the case of a disagreement within the network.[38]

---

[36] Vitalik Buterin, 'Notes on Blockchain Governance' (*Vitalik Buterin's website*, 17 December 2017), https://vitalik.ca/general/2017/12/17/voting.html.

[37] O' Neil referred to Bitcoin governance as a form of domination based on charismatic authority: Mathieu O'Neil, 'Hacking Weber: Legitimacy, Critique, and Trust in Peer Production' (2014) 17(7) *Information, Communication and Society*, 872.

[38] Odysseas Sclavounis, 'Understanding Public Blockchain Governance' (*Oxford Internet Institute*, 17 November 2017) https://www.oii.ox.ac.uk/blog/understanding-public-blockchain-governance/.

D. Law, market, and social forces

To sum up this discussion, the blockchain code, as opposed to any other type of code, demonstrates a far more powerful regulatory capacity and capability to resist the influence of other modalities. The blockchain code regulates the behaviour of individuals directly—substituting itself for the law—but, at the same time, it has relevant effects on the other modalities. Not only does the code influence the modalities of interaction between the participants to the network (i.e. social forces or norms), but it also influences the market dynamics that inform the functioning of the system (i.e. market forces). At the same time, the decentralized nature of the architecture makes the blockchain code particularly impervious to the direct effects of the law. The only social forces capable of impacting upon its way of being stem from within: they highlight new internal mechanisms capable of limiting the 'power' of the code.

The above necessitates a reflection on the role of the law and of the public authorities. The code does not only pose a problem for the public authorities insofar as it cancels that entire system of guarantees provided by the law of contracts; it also structures the dynamics of multiple markets upstream and/or downstream of the ledger.

Hence, possible distortive effects on the market, due to the architecture, could become a public policy problem, which could call the regulator into question. It is in this case that the particular decentralized and closed-off 'organization' of the system weakens the impact of public action. In particular, the difficulty for the public authorities lies in the fact that the technological architecture appears to be conceptually inseparable at the functional level from the network of individuals who organize it and who, at the same time, contribute to its modification.[39] Therefore, if it is true that the public authorities can indirectly regulate the architecture in any case by exploiting the market, it is also true that each modification to the same architecture must be approved by the community. This happens through those mechanisms of governance, whether informal or formalized in the code, which regulate their co-existence. In other words, the community becomes the filter for any changes to the code.

IV. Interoperability and Distributed Ledger Technologies

A. Interoperability at a glance

We have observed the complex blockchain ecosystem in light of the framework offered by Lawrence Lessig so far. At this point the framework shall be analysed in order to consider a further concept into which research literature has not yet delved but which is essential for the future and full development of the ecosystem: interoperability among distributed-ledger technologies. Understood as a technical and economic concept, 'interoperability' can be defined as the capacity of a system, product, or service to communicate and function together (that is, to be compatible) with other systems, products, or services which are technically different.[40] This interoperability is the result of a series of choices that depend on the type of good or service and on the underlying market dynamics. In fact, there are existing goods and/or services that have no value if consumed individually but do, and only, generate value if and when they are combined with other products or services. For example, consider telecommunication or social media services. For them, the market is characterized by positive network externalities, i.e. the utility that a consumer gets from the relevant certain good or service is proportional to the number of other consumers benefitting from the

[39] ibid.
[40] Wolfgang Kerber and Heike Schweitzer, 'Interoperability in the Digital Economy' (2012), Marburg Centre for Institutional Economics Paper 2/2017, 3, https://www.uni-marburg.de/fb02/makro/forschung/magkspapers/paper_2017/12-2017_kerber.pdf.

same good or service. Katz and Shapiro distinguish two types of network externalities: direct and indirect. The former depends on the number of consumers who benefit from the same product or service; the latter depends on the increase in goods and services which are complementary to the first, thereby increasing its value.[41] The nature of interoperability or non-interoperability of a good or service is the result of a strategic choice by a company in the market. Companies with larger networks tend to offer goods or services that are incompatible (i.e. non-interoperable) with the goods and services of competing undertakings. These companies do this to maintain their dominant position and to exploit direct network externalities. Conversely, companies with smaller networks seek to produce technologies that are highly compatible with other products or services (i.e. interoperable) in order to exploit the possible indirect network externalities.

B. Blockchain non-interoperability

The current blockchain architecture is not interoperable. Each blockchain system is closed off to its surrounding environment and does not communicate with other systems. This condition restricts the potential of the blockchain so that it operates only within the one relevant blockchain system: any member's transactions of a specific blockchain system, for example Bitcoin, are only recognized by other members of the same system. For members of any other system, for example Ethereum, there is no trace on the Ethereum blockchain of that specific transaction on the Bitcoin blockchain system; it is as if the transaction had never occurred and, thus, it has no binding force within its own (i.e. within the Ethereum) system.

There are multiple reasons for the lack of interoperability. Although a blockchain system is hard to compare to a company, due to the absence of unified management and coordination, all of the subjects which form a part of it are motivated by individual reasons and so conduct themselves opportunistically. Developers and miners of a certain blockchain system seek to maximize (market) profits.

Each individual's behaviour is guided by the expectation that enlarging the network will cause a correlated increase in both its value and in the monetary assets (i.e. tokens) held in the system. At the same time, the user's choice to enter into one blockchain system over another often significantly depends upon the relevant user's expectations regarding the future breadth of the network. Project developers and promoters are then motivated by the desire to maintain or increase their own political power within the system. They organize the system's architecture in pursuance of a specific aim, they work hard to promote the project and, as holders of top-level positions in the internal governance, they will adopt any measure to keep such. All of these factors make it disadvantageous for members of a specific blockchain to make their ledgers interoperable with other ledgers.

Apart from the absence of economic incentives, there is another rationale which discourages the adoption of the same protocol by two separate blockchain systems: the lack of trust among network members of different infrastructures. As we have seen, each blockchain system is made up of an infrastructure of nodes, which corresponds to a network of persons. Given that transactions are verified through the interaction of nodes, the network performs an essential function for the operation of the infrastructure: it is solely reliant on itself and the nodes comprising it. In this sense, interoperability would contradict the system's operating rules. The above discussion leads to the following conclusion: the interoperability of the ledger, beyond being a technical impossibility, results from a series of intentional choices to defend a given blockchain system and from its operating dynamics. Thus, the ledger is non-interoperable.

---

[41] Michael L. Katz and Carl Shapiro, 'Network Externalities, Competition and Compatibility' (1985) 75(3), *American Economic Review*, 424.

With the non-interoperability of the blockchain framed as a social problem, which finds its emergence point in the code, we must now concentrate on the effects that this limitation in the blockchain architecture has on the law and the market.

In relation to the effects of the non-interoperability on the law, the following examples should be considered. David may want to enter into a service agreement with Alice by which he pays to Alice a monthly fee (in ETH on Ethereum network) in exchange for having access to some data stored in the Bitcoin network by Alice. Or, for example, Charlie may want to lend money (in ETH) to Bob under the condition that Bob will pledge as collateral an asset registered in the Bitcoin network. Or simply, Alice, Bob, David, and Charlie may want to exchange private information recorded on different blockchains.

For various reasons, 'any information, goods and value [for] which (unencrypted, encrypted or hashed) data is tracked and stored in a blockchain system could become of interest to other people (or applications) outside that system'. And for various reasons, an individual could be interested that such information is recognized and validated by the system of which it forms a part. For instance, a protocol could be the only one to have implemented a certain feature or, for security and trust reasons, a party could be uninterested in entering the blockchain system of its contractual counterparty. However, in the absence of interoperability between protocols, these rules of interest cannot be achieved. In this sense, the non-interoperability of the protocols neither responds to the needs of international commerce nor does it bolster the principle of contractual autonomy. In fact, individuals can only subscribe to the contractual models permitted by the applications developed for, and on the basis of, a specific ledger. Only those typical agreements defined in the ledger protocol, by its developers, have citizenship in the relevant environment.

In relation to the impact upon the market, non-interoperability could strengthen technological lock-ins and could block the competitive and prosperous development of a market for the downstream applications of the ledger. The problem is similar to the one tackled by the supporters of net-neutrality,[42] who have fought against differential internet speed over the past several years. In that case, the subject of debate was the discriminatory behaviour of the internet service providers ('ISPs') in relation to the content services of the downstream market of the physical accessibility infrastructure. Through complex traffic management practices, ISPs tended to block or slow down competing services as opposed to the traditional communications services offered by their own business divisions. This behaviour was justified by the need to guarantee the content quality given the infrastructure's limited capacity. However, it caused harm to new market entrants who were not willing to pay for traffic prioritization. Once legislators recognized the principle of net neutrality and intervened,[43] the debate shifted to the discriminatory practices of the over-the-top media services that adopted non-interoperable standards with the potential to damage competition on the market.[44] Similarly, the non-interoperability among ledgers, in the case where this results in

---

[42] According to Tim Wu: 'Network neutrality is best defined as a design principle. The idea is that a maximally useful public information network aspires to treat all content, sites, and platforms equally': Tim Wu, 'Network Neutrality: Broadband Discrimination' (2003) 2 *Journal of Telecommunications and High Technology Law*, 141; According to Suzanne Crawford, "*A neutral Internet must forward packets on a first-come, first served basis, without regard for QoS considerations*": Suzanne P. Crawford, 'Transporting Communications' (2009) 89 *Boston University Law Review*, 871.

[43] Regulation (EU) 2015/2120 of the European Parliament and of the Council of 25 November 2015 laying down measures concerning open internet access and amending Directive 2002/22/EC on universal service and users' rights relating to electronic communications networks and services and Regulation (EU) No. 531/2012 on roaming on public mobile communications networks within the Union.

[44] José Marino García, Aurelia Valiño Castro, and Antonio Jesús Sánchez Fuentes, 'Price Discrimination of OTT Providers under Duopolistic Competition and Multi-Dimensional Product Differentiation in Retail Broadband Access' (2017) Public Economics, Governance and Decentralization Paper 1607, Universidade de Vigo, Governance and Economics Research Network ('GERN') https://econpapers.repec.org/paper/govwpaper/1607.htm.

the emergence of a dominant system capable of raising the standards would prejudice the natural development of the market of underlying applications, thereby damaging innovation.

C. Technical and business solutions hold complex social, economic, and legal implications

Since the outset, the problem of non-interoperability in blockchain has divided developers and influential individuals of the industry. Three alternative solutions have been advanced. Some base their force on the power of a particular community or market operator, others on the development of the code.

The first approach is proposed by the likes of Ethereum Enterprise Alliance[45] and Hyperledger Fabric,[46] which advocate that a dominant blockchain will take over the others and that different networks will be run on top of this blockchain. These enterprises aim to offer blockchain-as-a-service ('BaaS') applications for the industry and, although differing in their business approaches, promote a specific protocol.

The second method offers a network approach to link any two different blockchains via new, 'intermediate' blockchains that—thanks to special nodes and adapters—create a bridge between them at the 'transaction level'. Wanchain, Cosmos, Polkadot,[47] and AION are examples of this model. With respect to the first model, this second model favours the creation of a new technological architecture in third position, supported by its own community and by a new market: that of intermediary blockchain systems for inter-ledger communications.

A third alternative method is based on a layer approach. It connects different blockchains at the application level, instead of the transaction level, by decoupling the business logic from the underlying ledger. In this case, there is no need to route the information across ledgers, since all the ledgers are directly connected in the application layer. The information is retrieved from different ledgers, standardized and grouped in a 'message layer', then ordered in a 'filtering and ordering layer'. A blockchain program interface defines the rules, set by blockchain B user, for blockchain A user to follow in order to read and/or write messages in/from blockchain B without the need of intermediate blockchains. Overledger[48] by Quant Network is an example of this type of blockchain operating system. Unlike the first and second models, this approach did not come about in order to promote or create a specific blockchain infrastructure, but to offer particular types of software applications which make interoperability possible downstream of the ledger.

All these solutions present issues of an economic, legal, and/or social nature.

(The first solution to the issue of non-interoperability is unconvincing for two reasons. First, it is doubtful that a single blockchain can gain significant enough levels of traction with firms so to impose itself above all other competitors. In fact, as far as the network effects of a given blockchain system are concerned, the infrastructure upon which they rely is not only comprised of telephone wires and trellises, as in the case of telecommunications, but of natural persons who could, for opportunistic reasons, decide to exit the network and develop their own blockchain systems. This is possible due to low costs concerning the reproduction of the code and the code's high level of malleability and adaptability. For example, if half the Ethereum nodes decided to substitute the Ethereum protocol with another protocol in a

---

[45] Ethereum Enterprise Alliance, 'Introduction and Overview' (*Ethereum Enterprise Alliance* February 2017) https://entethalliance.org/wp content/themes/ethereum/img/intro-eea.pdf.

[46] Hyperledger Architecture, Volume II, (*Hyperledger*) https://www.hyperledger.org/.

[47] Polkadot Whitepaper (*Polkadot*) https://github.com/w3f/polkadot-white-paper.

[48] Gilbert Verdian, Paolo Tasca, Colin Paterson and Gaetano Mondelli, 'Quant Overledger ®' (*Quant*, 18 January 2018) https://objects-us-west-1.dream.io/files.quant.network/Quant_Overledger_Whitepaper_v0.1.pdf.

very short time period, the Ethereum chain would break in the same way as it did when the hard fork emerged from the Ethereum Classic. The possibility of this happening is inversely proportional to the degree to which internal governance is centralized but, in any case, revolutions can happen. For this reason, it is difficult for one particular protocol to impose itself as the de facto standard.

The second reason is that, even in the case where a specific system manages to autonomously gain a prevalent ledger position, the competition of the downstream market could be jeopardized. As set forth in section IV.B ('Blockchain non-interoperability'), the internal governance of a given system could decide to favour certain applications over others, to the latter's disadvantage. This is a real problem when one considers that both the Ethereum Enterprise Alliance and the Linux Foundation are legal entities with their own governing bodies, within which there are large stakeholders operating in various sectors. Given the network's limited capacity, due to the long-standing problem of scalability, it is not so unrealistic to imagine that some applications would end up being treated differently by the system. Consequently, that specific dominant infrastructure could risk assuming a gatekeeper's position for access to the market underlying the applications. In any case, whether a given system can become dominant and whether this hypothetical imposition can cause prejudices in the downstream markets will depend, for the most part, on the internal governance rules adopted.

The second solution provided is equally unconvincing. There are essentially two reasons for this. First, the same problems that plague the first solution would also arise here: given the lack of entry barriers, many blockchain systems could emerge, causing the fragmentation of the market; even where, for example, Polkadot imposed itself above the others, this situation would foster abuse in the downstream markets and—unlike the first solution— also in the upstream markets. In addition to discrimination in the application layer, for instance, Polkadot could decide to communicate with Ethereum and not do so with NEO, which has always been considered to be a similar blockchain system in terms of the application potential that allows the implementation, and this would unjustifiably damage the latter system to the former system's advantage. Second, this would raise the issue of how to build people's trust in the system. The problem of trust is extremely topical in markets characterized by imbalances of information and, for this reason, it arises also in the area of contractual interactions between parties belonging to different blockchain systems. This is because a member of a given blockchain code tends to know and trust only his own system: another system could, in fact, reveal security leaks or bugs in the code and, therefore, fail to guarantee a positive outcome in the transaction. This lack of trust would then be exacerbated by the existence of specific, and often complex, rules of governance of the intermediary system, which may or may not be shared by the member in another system. Polkadot uses a governance system based on the stakeholders' vote and on the principle of majority decision-making. Decision-making powers are granted to a specific body, the 'Board', an on-chain entity whose members are elected through an approval procedure and which shall propose referendums capable of affecting the system and thus, also single transactions.

The third solution provides an interesting compromise between the need to make persons, machines, or goods with citizenship in two different systems interact and the need to avoid that this must necessarily occur through the use of a particular blockchain infrastructure. To use an analogy, the Overledger software offered by Quant Network seeks to replicate for blockchain systems that have been done by Java Virtual Machine ('JVM') for software. Just as JVM operates as an interpreter for Java applications and allows their programmers to disregard the underlying operating system, Overledger aims to make the specificities of a given blockchain system neutral for all applications offering interledger services. This approach has the advantage of freeing up the entire potential of the blockchain to the application layer without requiring members to adhere to the operating and governance rules of a specific dominant, or intermediary, blockchain system. In other words, the user chooses the blockchain ecosystem in which it wishes to live and Overledger acts as a bridge between the two or more relevant ecosystems. Given the absolute neutrality of the software with respect to the overlying layer and the important linking function between networks, this solution limits the network effects of a system and possible situations of technological lock-in whilst favouring innovation and downstream market competition. For these reasons, it is believed that it can be favourably considered in blockchain systems, above all of those that are less popular and cannot boast an extensive network. In any case, as the debate on network neutrality has shown, market limitations can also happen through traditional over-the-top media services, acting as gatekeepers. This is certainly possible if an innovative technology develops to become the standard that is protected by intellectual property rights. Consequently, public authorities should keep a cautious eye on this solution.

V. Conclusion: The Paradox of Interoperability

The issue of interoperability cannot be construed as a simple technical and economic problem. It constitutes the point where tension between three distinct ways of being for the blockchain, which is intended as a regulatory technology, economic infrastructure, and model of social organization, emerges. These three concepts give rise to a fusion in the code that, just like a relentless dog with three heads, ends up structuring not only the technical operating rules of the system, but also the possibilities of interaction between members of the system, the logic of the underlying markets, and the social norms which guide the functioning of the community.

In Greek mythology, Cerberus monitored the underworld to stop the living from entering and the dead from leaving. Similarly, the blockchain code not only demarcates the impassable frontier between cyberspace and the real world but also that between the different blockchain systems. Hence, the idea of interoperability between ledgers gives rise to a paradox: that of trying to make two or more socio-technical-economic constructs communicate with each other, despite the fact that they were built by different communities to function as independent systems that do not communicate with each other. It would be wrong to reduce the interoperability between blockchain systems to a mere problem of standards. It is preferable to consider it a problem of reciprocal recognition between sovereign powers in their own space. Unlike the internet, where interconnection has always been a need of the entire cyberspace population, while it was the market that gave rise to monopolies, in blockchain the social forces exercise power in the opposite way, towards the closure and independence of their own system. This is reflected in initiatives that have thus far emerged to circumvent the problem of non-interoperability: they range from the emergence of a single prevalent system, to the affirmation of intermediary blockchain systems, to the adoption of a middleware software able to serve as an intermediary vessel for communication. All three models present solutions in line with the structural closure of the systems. To make an analogy with well-known concepts of international law: the first approach recalls the idea of a military conquest of one order over another; the second resembles the institution of a third-party organization which allows dialogue among equals; and the third is based on a principle similar to that of mutual recognition of the rules of different entities. The analogy is not so absurd, particularly in the case where one considers the internal limiting mechanisms present in one single system and the legal impacts of the non-interoperability among different networks. The game has already begun and it is still too early to say which of the three approaches will prevail. Public authorities will assist in the comparison from the side lines and sharpen the weapons for what promises to be not just a corrective action of the market but a true and actual fight between sovereign powers.

VI. Bibliography

Akins Benjamin, Chapman Jennifer L., and Gordon Jason, 'The Case for the Regulation of Bitcoin Mining as a Security' (2015) 19 *Virginia Journal of Law and Technology*, 669.

Black Julia, "Critical Reflections on Regulation" (2002) 27 *Australian Journal of Legal Philosophy*, 1.

Black Julia, 'Learning from Regulatory Disasters' (2014) 24 LSE Law, Society & Economy Working Papers.

Böhme Rainer, Christin Nicolas, Edelman Benjamin, and Moore Tyler, 'Bitcoin Economics, Technology, and Governance' (2015) 29(2) *Journal of Economics Perspectives*, 213.

Burk Dan L., 'Legal and Technical Standards in Digital Rights Management' (2005) 74(2) *Fordham Law Review*, 537.

Buterin Vitalik, 'Notes on Blockchain Governance' (Vitalik Buterin's Website, 17 December 2017) https://vitalik.ca/general/2017/12/17/voting.html, accessed on 8 January 2019.

Chief Scientific Adviser, 'Distributed Ledger Technology: Beyond Block Chain' (Crown 2016) UK Government Report.

Cohen Julie, 'Cyberspace as/and Space' (2007) 107 *Columbia Law Review*, 210

Clifford Jordan, 'Understanding the Block Size Debate, The Crux of the Issue' (*Medium*, 27 September 2017) https://medium.com/@jcliff/understanding-the-block-size-debate 351bdbaaa38, accessed on 8 January 2019.

Committee on the Financial Aspects of Corporate Governance, 'Report of the Committee on the Financial Aspects of Corporate Governance' (1992).

Crawford Suzanne P., 'Transporting Communications' (2009) 89 *Boston University Law Review*, 871.

Cunningham Alan, 'Decentralisation, Distrust and Fear of the Body —The Worrying Rise of Crypto-Law' (2016) 13(3) *SCRIPTed*, 235.

De Filippi Primavera and Hassan Samer, 'Blockchain Technology as a Regulatory Technology: From Code is Law to Law is Code' (2016) 21(12) *First Monday*, http://firstmonday.org/ojs/index.php/fm/article/view/7113/5657#author, accessed on 8 January 2019.

De Filippi Primavera and Loveluck Benjamin, 'The Invisible Politics of Bitcoin: Governance Crisis of a Decentralised Infrastructure' (2016) 5(3) *Internet Policy Review*, 1.

Ethereum Enterprise Alliance, 'Introduction and Overview' (*Ethereum Enterprise Alliance* February 2017) https://entethalliance.org/wp content/themes/ethereum/img/intro-eea.pdf, accessed 8 January 2019.

European Central Bank (ECB), 'Virtual Currencies Schemes—a Further Analysis' (2015), ECB Report.

García José Mario, Valiño Aurelia, Castro Antonio, and Sánchez Fuentes Jesús, 'Price Discrimination of OTT Providers under Duopolistic Competition and Multi-Dimensional Product Differentiation in Retail Broadband Access' (2017) Public Economics, Governance and Decentralization Paper 1607, Universidade de Vigo, Governance and Economics Research Network ('GERN') https://econpapers.repec.org/paper/govwpaper/1607.htm, accessed on 8 January 2019.

Gilbert Verdian, Paolo Tasca, Colin Paterson, and Gaetano Mondelli, 'Quant Overledger ®' (*Quant*, 18 January 2018) https://objects-us-west-1.dream.io/files.quant.network/Quant_Overledger_Whitepaper_v0.1.pdf, accessed 8 January 2019.

Goldsmith Jack and Wu Tim, *Who Controls the Internet? Illusions of a Borderless World* (Oxford University Press 2008).

Graber Christoph B., 'Internet Creativity, Communicative Freedom and a Constitutional Rights Theory Response to "Code is Law"' in *Transactional Culture in the Internet Age*, edited by Sean A. Pager and Adam Candeub (Edward Elgar Publishing 2012).

Hart Herbert L.A, *The Concept of Law* (first published 1961; Oxford University Press 2002).

Hildebrandt Mireille, 'Extraterritorial Jurisdiction to Enforce in Cyberspace? Bodin, Schmidt, Grotius in Cyberspace' (2013) 63(2) *The University of Toronto Law Journal*.

Hughes Sarah Jane and Middlebrook Stephen T., 'Advancing a Framework for Regulating Cryptocurrency Payments Intermediaries' (2015) 32 *Yale Journal*, 196.

Hyperledger Architecture, Volume II, (*Hyperledger*) https://www.hyperledger.org/, accessed on 8 January 2019.

Katz Michael L. and Shapiro Carl, '"Network Externalities", Competition and Compatibility' (1985) 75(3) *American Economic Review*, 424.

Kerber Wolfgang and Schweitzer Heike, 'Interoperability in the Digital Economy' (2012) Marburg Centre for Institutional Economics Paper 2/2017, 3, https://www.uni-marburg.de/fb02/makro/forschung/magkspapers/paper_2017/12-2017_kerber.pdf, accessed on 8 January 2019.

Kroll Joshua A., Davey Ian C., and Felten Edward W., 'The Economics of Bitcoin Mining, or Bitcoin in the Presence of Adversaries' (2013), *Proceedings of WEIS*, 1.

Latour Bruno, 'On Technical Mediation—Philosophy, Sociology, Genealogy' (1994) 3(3) *Common Knowledge*, 29 https://philpapers.org/rec/LATOTM, accessed on 8 January 2019.

Lessig Lawrence, *Code and Other Laws of Cyberspace* (Basic Books 1990).

Lessig Lawrence, 'The Law of the Horse: What Cyberlaw Might Teach' (1999) 113 *Harvard Law Review*, 501.

Newell Sue, Marabelli Marco, 'Strategic Opportunities (and Challenges) of Algorithmic Decision-Making: A Call for Action on the Long-Term Societal Effects of "datification"' (2015) 24 *Journal of Strategic Information Systems*, 3.

O'Neil Mathieu L., 'Hacking Weber: Legitimacy, Critique, and Trust in Peer Production' (2014) 17(7) *Information, Communication and Society*, 873.

O'Schields Reggie, 'Smart Contracts: Legal Agreements for the Blockchain' (2017) 21 *North Carolina Banking Institute*, 177.

Ou Elaine, 'Bitcoin's Anarchy Is a Feature, Not a Bug' (Bloomberg, 14 March 2018) https://www.bloomberg.com/view/articles/2018-03-14/bitcoin-blockchain-demonstrates-the-value-of-anarchy, accessed on 8 January 2019.

Polkadot Whitepaper (*Polkadot*) https://github.com/w3f/polkadot-white-paper, accessed 8 January 2019.

Samaniego Mayra and Deters Ralph, 'Blockchain as a Service for IoT' (2016) IEEE International Conference on Internet of Things (iThings) and IEEE Green Computing and Communications (GreenCom) and IEEE Cyber, Physical and Social Computing (CPSCom) and IEEE Smart Data (SmartData).

Satoshi Nakamoto, 'Bitcoin: A Peer-to-Peer Electronic Cash System' White Paper.

Sclavounis Odysseas, 'Understanding Public Blockchain Governance' (*Oxford Internet Institute*, 17 November 2017) https://www.oii.ox.ac.uk/blog/understanding-public-blockchain-governance/, accessed on 8 January 2019.

Swan Melanie, *Blockchain: Blueprint for a New Economy* (O'Reilly Media 2015).

Szabo Nick, 'Formalizing and Securing Relationships on Public Networks' (1997) 2(9) *First Monday*, https://journals.uic.edu/ojs/index.php/fm/article/view/548/469, accessed on 8 January 2019.

Tasca Paolo, 'Digital Currencies: Principles, Trends, Opportunities, and Risks' (7 September 2015) https://ssrn.com/abstract=2657598, accessed on 8 January 2019.

Tasca Paolo and Tessone Claudio, '"A Taxonomy of Blockchain Technologies". Principles of Identification and Classification' Ledger, [S.l.], v. 4, (February 2019) ISSN 2379-5980. http://ledger.pitt.edu/ojs/index.php/ledger/article/view/140/117, accessed on 25 March 2019. doi:https://doi.org/10.5195/ledger.2019.140.

Thiel Peter and Hoffman Reid, 'Technology and Politics' (January 2018) conference speech, Stanford.

Yeung Karen, 'Towards an Understanding of Regulation by Design' in *Regulating Technologies*, edited by Roger Brownsword and Karen Yeung (Hart 2008).

Winner Langdon, 'Do Artifacts Have Politics?' (1980) 109(1) *Daedalus* 121.

Wu Tim, 'Network Neutrality: Broadband Discrimination' (2003) 2 *Journal of Telecommunications and High Technology Law*, 141.

2

Blockchains, Private Ordering, and the Future of Governance

Jonathan Rohr and Aaron Wright

I. Introduction

In the ten years that have passed since the first bitcoins were mined, blockchain's potential to revolutionize banking, finance, and commerce has brought the technology into the mainstream. However, its promise does not stop with these payment-focused applications. With its ability to facilitate consensus within a group, blockchain provides new ways to coordinate a variety of interactions, commercial and non-commercial, between and among a large number of dispersed parties. This application of blockchain technology—the facilitation of group consensus—offers new ways to address the challenges of organizing and coordinating profit-seeking enterprises and holds out the possibility of fundamentally changing the means through which firms are governed. Governance, which was once the province of boards of directors, charters, bylaws, operating agreements, shareholder meetings, voting by proxy etc., can be incorporated into code and implemented automatically by the members of the blockchain network. Rather than just relying on traditional governance methods and mechanisms, organizers and promoters of business enterprises can now rely on code-based governance mechanisms for the management and coordination of their enterprises.

Blockchain's potential to change the way organizations are governed touches on both the familiar and unfamiliar. With regard to enterprises that are housed within traditional business organizations, smart contracts can be implemented to operationalize many current governance mechanisms. Blockchain-based voting systems, for example, can be implemented as a mechanism for conducting shareholder votes, by either streamlining the traditional system of shareholder voting by proxy or potentially eliminating the need for proxies at all. At the same time, blockchains allow people to organize and coordinate on a peer-to-peer basis in unprecedented ways. As the recent explosion of blockchain-based token sales or initial coin offerings ('ICOs') demonstrates, traditional entities are no longer viewed as a strict necessity for many entrepreneurs raising capital. These token sales involve the sale of blockchain-based tokens to the public as a way to raise funds for the development of new software applications, networks, and platforms. Rather than form a corporation, limited liability company (LLC), or other recognized form of business association to house their new enterprises, some organizers of token-based projects are opting to form loose associations with fellow software developers and technologists. Others are increasingly exploring an entirely new species of organization, 'decentralized organizations', in which governance is achieved through a set of blockchain-based smart contracts that are executed by the nodes of a blockchain's network. Teams sell blockchain-based tokens to members of the public to raise the funding needed to develop the project, and those tokens are coupled with smart contracts to bestow a variety of rights on their holders, including, in many instances, the right to use the platform or software that is under development.[1]

---

[1] Jonathan Rohr and Aaron Wright, 'Blockchain-Based Token Sales, Initial Coin Offerings, and the Democratization of the Public Capital Markets' (2018) 70 *Hastings Law Journal* (forthcoming), https://papers.ssrn.com/sol3/papers.cfm?abstract_id=3048104.

In what is perhaps the most high-profile example of an ICO involving a decentralized organization, an 'investor directed venture capital fund', confusingly named 'The Decentralized Autonomous Organization' ('DAO'), raised over $150 million worth of ether through the sale of blockchain-based tokens in 2016.[2] As a venture capital fund, its business was investment. However, unlike a traditional venture capital fund, participation in the DAO's investment decisions was not limited to a small number of upper- level managers. Instead, investment decisions were put to a vote of the holders of DAO tokens. Each token entitled its holder to participate in determining how the funds raised by the DAO would be invested. Broadly, tech developers seeking funding for a project could apply to the DAO for the funding for a project and, provided certain requirements were met (including approval by a group of individuals known as 'curators'), the funding decision was put to a vote of the holders of DAO tokens. If a sufficient number of tokens voted to fund a project, smart contracts transferred virtual currency from the DAO account to the account specified by the developer whose project was approved. The DAO was to receive a percentage of any income generated by the projects it funded.[3] The DAO had a short life—vulnerabilities in its code led to the theft of approximately one-third of the cryptocurrency it raised and then to its winding up.[4] But, the DAO and other decentralized organizations show that blockchain-based governance that does not rely on traditional business entities is possible. Could it be that we are witnessing the beginning of the end for traditional business associations and the governance arrangements we associate with them?

This chapter considers the future of traditional organizational forms in a world of blockchain-based governance. Despite the apparent threat that blockchain-based governance poses to the need for traditional business entities, the rise of blockchain and smart contracting as governance tools is actually consistent with a broader, decades-long trend in the development of American business law. This trend is 'private ordering', the ability for parties in a business enterprise to shape the rules governing that enterprise to their own needs. In the more than 100 years that have passed since the general incorporation statute became commonplace, American business law has developed in a way that offers significant freedom in the organization of business enterprises.[5] That trend has continued on in the twenty-first century, with a variety of legal developments that has increased the degree to which private ordering can take place.[6] Blockchain's governance applications are consistent with this trend insofar as blockchain facilitates private ordering by making a wider variety of governance arrangements and methods of organization possible.

As we show in this chapter, blockchain-based governance is consistent with the movement towards greater private ordering because to a large degree, it *is* privately ordered governance—parties devise governance arrangements (which may or may not resemble traditional arrangements), translate them into code, and then rely on automatic execution by the network responsible for maintaining the blockchain on which the code resides. Blockchain-based governance allows for degrees of private ordering that have not previously been possible and, in this sense, is consistent with the pro-private ordering direction of American business law, even if it has the potential for reducing reliance on the governance

---

[2] These tokens were eventually found by the Securities and Exchange Commission ('SEC') to constitute securities for purposes of American securities laws. *Report of Investigation Pursuant to Section 21(a) of the Securities Exchange Act of 1934: The DAO*, SEC Release No. 81207 (25 July 2017) https://www.sec.gov/litigation/investreport/34-81207.pdf .

[3] Christoph Jentzsch, 'Decentralized Autonomous Organization to Automate Governance', White Paper, https://download.slock.it/public/DAO/WhitePaper.pdf.

[4] SEC (n 2).

[5] William W. Bratton and Joseph A. McCahery, 'The Equilibrium Content of Corporate Federalism' (2006) 41 *Wake Forest Law Review* 619, 623.

[6] In 2000, for example, the Delaware legislature adopted legislation that allowed corporations to limit the scope of the corporate opportunity doctrine, an aspect of duty of loyalty, in their certificates of incorporation. Delaware General Corporation Law, Delaware Code, Title 8, s. 122(17).

arrangements offered by traditional business entities. The chapter concludes by considering the continued usefulness of those organizational forms in a world where blockchain-based governance is possible. Although blockchain-based governance may obviate the need for parties to rely on traditional business entities for the governance rule they supply, housing an enterprise in a traditional entity continues to offer the benefits of legal personhood, benefits which are not conferred by the blockchain.

II. Towards Greater Room for Private Ordering: The Development of American Business Law

To a remarkable degree, American business law reflects an 'enabling' approach,[7] which leaves parties significant room to organize business enterprises in the way they see fit.[8] The statutes that provide for the creation and governance of corporations and other business associations are largely comprised of 'default' provisions—rules which will apply if the parties do not specify otherwise (i.e. they require an opt-out)—and on occasion, enabling provisions, which apply if the parties specifically opt in.[9] Mandatory rules, though not unheard of, are not the norm in American business law.[10] Due to the fact that rules that are mandatory in one organizational form are not necessarily so in other organizational forms, even the mandatory rules that do exist can be worked around by choosing a different entity or otherwise planning around them.[11] Chief Justice Strine of the Delaware Supreme Court describes his State's approach to corporate law as 'flexible and enabling',[12] a significant statement given Delaware's outsized influence on American business law—most of the large, publicly traded corporations and alternative entities with a dispersed investor base are organized in the state and are, therefore, subject to its law under the internal affairs doctrine.[13] Although this enabling approach has dominated for decades, it has not always done so to this degree. The history of American business law is littered with the remains of rules which were once mandatory but are no longer so.[14]

The enabling approach to corporate law owes much to the jurisdictional competition for corporate charters that emerged in the late 1880s. New Jersey initially dominated this market by offering a largely enabling statute[15] but lost its position after it amended its corporate statute in 1913 to include a variety of new restrictions, including a prohibition on the formation of additional holding companies within the state.[16] Delaware, having already enacted a statute that paralleled the pre-1913 New Jersey statute, was well positioned to displace New Jersey as 'the place' to incorporate and did just that. Since then, the state's largely enabling approach to the law governing business organizations has had an outsized impact, on account

---

[7] Jens Dammann, 'The Mandatory Law Puzzle: Redefining American Exceptionalism in Corporate Law' (2014) 65 *Hastings Law Journal*, 441.

[8] Stephen M. Bainbridge, *The New Corporate Governance in Theory and Practice* (Oxford University Press 2008), 28.

[9] Reinier Kraakman, John Armour, Paul Davies et al., *The Anatomy of Corporate Law: A Comparative and Functional Approach* (3rd edn, Oxford University Press 2017), 18.

[10] Dammann (n 7), 441; Bainbridge, *The New Corporate Governance* (n 8), 30–31.

[11] Bernard S. Black, 'Is Corporate Law Trivial?: A Political and Economic Analysis' (1990) 84 *Northwestern University Law* Review, 542.

[12] Leo E. Strine, Jr, 'Delaware's Corporate-Law System: Is Corporate American Buying an Exquisite Jewel or a "Diamond in the Rough"? A Response to Kahan and Kamar's Price Discrimination in the Market for Corporate Law' (2001) 86 *Cornell Law Review* 1257, 1258.

[13] *VantagePoint Venture Partners 1996 v. Examen Inc.* [2005] 871 A.2d 1108 (Delaware Supreme Court).

[14] In their canonical account of the separation of ownership and control, Berle and Means bemoan the demise of a variety of formerly mandatory rules, including, for example, preemptive rights: Adolf A. Berle, Jr and Gardiner C. Means, *The Modern Corporation and Private Property* (The MacMillan Co. 1933), 144–48.

[15] Edward Q. Keasbey, 'New Jersey and the Great Corporations' (1899) 13 *Harvard Law Review*, 198.

[16] Charles Yablon, 'The Historical Race Competition for Corporate Charters and the Rise and Decline of New Jersey: 1880–1910' (2007) 32 *Journal of Corporation Law*, 323.

of both Delaware's success in attracting a large number of entity formations and its influence on other jurisdictions' law making.

Notwithstanding its roots in charter competition, an influential school of scholars and commentators have incorporated this enabling approach to corporate law into a robust and widely influential theory of the firm. Focusing largely on the voluntary nature of associating with others in a firm, these contractarian scholars and commentators argue that corporations are fundamentally contractual in nature and are nothing more than 'a set of implicit and explicit contracts establishing rights and obligations among the various inputs making up the firm'.[17] For contractarians, the statutes that provide for the formation and governance of business entities are simply form contracts that allow organizers to adopt 'off-the-rack' contractual terms, thereby saving the costs involved in negotiating and drafting a fully customized contract.[18] However, the contractual account is not merely descriptive. It has normative implications for both the content of these 'off-the-rack' contracts and the degree to which parties should be able to stray from them. As these state-supplied, off-the-rack contracts are primarily a vehicle for reducing transaction costs, contractarians argue that they should be comprised primarily of 'majoritarian' default rules that 'reflect the terms that the majority of well-informed parties would themselves most commonly choose'.[19] Or, as Easterbrook and Fischel put it in their canonical treatment of the contractual view of the firm, 'the terms people would have negotiated, were the costs of negotiating at arm's length for every contingency sufficiently low'.[20] Additionally, because these statutes are composed of rules that should be desirable to most, but not necessarily all, parties, those parties who prefer different terms should be able to adopt them in the absence of third-party effects or some market failure.[21] In the law and economics parlance, mandatory terms can be inefficient[22] so parties should be allowed to supply their own governance rules in place of the rules provided in the relevant statute.

Notably, this pro-private ordering view of business associations has had a significant impact on the ground. Delaware's judges speak in explicitly contractual terms when describing corporations' governing documents.[23] In the realm of corporate law, there has been a gradual relaxation of many of the most quintessential mandatory rules even into the twenty-first century. Fiduciary duties, for example, remain mandatory as a technical matter but can be voluntarily narrowed in the certificate of incorporation or through the action of management in the future. The duty of care, though not subject to elimination, can be largely neutralized through the adoption of an exculpation provision which insulates management against monetary liability for its breach.[24] Transactions between management and the corporation, which were once *void ab initio*, on account of the conflict of interest, can now be 'sanitized' and brought within the purview of the business judgment rule by disinterested members of the board of directors.[25] In 2000, Delaware adopted legislation allowing corporate charters to include provisions that limit the scope of the corporate opportunity doctrine, a longstanding component of the mandatory duty of loyalty.[26] In the realm of unincorporated business entities, the pro-private ordering approach is even more patent.

---

[17] Bainbridge, *The New Corporate Governance* (n 8), 28.

[18] Frank H. Easterbrook and Daniel R. Fischel, *The Economic Structure of Corporate Law* (Harvard University Press 1991), 12.

[19] Kraakman et al. (n 9), 18.   [20] Easterbrook and Fischel, *Economic Structure* (n 18), 15.

[21] ibid.

[22] Henry N. Butler and Larry E. Ribstein, 'Opting Out of Fiduciary Duties: A Response to the Anti-Contractarians' (1990) 65 *Washington Law Review*, 1.

[23] *Boilermakers Local 154 Ret. Fund. v. Chevron Corp.*, 73 A.3d 934, 940 (Del. Ch. 2013).

[24] Delaware General Corporation Law, Delaware Code, Title 8, s. 102(b)(7).

[25] ibid., s 144 (providing that such transactions are not void or voidable if certain procedures are followed); in *Re Wheelabrator Technologies Shareholder Litigation*, 663 A.2d 1194 (Delaware Court of Chancery 1995) (explaining the effect of sanitization on standard of review).

[26] Delaware General Corporation Law, Delaware Code, Title 8, s. 122(17).

Although these entities have long been recognized as providing considerable flexibility when it comes to devising governance structures, the Delaware legislature amended its limited liability company and limited partnership statutes in 2004 to include provisions explicitly stating the state's policies in favour of contractual freedom[27] and also expressly allowing for the elimination of fiduciary duties.[28] With this legislation, the Delaware legislature enunciated a strong and unmistakable preference for private ordering.

More recently, arguments in favour of private ordering have emerged that are not strictly rooted in a contractual description of business associations but which do draw on contractarian insights. For example, Professors Belinfanti and Stout apply systems theory to corporate law and conclude that this approach 'rejects central planning in favor of diversity and self-organization.'[29] Professors Goshen and Squire take a similar, pro-private ordering position that is grounded on 'principal costs.'[30] Taking issue with the longstanding focus on agency costs, Goshen and Squire point out that the involvement of principals in the operation of a firm will impose its own costs (e.g. costs related to a principal's lack of competence) and argue that each firm will have its own, unique combination of agency and principal costs. For Goshen and Squire, each firm will need its own, unique set of mechanisms for minimizing the total of these costs and the 'law's proper role is to allow firms to select from a wide range of governance structures, rather than to mandate some structures and ban others.'[31] Professor D. Gordon Smith and others have argued in favour of private ordering through the use of corporate bylaws as a means to increase shareholder empowerment, in effect allowing corporations to customize the traditional balance of power between the board and shareholders through implementation of firm-specific bylaw arrangements.[32] These more recent arguments in favour of private ordering acknowledged, at least implicitly, appeared to motivate much of the contractarian suspicion of mandatory terms—a recognition that no two firms are the same and concern over the ability of lawmakers to devise governance rules that work for all.

III. Blockchains, Private Ordering, and the Changing Landscape of Governance

Traditionally, the governance of business organizations has taken place 'in the boardroom', pursuant to rules provided by the legal system, the organization's governing documents (certificate of incorporation, bylaws, and other governing documents), relevant side agreements, and, in some instances, the listing standards of the exchanges on which the organization's securities trade. With blockchain, and specifically with blockchain-based smart contracts, organizations can implement all or parts of their governance rules and procedures into code, in effect, memorializing governance in a set of smart contracts that will be stored on a blockchain. As the DAO and other, more mainstream implementations of blockchain-based governance show,[33] some already have.

---

[27] Delaware Limited Liability Company Law, Delaware Code, Title 6, s. 18-1101(b); Delaware Limited Partnership Law, Delaware Code, Title 6, s. 17-1101(c).
[28] Delaware Limited Liability Company Law, Delaware Code, Title 6, s 18-1101(c); Delaware Limited Partnership Law, Delaware Code, Title 6, s. 17-1101(d).
[29] Tamara Belinfanti and Lynn Stout, 'Contested Visions: The Value of Systems Theory for Corporate Law' (2018) 16 *University of Pennsylvania Law Review* 579, 613.
[30] Zohar Goshen and Richard Squire, 'Principal Costs: A New Theory for Corporate Law and Governance' (2017) 117 *Columbia Law Review*, 767.
[31] ibid., 771.
[32] D. Gordon Smith, Matthew Wright, and Marcus Kai Hintze, 'Private Ordering with Shareholder Bylaws' (2011) 80 *Fordham Law Review*, 125.
[33] For example, Overstock, Inc. (which runs the popular retail website *Overstock.com*) has issued classes of common stock as well as debt securities whose ownership is tracked on a permissioned blockchain: Daniel DeConnick, 'Overstock Completes First Public Stock Issuance Using Blockchain' (2017) 36 *Review of Banking and Financial Law*, 416.

From a private ordering perspective, the emergence of blockchain-based governance is significant because of the ways that smart contracts can facilitate reliance on privately ordered governance arrangements. Specifically, smart contracts hold out the promise of removing many of the practical barriers that stand in the way of the adoption and implementation of a variety of individually tailored governance mechanisms. For example, using smart contracts to coordinate voting makes it possible to involve a larger number of individuals in decision making than is possible with other, more cumbersome and expensive systems for collecting and verifying votes. The availability of smart contract voting protocols may make it possible for some enterprises to adopt their own, individually tailored allocation of decision-making power between stakeholders.

In this section, we provide a brief discussion of some of the ways that blockchain-based governance facilitates private ordering.

A. Streamlined voting

Blockchains are best-known for the role they play in facilitating cryptocurrencies but this is just one application of their underlying function—storing information in a globally accessible, 'tamper-resistant, resilient, and non-repudiable manner'.[34] For cryptocurrencies, blockchains are used to store records of transactions but blockchains can store other information, including digitally signed votes and digitally signed proxy appointments. The consequences for shareholder voting (really any sort of organizational voting) are wide-ranging.[35]

First, by conducting and recording the vote on a blockchain, organizations can conduct votes (shareholder or otherwise) with increased transparency and avoid opportunities for contested elections, fraudulent behaviour, or simple mistakes.[36] On a blockchain, the voting process would generate a tamper-resistant registry of votes (or representations) of votes which can be tallied automatically. Once votes are recorded to a blockchain, it would be possible to verify the vote tallies by looking at the trail of blockchain-based transactions[37] and, depending on whether identities are correlated with the addresses used for voting, who voted in which way. Shareholder decisions could be public and audited by all members of the organization to ensure that procedural rules for decision making have been followed, thereby decreasing risks related to a miscalculated vote.

Second, the mechanics of voting would be streamlined and less cost-intensive, which could have wide-ranging effects. Votes would no longer require paper mailings or the securing of e-proxy services if administered on a blockchain.[38] Blockchain-based addresses (or identity systems tied to these addresses) would allow confirmable delivery of all necessary materials, facilitate the return and retention of proxy designations or any other information or documentation, and allow for the submission of votes. Voting could take place on an ongoing basis, not just at predetermined times of the year.[39] As blockchain-based voting systems mature, the cost of soliciting stakeholder input through a vote will likely decrease, potentially to the point that it becomes feasible for shareholders (or other dispersed stakeholders) to assume a greater role in the management of a wider variety of organizations that operate outside the technology sector. Ultimately, more regular and streamlined reliance on shareholder voting to make decisions could result in the regular adoption of *privately ordered*, firm-specific allocations of decision-making power.

---

[34] Primavera De Filippi and Aaron Wright, *Blockchain and the Law: The Rule of Code* (Harvard University Press 2018), 134.
[35] Anne Lafarre and Christoph Van der Elst, 'Blockchain Technology for Corporate Governance and Shareholder Activism' (2018) http://ssrn.com/abstract_id=3135209.
[36] De Filippi and Wright (n 34), 134.   [37] Lafarre and Van der Elst (n 35), 15–16.
[38] De Filippi and Wright (n 34), 134.   [39] Lafarre and Van der Elst (n 35), 18.

In short, widespread use of blockchain-based voting systems offers the potential for organizations to incorporate input from a wider group of stakeholders in a wider variety of situations and circumstances. The DAO and other decentralized autonomous organizations indicate that, for some enterprises, at least, this is a possibility. In the corporate realm, this could potentially empower shareholders to adopt bylaws or other provisions that limit the managerial authority of the board of directors in ways that are not yet practical. If taken to an extreme, these measures could draw into question a foundational principle of corporate governance, the allocation of managerial authority to the board of directors and its primacy.[40]

B. From *ex post* monitoring and enforcement to *ex ante* limitations

Governance through blockchain-based smart contracts also holds out the possibility of greater reliance on privately ordered, *ex ante* governance mechanisms and less on *ex post* monitoring and enforcement.

This trend is already underway in the realm of traditional governance. Shareholders and corporate boards are increasingly looking to bylaws to privately order the governance of large corporations[41] and large, publicly traded limited partnerships and limited liability companies rely on complicated operating agreements that eliminate fiduciary duties in favour of detailed provisions that govern a variety of specific situations, such as the approval of transactions that involve a conflict of interest.[42]

Smart contracts offer further opportunities to structure organizations in a more deterministic manner, with code detailing the *ex ante* rules for cooperation among a variety of constituents. For example, many organizations still struggle to implement appropriate safeguards to protect against the misappropriation or misuse of assets that belong to the organization by everyone from low-level employees to C-level executives and members of the board of directors.[43] Organizations (business or otherwise) can make misappropriation more difficult by allocating responsibilities and duties to different participants in ways that make unilateral transfer of organizational assets challenging.[44] Smart contracts governing the transfer of funds can be implemented to required multiple parties to 'sign off' on transactions in ways that make it difficult to falsify approvals. This application of smart contracting technology allows private ordering to shape governance at a level of detail typically reserved for enterprises of relatively limited size, such as a limited partnership whose operating agreement places limitations on the general partner's ability to enter into transactions that exceed a particular threshold. With this application, smart contracting allows parties to privately order a customized allocation of power amongst participants by restricting the possibility that participants will be able to consummate certain actions without the approval of others.

Blockchain's rigidity acts as another layer of controls here—*ex ante* limitations on conduct that are implemented as smart contracts are immutable in most instances, which means that those subject to the rules will not able to modify or annul them. By fostering a substitution of *ex ante* governance in this way, parties will have less need to invest in monitoring and enforcement. With less possibility for parties to act in their own self-interest, blockchain-based governance can decrease uncertainty and increase trust within an organization.

---

[40] Stephen M. Bainbridge, 'Director Primacy and Shareholder Disempowerment' (2006) 119 *Harvard Law Review* 1735, 1745.

[41] George S. Geis, 'Ex-Ante Corporate Governance' (2016) 41 *Journal of Corporate Law*, 609.

[42] Jonathan Rohr, 'Freedom of Contract and the Publicly Traded Uncorporation' (2017) 14 *New York University Journal of Law and Business* 247, 262.

[43] Jeffrey Doyle, Weili Ge, and Sarah McVay, 'Determinants of Weaknesses in Internal Control over Financial Reporting' (2007) 44(1) *Journal of Accounting and Economics*, 193–223.

[44] Eugene F. Fama and Michael C. Jensen, 'Separation of Ownership and Control' (1983) 26(2) *Journal of Law and Economics*, 301–25.

C. Decentralized organizations

The impact of blockchain technology on organizational governance is not limited to incremental improvements to existing organizational forms with targeted adoption of blockchain technology for specific functions. Rather, the application of blockchain technology to governance also makes it possible to create 'decentralized organizations', organizations that rely on blockchain technology and smart contracts as their primary or exclusive source of governance.[45] These organizations provide a laboratory for private ordering insofar as their governance scheme is privately ordered through smart contracts hosted on a blockchain. These smart contracts are not run on a centralized server but are, instead, executed by the network on which the code that compromises the smart contract is hosted.[46] In the case of decentralized organizations, smart contracts can be combined to form a web of coded relationships that, together, provide the rules under which the relevant organization will be governed.

Participation/affiliation with a decentralized organization is typically evidenced through a blockchain-based 'token' that is coupled with the smart contracts that govern the organization. The DAO (discussed in section I. Introduction), for example, issued DAO tokens to its investors. These tokens were the mechanism through which voting on funding decisions occurred and through which any returns would be remitted to investors. Individuals can either purchase tokens,[47] or receive them as a reward for some other contribution, such as computing power. Through smart contracts, tokens can be associated with specific rights in favour of their holders, such as the right to receive a portion of the organization's income or the right to use the network, software, or other services offered by the organization. Tokens can also be designed to provide their holders with the right to participate in certain organization decisions through a vote,[48] as was the case with the DAO.

With these capabilities, blockchain technology enables the creation of organizations that are governed with greater transparency and without reliance on a central authority.[49] Rather than rely on centralized decision makers, governance in a decentralized organization generally relies on group consensus achieved through crypto-economic systems that use smart contracts to aggregate the votes or preferences of token holders.[50] Organizations can also issue different types of tokens that entitle holders to different rights. For example, the same organization could issue one token that grants access to its software or platform, a second type of token that entitles the holder to a share of the organization's income, and a third type that grants the holder rights to participate in certain decisions.[51]

Decentralized organizations, thus, present the most expansive possibilities for private ordering, with parties collaborating through organizations that are not limited by geographic or jurisdictional borders. This could have consequences for our understanding of the outer boundaries of large firms. As Coase noted, technological advances 'like the telephone and telegraphy, which tend to reduce the cost of organizing spatially, ... tend to increase the size of the firm', particularly when these advances involve 'changes that improve managerial techniques'.[52] Like the telephone, blockchain-based governance techniques reduce the costs of organizing and hold out the promise of organizing larger groups of dispersed individuals within flatter and more decentralized organizations whose governance has been almost exclusively privately ordered without the aid of state-supplied associational forms.

---

[45] Carla Reyes, 'If Rockefeller Were a Coder' (forthcoming), 87 *George Washington Law Review*, https://papers.ssrn.com/sol3/papers.cfm?abstract_id=3082915.

[46] Arvind Narayanan and Steven Goldfelder, *Bitcoin and Cryptocurrency Technologies* (Princeton University Press 2016), 264–65.

[47] Rohr and Wright (n 1), 70.   [48] De Filippi and Wright (n 34), 137.

[49] Carla L. Reyes, Nizan Geslevich Packin, and Benjamin P. Edwards, 'Distributed Governance' (2017) 59 *William and Mary Law Review Online*, https://wmlawreview.org/distributed-governance

[50] De Filippi and Wright (n 34), 137.   [51] ibid.

[52] Ronald Henry Coase, *The Firm, the Market, and the Law* (University of Chicago Press 2012), 46.

IV. Blockchain-Based Governance in a Pro-Private Ordering Legal Landscape

Blockchain-supported smart contracting has the potential to empower types and degrees of private ordering that have simply not yet been possible, even if legally permissible. By removing many of the practical barriers that stand in the way of the implementation of particular governance mechanisms, blockchain-based governance holds out the potential for firms to better match their governance needs with the arrangements they adopt, whether they do so in the context of a traditional associational form or as a decentralized organization. In this sense, reliance on blockchain-based governance is consistent with the generally pro-private ordering orientation of American business law.

From a purely contractarian perspective, this could have consequences for the ongoing usefulness of traditional business associations. After all, under the contractarian view they are simply off-the-rack contracts.[53] If blockchain-based governance can remove the practical barriers to more extensive private ordering, maybe firms will not need to rely on the off-the-rack contracts made available to them. As the DAO and other token-based enterprises show, this is not mere conjecture. Already, organizers of some types of enterprises do not seem to feel any need to establish a formal legal entity.[54] The possibility that blockchain-based governance could eventually reduce, and maybe even displace, reliance on traditional business entities as a vehicle for governance cannot be dismissed.

However, focusing exclusively on the potential for blockchain to disrupt traditional internal governance ignores the other reasons underlying the formation of business entities. Certainly, capturing the variety of benefits that come with off-the-rack governance arrangements is one reason to form an entity. However, as single-member limited liability companies and single-shareholder corporations demonstrate, it is not the only reason. Even when governance rules are not needed, entity formation is a way to secure limited liability, to partition assets, and to enjoy the convenience of separate legal personhood (e.g. being able to sue in the entity's name).[55] And even if blockchain-based governance decreases the need to form business entities for governance purposes, it does not obviate the other reasons for entity formation, in particular, clear limited liability and the convenience of corporate personhood. For blockchain-based governance to go mainstream, participants will need a clear path to limited liability.[56] Contractual counterparties will want (legal) certainty with regard to with whom and with what they are transacting and which assets are available to satisfy contractual obligations. From a policy perspective, the most important question appears to be the degree to which lawmakers should accommodate the substitution of blockchain-based governance for traditional governance in legally recognized, limited liability entities. Should entrepreneurs who wish to deploy blockchain-based governance have a way to do so that offers clear, limited liability and the conveniences of separate legal personhood?

Perhaps unsurprisingly, state law efforts are already underway to adapt traditional business entities to blockchain-based governance. Both houses of Vermont's legislature recently passed an amendment to the state's limited liability company statute which would allow a limited liability company to designate itself a 'blockchain-based LLC'.[57] The legislation specifically empowers a blockchain-based LLC to 'provide for its governance, in whole or

---

[53] Bainbridge, *The New Corporate Governance* (n 8), 28.

[54] Some have argued that at least some decentralized organizations be treated as partnerships, the default business entity under American business law, but this is an awkward fit, see Reyes (n 45).

[55] Henry Hansmann and Reinier Kraakman, 'The Essential Role of Organizational Law' (2000) 110 *Yale Law Journal*, 387.

[56] Reyes (n 45).

[57] Vermont General Assembly, An Act Relating to Blockchain-Based Business Development, s. 269, https://legislature.vermont.gov/bill/status/2018/S.269.

in part, through blockchain technology'.[58] In other words, it specifically authorizes the creation of an LLC that substitutes 'blockchain technology' for traditional governance tools.
One might argue that, at most, this sort of legislation clarifies the status of something that is
already permitted—arguably, there is nothing in currently existing LLC statutes that would
prohibit a code-based operating agreement.[59] Even so, legislative recognition of blockchain-
based governance does lend it some legitimacy and offers a clear path for those relying on
blockchain-based governance to capture the benefits of legal personhood and clear limited
liability. As blockchain-based business enterprises become more mainstream, the availability
of a clear path to limited liability and legal personhood will become more important to
entrepreneurs and investors.[60]

These early efforts to combine blockchain-based governance with traditional business
entities raise a host of further questions related to the mainstreaming of blockchain-based
governance and its potential use outside of the token-based enterprises in which applications
of the technology are being developed. In the final section of this chapter, we analyse some of
these issues and discuss their significance on the ongoing development of blockchain-based
governance and its movement into the mainstream.

A. Gap filling

Traditional governance incorporates a variety of mechanisms that are applied to fill
'gaps' in the 'contract'. Fiduciary duties are, perhaps, the best-known gap fillers in traditional corporate law. Under the contractual view, fiduciary duties are a pragmatic way of
dealing with the impossibility of complete contracting.[61] Rather than specifying *ex ante*
a fiduciary's obligations in all situations, fiduciary duties supply general principles that
are enforced *ex post*. When legal decisionmakers are called upon to determine whether
a particular action violated a corporate director's duty of loyalty, they are both supplying
and applying a 'contractual' term.[62] Much of the debate surrounding private ordering in
the context of business associations has focused on the degree to which these mandatory
gap fillers should be subject to modification or elimination.[63] As discussed above, advocates for private ordering substantially won this debate in the context of unassociated
business associations and have made considerable inroads with piecemeal relaxations of
corporate fiduciary duties. However, even with regard to unassociated entities in which
contractual freedom reigns supreme, a mandatory gap filler—the duty of good faith and
fair dealing—remains.[64]

The ongoing role for gap-filling mechanisms is one of the issues raised by blockchain-
based governance. Without doubt, blockchain has the potential for more complete contracting by removing many of the practical barriers that stand in the way of the adoption of a
variety of *ex ante* governance arrangements. However, for now at least, the way those mechanisms are designed and the ways in which they are adopted are still directed by humans
who suffer from the bounded rationality and imperfect information that make complete
contracting impossible and gap fillers necessary.

---

[58] s. 269, https://legislature.vermont.gov/assets/Documents/2018/Docs/BILLS/S-0269/S-0269%20As%20Passed%20
by%20Both%20House%20and%20Senate%20Official.pdf.

[59] Lynn LoPucki, 'Algorithmic Entities' (2018) 95 *Washington University Law Review*, 887.

[60] Reyes (n 45).

[61] Frank H. Easterbrook and Daniel R. Fischel, 'Contract and Fiduciary Duty' (1993) 36 *Journal of Law and
Economics* 425, 427: 'The duty of loyalty replaces detailed contractual terms, and courts flesh out the duty of loyalty
by prescribing the actions the parties themselves would have preferred if bargaining were cheap and all promises
fully enforced.'

[62] Easterbrook and Fischel, *Economic Structure* (n 18), 92–94.   [63] Butler and Ribstein (n 22), 4.

[64] Delamere Code Ann., Title 6, § 18-1101(c) (2013); Delamere Code Ann., Title 6 § 17-1101(d) (2013). *See also*
Delamere Code Ann., Title 6, § 18-1101(b) (2013); Delamere Code Ann., Title 6 § 17-1101(c) (2013).

Thus, for reasons related to human, rather than technological, limitations, it may simply not be possible to provide for an organization's entire governance scheme on an *ex ante* basis, whether in code or on paper, without relying, to some degree, on open-ended standards and gap fillers. This is precisely the point that Chief Justice Leo E. Strine and Vice Chancellor Travis Laster made recently when they argued for reinstatement of a mandatory duty of loyalty for publicly traded unincorporated business associations.[65] According to Strine and Laster, both of whom have considerable experience adjudicating disputes involving operating agreements that have eliminated fiduciary duties, the contractarian experiment in allowing elimination of the gap filling duty of loyalty should be abandoned. Contracting parties need a more robust gap filler than the duty of good faith and fair dealing because they are not capable of contracting with sufficient completeness.[66]

Blockchain-based governance could attempt to incorporate terms that are intended to function as gap fillers. However, these terms, which are designed to leave the precise manner of performance unspecified, are not well suited for conversion into code, at least, not currently.[67] That could change at some point in the future. So, while blockchain-based governance certainly holds out the potential for allowing parties to rely more on *ex ante* governance mechanisms, this is not without limitation. Parties wising to rely on blockchain-based governance, even in the context of blockchain based LLC, will need to account for the gaps that remain in the arrangements they design and implement, at least for the time being.

B. Privately ordered securities—debt, equity, or something else?

Typically, when companies raise money from the public, they issue securities that take one of several, familiar forms—common stock, preferred stock, bonds, convertible bonds, etc.—that are commonly understood as debt, equity, or a hybrid of the two. Through the use of smart contracts and blockchain-based tokens, however, businesses have the ability to sell tokens to the public that combine rights in novel ways. Economic rights, participation rights, and utility rights can all be associated with tokens, which are then sold to the public in ways that are similar to a traditional initial public offering.[68] The recent explosion of ICOs has demonstrated the ability of blockchain-based enterprises to raise large sums of money through the sales of these tokens but, from a regulatory perspective, much uncertainty remains. Whether or not these tokens constitute securities is still an open question. The current Chairman of the Securities Exchange Commission (SEC) has indicated that, in his view, most are, but this has not yet been tested in litigation or in an enforcement action. Furthermore, even if these tokens are securities, their categorization for regulatory purposes is uncertain—they have been privately ordered in ways that make categorizing them according to the traditional equity/debt/hybrid framework difficult. A token, for example, can implicate interests related to both investment and consumption by entitling the holder to use a particular platform or network while also holding out the possibility of generating economic gains through resale on the secondary market.

This can matter for a variety of reasons. As an example, consider Section 12(g) of the Securities Act of 1934 and its application to blockchain-based tokens. Under Section 12(g) of the Securities Act of 1934, a company is required to register with the SEC and comply with ongoing disclosure requirements if it has more than $10 million in assets and a class of *equity* securities that are 'held of record' by either 2,000 persons or 500 persons who are not accredited investors.[69]

---

[65] Leo E. Strine and J. Travis Laster, 'The Siren Song of Unlimited Contractual Freedom' in *Research Handbook on Partnerships, LLCs and Alternative Forms of Business Organizations*, edited by Robert W. Hillman and Mark J. Loewenstein (Edward Elgar 2015), 12.
[66] ibid.   [67] De Filippi and Wright (n 34), 77.   [68] Rohr and Wright (n 1).
[69] 15 U.S.C. § 78l(g).

The ease with which blockchain-based business enterprises can amass more than $10 million in assets has become clear, as has the fact that most of the tokens are held by numerous purchasers (certainly more than 500 non-accredited investors) immediately after they are sold to the public. In the event a blockchain-based enterprise sells digital tokens that constitute equity securities, Section 12(g) may require registration at a very early stage in the life of the enterprise. Certainly, if a blockchain-based enterprise sells traditional securities that have simply been digitized, this issue is easy to resolve. However, when these enterprises issue non-traditional interests (e.g. a digital token that combines use with the potential for profit), it is not clear that they are securities in the first instance and, if they are, it is not clear that they are *equity* securities. Many of the tokens do not entitle the holder to any economic rights and, instead, represent the right to use a platform or software. If anything, this type of interest seems more like debt than equity, but it is not a perfect fit.

C. Market efficiency and transparency

One of the most obvious objections to the pro-private ordering, contractual view of the firm (at least when it comes to firms with a diverse and dispersed investor base, like publicly traded corporations) is the fact that the governance terms are offered on a purely 'take-it-or-leave-it' basis without negotiation or, in the case of most shareholders, any meaningful awareness of their content or operation. The vulnerability of investors under these circumstances is a longstanding argument in favour of mandatory terms that are designed to protect investors from the imposition of one-sided terms.[70] Perhaps unsurprisingly, contractarians' answer lies in the market, specifically the market's ability to price governance terms. In the words of Easterbrook and Fischel, 'all the terms in corporate governance are contractual in the sense that they are fully priced in transactions among the interested parties. They are thereafter tested for desirable properties; the firms that pick the wrong terms will fail in competition with other firms competing for capital. It is unimportant that they may not be 'negotiated'.'[71] In other words, the informational efficiency of capital markets means that investors get that for which they paid and it also prevents the imposition of unfair or one-sided terms because those terms will be priced into the firm's cost of capital. Under this contractarian account, mandatory terms are only appropriate when either private ordering imposes negative externalities or when 'the terms chosen by firms are both *unpriced* and systematically perverse'.[72] Of course, Easterbrook and Fischel overstate things a bit—there is a body of empirical evidence which shows that the market does *not* always fully price governance terms.[73] Instead, markets display differing degrees of informational efficiency.[74] They incorporate new information at different speeds and to different degrees but the underlying idea, that the price of a security is indicative of performance (which is impacted by governance) and there is no better indicator available, has ongoing salience for both debates surrounding contractual freedom and theories explaining a variety of current governance practices.[75]

In the context of blockchain-based governance, the degree to which the market will price governance terms and, therefore, the degree to which private ordering can be justified under the traditional contractarian position, remains an open question. The informational efficiency of a market is a function of information costs. When information costs are high,

---

[70] Jeffrey N. Gordon, 'The Mandatory Structure of Corporate Law' (1989) 89 *Columbia Law Review* 1549, 1556–62.

[71] Easterbrook and Fischel, *Economic Structure* (n 18), 17.   [72] ibid., 21.

[73] Lawrence A. Cunningham, 'Behavioral Finance and Investor Governance' (2002) 59 *Washington and Lee Law Review* 767, 774–76.

[74] *Halliburton v. Erica P. John Fund, Inc.* [2014] 134 Supreme Court 2398.

[75] Bainbridge, *The New Corporate Governance* (n 8), 57.

markets are likely to be less efficient.[76] Conversely, when information is acquired and processed easily, markets are likely to be more informationally efficient.[77] Certainly, with regard to traditional securities that have simply been 'tokenized', there are strong reasons to think that the market will be able to (accurately) price the terms, provided there is a way to 'translate' the code that reflects those governance terms into a format that can be understood by market participants and used to inform their purchasing decisions. Here, information costs should be relatively low as compared to their analog counterparts, provided purchasers are able to trust that the blockchain-based governance is an accurate reflection of the traditional governance terms that have simply been transferred from operating agreements, certificates of incorporation, and other relevant governing documents to blockchain-based smart contracts.

However, with regard to non-traditional arrangements that fall within the definition of 'security', there is potential for information costs to be significantly higher given that it will be more difficult for market participants to determine both what the code means and how novel private ordering mechanisms should be valued. As these instruments do not correlate directly to analog assets, purchasers will not be able to rely on previously accumulated experience and information and will be forced to determine (i) the meaning of the code; and (ii) its significance for pricing. Higher information costs bring questions relating to the informational efficiency of the market, which raises further questions related to the degree to which private ordering is actually appropriate.

It is clearly far too early to draw any conclusions on the informational efficiency of the market for digital tokens. Nevertheless, given the relationship between information costs, market efficiency, and private ordering, it may be appropriate to consider measures intended to lower purchasers' information costs, for example, by requiring that the operation of blockchain-based governance terms be described in a document written in 'plain English'. Even if such measures took the form of a mandatory rule, they would be pro-private ordering insofar as they would (hopefully) help to maintain the market conditions that are conducive to private ordering.

V. Conclusion

Blockchain's disruptive potential seems to obscure the ways in which the technology is actually consistent with existing policies and legal frameworks. As discussed in this chapter, there are early-stage indications that blockchain-based governance will have a significant impact on the way firms are governed, by both digitizing traditional governance mechanisms and by offering fundamentally new ways of organizing business enterprises, large and small. Despite the significant potential for change, this development is consistent with American business law's emphasis on private ordering. However, these changes call into question the degree to which American business law should accommodate blockchain-based governance within traditional business associations. While the increased reliance on privately ordered, blockchain-based governance could eventually lead to less reliance on the 'off-the-rack' governance arrangements offered by the traditional business entities, governance is only one reason parties adopt business entities. Asset partitioning, limited liability, and other conveniences of separate legal personhood are also reasons for forming a business entity, and based on the frequency with which single shareholder corporations and single-member limited liability companies occur, they appear to be relatively strong reasons. For this reason, we suspect that entrepreneurs and organizers wishing to adopt a system of blockchain-based

---

[76] Ronald J. Gilson and Reinier H. Kraakman, 'The Mechanisms of Market Efficiency' (1984) 70 *Virginia Law Review*, 549.

[77] ibid.

governance, even highly decentralized forms of blockchain-based governance, will want a way to secure a separate legal existence for their enterprises. The emergence and expansion of blockchain-based governance will present challenges as it intersects with traditional business law and the organizational forms that are at their core, but this should not be mistaken as an indication that blockchain-based governance is necessarily hostile to the policies underlying that body of law. Rather, when blockchain is viewed as a tool that allows parties to privately order their arrangements, its consistency with the American 'enabling approach' to business law becomes evident.

VI. Bibliography

Bainbridge Stephen M., 'Director Primacy and Shareholder Disempowerment' (2006) 119 *Harvard Law Review*, 1735.

Bainbridge Stephen M., *The New Corporate Governance in Theory and Practice* (Oxford University Press 2008).

Belinfanti Tamara and Stout Lynn, 'Contested Visions: The Value of Systems Theory for Corporate Law' (2018) 16 *University of Pennsylvania Law Review*, 579.

Berle Adolf A., Jr and Gardiner C. Means, *The Modern Corporation and Private Property* (The MacMillan Co. 1933).

Black Bernard S., 'Is Corporate Law Trivial?: A Political and Economic Analysis' (1990) 84 *Northwestern University Law Review*, 542.

Bratton William W. and McCahery Joseph A., 'The Equilibrium Content of Corporate Federalism' (2006) 41 *Wake Forest Law Review*, 619.

Butler Henry N. and Ribstein Larry E., 'Opting Out of Fiduciary Duties: A Response to the Anti-Contractarians' (1990) 65 *Washington Law Review*, 1.

Coase Ronald Henry, *The Firm, The Market and the Law* (University of Chicago Press 2012).

Cunningham Lawrence A., 'Behavioral Finance and Investor Governance' (2002) 59 *Washington and Lee Law Review*, 767.

Dammann Jens, 'The Mandatory Law Puzzle: Redefining American Exceptionalism in Corporate Law' (2014) 65 *Hastings Law Journal*, 441.

DeConnick Daniel, 'Overstock Completes First Public Stock Issuance Using Blockchain' (2017) 36 *Review of Banking and Financial Law*, 416.

De Filippi Primavera and Wright Aaron, *Blockchain and the Law: The Rule of Code* (Harvard University Press 2018).

Doyle Jeffrey, Ge Weili, and McVay Sarah, 'Determinants of Weaknesses in Internal Control over Financial Reporting' (2007) 44(1) *Journal of Accounting and Economics*, 193.

Easterbrook Frank H. and Fischel Daniel R., *The Economic Structure of Corporate Law* (Harvard University Press 1991).

Easterbrook Frank H. and Fischel Daniel R., 'Contract and Fiduciary Duty' (1993) 36 *Journal of Law and Economics*, 425.

Fama Eugene F. and Jensen Michael C., 'Separation of Ownership and Control' (1983) 26(2) *Journal of Law and Economics*, 301.

Geis George S., 'Ex-Ante Corporate Governance' (2016) 41 *Journal of Corporate Law*, 609.

Gilson Ronald J. and Kraakman Reinier H., 'The Mechanisms of Market Efficiency' (1984) 70 *Virginia Law Review*, 715.

Gordon Jeffrey N., 'The Mandatory Structure of Corporate Law' (1989) 89 *Columbia Law Review*, 1549.

Gordon Smith Dean, Wright Matthew, and Hintzee Marcus Kai, 'Private Ordering with Shareholder Bylaws' (2011) 80 *Fordham Law Review*, 125.

Goshen Zohar and Squire Richard, 'Principal Costs: A New Theory for Corporate Law and Governance' (2017) 117 *Columbia Law Review*, 767.

Hansmann Henry and Kraakman Reinier H., 'The Essential Role of Organizational Law' (2000) 110 *Yale Law Journal*, 387.

Jentzsch Christoph, 'Decentralized Autonomous Organization to Automate Governance', https://download.slock.it/public/DAO/WhitePaper.pdf, accessed on 8 January 2019.

Keasbey Edward Q., 'New Jersey and the Great Corporations' (1899) 13 *Harvard Law Review*, 264.

Kraakman Reinier, Armour John, Davies Paul, et al., *The Anatomy of Corporate Law: A Comparative and Functional Approach* (3rd edn, Oxford University Press 2017).

Lafarre Anne and Van der Elst Christoph, 'Blockchain Technology for Corporate Governance and Shareholder Activism' (2018) http://ssrn.com/abstract_id=3135209, accessed on 8 January 2019.

LoPucki Lynn, 'Algorithmic Entities' (2018) 95 *Washington University Law Review*, 887.

Narayanan Arvind and Goldfelder Steven, *Bitcoin and Cryptocurrency Technologies* (Princeton University Press 2016).

Reyes Carla, 'If Rockefeller Were a Coder' (forthcoming) 87 *George Washington Law Review*, https://papers.ssrn.com/sol3/papers.cfm?abstract_id=3082915, accessed on 8 January 2019.

Reyes Carla, Packin Nizan Geselvich, and Edwards Benjamin P., 'Distributed Governance' (2017) 59 *William and Mary Law Review Online*, https://wmlawreview.org/distributed-governance, accessed on 8 January 2019.

Rohr Jonathan, 'Freedom of Contract and the Publicly Traded Uncorporation' (2017) 14 *New York University Journal of Law and Business*, 247.

Rohr Jonathan and Wright Aaron, 'Blockchain-Based Token Sales, Initial Coin Offerings, and the Democratization of the Public Capital Markets' (2018) 70 *Hastings Law Journal*, 463, https://papers.ssrn.com/sol3/papers.cfm?abstract_id=3048104, accessed on 8 January 2019.

Securities Exchange Commission ('SEC'), *Report of Investigation Pursuant to Section 21(a) of the Securities Exchange Act of 1934: The DAO*, SEC Release No. 81207 (25 July 2017) https://www.sec.gov/litigation/investreport/34-81207.pdf, accessed on 8 January 2019.

Strine Leo E., Jr, 'Delaware's Corporate-Law System: Is Corporate American Buying an Exquisite Jewel or a "Diamond in the Rough"? A Response to Kahan and Kamar's Price Discrimination in the Market for Corporate Law' (2001) 86 *Cornell Law Review*. 1257.

Strine Leo E. and Laster J. Travis, 'The Siren Song of Unlimited Contractual Freedom' in *Research Handbook on Partnerships, LLCs and Alternative Forms of Business Organizations*, edited by Hillman Robert W. and Loewenstein Mark J. (Edward Elgar 2015).

Vermont General Assembly, An Act Relating to Blockchain Development, Vermont General Assembly, s. 269, https://legislature.vermont.gov/bill/status/2018/S.269, accessed on 8 January 2019.

Yablon Charles, 'The Historical Race for Corporate Charters and the Rise and Decline of New Jersey: 1880–1910' (2007) 32 *Journal of Corporation Law*, 323.

3

In Code(rs) We Trust

Software Developers as Fiduciaries in Public Blockchains

Angela Walch[*]

I. Introduction

'Those who are not expert developers or computer scientists who have invested a great deal of time in learning the design principles and codebase of a blockchain must place a great deal of faith in the expert developer community.'[1]

'A computer operates only in accordance with the information and directions supplied by its human programmers. If the computer does not think like a man, it is man's fault.'[2]

A decade into Bitcoin's existence, governance questions around it and other public blockchains abound. Do these 'decentralized' structures even have governance? If so, what does it look like? Who has power, and how is it channelled or constrained? Are power structures implicit or explicit? How can we improve upon the ad hoc governance structures of early blockchains? Is 'on-chain governance', like that proposed by Tezos and others, the path forward?

In August 2016, in the aftermath of the DAO theft and resulting Ethereum hard fork, I argued in *American Banker* that the core developers and significant miners of public blockchains function as fiduciaries of those who rely on these systems and should, therefore, be accountable as such.[3] The DAO episode provided a gripping real-world demonstration that certain people within nominally decentralized public blockchains were making decisions about other people's money and resources, yet this power was largely unacknowledged, undefined, and unaccountable.

In this chapter, I explore in greater depth my claim that certain developers of public blockchains act as fiduciaries,[4] as events since the DAO continue to point to the exercise of power within these systems without corresponding accountability.[5] With the peer-to-peer

[*] This paper was selected for presentation at the 2nd International Workshop—P2P Financial Systems 2016 at UCL on 8 September 2016. I would like to thank Samir Parikh, Aaron Wright, Patrick Murck, Ajit Tripathi, Tim Pastoor, Andrew Miller, Vlad Zamfir, Philipp Hacker, Drew Hinkes, Stephen Palley, Tim Swanson, Ciaran Murray, participants at the 2015 Southeastern Association of Law Schools Annual Conference New Scholars Program, the 2017 Blockchain and the Constitution of a New Financial Order: Legal and Political Challenges Conference at UCL, faculty workshops at Thurgood Marshall School of Law at Texas Southern University and Texas A&M Law School, the P2P Financial Systems 2016 Workshop, and the active crypto Twitterverse for helpful feedback and insights.

[1] Nick Szabo, 'Money, Blockchains, and Social Scalability' (*Unenumerated*, 9 February 2017) https://unenumerated.blogspot.com/2017/02/money-blockchains-and-social-scalability.html.

[2] *State Farm Mutual Auto Ins. v. Bockhorst*, 453 F 2d 533, 537 (10th Cir. 1972).

[3] Angela Walch, 'Call Blockchain Developers What They Are: Fiduciaries' (2016) *American Banker*, https://www.americanbanker.com/opinion/call-blockchain-developers-what-they-are-fiduciaries.

[4] In this chapter, 'developers' is used as shorthand for those involved in making decisions about the software that operates public blockchains. This group may include people who write software code, make decisions about policies that should be reflected in software code, review software code, etc. The term excludes miners and other nodes in the network that run the software.

[5] The governance of 'private' or 'permissioned' blockchains deserves its own careful scrutiny but is beyond the scope of this chapter. Private (i.e. permissioned) blockchains are data structures with a known and trusted group of transaction processors. 'Public' (i.e. 'permission-less') blockchains, like Bitcoin and Ethereum, are data structures for which anyone can become a transaction processor simply by running the applicable software.

computer network that operates these data structures through the running of software code, governance occurs through the software development and transaction verification processes. This chapter focuses on the software development process and compares the role of dominant software developers to a general definition of a fiduciary, finding many likenesses between the two. Recognizing that significant experimentation in governance is ongoing with public blockchains, I provide an initial outline of the core issues and questions raised by the fiduciary categorization.[6]

The age-old fiduciary concept may initially seem a poor fit for cutting-edge public blockchains, which are celebrated for enabling human coordination without the need to trust in a central party.[7] Indeed, the adjective 'trust*less*' is still regularly applied to these systems.[8] By contrast, the fiduciary concept is based fully on trust, one party entrusting another to make decisions on her behalf. Applying the fiduciary construct to public blockchains thus emphasizes that—even in public blockchains—we have not escaped the need to trust in other humans. Though some in the public blockchain space describe these systems as 'trust-minimized',[9] I see them as 'trust-shifting'; the need to trust in others has simply moved from its traditional place (e.g. the officers and directors of a *bona fide* corporation), leaving us to discern where it has landed. In these systems that operate money, smart contracts, and potentially many other critical human practices, people continue to lead and make important decisions on behalf of others; we just have to name them and decide how to treat them.

Understanding public blockchain governance is not merely an academic matter. Accurately describing the roles that various parties play in the governance of blockchain systems has implications for many different legal analyses related to these systems. A single important example is the application of securities laws to public blockchain systems.[10] If we do not press past a superficial description of public blockchain systems as 'decentralized', then we do not perceive the important decision makers within these systems, who wield significant power throughout the life of the blockchain.

In a broader sense, blockchain technology is being lauded as transformative for every human practice that uses recordkeeping (so, all of them). If blockchain technology achieves even a small portion of its projected potential, then it may soon undergird many critical infrastructures within our societies, ranging from property records, to payment and voting systems. And, if blockchain technology ends up enabling our most fundamental social infrastructures, then the governance processes for creating, maintaining, and altering the technology deserve careful scrutiny, as these processes will affect the resilience of the technology as well as any infrastructure that comes to rely on it.[11]

---

[6] In addition to developers, there are other parties who play important roles in a public blockchain system, including miners (transaction processors), nodes (those that do not actually process transactions), users, and exchanges (businesses that exchange one cryptocurrency for another cryptocurrency or a traditional sovereign currency like the US dollar). See, e.g., Jatinder Singh and Johan David Michels, 'Blockchain as a Service: Providers and Trust' (2017) Queen Mary, University of London, School of Law Legal Studies Research Paper No. 269/2017, https://ssrn.com/abstract=3091223. I plan to analyse the governance roles of these parties in later papers.

[7] Primavera De Filippi and Aaron Wright, *Blockchain and the Law: The Rule of Code* (Harvard University Press 2018), 2–3.

[8] ibid., 26.

[9] Nick Szabo, 'The Dawn of Trustworthy Computing' (*Unenumerated*, 11 December 2014), http://unenumerated. blogspot.com/2014/12/the-dawn-of-trustworthy-computing.html.

[10] Securities regulators around the world are evaluating how the tokens of blockchain systems fit into existing securities laws, with a number of prosecutions stemming from the initial coin offering mania that struck the cryptocurrency world in 2017. On 14 June 2018, a representative of the US Securities and Exchange Commission stated that it was unlikely that Bitcoin or Ethereum were securities due to their decentralized status because 'purchasers would no longer reasonably expect a person or group to carry out essential managerial or entrepreneurial efforts'. Speech by William Hinman, 'Digital Asset Transactions: When Howey Met Gary (Plastic)' (14 June 2018) Speech, https://www.sec.gov/news/speech/speech-hinman-061418.

[11] Angela Walch, 'The Bitcoin Blockchain as Financial Market Infrastructure: A Consideration of Operational Risk' (2015) 18 *New York University Journal of Legislation and Public Policy*, 83, considers the operational risks created by informal governance processes in Bitcoin and their implications for its suitability as financial market infrastructure. Angela Walch, 'Open-Source Operational Risk: Should Public Blockchains Serve as Financial Market

In section II, I describe the types of activities that software developers perform and explain how these activities function as a significant part of the governance of prominent public blockchains, like Bitcoin and Ethereum.[12] In section III, I evaluate the implications of this concentration of power in certain developers and apply Tamar Frankel's conception of a 'fiduciary' to their actions. In section IV, I discuss the pros and cons of treating these parties as fiduciaries of certain participants in the blockchains they manage. In section V, I discuss some of the complexities involved with the categorization, including the difficulties in precisely determining which individuals in a given blockchain function as fiduciaries and to whom they should owe corresponding duties. In section VI, I provide an overview of the continuing experimentation in public blockchain governance and of existing scholarly approaches. Finally, in section VII, I offer concluding thoughts and suggestions for further research.

As I perform this analysis, I am aware that analogizing software developers to fiduciaries is controversial, as treating these parties as fiduciaries directly contests the dominant narrative of decentralization of public blockchains and would almost certainly reduce innovation in the public blockchain space. However, sometimes consideration of taboo ideas is necessary to illuminate the trade-offs we make in our existing legal paradigm of protecting innovation by minimizing accountability. A discussion of the accountability of those who govern technology is particularly salient given the current, active debate over the governance of Facebook, Uber, and other technology companies that have significant effects on society.

II. Nominal Decentralization—De Facto Governance

In this section, I describe the role developers play in the governance of certain public blockchains and explore public blockchains' overstated reputation for decentralized software development, given that identifiable parties dominate (and therefore centralize) the process.[13]

One of the defining features of public blockchains is that they are said to be *decentralized*.[14] In theory, this means that there is no central entity that either creates or maintains them.[15] Rather, they operate on a peer-to-peer basis through the running of open-source software by a network of computers. The software development process for public blockchains is also said to be 'decentralized', as is typical of open-source software projects.[16] There is no central entity that is officially responsible for maintaining or updating the software. A mix of

---

Infrastructures?' in *Handbook of Blockchain, Digital Finance, and Inclusion*, edited by David Lee Kuo Chuen and Robert Deng (Vol. 2, Elsevier Academic Press 2017), explores the operational risks raised by the use of grassroots open-source software development practices in the use of public blockchains as financial market infrastructures.

[12] Each public blockchain has its own unique characteristics, so it is theoretically possible that some public blockchains may not have software developers who serve as fiduciaries. However, I am sceptical that the elimination of trusted software developers will actually occur, so believe the analysis in this chapter will be useful to the understanding of most, if not all, public blockchains.

[13] A great deal of experimentation is happening with public blockchains, with new variations introduced almost daily. This chapter does not specifically address each variation of governance but provides an overarching analytical framework. I highlight some recent variations of public blockchain governance in Part VI. It may be possible that new variations of public blockchains have no developers filling the role of fiduciaries, but I am sceptical that this will be the case.

[14] Adam E. Gencer, Soumya Basu, Ittay Eyal, Robbert van renesse, and Emin G. Sirer, 'Decentralization in Bitcoin and Ethereum Networks' (*arXiv.org*, 2018) https://arxiv.org/pdf/1801.03998.pdf.; Peter van Valkenburgh, 'What Could "Decentralization" Mean in the Context of the Law?' (*CoinCentreBlog*, 15 June 2018) https://coincenter.org/entry/what-could-decentralization-mean-in-the-context-of-the-law.

[15] Gencer (n 14). The mining networks of public blockchains, like Bitcoin and Ethereum, are quite centralized, which is relevant to the governance role miners play in these networks. More extensive discussion of this phenomenon is beyond the scope of this chapter.

[16] For a discussion of the software development process of public blockchains, see Walch, 'Open-Source Operational Risk' (n 11), 252–54.

volunteer and paid software developers write and update the software, determining how to revise the code through 'informal processes that depend on rough notions of consensus and that are subject to no fixed legal or organizational structure.'[17] The code is publicly available,[18] and anyone in the world may propose a change through a standardized proposal process. Indeed, many developers from across the globe have made proposals.

Furthermore, there may be people involved who help shape the code but do not actually write it—these may include people reviewing it or doing research and making recommendations about the policy and technical goals of the system. As mentioned earlier in footnote 4, my use of the term 'developer' in this analysis is intended to encompass those making decisions about the policy choices to be embedded in the code, how best technically to manifest those choices, and then actually crafting and reviewing the code to achieve those policy and technical choices. Within this group of contributors, importantly, not all participants are equal. For instance, in open-source software projects like public blockchains, a team of 'core developers' or 'maintainers' generally leads the software development process. This means that, although this group of people may not be united under the roof of an entity structure, they function as the leaders and decision makers in relation to the code.[19] This power manifests in the ways in which they differ from rank-and-file developers. With Bitcoin, for example, core developers, until recently, have had the ability to send emergency messages to all nodes in the network[20] and are the only developers who have 'commit access' that allow them to make actual changes to the software code,[21] i.e. other developers can propose changes but a core developer's password or access code is ultimately needed to put that change in a new code release. Prominent developers also shape how public blockchains are viewed by regulators and the public at large. Certain developers have met privately with various international regulators or leaders[22] and often comment publicly on what should happen with the particular blockchain they represent and the technology as a whole.[23]

---

[17] Shawn Bayern, 'Of Bitcoins, Independently Wealthy Software and the Zero-Member LLC' (2014) 108 *Northwestern University Law Review Online*, 257, 259.

[18] The GitHub pages for Bitcoin and Ethereum, the two most prominent public blockchains, are found at https://github.com/bitcoin/bitcoin and https://github.com/ethereum/, respectively.

[19] Vitalik Buterin, creator of Ethereum, stated in a January 2017 interview about Ethereum's governance: 'It is kind of technocratic in some ways, because right now there is a small group of people that really deeply understand all the different Ethereum technical considerations—a lot of decisions do tend to get made by a small group. But in the longer term that is definitely something we are looking to democratize.' This statement is from Joon Ian Wong, 'Ethereum's Inventor on How "Initial Coin Offerings" are a New Way to Fund the Internet' (*Quartz*, 14 September 2017), Interview with Viterik Buterin, https://qz.com/1075124/ethereum-founder-vitalik-buterin-discusses-initial-coin-offerings-the-consensus-algorithm-and-the-most-interesting-apps/.

[20] Andreas M. Antonopoulos, *Mastering Bitcoin: Unlocking Digital Cryptocurrencies* (2nd edn, O'Reilly 2017), 157: the emergency message power 'allow[ed] the core developer team to notify all Bitcoin users of a serious problem in the Bitcoin network, such as a critical bug that require[s] user action'. The password that allowed the sending of the network-wide emergency messages was held only 'by a few select members of the core development team'. Also see Arthur Gervais, Ghassan O. Karame, Srdjan Capkun, and Vedran Capkun, 'Is Bitcoin a Decentralized Currency?' (2014) http://eprint.iacr.org/2013/829.pdf, which argues that giving the emergency alert power only to the core developers 'gives these entities privileged powers to reach out to users and urge them to adopt a given Bitcoin release'.

[21] Tom Simonite, 'The Man Who Really Built Bitcoin' (2014) *MIT Technology Review*, http://www.technologyreview.com/featuredstory/527051/the-man-who-really-built-bitcoin/, describes how only the core developers have the power to 'change the code behind Bitcoin and merge in proposals from other volunteers'. Also see Gervais et al. (n 20), 6: 'this [software development process] limits the impact that users have, irrespective of their computing power, to affect the development of the official Bitcoin [software]'.

[22] For example, Gavin Andresen met with the Central Intelligence Agency in the United States when he served as the lead developer of Bitcoin in 2011. Vitalik Buterin, the creator of Ethereum, met with Russian president Vladimir Putin in 2017 as sourced from Ilya Khrennikov, 'Vladimir Putin is Getting Interested in Bitcoin's Biggest Rival' (*Bloomberg*, 6 June 2017) https://www.bloomberg.com/news/articles/2017-06-06/putin-eyes-bitcoin-rival-to-spur-economic-growth-beyond-oil-gas.

[23] Quoting of Bitcoin core developer Wladimir van der Laan on plans for funding Bitcoin software development found in Stan Higgins, 'Bitcoin Core Opens Doors to Outside Funding with Sponsorship Program' (*CoinDesk*, 6 April 2016) http://www.coindesk.com/bitcoin-core-opens-doors-to-outside-funding-with-sponsorship-program/;

Power is often most visible during a crisis and examining what has happened in crisis moments of public blockchains shows us the power that a small group of developers wields. Below, I briefly describe Bitcoin's March 2013 hard fork and Ethereum's July 2016 hard fork. A 'hard fork' occurs when at least two non-compatible versions of software are running on a network, meaning that different ledgers are being generated by different portions of a previously cohesive network.[24] Hard forks are significant moments in public blockchains as they result in two separate networks; if the hard fork is unintentional, it can require human discretion and action for the networks (and their ledgers) to reunite.[25]

A. Bitcoin's March 2013 hard fork

In March 2013, Bitcoin experienced a hard fork in the network, with the effect that two separate ledgers were being maintained by different computers within the network.[26] The fork happened because nodes within the network were running two different versions of the Bitcoin software; some had upgraded to a new release whilst others had not yet done so. When the software developers realized that the fork was occurring, they quickly contacted miners on the network to persuade them to support one of the two disparate ledgers. This required some of the miners to downgrade to the prior software version, 'sacrificing significant amounts of money' as a result.[27] With that change made, the network gradually returned to a single ledger.

This episode spotlights the exercise of power by both the key developers and miners with a significant amount of hashing power. The developers were able to correspond with, and persuade, particular miners to alter the software they were running, which had the effect of creating a 'winning' ledger. The developers involved also chose which ledger should be authoritative; this created financial winners and losers amongst the miners, based on which ledger fragment they had been processing during the fork. Miners with a threshold percentage of power within the network were able to sway the outcome through their choice of which version of the software to run. The more network power, essentially, the more 'votes' a miner could cast, and the more lobbying required by developers to obtain the result they sought.

B. Ethereum's July 2016 hard fork

The Ethereum blockchain faced an existential crisis in the summer of 2016 when the DAO, an application built on top of its blockchain platform, suffered a \$50+ million theft.[28] Presented with the choice of allowing the thief to keep the stolen ether to preserve the ledger's 'immutability' or to craft new code that would reverse the objectionable transactions, the Ethereum

---

transcribing of an interview with Vitalik Buterin about public blockchain governance and funding found in Wong (n 19).

[24] A 'hard fork' (i.e. a split into more than one network) can result from the use of incompatible software by different portions of a public blockchain network, whereas a 'soft fork' results from the release of new software to the network that is compatible with prior versions so that the network continues to produce a single blockchain record. Bruno Biais, Christophe Bisière, Matthieu Bouvard, and Catherine Casamatta, 'The Blockchain Folk Theorem' (2018) Toulouse School of Economics Working Paper No. 17-817, 14, https://www.tse-fr.eu/sites/default/files/TSE/documents/doc/wp/2017/wp_tse_817.pdf.

[25] For a more in-depth discussion of hard forks of public blockchains, see Walch, 'Open-Source Operational Risk' (n 11), 259–66; Biais et al. (n 24), 13–17.

[26] Walch, 'The Bitcoin Blockchain as FMI' (n 11), 873; Biais (n 24), 14–16.

[27] Walch, 'The Bitcoin Blockchain as FMI' (n 11), 873.

[28] Joon Ian Wong and Ian Kar, 'Everything You Need to Know About the Ethereum "Hard Fork"' (*Quartz*, 18 July 2016) https://qz.com/730004/everything-you-need-to-know-about-the-ethereum-hard-fork/.

developers decided to pursue a hard fork that would recover the funds.[29] They determined how to code revised software that would achieve the fork as well as persuaded a majority of the network's hashing power (held and exercised by miners) to adopt the revised software. The preparations for the hard fork included explanatory missives from the core developers and an advance poll of the Ethereum miners to see how likely the hard fork was to succeed.[30] Only a very small percentage of ether holders or miners voted in the advance polls but the Ethereum developers decided to proceed with the hard fork.[31]

It worked. Enough miners upgraded to the revised software, and the ledger followed them, taking the Ethereum name and primary developers with it. However, a splinter group of software developers and miners decided to keep the original ledger (reflecting the theft) going. Dubbing the surviving chain 'Ethereum Classic', this group issued a Declaration of Independence from Ethereum[32] and has since been operating a competing blockchain.

This hard fork demonstrates the power exercised by certain developers and significant miners. The developers made the decision whether to treat the hack of the DAO application as theft (meaning that it should have some sort of remedy) or as an exploitation of code intended to run without human involvement (meaning no remedy would be appropriate). The proposal to engage in the hard fork split the Ethereum community, with some arguing passionately for immutability no matter what, and others arguing that the hacker must be punished. Allegations that the dominant developers recommended the hard fork because some of their own money had been stolen in the hack[33] made the rounds on Twitter and Reddit.[34]

The passion, drama, and anger surrounding the Ethereum hard fork show how much was at stake for the Ethereum community, for investors in ether, and for those who built applications and companies atop the Ethereum blockchain. Yet only a small number of developers and miners in this 'decentralized' system decided what the resolution of the DAO hack would be, in effect determining the financial fortunes of all those relying on the Ethereum blockchain, whether or not they had invested in the DAO.[35]

These examples of power reveal that centralized decision making exists within nominally decentralized public blockchains.[36] There are countless other examples demonstrating the exercise of power by a small subset of developers—arguably every single bit of code actually

---

[29] ibid. [30] ibid.

[31] Vitalik Buterin, 'Notes on Blockchain Governance' (Vitalik Buterin's website, 17 December 2017) https://vitalik.ca/general/2017/12/17/voting.html.

[32] Ethereum Classic, 'The Ethereum Classic Declaration of Independence, 20 July 2016', https://ethereumclassic.github.io/assets/ETC_Declaration_of_Independence.pdf.

[33] Ray Jones, 'Ethereum Protocol Developer Holds $114,877 Worth of DAO Tokens' (*Reddit*, 29 June 2016) https://www.reddit.com/r/ethereum/comments/4qiqq8/ethereum_protocol_developer_holds_114877_worth_of/d4th8ce/: 'The simplest solution would be for all people in positions of influence who are in favor of a hard fork to openly declare their DAO token holdings.' Aakil Fernandes, 'Ethereum Protocol Developer Holds $114,887 of DAO Tokens' (*Reddit*, 29 June 2016) https://www.reddit.com/r/ethereum/comments/4qiqq8/ethereum_protocol_developer_holds_114877_worth_of/d4tm9o5/: 'We *should* care when people have conflicts of interest. That applies to lawyers, judges, bankers, politicians and yes it applies to developers. Humans are humans.'

[34] See, e.g., Justin Camarena, 'I'd agree with a rollback for protocol level hacks ... But this isn't that at all. Core devs own DAO' (*Twitter*, 17 June 2016) https://twitter.com/juscamarena/status/744008754459475968; Justin Camarena, 'they are unfairly slanted to HF'ing to regain their money ... might as well just have a private chain' (*Twitter*, 17 June 2016) https://twitter.com/juscamarena/status/744008863091941376; Fernandes (n 33).

[35] A counter-argument to the argument that Ethereum developers and miners exercised power is that parties who did not wish to proceed were able to continue with the Ethereum Classic blockchain. However, Ethereum Classic had much less mining power devoted to it, making it more vulnerable to attack, and it had to assemble a new slate of software developers to keep it going.

[36] Some may argue that these examples of power exercised in connection with a hard fork are no longer relevant because they happened in 2013 and 2016, respectively. However, nothing relevant appears to have changed about the software development governance models in Bitcoin or Ethereum since these events.

released to the network is an exercise of power. Since the moment these public blockchains were created (including the idea development and creation process), small groups of people have been making decisions about which policies should be reflected in the code (e.g. a limited or unlimited number of tokens? Transaction fees or the creation of new tokens?) and how those policy choices should technically be achieved through the code. These decisions have impacted upon significant numbers of people, and the more widely used public blockchains become, whether as cryptocurrencies or as infrastructure undergirding other systems, the greater will be the number of people who rely on the decision making of a small set of developers.

III. If It Looks Like a Fiduciary ...

In section I, I described how developers exercise power within public blockchains. In this section, I explore the implications of this concentration of power and analogize these central decision makers to fiduciaries.[37] When using a general definition of 'fiduciary', certain developers of public blockchains bear a strong resemblance.[38]

The fiduciary concept is ancient and is fundamentally based on the concept of 'trust'. Familiar fiduciaries include doctors, lawyers, financial advisors, trustees, and corporate officers and directors.[39] We frequently put our fate in the hands of others—others whom we count on to provide considered and competent advice, perform tasks we cannot do for ourselves (like open-heart surgery!) and to manage our funds or investments to our benefit. We expect these parties to put our interests before their own in this role and to perform their duties competently and honestly.

Tamar Frankel, the pioneering and leading scholar on fiduciary law, has written that all fiduciaries share the following attributes:

1) They offer mainly services (in contrast to products). The services that fiduciaries offer are usually socially desirable and often require expertise, such as healing, legal services, teaching, asset management, corporate management and religious services. 2) In order to perform these services effectively, fiduciaries must be entrusted with property or power. 3) Entrustment poses to 'entrustors' the risks that the fiduciaries will not be trustworthy. They may misappropriate the entrusted property, misuse the entrusted power or they will not perform the promised services adequately. 4) There is a likelihood that [a] the entrustor will fail to protect itself from the risks involved in fiduciary relationships; [b] the markets may fail to protect entrustors from these risks; and that [c] the costs for the fiduciaries of establishing their trustworthiness may be higher than their benefits from the relationships.[40]

Certain developers of public blockchains arguably resemble fiduciaries in all of the ways identified by Frankel. Below, I apply each of Frankel's factors in turn.

---

[37] Szabo, 'Money Blockchains' (n 1), analogized miners to fiduciaries and noted the significant trust placed in blockchain software developers: 'Miners are partially trusted fiduciaries, and those who are not expert developers or computer scientists who have invested a great deal of time in learning the design principles and codebase of a blockchain must place a great deal of faith in the expert developer community, much as non-specialists who want to understand the results of a specialized science do of the corresponding scientists.'

[38] This is not a jurisdiction-specific legal argument, but rather a consideration of the broad conception of a fiduciary. I am not claiming that in a particular jurisdiction, the core developers or dominant miners would be considered fiduciaries based on that jurisdiction's existing law.

[39] In recent years, legal scholars have examined whether expansion of the fiduciary category may be merited, including in the technology sector. See, e.g., Jack M Balkin, 'Information Fiduciaries and the First Amendment' (2016) 49 *University of California Davis Law Review*, 1183, who argues that tech companies holding personal data should be deemed 'information fiduciaries'. D. Theodore Rave, 'Politicians as Fiduciaries' (2013) 126 *Harvard Law, Review*671 argues that politicians function as fiduciaries. Ethan Leib, David L Ponet, and Michael Serota, 'A Fiduciary Theory of Judging' (2013) 101 *California Law Review*, 699, apply the fiduciary concept to judges.

[40] Tamar Frankel, *Fiduciary Law* (Oxford University Press 2011), 6.

A. Providing socially desirable services that often require expertise

Frankel's first factor is that fiduciaries provide services (as opposed to products) to the 'entrustors'[41] and that the services are typically 'socially desirable' and 'often require expertise'.

As described in section I, the software developers who work on public blockchains provide services to the users of that blockchain. These services include conducting research, reviewing the code, proposing conceptual changes to the code, reviewing changes proposed by other developers, drafting new code and revising existing code, security-testing new code, compiling code into new releases, and communicating about the project with other developers. There is certainly a conceptual question as to whether software code is a 'product',[42] but it is common practice that when companies license software to other parties, they can choose whether or not to provide the service (sold under a services or maintenance agreement) of ongoing software maintenance. While one could argue that the software itself is a product, the work that the developers do to maintain and change it is a service.

Furthermore, one could certainly argue (and I imagine that all software developers working on these blockchains would agree or they would not be working on these projects) that the services provided are 'socially desirable'. If one believes that public blockchains offer some benefits to the public or to their users, then the services performed to create and maintain them are arguably 'socially desirable'. In addition, the services provided by the software developers clearly 'require expertise'. Only those skilled in designing, reading, evaluating, and crafting software code can perform these services. Although the project is open-source, which typically means that the development process is open to anyone who wants to contribute, only developers who have at least a minimum amount of expertise in the relevant software languages and design techniques can realistically participate. And, only those who have earned the privilege of 'commit access' have the privilege of making changes to the actual code that will be released for use in the system.

B. Entrusted with property or power

According to Frankel, the second hallmark of a fiduciary is the ability to use his or her discretion on behalf of entrustors, as 'fiduciaries must be entrusted with property or power'.[43]

Developers exercise discretion on behalf of others in virtually every task they perform in connection with their blockchains. From decisions about which changes should be put into a new software release (reflecting both policy and technical choices) to decisions about the stance to take when speaking to regulators on behalf of the blockchain, developers are constantly making impactful choices.[44] In the 2013 Bitcoin hard fork, leading developers determined which of the forked ledgers should be recognized as true and persuaded particular miners to achieve their goals. In the 2016 Ethereum hard fork, key developers decided to treat the DAO hack as a theft and to reverse the transaction by issuing a new release of the code. In each of these cases, based on the developers' decisions, some people lost money.

Holders of public blockchain tokens and those who built businesses on top of these public blockchains did not get to explicitly approve these decisions[45]—once they chose to participate in the blockchain, the only way to escape the developers' power would be to abandon

---

[41] ibid., Introduction. I use Frankel's terminology, which she uses to refer to those whom fiduciaries serve: 'they entrust to fiduciaries property and power'.

[42] See David Berke, 'Products Liability in the Sharing Economy' (2016) 33 *Yale Journal on Regulation*, 609–18, which provides a recent description of the legal status of software as a product for products liability purposes.

[43] Frankel (n 40), 6 and 26.

[44] Note that some of the variations on public blockchain governance described in Part V incorporate 'on-chain' governance (e.g. Tezos), which provides for holders of the applicable token to vote on software changes. This may not affect the fiduciary analysis as any voter who is not an expert in the relevant technology or code will likely rely on the recommendations of an expert to cast a vote.

[45] ibid.

the investment (whether in the cryptocurrency or the blockchain-related business) or to persuade a group of people to create a new token by forking off the original blockchain (as happened with Bitcoin Cash and Bitcoin Gold in 2017).[46] Unfortunately, the developers' decisions could reduce the value of an investment in the blockchain to zero before an investor is able to get out (by selling the cryptocurrency to a willing buyer). Much is made of token-holders' 'right to exit' via the forking process or selling the token;[47] however, the ability to exit should not be relevant to the fiduciary analysis—shareholders of publicly registered stock can always exit by selling the stock, yet they are still owed fiduciary duties by officers and directors of the company.

One could also argue that developers are in some ways entrusted with property, given the trend to view cryptocurrency tokens as commodities or digital assets.[48] Developers are essential to maintaining the existence of these digital assets—if they mess up the coding (deliberately or unintentionally), the digital asset could cease to exist, analogous to what happened with the famous Parity bug in 2017, when millions of dollars of the cryptocurrency ether became inaccessible.[49] In this way, developers are important caretakers of other people's money.

C. Risk to entrustors that fiduciaries may not be trustworthy

Frankel's third indicator of a fiduciary is that 'entrustment poses to entrustors the risks that the fiduciaries will not be trustworthy. They may misappropriate the entrusted property, misuse the entrusted power or they will not perform the promised services adequately.'[50] This factor deals with both trustworthiness (the possibility of exploitation by the fiduciary) and competence (performing the promised service to an acceptable standard).

There are many ways in which developers could exploit their positions or fail to act with competence, in both cases harming those who rely on the relevant blockchain.

As with any position of power, conflict-of-interest situations can and do arise for key developers. These crop up most obviously with their compensation. Although open-source software is generally developed by software developers in their spare time as an unpaid hobby, the public blockchains of Bitcoin and Ethereum have worked differently. Keeping multibillion-dollar systems working 24/7 is too demanding for hobbyists, so people involved with Bitcoin and Ethereum have found ways of paying important developers for their time. With Ethereum, a Swiss non-profit company called the 'Ethereum Foundation' was created and crowd-funded through the first initial coin offering ('ICO'), and pays for the salaries of some developers, along with other administrative and advisory staff.[51] With Bitcoin, there have

---

[46] Recent 51% attacks against Bitcoin Gold, a forked network from the original Bitcoin chain, demonstrate that a forked network may have different (in this context, lesser) properties than the original network, including potentially less security if it has less mining power devoted to it or less experienced software developers. See Daniel Oberhaus, 'Cryptocurrency Miners are Sabotaging Blockchains for Their Personal Gain' (*Motherboard*, 25 May 2018) https://motherboard.vice.com/en_us/article/a3a38e/what-is-a-51-percent-attack-silicon-valley-bitcoin-gold-verge-monacoin-cryptocurrency.

[47] E.g. Jeffery Atik and George Gerro, 'Hard Forks on the Bitcoin Blockchain: Reversible Exit, Continuing Voice' (2018) 1 *Stanford Journal of Law and Public Policy*, analyse the availability of shareholder concepts of voice and exit in hard forks of the Bitcoin blockchain.

[48] See *In re Coinflip Inc.*, CFTC Docket No. 15-29 (17 September 2015); *Commodity Futures Trading Commission v. McDonnell*, F. Supp.3d 213 (E.D. NY) (2018); Chris Burniske and Jack Tatar, *Cryptoassets: The Innovative Investor's Guide to Bitcoin and Beyond* (McGraw-Hill 2018).

[49] See Giuseppe Destefanis, Michele Marchesi, Marco Ortu et al., 'Smart Contracts Vulnerabilities: A Call for Blockchain Software Engineering' (2018) IEEE Conference paper, http://dspace.stir.ac.uk/bitstream/1893/27135/1/smart-contracts-vulnerabilities-3.pdf, which conducts a case study of the Parity wallet hack and proposes a special category of 'Blockchain Software Engineering' with higher standards than non-blockchain software development.

[50] Frankel (n 40), 6.

[51] See Joseph Young, 'Vlad Zamfir: Sharding is the Only True Blockchain Scaling Solution' (*BinaryDistrict*, 13 November 2017) https://journal.binarydistrict.com/vlad-zamfir-sharding-is-the-only-true-blockchain-scaling-solution-/: 'Although initial coin offerings (ICOs) and independent blockchain projects have created many millionaire Ethereum developers, Zamfir explained that most Ethereum core developers earn salaries that are much

been a variety of ways of compensating the core developers, including having them work at the MIT Media Lab, for private companies within the Bitcoin ecosystem (e.g. Blockstream, BitPay), and/or under a sponsorship model.[52]

As I have previously argued,[53] this compensation structure sets up a clear conflict of interest for developers, who may feel pressured to make decisions about the blockchain that favour their salary payer's interests. A quick scan of Twitter, Reddit, or any blockchain message board reveals that there are vastly different opinions on virtually every decision that a developer might make, meaning that conflicts of interest among the key developers are relevant to anyone relying on the applicable blockchain.

This is not purely hypothetical. Leading developers have been accused of being improperly influenced by those who pay their salaries[54] or by their own financial interests.[55] A risk of exploitation of the position could also arise through key developers' interactions with regulators or policy makers on behalf of the blockchain. For instance, Ethereum founder Vitalik Buterin famously met with Vladimir Putin and Gavin Andresen met with the Central Intelligence Agency/Federal Bureau of Investigation when he was the leading core developer of Bitcoin.[56] Meetings with regulators or policy makers may not be open to the public, so users of the blockchain must simply trust that the developers are acting in users' interests rather than their own in these meetings.

There are infinite ways in which key developers could fail to act with competence on behalf of those who rely on the blockchain. A few quick examples include failing to discover and fix a security flaw in the code, misjudging the risks of a proposed change to the software, or acting in a way that causes regulators to lose faith in the blockchain, all of which could seriously damage those relying on the blockchain.

It is clear that users of blockchain tokens and any financial products based on them, as well as those building businesses in connection with a blockchain, are vulnerable to both untrustworthiness and lack of competence by key developers, particularly those users who do not have expertise in blockchain software development.

D. Difficulty or failure of entrustors to protect themselves from fiduciary risks

Frankel's fourth characteristic of fiduciaries is:

> there is likelihood that [a] the entrustor will fail to protect itself from the risks involved in fiduciary relationships; [b] the markets may fail to protect entrustors from these risks; and that [c] the costs for the fiduciaries of establishing their trustworthiness may be higher than their benefits from the relationships.[57]

This factor deals with the vulnerability of entrustors to fiduciaries and the likelihood that neither they nor markets will provide protection from this vulnerability.

It is likely that in public blockchains, certain entrustors will fail to protect themselves from the risks involved in a fiduciary relationship with developers. This is due to the expertise

---

lower than the market standard. "I agree with the general statement that core developers are not sufficiently incentivized", he noted. "Some Ethereum developers are paid by the Ethereum foundation, but at what are now below market salaries. I think core developers provide a huge amount of value as a public good", added Zamfir. "Public goods are inherently difficult to fund, because the non-excludable nature of their benefits means that even those who don't pay get to enjoy the benefits."'

[52] Walch, 'The Bitcoin Blockchain as FMI' (n 11), 878–79.　　[53] ibid.

[54] See, e.g., Whalecalls, 'Fact or FUD: Blockstream, Inc. is the Main Force Behind Bitcoin (and Taken Over)' (*Medium*, 1 December 2017) https://medium.com/@whalecalls/fud-or-fact-blockstream-inc-is-the-main-force-behind-bitcoin-and-taken-over-160aed93c003, discusses the common statement that the company Blockstream controls Bitcoin software development because it employs several core developers.

[55] See nn 33 and 34.　　[56] See n 22.　　[57] Frankel (n 40), 6.

barrier between blockchain software developers and users who cannot evaluate software code themselves. In 'permissionless' systems like public blockchains, there is nothing that prevents people who lack software expertise from becoming involved with a given blockchain, whether through the purchase of tokens or token-based financial products, or by investing in or creating a business tied to the blockchain. Anyone who lacks expertise in the particular code of the blockchain (some of which are coded in newly developed software languages like OCaml)[58] will have a difficult time protecting themselves from the actions of developers, as they are unable to meaningfully evaluate the software code and any proposed changes to it. They simply have to count on the developers to make good policy and technical decisions. The counter-argument to this is that if non-technical people want to use public blockchains, they should be willing to pay to have the code vetted and warrantied for them or accept that any use of the blockchain is *caveat emptor*. This may be somewhat persuasive when talking about direct purchasers of public blockchain tokens but is unpersuasive in the case of public blockchains serving as infrastructure, when people do not have a meaningful choice about their reliance on the blockchain. It is also impractical for entrustors to vet the loyalty and character of each influential developer of a public blockchain in order to evaluate whether they have a conflict of interest on certain issues.

Furthermore, 'fiduciaries that serve numerous entrustors in a standardized manner [as is the case with developers of public blockchains] acquire power that is greater than the power of fiduciaries that serve individuals'.[59] This is true in public blockchains because the decisions and actions of developers affect an entire blockchain system, rather than a single person. Moreover, 'the entrustors' ability to control their fiduciaries is weakened with the rise in the entrustors' number. The entrustors may not be well organized and may have different interests and different ideas about the benefits that their fiduciaries must pursue.'[60] This manifests in public blockchains as entrustors (token holders, businesses providing blockchain-related services, and systems building atop a blockchain) have extremely divergent views on the decisions and actions developers should take, which may dilute the control they exercise over developers.

There are arguments on both sides as to whether the market is likely to protect entrustors from the risks involved in trusting developers. One could argue that users of tokens who can evaluate software code will serve as market guidance to the entrustors who cannot evaluate code, as code-savvy people will signal their belief in the software code quality and the philosophy embedded in it by using the applicable token, or by building businesses related to the token. If tech-savvy people do not believe in the quality of the developers or their code, they will avoid a particular blockchain and non-tech-savvy people will pick up on these signals and also avoid that blockchain. Unfortunately, however, this argument seems to have been disproven by events in the cryptocurrency and ICO space in 2017–2018. Investors have poured billions into ICOs, though in many cases, little detail has been provided on the technology or the development team behind the technology.[61] Despite warnings from numerous regulators and policy makers, many scams have occurred, suggesting that market signals may not enable entrustors to responsibly evaluate a public blockchain and its developers.[62]

Finally, the costs for software developers serving as fiduciaries of establishing their trustworthiness may be higher than their benefits from the relationship. This may be particularly true in public blockchains that rely on grassroots open-source software governance, with uncertainties of how the work of software developers is funded.[63] Developers

---

[58] Tezos is coded in OCaml.   [59] Frankel (n 40), 11.   [60] ibid.
[61] David Floyd, '$6.3 Billion: 2018 ICO Funding Has Passed 2017's Total' (*CoinDesk*, 19 April 2018) https://www.coindesk.com/6-3-billion-2018-ico-funding-already-outpaced-2017/.
[62] See De Nikhilesh, 'SEC Halts Mayweather-Endorsed ICO, Charges Founders with Fraud' (*CoinDesk*, 2 April 2018) https://www.coindesk.com/sec-halts-mayweather-endorsed-ico-charges-founders-fraud/.
[63] Walch, 'Open-Sourced Operational Risk' (n 11), 256–59.

must spend significant time and effort gaining credibility and respect for their competence in order to be granted 'commit access' rights. Yet, as discussed in section IIIC, the mechanics of compensation for these efforts are uncertain and evolving, with no established way of paying developers for their extensive time and effort. A recent example of this phenomenon occurred in the Zcash public blockchain when a key developer threatened to quit working on Zcash wallet software (for which he was the sole maintainer and which could potentially affect thousands of users) and to create a competing blockchain because he was not being paid for his work, resulting in money quickly being contributed to the developer.[64]

* * *

Once we acknowledge that certain developers resemble fiduciaries, even if there is not a perfect likeness, the instincts that people have had all along make sense. For instance, there has been discussion about the need for increased transparency from the Ethereum Foundation, which apparently funds development of Ethereum, but provides very little public information about its structure, governance, or funding.[65] This instinct towards transparency suggests that the developers realize that they are acting on behalf of others and owe those they represent transparency about their actions. There have been comments from key developers that indicate they appreciate the heavy responsibility they bear to keep the blockchain running.[66] Recently, one of six core developers of Ethereum software resigned from his role because he was concerned about personal legal risk.[67] Finally, discussions about the compensation of core developers and commentary about conflicts of interest suggest that some have recognized the power certain developers exercise in relation to users.[68]

If certain people are functioning as fiduciaries, the question becomes 'What do we want to do about it?' From a policy perspective, there are clear arguments that those who act as fiduciaries should be legally accountable as fiduciaries. However, treating these parties as fiduciaries with concomitant liability would go against our existing liability framework for software systems, which generally enables those who create software to disclaim liabilities for its flaws or harms it causes[69] and has been resistant to characterizing those creating, designing, or building software as professionals subject to claims of professional malpractice.[70]

---

[64] Rachel O'Leary, 'Zcash Pays Off Developer to Avoid Blockchain Split' (*CoinDesk*, 22 June 2018) https://www.coindesk.com/zcash-pays-off-angry-developer-avoid-blockchain-split/.

[65] See Ethereum Foundation Website, https://ethereum.org/foundation. It lists three members of the Ethereum foundation but provides no information concerning governance, funding, or relationship to Ethereum software development. For discussion of lack of transparency, see Bob Summerwill, Tweets on Ethereum Foundation opacity (*Twitter*, 29 December 2017) https://twitter.com/BobSummerwill/status/946760015322398720. These state that 'there is no public list of who works for the Ethereum Foundation. There is no list of the projects which the Foundation funds or how much it funds them. There is no public information on the governance of the EF ... There is no public information on the legal entities within or funded by the EF. There is no public information on the composition of the board of the EF or voting structure. There is no public information on who advises the EF.'

[66] See Jonas Schnelli (Bitcoin core developer), Tweets (*Twitter*, 15 November 2017) https://twitter.com/_jonasschnelli_/status/930680174697381888: '4 developers have currently commit access: @orionwl @pwuille @MarcoFalke and myself. It's a burden. It's for those who are willing to review and test code and keep up with the ~80 github comments per day. It's not always fun and it's certainly not a privilege.'

[67] Rachel O'Leary, 'Ethereum Developer Resigns as Code Editor Citing Legal Concerns' (*CoinDesk*, 15 February 2018) https://www.coindesk.com/ethereum-developer-resigns-as-code-editor-citing-legal-concerns/.

[68] See nn 33 and 34.

[69] For a recent overview of the 'unusual liability cocoon' that software vendors enjoy, see Marian Reidy and Bartlomiej Hanus, 'It is Just Unfair Using Trade Laws to Out Security Software Vulnerabilities' (2017) 48 *Loyola University Chicago Law Journal*, 1111–14.

[70] Michael D. Scott, *Scott on Information Technology Law* (3rd edn, 2nd Supplement, Aspen 2018), Section 15.09[A]: 'whether computer designers or programmers are professionals in the legal sense is still an open question'.

IV. Costs and Benefits of Fiduciary Characterization

Although there are many ways that dominant developers resemble fiduciaries, the analysis here would be incomplete without considering the costs and benefits of such a categorization. In this section, I provide an initial sketch of these costs and benefits (in a non-quantitative sense) and leave exhaustive exploration of them to future work.

A. Benefits

The benefits of the fiduciary categorization go back to the roots of the fiduciary relationship: society gains when people can enter into relationships of trust, knowing that the trusted party has certain underlying obligations to them. These benefits include:

1. ensuring that the fiduciary takes the performance of his or her services seriously, and, thus, performs them with deliberation and care;

2. reducing harms caused by people, on whom others rely, acting without care or competence, or exploiting those that rely on them;

3. increasing efficiency and economic activity due to a reduction in the investigation and due diligence that has to be done before every transaction with a fiduciary[71]—if one has fiduciary duties, the entrustor does not have to exhaustively research the person before entering into a transaction with him or her;

4. the creation of an accountability standard that matches the seriousness of the services performed by the fiduciary.

Connecting these benefits more closely with public blockchains, characterizing certain developers as fiduciaries would theoretically have the following impacts.

(a) Developers would seriously consider the consequences of their policy and technical choices, obtain advice from expert sources when needed and use great care in drafting and reviewing code and all other actions they take whilst acting on behalf of the blockchain.

(b) Greater care would result in better decisions by developers, about both conflicts of interest and substantive coding matters, meaning that those relying on the blockchain would likely be harmed less.

(c) Less particularized due diligence of individual developers would be needed by those relying on the blockchain, meaning users would not have to keep track of the current cast of developers and do exhaustive research on each one in an ongoing evaluation of continued participation in the blockchain. This would minimize the resources needed to evaluate participation in the blockchain, which, in turn, would increase efficiencies.

(d) There would be an acknowledgement that certain developers are making high-stakes decisions on critical matters, such as finance and money, on behalf of others and so are accountable in a way that more closely approximates the stakes involved. (As mentioned in the concluding paragraph of section III, it is notoriously difficult to hold anyone liable for problems caused by software, in part due to the 'economic loss' rule in tort law and in part because software licenses generally disclaim all liability for anything related to the software.)[72]

---

[71] Frankel (n 40), 271–72.   [72] See Reidy and Hanus (n 69).

B. Costs

Of course, there are reasons not to view any developers as fiduciaries, many of which are commonly made against the idea of regulation itself.

1. The primary argument against categorizing certain developers as fiduciaries is that the categorization could inhibit innovation. If these parties have to be worried about the effects that their actions would have on others, this will stifle their creativity and hold back development in the area because people will be afraid to try things that might go wrong. It is too early to intervene in the development of blockchain technology.

2. We need not worry about the governance of public blockchains because they are 'platform' technologies and legal intervention is only appropriate at the application level or with intermediaries, such as wallet companies or exchanges.

3. A fiduciary characterization is too extreme and too high a duty to place on these people. It would not be fair to treat them as fiduciaries based on what they are doing here.

4. Given the large pool of potential beneficiaries who will have differing interests, it would be impossible to tell when developers have met the fiduciary standard. A more general duty to the public owed by certain developers may be more appropriate for these public infrastructural technologies.

5. Treating certain developers as fiduciaries could deter them from participating in what may be socially beneficial projects as they will fear potential liability.

6. Protecting those who rely on public blockchains through a fiduciary categorization is paternalistic and discourages people from doing proper due diligence when evaluating their participation in public blockchains. This discourages self-reliance and personal accountability in decision making.

7. It would be unfair to set such a high standard for developers as participants in these public blockchains may not have had such accountability expectations when they decided to participate.

8. Developers are not compensated at a level consistent with the high accountability standard of a fiduciary. If their accountability risks increase, they will demand more money to provide the services.

9. Too little is at stake now with public blockchains to bother with a fiduciary standard of performance by developers.

Perhaps, in the end, the costs of the fiduciary categorization to innovation are balanced in the aggregate by the harms that are avoided by, and investigations that entrustors would otherwise have to do before, relying on the fiduciary's actions. Further research in this domain would be useful.

V. Sorting Out the Details

To say that a man is a fiduciary only begins the analysis; it gives direction to further inquiry. To whom is he a fiduciary? What obligations does he owe as a fiduciary? In what respect has he failed to discharge these obligations? And what are the consequences of his deviation from his duty?[73]

As Justice Frankfurter noted in *SEC v. Chenery Corp.* in 1943, one does not conclude an analysis by simply stating that a party is a fiduciary.[74] For any given public blockchain, a tailored

---

[73] *SEC v. Chenery Corp.*, 318 U.S. 80 (1943), 85–86.   [74] ibid.

evaluation would be necessary to determine whether a particular developer is acting as a fiduciary.

In this section, I identify some of the nuances and practical matters that would need to be considered and resolved if a legislature or a court were evaluating whether to treat particular software developers of a public blockchain as fiduciaries. In some instances, I suggest appropriate resolutions but further work beyond the scope of this short chapter is necessary to draw firmer conclusions.

A. Who are the fiduciaries?

I have suggested that certain developers resemble fiduciaries in their role in public blockchains but this does not resolve the question. It seems problematic to consider *any and every* software developer who participates in blockchain code development to be a fiduciary as only a small subset (probably including the core developers) actually determine what makes it into the released code. Similarly, it would be problematic to focus solely on those who craft the code, ignoring those who may determine the policy choices to be reflected in the code, which is why I have incorporated these types of parties into my use of the term 'developer' in this chapter.[75] In a spectrum of 'fiduciary-ness', those developers who make the most decisions on behalf of others look a lot like fiduciaries, while those who occasionally make code proposals do not. Fiduciary developers would likely include developers who initially design and/or launch the system, those involved in decision making around new releases of software, including policy and technical choices as well as code review, and those who make decisions about how to address a crisis faced by the system (e.g. a critical bug or an attack on the system).

B. Who are the entrustors?

Thus far, I have been somewhat vague about who, precisely, are the parties to whom key developers would act as fiduciaries. In Frankel's parlance, who are the 'entrustors'?

There are a variety of parties who inhabit a blockchain ecosystem. In addition to the software developers and miners already identified, there are owners of the native tokens (cryptocurrencies) of a blockchain (e.g. bitcoins and ether), businesses that service those who own and trade in cryptocurrencies (exchanges, wallets, payment processors, financiers), and companies that are using the underlying blockchain as a platform for other forms of recordkeeping, such as trading or property records. All of these parties rely on the successful ongoing operation of the relevant public blockchain. In the future, a wider swath of the public could unknowingly rely on the operation of public blockchains, if they become part of underlying recordkeeping infrastructures that are not seen by the public.[76] Further, as Bitcoin, Ethereum, and other tokens are now being described as 'crypto-assets' with financial products like futures being tied to them, the holders of these cryptocurrency-based financial products also rely on developers.

The trick here will be to determine which of these groups are considered 'entrustors' and entitled to the protections of, and obligations imposed by, fiduciary duties. Users of the applicable cryptocurrency appear to have the most reliance on the blockchain, but there are arguments that the other businesses within the ecosystem do as well. Ultimately, the fact that the public could be impacted if public blockchains become infrastructure, or if cryptocurrencies become systemically important to the financial system, may mean that

---

[75] See n 4.
[76] There is much discussion about how blockchains will ultimately just be invisible to the public, much as the internet infrastructure is largely opaque to the public now.

these fiduciary duties run to the public at large, similar to how certified public accountants are obligated to act to 'serve the public interest [and] honor the public trust'[77] or perhaps through the common law doctrine of public trust, which 'imposes on governing bodies fiduciary duties toward the public'.[78] With much discussion of how public blockchains are analogous to sovereign entities,[79] the doctrine of public trust may also be a useful lens through which to view their governance processes.[80] A full spelling-out of these arguments is beyond the scope of this chapter but is an important area for further research.

C. What are the duties owed?

As Justice Frankfurter noted, we must ask what obligations one owes as a fiduciary. Again, deeper analysis is merited but the basic fiduciary duties of care and loyalty are a good starting point. Since leading developers look a lot like officers or directors of a corporation (if one views tokens as shares of stock in the corporation) having analogous fiduciary duties may make sense. A more fulsome analysis would look at whether the protections of the 'business judgment rule' used in the corporate setting would be appropriate here.[81]

The duties of care and loyalty fall in neatly with the fiduciary definition provided by Frankel above. As discussed in section III, both competence (as part of the duty of care) and acting on behalf of the entrustor rather than oneself (as part of the duty of loyalty) are expectations that leading developers are probably already trying to live up to, and blockchain users expect them to uphold.

D. How might fiduciary status of developers arise?

Perhaps the most difficult question to answer around the fiduciary characterization is how exactly the status would arise. As Frankel has noted, 'one cannot find a clear answer to the question of whether a relationship is fiduciary'.[82] Yet software developers and public blockchain advocates are quick to point to the open-source software licenses under which public blockchain software is issued, which generally disclaim liability for any claims arising from the software.[83] Furthermore, foundations associated with public blockchains may separately attempt to disclaim liability for claims related to the blockchain for the foundation

---

[77] American Institute of CPAs Code of Conduct, Section ET 53 Article II https://www.aicpa.org/research/standards/codeofconduct.html.

[78] See Frankel (n 40), 36 ('in the case of professional services, entrustors may include not only particular persons or groups but also the public and society'), 36–37 ('The fiduciary relationship of financial intermediaries may sometimes include a relationship to the financial system'), and 125.

[79] See Marcella Atzori, 'Blockchain Technology and Decentralized Governance: Is the State Still Necessary?' (2017) 6 *Journal of Governance and Regulation*, 45, who analyses claims of blockchains to represent new forms of governance as alternatives to sovereign states; Sarah Manski and Ben Manski, 'No Gods, No Masters, No Coders? The Future of Sovereignty in a Blockchain World' (2018) 29 *Law Critique*, 151, who discuss claims of sovereignty around blockchains.

[80] See Frankel (n 40), 279–87 for a discussion of government officials' fiduciary duties to the public. See also Ethan J. Leib, David L. Ponet, and Michael Serota, 'Translating Fiduciary Principles into Public Law' (2013) 126 *Harvard Law Review Forum*, 91, for an overview of the 'burgeoning field' of 'fiduciary political theory'.

[81] The fluctuating scrutiny of directors' actions in corporate law depending on the significance of the event may have resonance for developer fiduciary status. Director actions receive enhanced scrutiny when they relate to facilitating or fending off a change of control, for instance, which is analogous to a hard fork in a public blockchain. See *Revlon Inc v. MacAndrews and Forbes Holdings, Inc.*, 506 A 3d 173 (Delamere 1986); *Unocal Corp. v. Mesa Petroleum Co.*, 493 A 2d 946 (Delamere 1985). Carla Reyes notes this analogy in a draft paper, Carla Reyes, 'Corporate Crypto Governance' (26 January 2018) Blockchain Works-in-Progress Workshop, at Cardozo Law School.

[82] Frankel (n 40), 77.

[83] See, e.g., MIT License, https://opensource.org/licenses/MIT; GNU General Public License, https://www.gnu.org/licenses/gpl-3.0.en.html.

and any software developers employed by or contracted with the foundation.[84] One could argue that any potential liability as a fiduciary is already disclaimed so there is little point in discussing the matter further.

However, the presence of legal disclaimers in these documents does not resolve the question. Fiduciary duties can arise in a number of ways—by contract, by statute,[85] by acting as a fiduciary in the eyes of a court, or by status. Indeed, there is an ongoing debate in fiduciary law over whether fiduciary categorization is based solely on contract (and may be contracted out of by the parties) or whether there are situations in which fiduciary status arises by virtue of relationship or status and may not be disclaimed.[86] This has implications for the treatment of developers in public blockchains.

If one views fiduciary status as being purely contract-based, then one could argue that a broad liability disclaimer and failure to affirmatively create a fiduciary relationship by contract would mean no fiduciary status or liability could attach to a developer. One may attempt to argue that the contract between users and developers implies a fiduciary status[87] but it may be difficult to persuade a court of such. However, there is no certainty that the open-source software licenses will be enforced[88] and there are questions about which particular parties would be bound to the licenses. Not all owners of bitcoins, ether, or other cryptocurrencies actually run the software themselves and many may never see the related open-source software license. They may obtain their cryptocurrencies through intermediaries, like exchanges, or they may be exposed to what happens to cryptocurrencies through derivatives like futures contracts or investment funds. This raises questions about whether a given user of a cryptocurrency was on notice of the license terms and is, therefore, bound to them. Overall, though, it could be difficult to show that a fiduciary relationship was established by contract between developers and entrustors (whoever those entrustors are).

However, we may not need to show a contract establishing a fiduciary relationship for developers to be treated as fiduciaries, and even if the liability disclaimers around the software are upheld, they may not apply to breach of fiduciary claims.[89] A court could view developers to be acting as fiduciaries, due to the characteristics identified in section III, and be willing to treat them as such. Courts are generally reluctant to create new types of fiduciaries but it does happen, often over a period of time.[90] Frankel has identified spouses, mediators,

---

[84] See, e.g., Ethereum Legal Agreement, (*ethereum.org*), https://www.ethereum.org/agreement, which disclaims liability for both the Ethereum Foundation and software developers employed by or contracted with the Ethereum Foundation.

[85] For example, the Employee Retirement Income Security Act of 1974 (ERISA) 29 USC 1002(21)(A) statute deems certain parties to be fiduciaries.

[86] For the contractarian view, see Frank H. Easterbrook and Daniel R. Fischel, 'Contract and Fiduciary Duty' (1993) 36 *Journal of Law and Economics*, 425; Henry N. Butler and Larry E. Ribstein, 'Opting Out of Fiduciary Duties: A Response to the Anti-Contractarians' (1993) 65 *Washington Law Review*, 1. For the anti-contractarian view and a summary of the contract/status debate, see Frankel (n 40), 229–39.

[87] See Dirk Zetzsche, Ross Buckley, and Douglas Arner, 'The Distributed Liability of Distributed Ledgers: Legal Risks of Blockchain' (2018) *University of Illinois Law Review*, 1392–96, which analyses contract-based claims against parties involved with public blockchains, including developers.

[88] There has been little case law around the enforceability of open-source software licenses (and their liability disclaimers) thus far.

[89] See *Northeast Gen. Corp. v. Wellington Adv.*, 82 NY 2d 158, 172. Hancock, J., dissenting: 'It is fundamental that a fiduciary duty "is not dependent solely upon an agreement or contractual relation between the fiduciary and the beneficiary but results from the relation.' See Deborah DeMott, 'Beyond Metaphor: An Analysis of Fiduciary Obligation' (1988) *Duke Law Journal*, 887: 'contractual obligations are controlled by the parties' manifest intention; fiduciary obligation sometimes operates precisely in opposition to intention as manifest in express agreements. The terms of an express agreement are surely not irrelevant to the fiduciary obligation analysis, but once a court concludes that a particular relationship has a fiduciary character, the parties' manifest intention does not control their obligations to each other as dispositively as it does under a contract analysis.'

[90] See *Lash v. Cheshire County Savings Bank*, 474 A 2d 980 (NH 1984), which found a fiduciary relationship between a bank official and a bank customer in connection with confidential information entrusted by the customer to the official despite no explicit contractual agreement regarding the fiduciary nature of the relationship; *Martinelli Bridgeport Roman Catholic Diocesan Corp.*, 10 F Supp 2d 138 (D Conn 1998), which found a fiduciary relationship between a church and its parishioner based on 'an approach [of examining] the power relationship

and mortgage brokers among others, as emerging fiduciaries,[91] and more recently, Jonathan Zittrain and Jack Balkin have proposed treating tech companies who hold personal data as 'information fiduciaries'.[92] As I have argued throughout this chapter, there are many reasons why courts might be willing to view certain developers of public blockchains as fiduciaries, including the superior expertise and skill needed for public blockchain software design and development,[93] as well as the fact that public blockchains purport to embed and transfer value (cryptoassets or cryptocurrencies) for an entire blockchain system, thereby making developers' actions highly consequential for potentially large numbers of people.

Finally, developers could be deemed fiduciaries of a public blockchain by statute. With virtually every law-making body and regulatory agency worldwide considering how to treat blockchain technology and cryptoassets/cryptocurrencies, this is not an impossibility. As developers continue to take fiduciary-type actions within public blockchains and with the current questioning over power and ethics in the tech sector generally such a statutory designation becomes more likely.

E. How would a breach of duty be identified?

Identifying a breach of duty here would be challenging but perhaps no more challenging than it is in other complex tort problems. One of the primary challenges would be establishing that a particular action caused harm. It can be hard to identify which lines of code cause a problem as there are complex interactions that occur in the running of the software. Even once the problematic code is located, it may be difficult to pin it to a particular developer. What happens if a portion of code is fine until a later update makes it problematic? Furthermore, what happens if a core developer recommends a hard fork that turns out to do great damage to the blockchain and its users?

Presumably, if such a fiduciary standard existed, those subject to the standard would document their investigation of issues and the rationale for their decisions, much like lawyers regularly do. This type of behaviour would help to demonstrate that the fiduciary had fulfilled its responsibilities. Of course, taking action to avoid liability arguably leads to wasted efforts demonstrating compliance with the standard and could steal time from more productive use. However, a good amount of documentation around the process of proposing and evaluating changes to software code is a common part of open-source software development through sites like GitHub, so there may be few significant changes required in practice.

F. What are the consequences of a breach of the duty?

The consequences of a breach of such a fiduciary duty would arguably be that the 'entrustors' (whichever parties are deemed to fall in that bucket) would have a cause of action against the fiduciaries for the breach.[94] This means that fiduciary developers could, depending on who is deemed an entrustor, be subject to liability claims from an enormous number of people—users of the applicable cryptocurrency, potentially along with businesses building

and its potential for abuse'. For a discussion on how courts recognize new types of fiduciaries, see Frankel (n 40), 220–22.

[91] Frankel (n 40), 53–58.

[92] Jack M. Balkin and Jonathan Zittrain, 'A Grand Bargain to Make Tech Companies Trustworthy' (*The Atlantic*, 3 October 2016) https://www.theatlantic.com/technology/archive/2016/10/information-fiduciary/502346/.

[93] Destefanis et al. (n 49).

[94] Claims for breach of fiduciary duty are sometimes treated as tort claims and other times as contract claims, with a wide variety of remedies possible. Depending on the situation, monetary damages (compensatory or punitive), equitable remedies (like injunctions), rescission, or disgorgement of any profits made by the fiduciary as part of breaching the duty, may be available. See Dan Dobbs, Paul Hayden, and Ellen Bublick, *Dobbs' Law of Torts*, (2nd edn, Thomson West, June 2017 update), Section 699.

on and servicing the blockchain. Despite any cryptocurrency that they may have previously managed to cash out, it would likely be very difficult for any of these fiduciary developers to satisfy their liabilities—the cost of making whole an entire blockchain would simply be too great. This situation—the fact that the economic (or other) harms caused by parties deemed fiduciaries may be too great for them to cover—could cast doubt over whether the fiduciary categorization is worthwhile, if the entrustors are unlikely to ever be made whole.

Working out the consequences of a breach of fiduciary duty may lead to varying proposals, such as requiring some sort of malpractice insurance or directors' and officers' (D&O) insurance or bond for those with the fiduciary duties, or requiring a certification or licensure to engage in high-stakes, high-trust positions like those of leading developers. Indeed, a recent computer science paper called for a higher standard of software engineering for blockchain software development, given its particularly difficult nature and the high stakes involved with errors.[95]

Potential for liability claims may also incentivize developers to form a more traditional legal organizational structure for a public blockchain, such as a corporation or limited liability company. (Of course, adopting a traditional legal structure goes fundamentally against the core ideal of decentralized governance in public blockchain systems.)

G. Could a fiduciary standard be enforced?

Many who work with public blockchains do so based on an ideology of libertarianism or even anti-government or anarchic beliefs. Escaping government altogether through the technology is of great significance; a duty does not have any bite unless it is able to be enforced.

Enforcement of a fiduciary duty, when the fiduciaries are spread across the globe and perform their services from numerous different jurisdictions, would be complicated. Threading this needle would require recognition of the fiduciary relationship by the appropriate legal authorities as well as actually tracking down the people involved, some of whom may perform their services anonymously. Attempting to bring accountability to infrastructures on which the public relies could drive those wishing to avoid accountability further into the shadows. However, those who wish to legitimize the technology may be willing to step up and acknowledge the appropriateness of accountability in this area.

Opinions diverge on whether nation states can actually hold parties operating public blockchain systems accountable.[96] The matter remains unsettled but states have been able to enforce laws in cyberspace so I would expect them to work out a way to do the same in 'blockchain space'.

* * *

As always, the devil is in the details and many questions still need answers before this issue is resolved. Most of the questions will not have clear answers; rather, they will require a careful balancing of costs and benefits, fairness, public policy concerns, etc. However, the inquiries remain worthwhile despite the challenges they present.

VI. Ongoing Experiments in Governance and Accountability

The public blockchain world is incredibly fast-moving, with new blockchain systems constantly being created and existing ones working to fix governance issues as they are revealed. A number of blockchain systems have now explicitly incorporated governance into their

---

[95] Destefanis et al. (n 49).

[96] DeFilippi and Wright (n 7), 181–83, discuss government regulation of blockchain software developers and enforcement challenges.

designs from the outset; some of these new systems may structure the power of software developers differently than Bitcoin or Ethereum. Additionally, legal scholars, along with researchers in the blockchain community, have begun to weigh in with initial analyses of and proposals for public blockchain governance.

Tezos,[97] EOS,[98] Decred,[99] and Dfinity[100] are examples of public blockchains using or planning to use alternative governance processes, with variations in the powers of validators in the network or how changes to software are made. After starting out eschewing the need for governance entirely, those working on public blockchain networks have recognized the critical role governance plays in a system's success.[101] A field of study called 'cryptoeconomics' is being developed to design incentive structures intended to result in transaction processors providing security (resistance to attack) for a blockchain.[102] These 'consensus mechanisms' (or, rules for coming to agreement) for transaction processors play a significant role in the governance of public blockchain systems, indicating just how rich, complex, and nascent this area of study remains.

Legal scholars have begun to grapple with the governance questions raised by public blockchains. For example, Philipp Hacker has proposed fitting a corporate governance framework onto blockchains.[103] Carla Reyes has proposed that a business trust may be a suitable form of legal entity for blockchain developers and other players in the system to take advantage of limited liability without having to formally create a corporation or limited liability company.[104] Each of these analyses, in acknowledging the role that software developers play in the governance process of public blockchains, implicitly acknowledges that certain software developers fulfil roles of trust and power in public blockchain systems.[105]

All of this is to say that public blockchain governance and the theorizing around it remain works in progress. Nevertheless, I feel pretty comfortable predicting that systems based on software will continue to require software developers to create code (with all the processes, decisions, and judgement calls that are involved). (And yes, I hear those of you saying, 'But AI …').

VII. Broader Implications and Concluding Thoughts

This chapter focuses on the behaviours of software developers in the public blockchain context. They provide a neat example of a potentially new type of fiduciary acting in today's world and my hope is that this chapter opens the door to further research on the matter and also alerts regulators and policy makers to the need to press hard on the 'decentralized' reputation of public blockchains.

---

[97] Tezos website, https://tezos.com/.   [98] EOS website, https://eos.io/.

[99] Decred website, https://www.decred.org/.   [100] Dfinity website, https://dfinity.org/.

[101] See, e.g., Fred Ehrsam, 'Blockchain Governance: Programming Our Future' (*Medium*, 17 November 2017) https://medium.com/@FEhrsam/blockchain-governance-programming-our-future-c3bfe30f2d74; Vlad Zamfir, 'Against On-Chain Governance' (*Medium*, 1 December 2017) https://medium.com/@Vlad_Zamfir/against-on-chain-governance-a4ceacd040ca.

[102] See Josh Stark, 'Making Sense of Cryptoeconomics' (*Medium*, 28 August 2017) https://medium.com/l4-media/making-sense-of-cryptoeconomics-c6455776669. A helpful compilation of resources on cryptoeconomics is available at https://github.com/jpantunes/awesome-cryptoeconomics.

[103] See Philip Hacker, chapter 7 in this volume.

[104] Carla Reyes, 'If Rockefeller Were a Coder' (forthcoming) 87 *George Washington Law Review*, https://papers.ssrn.com/sol3/papers.cfm?abstract_id=3082915.

[105] Other researchers have examined the potential liability of software developers of public blockchain systems. See Zetzsche et al. (n 87); Tim Swanson, 'Who are the Administrators of Blockchains?' (*OfNumbers Blog*, 19 October 2017) http://www.ofnumbers.com/2017/10/19/who-are-the-administrators-of-blockchains/; Ciaran Murray, 'Are Public Blockchain Systems Unlicensed Money Services Businesses In Disguise?' (*Rules of the Game Blog*, 12 October 2017) http://rulesofthegame.blog/2017/10/12/are-public-blockchain-systems-unlicensed-money-services-businesses-in-disguise/.

We must be vigilant as to how our legal and social concepts need to change as our technologies and practices change. As we experiment in technology and with new methods of
governance, our legal concepts need to expand to accommodate these experiments. It may
be helpful to focus on the function and activities performed by a party, rather than on what
they call themselves. If the developers had formed a corporation to launch and operate these
public blockchains (rather than having separate foundations to pay developers), no one
would question that the officers, directors, and controlling shareholders of that corporation
had fiduciary duties in their leadership roles and that the corporation should be accountable
for harms that it causes (like Volkswagen is accountable for its deceptive emissions code).
Yet, we seem mystified by the nominally decentralized governance and unable to see that a
spade is still a spade (is still a fiduciary).

Blockchain technology has jumped into the deep end very early in its life. The functions
that its proponents expect it to perform are critical, infrastructural functions in our societies. As coding becomes infrastructure building and maintenance, it is very much akin to
building bridges, or nuclear reactors, or national security structures. And those building
and maintaining and making decisions about these core infrastructures must take what they
are doing seriously. Blockchain developers must recognize that they are not just building
fun technology like Wikipedia or Napster, where a system failure has few significant social
consequences.

Furthermore, it is insufficient to focus exclusively on the companies building on top of
public blockchains. This approach ignores the people involved in creating and running the
network upon which others are building. The *foundations* of this new infrastructure are
being built by *people*, people who are making decisions that will impact the operation and
success of the new infrastructure. It takes a great deal of expertise to successfully implement
these decisions, much less to make the policy choices that the implementation reflects. These
are not simply technical decisions being made—there are also, inevitably, policy choices, risk
assessments, economic decisions, and ethical judgements happening.

The bottom line is that trust in particular, identifiable people remains fundamental to
using 'trustless' public blockchains. The crucial question is—are we willing to acknowledge
its existence?

VIII. Bibliography

American Institute of CPAs Code of Conduct, Section ET 53 Article II, https://www.aicpa.org/re-
search/standards/codeofconduct.html, accessed on 9 January 2019.
Antonopoulos Andreas M., *Mastering Bitcoin: Unlocking Digital Cryptocurrencies* (2nd edn,
O'Reilly 2017).
Atik Jeffery and Gerro George, 'Hard Forks on the Bitcoin Blockchain: Reversible Exit, Continuing
Voice' (2018) 1 *Stanford Journal of Law and Public Policy*, 24.
Atzori Marcella, 'Blockchain Technology and Decentralized Governance: Is the State Still Necessary?'
(2017) 6 *Journal of Governance and Regulation*, 45.
Balkin Jack M., 'Information Fiduciaries and the First Amendment' (2016) 49 *University of
California Davis Law Review*, 1183.
Balkin Jack M. and Zittrain Jonathan, 'A Grand Bargain to Make Tech Companies Trustworthy'
(*The Atlantic*, 3 October 2016) https://www.theatlantic.com/technology/archive/2016/10/
information-fiduciary/502346/, accessed on 9 January 2019.
Bayern Shawn, 'Of Bitcoins, Independently Wealthy Software and the Zero-Member LLC' (2014)
108 *Northwestern University Law Review Online*, 1485.
Berke David, 'Products Liability in the Sharing Economy' (2016) 33 Yale Journal on Regulation 603.
Bitcoin GitHub Page, https://github.com/bitcoin/bitcoin, accessed on 9 January 2019.
Biais Bruno, Bisière Christophe, Bouvard Matthiue, and Casamatta Catherine, 'The Blockchain
Folk Theorem' (2018) Toulouse School of Economics Working Paper No. 17-817, 14, https://

www.tse-fr.eu/sites/default/files/TSE/documents/doc/wp/2017/wp_tse_817.pdf , accessed on 9 January 2019.

Burniske Chris and Tatar Jack, *Cryptoassets: The Innovative Investor's Guide to Bitcoin and Beyond* (McGraw-Hill 2018).

Buterin Vitalik, 'Notes on Blockchain Governance' (*Vitalik Buterin's Website*, 17 December 2017) https://vitalik.ca/general/2017/12/17/voting.html, accessed on 9 January 2019.

Butler Henry and Ribstein Larry, 'Opting Out of Fiduciary Duties: A Response to the Anti-Contractarians' (1993) 65 *Washington Law Review*, 1.

Camarena Justin, 'I'd agree with a rollback for protocol level hacks ... But this isn't that at all. Core devs own DAO' (*Twitter*, 17 June 2016) https://twitter.com/juscamarena/status/744008754459475968, accessed on 9 January 2019.

Camarena Justin, 'they are unfairly slanted to HF'ing to regain their money ... might as well just have a private chain' (*Twitter*, 17 June 2016) https://twitter.com/juscamarena/status/744008863091941376, accessed on 9 January 2019.

Compilation Resource on Cryptoeconomics, https://github.com/jpantunes/awesome-cryptoeconomics, accessed on 9 January 2019.

De Filippi Primavera and Wright Aaron, *Blockchain and the Law: The Rule of Code* (Harvard University Press 2018).

De Nikhilesh, 'SEC Halts Mayweather-Endorsed ICO, Charges Founders With Fraud' (*CoinDesk*, 2 April 2018) https://www.coindesk.com/sec-halts-mayweather-endorsed-ico-charges-founders-fraud/ , accessed on 9 January 2019.

Decred website, https://www.decred.org/, accessed on 9 January 2019.

DeMott Deborah, 'Beyond Metaphor: An Analysis of Fiduciary Obligation' (1988) *Duke Law Journal*, 879.

Destefanis Giuseppe, Marchesi Michelle, Ortu Marco et al., 'Smart Contracts Vulnerabilities: A Call for Blockchain Software Engineering' (2018) IEEE Conference Paper, http://dspace.stir.ac.uk/bitstream/1893/27135/1/smart-contracts-vulnerabilities-3.pdf, accessed on 9 January 2019.

Dfinity Website, https://dfinity.org/, accessed on 9 January 2019.

Dobbs Dan, Hayden Paul, and Bublick Ellen, *Dobbs' Law of Torts*, (2nd edn, Thomson West, June 2017 update).

Easterbrook Frank and Fischel Daniel, 'Contract and Fiduciary Duty' (1993) 36 *Journal of Law and Economics*, 425.

Ehrsam Fred, 'Blockchain Governance: Programming Our Future' (*Medium*, 17 November 2017) https://medium.com/@FEhrsam/blockchain-governance-programming-our-future-c3bfe30f2d74, accessed on 9 January 2019.

Employee Retirement Income Security Act of 1974 (ERISA), 29 USC 1002(21)(A).

EOS website, https://eos.io/ , accessed on 9 January 2019.

Ethereum Classic, 'The Ethereum Classic Declaration of Independence, 20 July 2016' https://ethereumclassic.github.io/assets/ETC_Declaration_of_Independence.pdf, accessed on 9 January 2019.

Ethereum Foundation website, https://ethereum.org/foundation, accessed on 9 January 2019.

Ethereum GitHub page, https://github.com/ethereum/, accessed on 9 January 2019.

Ethereum Legal Agreement (*ethereum.org*) https://www.ethereum.org/agreement , accessed on 9 January 2019.

Fernandes Aakil, 'Ethereum Protocol Developer Holds $114,887 of DAO Tokens' (*Reddit*, 29 June 2017) https://www.reddit.com/r/ethereum/comments/4qiqq8/ethereum_protocol_developer_holds_114877_worth_of/, accessed on 9 January 2019.

Floyd David, '$6.3 Billion: 2018 ICO Funding Has Passed 2017's Total' (*CoinDesk*, 19 April 2018) https://www.coindesk.com/6-3-billion-2018-ico-funding-already-outpaced-2017/, accessed on 9 January 2019.

Frankel Tamar, *Fiduciary Law* (Oxford University Press 2011).

Gencer Adam E., Basu Soumya, Eyal Ittay, Renesse Robbert van, and Sirer Emin G., 'Decentralisation in Bitcoin and Ethereum Networks' (*arXiv.org*, 2018) https://arxiv.org/pdf/1801.03998.pdf., accessed on 9 January 2019.

Gervais Arthur, Karame Ghassan O., Capkun Srdjan, and Capkun Vedran, 'Is Bitcoin a Decentralized Currency?' (2014) http://eprint.iacr.org/2013/829.pdf, accessed on 9 January 2019.

GNU General Public License, https://www.gnu.org/licenses/gpl-3.0.en.html, accessed on 9 January 2019.

Hacker Philipp, 'Corporate Governance for Complex Cryptocurrencies? A Framework for Stability and Decision Making in Blockchain-Based Organizations', this volume, chapter 7.

Higgins Stan, 'Bitcoin Core Opens Doors to Outside Funding with Sponsorship Program' (*CoinDesk*, 6 April 2016) http://www.coindesk.com/bitcoin-core-opens-doors-to-outside-funding-with-sponsorship-program/ accessed on 9 January 2019.

Hinman William, 'Digital Asset Transactions: When Howey Met Gary (Plastic)' (Speech, 14 June 2018) https://www.sec.gov/news/speech/speech-hinman-061418, accessed on 9 January 2019.

Jones Ray, 'Ethereum Protocol Developer Holds $114,877 Worth of DAO Tokens' (*Reddit*, 29 June 2016) https://www.reddit.com/r/ethereum/comments/4qiqq8/ethereum_protocol_developer_holds_114877_worth_of/d4th8ce/, accessed on 9 January 2019.

Khrennikov Ilya, 'Vladimir Putin is Getting Interested in Bitcoin's Biggest Rival' (*Bloomberg*, 6 June 2017) https://www.bloomberg.com/news/articles/2017-06-06/putin-eyes-bitcoin-rival-to-spur-economic-growth-beyond-oil-gas, accessed on 9 January 2019.

Leib Ethan, Ponet David, and Serota Michael, 'A Fiduciary Theory of Judging' (2013) 101 *California Law Review*, 699.

Leib Ethan, Ponet David, and Serota Michael, 'Translating Fiduciary Principles into Public Law' (2013) 126 *Harvard Law Review Forum*, 91.

Manski Sarah and Manski Ben, 'No Gods, No Masters, No Coders? The Future of Sovereignty in a Blockchain World' (2018) 29 *Law Critique*, 151.

MIT License, https://opensource.org/licenses/MIT, accessed on 9 January 2019.

Murray Ciaran, 'Are Public Blockchain Systems Unlicensed Money Services Businesses in Disguise?' (*Rules of the Game Blog*, 12 October 2017) http://rulesofthegame.blog/2017/10/12/are-public-blockchain-systems-unlicensed-money-services-businesses-in-disguise/, accessed on 9 January 2019.

O'Leary Rachel, 'Ethereum Developer Resigns as Code Editor Citing Legal Concerns' (*CoinDesk*, 15 February 2018) https://www.coindesk.com/ethereum-developer-resigns-as-code-editor-citing-legal-concerns/, accessed on 9 January 2019.

O'Leary Rachel, 'Zcash Pays Off Developer to Avoid Blockchain Split' (*CoinDesk*, 22 June 2018) https://www.coindesk.com/zcash-pays-off-angry-developer-avoid-blockchain-split/, accessed on 9 January 2019.

Oberhaus Daniel, 'Cryptocurrency Miners are Sabotaging Blockchains for Their Personal Gain' (*Motherboard*, 25 May 2018) https://motherboard.vice.com/en_us/article/a3a38e/what-is-a-51-percent-attack-silicon-valley-bitcoin-gold-verge-monacoin-cryptocurrency, accessed on 9 January 2019.

Rave D. Theodore, 'Politicians as Fiduciaries (2013) 126 *Harvard Law Review*, 671.

Reidy Marian and Hanus Bartlomiej, 'It is Just Unfair Using Trade Laws to Out Security Software Vulnerabilities' (2017) 48 *Loyola University Chicago Law Journal*, 1099.

Reyes Carla, 'Corporate Crypto Governance' (26 January 2018) Working Paper presented at Blockchain Works-in-Progress Workshop at Cardozo Law School.

Reyes Carla, 'If Rockefeller Were a Coder' (forthcoming) 87 *George Washington Law Review*, https://papers.ssrn.com/sol3/papers.cfm?abstract_id=3082915, accessed on 9 January 2019.

Schnelli Jonas, Tweets (*Twitter*, 15 November 2017) https://twitter.com/_jonasschnelli_/status/930680174697381888, accessed on 9 January 2019.

Scott Michael, *Scott on Information Technology Law* (3rd edn, 2nd Supplement, Aspen 2018).

Simonite Tom, 'The Man Who Really Built Bitcoin' (2014) *MIT Technology Review*, http://www.technologyreview.com/featuredstory/527051/the-man-who-really-built-bitcoin/, accessed on 9 January 2019.

Singh Jatinder and Michels Johan D., 'Blockchain as a Service: Providers and Trust' (2017) Queen Mary, Univeristy of London, School of Law Legal Studies Research Paper No. 269/2017, https://ssrn.com/abstract=3091223 , accessed on 9 January 2019.

Stark Josh, 'Making Sense of Cryptoeconomics' (*Medium*, 28 August 2017) https://medium.com/l4-media/making-sense-of-cryptoeconomics-c6455776669, accessed on 9 January 2019.

Summerwill Bob, Tweets on Ethereum Foundation opacity, (*Twitter*, 29 December 2017) https://twitter.com/BobSummerwill/status/946760015322398720, accessed on 9 January 2019.

Swanson Tim, 'Who are the Administrators of Blockchains?' (*OfNumbers Blog*, 19 October 2017) http://www.ofnumbers.com/2017/10/19/who-are-the-administrators-of-blockchains/, accessed on 9 January 2019.

Szabo Nick, 'The Dawn of Trustworthy Computing' (*Unenumerated*, 11 December 2014) http://unenumerated.blogspot.com/2014/12/the-dawn-of-trustworthy-computing.html, accessed on 9 January 2019.

Szabo Nick, 'Money, Blockchains and Social Scalability' (*Unenumerated*, 9 February 2017) https://unenumerated.blogspot.com/2017/02/money-blockchains-and-social-scalability.html, accessed on 9 January 2019.

Tezos website, https://tezos.com/, accessed on 9 January 2019.

Van Valkenburgh Peter, 'What Could "Decentralization" Mean in the Context of the Law?' (*CoinCentreBlog*, 15 June 2018) https://coincenter.org/entry/what-could-decentralization-mean-in-the-context-of-the-law, accessed on 9 January 2019.

Walch Angela, 'The Bitcoin Blockchain as Financial Market Infrastructure: A Consideration of the Operational Risk' (2015) 18 *New York University Journal of Legislation and Public Policy*, 837.

Walch Angela, 'Call Blockchain Developers What They Are: Fiduciaries' (2016) *American Banker*, https://www.americanbanker.com/opinion/call-blockchain-developers-what-they-are-fiduciaries, accessed on 9 January 2019.

Walch Angela, 'Open-Source Operational Risk: Should Public Blockchains Serve as Financial Market Infrastructures?' in *Handbook of Blockchain, Digital Finance and Inclusion*, edited by David Lee Kuo Chuen and Robert Deng (Vol. 2, Elsevier Academic Press 2017).

WhaleCalls, 'Fact or FUD: Blockstream, Inc. is the Main Force Behind Bitcoin (and Taken Over)' (*Medium*, 1 December 2017) https://medium.com/@whalecalls/fud-or-fact-blockstream-inc-is-the-main-force-behind-bitcoin-and-taken-over-160aed93c003, accessed on 9 January 2019.

Wong Joon Ian, 'Ethereum's Inventor on How "Initial Coin Offerings" are a New Way to Fund the Internet' (*Quartz*, Interview with Vitalik Buterin, 14 September 2017) https://qz.com/1075124/ethereum-founder-vitalik-buterin-discusses-initial-coin-offerings-the-consensus-algorithm-and-the-most-interesting-apps/, accessed on 9 January 2019.

Wong Joon Ian and Kar Ian, 'Everything You Need to Know About the Ethereum "Hard Fork"' (*Quartz*, 18 July 2016) https://qz.com/730004/everything-you-need-to-know-about-the-ethereum-hard-fork/ , accessed on 9 January 2019.

Young Joseph, 'Vlad Zamfir: Sharding is the Only True Blockchain Scaling Solution' (*BinaryDistrict*, 13 November 2017) https://journal.binarydistrict.com/vlad-zamfir-sharding-is-the-only-true-blockchain-scaling-solution-/, accessed on 9 January 2019.

Zamfir Vlad, 'Against On-Chain Governance' (*Medium*, 1 December 2017) https://medium.com/@Vlad_Zamfir/against-on-chain-governance-a4ceacd040ca, accessed on 9 January 2019.

Zetzsche Dirk, Buckley Ross, and Arner Douglas, 'The Distributed Liability of Distributed Ledgers: Legal Risks of Blockchain' (2018) *University of Illinois Law Review*, 1361.

PART II

BLOCKCHAIN AND THE FUTURE OF MONEY

4

Old Utopias, New Tax Havens

The Politics of Bitcoin in Historical Perspective

Stefan Eich[*]

I. Introduction

Cryptocurrencies are frequently framed as future-oriented, technological innovations that decentralize money, thereby liberating it from centralized governance and the political tentacles of the state. As I argue in this chapter, almost every single aspect of this picture is either straightforwardly false or highly misleading. Instead of associating cryptocurrencies with a futuristic technology that lifts money above politics, I take a contrarian view by placing the political vision behind cryptocurrencies in the historical context of the global politics of money after the collapse of the 'Bretton Woods' system.[1] This has a number of implications. Most importantly, instead of accepting the self-presentation of cryptocurrencies as a technological innovation that removes money from politics, recovering their broader historical and political context allows us to see cryptocurrencies as part of a struggle over the political status of money in an age of financialization. After all, cryptocurrency enthusiasts themselves often frame their own ambition to decentralize the issuance of money as a major *political* attraction. Instead of a hub-and-spokes model of a central bank that supports a cluster of commercial banks, cryptocurrency supporters hail the advent of a decentralized monetary system in which issuance is externally fixed and payments are settled through the public ledger of a blockchain.

In this chapter I follow up on this vision by interrogating its underlying political theory. By shedding light on the political visions that tend to undergird cryptocurrencies we can critically examine the frequent gap between public vision, implicit politics, and actual implementation. As I will argue, the attempt to remove money from political control is itself a supremely political act that raises profound questions of legitimacy. Instead of taking this vision at face value, I propose that cryptocurrencies are suspended between two contradictory goals: a radical political attempt to depoliticize the appearance of money, and a seductive use of cryptocurrencies as speculative assets beyond the regulatory grasp of monetary and fiscal authorities. Ironically, while the preferential tax and regulatory treatment of cryptocurrencies hinges on their self-professed status as currencies, the price swings of recent years precisely undermine this claim to being currencies. To highlight this contradiction and place it into a concrete historical context, I look specifically at the example of Bitcoin, still the most popular and valuable cryptocurrency.

Caught between these contradictory aspirations as both currencies and speculative assets, cryptocurrencies are at best prone to become victims of their own success. Not only are regulators likely to step in to contain financial fraud, regulate systemic risks, and tax speculative gains, but established financial actors have already begun to integrate cryptocurrencies into their business models. After all, blockchain algorithms are made and as such they reflect the intentions of their authors. There is nothing inherent in blockchain technology that rules

[*] I am grateful to Georgios Dimitropoulos, David Singh Grewal, Philipp Hacker, Ioannis Lianos, Helen Mavroidis, Jedediah Purdy, and Adam Tooze for comments and discussions.

[1] See Primavera De Filippi and Aaron Wright, *Blockchain and the Law: The Rule of Code* (Harvard University Press 2018).

out centralization, regulatory oversight, or democratic governance. Nor is there anything in cryptocurrencies that would prevent them from becoming appendices to the existing global shadow banking system. Unsurprisingly, both central banks and commercial banks have already developed blockchain protocols that combine a decentralized ledger with the possibility of centralized oversight and control. In either case, whatever scenario will emerge does not depend on technological inevitabilities but on political acquiescence and ultimately questions of power.

While cryptocurrencies are a recent development, political attempts to remove money from political control are a central, perhaps constitutive, feature of liberal modernity. One could therefore tell an even longer story involving the contested political status of money in modernity, as I have done elsewhere. In this chapter, however, I place cryptocurrencies in the narrower historical context of the ad hoc global politics of money after the collapse of the Bretton Woods system in the 1970s. In particular, I distinguish between three periods: first, an initial phase of the politicization of money (1973–1979); followed by the emergence of a global politics of disinflation that came to be hailed as the 'Great Moderation' (1980–2008); and finally, our current period in the wake of the Financial Crisis of 2008, which revealed the fragility of many of the presuppositions of the 'Great Moderation' and returned us to the unresolved questions of the 1970s (2008–present).

To grasp the peculiar politics underlying most currently existing cryptocurrencies it is thus important to see their rise as a post-Financial Crisis restaging of the contentious political demands for monetary depoliticization and privatization during the late 1970s. The insistence on technological novelty associated with cryptocurrencies can easily obscure the ways in which their underlying visions resemble those of earlier arguments, in particular Friedrich August Hayek's argument for the 'denationalization' of money.[2] At the time, this utopian vision of the privatization of money contended with Third World demands for the politicization and democratization of global money, which were subsequently largely displaced. The ad hoc system that emerged instead did not do away with the sovereign prerogative to issue money—indeed, as the Financial Crisis revealed, in many ways it further strengthened it—but it self-consciously depoliticized the appearance of money and encouraged the development of a global monetary system based on the principle of capital mobility. It was only in the wake of the 2008 Financial Crisis that conflicting demands for either the depoliticization or the democratization of money resurfaced. This was the concrete context for the emergence of cryptocurrencies that promised to remove money from both the state and banks. To understand the origins of this promise, it is necessary to return to the 1970s.

II. Two Utopias

On 11 December 1974, Friedrich Hayek stepped up to the lectern at the Stockholm School of Economics to deliver his obligatory prize lecture for the Nobel Memorial Prize in Economic Sciences he had been awarded the previous night. As Hayek announced in his opening lines, the chief practical problem across the Western world was the spectre of inflation.[3] This had made his choice of topic easy, indeed almost inevitable. The problem of inflation, Hayek exhorted, threatened Western civilization at its very foundation. 'Economists', he explained,

---

[2] Friedrich August Hayek, *Denationalisation of Money* (London: The Institute of Economic Affairs 1976), 70. Enlarged version reprinted as Friedrich August Hayek, 'The Denationalization of Money: An Analysis of the Theory and Praxis of Concurrent Currencies [1978]' in *Good Money, Part II. The Collected Works of F. A. Hayek*, edited by Stephen Kresge (Volume 6, University of Chicago Press 1999), 128–229.

[3] Friedrich August Hayek, 'The Pretence of Knowledge. Lecture to the Memory of Alfred Nobel, December 11, 1974' in *New Studies in Philosophy, Politics, Economics and the History of Ideas* (University of Chicago Press and Routledge & Kegan Paul 1978), 23. For an account of Hayek's visit to Sweden, see Bruce Caldwell, 'Hayek's Nobel' (2016) 21 *Advances in Austrian Economics*, 23.

'are at this moment called upon to say how to extricate the free world from the serious threat of accelerating inflation'. But they were failing. As a profession, 'we have made a mess of things'. Blaming the inflation on epistemological hubris, Hayek launched a fundamental challenge to Keynesian national welfarism and placed stable money at the heart of his liberalism. Money, Hayek had already explained in *The Road to Serfdom* (1944), 'is one of the greatest instruments of freedom ever invented by man'.[4]

Spurred on by the inflation of the 1970s and utilizing the prestige of the Nobel Prize, Hayek returned to his monetary writings from the interwar period and updated them with startlingly radicalized conclusions. As he declared in 1975, in a lecture at a London-based free market think tank, 'the cause of waves of unemployment is not "capitalism" but governments denying enterprise the right to produce good money'.[5] Economic crisis and inflation were a result of 'the exclusion of the most important regulator of the market mechanism, money, from itself being regulated by the market process'.[6] The lecture, soon expanded into a pamphlet and published in 1976 as *The Denationalization of Money*, entered wide circulation on the back of Hayek's Nobel fame. Given the inflation shock of the 1970s, the time had now come to eliminate the government monopoly of money and fully privatize its issuance. No government with direct control over money could ever be trusted not to abuse it. While Hayek blamed the inflationary malaise on Keynes's influence specifically, his critique now extended to the political control over money more generally. Money, Hayek insisted, was simply too dangerous an instrument to be left to the state and the 'fortuitous expediency' of politicians or indeed economists. 'Our only hope for a stable money', he exclaimed, 'is indeed now to find a way to protect money from politics'.[7]

Over the subsequent years, as inflation soared once more to more than 10% in the United States and more than 20% in Britain, Hayek dedicated himself to spreading the gospel. As he explained in 1979, the deprivation of governments of their monopolistic control of money was the only 'possible escape from the fate which threatens us'.[8] Left unchecked, inflation will 'lead to the destruction of our civilization'.[9] His call for the privatization of the monetary order dovetailed in this regard with his other constitutional recommendations, including a proposal to raise the voting age for a second legislative chamber to forty-five.[10] As Hayek stressed, 'my radical proposal concerning money will probably be practicable only as part of a much more far-reaching change in our political institutions, but an essential part of such a reform which will be recognized as necessary before long'.[11] Both parts were needed 'if we are to escape the nightmare of increasingly totalitarian powers'.[12]

Hayek had not been the sole recipient of the Nobel Prize in Economics in 1974. In the heated political climate of the early 1970s, the Swedish Academy of Sciences instead jointly awarded the 1974 Prize to Hayek and the Swedish economist Gunnar Myrdal for their 'pioneering work in the theory of money' as well as their 'penetrating analysis' of the interdependence of economic, social, and institutional phenomena.[13] Two radically divergent

---

[4] Friedrich August Hayek, 'The Road to Serfdom' in *The Collected Works of F. A. Hayek*, edited by Bruce Caldwell (Volume 2, University of Chicago Press 2007), 125. In *The Constitution of Liberty* (1960), Hayek similarly stressed the importance of 'the monetary framework' for any classically liberal position: Friedrich August Hayek, 'The Constitution of Liberty [1960]' in *The Collected Works of F. A. Hayek*, edited by Bruce Caldwell and Ronald Hamowy (Volume 17, University of Chicago Press 2011), 451–65.

[5] Hayek, *Denationalisation of Money* (n 2), epigraph on cover page.

[6] Hayek, 'The Denationalization of Money' (n 2), 202.

[7] Friedrich August Hayek, 'Choice in Currency' in *The Collected Works of F. A. Hayek*, edited by Stephen Kresge (Volume 6, University of Chicago Press 1999), 120, 125.

[8] Friedrich August Hayek, *Law, Legislation and Liberty: The Political Order of a Free People* (Volume 3, University of Chicago Press 1979), xiii–xiv.

[9] Hayek, 'The Denationalization of Money' (n 2), 186.   [10] Hayek, *Law, Legislation and Liberty* (n 8), 113.

[11] Hayek, 'The Denationalization of Money' (n 2), 186.

[12] Friedrich August Hayek, 'Consolidated Preface' in *Law, Legislation and Liberty. A New Statement of the Liberal Principles of Justice and Political Economy* (Volumes 1–3, Routledge & Kegan Paul 1982), xx.

[13] The Sveriges Riksbank Prize in Economic Sciences in Memory of Alfred Nobel 1974, https://www.nobelprize. org/prizes/economic-sciences/1974/press-release.

visions of money were on offer. When giving his own Nobel lecture, Myrdal agreed with Hayek about the constraints of national welfarism and the pressing global crisis.[14] However, instead of veering towards a vision of competing private currencies in a world of liberalized global trade, Myrdal proposed an internationalization of the post-war welfare state.[15] Decolonization posed a profound challenge to the unequal welfarist settlement of the post-war world. As Myrdal reminded his audience in Stockholm, 'the underdeveloped countries are therefore now proclaiming the necessity of not only increased aid but fundamental changes of international economic relations. By their majority votes they can in the United Nations carry resolutions like the Declaration on the Establishment of a New International Economic Order ("NIEO").'[16] In aligning himself with the demands of the NIEO, which had successfully passed its UN resolution in May 1974, Myrdal insisted that 'what the poor masses need is not a little money [but] fundamental changes in the conditions under which they are living and working'. The present calamitous situation in the world—and here Myrdal was thinking as much of famines as of inflation—posed a fundamental moral problem that required a comprehensive political reform of the international economic and monetary system.

In 1980, as Hayek was on the lecture circuit promoting his vision of a world of only private monies, a coalition more to Myrdal's liking was gathering in the Tanzanian city of Arusha. Instigated by the President of Tanzania, Julius Nyerere, and the Jamaican Prime Minister Michael Manley, the South–North Conference on 'The International Monetary System and the New International Order' met in the vast Arusha International Conference Center from 30 June to 3 July 1980 to discuss the future of the international monetary system.[17] While the NIEO had burst onto the international scene in the immediate wake of the collapse of the Bretton Woods system, it had in many ways still been an outgrowth of the anti-colonial trade struggles of the 1950s and 1960s.[18] Though the NIEO had made references to the need for monetary reform, these were fleeting. By the end of the 1970s, however, the monetary dimension had fully asserted itself internationally. As the experience of peacetime inflation traumatized Europe and North America, the Global South was hit even harder and in the case of Jamaica and Tanzania had just received a first taste of the 'structural adjustment' policies championed by the International Monetary Fund ('IMF').

Within sight of Mount Kilimanjaro, the Arusha conference was in this context meant both as an expression of solidarity with Jamaica and Tanzania as well as a call for a UN conference on international monetary reform.[19] Confronted with the technocratic imperatives of the IMF, the participants pointed instead to the inescapable politics of money. 'Money is power', declared the signatories of the resulting Arusha Initiative. 'Those who wield power control money. Those who manage and control money, wield power. An international monetary system is both a function and an instrument of prevailing power structures.'[20] As the

---

[14] Gunnar Myrdal, 'The Equality Issue in World Development' (March 1975) Lecture to the memory of Alfred Nobel.

[15] Adom Getachew, *Worldmaking after Empire: The Rise and Fall of Self-Determination* (Princeton University Press 2019); Gunnar Myrdal, *Beyond the Welfare State: Economic Planning and its International Implications* (Yale University Press 1960).

[16] Myrdal, 'The Equality Issue in World Development' (n 14). For the NIEO resolution, see United Nations General Assembly, 'Declaration on the Establishment of a New International Economic Order' (1 May 1974) Resolution A/RES/S-6/3201.

[17] The proceedings were published as 'The Arusha Initiative. A Call for a United Nations Conference on International Money and Finance' (1980) 2 *Development Dialogue (Uppsala)* (henceforth 'The Arusha Initiative'). The Swedish Dag Hammarskjöld Foundation had partially helped to fund the gathering.

[18] Getachew (n 15), Ch. 5; as well as the special NIEO issue of *Humanity: An International Journal of Human Rights, Humanitarianism and Development* (Spring 2015) 6(1). In his contribution, Bret Benjamin describes the NIEO as the 'bookend to Bandung', 33–46.

[19] Vijay Prashad, *The Darker Nations: A People's History of the Third World* (The New Press 2007), 191. For the Fund's perspective on the Arusha Initiative, see Jim Boughton, *Silent Revolution: The International Monetary Fund 1979–1989* (International Monetary Fund 2001), 588–601.

[20] The Arusha Initiative (n 17), 12.

Arusha Statement pointed out, while the stabilizing elements of the Bretton Woods order had collapsed in the course of the 1970s, the IMF and the World Bank remained standing and continued to reflect the power balances of an international order in which the majority of Third World countries had not yet existed.[21] While the UN General Assembly had since been enlarged, the IMF continued to resemble a hierarchical world more akin to the Security Council. Although the Third World counted close to one hundred countries that included more than two-thirds of the world's population, its cumulative voting share at the IMF amounted to no more than 35% and thus less than the 40% of the five leading industrial powers alone.

Even worse, in the course of the 1970s, as the United States abandoned the embedded multilateralism of the post-war period for unilateralism, the IMF had become even more beholden to the G7 than ever before. As the Third World countries had declared the previous year when meeting in Jamaica in October 1979, 'the IMF, acting on behalf of the major industrialized capitalist countries, has assumed a growing role as a financial and economic policeman in Third World countries'.[22] In addition to the previous political imbalances of the Bretton Woods system, during the 1970s a new tendency had 'emerged for the Fund [IMF] to exercise a major influence on the process of internal decision-making in a number of the Third World countries'.[23] The Bretton Woods system, imperfect as it had been, had imploded into an ad-hoc non-system that invited an evasion of responsibilities and heightened opportunism. The dollar's dual role as both the domestic currency of the United States as well as the international reserve (and shadow banking) currency of choice had already marked the post-war period. The collapse of Bretton Woods had not ended this 'exorbitant privilege' but informalized it and lifted most obligations previously associated with it.[24] Given the growing destabilizing effect of largely unregulated flows of so-called 'Eurodollars' under conditions of floating exchange rates and increasing capital mobility, the dollar's mark on the rest of the world was deepened in unpredictable ways.[25]

The Arusha Initiative's emphasis on the burden of hierarchical imbalances imposed by this informal international monetary system was in this light both an insistence on money's political nature and an attempt to counter claims to neutral technical expertise asserted by the Fund's 'money doctors'. The IMF, the Arusha signatories explained, 'claims to have a "scientific" basis for these policies and to be an objective and neutral institution charged with the "technical" function of "helping" countries to overcome their financial difficulties'.[26] However, all available evidence, including the Fund's own internal documentation (which Nyerere leaked to the international press), pointed the other way. The IMF was neither purely scientific, nor neutral. Instead, it systematically applied double standards to otherwise similar situations and was deeply ideological in the way it framed underdevelopment as a lack of private markets. In reducing the international politics of money to seemingly scientific theories of underdevelopment and domestic structural reforms, the IMF was a de-politicization machine.[27] Its denial of the political nature of money was the capstone of these efforts. As the Arusha Statement declared perceptively, precisely in denying the politics of money the IMF 'has proved to be a basically political institution'.[28]

---

[21] ibid., 12.

[22] As cited in Prashad (n 19), 66: 'The Terra Nova Statement on the International Monetary System and the Third World' (1980) 1 *Development Dialogue*, 29.

[23] ibid., (22), 2.

[24] Barry Eichengreen, *Exorbitant Privilege. The Rise and Fall of the Dollar* (Oxford University Press 2011); Benjamin Cohen, *Currency Power: Understanding Monetary Rivalry* (Princeton University Press 2015).

[25] Harold James, *Making the European Monetary Union* (Harvard University Press 2012), 9–10 and 146–80; Jeffry Frieden, *Banking on the World* (Harper and Row 1987), Ch. 4.

[26] The Arusha Initiative (n 17), 12–13.

[27] James Ferguson, *The Anti-Politics Machine: 'Development', Depoliticization, and Bureaucratic Power in Lesotho* (University of Minnesota Press 1994).

[28] The Arusha Initiative (n 17), 14.

The monetary disorder of the 1970s was neither inevitable nor accidental. The 'present monetary non-system,' the Arusha Initiative explained, was 'man-made and can consequently be redressed by political decisiveness and action'.[29] What was needed was not technical fixes and domestic programmes to adjust to the new logic of discipline but a political reform of the international monetary constitution. The abrogation of political agency in international monetary matters was in this regard an embarrassment to human rationality and ingenuity. The only viable response against it was for money to 'be demystified and exposed to public debate and scrutiny'.[30] The necessary political decisions would have to be taken 'by governments acting in a collective and democratic manner'.[31] Unlike the redistributive commodity confrontation of the NIEO, it was furthermore not clear that international monetary reform was a zero-sum game. After all, South and North both had an interest in creating a truly stable international monetary system that would be better equipped to address the issue of inflation. The Arusha Declaration ended in this spirit by urging 'the governments of East and West to pursue together their common interest in a universal and democratic monetary system'.[32]

Both Hayek and the Arusha Initiative detected political forces behind the ad-hoc international monetary order of the 1970s. However, their respective assessments of the politics of money could hardly have diverged more strongly. Where Hayek saw states abusing their monetary monopoly to create inflation, the signatories in Arusha saw developed countries bending the post-Bretton Woods monetary order to their interest. Hayek's call for the removal of money from politics thus found its exact counterpart in the Arusha Initiative's attempt to raise an awareness of money's political purpose.

In the end, both Hayek's vision of competing private currencies and the Arusha vision of a post-colonial international monetary constitution were disappointed. Nonetheless, it was Hayek who had the last laugh. What won the day was a continuation of the ad-hoc system of informal American global money and floating fiat currencies but now operated by the semi-depoliticized, technocratic rule of experts in formally independent central banks. Few observers during the 1970s would have expected this development. States were nominally left in control of currencies but abrogated many of their political responsibilities.[33] This was not Hayek's vision of pure private money. However, it approximated his goal since it depoliticized economic relations, ensured price stability, and enforced economic discipline. Furthermore, the new system was complemented by an unprecedented level of private credit money in the form of new financial instruments that circled the globe, often beyond the direct reach of governments. In particular the establishment of the free movement of capital in the course of the 1980s was essential to this.[34] Moreover, if the new politics of disinflation self-consciously imposed constraints on collective bargaining and real wage growth, it simultaneously opened the taps of private consumer credit. None of this was lost on Hayek and when he was asked to address Visa credit cards executives in Athens in September 1981, he used the opportunity to remind them of the significance of private credit acting as a unit of account beyond the state.[35]

The international monetary order that arose out of the 1970s consequently took the Arusha Statement's insistence on money's political nature seriously but derived from it Hayek's objectives of discipline and price stability. The age of floating national fiat currencies unexpectedly produced a new politics of monetary depoliticization. To Hayek's surprise, the lesson of the 1970s thus illustrated the way in which a self-reflexive modernity could end up

---

[29] ibid., 15–16 and 21–22.   [30] ibid., 21.   [31] ibid., 11.   [32] ibid., 21–22.

[33] Stefan Eich and Adam Tooze, 'The Great Inflation' in *Vorgeschichte der Gegenwart*, edited by Anselm Doering-Manteuffel, Lutz Raphael, and Thomas Schlemmer (Vandenhoeck and Ruprecht 2015) 173–96.

[34] Rawi Abdelal, *Capital Rules. The Construction of Global Finance* (Harvard University Press 2007).

[35] Friedrich August Hayek, 'The Future Unit of Value' (14 September 1981), Visa International Annual Conference, Papers of Friedrich A. Hayek, Hoover Institute, Stanford University, Box 131, Folder 5.

defining itself in a foreclosure of its own agency. For better or worse, democracies turned out to be remarkably able and willing to bind themselves. If the collapse of Bretton Woods had repoliticized money, one expression of this new politics of money consisted in its own disavowal.[36] Where inflation and the politics of money had dominated the immediate post-Bretton Woods years, with the successful assertion of a newly depoliticized appearance of money during the 1980s, the politics of money—and with it Myrdal's call for a welfare world and Third World demands for international monetary reform—faded from view.

III. The Financial Crisis and the Birth of Bitcoin

Until the Financial Crisis of 2008, the contours of the depoliticized anti-inflationary system that had unexpectedly emerged out of the late 1970s were rarely questioned. Low inflation rates, enforced by independent central banks, were instead hailed as having paved the way to the 'Goldilocks economy' of the Great Moderation.[37] But as the world's central banks and treasuries had to step into the breach in 2008 to undertake sprawling rescue actions to prevent an imminent collapse of the global financial system, two myths rapidly unravelled. Most immediately, the Crisis revealed the widely held belief of money as neutral as an illusion. While the appearance of money had been naturalized during the Great Moderation as a depoliticized tool of scarcity, it was now revealed once more as fickle and malleable. The state, seemingly obsolete before the Crisis, had to backstop the financial system by socializing its losses. In the European context, where the vision of depoliticized money had paved the way for deeper integration in the form of a currency union without matching political mechanisms of adjustment, the Eurocrisis revealed the apolitical design of the Euro and policy-makers' refusal to politically restructure debts as a tragic flaw that pitted nations against each other instead of bringing them closer together.[38]

But if money turned out to be more political than many had come to assume, the Crisis also rapidly undermined any presumption that money was still straightforwardly privy to the sovereignty of states and accountable to politics. Currency had in large parts been replaced by private global money. As central banks sought to exercise control over the money supply and the credit system, they saw themselves confronted with a vast and arcane global financial structure that was at least in part beyond their control. Since the late 1970s, economic globalization and the international integration of financial markets have severely constrained formal state competencies in monetary and financial matters and led, as scholars of International Political Economy have traced, to a 'deterritorialization' of money.[39] Where the literature of the 1970s had offered state-centric analyses of power,[40] the same scholars have since sketched market-centric accounts of globalization and financialization.[41] If the crisis thus revealed money to be inescapably political, politics found itself at the same time short-changed in its ability to govern the new money.

It had, of course, been states themselves that had tied themselves to the mast of monetary depoliticization in the hope of deflecting responsibility from the painful disinflationary

---

[36] David Grewal, *Network Power: The Social Dynamics of Globalization* (Yale University Press 2008), 105.

[37] Ben Bernanke, 'The Great Moderation' (20 February 2004) Meeting of the Eastern Economic Association.

[38] For a reading of the Eurocrisis that blames not structural causes but bad crisis management and, in particular, the unwillingness to restructure debt, see Martin Sandbu, *Europe's Orphan: The Future of the Euro and the Politics of Debt* (Princeton University Press 2015).

[39] Claus Zimmermann, 'The Concept of Monetary Sovereignty Revisited' (2013) *European Journal of International Law*, 799–800; Benjamin Cohen, 'The New Geography of Money' in *Global Monetary Governance* (Routledge 2008), 207–24.

[40] Susan Strange, *Sterling and British Policy* (Oxford University Press 1971); Benjamin Cohen, *The Future of Sterling as an International Currency* (Macmillan 1971).

[41] Susan Strange, *Mad Money: When Markets Outgrow Governments* (University of Michigan Press 1998); Benjamin Cohen, *The Geography of Money* (Cornell University Press 1998).

economic choices of the late 1970s and early 1980s. But in the 2008 Financial Crisis, as states sought to loosen these bonds in order to regain their agency, they found themselves as an Odysseus whose crew now refused to untie him. In the Eurozone, the realization of money's political dimension was similarly accompanied by states coming to the painful realization that the tools of monetary policy were no longer available to them when they needed them most, while the European Central Bank proved inept in fully living up to its new responsibilities.

Despite these constraints, central banks acted swiftly and enacted historically unprecedented rescue measures that ranged from bailing out financial institutions to extending vast international swap lines to favoured central banks around the world.[42] This new assertion of political agency left central banks in a perilous position. As Adam Tooze has pointed out, it was always a telling contradiction of neoliberalism that its emphasis on discipline was coupled to the elevation of a select group of central bankers to captains of global prosperity.[43] Faced with financial meltdown, the depoliticized rule-based model of neoliberal governance that had promised to disentangle politics and economics was revealed as hinging on the ability of experts with largely undefined mandates to directly intervene in the financial system. As a flipside of their increased importance, central banks now found themselves in the political limelight without being quite able to fess up to their own agency. They had become central planners that dare not speak their name.[44] The newly visible agency of central banks uncomfortably raised the possibility of political choices in a system that was supposedly without alternatives. The recognition that central bankers could create money at will with the click of a proverbial button provoked starry-eyed amazement from those toiling under the weight of austerity during the Great Recession.

With the myth of apolitical money eroded, the divergent visions of the 1970s have made a concealed comeback. Reminded of the ability of central banks to create money at will, since the Financial Crisis there have been once more a number of proposals that aspire to complete the Hayekian call for denationalized and privatized monies removed from the control of the state. Though it undoubtedly shaped the anti-inflationary turn that won the day, Hayek's vision of competing private currencies ultimately failed to gain traction. With the depoliticizing successes of the Great Moderation and the rise of global credit money beyond governments' direct control, it rapidly lost its urgency. But the idea never quite died. It remained a secret fantasy of those with libertarian leanings. Even among central bankers, whom Hayek had after all castigated as doing the devil's work, it was nurtured. In 1996, Alan Greenspan, the then Chairman of the Federal Reserve and just reappointed by President Clinton, marvelled at how the technological innovations under way could bring back the possibility of private money. 'We could envisage proposals in the near future', he explained, 'for issuers of electronic payment obligations, such as stored-value cards or "digital cash"'.[45] In the midst of the Financial Crisis, with the traditional banking system under threat and governments' contested role in monetary matters once more on full display, the possibility suddenly became concrete.[46] Hayek's vision resurfaced electronically.

On 1 November 2008, mere weeks after the collapse of Lehman Brothers, a pseudonymous Satoshi Nakamoto posted a paper on an online messaging board that contained a technical proposal for an electronic crypto-currency dubbed 'Bitcoin'. In the code of the first Bitcoin block, Nakamoto included a short message:

---

[42] Adam Tooze, *Crashed. How a Decade of Financial Crises Changed the World* (Viking 2018), 166–219.

[43] Adam Tooze, 'Just Another Panic' (2016) 97 *New Left Review*, 129; Tooze, *Crashed* (n 38), 1–22, 141–201.

[44] J. W. Mason, 'The Fed Doesn't Work for You' (Jacobin, January 2016) https://www.jacobinmag.com/2016/01/federal-reserve-interest-rate-increase-janet-yellen-inflation-unemployment/.

[45] As cited by Nathaniel Popper, *Digital Gold. The Untold Story of Bitcoin* (Harper Collins 2015).

[46] Benjamin Cohen, 'Electronic Money: New Day or False Dawn?' (2001) 8(2) *Review of International Political Economy*, 221.

The Times 03/Jan/2009
Chancellor on brink of second bailout for banks

Meant to serve as a time stamp, the message also embodied Bitcoin's ethos and motivation. From the start, its mysterious founder (or those operating behind his pseudonym) and its fervent enthusiasts envisioned the new electronic currency as a digital analogue to gold; a universal money beyond human control. Where Hayek had sought to take money away from the state, Bitcoin now aimed to remove it both from the state and from banks. This was money for an age in which trust had collapsed. What made Bitcoin unique, Nakamoto explained, was that it was 'a system for electronic transactions without relying on trust ... The real problem with conventional currency is all the trust that is required to make it work.'[47]

Behind this dark vision of the fragility of human trust and reason, one can easily detect Hayek's mirage of superior private monies administered by markets. However, where Hayek could innocently think of banks as ideal tools for the privatization of money, from Nakamoto's perspective at the height of the Financial Crisis banks were just as tainted as governments. After all, banks had failed to function as intended, instead bringing the financial system within inches of fatal collapse. Even worse, as the waves of bailout proved, it was not entirely obvious that banks issuing credit were indeed fully private institutions. When it mattered, they either received public support from central banks or, in many cases, were straightforwardly nationalized. As Nakamoto argued, a denationalized, privatized currency for the twenty-first century would have to exist outside the banking system. Despite such crucial differences, the Hayekian aspiration to denationalize money is never far from Bitcoin's surface. Nor is the nostalgia of metal money. As already suggested by the apt metaphor of 'mining', despite being cast in technological futurism, Bitcoin also always looks back nostalgically to a world of metal money.[48] Driven by an attempt to induce economic discipline and a quest for the intensified commodification of money, Bitcoin is a project of artificial scarcity.[49]

IV. The Politics of Bitcoin

As much as blockchain systems may aspire to 'create order without law', as De Filippi and Wright put it, these visions are not beyond politics.[50] Instead, cryptocurrencies are highly political projects in their own right. From the beginning, Bitcoin presented itself in the garb of a transformative utopian project, with roots in cypher-punk, anarchist, and libertarian promises of technology. Robbing governments and banks of their ability to control money would create on this view a world in which states had lost control over tax revenue and credit creation, thereby left unable to finance wars.[51] In this section, I take a closer look at this political vision with reference to the example of Bitcoin and subject it both to internal and external critiques. To summarize, first, Bitcoin's colourful paeans to decentralization, competition, and efficiency stand in stark contrast to its actual workings. Instead of a decentralized, efficient currency, Bitcoin is today mostly a speculative asset with few if any uses

---

[47] Satoshi Nakamoto, 'Bitcoin: A Peer-to-Peer Electronic Cash System' (2008), 8.

[48] One entrepreneur—Anthem Hayek Blanchard, whose first name is the title of an Ayn Rand novel while his middle name speaks for itself—has even since combined all three elements in the form of a digital currency backed by a gram of gold. Its name? 'HayekCoin.' Henry Sanderson, 'Digital Currencies: A Gold Standard for Bitcoin' (*Financial Times*, 15 May 2015).

[49] As computing power becomes more powerful, the mathematical problem that needs to be solved in order to 'mine' an additional Bitcoin is designed to become automatically more complicated. Bitcoin is also irreversibly programmed to stop 'mining' once there are 21 million Bitcoins (as of March 2018, around 16 million had been generated).

[50] De Filippi and Wright (n 1), 5. See also Primavera De Filippi and Benjamin Loveluck, 'The Invisible Politics of Bitcoin: Governance Crisis of a Decentralized Infrastructure' (2016) 5(3) *Internet Policy Review*, 1–28.

[51] Popper (n 44), xx–xv.

as currency but a substantial energy footprint generated by an oligopolistic set of miners. Second, even in as far as Bitcoin succeeds in privatizing money (or in particular if it were to succeed more generally), this would amount to a de-democratization of an essential public good. It is not clear why any regulatory authority or democratically legitimated body should accept such a proposal.

The central claim of blockchain technology is that it 'addresses the centuries-old problem of trust'.[52] The 'decentralized trust' of the ledger offers on this account a technological solution to the fragility of human relations. However, while vowing to exist without trust and hierarchy, existing cryptocurrencies have quickly given rise to informal structures of de facto governance that can be neither checked nor changed. Despite their self-presentation as currencies beyond the fickle bonds of human trust, existing cryptocurrencies have shown themselves moreover to be heavily dependent on the trust of their respective community of adopters. After all, the quality of the ledger is only ever as good the quality of its members. As Nathaniel Popper has documented, it was only the mutual trust of the early Bitcoin community members that allowed it to take off in the first place.[53] This entailed both networks of collective trust, as well as highly personalized trust in selecting Bitcoin opinion leaders, such as Roger Ver, the early cryptocurrency advocate humbly known as 'Bitcoin Jesus'. Just as the politics of money is inescapable, even a blockchain payment system requires trust: trust in the integrity of the underlying code, trust in any authority deciding about the exception (such as a 'fork' in the blockchain) and trust in the liquidity of the respective asset. While the pure theory of blockchain systems speaks only of 'decentralized trust', personal authority and trust in individual reputation has been crucial to the success of various existing cryptocurrencies.

Once more, existing cryptocurrencies paint a picture that deviates markedly from reality. Bitcoin's mining algorithm, for example, highly favours large conglomerates of miners. As a result, neither the generation of Bitcoins nor the confirmation of Bitcoin payments is truly decentralized. Instead, its mining and the processing of payments tends to be heavily centralized, with a small number of extremely large miners operating in an oligopolistic structure that strikingly resembles that of the global banking system.[54] Faith in decentralization has obscured the ongoing existence of hidden central authorities, the trusting influence of individual opinion leaders, and more generally the oligopolistic forces of network power.[55] Cryptocurrencies continue to rely on centralized forms of authority that are tacitly embedded in the design of the original algorithm but systematically obscured in the form of market power.[56]

If decentralization is one important rhetorical pillar of the Bitcoin vision, the implicit promise of efficiency is another. But again, due to the way in which Bitcoin intentionally produces artificial scarcity through the solving of cryptographic puzzles there is an enormous waste of resources that produces a breath-taking energy footprint. To estimate Bitcoin's energy use we can begin with the total computing power of the entire Bitcoin network. In early 2018, total Bitcoin computing power stood at around 26 quintillion hashes per second.[57] These can come either from highly efficient, professional mining computers or from less efficient, older computers. Assuming that the entire computing power derives from the most efficient mining computers available, researchers have arrived at an absolute minimum

---

[52] Michael Casey and Mariana Dahan, 'Blockchain Technology: Redefining Trust for a Global, Digital Economy' (14 June 2016) https://medium.com/mit-media-lab-digital-currency-initiative/blockchain-technology-redefining-trust-for-a-global-digital-economy-1dc869593308#.9fyo6ynbv.

[53] Popper (n 44), 77–80 and 142.

[54] At the end of 2017, less than 1,000 or so accounts owned 40% of Bitcoin. Olga Kharif, 'The Bitcoin Whales: 1,000 People Who Own 40 Percent of the Market' (*Bloomberg*, 8 December 2017).

[55] Grewal (n 36).

[56] Such hidden centralized authority has become visible most palpably in the case of hard forks: De Filippi and Wright (n 1).

[57] Alex de Vries, 'Bitcoin's Growing Energy Problem' (May 2018) 2 *Joule*, 801–09.

estimate of Bitcoin's energy consumption. As of March 2018, this absolute lower bound was 2.55 GW.[58] For comparison, this is roughly as much energy as Ireland consumes.[59] Once we account for less efficient equipment and include the energy necessary to cool the computers, the estimate quickly rises to 8 GW.[60] This range suggests that Bitcoin's energy consumption is currently comparable to that of a medium-sized European country. (Nathan Ensmenger even estimates that Bitcoin today uses as much energy as the whole of Germany.)[61] This is likely to rise quickly thanks to the inbuilt increase in difficulty of the underlying crypto-graphic task. As of 2018, Bitcoin's energy footprint was on track to soon overtake the total amount of energy generated by all the world's solar panels.[62] The metaphor of 'mining' Bitcoin thus turns out to be a painfully accurate description of its environmental impact. To be sure, it is possible to envision a cryptocurrency without such an enormously wasteful energy footprint but these would have to abandon precisely the pledge to cryptographically enforced artificial scarcity so prized by those who are looking for a speculative asset with a fixed supply or a currency with an in-built deflationary bias.

These discrepancies between Bitcoin's outward self-presentation as a decentralized cur-rency beyond politics and its actual political impact as a wasteful speculative asset are not just caveats or exceptions. They point to a larger issue by serving as a reminder of the in-escapability of politics and the way in which Bitcoin relies on recurrent attempts to hollow-out existing public goods, from money to energy. Existing cryptocurrencies do not break with politics. Instead they aspire to cut themselves off from the shared provision of public goods and the democratic ideal of collective self-rule. To be sure, the politics of Bitcoin is a peculiar one in as far that it tends to deny its own political nature. However, this, in itself, is nothing puzzling or new. Some of the most powerful political movements—not least clas-sical liberalism—have tended to naturalize their political claims or hide them behind invo-cations of nature, history, and other forces that seem to be precisely beyond human control. To insist then that there can be no such thing as apolitical money is to refuse to take at face value the anti-political rhetoric of Bitcoin and to understand it instead as a powerful, if per-nicious, political strategy in its own right.

V. Conclusion

The depoliticized vision of electronic money embodied by Bitcoin rose to prominence in the context of the re-politicization of money during the 2008 Financial Crisis. Taking seriously this context allows for re-situating the rise of cryptocurrencies as an echo of the unresolved political contestations of the 1970s over the politicization and depoliticization of money, contestations that the Great Moderation had subdued and obscured. Only the post-Crisis collapse of the depoliticizing facade of money opened up the space for Bitcoin's proposal to shield money against political discretion. Appreciating this framing allows us to become more attentive to cryptocurrencies' peculiar politics of depoliticization in the liminal space between private money and speculative asset. While cryptocurrencies are frequently framed as an escape from the politics of money, I have argued that this is highly misleading. Not only do cryptocurrencies engender their own politics, they also rely constitutively on the acquies-cence of states, central banks and other regulatory authorities. Cryptocurrencies are highly

---

[58] ibid., 801.

[59] International Energy Agency, 'World Energy Statistics 2017', https://www.iea.org/publications/freepublications/publication/KeyWorld2017.pdf.

[60] de Vries (n 56), 801. See also Karl O'Dwyer and David Malone, 'Bitcoin Mining and Its Energy Footprint' (2014) ISSC 2014/CIICT. Ironically, it is most profitable to mine Bitcoin in socialist countries with highly subsidized energy, such as China and Venezuela.

[61] Nathan Ensmenger, 'Dirty Bits: An Environmental History of Computing' (16 March 2016), Talk at Yale University. See also Ingrid Burrington, 'The Environmental Toll of a Netflix Binge' (*The Atlantic*, 2015).

[62] de Vries (n 56), 801–09.

unlikely to replace fiat currencies any time soon, but they will deepen the global prolifer-ation of tax havens, regulatory arbitrage, and shadow banking. Rather than revolutionizing the global monetary infrastructure for the better, cryptocurrencies have instead emerged as highly risky, speculative financial games.[63] High transaction costs and long processing times have meanwhile rendered Bitcoin virtually impracticable as a payment system.[64] Instead of a new form of money, most cryptocurrencies now function as decentralized gambling machines masquerading as a technological breakthrough.[65] Cryptocurrencies' insistence on their status as currencies looks from this perspective less like a noble ambition than a self-serving attempt to starve off securities regulation, money-laundering rules, and the tax-ation of capital gains. After all, the success of cryptocurrencies as speculative assets would be unthinkable without their extremely light, preferential regulatory treatment that has rendered them highly desirable for purposes of financial fraud, price manipulation, and an extraordinary mis-selling of risky securities to ill-informed retail investors. The price rise of 2017 exposed this strategy to an ironic predicament. While light regulatory treatment of cryptocurrencies hinges on their nominal status as currencies, their success as speculative assets undermines precisely such claims.

It is worth stepping back at this point to recall the stakes involved. The Financial Crisis constituted a powerful reminder of the political dimension of money. Since the crisis the seeming alchemy of fiat money, so successfully repressed before, has once more stirred up a wariness and anxiety about the effervescence of modern credit money. Faced with the fic-titious nature of credit money it is tempting to be suspicious of its Faustian character. Calls for rooting money in an unalterable algorithm mirror in this context the earlier seductions of rooting money in a precious commodity. Both respond to the same underlying anxiety by promising to remove money from human control. But this impulse should make us pause. Appreciating the inescapable politics of cryptocurrencies points us instead towards the un-resolved nature of the ad hoc global monetary order that emerged haphazardly since the end of the Bretton Woods system. The Financial Crisis not only witnessed cryptocurrencies' re-staging of earlier attempts to depoliticize money, but it also opened up renewed calls for global monetary reform that echo the unsuccessful demands of the Global South during the late 1970s. The dystopian challenge of cryptocurrencies offers, in this sense, also an oppor-tunity to openly reflect about the kind of monetary order we want and the kind of currency that can live up to our political ideals.

VI. Bibliography

Abdelal Rawi, *Capital Rules. The Construction of Global Finance* (Harvard University Press 2007).
Bernanke Ben, 'The Great Moderation' (26 February 2004) Meeting of the Eastern Economic Association.
Boughton Jim, *Silent Revolution: The International Monetary Fund 1979–1989* (International Monetary Fund 2001).
Bret Benjamin, 'Bookend to Bandung: The New International Economic Order and the Antimonies of the Bandung Era' (2015) 6(1) *Humanity: An International Journal of Human Rights, Humanitarianism and Development*, 33–46.
Burrington Ingrid, 'The Environmental Toll of a Netflix Binge' (2015) *The Atlantic*.

---

[63] J. P. Koning, 'Bitcoin as a Novel Financial Game' (6 June 2016) *American Institute for Economic Research* https://www.aier.org/article/sound-money-project/bitcoin-novel-financial-game.

[64] In a tell-tale sign, in January 2018, the North American Bitcoin Conference was forced to suspend pay-ments in Bitcoin because these had become too slow and expensive: Aaron Mak, 'The North American Bitcoin Conference is No Longer Accepting Bitcoin Payments for Tickets' (*Slate*, 2018) https://slate.com/technology2018/01/the-most-important-blockchain-conference-of-the-year-won't-take-bitcoin-for-last-minute-sales.html.

[65] Lynn Parramore, 'Jim Chanos on Fraud' *Institute for New Economic Thinking* (2018) https://www.ineteconomics.org/perspectives/blog/jim-chanos-cryptocurrency-is-a-security-speculation-game-masquerading-as-a-technological-breakthrough.

Caldwell Bruce, 'Hayek's Nobel' (2016) 21 *Advances in Austrian Economics*, 1–19.

Casey Michael and Dahan Mariana, 'Blockchain Technology: Redefining Trust for a Global, Digital Economy' (14 June 2016) https://medium.com/mit-media-lab-digital-currency-initiative/blockchain-technology-redefining-trust-for-a-global-digital-economy-1dc869593308#.9fyo6ynbv, accessed on 10 January 2019.

Cohen Benjamin, *The Future of Sterling as an International Currency* (Macmillan 1971).

Cohen Benjamin, *The Geography of Money* (Cornell University Press 1998).

Cohen Benjamin, 'Electronic Money: New Day or False Dawn?' (2001) 8(2) *Review of International Political Economy*, 197–225.

Cohen Benjamin, 'The New Geography of Money' in *Global Monetary Governance* (Routledge 2008).

Cohen Benjamin, *Currency Power: Understanding Monetary Rivalry* (Princeton University Press 2015).

De Filippi Primavera and Loveluck Benjamin, 'The Invisible Politics of Bitcoin: Governance Crisis of a Decentralized Infrastructure' (2016) 5(3) *Internet Policy Review*.

De Filippi Primavera and Wright Aaron, *Blockchain and the Law: The Rule of Code* (Harvard University Press 2018).

Eich Stefan and Tooze Adam, 'The Great Inflation' in *Vorgeschichte der Gegenwart*, edited by Anselm Doering-Manteuffel, Lutz Raphael, and Thomas Schlemmer (Vandenhoeck and Ruprecht 2015).

Eichengreen Barry, *Exorbitant Privilege. The Rise and Fall of the Dollar* (Oxford University Press 2011).

Ensmenger Nathan, 'Dirty Bits: An Environmental History of Computing' (16 March 2016) Talk at Yale University.

Ferguson James, *The Anti-Politics Machine: 'Development', Depoliticization, and Bureaucratic Power in Lesotho* (University of Minnesota Press 1994).

Frieden Jeffry, *Banking on the World* (Harper and Row 1987).

Getachew Adom, *Worldmaking after Empire: The Rise and Fall of Self-Determination* (Princeton University Press 2019).

Grewal David, *Network Power: The Social Dynamics of Globalization* (Yale University Press 2008).

Hayek Friedrich August, 'The Pretence of Knowledge. Lecture to the Memory of Alfred Nobel, December 11, 1974' in *New Studies in Philosophy, Politics, Economics and the History of Ideas* (University of Chicago Press and Routledge & Kegan Paul 1978).

Hayek Friedrich August, *Law, Legislation and Liberty: The Political Order of a Free People* (Volume 3, University of Chicago Press 1979).

Hayek Friedrich August, 'The Future Unit of Value' (14 September 1981) Visa International Annual Conference, Papers of Friedrich A. Hayek, Hoover Institute, Stanford University, Box 131, Folder 5.

Hayek Friedrich August, 'Consolidated Preface' in *Law, Legislation and Liberty. A New Statement of the Liberal Principles of Justice and Political Economy* (Volumes 1–3, Routledge & Kegan Paul 1982).

Hayek Friedrich August, 'Choice in Currency' in *The Collected Works of F. A. Hayek*, edited by Stephen Kresge (Volume 6, University of Chicago Press 1999).

Hayek Friedrich August, 'The Denationalization of Money: An Analysis of the Theory and Praxis of Concurrent Currencies [1978]' in *Good Money, Part II. The Collected Works of F. A. Hayek*, edited by Stephen Kresge (Volume 6, University of Chicago Press 1999).

Hayek Friedrich August, 'The Road to Serfdom' in *The Collected Works of F. A. Hayek*, edited by Bruce Caldwell (Volume 2, University of Chicago Press, 2007).

Hayek Friedrich August, 'The Constitution of Liberty [1960]' in *The Collected Works of F. A. Hayek*, edited by Bruce Caldwell and Ronald Hamowy (Volume 17, University of Chicago Press 2011).

International Energy Agency, 'World Energy Statistics 2017', https://www.iea.org/publications/freepublications/publication/KeyWorld2017.pdf, accessed on 10 January 2019.

James Harold, *Making the European Monetary Union* (Harvard University Press 2012).

Kharif Olga, 'The Bitcoin Whales: 1,000 People Who Own 40 Percent of the Market' (*Bloomberg*, 8 December 2017).

Koning J.P., 'Bitcoin as a Novel Financial Game' (2018) *American Institute for Economic Research* https://www.aier.org/article/sound-money-project/bitcoin-novel-financial-game.

Mak Aaron, 'The North American Bitcoin Conference is No Longer Accepting Bitcoin Payments for Tickets' (2018) *Slate* https://slate.com/technology/2018/01/the-most-important-conference-of-the-year-won't-take-bitcoin-for-last-minute-sales.html.

Mason J.W., 'The Fed Doesn't Work for You' (2016) *Jacobin* https://www.jacobin.com/2016/01/federal-reserve-interest-rate-increase-janet-yellen-inflation-unemployment/.

Myrdal Gunnar, *Beyond the Welfare State: Economic Planning and Its International Implications* (Yale University Press 1960).

Myrdal Gunnar, 'The Equality Issue in World Development' (March 1975) Lecture to the memory of Alfred Nobel.

Nakamoto Satoshi, 'Bitcoin: A Peer-to-Peer Electronic Cash System' (2008).

O'Dwyer Karl and Malone David, 'Bitcoin Mining and Its Energy Footprint' (2014) ISSC 2014/CIICT.

Parramore Lynn, 'Jim Chanos on Fraud' (2018) *Institute for New Economic Thinking* https://www.ineteconomics.org/perspectives/blog/jim-chanos-cryptocurrency-is-a-security-speculation-game-masquerading-as-a-technological-breakthrough.

Popper Nathaniel, *Digital Gold. The Untold Story of Bitcoin* (Harper Collins 2015).

Prashad Vijay, *The Darker Nations: A People's History of the Third World* (The New Press 2007).

'The Arusha Initiative. A Call for a United Nations Conference on International Money and Finance' (1980) 2 *Development Dialogue (Uppsala)*, 11–23.

Sandbu Martin, *Europe's Orphan: The Future of the Euro and the Politics of Debt* (Princeton University Press 2015).

Sanderson Henry, 'Digital Currencies: A Gold Standard for Bitcoin' (*Financial Times*, 15 May 2015).

Strange Susan, *Sterling and British Policy* (Oxford University Press 1971).

Strange Susan, *Mad Money: When Markets Outgrow Governments* (University of Michigan Press 1998).

Sveriges Riksbank Prize in Economic Sciences in Memory of Alfred Nobel 1974, http://www.nobelprize.org/nobel_prizes/economic-sciences/1974/press-release, accessed on 29 January 2019.

'The Terra Nova Statement on the International Monetary System and the Third World' (1980) 1 *Development Dialogue*, 29–34.

Tooze Adam, 'Just Another Panic' (2016) 97 *New Left Review*, 129–38.

Tooze Adam, *Crashed. How a Decade of Financial Crises Changed the World* (Viking 2018).

United Nations General Assembly, 'Declaration on the Establishment of a New International Economic Order' (1 May 1974) Resolution A/RES/S6/3201.

Vries Alex de, 'Bitcoin's Growing Energy Problem' (May 2018) 2 *Joule*, 801–9.

Zimmermann Claus, 'The Concept of Monetary Sovereignty Revisited' (2013) *European Journal of International Law*, 797–818.

5

Monetary Policy in the Digital Age

*Claus D. Zimmermann**

I. Introduction

The term 'virtual currencies', and the synonymous term 'digital money', refer to digital representations of value, issued by private developers and denominated in their own units of account.[1] As defined by the International Monetary Fund ('IMF'), virtual currencies 'can be obtained, stored, accessed, and transacted electronically, and can be used for a variety of purposes, as long as the transaction parties agree'.[2] Their scope goes from simple IOUs of issuers (such as mobile coupons) to virtual currencies backed by assets such as gold, to cryptocurrencies such as Bitcoin.[3]

The potential of digital money to replace state-issued fiat money as the predominant means of payment for retail goods combined with its ability to flow freely across international borders is attracting much attention among central bankers, the media, and scholars. One of the central concerns is that central banks could gradually lose control over the monetary aggregates via which they regulate the money supply for purposes of conducting monetary policy.

After discussing the contemporary scope of monetary policy and the potential impact of virtual currencies on its conduct (section II), this chapter succinctly examines the main regulatory challenges for monetary policy arising from the growing importance of digital money (section III), prior to presenting its conclusions (section IV).

II. Contemporary Monetary Policy and the Impact of Virtual Currencies

This section opens with an important preliminary analysis: do virtual currencies amount to 'money' in an economic and/or legal sense (section A)? It then discusses the contemporary scope of monetary policy, from the perspective of its tools and objectives (section B). Finally, it assesses the potential of virtual currencies to affect any of the so-called 'monetary aggregates' into which the money supply in a given economy is usually broken down for the purpose of conducting monetary policy (section C).

A. Virtual currencies: do they amount to 'money' in an economic and/or legal sense?

The basic concept of what amounts to 'money' has traditionally been significantly larger in economics than in law.

---

* This paper exclusively represents the author's personal views and not those of Sidley Austin LLP or any of the firm's clients. This chapter benefited greatly from comments by participants in the workshop 'Blockchain and the Constitution of a New Financial Order: Legal and Political Challenges', held at UCL Faculty of Laws on 19 June 2017. The final manuscript of this chapter was completed on 1 August 2018; any subsequent developments could not be taken in account.

[1] The technical and legal specificities of some outstanding virtual currency schemes in what is a rapidly evolving landscape are addressed as part of other chapters in this book.

[2] IMF Staff Discussion Note, 'Virtual Currencies and Beyond: Initial Considerations' (2016) https://www.imf.org/external/pubs/ft/sdn/2016/sdn1603.pdf, [8].

[3] ibid.

1. Economic perspective

For economists, money is everything that is generally accepted as payment for goods and services and/or as repayment of debts.[4] The three essential functions ascribed to money by economists are: (i) money as a unit of account; (ii) money as a means of exchange; and (iii) money as a store of value. In economic terms, the money stock or money supply designates the total amount of money available in an economy at a given time. However, there is no single accepted economic definition of which assets are included under the general term 'money'.[5]

From an economic perspective, it appears safe to say that, at present, virtual currencies do not (yet) completely fulfil the three economic roles associated with money.

a. Unit of account

According to the IMF,[6] there is currently not much evidence that virtual currencies are being used as a self-standing unit of account. Put differently, instead of being used as a direct measure for the value of goods and services, virtual currencies instead represent a value in fiat currency based on the exchange rate with a given virtual currency. This produces a situation in which retailers accepting payment in virtual currencies usually quote prices in fiat currency with the virtual-currency price being based on the exchange rate at a particular point in time.

b. Medium of exchange

As convincingly analysed by the IMF,[7] the current small size and limited acceptance network of virtual currencies significantly restricts their use as a medium of exchange. The problem here is that without legal tender status, a virtual currency can only be accepted to the extent that two parties agree to use it. Thus, the number and volume of transactions in virtual currencies remain small. Importantly, this continues to be the case despite the rapid growth of payments that are based on virtual currencies as a medium of exchange. Indeed, according to the IMF, by the end of 2016, US currency in circulation was US$ 1.4 trillion, while US money supply (M2) was about US$ 12 trillion. By contrast, the total market value of virtual currencies was a mere US$7 billion.[8]

c. Store of value

According to the IMF,[9] the high price volatility of virtual currencies strongly limits their ability to serve as a reliable store of value. Indeed, until now, the prices of virtual currencies have been highly unstable and are typically characterized by huge price fluctuations. Importantly, the volatility of virtual currencies so far appears to be much higher than for national currencies.

---

[4] For detail on the economic concept of money, see Frederic Mishkin, *The Economics of Money, Banking, and Financial Markets* (Business School 2nd edn, Addison Wesley 2009); John Smithin, *What is Money?* (Routledge 2000); and James Tobin, 'Money' in *The New Palgrave Dictionary of Economics*, edited by Steven Durlauf and Lawrence Blume (2nd edn, Palgrave Macmillan 2008).

[5] John Black describes this dilemma as follows: '[w]hile notes and coins are legal tender [ie, forms of money that creditors are obliged, by law, to accept in settlement of a debt] and must be included in any definition [of money supply], and bank deposits repayable on demand are unlikely to be excluded, there are various types of deposit in non-bank financial intermediaries such as building societies, and various forms of highly liquid security, which can be included or excluded in various ways. Even unused postage stamps and uncashed postal orders could be used as money, though they are not included in any current definition.' Sourced from John Black, *Oxford Dictionary of Economics* (2nd edn, Oxford University Press 2003), 305–06.

[6] See IMF (n 2), [20].   [7] ibid.   [8] ibid., [20].   [9] ibid.

2. Legal perspective

In the realm of the law, three different theories exist for what constitutes money. It is insightful to take a look whether virtual currencies qualify as 'money' under any of these legal theories.

a. State theory of money

According to the still dominant state theory of money, which was developed to a large extent by Mann, only that which is recognized as 'money' under the law of the issuing jurisdiction has the legal quality of money.[10] It is not only the state's monopoly in issuing notes and coins, but in a larger sense the state's predominant role in establishing a monetary system that the state theory of money is built upon.[11] Mann's thoughts on the subject appear to have been informed by the writings of German economist Knapp who, as early as 1905, wrote that only chattels issued by the legal authority of the state could acquire the character of 'money' and that the value to be attributed to them is fixed by law, rather than by reference to the materials employed in the process of production.[12]

The state theory of money has traditionally been analysed as a corollary of the sovereign power over currency, and its global acceptance has even led to it being indirectly recognized in several modern constitutions, such as Article 1, section 8, paragraphs 5 and 6 of the US Constitution and Article 73(4) of the German Grundgesetz (in both cases by vesting the exclusive legislative authority in monetary matters in the federal state).[13] The widely acknowledged downside of the state theory of money is that, under this theory, only a tiny percentage of the actual money stock in a modern economy qualifies as 'money' in a strictly legal sense.

In light of the above, it is safe to say that, from a legal perspective, virtual currencies do not amount to 'money' under the state theory of money. The same is true, by the way, for scriptural and electronic money as the largely dominant payment instruments these days. Scriptural money, and therewith the huge bulk of all bank deposits, does not amount to money but to credit according to the state theory of money, which regards electronic money merely as a specific technique for using scriptural money.[14]

b. Societary theory of money

In order to overcome the widening gap between economic reality and the legal concept of money, very early on a 'societary' theory of money emerged in the legal literature with von Savigny (1779–1861) in the nineteenth century and Nussbaum (1877–1964) in the middle of the twentieth century being its first major proponents.[15] According to this theory, it is not a formal decision by the state, but the attitude taken by society—as expressed in the practices of commercial life—which is relevant in deciding what counts as money. In his famous treatise 'Money in the Law—National and International', Nussbaum argued convincingly as follows:

> in the phenomenon of money the attitude of society, as distinguished from state, is paramount.... [A]s a matter of legal theory, ... the Societary process which gives life to money is

---

[10] See Charles Proctor, *Mann on the Legal Aspect of Money* (7th edn, Oxford University Press 2012), 15.

[11] On this point, see also ibid., 15.

[12] On this point, see also ibid., 16, referring to George Knapp, *Staatliche Theorie des Geldes* (4th edn, Duncker and Humblot 1923).

[13] For these and additional references to modern constitutions indirectly recognizing the state theory of money, see Rosa Lastra, *Legal Foundations of International Monetary Stability* (Oxford University Press 2006), 18, n 52.

[14] For detail, see Geneviève Burdeau, 'L'Exercice des Compétences Monétaires par les États' (1988) 212 *Recueil des Cours*, 234–36.

[15] On this point, see Dominique Carreau, 'Le Système Monétaire International Privé (UEM et euromarchés)' (1998) 274 *Recueil des Cours*, 367.

not exactly a process of 'customary law'. It does not engender new canons of law. Similarly, as in the emergence of new types of negotiable instruments the process only widens the range of things to which a pre-existing body of rules—in this case of rules of monetary conduct—may be applied. By no means does the [S]ocietary theory of money deny the fact that normally the modern state exercises full power over the currency. But legal theory has to take care also (and in a sense primarily) of abnormal and controversial situations. This test the State [t]heory of money cannot stand.[16]

Nussbaum's analysis still seems perfectly valid and, if anything, appears to have gained in power over the past decades. The state theory of money certainly provides a coherent definition of what constitutes money in a strictly formal sense. However, its increasing inability to be properly recognized as money in the legal sense, most monetary aggregates that form the monetary stock in a modern economy and which are the objects of monetary policy, clearly indicates that the state theory of money has to a large extent become outdated.

Scriptural money and timeless, yet increasingly widespread, phenomena such as local or regional currencies,[17] as well as powerful new phenomena, such as virtual or digital currencies easily qualify as 'money' under the broad scope of the societary theory of money.

c. Institutional theory of money

A few words need to be said with respect to a 'third' theory of money, the so-called 'institutional' theory of money, which has more recently been introduced into the legal literature by Antonio Sáinz de Vicuña, a former general counsel of the European Central Bank ('ECB').[18] The institutional theory of money is based on the presupposition that the concept of legal tender underpinning the state theory of money has become outdated as a consequence of the overwhelming use of scriptural money in today's economy.[19] As elaborated by Sáinz de Vicuña:

> the concept of money, in a situation of global markets and modern communication technologies, is now inseparable from the institutional set-up of the central banks (that is, their independence, mandate, and instrumentaria) and from the normative framework under which central banks, credit institutions, financial infrastructures (for example, payments systems), and markets operate, which ensures the stability and the functionality of money. The value of money no longer depends on the will of the individual sovereigns.[20]

However, as a 'third' legal theory of money, the institutional theory of money does not appear to be substantially different from the societary theory of money as refined by Nussbaum. As noted above, the societary theory perfectly recognizes that the definition of the monetary system remains the prerogative of the state and does not take a merely functional approach, contrary to what some authors have claimed.[21]

---

[16] Arthur Nussbaum, *Money in the Law—National and International* (The Foundation Press 1950), 8.

[17] Local or regional currencies, often also referred to as community currencies, are currencies that are not legal tender, are intended to be used in parallel to the respective national currency and only trade in a rather limited geographical area (usually not across borders). At present, close to 3,000 different local or regional currencies are known to exist worldwide, many of them operating as scrips or vouchers that can be exchanged into national currency. From an economic perspective, local or regional currencies tend to circulate more quickly than regular currency since they usually operate on the basis of a demurrage charge, i.e. their nominal value decreases over time making it more attractive to actually spend the money.

[18] This institutional theory of money was first proposed by Sáinz de Vicuña in a paper presented at a meeting of the Committee on International Monetary Law of the International Law Association (MOCOMILA) in Tokyo on 1 April 2004. A brief discussion of that paper and the institutional theory of money outlined therein can be found in Lastra (n 13), 21, n 34. Sainz de Vicuña has more recently provided an updated analysis of his institutional theory of money in Antonio Sáinz de Vicuña, 'An Institutional Theory of Money' in *International Monetary and Financial Law: The Global Crisis*, edited by Mario Giovanoli and Diego Devos (Oxford University Press 2010), 517. For a nuanced discussion of that article, see Proctor (n 10), 25–30.

[19] For detail, see Vicuña (n 18), 521–23.   [20] ibid., 519.   [21] See Proctor (n 10), 24.

Interestingly, even though the institutional theory of money appears in many ways a mere expression of the societary theory, it appears less certain whether virtual currencies would qualify as 'money' under the institutional theory of money with its much stronger focus on the institutional and normative framework in which modern monetary policy is being conducted. One could plausibly argue that as long as most states and their central banks have not made the important step to regulate the use of virtual currencies, the latter somehow remain under the radar of the institutional theory of money.

B. The contemporary scope of monetary policy—tools and objectives

Depending on their respective—explicit or implicit—mandate, most central banks around the world aim to achieve 'monetary stability',[22] which can be regarded as a synonym for 'price stability'.[23] Importantly, although central banks often also seek to achieve not only the stability of domestic prices but also external price stability, i.e. a stable exchange rate, it is economically inconsistent in the medium- or long-term to simultaneously pursue both objectives. In addition, some central banks, notably the US Federal Reserve System ('Fed'), also aim to achieve a desired level of growth in real activity as part of their monetary policy.

The setting of key interest rates, such as the Federal Funds Target Rate determined by the Federal Open Market Committee in the United States, the Bank of England Base Rate set by the Bank of England's Monetary Policy Committee, or the key interest rates determined by the Governing Council of the European Central Bank ('ECB'), is one of three main tools of monetary policy.[24] The other two key tools of monetary policy are open market operations (by which the quantity of money in circulation is managed through the purchase and sale of financial instruments such as treasury bills and foreign currency) and reserve requirements (by which central banks determine the minimum reserves, under the form of vault cash or deposits with the central bank, that each commercial bank must hold of customer deposits and notes). Besides that, the regulation of the banking system (and the availability and cost of credit) and of the payments system (clearing and settlement) are increasingly important, additional tools for controlling the money supply in a modern economy.[25]

These days, the tools of monetary policy are usually divided into conventional (or traditional) and unconventional tools. The setting of key interest rates stands at the centre of what is commonly referred to as the *conventional* tools of monetary policy. Thus, in normal, non-crisis times, the central bank is neither involved in direct lending to the government or the private sector nor in the direct purchasing of government bonds, corporate debts, or other types of debt instruments. Usually, it is enough for the central bank to steer the level of the key interest rates and to adjust the supply of central bank money through open market operations to manage the liquidity conditions in money markets.

Now, as evidenced by the recent Global Financial Crisis, in addition to these conventional, traditional, tools, *unconventional* tools have become increasingly prominent in the conduct of monetary policy. The most important ones to mention are quantitative easing and so-called credit easing, both of which aim to ease financing conditions when the conventional

---

[22] *Financial* stability, the other key objective pursued by most central banks besides that of *monetary* stability, is not strictly speaking a monetary or interest rate policy objective.

[23] The Governing Council of the ECB, for example, has clarified that, in pursuing price stability as the ECB's primary policy objective, it seeks to keep inflation below, but close to, 2% over the medium term.

[24] These days, the majority of modern economies have delegated the conduct of monetary policy to independent central banks.

[25] A given monetary policy is commonly referred to as being contractionary if it reduces the size of the money supply, notably by raising key interest rates. By contrast, an expansionary policy increases the money supply in the economy, notably by decreasing interest rates. Similarly, a monetary policy referred to as being accommodative is one that is intended to create economic growth while a tight policy would be one that is intended to reduce inflation.

tools no longer work, i.e. most importantly, when short-term interest rates are already at or close to zero and can therefore no longer be lowered to stimulate the economy.

As noted at the beginning of this subsection, achieving monetary stability is usually the main objective of monetary and, more specifically, interest rate policies as conducted by central banks. It emerges from a detailed study of central bank objectives undertaken by François Gianviti, a former general counsel of the IMF, that in most central banking laws worldwide, monetary stability is defined as the stability of domestic prices.[26] As explained in detail by Gianviti, this is due to the economic reality that *external* price stability (in terms of the exchange rate with a given major currency) and *domestic* price stability are, in fact, two distinct objectives, that are incompatible with each other in the long run.[27] For example, a central bank increasing its monetary base in order to prevent its currency from appreciating in line with economic fundamentals, thereby aiming to maintain an unrealistic currency peg, will in the long run fuel inflation, thereby endangering domestic price stability.

Gianviti's survey shows that most countries do not explicitly and precisely define their understanding of the notion of 'domestic price stability', unless the country concerned is one that has a specific procedure in place for the formulation of an explicit inflation target or some other form of quantified price objective.[28] In countries lacking a formal definition of the objective of domestic price stability, the understanding of that objective is subject to the central bank's case-by-case interpretation and, to the extent that the central bank is not entirely independent,[29] to the approval and review by the government.[30] However, Gianviti's survey identifies a global trend towards the adoption of quantified price objectives as opposed to letting central banks conduct monetary policy without publicly announcing specific objectives.[31]

Gianviti's study indicates that there now seems to be common agreement on what is understood by the objective of domestic price stability. Thus, while domestic prices are those of domestic goods and services, asset prices are not usually covered by the term. As regards 'stability', there appears to be broad consensus that, while a total absence of inflation would discourage investment and thus stifle economic growth, an annual price increase of 2% would still be considered consistent with the objective of price stability.[32]

Consequently, some countries have adopted inflation ceilings whilst others have considered the setting of inflation targets to be the preferable approach.[33] An inflation target may take the form of a 'point inflation target', i.e. a specific percentage increase of consumer prices, such as the Bank of England's inflation target of 2.0%,[34] or of a 'target inflation range' which seems to be the more common approach and which is adhered to, for example, in Canada and Sweden.[35] An interesting example in that context is the approach taken by the Governing Council of the ECB. It has shifted over the years from a quantitative definition of price stability that amounted to an outright inflation ceiling of 2% to a hybrid definition of price stability that it seems appropriate to qualify as a 'targeted inflation ceiling'. Thus, the Governing Council of the ECB clarified in 2003 that, in pursuing domestic price stability as

---

[26] F. Gianviti, 'The Objectives of Central Banks' in *International Monetary and Financial Law: The Global Crisis*, edited by Mario Giovanoli and Diego Devos (Oxford University Press 2010), 449–83 and 468.

[27] ibid., 473.   [28] ibid., 468.

[29] For an insightful analysis of the theory and practice of central banks independence, see Lastra (n 13), 41–61. On the economic rationale for central bank independence, see Stanley Fischer, 'Central-Bank Independence Revisited' (1995) 85(2) *The American Economic Review*, 201, as well as the various references listed therein.

[30] Gianviti (n 26), 468–69.   [31] ibid., 472.   [32] ibid., 470.

[33] On the reasons that led to the widespread adoption of inflation targeting towards the end of the twentieth century, see Frederic Mishkin, 'Inflation Targeting: True Progress or Repackaging of an Old Idea' in *The Swiss National Bank 1907–2007* (Swiss National Bank 2007), 599–623.

[34] Bank of England, Inflation Report of February 2018, https://www.bankofengland.co.uk/inflation-report/2018/february-2018.

[35] Gianviti (n 26), 471.

the ECB's primary policy objective, it seeks to keep inflation below, but close to, 2% over the medium term.[36]

Despite this significant degree of convergence of the ways in which the objective of price stability is being pursued by central banks, it is important to stress that the remaining differences are not limited to scenarios where a country accords priority to external price stability as opposed to focusing on inflation. Hence, it makes a huge difference whether a central bank adheres to an inflation ceiling of 2%, which will be met even with zero inflation, or if it aims to achieve a target inflation rate of 2%, which means neither more nor less. Inflation targeting may thus be considered as having a built-in bias for a consistently moderate level of inflation, which is favourable, at least in the short-term, to growth and employment.[37]

This leads directly to what is arguably the contemporary key difference between interest rate policies pursued by different central banks. While the formal adoption of an inflation target (or target range) amounts to an implicit acknowledgement that the central bank wishes to contribute, via the way it conducts monetary policy, to economic growth and employment, some central banks, as noted earlier, also aim to achieve a desired level of growth in real activity as part of their monetary policy. These different approaches explain to a large extent the existing discrepancies in interest rate policies conducted on opposite sides of the Atlantic.

The different responses of the Fed and the ECB to the onset of the 2007–2012 economic and financial Crisis are highly insightful in this context. The Fed reacted with a series of interest rate cuts aimed at saving employment, while the ECB kept interest rates unchanged for much longer in order not to endanger price stability. This illustrates that the current lack of harmonization in the way interest rates policies are being conducted by central banks may lead to major differences in how similar economic problems are tackled across different countries.

Finally, as regards the other key objective pursued by most central banks, the objective of financial stability, that objective is strictly speaking neither a monetary nor interest rate policy objective. Many different definitions have been advanced in the economics literature for financial stability. Usually, the concept is approached in an indirect manner by defining the opposite of financial stability, i.e. financial *instability*. A broad and systemic approach defines financial instability as the prevalence of a financial system that is unable to ensure, in a lasting way and without major disruptions, an efficient allocation of savings to investment opportunities.[38] Financial regulation on minimum capital ratios for commercial banks is the main, but not exclusive, tool for avoiding financial instability.

Although a common position on the precise interdependence of monetary stability and financial stability does not seem to exist in the economics literature, it appears to be broadly admitted that both phenomena are intrinsically linked and reinforce each other, which seems equally true for the two instability scenarios.[39] Thus, as pointed out by Gianviti, while in most cases, securing financial stability will be supportive of achieving monetary stability, a central bank may face a conflict of objectives in the conduct of its monetary and interest rate policies once it becomes engulfed in a financial crisis.[40] Gianviti cites the example of a major financial crisis in which the central bank, in order to safeguard a financial system on the verge of collapsing, decides to bail out numerous, systemically important, financial institutions, partly without collateral, on top of lowering its interest rates and injecting short-term liquidity into the banking system. In addition, the central bank may even be exposed

---

[36] For detail on the ECB's definition of price stability, see https://www.ecb.europa.eu/mopo/strategy/pricestab/html/index.en.html.

[37] Gianviti (n 26), 471.

[38] Otmar Issing, 'Monetary and Financial Stability: Is There a Trade-Off?' (28–29 March 2003) Conference on 'Monetary Stability, Financial Stability and the Business Cycle', held at the Bank for International Settlements.

[39] ibid.   [40] Gianviti (n 26), 481.

to significant public pressure to purchase large amounts of government bonds to finance budget deficits arising from countercyclical measures taken to mitigate the crisis.[41] In the long run, the injected amounts of central bank money, all injected in the name of financial stability, may endanger monetary stability in the sense of domestic price stability.

Based on the above, it would be wrong to conclude that central banks should not aim to safeguard financial stability in addition to pursuing their monetary policy objective(s), in particular, as both monetary and financial stability will, in most cases, mutually reinforce each other. However, while a sovereign state is free to determine in the statutes of its central bank that the objective of monetary stability takes priority over that of financial stability, such an order of priority would effectively have to be abandoned in the case of a severe crisis. Although, strictly speaking, financial stability is not an objective of monetary and interest rate policies, the central bank of a modern economy has little choice but to pursue both these objectives simultaneously. This seems true despite the above-mentioned potential for conflict between both objectives. This clearly distinguishes the pair of financial/monetary stability from the wholly separate choice as to whether or not to pursue an economic growth objective as part of monetary policy on top of the objective of price stability.

C. The potential of virtual currencies to affect any of the monetary aggregates

For the purpose of conducting monetary policy, the money supply in a given economy is usually broken down into more or less narrowly defined 'monetary aggregates', the main ones of which are M0, M1, M2, and M3 (with M0 (notes and coins) being the narrowest aggregate and M3 (extending to various types of deposits like savings and demand deposits) being the largest.

Most major central banks no longer rely on official M0 aggregates, although they continue to publish the quantity of notes and coins in circulation. The ECB, for example, relies on the following three monetary aggregates: Narrow Money ('M1'), which is defined as the sum of currency in circulation and overnight deposits; Intermediate Money ('M2'), which is defined as M1 plus deposits with an agreed maturity of up to two years and deposits redeemable at a period of notice of up to three months; and Broad Money ('M3'), which is defined as M2 plus repurchase agreements and money market fund shares/units and debt securities of up to two years.[42] The US Fed, having discontinued publication of the M3 monetary aggregate on 23 March 2006, publishes weekly figures for M1 and M2.[43] Finally, in the United Kingdom, the Bank of England, following the implementation of the May 2006 Money Market Reform publishes figures for notes and coins and reserve balances as well as a broad money aggregate ('M4') that measures the money supply in the United Kingdom. In addition, the Bank of England publishes a UK estimate of the important monetary aggregate M3 as defined by the ECB.

Virtual currencies, to the extent that they are designed to substitute central bank currency, could, at least, in theory, replace the entire stock of central bank currency. Central bank currency is a component in all monetary aggregates; therefore, a change in the demand for central bank currency has at least the theoretical potential to affect these aggregates.

The largest impact, however, of a steady rise in the importance of virtual currencies, would be on the narrowly defined stock of money, M1, which in most countries consists of central bank currency in circulation, travellers' checks in the hands of the public, and demand deposits. At

---

[41] ibid., 481.

[42] For detail on the ECB's definition of euro area monetary aggregates, see ECB, http://www.ecb.europa.eu/stats/money_credit_banking/monetary_aggregates/html/hist_content.en.html.

[43] US Federal Reserve, https://www.federalreserve.gov/releases/h6/.

least in theory, other monetary aggregates, such as M2 or M3, could also be impacted. However, since central bank currency has less weight in these aggregates, they would be less affected.

With the above discussion of the contemporary scope of monetary policy and the potential impact of virtual currencies on its conduct in mind, this chapter now turns to a succinct examination of the main regulatory challenges for monetary policy arising from the growing importance of digital money.

III. Regulatory Challenges for Monetary Policy Arising from Virtual Currencies

From a monetary policy perspective, it is interesting to assess virtual currency systems in light of certain critical features that stable monetary regimes are typically expected to provide. A detailed analysis, part of a broader research effort undertaken by the IMF in 2015–2016 for the World Economic Forum, provides particularly helpful insights in this regard.[44] To the extent that virtual currency systems possess or lack relevant features that normally characterize stable monetary systems, specific regulatory challenges arise for the conduct of monetary policy in the digital age.

Specifically, according to the IMF's analysis,[45] stable monetary regimes are typically expected to provide a significant level of resilience against the following three types of monetary stability risks or concerns that are considered to be of key importance. The first risk is that of structural deflation. The second risk is that of lacking the requisite flexibility to respond to temporary shocks to money demand and thus to smooth the business cycle. The final risk is that of lacking the capacity to function as a lender of last resort ('LOLR').

The following sections succinctly address each of these three risks that arise from virtual currency systems under a monetary policy perspective.

A. Risk 1: structural deflation

In economics, the term 'deflation' designates a decrease in the general price level of goods and services. Put differently, whereas inflation reduces the real value of money over time, deflation increases it. A modest level of *inflation* (the optimum level of which is commonly regarded as being close to, but below, 2% per year) acts as an incentive to invest, and thus as a stimulant for economic growth. By contrast, most economists agree that even a modest level of *deflation* is problematic as it increases the real value of debt. Unless deflation is due to an exceptional event, such as a one-off economic shock, if it is due to the underlying economic fundamentals it is referred to as 'structural deflation'.

As pointed out by the IMF, the nearly fixed supply of existing virtual currency systems, particularly of many cryptocurrencies, has the potential to result in structural deflation in the same way as under a 'gold standard', i.e. a system where the standard economic unit of account is based on a fixed quantity of gold as a rare raw material.[46] As explained by the IMF, typically, the demand for money grows in line with the growth of the economy. When the supply of money is nearly fixed, continued growth of the demand for money leads to structural deflation.[47] It is useful to keep in mind that, as highlighted by Redish and Bordo, this was also the main reason why the gold standard and sterling or US dollar-based international reserve systems had to be reformed to no longer rely on limited reserves.[48]

---

[44] IMF (n 2).   [45] ibid., [60].   [46] ibid., [61].   [47] ibid.
[48] See Angela Redish, 'Anchors Aweigh: The Transition from Commodity Money to Fiat Money in Western Economies' (1993) 26(4) *Canadian Journal of Economics*, 777–95. See also Michael Bordo, 'The Classical Gold Standard: Some Lessons for Today' (1981) *Federal Reserve Bank of St. Louis Review*, 2–17.

In its analysis, the IMF comes to the rather sceptical conclusion that modern monetary regimes with a flexible money supply have a major advantage over virtual currencies in this regard.[49]

However, from a purely technical perspective, one should always keep in mind, that there is no obvious reason why future virtual currency systems could not be designed in a manner that allows for an expansion in money supply, in line with transaction volumes, thereby helping to overcome their deflationary bias in a growing economy.[50] Ultimately, this is merely an issue of (i) technical innovation; and (ii) obtaining appropriate regulatory authorization where necessary. It therefore seems quite likely that it is only a matter of time until virtual currency systems will be designed in a manner that will allow for a sufficient expansion in money supply to avoid the risk of structural deflation.

B. Risk 2: lacking flexibility to respond to temporary shocks to money demand

According to the IMF, in an economy with a high share of virtual currencies, monetary policy could see its ability to manage the business cycle significantly diminished.[51] This concern is of particular relevance for those countries which have a tradition of strongly relying on monetary policy as a steering tool for obtaining desired levels of growth in real activity such as, notably, the United States.

In this regard, some of the challenges would be similar to those faced by countries that are 'dollarized', i.e. countries that do not or no longer issue their own currencies but rely on the currency of another country as legal tender. That situation can occur either as the result of a deliberate policy choice or as a result of a de facto choice by economic operators to utilize a strong external currency, such as the US dollar or the euro, over the domestic currency.[52]

As highlighted by the IMF in its analysis, the current generation of virtual currencies does not allow for an expansion of the money supply as a policy choice by the central bank in response to negative demand shocks.[53] For the IMF, the major risk associated with this situation is that it 'would tend to exacerbate recessions and could lead to a deflationary spiral, as during the Great Depression under the [former] gold standard'.[54]

At present, it seems, at best, unclear whether the limited capacity of virtual currency systems to allow for a quick expansion of the money supply can be overcome by future generations of digital money. According to the IMF's sceptical conclusion, there currently is 'no obvious way to program [virtual currency] supply rules to respond appropriately to all conceivable macroeconomic shocks'.[55]

In the same vein, as opined by Janet Yellen, the then Chair of the US Fed in a speech given in 2015, even largely rule-based inflation-targeting regimes still require a great deal of judgement, especially in the face of large or qualitatively different shocks.[56] The IMF considers that even substantially improved supply-rule programmes for virtual currencies that incorporate various contingency plans will probably not be flexible enough, particularly in view of ongoing structural changes in the economy.[57]

---

[49] IMF (n 2), [61].   [50] ibid.   [51] ibid., 62.

[52] Kosovo, Monaco, and Montenegro are examples of fully dollarized economies using the euro. Notable examples of countries relying exclusively on the US dollar are the British Virgin Islands, Ecuador, El Salvador, and Panama.

[53] IMF (n 2), [62].   [54] ibid.   [55] ibid.

[56] Janet Yellen, 'Normalizing Monetary Policy: Prospects and Perspectives' (27 March 2015), Speech at 'The New Normal Monetary Policy' research conference held at the Federal Reserve Bank of San Francisco, California.

[57] IMF (n 2), [62], n 58.

C. Risk 3: lacking capacity to function as an LOLR

A third major risk identified by the IMF is that it is difficult to conceive how virtual currency systems should be able to fulfil the important function of central banks to act as LOLR,[58] i.e. to provide systemically, vital emergency liquidity in situations in which it would be irrational for private lenders to provide support.

The importance of institutions that can act as LOLR and provide emergency liquidity has again been powerfully illustrated during the recent Global Financial Crisis. According to the IMF's analysis, 'even with flexible supply rules, it is difficult to conceive how a decentralized virtual currency scheme could generate the type of large-scale liquidity response that is needed during a financial crisis'.[59]

The IMF concludes that experience and economic theory suggests that a public agency is needed to solve the externalities and coordination failures that arise in such cases.[60] In other words, the main limitations in this regard are not of a technical nature, i.e. of a nature that could potentially be overcome by the private actors behind the currently existing virtual currency systems. Rather, they fundamentally stem from the economic incentives that arise from the essence of virtual currency systems as a creation of private actors.

IV. Conclusion

As highlighted by the Bank for International Settlements ('BIS'), were virtual currencies to be adopted and used much more widely, this could have a real impact on the demand for existing monetary aggregates and thus the conduct of monetary policy.[61] At present, however, despite the recent hype over Bitcoin and other cryptocurrencies, the degree to which virtual currencies are being used 'appears too low for these risks to materialize'.[62]

Furthermore, it seems plausible that the BIS is right with its assessment that the future impact of virtual currencies on the conduct of monetary policy will likely show many similarities with the impact of e-money.[63] Thus, the effect of digital money on the implementation of monetary policy will essentially depend on two things. First, it will depend on the extent to which the availability of virtual currency systems provokes a change in demand for bank reserves (e.g. a substitution towards digital currencies, away from the existing banking system for deposits and payments). Second, it will depend on the precise degree of economic and financial interconnection between the users of sovereign currency and the users of the digital currency.[64] As concluded by the BIS, only 'if the substitution is large and the interconnection is weak, then may monetary policy [gradually] lose efficacy'.[65]

After discussing the contemporary scope of monetary policy and the potential impact of virtual currencies on its conduct, this chapter has highlighted the main regulatory challenges for monetary policy arising from the growing importance of digital money. It is safe to say that the nature of these regulatory challenges will require a regular re-assessment to account for new circumstances in a rapidly changing environment.

That being said, from a monetary policy perspective, introducing major legal restrictions that limit or prevent the proliferation of virtual currencies would, at present, seem exaggerated. This seems particularly true in light of the ongoing efforts to further deregulate and improve the efficiency of the financial sector. These efforts stem from the fact that central bank currency is an expensive medium of exchange.[66] For example, in the United States, the estimated annual cost of consumers, retailers, banks and the government to handle cash is

---

[58] ibid., [63].   [59] ibid.   [60] ibid.

[61] See BIS Committee on Payments and Market Infrastructures, 'Digital Currencies' (*Bis.org*, November 2015) https://www.bis.org/cpmi/publ/d137.pdf, 16.

[62] ibid.   [63] ibid.   [64] ibid.   [65] ibid.

[66] See Marke Slovinec, 'Digital Money and Monetary Policy' (2006) XIV *BIATEC*, 14.

approximately US$ 200 billion,[67] which includes costs associated with processing and ac-counting of money, storage, transport, and security.

At present, it appears appropriate to adhere to the IMF's conclusion that the appeal for, and the risks arising from, virtual currency systems may be greater for countries where con-fidence in monetary policy is low.[68] This leads the IMF to the convincing conclusion that without regulatory measures and other interventions, virtual currency systems will likely be more widely adopted in countries with less credible monetary policy, i.e. in essence, a less credible commitment to price stability.[69] This, in turn, strongly indicates that a harmonized, internationally concerted approach to regulating virtually currency schemes, potentially under the IMF's leadership, would seem superior to individual economies issuing their own regulations.

V. Bibliography

Bank of England, Inflation Report of February 2018, https://www.bankofengland.co.uk/inflation-report/2018/february-2018, accessed on 10 January 2019.

Bank for International Settlements (BIS) Committee on Payments and Market Infrastructures, 'Digital Currencies' (*Bis.org*, November 2015) https://www.bis.org/cpmi/publ/d137.pdf, accessed on 10 January 2019.

Black John, *Oxford Dictionary of Economics* (2nd edn, Oxford University Press 2003).

Bordo Michael, 'The Classical Gold Standard: Some Lessons for Today' (1981) 63(5) *Federal Reserve Bank of St Louis Review*. 2.

Burdeau Geneviève, 'L'exercice des Compétences Monétaires par les États' (1988) 212 *Recueil des Cours*, 211.

Carreau Dominique, 'Le Système Monétaire International Privé (UEM et euromarchés)' (1998) 274 *Recueil des Cours*, 367.

Chakravorti Bhaskar and Mazzotta Benjamin, 'The Cost of Cash in the United States' (2013) Institute for Business in the Global Context The Fletcher School, Tufts University, http://fletcher.tufts.edu/CostofCash/~/media/Fletcher/Microsites/Cost%20of%20Cash/CostofCashStudyFinal.pdf, accessed on 10 January 2019.

European Central Bank ('ECB'), Definition of Euro Area Money Aggregates, http://www.ecb.europa.eu/stats/money_credit_banking/monetary_aggregates/html/hist_content.en.html, accessed on 10 January 2019.

European Central Bank ('ECB'), Definition of Price Stability, https://www.ecb.europa.eu/mopo/strategy/pricestab/html/index.en.html, accessed on 10 January 2019.

Fischer Stanley, 'Central-Bank Independence Revisited' (1995) 85(2) *The American Economic Review*, 201.

German Grundgesetz, Article 73(4).

Gianviti François, 'The Objectives of Central Banks' in *International Monetary and Financial Law: The Global Crisis*, edited by Mario Giovanoli and Diego Devos (Oxford University Press 2010).

IMF Staff Discussion Note, 'Virtual Currencies and Beyond: Initial Considerations' (2016) https://www.imf.org/external/pubs/ft/sdn/2016/sdn1603.pdf, accessed on 10 January 2019.

Issing Otmar, 'Monetary and Financial Stability: Is There a Trade-off?' (28–29 March 2003) ECB Conference on 'Monetary Stability, Financial Stability and the Business Cycle' held at the Bank for International Settlements.

Knapp Georg, *Staatliche Theorie des Geldes* (4th edn, Duncker and Humblot 1923).

Lastra Rosa, *Legal Foundations of International Monetary Stability* (Oxford University Press 2006).

---

[67] Bhaskar Chakravorti and Benjamin Mazzotta, 'The Cost of Cash in the United States' (2013) Institute for Business in the Global Context The Fletcher School, Tufts University, http://fletcher.tufts.edu/CostofCash/~/media/Fletcher/Microsites/Cost%20of%20Cash/CostofCashStudyFinal.pdf, 35.

[68] IMF, (2), at [64].   [69] Ibid.

Mishkin Frederic, 'Inflation Targeting: True Progress or Repackaging of an Old Idea' in *The Swiss National Bank 1907–2007* (Swiss National Bank 2007).

Mishkin Frederic, *The Economics of Money, Banking, and Financial Markets* (Business School 2nd edn, Addison Wesley 2009).

Nussbaum Arthur, *Money in the Law—National and International* (The Foundation Press 1950).

Proctor Charles, *Mann on the Legal Aspect of Money* (7th edn, Oxford University Press 2012).

Redish Angela, 'Anchors Aweigh: The Transition from Commodity Money to Fiat Money in Western Economies' (1993) 26(4) *The Canadian Journal of Economics*, 777.

Slovinec Marko, 'Digital Money and Monetary Policy' (2006) XIV *BIATEC*, 12.

Smithin John, *What is Money?* (Routledge 2000).

Tobin James, 'Money' in *The New Palgrave Dictionary of Economics*, edited by Steven Durlauf and Lawrence Blume (2nd edn, Palgrave Macmillan 2008).

US Constitution, Article 1, Section 8, Paragraphs 5 and 6.

US Federal Reserve, https://www.federalreserve.gov/releases/h6/ , accessed on 10 January 2019.

Vicuña Antonio Sáinz de, 'An Institutional Theory of Money' in *International Monetary and Financial Law: The Global Crisis*, edited by Mario Giovanoli and Diego Devos (Oxford University Press 2010).

Yellen Janet, 'Normalizing Monetary Policy: Prospects and Perspectives' (27 March 2015), Speech at 'The New Normal Monetary Policy' research conference held at the Federal Reserve Bank of San Francisco, California.

6

Global Currencies and Domestic Regulation

Embedding through Enabling?

*Georgios Dimitropoulos**

I. Introduction

The concepts of virtual currencies and cryptocurrencies are not strictly identical. 'Virtual currencies' have been defined by the European Central Bank as a 'digital representation of value, not issued by a central bank, credit institution or e-money institution, which, in some circumstances, can be used as an alternative to money.'[1] The term 'cryptocurrency' is used to refer to any virtual currency that relies on peer-to-peer cryptography for the validation of value transfers.[2] The term 'altcoin' is also very often used in this context, mostly to describe virtual currencies except for the 'dollar' of the cryptocurrencies: the bitcoin. The bitcoin is

> a non-fiat cryptographic electronic payment system that purports to be the world's first cryptocurrency. In other words, it is a peer-to-peer, client-based, completely distributed currency that does not depend on centralised issuing bodies (i.e. a 'sovereign') to operate. The value is created by users and the operation is distributed using an open source client that can be installed on any computer or mobile device.[3]

The software Bitcoin uses is completely open source and anyone can download it, modify it, and consequently create their own version of the software, which then becomes a new virtual currency regime; this has led to an explosion of altcoins. There are no limits to the number of altcoins that can be developed and released;[4] in practice there are only a few real alternatives that implement minor or major changes to the Bitcoin software.[5]

Cryptocurrencies and other virtual currencies have been gaining greater relevance since 2008, when two interrelated incidents took place: the Global Financial Crisis, and the introduction of Bitcoin. On 3 March 2017, the Bitcoin price exceeded the price of gold.[6] One bitcoin now costs more than an ounce of gold. Accordingly, the literature on the legal aspects of cryptocurrencies has been expanding with an obvious focus on Bitcoin.[7] The issue of

* I would like to thank Stefan Eich, Philipp Hacker, and Ioannis Lianos for comments and discussions on this and related topics, as well as the participants at the 'Blockchain and the Constitution of a New Financial Order: Legal and Political Challenges' conference at UCL. The usual disclaimer applies.

[1] European Central Bank, *Virtual Currency Schemes—A Further Analysis* (February 2015).

[2] Most cryptocurrencies are not completely anonymous; they are rather pseudonymous; see Edward Murphy, Maureen Murphy, and Michael Seitzinger, 'Bitcoin: Questions, Answers, and Analysis of Legal Issues' (Congressional Research Service, 13 October 2015) http://fas.org/sgp/crs/misc/R43339.pdf, 3.

[3] Andres Guadamuz and Chris Marsden, 'Blockchains and Bitcoin: Regulatory Responses to Cryptocurrencies' (2015) 20 *First Monday*.

[4] 'The internet of money will be less concerned with creating one coin to rule them all, than it will be about finding one rule to coin them all'; see World Government Summit, *The Future of Money: Back to The Future—The Internet of Money* (2017), 7.

[5] These are known as 'forks'; see Adam Hayes, 'The Decision to Produce Altcoins: Miners' Arbitrage in Cryptocurrency Markets' (2015) https://papers.ssrn.com/sol3/papers.cfm?abstract_id=2579448.

[6] Its price closed at $1,268 on that Thursday while the price of a troy ounce of gold was $1,233.

[7] Reuben Grinberg, 'Bitcoin: An Innovative Alternative Digital Currency' (2012) 4 *Hastings Science & Technology Law Journal*, 159; Tracey Anderson, 'Bitcoin—Is It Just a Fad? History, Current Status and Future of the Cyber-Currency Revolution' (2014) 29 *Journal of International Banking Law and Regulation*, 428; Alexandre

regulation of cryptocurrencies has been prominent,[8] again with a focus on Bitcoin.[9] The views in the legal commentary range from scholars against,[10] in favour, and in favour of minimal regulation.[11] Given the great importance that cryptocurrencies and other virtual currencies are gaining globally, the purpose of this chapter is to discuss the question of their regulation from a comparative perspective.

There is a discrepancy in how different countries around the word deal with cryptocurrencies. A comparative look at cryptocurrency regulation even reveals a paradoxical regulatory landscape: on the one side, some jurisdictions try to restrict their use—reaching from complete bans on the use of cryptocurrencies to restrictions on use to more spot-on restrictions; on the other side, some governments have been trying to enable the operations of Financial Technology (FinTech) companies, including virtual currency start-ups, in their jurisdictions by using innovative regulatory instruments, such as 'innovation hubs', and 'regulatory sandboxes'. More loose regulatory standards apply to them than for conventional financial institutions.

According to the political economist of the twentieth century, Karl Polanyi, the market system necessarily produces two antithetical movements in society: one in favour of market expansion (and equally against government intervention in the economy), and one in favour of protective measures (and equally against market expansion);[12] the market system progresses through the support of a movement in favour of free trade, on the one side, and the support of interventionist measures by a collectivist counter-movement, on the other, in an effort to embed the market into institutions of society.[13] The Polanyian concept of the 'double movement' has gained traction again after the financial and economic Crisis of 2008. Economic and financial expansion through cryptocurrencies and responses to their expansion can be explained in similar terms.

In a way, the virtual and cryptocurrency system disrupts the narrative of the double movement but produces the same effects in society as the double movement does. Bitcoin and other virtual currencies have been produced by libertarians, anarchists, and other opponents of the global financial system in an effort to by-pass the institutions of the financial markets,

---

Mallard, Cécile Méadel, and Francesca Musiani, 'The Paradoxes of Distributed Trust: Peer-to-Peer Architecture and User Confidence in Bitcoin' (2014) 4 *Journal of Peer Production*; Primavera De Filippi and Aaron Wright, *Blockchain and the Law: The Rule of Code* (Harvard University Press 2018).

[8] Andres Guadamuz, 'Virtual Currency and Virtual Property Revisited (*Technollama.co.uk*, 11 February 2013) http://bit.ly/1MaeW4N; Pirmavera De Filippi, 'Bitcoin: A Regulatory Nightmare to a Libertarian Dream' (2014) 3 *Internet Policy Review*; Global Legal Research Directorate and Law Library of Congress Staff, 'Regulation of Bitcoin in Selected Jurisdictions' (2014) https://www.loc.gov/law/help/bitcoin-survey/regulation-of-bitcoin.pdf; Stephen Middlebrook and Sarah Jane Hughes, 'Regulating Cryptocurrencies in the United States: Current Issues and Future Directions' (2014) 40 *William Mitchell Law Review*, 813; Jerry Brito, Houman B. Shadab, and Andrea Castillo O'Sullivan, 'Bitcoin Financial Regulation: Securities, Derivatives, Prediction Markets, and Gambling' (2014) 16 *Columbia Science and Technology Law Review*; Nicholas Plassaras, 'Regulating Digital Currencies: Bringing Bitcoin within the Reach of the IMF' (2013) 14 *Chicago Journal of International Law*, 377; Andy Yee, 'Internet Architecture and the Layers Principle: A Conceptual Framework for Regulating Bitcoin' (2014) 3 *Internet Policy Review*, 1; Kevin Tu and Michael Meredith, 'Rethinking Virtual Currency Regulation in the Bitcoin Age' (2015) 90 *Washington Law Review*; Omri Y. Marian, 'A Conceptual Framework for the Regulation of Cryptocurrencies' (2015) 82 *University of Chicago Law Review Online*, 53; Guadamuz and Marsden (n 3); Jeffrey Matsuura, *Digital Currency: An International Legal and Regulatory Compliance Guide* (Bentham e-Books 2016).

[9] Joshua Doguet, 'Nature of the Form: Legal and Regulatory Issues Surrounding the Bitcoin Digital Currency System' (2013) 73 *Louisiana Law Review*, 1119.

[10] Nikolei Kaplanov, 'Nerdy Money: Bitcoin, the Private Digital Currency, and the Case against its Regulation' (2012) 25 *Loy Consumer Law Review*, 111; Joseph Stiglitz, 'Bitcoin Ought to Be Outlawed' (World Economic Forum, 30 November 2017) https://www.weforum.org/agenda/2017/11/joseph-stiglitz-bitcoin-ought-to-be-outlawed/.

[11] Daniela Sonderegger, 'A Regulatory and Economic Perplexity: Bitcoin Needs just a Bit of Regulation' (2015) 47 *Washington University Journal of Law and Policy*, 175.

[12] Karl Polanyi, *The Great Transformation: The Political and Economic Origins of Our Time* (Beacon Press 1944, 1957, 2001), 79–80 and 136–40.

[13] The fist mention of the idea of 'embeddedness' of economic institutions into social relations is in ibid., 60.

the central banks, and the commercial banks.[14] For possibly the first time in the history of capitalism, the protective counter-movement identified and analysed by Polanyi has contributed to the further commodification of one of the factors of production, meaning capital, and the creation of a truly global market for money, thus replacing and even moving beyond the gold standard of the nineteenth and twentieth centuries.

If one takes Polanyi seriously, this can have destructive results on national societies, since they may eventually be deprived of the national and cultural institution of their currency. This might explain the emergence of a counter-movement to the counter-movement, which has developed in order to tackle the potential negative effects of cryptocurrencies on economy and society by introducing interventions in favour of social protection; this can be dubbed as the 'anti-countermovement'.[15] The anti-countermovement has appeared in countries like the United States that follow the market economy system, and countries like China and Russia that follow their own versions of market economy.

The emergence of the anti-countermovement explains the varying responses by countries around the world to virtual currencies. The anti-countermovement may take the disguise of the countermovement and try to block the spread of cryptocurrencies: this is the restricting approach to the regulation of virtual currencies. Other forces of the anti-countermovement may try to 'domesticate' the global currencies. In this case, the anti-countermovement views virtual currencies as a technology, and tries to embed them into the domestic legal order through enabling their technology in its own jurisdiction. The following question thus emerges: can enabling constitute a sufficient means of embedding? This chapter suggests that the answer may be positive if one condition is satisfied: the sufficient regulation of the new intermediaries of the cryptocurrency economy.

The remainder of this chapter is organized as follows. Section II discusses measures taken to regulate cryptocurrencies from a comparative perspective with a focus on command and control and other intermediate measures. Section III discusses the legal nature of cryptocurrencies, explaining that cryptocurrencies may be perceived as money, or a commodity. It further shows how the regulatory question is complicated in some jurisdictions given the dual nature of cryptocurrencies, namely not only as currency, but also as technology, revealing a schizophrenic approach to regulation of cryptocurrencies. Section IV provides an explanation to this schizophrenic approach by tapping into the theory of Karl Polanyi on the embeddedness of markets in societal institutions and the double movement in market society.

II. Regulatory Approaches to Cryptocurrencies

The idea of creating a currency that relies on a different paradigm to traditional money presents legislators and regulators around the world with very difficult regulatory challenges. The present section makes a case for understanding cryptocurrencies and other virtual currencies as global currencies and then deals with both the command-and-control and the intermediary approaches to cryptocurrency regulation.

A. Cryptocurrency as global currency

There are many similarities between physical currencies and virtual currencies. Virtual currency is a digital representation of value that can be traded online and has at least some of

---

[14] Satoshi Nakamoto, 'Bitcoin: A Peer-to-Peer Electronic Cash System' (31 October 2008) https://bitcoin.org/bitcoin.pdf; De Filippi (n 8), 1.

[15] The coming of the gold standard in the nineteenth century had equally led at the time to the spread of protectionist institutions and measures; see Polanyi (n 12), 223.

the generally recognized functions of money; it operates as a store of value, a medium of exchange, and as a unit of account—but unlike physical money, virtual currency does not have a legal tender status in any legal order.[16] They are both means of payment that are nowadays invariably accepted by many companies like *Amazon, eBay, Expedia.com, Microsoft,* the *App Store,* etc., while there are examples of government agencies that have started accepting cryptocurrencies by citizens, for example the Swiss town of Zug, which accepts Bitcoin payments for municipality services.[17]

There are obviously also many differences between traditional currencies and cryptocurrencies, but the key difference may be the domestic nature of the former as opposed to the global nature of the latter. Their immaterial as well as their decentralized nature make cryptocurrencies genuinely global, whereas traditional (and fiat) currency is generally a national currency. This is an aspect of cryptocurrencies that has been less discussed in the relevant literature. The main issues arising around the regulation of cryptocurrencies are connected to their global nature.

Currency and monetary units have traditionally been physical units. The British 'pound', the 'peso', and the Israeli 'shekel' derive from units of weight.[18] Other currencies are indicative of the material they are made of; for example, the 'rupee' used in India and countries that have been influenced by the Indian system, comes from a Sanskrit word for silver. Cryptocurrencies are built on codes rather than tangible materials. However, even in the twentieth century, 'money moved from being the physical representation of a valuable commodity to an intangible symbol of trust'.[19] This is what is known as 'fiat money'. In a way, virtual currencies form part of a larger, more recent trend towards the digitization of money and the economy more generally, and the use of data rather than tangible instrumentalities in modern economic transactions.[20]

Additionally, a central authority like the King or the Crown has traditionally exercised the regulation of currency; this is expressed in currency designations like 'riyal' (Saudi Arabia, Qatar), 'rial' (Iran, Oman), 'riel' (Cambodia), 'real' (Brazil).[21] The more recent trend, which expanded in the twentieth century, has been to entrust the power to regulate money to central banks or federal reserves. According to Article 25(1) of the Bank of Canada Act, for example, the Central Bank of Canada has the 'sole right of note issue'.[22] Cryptocurrencies are not controlled by a central authority. They are based on a system of production and management that is fundamentally decentralized. There is no issuing body and no central authority in charge of the currency; virtual currencies are managed by the network of peers participating in the global system.

The immaterial, decentralized nature of virtual currencies makes them fundamentally global.[23] They are actually designed for a transnational use via the internet.[24] Virtual

---

[16] See Allen & Overy, *Virtual Currencies: Mining the Possibilities* (2015), 3: 'VCs [virtual currencies] are not legal tender, which means the following features are not fulfilled: (a) mandatory acceptance, i.e., that the creditor of a payment obligation cannot refuse currency unless the parties have agreed on other means of payment; (b) acceptance at full face value, i.e., the monetary value is equal to the amount indicated; and (c) that the currency has the power to discharge debtors from their payment obligations". See European Banking Authority ('EBA'), 'EBA Opinion on "Virtual Currencies"' (4 July 2014) EBA/Op/2014/08, https://eba.europa.eu/documents/10180/657547/EBA-Op-2014-08-+Opinion+on+Virtual+Currencies.pdf.

[17] CryptoCoin News (CCN), 'Swiss Town Zug Continues Allowing Bitcoin Payments for Municipal Services' (*CCN.com*, 19 December 2016) https://www.ccn.com/swiss-town-zug-continues-allowing-bitcoin-payments-municipal-services/.

[18] Alec Ross, *The Industries of the Future* (Simon & Schuster 2016), 76.

[19] World Government Summit, *The Future of Money* (n 4), 4.   [20] ibid.

[21] See T. Daniel Seely, 'Currency Names Summary' (*LinguistList.org*, 22 August 1995) https://linguistlist.org/issues/6/6-1145.html.

[22] 'The Bank has the sole right to issue notes and those notes shall be a first charge on the assets of the Bank'; see Article 25(1) of the Bank of Canada Act (R.S.C., 1985, c. B-2); see also Council Regulation (EC) No. 974/98 of 3 May 1998 on the introduction of the Euro.

[23] Paul Ford, 'Bitcoin May Be the Global Economy's Last Safe Haven' (*Bloomberg.com*, 28 March 2013) https://www.bloomberg.com/news/articles/2013-03-28/bitcoin-may-be-the-global-economys-last-safe-haven.

[24] Plassaras (n 8), 388.

currencies are by design currencies made to operate without the need for and beyond the national states.[25] Cryptocurrency holders have to engage in fewer transactions than the traditional currency holder in order to conduct commerce in jurisdictions outside their own.[26] 'In this sense, digital currencies are "universal" in that they can operate *outside* a system that uses multiple currencies, thereby avoiding the transaction costs associated with currency exchange.'[27] Some proponents of the system even suggest that, in the future, virtual currencies may even replace the increasingly mistrusted sovereign currencies.[28]

The global nature of cryptocurrencies has important advantages for the payer. There are no foreign exchange costs when using virtual currencies, as opposed to national currencies that need to be converted.[29] Virtual currencies are thus an extremely useful and efficient tool for cross-border payments and other money transfers.[30] The only incurred costs are the ones to convert the cryptocurrency into a national currency in case the receiver does not wish to keep the virtual currency for future usage.[31] Payees enjoy the same advantages, since virtual currencies have a global outreach which allows products to be sold to consumers located anywhere in the world.[32]

The new virtual currencies might thus present a better alternative for the promotion of the global market system than the traditional favourite of the market system itself, the gold standard. Since at least the 1820s, economic liberalism has maintained three classical tenets: (i) a labour market—labour should find its price on the market; (ii) the (international) gold standard—the creation of money should be subject to an automatic mechanism; and (iii) free trade—goods should be free to flow from country to country without hindrance or preference.[33] The gold standard is a monetary system in which the unit of account is based on a fixed quantity of gold. The international gold standard that was in force for the greater part of the nineteenth and twentieth centuries was a commitment by participating countries to fix the prices of their national currencies in terms of a specified amount of gold. National money was freely converted into gold at the fixed price.[34] The gold standard was the medium by which the system of market liberalism wanted to extend the supposedly self-regulated market throughout the entire world. According to the theory, the currency of each nation should be backed by gold; a deficit in the balance of payments of a country would lead to gold flowing out of the nation, leading to a contraction in the money supply, an equivalent rise in interest rates, a fall in prices and wages, and thus a rise in exports. For various reasons that fall outside the scope of this analysis, the system collapsed twice in the twentieth century.

Cryptocurrencies could potentially operate as a more efficient alternative to the gold standard; they abolish almost all transaction costs for the conversion of national currency to the new global currency; they may thus enhance economic liberalism through the facilitation of global trade. Alternatively, one or more virtual currencies may in the future operate as the new gold standard for the twenty-first century; namely, the digital commodity called cryptocurrency may, in the future, replace the physical commodity of gold.[35]

B. Types of regulation

In response to these and other anxieties, an anti-countermovement in favour of the introduction of social protection measures has appeared. Different countries around the world

---

[25] ibid., 405.   [26] ibid.   [27] ibid., 388–89.
[28] Adam James, 'Will Cryptocurrency Replace National Currencies by 2030?' (*Bitcoinist.com*, 2 March 2018) https://bitcoinist.com/will-cryptocurrency-replace-national-currencies-by-2030/.
[29] European Central Bank (n 1), 19.   [30] ibid.   [31] ibid.   [32] ibid.
[33] Polanyi (n 12), 141.
[34] See Michael Bordo, 'Gold Standard' (*Econlib.org*) http://www.econlib.org/library/Enc/GoldStandard.html.
[35] See also section III.B below.

have started developing legal frameworks for the regulation of cryptocurrencies. These countries have realized the potentially disruptive nature of cryptocurrencies functioning as currencies and have mainly developed three approaches to their regulation: the indifference approach (under B.1.), the command-and-control approach (under B.2.), and various intermediate approaches (under B.3.).

1. The indifference approach

The majority of countries have so far had difficulties in grappling with cryptocurrencies, either because they have not identified the potentially very important impact on their financial systems or because they have considered the potential impact of global currencies but have not qualified it as a significant risk at this stage of their development. For example, the UK Government stated in 2013 that Bitcoin is unregulated,[36] while other authorities such as the European Banking Authority (EBA) have said that there needs to be a coordinated supra-national response by regulators around the world, given the global nature of virtual currencies.[37]

2. The command-and-control approach

Some countries have adopted an approach of direct, or command-and-control regulation to cryptocurrencies, known from other fields of regulation. China has been the main example of a jurisdiction to attempt a major ban on the use of Bitcoin and other global currencies. Partly in response to claims of theft and fraud affecting Chinese citizens using Bitcoin, the People's Bank of China and four other central government agencies jointly issued the 'Notice on Precautions against the Risks of Bitcoins'[38] in order to 'protect the public's property rights, to protect RMB's official currency status, to prevent money laundering risk and to protect financial stability'.[39] The statement reads as follows:

> it is required that, at this stage, financial and payment institutions may not use Bitcoin pricing for products or services, may not buy or sell Bitcoins, may not act as a central counterparty in Bitcoin trading, may not offer insurance products associated with Bitcoin, may not provide direct or indirect Bitcoin-related services to customers, including: registering, trading, settling, clearing or other services; accepting Bitcoin or use of Bitcoin as a clearing tool; trading Bitcoin with Chinese Yuan Renminbi ('CNY') or foreign currencies; storing, escrowing, and mortgaging in Bitcoin; issuing Bitcoin-related financial products; and using Bitcoin as a means of investment for trusts and funds.[40]

This is not a direct prohibition of Bitcoin in China, as Bitcoin and other cryptocurrencies can still 'exist' and be used. The Chinese Government has simply banned certain financial institutions from handling transactions in cryptocurrencies and puts restrictions on the way in which financial institutions may use cryptocurrencies. The Notice practically restricts most of the money-like functions of Bitcoin as it cannot be used to clear settlements or to make payments, since banks and payment institutions in China are prohibited from dealing in bitcoins. The Notice further requires strengthening the oversight of internet websites providing Bitcoin registration, trading, and other services.[41] Moreover, in September 2017, a

---

[36] UK Parliament, 'Banking: Bitcoins' (Parliamentary debate, House of Lords, 18 December 2013) 4013, http://www.publications.parliament.uk/pa/ld201314/ldhansrd/text/131218w0001.htm.
[37] European Banking Authority (n 16).
[38] People's Bank of China, Ministry of Industry and Information Technology, China Banking Regulatory Commission, China Securities Regulatory Commission, and China Insurance Regulatory Commission, 'Notice on Precautions against the Risks of Bitcoins' (2013), YIN FA, 2013, No. 289, www.it.gov.cn/n1146295/n1652858/n1652930/n3757016/c3762245/content.html (in Chinese).
[39] ibid.   [40] ibid., § 2.   [41] ibid., §§ 3–4.

Committee led by the Central Bank of China announced an immediate ban on fund raising for new cryptocurrency ventures, known as Initial Coin Offerings ('ICOs') 'or token sales'.[42]

Another interesting example of the application of a command-and-control approach to cryptocurrency regulation is that taken in the United Arab Emirates (UAE), where the Central Bank of the country issued a circular on electronic payment systems.[43] Section D.7.3. of the circular contains the following provision for virtual currencies: 'All Virtual Currencies (and any transactions thereof) are prohibited.' This has created huge uncertainty in the emerging start-up market of Dubai and Abu Dhabi. In a statement to a major newspaper, the Governor of the UAE Central Bank said that the Central Bank is working on a regulatory framework for cryptocurrencies and that:

> these regulations do not cover 'virtual currency', which is defined as any type of digital unit used as a medium of exchange, a unit of account or a form of stored value. In this context, these regulations do not apply to bitcoin or other crypto-currencies, currency exchanges or underlying technology such as Blockchain.[44]

At the same time, the Dubai Supreme Legislation Committee has issued a press release proclaiming that 'the UAE should be among the first in the region, and the world, to establish a legislative framework and a financial and organizational structure for this technology'.[45] Blockchain start-ups already operate in the UAE. The Dubai start up BitOasis, for example, operates a Bitcoin wallet and exchange. Dubai has long been planning to run all its government services on the blockchain. The government of Dubai, moreover, recently announced that it will introduce its own blockchain-based cryptocurrency, called 'emCash', to facilitate transactions in the public and private sectors in the country.[46]

3. Intermediate approaches

Other countries have adopted softer approaches to the regulation of global currencies. Three main strategies can be identified: (i) subjecting them to related 'neighbouring' regulatory regimes; (ii) issuing warnings; and (iii) imposing taxation. These intermediate regulatory approaches recognize the need to regulate cryptocurrencies, accepting at the same time their existence in the respective legal orders.

One of the first measures to be adopted in the United States with regard to cryptocurrencies was the imposition of an anti-money laundering regime. The Financial Crimes Enforcement Network ('FinCEN') issued in 2013 a Guidance specifying that 'decentralized currencies' should comply with money laundering regulations.[47] While a user of virtual currency is not a Money Services Business ('MSB') under FinCEN's regulations and therefore not subject to MSB registration, reporting, and recordkeeping regulations, an administrator or exchanger of virtual currency is regarded as an MSB and should generally be considered as a 'money

---

[42] See Kenneth Rapoza, 'China's "Bitcoin Ban" No Match for Stateless Cryptocurrency Market' (*Forbes.com*, 18 October 2017) https://www.forbes.com/sites/kenrapoza/2017/10/18/chinas-blockchain-bitcoin-ban-no-match-for-stateless-cryptocurrency-market/#2032415e2de6.

[43] Central Bank of the United Arab Emirates, 'Regulatory Framework for Stored Values and Electronic Payment Systems' (2017).

[44] *Gulf News*, 1 February 2017.

[45] (Dubai) Supreme Legislation Committee, 'Workshop on the Present and Future of Legislative and Legal Frameworks of "Bitcoin"' (*slc.dubai.gov*, 16 November 2016) http://slc.dubai.gov.ae/en/AboutDepartment/News/Lists/NewsCentre/DispForm.aspx?ID=260.

[46] Government of Dubai, 'Dubai Economy Launches Partnership to Expedite emCash' (*Altcoin News*, 26 September 2017) https://www.cryptocoinsnews.com/emcash-dubais-first-official-state-cryptocurrency/.

[47] US Department of the Treasury, Financial Crimes Enforcement Network, 'Application of FinCEN's Regulations to Persons Administering, Exchanging, or Using Virtual Currencies' (18 March 2013) FIN-2013-G001, https://www.fincen.gov/sites/default/files/shared/FIN-2013-G001.pdf, (henceforth 'FinCEN').

transmitter'. At the same time, an administrator or exchanger is neither a provider or a seller of prepaid access nor a dealer in foreign exchange, under the regulations of FinCEN.

The US Securities and Exchange Commission ('SEC') has successfully placed cryptocurrencies under its regulatory ambit by imposing sanctions on unauthorized traders operating securities online for Bitcoin and Litecoin.[48] According to the SEC, investments in the currencies are securities for the purposes of US securities laws.[49] In a 2013 decision the US District Court followed the interpretation of the SEC.[50] The same approach has been adopted by the SEC with regard to ICOs.[51]

The SEC has also been involved in cryptocurrency regulation in the form of warnings, having issued a statement warning investors about the dangers of investing in Bitcoin.[52] The SEC raises the issues of the potential loss of bitcoins, the lack of recourse if something does not go as planned, and security concerns. The European Banking Authority ('EBA') also issued a warning in 2013 regarding cryptocurrencies raising the issues of monetary loss due to fraud, price instability, theft, and users' inexperience, which makes consumers unable to adequately assess the risk of purchasing and using cryptocurrencies.[53] Many agencies in EU Member States followed the lead of the EBA and have issued similar warnings.[54]

In their anxiety to deal with the global phenomenon of cryptocurrencies, many more countries have introduced various taxation schemes for cryptocurrencies.[55] In the United States again, the Internal Revenue Service ('IRS') issued a Notice clarifying that while virtual currencies are used by consumers in the same way as legal tender, the disposition of Bitcoin is, unlike cash, a taxable transaction to the consumer.[56] According to the IRS Notice, cryptocurrency is 'property' in the hands of a taxpayer, which means that its disposition is a taxable event to the extent that the cryptocurrency's value has changed since its acquisition by the taxpayer.[57] As no traditional intermediaries are involved in the transactions, the collection of such tax is only possible to the extent that the taxpayer voluntarily reports the transactions.

Australia is an interesting example of a country that used to subject both parties to a transaction with the use of Bitcoin to Goods and Service Tax ('GST'); once for the goods and

---

[48] See US Securities Exchange Commission ('SEC'), 'SEC Sanctions Operator of Bitcoin-Related Stock Exchange for Registration Violations' (*Sec.gov*, 8 December 2014) https://www.sec.gov/news/press-release/2014-273.

[49] See also US Securities Exchange Commission ('SEC'), 'Final Judgment Entered against Trendon T. Shavers, a/k/a "Piratreat40"—Operator of Bitcoin Ponzi Scheme Ordered to Pay More than $40 Million in Disgorgement and Penalties' (*Sec.gov*, 22 September 2014), SEC Litigation Release No. 23090, https://www.sec.gov/litigation/litreleases/2014/lr23090.htm; cf. also Ruoke Yang, 'When is Bitcoin a Security under US Securities Law?' (2013) 18 *Journal of Technology Law & Policy*, 99.

[50] *SEC v. Shavers and Bitcoin Savings and Trust*, Case No. 4:13-CV-416 (E.D.Tex.) (6 August 2013).

[51] US Securities Exchange Commission ('SEC'), 'Report of Investigation Pursuant to Section 21(a) of the Securities Exchange Act of 1934: The DAO' (25 July 2017), Release No. 81207; see also US Securities Exchange Commission ('SEC'), 'Investor Bulletin: Initial Coin Offerings' (*Sec.gov*, 27 July 2017) https://www.investor.gov/additional-resources/news-alerts/alerts-bulletins/investor-bulletin-initial-coin-offerings. SEC Chairman Jay Clayton has differentiated between the regulation of cryptoassets as means of exchange, securities, and/or commodities; see SEC Chairman Jay Clayton, 'Statement on Cryptocurrencies and Initial Coin Offerings' (*Sec.gov*, 11 December 2017) https://www.sec.gov/news/public-statement/statement-clayton-2017-12-11.

[52] US Securities Exchange Commission ('SEC'), 'Investor Alert: Bitcoin and Other Virtual Currency-Related Investments' (*Sec.gov*, 7 May 2014) https://www.sec.gov/oiea/investor-alerts-bulletins/investoralertsia_bitcoin.html.

[53] European Banking Authority ('EBA'), 'EBA Warns Consumers on Virtual Currencies' (*eba.europa.eu*, 13 December 2013) http://www.eba.europa.eu/-/eba-warns-consumers-on-virtual-currencies.

[54] See the detailed analysis of the European Central Bank (n 1), 30–32. See, e.g., the warning of the Bank of rance, 'Les dangers liés au développement des monnaies virtuelles: l'exemple du bitcoin' (*banque-france.fr*, 5 December 2013) Focus No. 10 https://publications.banque-france.fr/les-dangers-lies-au-developpement-des-monnaies-virtuelles-lexemple-du-bitcoin.

[55] See generally Omri Y. Marian, 'Are Cryptocurrencies Super Tax Havens?' (2013) 112 *Michigan Law Review*, 38; Aleksandra Bal, 'Stateless Virtual Money in the Tax System' (2013) 53 *European Taxation*, 351.

[56] Internal Revenue Service ('IRS'), 'Virtual Currency Guidance' (*IRS.gov*, 25 March 2014) IRS Notice 2014-21, http://www.irs.gov/pub/irs-drop/n-14-21.pdf.

[57] ibid.

services on the purchase and again for the virtual currency used in the transaction, since the Australian Tax Office designated Bitcoin in 2014 as an 'intangible asset' rather than a currency.[58] This double taxation regime reportedly led to several cryptocurrency start-ups leaving the country. As promised in 2016 by the Federal Government,[59] the double taxation regime was abolished as of 1 July 2017.[60]

In Germany, federal agencies have also considered the tax treatment of bitcoins. The Ministry of Finance discussed in a statement the possibility of a Value Added Tax for Bitcoin transfers, the lack of income tax effects for the underlying transaction when bitcoins are used as a means of payment and the lack of long-term capital gains liability for bitcoins that are held for longer than one year,[61] but has not taken any action yet.

III. The Legal Nature of Global Currencies: Money, Commodity, Technology

The response of different jurisdictions to the question of regulation of cryptocurrency goes back to how each country understands their nature.[62] Two principal approaches can be identified: cryptocurrency as money and cryptocurrency as commodity. Some countries treat them as both money and as a commodity. Thus, it has to be noted that the unidentified nature of cryptocurrencies does not always operate in favour of the creators, intermediaries, users, and others. Regulatory uncertainty very often means more regulation rather than less.

By identifying cryptocurrencies as money, or commodity, these countries still identify them as currency. As will be discussed later in the chapter, some countries take an approach that sometimes leads to a schizophrenic situation with regard to the regulation of cryptocurrencies in one jurisdiction. This has got to do with an understanding of cryptocurrency not as a currency, but as a technology.

A. Global currency as money

1. A comparative perspective

Various regulators around the world deal with cryptocurrency as money. In the United States, according to FinCEN,

> [i]n contrast to real currency, 'virtual' currency is a medium of exchange that operates like a currency in some environments but does not have all the attributes of real currency. In particular, virtual currency does not have legal tender status in any jurisdiction. [FinCEN] guidance addresses 'convertible' virtual currency. This type of virtual currency either has an equivalent value in real currency or acts as a substitute for real currency.[63]

---

[58] See Australian Taxation Office, 'Goods and Services Tax Ruling' (*law.ato.gov*, 17 December 2014) GSTR 2014/ 3, http://law.ato.gov.au/atolaw/view.htm?docid=GST/GSTR20143/NAT/ATO/00001&PiT=20141217000001.

[59] Australian Government, The Treasury, 'Australia's FinTech Priorities' (2016) https://fintech.treasury.gov.au/ australias-fintech-priorities/.

[60] Australian Taxation Office, 'Goods and Services Tax Ruling' (n 58); see also Australian Taxation Office, 'Tax Treatment of Cryptocurrencies in Australia—Specifically Bitcoin' (*law.ato.gov*, 21 December 2014) https://www. ato.gov.au/General/Gen/Tax-treatment-of-crypto-currencies-in-Australia---specifically-bitcoin/.

[61] Franz Nestler, *Deutschland erkennt Bitcoins als privates Geld an* [*Germany Recognizes Bitcoins as Private Money*] (*faz.net*, 16 August 2013) Frankfurter Allgemeine Zeitung, http://www.faz.net/aktuell/finanzen/devisen-rohstoffe/digitale-waehrung-deutschland-erkennt-bitcoins-als-privates-geld-an-12535059.html.

[62] See also Noah Vardi, 'Bit by Bit: Assessing the Legal Nature of Virtual Currencies' in *Bitcoin and Mobile Payments: Constructing a European Union Framework*, edited by Gabriella Gimigliano (Palgrave Macmillan 2016).

[63] FinCEN (n 47).

This definition brings cryptocurrencies very close to actual money but does not really equate them.[64]

A similar approach is taken by BaFin, the German Federal Financial Supervisory Authority (*Bundesamt für Finanzdienstleistungen*). BaFin issued a communication on bitcoins in December 2013,[65] according to which bitcoins are legally binding financial instruments in the form of units of account that are similar to foreign currencies.[66] Accordingly, bitcoins are units of value that are not expressed in the form of legal tender. Instead, they have the function of private means of payment within private trading exchanges operating as a private substitute for money in private transactions. At the current stage of their development, the way in which they are being offered and accepted as payment or the way they are mined does not require bank supervisory licensing according to German law; the necessity of licensing is mentioned as a possibility under certain circumstances in the future.

In France, the Bank of France has adopted a relatively negative stance towards the development of cryptocurrencies.[67] The French judiciary acknowledged in a way the nature of cryptocurrencies as money.[68] The judgment of the Commercial Court of 6 December 2011, confirmed by the Court of Appeal of Paris on 26 September 2013, clarified that the Macaraja company, a Bitcoin intermediary between the MtGox platform and buyers and sellers of MtGox, is a 'financial intermediary', and thus subject to the licensing and approval obligations for its operations by the *Autorité de Contrôle Prudentiel*; an approval which was not requested by Macaraja.[69] These judgments show that certain services related to virtual currencies in France might be considered as financial services, and thus cryptocurrencies may be perceived as money.

In the United Kingdom, Her Majesty's Revenue and Customs ('HMRC') issued a statement laying out its position on the tax treatment of income received from, and charges made in connection with, activities involving Bitcoin and other similar cryptocurrencies.[70] HMRC recognizes that this is an evolving regulatory area and is expecting that at some point there will be an EU-wide effort to define and clarify cryptocurrencies in general. HMRC has, in the meantime, decided to treat income from sales of goods and services through Bitcoin in the same manner as it does any other sales. With regard to other income, HMRC issued the following guidelines for the time being:

1. Income received from Bitcoin mining activities will generally be outside the scope of VAT on the basis that the activity does not constitute an economic activity for VAT purposes because there is an insufficient link between any services provided and any consideration received.

2. Income received by miners for other activities, such as for the provision of services in connection with the verification of specific transactions for which specific charges are

---

[64] The US anti-money laundering regime applies to any 'value that substitutes for currency'; see 31 CFR § 1010.100(ff)(5)(i)(A).

[65] Jens Münzer, 'Bitcoins: Aufsichtliche Bewertung und Risiken für Nutzer' (*Bafin.de*, 19 December 2013) https://www.bafin.de/SharedDocs/Veroeffentlichungen/DE/Fachartikel/2014/fa_bj_1401_bitcoins.html; see, for more information in English, https://bitcoinmagazine.com/articles/regulation-bitcoins-germany-first-comprehensive-statement-bitcoins-german-federal-financial-supervisory-authority-bafin-1391637959/.

[66] See the first sentence of Section 1(11) German Banking Act, German Banking Act (Kreditwesengesetz [Banking Act], updated 9 September 1998), Bundesgesetzblatt I at 2776, as amended, http://www.gesetze-im-internet.de/kredwg/index.html.

[67] See Bank of France (n 54).

[68] Commercial Court of Créteil (6 December 2011) SAS Macaraja c/SA Crédit Industriel et Commercial, Tribunal de commerce [Commercial Tribunal] Crétail, 2nd ch. (6 December 2011); confirmed by the Court of Appeal of Paris (26 September 2013) https://www.doctrine.fr/d/CA/Paris/2013/RD2AE0AF6A196D83C06B9.

[69] CA de Paris, pôle 5, ch. 6 (26 September 2013), *Macaraja* c/Crédit industriel et commercial.

[70] Her Majesty's Revenue and Customs, 'Bitcoin and Other Similar Cryptocurrencies' (*Gov.uk*, 3 March 2014) Revenue and Customs Brief, 9, https://www.gov.uk/government/publications/revenue-and-customs-brief-9-2014-bitcoin-and-other-cryptocurrencies.

made, will be exempt from VAT under Article 135(1)(d) of the EU VAT Directive as falling within the definition of "transactions, including negotiation, concerning deposit and current accounts, payments, transfers, debts, cheques and other negotiable instruments".

3. When Bitcoin is exchanged for Sterling or for foreign currencies, such as Euros or Dollars, no VAT will be due on the value of the Bitcoins themselves.

4. Charges (in whatever form) made over and above the value of the Bitcoin for arranging or carrying out any transactions in Bitcoin will be exempt from VAT under Article 135(1)(d) as outlined at 2 above. Treatment of cryptocurrencies is brought into line with the treatment of money and could be considered as an official recognition of cryptocurrency status as yet another currency in the eyes of the law.

The jurisdictions studied in this section show a tendency towards the recognition of cryptocurrency as money for various regulatory purposes. As has been already mentioned, this classification is not always to the benefit of the developers and the users. What remains to be seen is the exact classification of cryptocurrencies under the domestic regulatory systems, namely whether cryptocurrencies will eventually be regulated as domestic money or as foreign exchange. Some countries will refrain from making explicit statements one way or the other; some others less so. In Australia, for example, under paragraph 2 of the new Goods and Services Tax Ruling 2014/3W, 'digital currency will have the equivalent treatment to money and in certain circumstances supplies of digital currency will be treated as financial supplies'. The Court of Justice of the EU has taken a similar stance with regard to Bitcoin and other virtual currencies, which will be dealt with in the following subsection.

2. *The CJEU judgment in the case C-264/14*

The issue of the nature of cryptocurrencies has been dealt with in a 2015 judgment of the Court of Justice of the European Union (CJEU) in a request for a preliminary ruling from the Swedish Supreme Administrative Court.[71] This request relates to the interpretation of Articles 2(1) and 135(1) of the VAT Directive.[72] The request has been made in proceedings between the Swedish tax authority ('Skatteverket') and David Hedqvist, a Swedish citizen, concerning a preliminary decision given by the Swedish Revenue Law Commission ('Skatterättsnämnden') on whether transactions to exchange a traditional currency for Bitcoin or vice versa should be subject to Value Added Tax ('VAT').

Hedqvist wished to provide services through a company based in Sweden consisting of the exchange—namely purchase and sale—of traditional currency, such as the Swedish crown, for virtual currencies with bidirectional flow, such as Bitcoin, and vice versa. The company of Hedqvist would be remunerated for supplying the service by a consideration equal to the margin that it would include in the calculation of the exchange rate at which it would be willing to sell and purchase the currencies. Before starting to carry out the transactions, Hedqvist requested a preliminary decision from the Revenue Law Commission in order to establish whether VAT must be paid on the purchase and sale of Bitcoin. In a decision of 14 October 2013, the Revenue Law Commission found, on the basis of the judgment of the CJEU in First National Bank of Chicago,[73] that this type of service is an exchange service effected 'for consideration' under the VAT Directive. The Revenue Law Commission held, however, that the exchange service was covered by the exemption under Chapter 3, paragraph 9, of the Law on VAT. The Swedish Tax Authority appealed against the Revenue

---

[71] Judgment of the Court in Case C-264/14 (22 October 2015).
[72] Council Directive 2006/112/EC (28 November 2006), OJ 2006 L 347, 1 on the common system of value added tax ('VAT' Directive).
[73] Case C-172/96, *First National Bank of Chicago*, EU:C:1998:354.

Law Commission's decision to the Supreme Administrative Court, arguing that the relevant service is not covered by the exemption under Chapter 3, paragraph 9 of the Law on VAT.

The referring court asked the CJEU two questions: first, whether Article 2(1) of the VAT Directive is to be interpreted as meaning that transactions in the form of the exchange of virtual currency for traditional currency and vice versa, which is effected for consideration added by the supplier when the exchange rates are determined, constitutes the supply of a service effected for consideration. Article 2(1) of the VAT Directive provides that the supply of goods and services for consideration within the territory of a Member State by a taxable person acting as such is to be subject to VAT. If an affirmative response is given to this question, the second question asks whether Article 135(1) of the VAT Directive must be interpreted as meaning that the exchange transactions are tax exempt.

According to the CJEU, for the purposes of the VAT Directive, Bitcoin is a virtual currency with bidirectional flow, and cannot thus be characterized as 'tangible property' within the meaning of Article 14 of the VAT Directive;[74] Bitcoin has no purpose other than to be a means of payment.[75] As the Court notes in paragraph 25, the same applies to traditional currencies, since this involves money, which is legal tender.[76] The underlying transactions consist of the exchange of different means of payment, and thus do not fall within the concept of 'supply of goods' of Article 14 of the Directive.[77] The Court thus denies the tangible property nature and the nature as goods of virtual currencies and moves on to equate them to traditional currencies. The exchange from and to Bitcoin from traditional currencies constitutes rather the 'supply of services' within the meaning of Article 24 of the VAT Directive.[78] Services are subject to VAT under the VAT Directive regime only in the case that there is a direct link between the services supplied and the 'consideration' received by the taxable person.[79] Thus the service of exchange of bitcoins from and to traditional currency in return for payment constitutes the supply of services for consideration within the meaning of Article 2(1)(c) of the VAT Directive.[80]

With regard to the second question, the Court moves on to discuss whether transactions related to bitcoins fall under the exemptions of Article 135(1) of the VAT Directive. The transactions referred to in Article 135(1)(d) of the VAT Directive concern services or instruments that operate as a way of transferring money.[81] The Court recognizes that Bitcoin is 'a contractual means of payment', and thus it 'cannot be regarded as a current account or a deposit account, a payment or a transfer'.[82] Moreover, unlike a debt, cheques and other negotiable instruments, Bitcoin is a direct means of payment between operators that accept the virtual currency.[83] For this reason, transactions involving bitcoins and their conversion from and to national currencies do not fall within the scope of the exemptions provided for under Article 135(1)(d) of the VAT Directive.[84]

On the other side, Article 135(1)(e) of the VAT Directive provides that Member States are exempt from VAT transactions involving 'currency [and] bank notes and coins used as legal tender'. According to the Court, following the Opinion of Advocate General Kokott,[85] the different language versions of the Article do not allow it to be determined without ambiguity whether the provision applies only to transactions involving traditional currencies

---

[74] Case C-264/14 (n 71), [24].   [75] Case C-264/14, AG Opinion, [17].
[76] Case C-264/14 (n 71), [25].   [77] ibid., [26].   [78] ibid.
[79] See judgments in Cases C-53/09 and C-55/09, *Loyalty Management UK and Baxi Group*, EU:C:2010:590, [51] and the case-law cited, and Case C-283/12, *Serebryannay vek*, EU:C:2013:599, [37]; see Council Directive 2006/112/EC (n 72) on the supply of services effected 'for consideration'.
[80] Case C-264/14 (n 71), [31].
[81] See Case C-461/12, *Granton Advertising*, EU:C:2014:1745, [37]–[38]). It has to be noted that transactions that involve money itself are the object of a specific provision, namely that of Article 135(1)(e) of Council Directive 2006/112/EC (n 72); see AG Opinion (n 75), points 51 and 52.
[82] Case C-264/14 (n 71), [42].   [83] ibid.   [84] ibid., [43].
[85] AG Opinion (n 75), [31]–[34].

or whether it is also intended to cover transactions involving another currency.[86] For this reason, the Court moves beyond textual interpretation and interprets the relevant provision in the light of the context in which it is used and the aims of the VAT Directive.[87] Under a contextual and teleological interpretation of the provision, transactions in 'virtual' or 'non-traditional' currencies like bitcoins should be perceived as financial transactions.[88] Applying an *effet utile* approach, the Court says that interpreting the provision of Article 135(1)(e) as including only transactions involving traditional currencies would partly deprive it of its effect.[89] As the Court very characteristically states in paragraph 52: '… it is common ground that the "bitcoin" virtual currency has no other purpose than to be a means of payment and that it is accepted for that purpose by certain operators'. Bitcoin exchange services are thus covered by the exemption of Article 135(1)(e) of the VAT Directive.[90] Consequently, exchange of traditional currencies for Bitcoin and vice versa, performed in return for payment of a sum equal to the difference between, on the one hand, the price paid by the operator to purchase the currency and, on the other hand, the price at which he sells that currency to his clients, are transactions exempt from VAT, within the meaning of Article 135(1)(e) of the VAT Directive.[91]

This is an extremely important decision concerning the nature of Bitcoin and other cryptocurrencies in the EU legal order. It both implicitly and explicitly recognizes its nature as some sort of money. First, it is very interesting to note that the Court uses the terms 'traditional currency' for national currencies such as the Swedish crown, and 'virtual currency' or 'non-traditional currency' for Bitcoin. According to the Court in paragraph 49, non-traditional currencies are 'currencies other than those that are legal tender in one or more countries, insofar as those currencies have been accepted by the parties to a transaction as an alternative to legal tender and have no purpose other than to be a means of payment'. Second, it denies them the nature of a good. Third, by applying a contextual and teleological interpretation of the relevant provision of the VAT Directive, it concludes by also applying the provisions that apply to traditional money to a cryptocurrency like Bitcoin.

B. Global currency as a commodity

Various regulators have taken different approaches to regulation of cryptocurrencies to the one that the CJEU has taken in its judgment. Janet Yellen, the Chair of the Board of Governors of the US Federal Reserve System, noted at a Senate Banking Committee hearing that '[i]t's important to understand that [the bitcoin] is a payment innovation that's happening outside the banking industry' and that 'the Federal Reserve simply does not have the authority to regulate bitcoin in any way'.[92] Echoing Yellen's understanding of the nature of virtual currencies, many regulators treat the new global currencies as commodities. This approach fails to understand cryptocurrency as money but recognizes the need for regulation. Bank of England economists have equally identified virtual currencies as commodities:

> in contrast to commonly used forms of money such as banknotes or bank deposits, digital currencies are not a claim on anybody. In this respect, they can therefore be thought of as a type of commodity. But unlike physical commodities such as gold, they are also intangible assets, or digital commodities. Digital currencies have meaning only to the extent that participants agree

---

[86] Case C-264/14 (n 71), [46].

[87] ibid., at [47]; see also Case C-455/05, *Velvet & Steel Immobilien*, EU:C:2007:232, [20] and the case law cited, and Case C-189/11, *Commission v. Spain*, EU:C:2013:587, [56].

[88] Case C-264/14 (n 71), [49].   [89] ibid., [51].   [90] ibid., [53].   [91] ibid., [57].

[92] See Janet Yellen, 'Fed will Steer Clear of Bitcoin' (*Fortune.com*, 27 February 2014) http://fortune.com/2014/02/27/janet-yellen-fed-will-steer-clear-of-bitcoin/.

that they have meaning …That agreement takes the form of a public ledger and a process for how changes to it are made, including the creation of new currency.[93]

In China, the Central Bank, together with the other four central government agencies in the 'Notice on Precautions against the Risks of Bitcoins',[94] denied Bitcoin the nature of money, and cryptocurrencies' ability to circulate in the market as a money.[95] It explicitly classified Bitcoin as a 'specially-designated virtual commodity or good'. Bitcoin operators and users can thus trade the global currency as a commodity, leaving out most other functions.

Despite the adverse effect this strict approach has had on the use of Bitcoin in China,[96] it is still being traded in the country. The yuan is actually the top trade exchange currency in the Bitcoin economy.[97] The underlying rationale may be the same as the legal justification for the ban on the use of Bitcoin by financial institutions in China. Chinese citizens trading in bitcoin might be keeping bitcoins as a form of investment in a valuable commodity given the more limited opportunities for private investment in the country.[98]

Also, outside China it is very common on the Bitcoin market for users to hoard bitcoins instead of using them for purchases.[99] There might thus be a general trend for bitcoin to be used not as a means of exchange, but rather as a commodity, which users use to exchange bitcoins for cash and vice versa,[100] and/or for mid-to-long-term investment.

In the United States, only the US dollar is legal tender;[101] accordingly, only the Mint and the Federal Reserve can produce coins and currency. There are cases in which individuals have been convicted in the United States for minting (physical) private (local) currency in violation of the US legislative framework and the Constitution, namely Article I, Section 8, Clause 5, which delegates to Congress the power to coin money and to regulate its value.[102] It is probably for this reason that regulatory agencies in the United States have (also) classified virtual currencies as commodities.[103]

Taking advantage of the broad definition of a commodity under the Commodity Exchange Act 1936, the Commodity Futures Trade Commission ('CFTC') in the 'Derivabit Order' of September 2015 classified Bitcoin—as well as other cryptocurrencies—as a commodity for the purposes of commodities regulation.[104] Cryptocurrency derivatives, including futures, options, or swaps are thus subject to CFTC jurisdiction.[105] The CFTC concluded accordingly, first, that any options on Bitcoin or other cryptocurrencies are to be regulated as 'swaps'; second, that Bitcoin options trading platforms should be registered with the CFTC;

---

[93] Rableh Ali, John Barrdear, Roger Clews, and James Southgate, 'The Economics of Digital Currencies' (2014) Q3 *Quarterly Bulletin*, 3.
[94] People's Bank of China et al. (n 38).   [95] ibid., § 1.
[96] See Lulu Yilun Chen, 'Bitcoin Banned by Alibaba's Taobao after China Tightens Rules' (*Bloomberg.com*, 8 January 2014) http://bloom.bg/1J1fsVf.
[97] Joon Wong, 'China's Market Dominance Poses Questions about Global Bitcoin Trading Flows' (*CoinDesk. com*, 27 September 2014) http://bit.ly/1R3Pqj9.
[98] ibid.   [99] Guadamuz and Marsden (n 3).   [100] ibid.   [101] 31 U.S.C., § 5103.
[102] United States District Court for the Western District of North Carolina, Statesville Division, *US v. Bernard von NotHaus et al.*, http://www.lawandfreedom.com/site/constitutional/vonnothaus_amicus_appendix_a.pdf.
[103] Guadamuz and Marsden (n 3).
[104] See 7 U.S.C., §1a(9); see also *Board of Trade of City of Chicago v. SEC*, 677 F.2d 1137, 1142 (7th Cir. 1982) (very broad definition of a 'commodity'). In *Re Coinflip, Inc., d/b/a/Derivabit, et al.* (17 September 2015) Order Instituting Proceedings Pursuant to Sections 6(c) and 6(d) of the Commodity Exchange Act, Making Findings and Imposing Remedial Sanctions ('Derivabit Order'), CFTC Docket No. 15-29, http://www.cftc.gov/ucm/groups/public/@lrenforcementactions/documents/legalpleading/enfcoinfliprorder09172015.pdf. The Chairman of Commodity Futures Trading Commission ('CFTC') and CFTC Commissioner Wetjen had already publicly expressed the view that the CFTC has regulatory authority over Bitcoin and other cryptocurrencies; see US Senate Committee on Agriculture, Nutrition and Forestry, Testimony of Chairman Timothy Massad (*CFTC.gov*, 10 December 2014) http://www.cftc.gov/PressRoom/SpeechesTestimony/opamassad-6; Mark Wetjen, 'Bringing Commodities Regulation to Cryptocurrency' (2014) *Wall Street Journal*.
[105] Derivabit Order (n 104); see 7 U.S.C. §§ 1.3(hh) (definition of 'commodity option transaction'), 1a(47)(A)(i) (definition of 'swap' includes option contracts); 17 C.F.R. § 32.2.

and third, that the failure to do so constitutes a violation of the CFTC regulations and the Commodities Exchange Act.[106]

C. Global currency as a technology: the dual nature of cryptocurrencies and the schizophrenic approach to regulation

When identified as currency, virtual currencies are perceived either as money or as a commodity; overall when classified as currency, cryptocurrencies are regulated in rather restrictive ways. Both the command-and-control approach and the intermediate approaches identified in section II have the purpose of limiting the ways in which cryptocurrencies are used. Some other countries, or sometimes other regulators within the same countries, have been going about regulating cryptocurrencies in different ways. The difference in the regulatory approaches are largely related to how each country perceives the nature of cryptocurrencies.

Cryptocurrencies have a dual nature; there are thus two main ways in which cryptocurrencies are treated from a regulatory perspective: as currencies—money and commodity—and/or as a technology. The governments that view cryptocurrencies as a currency have adopted more restrictive regulatory approaches, whilst the governments that view them as a technology have adopted more favourable approaches to their presence in their jurisdiction.

1. Regulation as technology: innovation hubs and regulatory sandboxes

Increasingly, countries around the world have started adopting policies directed towards the promotion of FinTech start-ups, prominently also including start-ups developing the blockchain technology and cryptocurrencies. FinTech promotion policies involve predominantly two regulatory measures: (i) launching innovation hubs to help FinTech start-ups comply with the relevant laws and regulations; and, (ii) establishing regulatory sandboxes for new financial service participants,[107] including the lowering of licensing barriers for digital financial services participants reaching sometimes all the way to FinTech licensing exemptions. The regulatory sandbox allows businesses to test innovative products, services, business models, and delivery mechanisms in a more relaxed regulatory environment. The idea is to provide FinTech and start-up companies with more pathways to start testing the viability of innovative financial services before being subject to the regulations and regulatory costs associated with the development of standard financial products. The underlying idea is to strike a balance between facilitating innovation and competition, while at the same time ensuring consumer protection and the distribution of the benefits of innovative FinTech products to society at large.

These regulatory instruments are now used to promote cryptocurrencies and their underlying technology. The UK FCA's 'Project Innovate' is a very good example, since it operates an Innovation Hub and a Regulatory Sandbox. The Innovation Hub offers support to FinTech businesses, namely a dedicated team and contact for FinTech business that has the innovation potential and helps them understand the relevant regulatory framework and

---

[106] Derivabit Order (n 104). While the Derivabit Order mandated the cease of violations under the CEA, it did not impose any sanctions against Coinflip and its CEO, given that this has been the first time that Bitcoin and other cryptocurrencies have been identified as 'commodities' under the Commodities Exchange Act.

[107] See generally Pavel Shoust, 'Regulators and Fintech: Influence is Mutual?' (undated), http://pubdocs. worldbank.org/en/770171476811898530/Session-4-Pavel-Shoust-Regulatory-Sandboxes-21-09-2016.pdf;   Carlo De Meijer, 'Blockchain: Playing in the Regulatory Sandbox' (2016) https://www.finextra.com/blogposting/13055/blockchain-playing-in-the-regulatory-sandbox; Freehills Herbert Smith, 'Overview of Regulatory Sandbox Regimes in Australia, Hong Kong, Malaysia, Singapore, and the UK' (*law.ox.ac.uk*, 18 December 2016) https://www.law.ox.ac.uk/business-law-blog/blog/2016/12/overview-regulatory-sandbox-regimes-australia-hong-kong-malaysia.

how it applies to them; moreover, it offers assistance in preparing and making an application for authorization and dedicated contact for up to a year after an innovator business is authorized. Finally, the UK Innovation Hub signs co-operation agreements with regulators from other jurisdictions to coordinate their FinTech regulatory policies. Many of the projects under the FCA Regulatory Sandbox deal with blockchain technology-related products.

Very importantly as well, the UK FCA has created a Regulatory Sandbox allowing businesses to test innovative products, services, and business models. The Regulatory Sandbox allows innovative businesses to test products with reduced regulatory standards, mostly licensing exemptions and different time frames in comparison to traditional financial products. In exchange for more flexible standards, regulators tend to require applicant business to incorporate appropriate safeguards in their testing models, such as requiring the informed consent of consumers.

Since the United Kingdom took the lead in creating a special regulatory regime for FinTech in 2015, many more countries, especially in the Asia Pacific region, like Australia, Hong Kong, Malaysia, and Singapore, have followed its lead. The Australian Government has undertaken important initiatives in regulating cryptocurrency as a technology.[108] The Australian Securities and Investment Commission ('ASIC') has also launched an Innovation Hub to help FinTech start-ups on compliance matters; moreover, it established a regulatory sandbox for digital services participants. Australia's regulatory sandbox framework is comprised of three options for testing a new product or service without a license.[109] First, it relies on existing statutory exemptions or flexibility in the relevant regulatory framework like, for example, for certain foreign exchange services. Second, and very importantly, Australia is the first jurisdiction in the world to introduce a regulatory regime that gives the power to the regulator to release class waivers. Eligible businesses of the waived classes are only obliged to submit a notification of intent to test under the exemption to ASIC as well as some additional information on the notifying business without an individual application process. ASIC has used this power to issue a 'FinTech licensing exemption', which allows eligible FinTech companies to test certain specified products or services for up to twelve months with up to 100 retail clients without holding an Australian Financial Services ('AFS') or credit license.[110] This exemption from the ASIC regime does not mean a simultaneous exemption from other regulatory frameworks such as anti-money laundering. Third, for other services individual licensing exemptions can be provided from ASIC to facilitate product or service testing for businesses that are not eligible for the FinTech licensing exemption.[111] Individual exemptions of this nature are similar to the regulatory sandboxes established by financial services regulators in other jurisdictions, e.g. the United Kingdom. This option is open to existing licensees who wish to test an innovative product or service.

2. The concept of 'enabling law'

Cryptocurrencies and blockchain technology are subject to a completely different type of regulation when viewed by regulators as technology in comparison to when cryptocurrencies

---

[108] On the Australian initiatives see Australian Government, The Treasury, 'Backing Australian FinTech', http://fintech.treasury.gov.au/files/2016/03/Fintech-March-2016-v3.pdf (Commonwealth of Australia 2016).

[109] See Australian Securities and Investment Commission (ASIC), 'Testing Fintech Products and Services without Holding an AFS or Credit Licence', Regulatory Guidance 257 ('RG 257'); the FinTech licensing exemption was initially proposed in Australian Securities and Investment Commission (ASIC), Consultation Paper 260, 'Further Measures to Facilitate Innovation in Financial Services' ('CP 260').

[110] ASIC's Fintech Licensing exemption provided under Australian Securities and Investment Commission (ASIC), 'Corporations (Concept Validation Licensing Exemption) Instrument 2016/1175 and Australian Securities and Investment Commission (ASIC), Credit (Concept Validation Licensing Exemption) Instrument 2016/1176. On the eligibility criteria, see Sections C and D of RG 257 (n 109).

[111] See Australian Securities and Investment Commission (ASIC), 'Applications for Relief', Regulatory Guide 51 ('RG 51').

are viewed as a currency. They are subject to a type of law that enables the operations of FinTech companies and the development of the new technology rather than restraining it. The prevalent motive is to attract financial, social, and human capital to a jurisdiction with the purpose of producing new value propositions that should be beneficial to the consumer. Innovation hubs and regulatory sandboxes support companies that want to bring their products to market but are confronted with regulatory uncertainty. Moreover, it gives the opportunity to regulators to be in touch with global FinTech companies to create an environment favourable to them.

Embedding in society takes place here through a legal framework that enables the operations of the relevant companies, rather than restricting them. Embedding through enabling pre-supposes a different understanding of the law as well as how the law operates.[112] Usually the law is considered to have a predominantly backward-looking and constraining dimension. The law in the era of the new embeddedness has the function of trying to bring the technology of the global currency to a certain national jurisdiction.

Various governments around the world are thus competing to attract global capital. At the same time, different agencies within one country are competing with each other, depending on their understanding of cryptocurrency as currency or technology, and consequently as to which camp they support: the liberal movement or the collectivist.

IV. Embedding through Enabling

The final section of the chapter discusses the dilemma between embedding cryptocurrencies into a domestic regulatory framework by regulating them or allowing both their market and underlying technology to develop outside the scope of domestic regulatory intervention. The advantages of embedding cryptocurrencies into a domestic legal order may be offset by the advantages brought about by allowing a new innovative technology such as blockchain technology to flourish without the restraints of regulation. This is discussed in section IV.A. The new perils of enabling cryptocurrencies through domestic legislation are discussed in section IV.B. Section IV.C ends with a discussion of the possibilities to mitigate the dangers of enabling cryptocurrencies through the regulation of the intermediaries of the cryptocurrency market.

A. The advantages and disadvantages of domestic embeddedness of cryptocurrencies

From a national government's point of view, there are many reasons in favour of regulating cryptocurrencies and embedding them into a certain domestic legal order. The most obvious set of reasons derives from the risk of crime to which this new currency opens the gateway. The only truly public feature of the cryptocurrency ledger is the documentation of ownership and transfers. The owners themselves are not identified by name on the ledger but rather by a set of letters and numbers representing their public cryptocurrency address. The public cryptocurrency address together with the private key that proves ownership of that address constitute the owner's cryptocurrency 'wallet'. This relatively high level of anonymity makes it difficult for regulators to identify individuals who use the protocol

---

[112] According to Max Weber, law does not consist only of coercive rules, especially in the framework of the economy, but also of 'legal empowerment rules' and 'enabling laws'; see Max Weber, *Economy and Society*, edited by Guenther Roth and Claus Wittich (University of California Press 1978), 730–31; see also Friedrich Kratochwil and John Gerard Ruggie, 'International Organization: A State of the Art on an Art of the State' (1986) 40 *International Organization*, 753 (rules are not only regulative, but also constitutive); Georgios Dimitropoulos, 'Compliance through Collegiality: Peer Review in International Law' (2016) 37 *Loyola LA International and Competition Law Review*, 275.

for illicit value transfers. Cryptocurrencies are thus very often used for money laundering purposes.[113] This creates problems of enforcement of financial sanctions. It may also lead to tax evasion.

Additionally, cryptocurrency users are exposed to various consumer risks given the price volatility of cryptocurrencies. A related but more systemic issue is that of monetary and financial stability—a problem mostly of the future. This obviously also creates issues of trust in currency generally.

Another set of issues is derived from the new intermediaries of the virtual currency environment. It may well be the case that the cryptocurrency system circumvents traditional national financial intermediaries like central and commercial banks; at the same time, it introduces new intermediaries. These new intermediaries are exposed to novel problems such as the risk of hacking. The Mt Gox scandal—where hackers stole 850,000 bitcoins in February 2014 that were worth approximately $500 million from Mt Gox, a Bitcoin exchange database handling at the time up to 70% of all Bitcoin transactions—has showcased very vividly the technological risks to which cryptocurrency users are exposed.

From a more global perspective, the main reasons leading to the justification of domestic regulation—and potentially also of international regulation—of virtual currencies are related to the new inequalities that they may create. Cryptocurrencies may foment at least three new sources of inequality. First, they create a sharp divide between those with access to the internet and those without. Bitcoin has been created as the currency of a specific community of people and is very largely used by the same community. Cryptocurrencies as a new form of global currency may eventually turn out to be the currency of the privileged parts of the global population with access to the internet. This brings us to the second source of concern, namely the divide between the ones that know how to code and those that do not. Bitcoin is peculiar in the production of new value in the system in that new bitcoins are generated as a reward and at the same time as an incentive for the guardians of the decentralized system, the 'miners', namely the programmers that verify whether the transactions on the blockchain are accurate. Not everybody has the knowledge, capabilities, or the desire to code and become a miner; the production of new wealth is thus reserved either to the individuals that belong to the first community that established Bitcoin as a club privilege or to new mining companies that are involved in the business of producing new bitcoins.[114] The third possible source of inequality is that caused by the geography as well as the natural and climatic conditions prevalent in a country. Mining takes significant computing power. Greater computing power can generally be achieved in countries with a colder rather than a warmer climate. Huge parts of the world are by default excluded from the cryptocurrency map as a natural locus for mining, such as the Middle East, large parts of Latin America, Central Africa, or even the Mediterranean. This creates new comparative advantages for the cooler countries in northern Europe and north America.

These are all reasons why governments around the world are and should be assuming their responsibility for regulating cryptocurrencies. There are also reasons that should make regulators think twice before moving towards their embeddedness. The most important reasons against regulation are related to the nature of cryptocurrencies as technology. As opposed to national currencies, cryptocurrencies rely on algorithm-generated trust. Regulation might reduce trust in the technology and mathematics, which might eventually lead to the dissolution of the currencies. Moreover, there is inherent uncertainty as to how to regulate new technologies, as well as fundamental difficulties in regulating a new technology.

---

[113] Financial Action Task Force ('FATF'), 'Virtual Currencies: Key Definitions and Potential AML/CFT Risks' (2014) Report.

[114] Evan Faggart, 'Bitcoin Mining Centralization: The Market is Fixing Itself' (*Coin Brief*, 2014) https://99bitcoins.com/bitcoin-mining-free-market/.

The uncertainty surrounding the development potential of new technologies, namely the fact that we do not yet know how they will develop and be used in the future, makes regulation of new technologies very difficult. Regulation may thus be an obstacle to innovation.[115] Regulatory responses to cryptocurrencies threaten to increase the cost of compliance and/or slow the development or adoption of beneficial innovations.[116] Government intervention in cryptocurrency might stall a necessary wave of technological development and innovation that, through spill-over effects, may benefit various sectors of the economy and, eventually, society at large.[117]

Even the not-so-ardent proponents of cryptocurrencies praise Bitcoin for having brought to light and having made possible the broad use of its background technology: the blockchain technology. Blockchain technology may potentially have many more future uses than supporting cryptocurrencies. Blockchain technology makes possible many new applications with a possibly disruptive impact on social life such as smart contracts, managing registers of assets, and the operation of autonomous agents. Countries like Estonia, Georgia, Ghana, Honduras, and Dubai in the UAE are purporting to become 'blockchained' governments, basing essential government operations, like land registries, on blockchain.[118] Moreover, even if Bitcoin fails as a currency, some predict that the platform and relevant technology might stay for the facilitation of digital transactions of conventional currencies.

B. The perils of embedding through enabling

The concept of embeddedness, as defined by Karl Polanyi and used by other economists and economic sociologists, refers to the fact and need for every economic activity to be embedded within institutions of society, like institutions of kinship, religion, politics, etc. that keep economic activity under certain control.[119] In pre-nineteenth-century societies, there were no purely economic institutions outside of the frame of other societal institutions. In the market society that appeared in the nineteenth century, the economic system gained a certain degree of independence, leading largely to this system being disembedded from society, with catastrophic effects that eventually, according to Polanyi, led to the disaster of the two world wars. In the final chapter of his book, Polanyi expressed the hope that post-World War II society would develop the appropriate institutions to re-embed the economy,[120] which was largely the case during the *trente glorieuses* with the various social protection programmes and schemes of the post-World War II welfare state. This changed in the 1990s, leading up to the 2008 Global Financial Crisis. The crisis led to a new process of the embedding and dis-embedding of market forces; Bitcoin and other digital currencies are a peculiar case of an effort to dis-embed money from the mainstream financial system and possibly (re-)embed

---

[115] See e.g. Organisation for Economic Co-operation and Development (OECD), 'Regulatory Reform and Innovation' https://www.oecd.org/sti/inno/2102514.pdf; Jacques Pelkmans and Andrea Renda, 'Does EU Regulation Hinder or Stimulate Innovation?' (2014) Centre for European Policy Studies Special Report No. 96; Luke Stewart, 'The Impact of Regulation on Innovation in the United States: A Cross-Industry Literature Review' (2010) https://www.itif.org/files/2011-impact-regulation-innovation.pdf; Knut Blind, 'The Impact of Regulation on Innovation' (2012) Nesta Working Paper 12/02.

[116] See with regard to artificial intelligence, Executive Office of the President, National Science and Technology Council Committee on Technology, 'Preparing for the Future of Artificial Intelligence' (October 2016).

[117] See Tim Worstall, 'Exactly What We Don't Need—Regulation of AI and Technology' (*Forbes.com*, 12 October 2016) http://www.forbes.com/sites/timworstall/2016/10/12/exactly-what-we-dont-need-regulation-of-ai-and-technology/#4bc0361f5121 (with reference to the regulation of Artificial Intelligence). See generally Joseph Stiglitz and Bruce Greenwald, *Creating A Learning Society: A New Approach to Growth, Development and Social Progress* (Columbia University Press 2014).

[118] World Government Summit, *Building the Hyperconnected Future on Blockchains* (2017).

[119] See e.g. Mark Granovetter, 'Economic Action and Social Structure: The Problem of Embeddedness' (1985) 91 *American Journal of Sociology*, 487.

[120] Polanyi (n 12), 257–68.

it into new communities, such as the communities of IT specialists. It is in this process that money may accidentally face a new phase of extreme dis-embeddedness, and economic liberalism may spread and expand its role and the remit of the market process. This process may be unique in the history of money by making it independent from any context, except for that of the new virtual world of the internet.

This explains the backlash from societal and governmental forces in the form of the anti-countermovement, in an effort to protect the vulnerable parties of virtual currency transactions and the institutions of the welfare state, by introducing legislation on anti-money laundering, the raising of taxes on cryptocurrencies, etc. We have largely observed two ways in which re-embeddedness takes place: the constraining and the enabling. The constraining approach to re-embeddedness is largely also what Polanyi had in mind when describing the collectivist counter-movement of the nineteenth and twentieth centuries and takes place through command-and-control measures, and softer mechanisms of direct regulation, like warnings and taxes. Enabling is a novel effort of embedding which is characteristic of a society that has reached the extent of globalization and digitization of our contemporary society.

Embedding through enabling raises at least two major concerns at the global and domestic level of governance that need to be mitigated. The following two subsections discuss them before moving on to the discussion on how to mitigate the dangers.

1. More finance

The interplay between constraining and enabling regulation is very interesting from a more global and systemic point of view. Since the Global Financial and Economic Crisis, there is a general tendency at the global, the regional, and the domestic governance levels to constrain more conventional finance.[121] At the same time, the 'dollar' of global currencies, Bitcoin, made its appearance on the internet and the global money market and a similar trend to enable digital and virtual finance and financial technology more generally has been growing. This has been reflected in the implementation of a new type of law through the establishment of innovation hubs and regulatory sandboxes.

This raises the question of the viability of restraining conventional finance. As the UK FCA defines it, a regulatory sandbox is a 'safe space in which businesses can test innovative products, services, business models and delivery mechanisms without immediately incurring all the normal regulatory consequences of engaging in the activity in question'.[122] Both conventional financial institutions and new start-ups now receive incentives from different regulators globally to work around conventional finance restrictions and develop new products that are potentially no less dangerous for consumers than the products developed by conventional financial institutions.

The FinTech industry seems to be in an odd and contradictory position where regulatory agencies, on the one hand, insist that the world of finance has to be tightly regulated and constrained, while simultaneously engaging in neo-mercantilist and anti-embeddedness strategies of attracting investment in emerging FinTech hubs. This is difficult to reconcile and the schizophrenic approach to the regulation of cryptocurrencies will be characteristic of the field in the years to come as well. In the long run, these developments may eventually lead to an overall less regulated field of finance.

---

[121] Kevin Davis, 'Regulatory Reform Post the Global Financial Crisis: An Overview' (9 March 2011) https://kevindavis.com.au/secondpages/Miscellaneous/Regulatory%20Reform%20Post%20GFC-%20Overview%20Report.pdf.

[122] Financial Conduct Authority ('FCA'), Regulatory Sandbox 2 (*FCA.org*, November 2015) https://www.fca.org.uk/publication/research/regulatory-sandbox.pdf.

2. Clash of agencies

There is a second way in which regulation of global currencies through enabling undermines policy-making by the state. This goes to the core function of government and governance. Given their unregulated and undefined nature, global currencies may fall within the competence of many different regulators of a country;[123] cryptocurrencies leave open space for several agencies to capture the empty regulatory space and regulate global currency as money, commodity, or technology.

This has already led to the schizophrenic approach to regulation of cryptocurrencies involving multiple agencies in their regulation. In the future, this situation might end up with an even greater clash of agencies within some countries as to which regulator will regulate them and what regulatory approach should be taken.[124] Different national agencies may have different aims; the Ministry of Economics may typically want to create economic hubs via enabling regulation. On the other side, Ministries of Finance and Central Banks will have an interest in financial stability; the banking and financial supervision authorities may be willing to minimize the risk for market participants and consumers; anti-money laundering agencies will be willing to assume their powers to enforce the anti-money laundering legislation; and commodities regulators might be entering the regulatory arena as well, as is the case in the United States. The interplay between the liberal and the collectivist countermovement are thus replayed within the domestic governments as a struggle for regulatory and deregulatory power and competence among different agencies. At the moment, the result is an odd mixture of constraining and enabling regulation.

This can be exemplified by the US example, where several agencies have claimed jurisdiction over cryptocurrencies. The Derivabit Order of the CFTC classifies Bitcoin and other cryptocurrency derivatives as commodities. The IRS considers Bitcoin to be 'property' for US federal tax purposes;[125] FinCEN treats virtual currency as 'money' for purposes of the money services business ('MSB') regulations.[126] The SEC has successfully argued that Bitcoin-denominated investments are 'securities' that can be regulated under the US securities laws.[127]

This creates significant regulatory confusion, which is greater than regulatory uncertainties caused by exclusively domestic phenomena. This undermines the power of the state to regulate. It may be undermining as well the 'symbolic power' of the state,[128] namely the perception of the state and its institutions in the eyes of its citizens, further impacting upon its capacity to regulate. This may have catastrophic results, especially in countries with less-established institutions, or when the authority of the state is also undermined by external factors, like an economic and financial crisis, or national security emergencies.

C. Mitigating the dangers of embedding through enabling: intermediary regulation

Many national regulators have either found themselves or will, sooner rather than later, find themselves before the question of how to regulate cryptocurrencies. They will have to face the dilemma on whether to adopt restraining or enabling policies on cryptocurrencies. On the one side, in an era of austerity and constrained public budgets, no government can afford

---

[123] Ross Leckow, 'Virtual Currencies—the Regulatory Challenges' (6 June 2017) http://yalejreg.com/nc/virtual-currencies-the-regulatory-challenges-by-ross-leckow/.

[124] This actually would most probably happen to countries with presidential, rather than parliamentary, systems of government such as the United States, where the (independent) agencies can pursue different agendas than the ones of the departments/ministries.

[125] IRS (n 56).   [126] See FinCEN (n 47).   [127] See n 51.

[128] Pierre Bourdieu, Loic Wacquant, and Samar Farage, 'Rethinking the State: Genesis and Structure of the Bureaucratic Field' (1994) 12 *Sociological Theory*, 1.

to have incomes and other funds untaxed and laundered into illicit and other activities; on the other side, in an era of fierce competition to attract foreign capital, no government can afford not to adopt policies attracting FinTech and other tech start-ups to their jurisdiction.

The solution to the regulatory dilemma will have to be a combination of the restricting and the facilitating approaches to regulation, on the one hand, developing strategies to promote the relevant background technology that may eventually be of great use also for other areas of public and social life, but at the same time regulating the enabling ecosystem and the markets around cryptocurrencies. The regulatory efforts should, as much as possible, be directed towards preserving the positive aspects of cryptocurrencies, while at the same time mitigating the systemic risks, as well as the risk for individual users.

Some commentators argue that blockchain technology has the potential to eliminate financial intermediaries,[129] which might lead to the loss of the ability of the legal system to use intermediaries as agents for regulation.[130] This is not necessarily the case, though. The cryptocurrency market has developed and most people will still rely on intermediaries when using cryptocurrencies:[131] trading platforms and exchanges of cryptocurrencies to fiat currencies, digital wallet service providers, payment systems and pricing indices, and other clearinghouses for cryptocurrency transactions.[132] Studies have shown, for example, that Mt Gox had intervened in 90% of all Bitcoin transactions ever recorded[133] before closing. Novel types of intermediaries are also being created. 'Tumblers' (or 'mixers') offer services that obscure the origin of virtual currencies, which can hinder the ability to trace virtual currencies to illicit sources. Bitcoin users usually rely on intermediaries to purchase bitcoins; these intermediaries often require identifying information to open an account. Authorities and/or hackers can potentially use this personal data to de-anonymize the user.[134] In order to preserve the anonymity of the users, new intermediary services have been created that allow users to mix their coins, swap them, and change them from one address to another.[135] This achieves some further anonymity, but adds one more intermediary between the user and the currency.

Intermediary intervention can only be expected to increase as the proportion of cryptocurrencies in the global economy increases. The Bitcoin model of production of new currency presents an effort to replicate scarcity on the market. Late adopters and other interested individuals that have no capabilities in coding will not be able to produce new coins through mining; the Bitcoin economy will thus rely mostly on users buying bitcoins with fiat currency through exchanges, namely through the intervention of intermediaries.[136] Finally, existing payment systems intermediaries like PayPal have included Bitcoin in their services.[137] These new intermediaries can also be used as 'regulatory agents'.[138]

During the first few years of the existence of cryptocurrencies, the lack of any meaningful regulation or enforcement meant that intermediaries were left to self-regulation through terms of use and policies.[139] These new intermediaries can be subjected to traditional models

---

[129] Brito et al. (n 8), 216–18.   [130] See Yee (n 8).   [131] ibid.

[132] See Tyler Moore and Nicolas Christin, 'Beware of the Middleman: Empirical Analysis of Bitcoin-Exchange Risk' in *Financial Cryptography*, edited by Ahmad-Reza Sadeghi (Springer 2013), 26; see also Marian, 'A Conceptual Framework' (n 8), 58.

[133] Dorit Ron and Ali Shamir, 'Quantitative Analysis of the Full Bitcoin Transaction Graph' (2012), Report 2012/584, Cryptology ePrint Archive, http://eprint.iacr.org/2012/584.

[134] Malte Möser, 'Anonymity of Bitcoin Transactions' (2013), Münster Bitcoin Conference, https://pdfs. semanticscholar.org/e1ae/d9296c3af9139f48d15e043e2e8beab55409.pdf.

[135] ibid., 9.   [136] Guadamuz and Marsden (n 3); Moore and Christin (n 132), 25–33.

[137] See Ryan Mac, 'PayPal Takes Baby Step toward Bitcoin, Partners with Cryptocurrency Processors' (*Forbes.com*, 23 September 2014) http://www.forbes.com/sites/ryanmac/2014/09/23/paypal-takes-small-step-toward-bitcoinpartners-with-cryptocurrency-processors.

[138] Marian, 'A Conceptual Framework' (n 8), 66.

[139] Lam Pak Nian and David Lee Kuo Chuen, 'A Light Touch of Regulation for Virtual Currencies' in *Handbook of Digital Currency: Bitcoin, Innovation, Financial Instruments, and Big Data*, edited by David Lee Kuo Chuen (Elsevier 2015), 315.

of intermediary regulation, like constraining regulation,[140] while leaving the software developers unregulated.[141] This has already been the case in many countries around the world. As discussed above, FinCEN has subjected certain cryptocurrency service providers to its regime as money transmitters,[142] and the IRS requires certain cryptocurrency clearing organizations to provide information to the IRS and their service recipients,[143] etc.

In a very interesting move, the New York State Department of Financial Services has imposed separate licensing requirements on intermediary service providers of cryptocurrencies. The 'BitLicense' framework creates a very comprehensive licensing regime for a very wide range of virtual currency intermediaries, including exchanges, wallets, dealers, and administrators.[144] The new rules require registration and licensing for certain cryptocurrency service providers. This now seems to be the preferred approach in the United States, where a 'Regulation of Virtual Currency Businesses Act' Committee has been established under the Uniform Law Commission in 2014.[145] This Committee made a proposal for the regulation of virtual currencies, which is similar to the one that has already been adopted in New York.

In France, the Ministry of Finance has issued a report showing a clear regulatory path for the future regulation of cryptocurrencies. The recommendations of the French Ministry include many obligations for intermediaries, including limiting anonymity by making it mandatory for intermediaries and exchanges to require proof of identity upon opening an account, and regulating at the European and international level platforms that exchange virtual currencies against official currencies.[146]

It will be interesting to see to what extent the steps taken by some countries with regard to registering and licensing global currency intermediaries will act as a deterrent against the creation and establishment of new intermediaries in these countries.

V. Conclusion

This chapter aimed to reveal the regulatory paradox of cryptocurrencies. Governments make efforts to restrain them, while these measures are sometimes combined with efforts to enable them by creating the environment necessary for the development of the technology. Cryptocurrencies are designed to play the role that currencies have traditionally played in economies since the beginning of civilization but in new immaterial forms and by new actors. The push for innovation and innovative products brought about by the financial crisis has led to the creation of policies to promote this type of innovation and innovative products. FinTech companies operate now in competition with traditional financial institutions.

The paradoxical regulatory approach to cryptocurrencies is inextricably linked to their nature; they are both a currency and a technology. The dual nature of cryptocurrencies has led governments around the world to adopt a schizophrenic approach to their regulation and a paradoxical interplay between restricting and enabling them—restricting their use, while enabling the underlying technology. The restricting approach tries to put limits on the use of cryptocurrencies in the way the law has traditionally exercised its influence and power on social phenomena. Enabling approaches create the necessary conditions for the

---

[140] Ross (n 18).

[141] On the politics of self-regulation, see Primavera De Filippi and Benjamin Loveluck, 'The Invisible Politics of Bitcoin: Governance Crisis of a Decentralised Infrastructure' (2016) 5 *Internet Policy Review*.

[142] FinCEN (n 47), 3.   [143] IRS (n 56).

[144] New York Codes, Rules and Regulations ('NYCRR'), 'Part 200 Virtual Currencies', http://www.dfs.ny.gov/legal/regulations/adoptions/dfsp200t.pdf.

[145] Some other states also seem to be following the same path; see California: California Legislature, 'Virtual Currency' (27 February 2015), Assembly Bill 1326.

[146] See Ministère des Finances et des Comptes Publics, Réguler les monnaies virtuelles, (2014) Recommendations 1 and 4.

development of the relevant technologies and the necessary regulatory environment for the flourishing of cryptocurrency start-ups.

It has been, and will be, very difficult for governments to sort out their policy-making priorities. Should they be giving priority to the traditional trust of and in money, or to the promotion of new products, including FinTech products? As the interplay of the double movement has shown in this context, embedding through enabling will only work if combined with the appropriate measures to protect citizens from the risks of the new global currencies.

VI. Bibliography

Ali Robleh, Barrdear John, Clews Roger, and Southgate James, 'The Economics of Digital Currencies' (2014) Q3 *Quarterly Bulletin*, 276.

Allen & Overy, *Virtual Currencies: Mining the Possibilities* (Allen & Overy 2015).

Anderson Tracey, 'Bitcoin—Is It Just a Fad? History, Current Status and Future of the Cyber-Currency Revolution' (2014) 29 *Journal of International Banking Law and Regulation*, 373.

Australian Government, The Treasury, 'Australia's FinTech Priorities' https://fintech.treasury.gov.au/australias-fintech-priorities/, accessed on 10 January 2019.

Australian Government, The Treasury, 'Backing Australian FinTech' (2016) http://fintech.treasury.gov.au/files/2016/03/Fintech-March-2016-v3.pdf, accessed 11 January 2019.

Australian Securities and Investments Commission (ASIC), 'Applications for Relief', Regulatory Guide 51.

Australian Securities and Investments Commission (ASIC), Corporations (Concept Validation Licensing Exemption) Instrument 2016/1175.

Australian Securities and Investments Commission (ASIC), Credit (Concept Validation Licensing Exemption) Instrument 2016/1176.

Australian Securities and Investments Commission (ASIC), Consultation Paper 260, 'Further Measures to Facilitate Innovation in Financial Services' ('CP 260').

Australian Securities and Investments Commission (ASIC), 'Testing Fintech Products and Services without Holding an AFS or Credit Licence' (2016) Regulatory Guide 257.

Australian Taxation Office, 'Goods and Services Tax Ruling' (*law.ato.gov*, 17 December 2014) GSTR 2014/3, http://law.ato.gov.au/atolaw/view.htm?docid=GST/GSTR20143/NAT/ATO/00001&PiT=20141217000001 , accessed on 10 January 2019.

Australian Taxation Office, 'Tax Treatment of Cryptocurrencies in Australia – Specifically Bitcoin' (*law.ato.gov*, 21 December 2014) https://www.ato.gov.au/General/Gen/Tax-treatment-of-crypto-currencies-in-Australia---specifically-bitcoin/, accessed on 10 January 2019.

Bal Aleksandra, 'Stateless Virtual Money in the Tax System' (2013) 53 *European Taxation*, 351.

Bank of France, 'Les dangers liés au développement des monnaies virtuelles: l'exemple du bitcoin' (*banque-france.fr*, 5 December 2013) Focus No. 10, https://publications.banque-france.fr/les-dangers-lies-au-developpement-des-monnaies-virtuelles-lexemple-du-bitcoin, accessed on 10 January 2019.

Blind Knut, 'The Impact of Regulation on Innovation' (2012) Nesta Working Paper 12/02.

Bordo Michael, 'Gold Standard' (*Econlib.org*) http://www.econlib.org/library/Enc/GoldStandard.html, accessed on 10 January 2019.

Bourdieu Pierre, Wacquant Loic, and Farage Samar, 'Rethinking the State: Genesis and Structure of the Bureaucratic Field' (1994) 12 *Sociological Theory*, 1.

Brito Jerry, Shadab Houman B., and Castillo O'Sullivan Andrea, 'Bitcoin Financial Regulation: Securities, Derivatives, Prediction Markets, and Gambling' (2014) 16 *Columbia Science and Technology Law Review*, 1.

California Legislature, 'Virtual Currency' (27 February 2015), Assembly Bill 1326.

Central Bank of the United Arab Emirates, 'Regulatory Framework for Stored Values and Electronic Payment Systems' (2017).

Chen Lulu Yilun, 'Bitcoin Banned by Alibaba's Taobao after China Tightens Rules' (*Bloomberg.com*, 8 January 2014) http://bloom.bg/1J1fsVf, accessed on 10 January 2019.

Clayton, Jay, 'Statement on Cryptocurrencies and Initial Coin Offerings' (*Sec.gov*, 11 December 2017) https://www.sec.gov/news/public-statement/statement-clayton-2017-12-11, accessed on 10 January 2019.

Commercial Court of Créteil (6 December 2011) SAS Macaraja c/SA Crédit Industriel et Commercial, Tribunal de commerce [Commercial Tribunal] Crétail, 2nd ch. (December 2011); confirmed by the Court of Appeal of Paris (26 September 2013) https://www.doctrine.fr/d/CA/Paris/2013/RD2AE0AF6A196D83C06B9, accessed on 10 January 2019.

CryptoCoinsNews (CCN), 'Swiss Town Zug Continues Allowing Bitcoin Payments for Municipal Services' (*CCN.com*, 19 December 2016) https://www.ccn.com/swiss-town-zug-continues-allowing-bitcoin-payments-municipal-services/, accessed on 10 January 2019.

Davis Kevin, 'Regulatory Reform Post the Global Financial Crisis: An Overview' (9 March 2011) https://kevindavis.com.au/secondpages/Miscellaneous/Regulatory%20Reform%20Post%20GFC-%20Overview%20Report.pdf, accessed on 10 January 2019.

De Meijer Carlo, 'Blockchain: Playing in the Regulatory Sandbox' (2016) https://www.finextra.com/blogposting/13055/blockchain-playing-in-the-regulatory-sandbox, accessed on 19 January 2019.

De Filippi Primavera, 'Bitcoin: A Regulatory Nightmare to a Libertarian Dream' (2014) 3 *Internet Policy Review*.

De Filippi Primavera and Loveluck Benjamin, 'The Invisible Politics of Bitcoin: Governance Crisis of a Decentralised Infrastructure' (2016) 5 *Internet Policy Review*.

De Filippi Primavera and Wright Aaron, *Blockchain and the Law: The Rule of Code* (Harvard University Press 2018).

Dimitropoulos Georgios, 'Compliance through Collegiality: Peer Review in International Law' (2016) 37 *Loyola LA International and Competition Law Review*, 275.

Doguet Joshua, 'Nature of the Form: Legal and Regulatory Issues Surrounding the Bitcoin Digital Currency System' (2013) 73 *Louisiana Law Review*, 1119.

(Dubai) Supreme Legislation Committee, 'Workshop on the Present and Future of Legislative and Legal Frameworks of "Bitcoin"' (*slc.dubai.gov*, 16 November 2016) http://slc.dubai.gov.ae/en/AboutDepartment/News/Lists/NewsCentre/DispForm.aspx?ID=260, accessed on 10 January 2019.

European Banking Authority ('EBA'), 'EBA Warns Consumers on Virtual Currencies' (*eba.europa.eu*, 13 December 2013) http://www.eba.europa.eu/-/eba-warns-consumers-on-virtual-currencies, accessed on 10 January 2019.

European Banking Authority ('EBA'), 'EBA Opinion on "Virtual Currencies"' (4 July 2014), EBA/Op/2014/08, http://bit.ly/1HOuUT5, accessed on 10 January 2019.

European Central Bank ('ECB'), *Virtual Currency Schemes—A Further Analysis* (February 2015).

Executive Office of the President, National Science and Technology Council Committee on Technology, 'Preparing for the Future of Artificial Intelligence' (October 2016).

Faggart Evan, 'Bitcoin Mining Centralization: The Market is Fixing Itself' (*Coin Brief*, 2014) https://99bitcoins.com/bitcoin-mining-free-market/, accessed on 10 January 2019.

Financial Action Task Force ('FATF'), 'Virtual Currencies: Key Definitions and Potential AML/CFT Risks' (2014) Report.

Financial Conduct Authority ('FCA'), Regulatory Sandbox 2 (*FCA.org*, November 2015) https://www.fca.org.uk/publication/research/regulatory-sandbox.pdf, accessed on 10 January 2019.

Ford Paul, 'Bitcoin May Be the Global Economy's Last Safe Haven' (*Bloomberg.com*, 28 March 2013) https://www.bloomberg.com/news/articles/2013-03-28/bitcoin-may-be-the-global-economys-last-safe-haven, accessed on 10 January 2019.

German Banking Act (Kreditwesengesetz [Banking Act], updated 9 September 1998), Bundesgesetzblatt I at 2776, as amended, http://www.gesetze-im-internet.de/kredwg/index.html, accessed on 10 January 2019.

Global Legal Research Directorate and Law Library of Congress Staff, 'Regulation of Bitcoin in Selected Jurisdictions' (2014) https://www.loc.gov/law/help/bitcoin-survey/regulation-of-bitcoin.pdf, accessed on 10 January 2019.

Government of Dubai, 'Dubai Economy Launches Partnership to Expedite emCash' (*Altcoin News*, 26 September 2017) https://www.cryptocoinsnews.com/emcash-dubais-first-official-state-cryptocurrency/, accessed on 10 January 2019.

Granovetter Mark, 'Economic Action and Social Structure: The Problem of Embeddedness' (1985) 91 *American Journal of Sociology*, 481.

Grinberg Reuben, 'Bitcoin: An Innovative Alternative Digital Currency' (2012) 4 *Hastings Science & Technology Law Journal*, 159.

Guadamuz Andres, 'Virtual Currency and Virtual Property Revisited' (*Technollama.co.uk*, 11 February 2013) http://bit.ly/1MaeW4N, accessed on 10 January 2019.

Guadamuz Andres and Marsden Chris, 'Blockchains and Bitcoin: Regulatory Responses to Cryptocurrencies' (2015) 20 *First Monday*.

Hayes Adam, 'The Decision to Produce Altcoins: Miners' Arbitrage in Cryptocurrency Markets' (2015) https://papers.ssrn.com/sol3/papers.cfm?abstract_id=2579448, accessed on 10 January 2019.

Her Majesty's Revenue and Customs ('HMRC'), 'Bitcoin and Other Similar Cryptocurrencies' (*Gov.uk*, 3 March 2014) Revenue and Customs Brief, 9, https://www.gov.uk/government/publications/revenue-and-customs-brief-9-2014-bitcoin-and-other-cryptocurrencies, accessed on 10 January 2019.

Herbert Smith Freehills, 'Overview of Regulatory Sandbox Regimes in Australia, Hong Kong, Malaysia, Singapore, and the UK' (*law.ox.ac.uk*, 18 December 2016) https://www.law.ox.ac.uk/business-law-blog/blog/2016/12/overview-regulatory-sandbox-regimes-australia-hong-kong-malaysia, accessed on 10 January 2019.

Internal Revenue Service ('IRS'), 'Virtual Currency Guidance' (*IRS.gov*, 25 March 2014) IRS Notice 2014-21, http://www.irs.gov/pub/irs-drop/n-14-21.pdf, accessed on 10 January 2019.

James Adam, 'Will Cryptocurrency Replace National Currencies by 2030? (*Bitcoinist.com*, 2 March 2018) https://bitcoinist.com/will-cryptocurrency-replace-national-currencies-by-2030/, accessed on 10 January 2019.

Kaplanov Nikolei, 'Nerdy Money: Bitcoin, the Private Digital Currency, and the Case against Its Regulation' (2012) 25 *Loy Consumer Law Review*, 111.

Kratochwil Friedrich and Ruggie John Gerard, 'International Organization: A State of the Art on an Art of the State' (1986) 40 *International Organization*, 753.

Leckow Ross, 'Virtual Currencies—the Regulatory Challenges' (6 June 2017) *Yale Journal on Regulation: Notice &Comment*, http://yalejreg.com/nc/virtual-currencies-the-regulatory-challenges-by-ross-leckow/.

Mac Ryan, 'PayPal Takes Baby Step toward Bitcoin, Partners with Cryptocurrency Processors' (*Forbes.com*, 23 September 2014) http://www.forbes.com/sites/ryanmac/2014/09/23/paypal-takes-small-step-toward-bitcoinpartners-with-cryptocurrency-processors, accessed on 10 January 2019.

Mallard Alexandre, Méadel Cécile, and Musiani Francesca, 'The Paradoxes of Distributed Trust: Peer-to-Peer Architecture and User Confidence in Bitcoin' (2014) 4 *Journal of Peer Production*.

Marian Omri Y., 'Are Cryptocurrencies Super Tax Havens?' (2013) 112 *Michigan Law Review*.

Marian Omri Y., 'A Conceptual Framework for the Regulation of Cryptocurrencies' (2015) 82 *University of Chicago Law Review Online*, 53.

Matsuura Jeffrey, *Digital Currency: An International Legal and Regulatory Compliance Guide* (Bentham e-Books 2016).

Middlebrook Stephen and Hughes Sarah Jane, 'Regulating Cryptocurrencies in the United States: Current Issues and Future Directions' (2014) 40 *William Mitchell Law Review*, 813.

Ministère des Finances et des Comptes Publics, Réguler les monnaies virtuelles (2014).

Moore Tyler and Christin Nicolas, 'Beware of the Middleman: Empirical Analysis of Bitcoin-Exchange Risk' in *Financial Cryptography*, edited by A-R Sadeghi (Springer 2013).

Möser Malte, 'Anonymity of Bitcoin Transactions' (2013) Münster Bitcoin Conference, https://pdfs.semanticscholar.org/e1ae/d9296c3af9139f48d15e043e2e8beab55409.pdf, accessed on 10 January 2019.

Münzer Jens, 'Bitcoins: Aufsichtliche Bewertung und Risiken für Nutzer' (*Bafin.de*, 19 December 2013) https://www.bafin.de/SharedDocs/Veroeffentlichungen/DE/Fachartikel/2014/fa_bj_1401_bitcoins.html; English version: https://bitcoinmagazine.com/articles/regulation-bitcoins-germany-first-comprehensive-statement-bitcoins-german-federal-financial-supervisory-authority-bafin-1391637959/, both accessed on 10 January 2019.

Murphy Edward, Murphy Maureen, and Seitzinger Michael, 'Bitcoin: Questions, Answers, and Analysis of Legal Issues' (Congressional Research Service, 13 October 2015) http://fas.org/sgp/crs/misc/R43339.pdf, accessed on 10 January 2019.

Nakamoto Satoshi, 'Bitcoin: A Peer-to-Peer Electronic Cash System' (31 October 2008) https://bitcoin.org/bitcoin.pdf, accessed on 10 January 2019.

Nestler Franz, 'Deutschland erkennt Bitcoins als privates Geld an' ['Germany Recognizes Bitcoins as Private Money'], (*faz.net*, 16 August 2013) Frankfurter Allgemeine Zeitung, http://www.faz.net/aktuell/finanzen/devisen-rohstoffe/digitale-waehrung-deutschland-erkennt-bitcoins-als-privates-geld-an-12535059.html, accessed on 10 January 2019.

New York Codes, Rules and Regulations ('NYCRR'), 'Part 200 Virtual Currencies', http://www.dfs.ny.gov/legal/regulations/adoptions/dfsp200t.pdf, accessed on 10 January 2019.

Nian Lam Pak and Lee David Kuo Chuen, 'A Light Touch of Regulation for Virtual Currencies' in *Handbook of Digital Currency: Bitcoin, Innovation, Financial Instruments, and Big Data*, edited by David Lee Kuo Chuen (Elsevier 2015).

Organisation for Economic Co-operation and Development (OECD), 'Regulatory Reform and Innovation', https://www.oecd.org/sti/inno/2102514.pdf, accessed on 10 January 2019.

Pelkmans Jacques and Renda Andrea, 'Does EU Regulation Hinder or Stimulate Innovation?' (2014) Centre for European Policy Studies Special Report No. 96.

People's Bank of China, Ministry of Industry and Information Technology, China Banking Regulatory Commission, China Securities Regulatory Commission, and China Insurance Regulatory Commission, 'Notice on Precautions against the Risks of Bitcoins' (2013) YIN FA, 2013, No. 289, www.miit.gov.cn/n1146295/n1652858/n1652930/n3757016/c3762245/content.html (in Chinese), accessed on 10 January 2019.

Plassaras Nicholas, 'Regulating Digital Currencies: Bringing Bitcoin within the Reach of the IMF' (2013) 14 *Chicago Journal of International Law*, 377.

Polanyi Karl, *The Great Transformation: The Political and Economic Origins of Our Time* (Beacon Press 1944, 1957, 2001).

Rapoza Kenneth, 'China's "Bitcoin Ban" No Match for Stateless Cryptocurrency Market' (*Forbes.com*, 18 October 2017) https://www.forbes.com/sites/kenrapoza/2017/10/18/chinas-blockchain-bitcoin-ban-no-match-for-stateless-cryptocurrency-market/#2032415e2de6, accessed on 10 January 2019.

Re Coinflip, Inc., d/b/a/Derivabit, et al. (17 September 2015) Order Instituting Proceedings Pursuant to Sections 6© and 6(d) of the Commodity Exchange Act, Making Findings and Imposing Remedial Sanctions ('Derivabit Order'), CFTC Docket No. 15-29, http://www.cftc.gov/ucm/groups/public/@lrenforcementactions/documents/legalpleading/enfcoinfliprorder09172015.pdf, accessed on 11 January 2019.

Ron Dorit and Shamir Adi, 'Quantitative Analysis of the Full Bitcoin Transaction Graph' (2012) Report 2012/584, Cryptology ePrint Archive, http://eprint.iacr.org/2012/584, accessed on 10 January 2019.

Ross Alec, *The Industries of the Future* (Simon & Schuster 2016).

Seely T. Daniel, 'Currency Names Summary' (*LinguistList.org*, 22 August 1995) https://linguistlist.org/issues/6/6-1145.html, accessed on 10 January 2019.

Shoust Pavel, 'Regulators and Fintech: Influence is Mutual?' (undated) http://pubdocs.worldbank.org/en/770171476811898530/Session-4-Pavel-Shoust-Regulatory-Sandboxes-21-09-2016.pdf, accessed on 10 January 2019.

Sonderegger Daniela, 'A Regulatory and Economic Perplexity: Bitcoin Needs just a Bit of Regulation' (2015) 47 *Washington University Journal of Law and Policy*, 175.

Stewart Luke, 'The Impact of Regulation on Innovation in the United States: A Cross-Industry Literature Review' (2010) https://www.itif.org/files/2011-impact-regulation-innovation.pdf, accessed on 10 January 2019.

Stiglitz Joseph, 'Bitcoin Ought to be Outlawed' (World Economic Forum, 30 November 2017) https://www.weforum.org/agenda/2017/11/joseph-stiglitz-bitcoin-ought-to-be-outlawed/, accessed on 10 January 2019.

Stiglitz Joseph and Greenwald Bruce, *Creating a Learning Society: A New Approach to Growth, Development and Social Progress* (Columbia University Press 2014).

Tu Kevin and Meredith Michael, 'Rethinking Virtual Currency Regulation in the Bitcoin Age' (2015) 90 *Washington Law Review*, 271.

UK Parliament, 'Banking: Bitcoins' (Parliamentary debate, House of Lords, 18 December 2013) 4013, http://www.publications.parliament.uk/pa/ld201314/ldhansrd/text/131218w0001.htm, accessed on 10 January 2019.

United States District Court for the Western District of North Carolina, Statesville Division, *US v. Bernard von NotHaus et al.*, http://www.lawandfreedom.com/site/constitutional/vonnothaus_amicus_appendix_a.pdf, accessed 10 January 2019.

US Department of the Treasury, Financial Crimes Enforcement Network, 'Application of FinCEN's Regulations to Persons Administering, Exchanging, or Using Virtual Currencies' (18 March 2013) FIN-2013-G001, https://www.fincen.gov/sites/default/files/shared/FIN-2013-G001.pdf, accessed on 10 January 2019.

US Securities Exchange Commission ('SEC'), 'Investor Alert: Bitcoin and Other Virtual Currency-Related Investments' (*Sec.gov*, 7 May 2014) https://www.sec.gov/oiea/investor-alerts-bulletins/investoralertsia_bitcoin.html, accessed on 10 January 2019.

US Securities Exchange Commission ('SEC'), 'Final Judgment Entered against Trendon T. Shavers, a/k/a "Pirateat40"—Operator of Bitcoin Ponzi Scheme Ordered to Pay More than $40 Million in Disgorgement and Penalties' (*Sec.gov*, 22 September 2014), SEC Litigation Release No. 23090, https://www.sec.gov/litigation/litreleases/2014/lr23090.htm, accessed on 10 January 2019.

US Securities Exchange Commission ('SEC'), 'SEC Sanctions Operator of Bitcoin-Related Stock Exchange for Registration Violations' (*Sec.gov*, 8 December 2014) https://www.sec.gov/news/press-release/2014-273, accessed on 10 January 2019.

US Securities Exchange Commission ('SEC'), 'Report of Investigation Pursuant to Section 21(a) of the Securities Exchange Act of 1934: The DAO' (25 July 2017) Release No. 81207.

US Securities Exchange Commission ('SEC'), 'Investor Bulletin: Initial Coin Offerings' (*Sec.gov*, 27 July 2017) https://www.investor.gov/additional-resources/news-alerts/alerts-bulletins/investor-bulletin-initial-coin-offerings, accessed on 10 January 2019.

US Senate Committee on Agriculture, Nutrition & Forestry, Testimony of Chairman Timothy Massad (*CFTC.gov*, 10 December 2014) http://www.cftc.gov/PressRoom/SpeechesTestimony/opamassad-6, accessed on 10 January 2019.

Vardi Noah, 'Bit by Bit: Assessing the Legal Nature of Virtual Currencies' in *Bitcoin and Mobile Payments: Constructing a European Union Framework*, edited by Gabriella Gimigliano (Palgrave Macmillan 2016).

Weber Max, *Economy and Society*, edited by Guenther Roth and Claus Wittich (University of California Press 1978).

Wetjen Mark, 'Bringing Commodities Regulation to Cryptocurrency' (2014) *Wall Street Journal*.

Wong Joon, 'China's Market Dominance Poses Questions about Global Bitcoin Trading Flows' (*CoinDesk.com*, 27 September 2014) http://bit.ly/1R3Pqj9, accessed on 9 January 2019.

World Government Summit, *Building the Hyperconnected Future on Blockchains* (2017).

World Government Summit, *The Future of Money: Back to the Future—The Internet of Money* (2017).

Worstall Tim, 'Exactly What We Don't Need—Regulation of AI and Technology' (*Forbes.com*, 12 October 2016) http://www.forbes.com/sites/timworstall/2016/10/12/exactly-what-we-dont-need-regulation-of-ai-and-technology/#4bc0361f5121, accessed on 10 January 2019.

Yang Ruoke, 'When is Bitcoin a Security under US Securities Law?' (2013) 18 *Journal of Technology Law & Policy*, 99.

Yee Andy, 'Internet Architecture and the Layers Principle: A Conceptual Framework for Regulating Bitcoin' (2014) 3 *Internet Policy Review*.

Yellen Janet, 'Fed will Steer Clear of Bitcoin' (*Fortune.com*, 27 February 2014) http://fortune.com/2014/02/27/janet-yellen-fed-will-steer-clear-of-bitcoin/, accessed on 10 January 2019.

7

Corporate Governance for Complex Cryptocurrencies?

A Framework for Stability and Decision Making in Blockchain-Based Organizations

Philipp Hacker*

I. Introduction

In February 2016, a group of high-level experts, including the Chief Economist of the Bank of England, recommended the use of complexity theory for the predictive modelling of behaviour and outcomes on financial markets.[1] Complex systems sit between simple order and chaos; hence, they are defined, inter alia, by a tension between regularity and unpredictability. In recent years, scholarship has identified an increasing number of social systems—from the health system and traffic management to economic organizations and financial markets—that exhibit such complex patterns.

In its first part, this chapter seeks to apply complexity theory to a novel type of financial infrastructure: blockchain-based organizations. These fall into two main types that often, however, overlap:[2] on the one hand, they include *cryptocurrencies*, such as Bitcoin or Ethereum, that provide a means of payment. On the other hand, particularly Ethereum is also increasingly used as a basis for a broad array of *token-based ventures*, such as utility and investment tokens, built on top of Ethereum. The recent rise in token sales (also called initial coin offerings, 'ICOs'), with more than $5 billion raised in 2017 alone through this channel, testifies to this staggering development.[3] Token-based ventures (also called 'decentralized applications') include, for example, decentralized storage applications (Filecoin)[4] or mobile messaging platforms (Status). Complexity economics has already been successfully applied to the detection of bubbles in Bitcoin prices, for example.[5] Arguably, the complexity inherent in these systems spawns deep governance problems that call for novel responses.

* This chapter benefitted from comments by Stefan Eich, Hermann Elendner, Florian Glatz, Steven Klein, Patrick Leyens, Hilton Root, Angela Walch and Aaron Wright, as well as audiences at the European University Institute, at the 'Digital Currencies, Digital Finance and the Constitution of a New Financial Order' conference in Athens and at the workshop on 'Blockchain and the Constitution of a New Financial Order' at UCL. All errors remain entirely my own.

[1] Stefano Battiston J. Doyne Farmer, Andreas Flache et al., 'Complexity Theory and Financial Regulation. Economic Policy Needs Interdisciplinary Network Analysis and Behavioral Modeling' (2016) 351 *Science*, 818.

[2] See for a more detailed explanation Philipp Hacker and Chris Thomale, 'Crypto-Securities Regulation: ICOs, Token Sales and Cryptocurrencies under EU Financial Law' (2017) 15 *European Company and Financial Law Review* 645, https://papers.ssrn.com/sol3/papers.cfm?abstract_id=3075820; Jonathan Rohr and Aaron Wright, "Blockchain-Based Token Sales, Initial Coin Offerings, and the Democratization of Public Capital Markets" (forthcoming) 70 *Hastings Law Journal*, <https://papers.ssrn.com/sol3/papers.cfm?abstract_id=3048104>.

[3] See Chapter 12 by Hacker and Thomale in this volume.

[4] Protocol Labs, 'Filecoin: A Decentralized Storage Network' (2017) Updated White Paper.

[5] Eng-Tuck Cheah and John Fry, 'Speculative Bubbles in Bitcoin Markets? An Empirical Investigation into the Fundamental Value of Bitcoin' (2015) 130 *Economics Letters*, 32; Eng-Tuck Cheah and John Fry, 'Negative Bubbles and Shocks in Cryptocurrency Markets' (2016) 47 *International Review of Financial Analysis*, 343; David Garcia,

In its second part, this chapter maps out regulatory implications of the complexity analysis and adapts a corporate governance framework to blockchain-based organizations. Improving the governance of these systems is crucial not only for the future of cryptocurrencies as a means of payment but also for token sales and decentralized applications funded by them. First, these applications need a solid, predictable environment on which to run their code. Second, as the controversies surrounding Tezos tokens show,[6] token-based ventures operating on top of the Ethereum blockchain are themselves beset by significant governance problems. Arguably, token-based ventures often very much look like companies with their principals (investors) and agents (management), rather than open currency networks.[7] Therefore, the corporate governance perspective befits them even more than the underlying cryptocurrency protocols like Bitcoin or Ethereum. The chapter suggests the development of a 'Blockchain Governance Code' and the compulsion of cryptocurrencies to comply with it or to explain their reasons for not doing so. The European Parliament, in its resolution on virtual currencies, warned that regulation 'may not be adapted to a state of affairs which is still in flux', and therefore called for proportionate, 'smart regulation' tailored to cryptocurrencies without stifling innovation;[8] the solution offered here is very much in line with these requirements. 'Testing' regulation in the form of a comply-or-explain approach is likely to generate, over time, information and a better understanding, for regulators, of where the relevant problems lie.[9] Arguably, a coherent and transparent governance mechanism can strengthen elements of regularity and stability within cryptocurrencies, protecting those already owning cryptocoins, making such currencies more attractive for novel users, and encouraging financial stability more broadly as cryptocurrencies and token-based ventures become more interconnected with the traditional financial system. Transparency and stability on the platform level will likely prove crucial as an increasing number of decentralized applications, such as smart contracts or token-based investment vehicles, are added onto blockchain platforms.

The remainder of the chapter is organized as follows. Section II provides a very brief overview of complexity theory and its applications. Section III offers a short introduction to blockchain-based systems and argues that they should be understood as complex systems. Section IV explores the regulatory consequences of this novel analysis by adapting corporate governance schemes to cryptocurrency regimes and token-based ventures. Section V concludes.

II. Chaos and Complexity Theory

Complexity, as an intermediate concept, sits between simple order, on the one hand, and chaos, on the other. While in simply ordered systems, future development can be assessed fairly precisely (at least probabilistically),[10] chaos is defined by largely unpredictable behaviour which, however, still shows some regularity or structure (and therefore can be distinguished from mere chance).[11] An example of simple order would be a snooker table on

---

Claudia Tessone, Pavlin Mavrodiev, and Nicolas Perony, 'The Digital Traces of Bubbles: Feedback Cycles between Socio-Economic Signals in the Bitcoin Economy' (2014) 11 *Journal of the Royal Society Interface*.

[6] See Marc Hochstein, 'Tezos Founders on ICO Controversy: "This Will Blow Over"' (*CoinDesk.com*, 25 October 2017) https://www.coindesk.com/tezos-founders-ico-controversy-will-blow/.

[7] See, e.g., Us Securities Exchange Commission ('SEC'), 'Report of Investigation Pursuant to Section 21(a) of the Securities Exchange Act of 1934: The DAO' (25 July 2017) Release No. 81207, 12–15.

[8] European Parliament Resolution, 'Virtual Currencies' (26 May 2016) 2016/2007(INI), Articles 4, 14, and 18.

[9] Patrick Leyens, 'Comply or Explain' (2016) *ZEuP*, 419.

[10] Michael Strevens, *Bigger Than Chaos. Understanding Complexity through Probability* (Harvard University Press 2003), 5.

[11] ibid., 6; Cars Hommes, *Behavioral Rationality and Heterogeneous Expectations in Complex Economic Systems* (Cambridge University Press 2013), 54–58; David Levy, 'Chaos Theory and Strategy: Theory, Application, and Managerial Implications' (1994) 15 *Strategic Management Journal*, 168.

which a ball is hit. Of chaos, the development of weather systems is the best-known example.[12] Complexity shows elements of both of these extreme cases; of structural regularity and of unpredictability.

A. Properties of complex systems

Complexity theory models system–environment relationships with a focus on the interaction between system members and their spontaneous self-organization.[13] Complexity models are dynamic, describing the evolution of systems as iterative processes, where the outcome of one cycle is simultaneously the start of the next.[14]

Complex systems exhibit a variety of properties that distinguish them from ordinary, simply ordered systems. First, and most importantly, some sort of order (recurring patterns) exists but the system over time generates outcomes that are non-linear and a priori unpredictable.[15] Second, often the system exhibits feedback effects: local interactions have global effects,[16] which in turn may influence local interactions (positive or negative feedback). Third, complex systems are marked by significant variance, i.e. actors are highly heterogeneous.[17] They may, for example, differ in their goals, motivations, or degrees of rationality.

B. Applications of complexity theory

Complexity theory was first introduced in the study of biological systems.[18] Since the 1990s, chaos and complexity theory have been increasingly applied to the social sciences as well.[19] Particularly, organizations were fruitfully modelled as complex institutions.[20] From there, it was but a small step to an application in economics.[21] After the stock market crash of 19 October 1987, academics began turning to non-linear models, found in non-linear dynamics and complexity theory, to explain the interaction of market participants and of financial markets, in particular.[22] Specifically, those theories are better able to model sudden changes of behaviour and stark movements, such as those witnessed during financial crashes, than conventional, linear models.[23] They may thus provide some much-needed structure for such seemingly random events. The contribution made by Stefan Battiston et al.[24] is, as far as can be seen, the first to apply the insights of complexity and chaos theory not only to the modelling of financial markets but explicitly to financial regulation. The moment of its appearance is suggestive: the Global Financial Crisis has made it clear that the models used to inform financial regulation before were inadequate.[25]

---

[12] William Baumol and Jess Benhabib, 'Chaos: Significance, Mechanism, and Economic Applications' (1989) 3 *Journal of Economic Perspectives*, 92; David Byrne, *Complexity Theory and the Social Sciences* (Routledge 1998), 23 and 28.

[13] Mitchell Waldrop, *Complexity. The Emerging Science at the Edge of Order and Chaos* (Simon & Schuster 1992), 11; Strevens (n 10), 7.

[14] Tim Blackman, 'Complexity Theory' in *Understanding Contemporary Society: Theories of the Present*, edited by Gary Browning, Abigail Halcli, and Frank Webster (SAGE 2000), 145.

[15] ibid., 140.   [16] ibid., 142.   [17] Hommes (n 11), 8–10; Strevens (n 10), 10–11.

[18] Stuart Kauffman, *At Home in the Universe. The Search for Laws of Self-Organization and Complexity* (Oxford University Press 1995), Chapter 1.

[19] David Harvey and Michael Read, 'The Evolution of Dissipative Social Systems' (1994) 17 *Journal of Social and Evolutionary Systems*, 373.

[20] R. Thiétart and B. Forgues, 'Chaos Theory and Organization' (1995) 6 *Organization Science*, 19.

[21] Baumol and Benhabib (n 12).

[22] David Hsieh, 'Chaos and Nonlinear Dynamics: Application to Financial Markets' (1991) 46 *Journal of Finance*, 1839; Edgar Peters, *Fractal Market Analysis. Applying Chaos Theory to Investment and Economics* (Wiley 1994).

[23] Hsieh (n 22), 1839.   [24] Battiston et al. (n 1).   [25] Battiston et al. (n 1), 819.

III. Complex Cryptocurrencies and Imperfect Governance

This chapter claims that complexity theory not only fits traditional modes of banking and finance but also novel financial ecosystems, such as blockchain-based cryptocurrencies, and may deliver important insights into their regulation. Cryptocurrencies, such as Bitcoin and Ethereum, and token-based ventures running on permissionless blockchain technology are excellent candidates for complexity theory insofar as they are to a large extent self-organized; there is a high degree of interconnectedness of the different independent agents.[26] As we shall see, however, centralizing elements become ever more important in times of crisis. This tension between decentralization and re-centralization, and between regularity and unpredictability, becomes apparent most prominently in the contested governance of cryptocurrencies, to which we turn (sections B and C below), after a brief introduction of the technology behind blockchain.

A. The functioning of blockchain-based systems

Using a public–private key encryption protocol, a blockchain logs pieces of information, such as transactions between two users (e.g. a monetary payment), on a decentralized list (the 'ledger') that is stored in its entirety on many users' computers (so-called 'nodes').[27] New pieces of information are validated by the nodes in a mathematically secured way—creating a list (chain) of transaction blocks.[28] A decentralized consensus mechanism decides which chain is authentic in cases of discrepancy between different variants of the distributed ledger. Chains grow at the rate at which new blocks are added and confirmed by the community of nodes. Therefore, the longest chain, backed by the majority of users (more precisely, their computing power), is considered the consensus chain.[29] A blockchain, hence, does not rely on any 'trusted third party', such as a central bank, to decide on the validity of records on the ledger.[30]

In the context of cryptocurrencies (also called 'digital or virtual currencies'),[31] and of decentralized applications built on top of them (such as Filecoin, Status, etc.),[32] a *permissionless* variety of blockchain is most often used;[33] utility or investment tokens are generally offered on Ethereum under its ERC20 token standard.[34] The theoretical attractiveness of

---

[26] cf. also, for the financial system as such Battiston et al. (n 1), 818.

[27] More precisely, these functions are only fulfilled by full nodes (as opposed to lightweight nodes); see Andreas M. Antonopoulos, *Mastering Bitcoin: Unlocking Digital Cryptocurrencies* (O'Reilly 2014), 6; the term 'node' will imply 'full node' in this chapter.

[28] See the 'founding document' of blockchain: Staoshi Nakamoto, 'Bitcoin: A Peer-to-Peer Electronic Cash System' (31 October 2008) https://bitcoin.org/bitcoin.pdf; for an introductory overview, see also Jan Witte, 'The Blockchain: A Gentle Introduction' (2016) Working Paper, https://ssrn.com/abstract=2887567.

[29] Even more precisely, it is the chain with greatest cumulative proof-of-work difficulty, see Antonopoulos (n 27), 198–200.

[30] Nakamoto (n 28), 1.

[31] All cryptocurrencies use cryptographic techniques to function; the terminological differences between them and other digital or virtual currencies are not important for this chapter. See, e.g., Lam Pak Nian and David Lee Kuo Chuen, 'Introduction to Bitcoin' in *Handbook of Digital Currency*, edited by David Lee Kuo Chuen (Elsevier 2015), 6–7, hence the term "cryptocurrencies" will be used, which denotes Bitcoin, Ethereum and other blockchain-based, decentralized currencies studied in this Chapter.

[32] For an overview of these applications, see, e.g., Hacker and Thomale (n 2), 11–13; Rohr and Wright (n 2), 12–24.

[33] 'Permissionless' (also called 'public') blockchains can be joined by anyone at any time, typically under conditions of pseudonymity or anonymity, and any user can add transactions and update the chain by mining (BitFury Group and Jeff Garzik, 'Public versus Private Blockchains: Part II: Permissionless Blockchains' (2015), 2). This chapter focuses on permissionless blockchains as they are employed by cryptocurrencies.

[34] Rohr and Wright (n 2), 12 et seq.

permissionless blockchains like Ethereum resides precisely in their openness.[35] They allow everyone to join, run a node, and participate fully in the updating of the chain.

B. Imperfect governance structures

As a nascent strand of literature shows, however, permissionless blockchains also exhibit significant governance problems.[36] Governance is a key concept in studies on the internet ecosystem,[37] but it can be fruitfully applied to blockchain ecosystems as well. It is generally understood as a system shaping coordination between different actors. Governance becomes particularly notable in times of crisis.[38] In the case of cryptocurrencies, these critical moments particularly arise when there is a need for a change of the code protocol that governs transactions on the blockchain. The protocol of each blockchain-based organization specifies exactly how certain transactions are executed, how new coins are created, at what speed the chain is updated, etc. Protocol changes thus alter the 'rules of the game' according to which transactions can be accomplished and the system functions. As the following brief case studies show, imperfect governance structures become particularly visible in the process leading to major breaks in the protocol structure, so-called 'hard forks'.[39]

What is perhaps most striking about the constructive feature of cryptocurrencies is not the high degree of specification in *applying* the protocol to transactions but the opacity and informality when it comes to the *updating* of the protocol itself.[40] There are no clear guidelines in place describing how the protocol itself can be changed, particularly when conflicting views have to be reconciled.[41] In stark contrast to the exactness of the protocol itself, governance mechanisms are thus almost entirely lacking when it comes to changing the rules of the game in moments of dispute.

For example, the reference implementation of the Bitcoin protocol, openly accessible at the code platform GitHub, is maintained by a small group of people (its core developers).[42] While anyone may make proposals for updating the code, only the core developers have the power to actually implement changes.[43] Non-linearity and unpredictability in changes to the protocol arguably result from the lack of a procedure to accommodate dissent within the community of developers and, more broadly, of users and stakeholders.[44] Core developers use 'informal processes that depend on rough notions of consensus and that are subject to

---

[35] Cf. Philipp Paech, ' The Governance of Blockchain Financial Networks' (2017) 80(6) *Modern Law Review* 7, 14, https://ssrn.com/abstract=2875487,.

[36] Arthur Gervais, Ghassen Karame, Vedran Capkun, and Srdjan Capkun, 'Is Bitcoin a Decentralized Currency?' (2014) 12(3) *IEEE Security & Privacy*, 54; Rainer Böhme, Nicolas Christin, Benjamin Edelman, and Tyler Moore, 'Bitcoin: Economics, Technology, and Governance' (2015) 29 *The Journal of Economic Perspectives*, 213; Angela Walch, 'The Bitcoin Blockchain as Financial Market Infrastructure: A Consideration of Operational Risk' (2015) 18 *New York University Journal of Legislation and Public Policy*, 865–82; Paech (n 35), 18–31 and 42–54; Primavera De Filippi and Benjamin Loveluck, 'The Invisible Politics of Bitcoin: Governance Crisis Of A Decentralised Infrastructure' (2016) 5(3) *Internet Policy Review*, 1; Don Tapscott and Alex Tapscott, *Blockchain Revolution* (Penguin 2016), Ch 11; World Economic Forum, 'Realizing the Potential of Blockchain' (2017), White Paper.

[37] See, e.g., Eric Brousseau, Meryem Marzouki, and Cécile Méadel, *Governance, Regulation and Powers on the Internet* (Cambridge University Press 2012).

[38] Jeanette Hofmann, Christian Katzenbach, and Kirsten Goliatz, 'Between Coordination and Regulation: Finding the Governance in Internet Governance' (2016) *New Media and Society*, 9.

[39] While soft forks are reversible and essentially implement changes to the protocol via voluntary software updates (just like updates for other computer programs), hard forks are irreversible and forced upon user communities by mandatory updates; cf. BitcoinWiki, https://en.bitcoin.it/wiki/Softfork; Antonopoulos (n 27), 199–204.

[40] On the difference between these two governance layers, see De Filippi and Loveluck (n 36), 10.

[41] ibid., 14.

[42] Gerald Dwyer, 'The Economics of Bitcoin and Similar Private Digital Currencies' (2015) 17 *Journal of Financial Stability*, 81; Gervais et al. (n 36), 55.

[43] Gervais et al. (n 36), 57; De Filippi and Loveluck (n 36), 13–14; see also the Chapter 3 by Walch in this volume.

[44] See GitHub, https://github.com/bitcoin/bips/blob/master/README.mediawiki.

no fixed legal or organizational structure.[45] They do, however, often coordinate their actions with operators of large mining pools;[46] these are entities that supply the computing power to validate transactions in the chain and that are rewarded for their efforts with newly 'minted' coins.[47] A small group of agents crucial for the development and maintenance of the network (core developers and operators of mining pools) may thus acquire true power to change the protocol, even when holding less than 50% of computing power,[48] and independent of their financial stakes in the currency. While these agents effectively regulate the crypto-economy, they are accountable to no one and users do not play any significant role in their appointment.[49]

C. Case studies

We shall now take a brief look at three specific examples: two hard forks by Bitcoin and Ethereum, which happened in March 2013 and July 2016, respectively; and the controversy surrounding the Bitcoin scaling debate which has led to yet two more hard forks in 2017, driven by disagreement over updating the rules on block sizes.

1. The Bitcoin hard fork of 2013

On 11 March 2013, the Bitcoin blockchain forked into two chains that were no longer mutually consistent.[50] Importantly, the new chain was growing faster than the old one. However, the core developers convinced the largest mining pool (BTC Guild)[51] and other major pools,[52] without any coordination with users, to back the shorter chain because it functioned under both old and new versions.[53] In doing so, they violated the basic blockchain rule of the authenticity of the longest chain.[54] Mining rewards worth $26,000 in the new chain were lost.[55] In this case, therefore, the operators of major mining pools and core developers informally colluded to take the blockchain into a novel, non-majoritarian, direction. While their intentions to quickly resolve the fork may have been laudable, the episode shows the vulnerability of the infrastructure to ad hoc coalitions of the willing.

2. The Ethereum hard fork of 2016

In this way, even transaction histories may be changed retroactively, sacrificing a second basic rule of blockchain: its irreversibility.[56] This is exactly what happened on 20 July 2016 in the Ethereum blockchain. As mentioned above, Ethereum is also configured to support networks of smart contracts known as token-based ventures.[57] These decentralized applications can take a broad variety of forms. In the specific instance, a German start-up programmed a smart contract running on Ethereum called 'The DAO', which was intended to function like

---

[45] Shawn Bayern, 'Of Bitcoins, Independently Wealthy Software, and the Zero Member LLC' (2014) 108 *Northwestern University Law Review Online*, 259.

[46] See Walch, 'The Bitcoin Blockchain' (n 36), 873.   [47] See Antonopoulos (n 27), 207–10.

[48] Gervais et al. (n 36), 55.   [49] ibid., 55.   [50] ibid., 56.

[51] Arvind Narayanan, 'Analyzing The 2013 Bitcoin Fork: Centralized Decision-Making Saved the Day' (26 July 2015) https://freedom-to-tinker.com/blog/randomwalker/analyzing-the-2013-bitcoin-fork-centralized-decision-making-saved-the-day/, Introductory Section and under Achtung!.

[52] ibid.

[53] Gervais et al. (n 36), 56; Vitalik Buterin, 'Bitcoin Network Shaken by Blockchain Fork' (*Bitcoin Magazine*, 12 March 2013) https://bitcoinmagazine.com/articles/bitcoin-network-shaken-by-blockchain-fork-1363144448.

[54] Buterin, 'Bitcoin Network Shaken' (n 53).   [55] ibid.

[56] See, on rewriting blockchain history, David Siegel, 'Understanding the DAO Attack' (*Coindesk.com*, 25 June 2016) http://www.coindesk.com/understanding-dao-hack-journalists/.

[57] Vitalik Buterin 'A Next Generation Smart Contract and Decentralized Application Platform' (2014) Ethereum White Paper.

a decentralized investment platform. Having collected a surprising equivalent of 150 million dollars in ethers, representing 15% of all outstanding ether, The DAO was hacked and deprived of one-third of its funds.[58] Overnight, ethers lost half of their value.[59]

In an unprecedented move, core Ethereum developers decided to effectively rewrite the history of their blockchain in order to undo the hack and restore the funds to all investors via a hard fork.[60] Similar measures are currently envisaged to undo the Parity bug.[61] The DAO fork was unique insofar as the blockchain, which is supposed to be an irreversible record of all transactions, was effectively changed in order to erase the consequences of the fundamental coding error which led to the greatest hack in the history of blockchain-based organizations.[62] The proposers of this rewriting of the Ethereum blockchain subjected their radical ideas to the majority vote of users by conditioning the hard fork on the approval by the majority of users.[63] The proposal was fiercely contested.[64] Only a minority of ether owners voted,[65] but in the end, the vast weighted majority of those users that did vote[66] and, after this, a similar majority of computing power of miners backed the hard fork.[67] Other than in the case of the unintentional Bitcoin fork discussed in section 1, the intentional Ethereum fork was thus subjected to a dual mechanism: first, a vote by users, and then, the (unavoidable and economic) vote of miners by virtue of their computing power, who decided on whether to back the old or the newly forked version.[68] Nevertheless, in a way difficult to foresee *ex ante*, the principle of the immutability of the chain was sacrificed.

3. Bitcoin hard forks without end: the ongoing block size debate

The ongoing controversy over the best way to fix a problem inherent in the current Bitcoin implementation provides a third example of potentially complex and unpredictable behaviour. Even after two hard forks in August and October 2017, creating Bitcoin Cash[69] and Bitcoin Gold,[70] the Bitcoin network is still facing its largest challenge for a stable and sustainable future: the scaling debate.[71] With its current configuration, the Bitcoin blockchain can only validate a limited number of transactions per block.[72]

---

[58] Siegel (n 56); Joon Ian Wong and Ian Klar, 'Everything You Need to Know about the Ethereum "Hard Fork"' (*Quartz*, 18 July 2016) http://qz.com/730004/everything-you-need-to-know-about-the-ethereum-hard-fork/.

[59] Luke Parker, 'Ethereum Hard Fork Results in Two Surviving Cryptocurrencies, Both Are Now Trading' (*BraveNewCoin.com*, 26 July 2016) https://bravenewcoin.com/news/ethereum-hard-fork-results-in-two-surviving-cryptocurrencies-both-are-now-trading/.

[60] Jeffrey Wilke, 'To Fork or Not to Fork' (*EthereumBlog.org*, 15 July 2016) https://blog.ethereum.org/2016/07/15/to-fork-or-not-to-fork/.

[61] Rachel O'Leary, 'Parity Says "No Intention" to Split Ethereum over Fund Recovery' (*CoinDesk.com*, 26 April 2018) https://www.coindesk.com/parity-says-no-intention-to-split-ethereum-over-fund-recovery/.

[62] Siegel (n 56).

[63] The vote was weighted by the ethers of the users, http://carbonvote.com/; see also Wilke (n 60).

[64] See, Reddit, 'Critical Update RE: DAO Vulnerability' (2016) https://www.reddit.com/r/ethereum/comments/4oiqj7/critical_update_re_dao_vulnerability/.

[65] Parker (n 59).   [66] In the end, 87% supported the hard fork: Parker (n 59).

[67] Even by 20 June 2016, 85% of miners were mining on the new fork: Vitalik Buterin, 'Hard Fork Completed' (*EthereumBlog.org*, 20 July 2016) https://blog.ethereum.org/2016/07/20/hard-fork-completed/.

[68] On the necessary backing by miners, see Wong and Klar (n 58).

[69] Alyssa Hertig, 'Bitcoin Cash: Why It's Forking the Blockchain and What That Means' (*CoinDesk.com*, 26 July 2017) https://www.coindesk.com/coindesk-explainer-bitcoin-cash-forking-blockchain/.

[70] Alyssa Hertig, 'Bitcoin Gold: What to Know about the Blockchain's Next Split' (*CoinDesk.com*, 23 October 2017) https://www.coindesk.com/bitcoin-gold-know-blockchains-next-split/.

[71] See, e.g., Ofir Beigel, 'Segwit vs. Bitcoin Unlimited and Bitcoin's Fork Explained Simply' (*99Bitcoins.com*, 27 March 27/2 April 2017) https://99bitcoins.com/bitcoin-fork-segwit-vs-bitcoin-unlimited-explained-simply/; Pete Rizzo, 'Making Sense of Bitcoin's Divisive Block Size Debate' (*CoinDesk.com*, 19 January 2016) http://www.coindesk.com/making-sense-block-size-debate-bitcoin/; De Filippi and Loveluck (n 36), 7–9.

[72] Arvind Narayanan and Steven Goldfelder, *Bitcoin and Cryptocurrency Technologies. A Comprehensive Introduction* (Princeton University Press, 2016), Chs 3.6 and 7.

The most notable implementation that would achieve increased block size is called Segregated Witness ('SegWit'). Without going into the details,[73] it is safe to say that the proposal that came closest to adoption, called SegWit2x, would have freed up space for transactions in the blocks and additionally raised the block size to 2 MB. SegWit2x would have been implemented by a hard fork around 16 November 2017 had enough miners backed it.[74] Observers agreed that, if anything, the threat of a hard fork seeking to take along the majority of the nodes of the legacy Bitcoin chain (and not only open a new chain as Bitcoin Gold and Cash did, respectively), infused significant uncertainty as to the future of the Bitcoin blockchain[75]—again testifying to its complex nature. Further complicating matters, the SegWit2x hard fork was called off at the last minute,[76] leaving users and app developers perplexed about the future of scaling on the Bitcoin blockchain.[77]

Arguably, however, all solutions enable, through different avenues, the steering of the Bitcoin currency by informal, already powerful groups. A greater block size would make it more difficult for conventional computers to process transactions in the first place, making those with significant computing power even more relevant.[78] There was a growing fear that under SegWit2x control would be effectively handed over to mining pool operators.[79] However, the alternative is also all but devoid of power problems. Earlier in 2017, the core developers held meetings with large mining pool operators, for example in China, to discuss possible solutions, raising the fear of collusion between the groups.[80] Core developers have also been accused of illegitimate censorship in the scaling debate.[81]

Again, it appears that a small group of technological leaders (miners and core developers) tried to leverage their position, assume informal power and, in opaque ways, influence the decision about the updating of the protocol. It was precisely this tendency that sparked the hard fork generating Bitcoin Gold, which aims to restore user power,[82] but has been dwarfed by the legacy Bitcoin chain in importance so far.[83]

4. Lessons from the hard forks

In all the cases discussed above, a clear imperfection of governance schemes is apparent. It allows for the coordinated actions of a few major stakeholders or developers to take control of the rules for constructing the blockchain. Of course, any person can make changes to the open-source software and thereby launch a new cryptocurrency. However, the important

---

[73] For an excellent technical introduction, see Aaron van Wirdum, 'Segregated Witness, Part 1: How a Clever Hack Could Significantly Increase Bitcoin's Potential' (*BitcoinMagazine.com*, 19 December 2015) https://bitcoinmagazine.com/articles/segregated-witness-part-how-a-clever-hack-could-significantly-increase-bitcoins-potential-1450553618/.

[74] Pete Rizzo, 'Understanding Segwit2x: Why Bitcoin's Next Fork Might Not Mean Free Money' (*CoinDesk.com*, 1 November 2017) https://www.coindesk.com/understanding-segwit2x-bitcoins-next-fork-might-different/.

[75] Laura Shin, "Will This Battle for the Soul of Bitcoin Destroy It?' (*Forbes.com*, 23 October 2017) https://www.forbes.com/sites/laurashin/2017/10/23/will-this-battle-for-the-soul-of-bitcoin-destroy-it/#c3f4e323d3c0; Ariel Deschapel, 'Why Segwit2x Is Doomed to Fail' (*CoinDesk.com*, 6 November 2017) https://www.coindesk.com/opinion-segwit2x-doomed-fail/ under 'Scheduled Chaos'; Rizzo, 'Understanding Segwit2x' (n 74).

[76] Alyssa Hertig, '2x Called Off: Bitcoin Hard Fork Suspended for Lack of Consensus' (*CoinDesk.com*, 8 November 2017) https://www.coindesk.com/2x-called-off-bitcoin-hard-fork-suspended-lack-consensus/.

[77] Pete Rizzo and Alyssa Hertig, 'Relief and Disbelief: Bitcoin Reacts to Sudden "2x" Suspension' (*CoinDesk.com*, 8 November 2017) https://www.coindesk.com/relief-disbelief-bitcoin-reacts-sudden-2x-suspension/.

[78] De Filippi and Loveluck (n 36), 8; Rizzo, 'Understanding Segwit2x' (n 74).

[79] Don Tapscott and Alex Tapscott, 'Realizing the Potential of Blockchain' (2017) World Economic Forum White Paper, 11; Beigel (n 71).

[80] J. P. Buntinx, 'Bitcoin Core Members Discuss Blockchain Consensus at Chinese Event' (*TheMerkle.com*, 11 December 2016) https://themerkle.com/bitcoin-core-members-discuss-blockchain-consensus-at-chinese-event/.

[81] John Blocke, '/r/Bitcoin Censorship, Revisited' (*Medium.com*, 27 February 2017) https://medium.com/@johnblocke/r-bitcoin-censorship-revisited-58d5b1bdcd64.

[82] See BitcoinGold, '/Roadmap', https://bitcoingold.org/.

[83] See CoinMarketCap, 'Bitcoin Gold [Futures]', https://coinmarketcap.com/currencies/bitcoin-gold/.

question is who is deciding on the development of the existing, successful cryptocurrencies (such as Bitcoin or Ethereum), in which users or investors have already acquired substantial amounts of coins. The three examples show that the decentralized structure is vulnerable to coalitions of the willing, which combine enough technological prowess, computing power, or force of persuasion to implement their proposals on the development of the blockchain.[84] This leads to erratic, unforeseen, and potentially radical changes of the system status as a reaction to external shocks or internal developments. This is exactly the kind of behaviour that complexity theory predicts for complex systems.

D. Complexity and cryptocurrencies

All in all, the case studies show that cryptocurrencies possess five properties that suggest they qualify as complex systems. First, a great degree of heterogeneity between the actors exists, in terms of their tech-savviness, rationality, motivations, and goals. Second, they exhibit a clear network character, being based on decentralized nodes. Third, the lack of altering rules for the blockchain protocols and the concomitant lack of governance schemes to deal with dissent, unforeseen events, or security breaches, leads to an inherent unpredictability of the future development of the protocols when coalitions of major players (core developers, operators of mining pools, etc.) can exert disproportionate power to unilaterally push updates they view as personally favourable or generally reasonable. Fourth, this abstract lack of governance has manifested itself in a series of concrete events in which major transitions in the protocol were conducted. This included the violation of perhaps the two most basic rules of blockchain, namely the invalidation of the significantly longer chain and the effective rewriting of the Ethereum blockchain. Finally, the value of cryptocoins is so volatile that some economists tend to categorize cryptocurrencies as investment assets rather than currencies.[85] Price volatility, however, is another instantiation of unpredictable behaviour exhibited by complex systems.[86]

The upshot of treating cryptocurrencies as complex systems is threefold. First, on the predictive level, if the analysis is correct, we should expect to see more unpredictable behaviour over time. This implies radical uncertainty for cryptocurrencies and token-based ventures built on top of them. Second, on the descriptive level, specific complexity analyses (e.g. agent-based models[87]) may better match the actual behaviour of the system than traditional economic analysis and help predict transitions from stable to unstable states.[88] Third, on the normative level, regulation should strive to strengthen elements of order and reduce uncertainty in the development of the system by tackling, where possible, the roots of complexity and unpredictability. This last point is precisely what the final part of the chapter is about.

IV. Regulating Blockchain-Based Organizations under Uncertainty

Complexity implies uncertainty concerning the future development of a system. Against this background, regulation can arguably take two different approaches. First, regulation may

---

[84] cf. Dwyer (n 42).
[85] Cheah and Fry (n 5), 33; David Yermack, 'Is Bitcoin a Real Currency: An Economic Appraisal' in *Handbook of Digital Currency*, edited by David Lee Kuo Chuen (Elsevier 2015), 32; Dirk Baur, Lee Adrian, and Hong Kihoon, 'Bitcoin: Currency or Investment?' (2014) Working Paper, https://ssrn.com/abstract=2561183.
[86] Cheah and Fry (n 5), 35; Battiston et al. (n 1), 819.
[87] See, e.g., Blake LeBaron, 'Agent-Based Computational Finance' in *Handbook of Computational Economics*, edited by Leigh Tesfatsion and Kenneth L. Judd (Volume 2, North-Holland 2006), 1187.
[88] Battiston et al. (n 1), 818 (see also n 2 there).

take uncertainty as given and attempt to *accommodate* it, for example through principles-based regulation.[89] Second, it may *reduce* uncertainty by installing institutional frameworks. This chapter takes the second approach. It suggests that uncertainty may be reduced, and elements of order strengthened, by the implementation of governance mechanisms. In this, it draws primarily on a comply-or-explain approach, which promises to cure the ills of re-centralization in blockchain-based systems while respecting the freedom to innovate and experiment.

A. Mitigating uncertainty: improving governance structures in blockchain-based organizations

David Yermack has shown, in an influential paper, how blockchain technology stands to up-root corporate governance mechanisms;[90] however, the inverse question of the adaptability of corporate governance rules to blockchain applications like cryptocurrencies has not yet been posed. Core developers and important miners wield powers that are comparable with those of the management of publicly traded companies; however, they are not subject to the same rules of scrutiny, transparency, and accountability faced by company managers. Blockchain governance rules could change that.

1. Reasons to improve governance through legal intervention

There are five reasons that speak in favour of the installation of concrete governance mechanisms for cryptocurrencies in general, and for drawing on corporate governance in particular. First, in general, governance mechanisms may rein in, to a certain extent, the spontaneous, uncoordinated, and unpredictable interaction of users and other stakeholders. Therefore, they can produce a shift from complexity towards a greater degree of order in the system, strengthening regularity and stability. This would likely be appreciated not only by most current users but also by potential future users, who at the moment refrain from getting involved with cryptocurrencies and token-based ventures precisely because of the described governance problems. It also protects third parties from ripple effects that are likely to become larger as cryptocurrencies gain market capitalization. Therefore, second, the introduction of governance rules takes the first steps towards a shift in the legal perspective on cryptocurrencies: from currency regulation to investor protection. This is particularly relevant in the context of novel tokens born out of ICOs that are, more often than not, perceived as investment opportunities by their holders.[91] As mentioned previously, economists have argued that, given their volatility, cryptocurrency tokens should be treated like investment assets and not like pieces of electronic currencies.[92] While this debate cannot be decided in this chapter,[93] it seems clear that at least some suitable measures of investor protection should be implemented to safeguard the interests of cryptocoin owners against those of other, more powerful stakeholders. Third, a clear designation of competences and procedures would break up the informal power structures that hold sway in cryptocurrency systems, and more generally in token-based systems[94] at the moment, presenting an opportunity to distribute power in a fairer and more transparent way. Fourth, *corporate* governance

---

[89] See, e.g., Julia Black, 'Forms and Paradoxes of Principles-Based Regulation' (2008) 3 *Capital Markets Law Journal*, 425, and Chapter 18 by Lianos in this volume.

[90] David Yermack, 'Corporate Governance and Blockchains' (2017) 21 *Review of Finance*, 7.

[91] See Saman Adhami, Giancarlo Giudici, and Stefano Martinazzi, 'Why Do Businesses Go Crypto? An Empirical Analysis of Initial Coin Offerings' (2017) Working Paper, 21, https://ssrn.com/abstract=3046209; more generally, Hacker and Thomale (n 2); Rohr and Wright (n 2).

[92] See n 85.   [93] See Chapter 12 by Hacker and Thomale in this volume.

[94] See Hochstein (n 6).

rules, as we will see in greater detail (section IV.B.), primarily work through a 'comply-or-explain' approach that delegates ultimate choice about the adoption of good governance rules to the regulated entity: it either has to comply with a corporate governance code or disclose why it does not comply with it. Blockchain-based systems would have the choice not to incur the cost of implementing robust governance structures, and to continue to experiment with minimal ones—if only they adequately and saliently inform the public about this decision. Particularly, smaller cryptocurrencies or token projects may therefore selectively opt out of the entire Blockchain Governance Code, or out of parts of it that they find disproportionately burdensome.[95] This framework therefore balances incentives for technical experimentation with user protection; mandatory governance rules, by contrast, should only be considered for those cryptocurrencies, or token-based ventures, that have gained significant importance in the financial system (see section IV.B.3. below). Fifth, it is currently often unclear which state(s)' law applies to cryptocurrencies or token-based projects.[96] An empirical study has found that users do appreciate a clear choice of a reference jurisdiction in token sales.[97] The elaboration of a Blockchain Governance Code would partially solve this problem. It would contain a minimal set of rules that applies to a cryptocurrency or token-based venture that adopts it. Drawing extensively on corporate governance, the next sections spell out what such a framework might look like.

2. External and internal governance: from corporate to crypto

Spurred on by the corporate scandals and board room abuses of the 1980s,[98] the literature on corporate governance analyses the optimal structure for decision making within companies.[99] It distinguishes between external and internal governance,[100] mirroring Albert Hirshman's distinction between exit and voice.[101]

a. The corporate framework

External governance is concerned with optimizing parameters that lie outside the company itself but that nevertheless have a decisive impact on managerial decision making within the company. Shareholders can sell their shares on the market ('exit').[102] Moreover, importantly, the market for corporate control disciplines the current management.[103]

Internal governance, by contrast, describes channels of influence by which shareholders can influence the management ('voice').[104] It comprises information rights, approval rights, and the core competence of the general meeting of shareholders to decide on fundamental matters pertaining to the company.[105] More generally, internal governance formulates a regime for a balance of power between different organs of the company (the board of directors, shareholders, supervisory board where applicable).

---

[95] Financial Reporting Council, 'UK Corporate Governance Code (UK 'CGC') (2016), [5], https://www.frc.org.uk/Our-Work/Codes-Standards/Corporate-governance/UK-Corporate-Governance-Code.aspx

[96] See Iris Barsan, 'Legal Challenges of Initial Coin Offerings ('ICO')' (2017) 3 *RTDF*, 63 et seq.

[97] Adhami et al. (n 91), 21 et seq.

[98] R. (Bob) Tricker, 'The Evolution of Corporate Governance' in *The SAGE Handbook of Corporate Governance*, edited by Thomas Clarke and Douglas Branson (SAGE 2012), 44–45.

[99] Stefan Grundmann, *European Company Law* (2nd edn, Intersentia 2012), § 14 [1]; cf. also Thomas Clarke and Douglas Branson, 'Introduction: Corporate Governance—and Emergent Discipline?' in *The SAGE Handbook of Corporate Governance*, edited by Thomas Clarke and Douglas Branson (SAGE 2012), 2–3.

[100] Grundmann (n 99), § 14 [11].

[101] Albert Hirshman, *Exit, Voice, and Loyalty: Responses to Decline in Firms, Organizations, and States* (Harvard University Press 1970).

[102] Grundmann (n 99), § 14 [35]–[36] and [40]–[42].

[103] Henry Manne, 'Mergers and the Market for Corporate Control' (1965) 73 *Journal of Political Economy*, 110.

[104] See R. (Bob) Tricker, *Corporate Governance* (2nd edn, Oxford University Press 2012), 86–88.

[105] Julian Velasco, 'Taking Shareholder Rights Seriously' (2007) 41 *UC Davis Law Review*, 605.

b. The comparability of corporations and blockchain-based organizations

Turning to blockchain, it may at first glance seem far-fetched to compare informal, open-source-based networks of agents in a blockchain-based system with the highly formalized processes involved in corporations. This difference is most pronounced, however, on a theoretical, rather than on a practical, level. It is true that orthodox corporate governance is built on principal agency or stewardship theory,[106] i.e. theories that presuppose a hierarchically structured company.[107] These theoretical foundations seem to be at odds with less hierarchical, network-type organizations such as cryptocurrencies or decentralized applications.[108] Nevertheless, the comparison is useful for four reasons. First, as the case studies have shown, abuses of power by a subgroup of actors can be detected within cryptocurrencies—as mentioned, similar incidents led to corporate governance rules in the 1980s. Second, both entities (corporations and cryptocurrency systems) have to overcome the challenge of coordinating, and stabilizing, the behaviour of a wide range of actors, some of whom assume—informally or formally—a centralizing management function (directors and core developers/potentially large miners) while others are rather diffused and may suffer from collective action problems (shareholders and cryptocoin owners). Despite the theoretically flat hierarchies of cryptocurrency networks, the case studies have shown that a de facto separation between ownership (of cryptocoins) and control (over protocol changes) exists—precisely like in publicly traded companies.[109] Third, as scholars have pointed out, the grounding of governance questions in human decision making which, in turn, is universally limited by cognitive capacity constraints, make non-hierarchical and hierarchical organizations comparable from a governance perspective.[110] Both types of organization need to separate tasks, and power, in order to prevent information overload of their members.[111] Fourth, tokens issued in token sales function not only as decentralized means of payment but also as alternative routes for financing entrepreneurial projects that, outside of the blockchain, would require the foundation of traditional companies.[112] Many of these for-profit token applications, therefore, share a number of characteristics with companies, or even investment funds, rather than with open-source networks. Hence, it has even been suggested that blockchain-based networks might, in themselves, be partnerships in a legal sense, particularly if users follow a joint purpose and share profits.[113] This reasoning would apply a fortiori to token systems launched by ICOs, particularly to investment tokens.[114]

Therefore, many of the problems corporate governance is supposed to solve reappear in cryptocurrency and decentralized application regimes. It is clear, however, that in the adaptation of corporate governance concepts to cryptocurrencies, we have to take account not only of the similarities, but also of the profound differences between these entities.

---

[106] Tricker, 'The Evolution of Corporate Governance' (n 98), 53–57.

[107] Shann Turnbull, 'The Limitations of Corporate Governance Best Practices' in *The SAGE Handbook of Corporate Governance*, edited by Thomas Clarke and Douglas Branson (SAGE 2012), 434.

[108] ibid., 434; see also David Craven, Nigel Piercy, and Shannon Shipp, "New Organizational Forms for Competing in Highly Dynamic Environments: The Network Paradigm' (1996) 7 *British Journal of Management*, 203.

[109] Eugene Fama and Michael Jensen, 'Separation of Ownership and Control' (1983) 26 *The Journal of Law and Economics*, 301.

[110] Turnbull, 'The Limitations of Corporate Governance' (n 107), 435.

[111] Shann Turnbull, *A New Way to Govern: Organizations and Society after Enron* (New Economics Foundation Pocketbook 2002), 5–6.

[112] See Hacker and Thomale (n 2); Rohr and Wright (n 2); and SEC, 'The DAO' (n 7).

[113] Dirk Zetzsche, Ross Buckley, and Arthur Douglas, 'The Distributed Liability of Distributed Ledgers: Legal Risks of Blockchain' (forthcoming), *University of Illinois Law* Review, 36 et seq., https://papers.ssrn.com/sol3/papers.cfm?abstract_id=3018214; Maximilian Mann, 'Die Decentralized Autonomous Organization—ein neuer Gesellschaftstyp?' (2017) 26 *NZG*, 1014, 1017.

[114] For this terminology, see Hacker and Thomale (n 2); Rohr and Wright (n 2).

c. The blockchain governance framework

To start with, we may also distinguish between an external and an internal governance perspective in the realm of cryptocurrencies and token-based ventures.[115] Concerning the external dimension, an analogy to a market for corporate control does not exist at the moment. There is no formal way to oust the core developer team by means of a 'takeover'. The introduction of such a feature by legal means would indeed provide a strong, disciplining incentive for core developers to act reasonably and in the interest of users. However, the technical specificities of each blockchain make it difficult to replace an entire core developer team. The difficulties of the developers of Bitcoin Unlimited to implement a version of their alternative cryptocurrency that is free from fundamental bugs testifies to this problem.[116] At this point, it becomes apparent that a cryptocurrency is not simply a company; it is also akin to a financial infrastructure. The introduction of a 'market for cryptocurrency control' would likely introduce *more* instability into the valuation and decision making of the currency than mitigate governance problems. While temporarily unstable companies can be tolerated easily in a market economy, inherently unstable financial infrastructures seem much less desirable. This reason applies less to token-based ventures such as Filecoin or Status that lack a primary financial component; however, it is often difficult to draw the line between those tokens with currency and those with internal utility functions.[117]

Therefore, other instruments of external governance should be pursued in the first place. One exit strategy for users is, of course, the simple sale of their cryptocoins.[118] To the extent that core developers are not directly responsible to users, this option does not exert direct pressure on core developers, only indirectly through the pricing mechanism if enough users sell simultaneously. However, there is another and more potent 'exit tool' that is lacking in corporate governance: the possibility to initiate a hard fork at any time.[119] Since cryptocurrencies, and many token-based ventures, are based on open-source software, anybody can create an alternative token that resembles the original one but changes a set of rules that users were discontented with.

However, as we have seen, unregulated hard forks create the very uncertainty that ought to be reduced. Therefore, a key challenge to external cryptocurrency governance is the development of a meaningful regime for hard forks. It must strike the difficult balance between safeguarding users' rights to exit and mitigating destabilizing consequences for those remaining with the original version of the token.[120]

Internal governance mechanisms, by contrast, give a voice to users. Most importantly, they would therefore clearly establish community referenda on fundamental matters pertaining to the cryptocurrency or token-based venture. These may comprise, for example, the violation of basic rules of public blockchains, hard forks, and other matters of vital interest to users. Section B will spell out in greater detail how such external and internal governance mechanisms could be implemented within the framework of existing cryptocurrencies and decentralized applications.

---

[115] See also Ying-Ying Hsieh, Jean-Philippe Vergne, and Sha Wang, 'The Internal and External Governance of Blockchain-Based Organizations: Evidence from Cryptocurrencies' in *Bitcoin and Beyond: Blockchains and Global Governance*, edited by M. Campbell-Verduyn (Routledge forthcoming) https://ssrn.com/abstract=2966973.

[116] Garrett Keirns, 'Bitcoin Unlimited Nodes Recover after Second Bug Exploit' (*CoinDesk.com*, 23 March 2017) http://www.coindesk.com/bitcoin-unlimited-releases-bug-patch-as-exploit-brings-down-nodes/.

[117] Hacker and Thomale (n 2), Part IV.B.1.b.ii.(5)(ii).

[118] See, for the selling of shares as a corporate governance instrument, Grundmann (n 99), § 14 [50].

[119] Cf. Linus Nyman and Juho Lindman, 'Code Forking, Governance, And Sustainability In Open Source Software' (2013) 3 *Technology Innovation Management Review*, 7.

[120] See section IV.B.2.f.

B. Implementation: the Blockchain Governance Code

Arguably, the greatest innovation in the theory and practice of corporate governance since the 1990s has been the elaboration of corporate governance codes.[121] Such codes have expanded across the globe into virtually all industrialized nations;[122] at the European level, the European Commission has recognized them as an effective tool for steering corporate governance through comply or explain. Hence, Article 46a of Directive 2006/46/EC mandated this approach for listed companies in the European Union.[123] In recent years, the comply-or-explain approach has been extended to a number of fields such as say on pay, insider trading, corporate takeover, and rating agency regulation.[124]

Admittedly, corporate governance codes have been criticized as ineffective and excessively focused on control and accountability.[125] However, it remains true that the strength of the comply-or-explain approach lies in offering a 'discretionary solution which nevertheless provides transparency'.[126] As such, it seems ideally suited for blockchain frameworks that currently lack transparency but that equally ought to preserve opportunities for experimentation and innovation.[127]

1. Preconditions for an effective Blockchain Governance Code

Before exploring the content of a Blockchain Governance Code, we have to briefly address the conditions for its effectiveness, as well as some principled objections. In this domain, two issues stand out. First, sufficient incentives must be in place for cryptocurrencies or token sellers to adopt the Code; this is mainly a question of competitive advantage. Second, to the extent that the Code encourages user participation and empowerment, we must credibly rule out user apathy.

Starting with the first and most important prerequisite, it is common ground that voluntary governance codes only work if those adopting them gain an advantage vis-à-vis their competitors;[128] otherwise, compliance costs counsel against their adoption. This requires that competition exists at all in the blockchain ecosystem. In oligopolistic markets such as, for example, the market for credit ratings, a governance code has largely failed to deliver behavioural change; the European legislator therefore switched from code-based self-regulation to command-and-control regulation in late 2008.[129]

However, from a competitive perspective, there are reasons to be more optimistic about the effectiveness of a potential Blockchain Governance Code. Competitors exist in sufficient numbers.[130] Technically, it is possible to start a novel cryptocurrency either via a hard fork[131] or a token sale.[132] Both possibilities are widely used currently. Other than in the case of companies, a hard fork specifically enables developers to copy an existing cryptocurrency

---

[121] R. (Bob) Tricker, 'The Evolution of Corporate Governance' (n 98), 45.

[122] For an empirical analysis, see Alessandro Zattoni and Francesca Cuomo, 'Why Adopt Codes of Good Governance? A Comparison of Institutional and Efficiency Perspectives' (2008) 16 *Corporate Governance: An International Review*, 1.

[123] Directive 2006/46/EC of the European Parliament and of the Council of 14 June 2006, OJ 2006 L 224/1 ('Annual Accounts Amendment Directive').

[124] Leyens, 'Comply or Explain' (n 9), 417–19.   [125] Clarke and Branson (n 99), 4–5 and 11.

[126] Grundmann (n 99), § 14 [12].

[127] Janet Yellen, Letter to Congressman Mick Mulvany (2015) 8, https://de.scribd.com/document/283714666/ Janet-Yellen-Response-to-US-Representative-Mick-Mulvaney-on-Bitcoin; see also Walch, 'The Bitcoin Blockchain' (n 36), 891.

[128] cf. Clarke and Branson (n 99), 5; Leyens, 'Comply or Explain' (n 9), 412.

[129] Niamh Moloney, *EU Securities and Financial Markets Regulation* (Oxford University Press 2014), 644–48; Leyens, 'Comply or Explain' (n 9).

[130] For a detailed analysis of competition issues surrounding blockchain, see Chapter 18 by Lianos in this volume.

[131] Nyman and Lindman (n 119).   [132] Hacker and Thomale (n 2); Rohr and Wright (n 2).

and change it only in one, decisive detail.[133] Hence, competitors offering highly substitutable goods or services can arise at any moment in an open-source community like the blockchain ecosystem. This generates specific competitive dynamics and credible threats of rivalry in case of dissent, as the recent Bitcoin hard forks have shown. These competitors are often not negligible fantasy products but are serious contenders: Ethereum Classic and Bitcoin Cash, having both arisen of hard forks, currently have the ninth and third highest market capitalization of all cryptocurrencies, respectively.[134] Litecoin, another Bitcoin spinoff, occupies the fifth rank.[135] Ethereum has a first-mover advantage concerning the hosting of ICOs and smart contracts but Eos and Neo are providing increasingly viable alternatives.[136]

Low switching costs between these competitors raise competitive pressure on incumbents. Cryptocurrency exchanges enable users to switch from one currency to the other. Rising liquidity in these exchanges makes convertibility ever more feasible;[137] and Bancor provides a decentralized app for inter-currency conversion.[138] Therefore, even though the market capitalization of Bitcoin and Ethereum is still unrivalled at the moment, competitive pressure seems to be mounting among cryptocurrencies.[139] This holds even more true for ICO-financed decentralized apps that are created almost on a daily basis.

Therefore, offering users a clear framework for governance, and a path to participation, is increasingly viewed as a distinguishing component that confers a competitive advantage. For example, the Tezos token was precisely designed to improve governance matters; ironically, the Tezos foundation has now been caught in a governance crisis of its own.[140] Its staggering success in the token sale, however, arguably testifies to the demand for governance solutions. Furthermore, Ethereum, as the following examples will show (section IV.B.2), already implements a number of desiderata of a governance code. If Ethereum was to endorse large parts of a Blockchain Governance Code, it could prompt competitors to follow suit.

Turning to the second issue, giving more power to users raises concerns of the adequacy of user participation in governance matters. After all, shareholder apathy is often cited as an example for the ineffectiveness of shareholder rights;[141] by analogy, user apathy needs to be confronted by a Blockchain Governance Code. There are at least two answers to this problem. First, mandatory user participation can, and should, be restricted to fundamental matters concerning the blockchain-based organization (section IV.B.2.e below). This runs in parallel to the largely accepted dogma in corporate law where shareholders equally vote on fundamental matters concerning the company.[142] Second, the online nature of blockchain technology makes user participation more feasible and more expectable; after all, those using the technology often (though not always) do so out of a desire to acquire voice and avoid a system steered by a central authority.[143] However, the explanations for departures from the Code would have to be disclosed in cognitively optimized ways, for example by using colour coding, to have an impact on user behaviour.[144]

---

[133] Narayanan and Goldfelder (n 72), Ch. 3.6; De Filippi and Loveluck (n 36), 8.

[134] CoinMarketCap, 'Cryptocurrency Market Capitalizations', https://coinmarketcap.com/.

[135] ibid.

[136] Max Moeller, 'Ethereum Competitors: Guide to the Alternative Smart Contract Platforms' (*Blockonomi. com*, 26 February 2018) https://blockonomi.com/ethereum-competitors/.

[137] J. P. Buntinx, 'Cryptocurrency ICO Education—the Basics' (*TheMerkle*, 6 June 2017) https://themerkle. com/cryptocurrency-ico-education-the-basics/); Rohr and Wright (n 2), 35 ('highly liquid'); eventually, with the increasing number of exchanges (there are more than 100 currently, see CoinMarketCap, 'Top 100 Cryptocurrency Exchanges by Trade Volume', https://coinmarketcap.com/rankings/exchanges/), liquidity is improving, too: Prableen Bajpai, 'Liquidity of Bitcoins' (*Investopedia*, 8 January 2018) http://www.investopedia. com/articles/investing/112914/liquidity-bitcoins.asp.

[138] Eyal Hertzog, Guy Benartzi, and Galia Benartzi, 'Bancor Protocol' (2017) White Paper.

[139] Hsieh et al. (n 115), 22.   [140] Hochstein (n 6).   [141] Velasco (n 105), 622.

[142] Velasco (n 105), 623.

[143] See, e.g., Jarred Hope, Chris Volosovskyi, Ricardo Hutchinson et al., 'The Status Network' (2017) White Paper, 6.

[144] See generally on the importance of understandable disclosure Philipp Hacker, 'Nudge 2.0: The Future of Behavioral Law and Economics, in Europe and Beyond' (2016) 24 *ERPL*, 313; for corporate governance

Therefore, although the success of a Blockchain Governance Code cannot be guaranteed, its effectiveness is sufficiently plausible. If, at the end, a governance code did not lead to significant behavioural change, the uptake rate and explanations for non-adoption still generate knowledge for regulators to base more coercive regulation on.[145]

2. *The content of a Blockchain Governance Code*

The content of a Blockchain Governance Code should be determined by a representative working group that comprises experts and stakeholders as well as user representatives. Eventually, this group could evolve into a self-regulatory organization, an 'ICANN for blockchains' (section IV.C below). Proposals for the Code's content can only be sketched in this chapter; however, the following guidelines can be offered. Overall, the Code should contain provisions on (i) the creation of organs that represent certain stakeholders; (ii) transparency, especially of decisions by core developers; (iii) fiduciary duties owed by core developers; (iv) foundational rules of blockchain-based cryptocurrencies; (v) rights of the user community; (vi) rules on hard forks; and (vii) rules for mining pool operators. Following the example of the UK Corporate Governance Code,[146] *Main Principles* as well as *Specific Rules* should be included in the Blockchain Governance Code. The former provides a general framework of good governance and guides the interpretation of the rules, which, in turn, spell out the implementation of the principles with greater precision.

a. Establishing organs: the group of core developers and the community of users

The UK Corporate Governance Code starts with the observation that '[e]very company should be headed by an effective board which is collectively responsible for the long-term success of the company'.[147] The cryptocurrency ecosystem, by contrast, has been characterized by loose and informal coalitions so far. The lack of formal authority has led to a lack of accountability and foreseeability—to complex behaviour at the expense of users (see section III). The first major challenge in the elaboration of a good governance scheme is thus the creation of clearly delineated organs whose members have certain rights and duties. This is a necessary precondition for formulating rights that one group of stakeholders has vis-à-vis another. Therefore, the first *Main Principle* of the Blockchain Governance Code ought to be: *Blockchain-based organizations must establish organs for core developers (responsible for the management of everyday affairs) and users (responsible for deciding fundamental matters).*

Borrowing a simple version of a principal–agent model from corporate governance, we may liken owners of cryptocoins to shareholders (i.e. to principals); and core developers to managers (i.e. to agents). This also implies that blockchain-based organizations should primarily cater to the interests of users who invest in them—and not to groups of miners or core developers. Such a perspective embodies the spirit of Nakamoto's Bitcoin White Paper, which introduced blockchain technology as a means to overcome the problem of trusted parties precisely to allow for decentralized but secure interaction between diffused users.[148] However, it does not prevent developers from taking external factors, such as financial stability and the concern of stakeholders other than users, into account, too (see section IV.B.2.c below).

Specific Rules can govern the formation of the respective organs. While everyone owning a cryptocoin (henceforth the term 'user' shall be restricted to these owners[149]) forms part

---

explanations specifically, see Articles 8–10 of Commission Recommendation 2014/208/EU (9 April 2014) on the quality of corporate governance reporting ('comply or explain'), OJ 2014 L 109/43.

[145] Patrick Leyens, 'Selbstbindungen an untergesetzliche Verhaltensregeln' (2015) 215 *AcP*, 614; Leyens, 'Comply or Explain' (n 9).

[146] UK CGC (n 95), 4 [2].   [147] ibid., section A.1.   [148] Nakamoto (n 28), 1.

[149] Note that one can own cryptocoins without running a node; see, for Bitcoin, Antonopoulos (n 27), 6.

of the community of principals, it is more difficult to clearly establish who should count as a core developer. Therefore, each cryptocurrency (Bitcoin, Ethereum, etc.) should appoint, as a first step, a group of core developers by majority vote of the community of users. In the case of token-based ventures (Filecoin, Status, Bancor, etc.), however, a development team is generally already identified in the White Paper; if this is the case, this team should form the initial core developer organ. From then on, new core developers should be appointed by a majority vote of the existing group of core developers.

This departs significantly from corporate governance practices where the influential Cadbury Report, for example, recommended as a key corporate governance improvement the establishment of a nomination committee with independent directors to propose new board member.[150] However, a nomination committee seems excessively burdensome for the cryptocurrency ecosystem in which many core developers still contribute to the project on a voluntary and unpaid basis. One must be careful not to create compliance costs that would deter most cryptocurrencies from applying the Code in the first place. This may be different for profit-driven token-based ventures. However, furthermore, existing developers, in the highly specialized field of blockchain-based organizations, have the expertise to know who has the requisite skills to fill a new position. Independent nomination procedures are therefore best reserved for a time when cryptocurrencies have gained even greater market capitalization or when token-based organizations have entered mainstream business. Vis-à-vis a vote by the user community, appointment by existing members allows for more flexible and faster appointments; however, as a balancing element, users should have a right of veto in the appointment of single new members to the group of core developers.

In sum, the two organs of a cryptocurrency or a token-based organization representing the two main stakeholders are the group of core developers, and the community of users (mirroring the board of directors, and the general meeting of shareholders), with a special, separate regime governing mining pool operators.

b. Transparency

Once the organs have been formed, specific rights and obligations can be attached to membership within them. A first and pressing requirement is to enhance the transparency of managerial decision making.[151] In corporate governance, this is achieved, inter alia, by board reports. In the words of the UK Corporate Governance Code: 'The board should present a fair, balanced and understandable assessment of the company's position and prospects.'[152] Transparency also ranks prominently in other corporate governance contexts, for example in financial reporting, risk management, and internal control mechanisms.[153] We can therefore formulate a second *Main Principle*: *The decision-making process of core developers should be transparent to users, particularly in matters pertaining to the update of the protocol.*

The *Specific Rules* should include the following. First, the group of core developers is obliged to maintain a list of current core developers that has to be published on a universally accessible website. Second, in corporate law, shareholders have a right to inspect books and records, which is perceived as a disciplining tool contributing to good corporate governance.[154] Similarly, users should have a right to demand information from core developers about past or present decisions that might affect the valuation of tokens or the rules governing transactions. Finally, core developers ought to report annually on the reasons for making updates to the protocols and on the extent to which miners have been involved in

---

[150] Committee on the Financial Aspects of Corporate Governance, *Report* (Gee 1992), [4.15]; R. (Bob) Tricker, 'The Evolution of Corporate Governance (n 98), 45; see now UK CGC (n 95), section B.2.

[151] Gervais et al. (n 36), 59.   [152] UK CGC (n 95), section C.1.   [153] ibid., section C.3.

[154] See, e.g., Lawrence Hamermesh, 'Twenty Years after Smith v. Van Gorkom: An Essay on the Limits of Civil Liability of Corporate Directors and the Role of Shareholder Inspection Rights' (2006) 45 *Washburn Law Journal*, 283.

managerial decisions (see section IV.B.2.g below). Ethereum is already publishing transcripts of core developer calls, showing that transparency is not prohibitively burdensome.[155]

c. Fiduciary duties

Fiduciary duties are another staple of corporate law owed by management.[156] Similarly, scholars have recently proposed that fiduciary duties should play a greater role in the regulation of data-driven environments.[157] Angela Walch has contended that blockchain core developers and significant miners should assume fiduciary duties towards users who (impliedly) entrust them with the power of maintaining the code and updating the chain.[158] Moreover, if some types of blockchain-based organizations are regarded as partnerships in a legal sense,[159] fiduciary duties may arise by default as a matter of company law.

This section discusses the fiduciary duties of core developers (section IV.B.2.g discusses rules for miners). Importantly, in corporate law, fiduciary duties are part of general corporate law and are (generally) mandatory in nature;[160] hence, they are not part of the corporate governance code. Nevertheless, I would like to submit that, in order to balance incentives for experimentation with accountability, fiduciary duties should in general be included in the Blockchain Governance Code, and thus subjected to the comply or explain framework. Only for particularly important blockchain-based organizations should they be made mandatory (see section IV.B.3 below).

In corporate law, the main question is to whom these duties are owed: only to shareholders, to all stakeholders, or even to the public at large and to the environment?[161] Similarly, we may ask whether core developers should owe fiduciary duties of loyalty and care to the community of users only; also to other stakeholders, such as exchanges, wallet designers, and employees; or whether they should even assume responsibility for, and act in the interest of, financial systemic stability.

In comparative corporate governance, the so-called enlightened shareholder value approach has lately gained prominence.[162] It posits that the interest of shareholders should be at the centre of the actions of management but that the interests of other stakeholders and the public at large can also be taken into account. The main argument for not strictly equating shareholder interests with stakeholder interests is that stakeholders typically maintain contractual relationships with the company that they can use to protect their interests.[163] Similarly, one may argue that cryptocurrency stakeholders (e.g. mining pool operators, exchanges, wallet providers, etc.) are powerful, centralizing intermediaries[164] who may, in contrast to users, contractually safeguard their interests. Nevertheless, questions of financial systemic stability should become increasingly important to managerial decision making as

---

[155] Tapscott and Tapscott, 'Realizing the Potential' (n 79), 15.

[156] R. (Bob) Tricker, *Corporate Governance* (n 104), 102–03.

[157] Jack Balkin, 'Information Fiduciaries and the First Amendment' (2016) 49 *UC Davis Law Review*, 1183; Jack Balkin, 'The Three Laws of Robotics in the Age of Big Data' (2017) 78 *Ohio State Law Journal*, 1217, 1227–31.

[158] Angela Walch, 'Call Blockchain Developers What They Are: Fiduciaries' (9 August 2016) *American Banker*, https://www.americanbanker.com/opinion/call-blockchain-developers-what-they-are-fiduciaries; for a detailed discussion, see her Chapter 3 in this volume.

[159] See Zetzsche et al. (n 113); Mann (n 113); Jonathan Macey, 'An Economic Analysis of the Various Rationales for Making Shareholders the Exclusive Beneficiaries of Corporate Fiduciary Duties' (1991) 21 *Stetson Law Review*, 23.

[160] Mads Adenas and Frank Woolridge, *European Comparative Company Law* (Cambridge University Press 2009), 271–75; under Delaware law, fiduciary duties are mere default rules, however, for LLCs and LPs see, generally, Mohsen Manesh, 'What Is the Practical Importance of Default Rules under Delaware LLC and LP Law?' (2012) *Harvard Business Law Review Online*, 121.

[161] See Macey (n 159).

[162] Grundmann (n 99), § 14 [20]; Paul Davies, 'Enlightened Shareholder Value and the New Responsibilities of Directors' (2005) Lecture at University of Melbourne Law School, http://law.unimelb.edu.au/__data/assets/pdf_file/0014/1710014/94-Enlightened_Shareholder_Value_and_the_New_Responsibilities_of_Directors1.pdf; Clarke and Branson (n 99), 3.

[163] Grundmann (n 99), § 14 [22].   [164] Gervais et al. (n 36), 55–56.

the market capitalization of a cryptocurrency rises. The centre of fiduciary duties, however, should be users who, other than most stakeholders, are not in a position to individually negotiate with the management to safeguard their interests.

Continuing this line of reasoning, a third *Main Principle* should be: *Core developers owe fiduciary duties to users.*

Specific Rules should include the following.[165] First, core developers owe a duty of loyalty to users; they have to act in their best interests. However, this does not prevent them from taking the interests of other stakeholders, and the financial system at large, into account in their decision making, provided they make these considerations transparent. Second, core developers owe a duty of care to users. They have to act competently and use adequate, state-of-the-art technical means to assure the smooth functioning of the blockchain, for payments (in the case of cryptocurrencies) or (additionally) for the product they are developing (storage app, messenger platform, etc.).

d. Adherence to foundational blockchain rules

In corporate law, the duty of good faith prevents managers from violating generally accepted basic corporate norms.[166] Similarly, the group of core developers should promise to adhere to the foundational rules of blockchain-based organizations. Particularly, this implies the fourth *Main Principle*: *The blockchain-based organization adheres to the following two basic rules. First, in case of conflicting chains coming into existence, the longer chain is regarded as the authentic one. Second, the information contained in the authentic chain cannot be retrospectively changed.*

As was shown in section III.C, both basic rules were effectively violated in the Bitcoin and the Ethereum hard fork, respectively. The first rule is crucial because it enshrines user sovereignty over the authenticity of the chain. The second rule prevents the circumvention of the first one and adds a decisive element of stability to validated transactions on the chain. Because both rules, eventually, flow from user power, exemptions from these rules ought to be treated as a matter of competence of the user community—to which we now turn.

e. Community vote on fundamental matters

The competence of the general assembly of shareholders to vote on fundamental matters pertaining to the company is a key component of internal governance by voice.[167] Analogously, the fifth *Main Principle* ought to be: *The community of users should have the right to vote on fundamental matters concerning the blockchain-based organization.*

This is a desideratum that is also voiced by the cryptocurrency community.[168] In fact, returning power to users corresponds precisely to the ethos of blockchain's founding document.[169] Fundamental matters are indeed best decided by all those directly concerned (i.e. the users), to prevent a deadlock. However, a majority vote must suffice for proposals to be adopted.

Specific Rules may list examples of fundamental matters. First, exceptions to the abovementioned foundational rules should only be permissible if the majority of users approve of them. As previously mentioned, Ethereum surveyed users, asking them to express their opinion about the hard fork violating the second foundational rule (no rewriting of the chain) before its implementation; the majority of participants had approved it.[170] Second, hard forks pushed by the group of core developers should be subject to user approval.

---

[165] See also Chapter 3 by Walch in this volume.
[166] Melvin Eisenberg, 'The Duty of Good Faith in Corporate Law' (2006) 31 *Delaware Journal of Corporate Law*, 24.
[167] Velasco (n 105), 610–14.
[168] cf. the proposals to reinforce user voice in Bitcoin Core, De Filippi and Loveluck (n 36), 9.
[169] Nakamoto (n 28), 1.   [170] See n 66.

Third, the question of whether a blockchain-based organization ought to comply with the Blockchain Governance Code should also be decided by the user community—after all, the Code seeks to improve governance first and foremost in the interest of users. As an exception, arguably, the non-adoption of parts of the Code may be decided by the group of core developers in utility or investment tokens if specific sections of the Code would render their projects impossible or highly unlikely to succeed.

These voting rules collectively guarantee that whenever the financial stake or the participation of users in the respective cryptocurrency is fundamentally affected, they cannot be overruled by collusion between core developers, potentially in conjunction with mining pool operators. Core developers, finally, would be under an obligation to set up the necessary technical infrastructure that allows for communication between users and for conducting voting procedures. Carbonvote shows that voting coupled to accounts is technically possible in a cost-effective way.

f. Rules on hard forks

'The right to fork code is built into the very definition of what it means to be an open source program.'[171] Nevertheless, as the case studies have shown, hard forks are another primary source of instability in cryptocurrency environments and can be identified as tipping points that, in the case studies, marked the transition from a stable to an unstable state of the system. Therefore, the Code should contain a sixth *Main Principle* on hard forks: *Rules governing hard forks must balance the users' right to exit with the interest of remaining users in the continued stability of the blockchain-based organization.*

By virtue of *Specific Rules*, those initiating a hard fork (users or developers) should be under an obligation to implement suitable measures to stabilize the value of existing tokens and to cooperate fully with all stakeholders (including wallet designers and exchanges) to guarantee a smooth transition into the newly created chain. They should also be required to install features that prevent unnecessary conflict between the old and the new chain, for example replay protection schemes.[172] While Bitcoin Cash offered such protection, the SegWit2x hard fork proposal lacked it, which significantly increased uncertainty for those willing to stay on the legacy chain before the proposed fork.[173] Finally, as seen previously, hard forks initiated by core developers should be subjected to user approval.[174]

g. Rules for mining pool operators

In the current state of large cryptocurrency systems like Bitcoin, individual miners usually join mining pools.[175] These are managed, on a technological level, by pool-mining protocols that coordinate the contributions of hundreds, or even thousands of miners.[176] Mining pools are (mostly) run by so-called mining pool operators.[177] These operators de facto wield large amounts of computing power—including the ability to direct these resources in support of specific chains in case there is a fork.[178] As it were, they bundle and exercise the 'voting rights' of individual miners, without the explicit authority to do so. In the summer of 2017, almost 95% of Bitcoin and almost 80% of Ethereum mining power was controlled by ten and six mining pools, respectively.[179]

---

[171] Nyman and Lindman (n 119), 8.

[172] Replay protection prevents an attacker from conducting the same transaction twice, once on the old and once on the new chain, after a chain split; see J. P. Buntinx, 'What is a Bitcoin Replay Attack?' (*TheMerkle*, 22 March 2017).

[173] Deschapel (n 75), under 'Unprecedented circumstance'.   [174] ibid., Part IV.B.1.e).

[175] Gervais et al. (n 36), 56; Joseph Bonneau, Andrew Miller, Jeremy Clark et al., 'SoK: Research Perspectives and Challenges for Bitcoin and Cryptocurrencies' (2015), Proceedings of the IEEE Symposium on Security and Privacy, 104, 108.

[176] Antonopoulos (n 27), 207–08.   [177] ibid., 209.   [178] Gervais et al. (n 36), 57.

[179] Loi Luu, Yaron Velner, Jason Teutsch, and Prateek Saxena, 'Smartpool: Practical Decentralized Pooled Mining' (2017), USENIX Security Symposium.

Therefore, mining pool operators occupy a middle ground between core developers and individual users. They do not directly form part of the management team, as they are not implementing updates to the code. However, they exert informal power and control through their miners' computing power. There is a growing concern that the use of that power may be diametrically opposed, at times, to the preferences of the user community.[180]

Hence, the seventh *Main Principle* ought to postulate: *Mining pool operators must refrain from covertly influencing core developers and must direct mining power responsibly.*

Specific Rules of transparency should apply to them for the adoption of, or other types of support for, new versions of reference implementations, particularly after a hard fork. This should prevent covert collusion between mining pool operators and core developers. Irresponsible use, in turn, arises primarily from the intentional exploitation of mining power for inappropriate ends. Thus, first, mining pool operators should be barred from supporting proposals or updates that violate the foundational rules of blockchain unless these violations have been approved by community vote. Second, they would have to provide detailed reasons for refusing to back an update that was approved by the community of users. Finally, the use of disproportionate computing power to launch a so-called 51% attack, exploiting a specific vulnerability in the blockchain set up,[181] would count as irresponsible. As concerns rise about the power of miners, a duty of responsible use legally binds mining pool operators that, until now, have been bound by their goodwill alone.

3. From comply and explain to mandatory compliance

One final lesson can be drawn from corporate governance. For those companies wishing to be listed on stock exchanges, the choice between comply and explain was sometimes replaced by mandatory compliance with the corporate governance code (through the listing rules of the respective stock exchanges).[182] The idea is that those companies whose shares are particularly frequently and publicly traded should adhere to the minimal requirements formulated by the applicable corporate governance code.

Similarly, those individual cryptocurrencies or token-based ventures that assume a certain weight in the financial system should be forced to comply with the Blockchain Governance Code. Arguably, this could be the case once a certain cryptocurrency is granted legal tender status or once a certain threshold of market capitalization is passed. In a similar vein, Angela Walch has argued that, once cryptocurrencies become large enough to be considered 'financial market infrastructures', they should be subject to financial stability rules of the international financial market architecture, for example the Principles for Financial Market Infrastructures.[183] Corporate governance mechanisms ought to be another building block in this regime.

C. The future of blockchain governance

The rise of the internet has shown how a decentralized structure, lacking governance mechanisms can be gradually transformed and subjected to self-regulation by an organization that brings together various stakeholders: the Internet Corporation for Assigned Names and Numbers ('ICANN'). Similarly, an 'ICANN for blockchains' may eventually be necessary to the extent that permissionless blockchains, and the cryptocurrencies and token-based ventures they give rise to, become more interconnected;[184] their respective coins more

---

[180] Rizzo (n 71); J. P. Buntinx, 'Jihan Wu Wants to Accelerate the Bitcoin Unlimited Hard Fork Regardless of Community Sentiment' (*News BTC*, 19 March 2017) http://www.newsbtc.com/2017/03/19/jihan-wu-wants-accelerate-bitcoin-unlimited-hard-fork-regardless-community-sentiment/.

[181] Antonopoulos (n 27), 211–13.   [182] Grundmann (n 99), § 14 [8].

[183] Walch, 'The Bitcoin Blockchain' (n 36), 854.

[184] cf. Tapscott and Tapscott, 'Realizing the Potential' (n 79), 17.

convertible through exchanges;[185] and governance problems are replicated in similar fashion within different blockchain-based organizations.[186] Indeed, the US Commodity Futures Trading Commission (CFTC) Commissioner has explicitly called for a self-regulatory body in the blockchain space.[187] Such a body could develop and update the Blockchain Governance Code and set further industry standards, while avoiding the pitfalls besetting ICANN.[188] In this, the Blockchain Governance Code should be viewed as a dynamic instrument; corporate governance codes also developed in an incremental way.[189]

Therefore, Blockchain Governance Codes should refrain both from regulatory excesses and from an overreliance on disclosure. In a first draft, not all of the problems that have arisen in corporate governance over the years need to or should be addressed. The law of blockchain-based organizations is a very young field that will benefit from an attempt to limit the number of legal provisions to those necessary to solve the most pressing of its current problems; otherwise, compliance costs will likely deter not only organizations from applying the Code but will also impede experimentation and socially beneficial innovation in the long run. A Blockchain Governance Code is an attempt to mitigate governance problems by means of soft law, applicable only if organizations voluntarily decide to adopt it, or if they surpass a threshold of financial importance. If, eventually, these strategies prove incapable of providing stability and user protection, nothing prevents regulators from introducing mandatory solutions later. In fact, in a number of areas such as say on pay, insider trading, takeover, and rating agency regulation, comply-or-explain approaches have been gradually replaced by mandatory regulation.[190] However, until we reach this point, it seems prudent first to introduce a comply-or-explain approach that gives greater leeway to the agents in the system to experiment and to adapt principles and rules to their specific needs.

V. Conclusion

Recent scholarship has discussed the opportunities, but increasingly also the limits, of blockchain-based architectures such as cryptocurrencies or token-based ventures for serving as a novel backbone of our financial system. The present chapter adds to this critical perspective by highlighting the instability and unpredictability that has so far proven to be inherent in major blockchain-based organizations such as Bitcoin and Ethereum. Importantly, it identifies imperfections in existing governance structures as a key source of violations of core blockchain rules that make predictions of the development of these systems highly uncertain.

This chapter therefore highlights the need to analyse, and optimize, decision-making frameworks in blockchain-based organizations. More specifically, it aims to make two novel contributions to the emerging discussion of the law of blockchain. First, it argues that it is analytically profitable to analyse blockchain-based organizations, in their existing format, as complex systems that exhibit both patterns of regularity and unpredictability. Second, legislators should use rules specifically designed to reduce uncertainty by strengthening the elements of order and regularity in a complex system. Based on the analysis of imperfect governance regimes, this chapter suggests adapting the theory and practice of corporate governance codes—and their concomitant 'comply-or- explain approach'—to the reality of

---

[185] See CoinMarketCap (n 137), listing 193 exchanges.
[186] Cf. Tapscott and Tapscott, 'Realizing the Potential' (n 79), 33.
[187] Brian Quintenz, 'Keynote Address by Commissioner Brian Quintenz before the DC Blockchain Summit' (2018) https://www.cftc.gov/PressRoom/SpeechesTestimony/opaquintenz.
[188] Jonathan Koppell, 'Pathologies of Accountability: ICANN and the Challenge of "Multiple Accountabilities Disorder"' (2005) 65 *Public Administration Review*, 94; Michael Geist, 'Fair.com? An Examination of the Allegations of Systemic Unfairness in the ICANN UDRP' (2002) 27 *Brooklyn Journal of International Law*, 903.
[189] R. (Bob) Tricker, 'The Evolution of Corporate Governance' (n 98), 45–47 and 50–52.
[190] Leyens, 'Comply or Explain' (n 9).

cryptocurrencies. In this, it proposes concrete measures to improve the external and internal governance in an attempt to strike a fair balance of power between different stakeholders. Arguably, this would strengthen elements of regularity and order in complex blockchain-based organizations, while allowing developers the discretion to experiment to the benefit of users and the financial system alike.

VI. Bibliography

Adenas Mads and Woolridge Frank, *European Comparative Company Law* (Cambridge University Press 2009).

Adhami Saman, Giudici Giancarlo, and Martinazzi Stefano, 'Why Do Businesses Go Crypto? An Empirical Analysis of Initial Coin Offerings' (2017) Working Paper, 21, https://ssrn.com/abstract=3046209, accessed on 11 January 2019.

Antonopoulos Andreas, *Mastering Bitcoin: Unlocking Digital Cryptocurrencies* (O'Reilly 2014).

Bajpai Prableen, 'Liquidity of Bitcoins', (*Investopedia*, 8 January 2018) http://www.investopedia.com/articles/investing/112914/liquidity-bitcoins.asp, accessed on 11 January 2019.

Balkin Jack, 'Information Fiduciaries and the First Amendment' (2016) 49 *UC Davis Law Review*, 1183.

Balkin Jack, 'The Three Laws of Robotics in the Age of Big Data' (2017) 78 *Ohio State Law Journal*, 1217.

Barsan Iris, 'Legal Challenges of Initial Coin Offerings ("ICO")' (2017) 3 *RTDF*, 54.

Battiston Stefano, Doyne Farmer J., Flache Andreas et al., 'Complexity Theory and Financial Regulation. Economic Policy Needs Interdisciplinary Network Analysis and Behavioral Modeling' (2016) 351 *Science*, 818.

Baumol William and Benhabib Jess, 'Chaos: Significance, Mechanism, and Economic Applications' (1989) 3 *Journal of Economic Perspectives*, 77.

Baur Dirk, Lee Adrian, and Hong Kihoon, 'Bitcoin: Currency or Investment?' (2014) Working Paper, https://ssrn.com/abstract=2561183, accessed on 11 January 2019.

Bayern Shawn, 'Of Bitcoins, Independently Wealthy Software, and the Zero Member LLC' (2014) 108 *Northwestern University Law Review Online*, 257.

Beigel Ofir, 'Segwit vs. Bitcoin Unlimited and Bitcoin's Fork Explained Simply' (*99Bitcoins.com*, 27 March 27/2 April 2017) https://99bitcoins.com/bitcoin-fork-segwit-vs-bitcoin-unlimited-explained-simply/, accessed on 11 January 2019.

BitcoinGold, 'Roadmap', https://bitcoingold.org/, accessed on 11 January 2019.

BitcoinWiki, https://en.bitcoin.it/wiki/Softfork, accessed on 11 January 2019.

BitFury Group and Garzik Jeff, 'Public versus Private Blockchains: Part II: Permissionless Blockchains' (2015).

Black Julia, 'Forms and Paradoxes of Principles-Based Regulation' (2008) 3 *Capital Markets Law Journal*, 425.

Blackman Tim, 'Complexity Theory' in *Understanding Contemporary Society: Theories of the Present*, edited by Gary Browning, Abigail Halcli, and Frank Webster (SAGE, 2000).

Blocke John, '/r/Bitcoin Censorship, Revisited' (*Medium.com*, 27 February 2017) https://medium.com/@johnblocke/r-bitcoin-censorship-revisited-58d5b1bdcd64, accessed on 11 January 2019.

Böhme Rainer, Christin Nicolas, Edelman Benjamin, and Moore Tyler, 'Bitcoin: Economics, Technology, and Governance' (2015) 29 *The Journal of Economic Perspectives*, 213.

Bonneau Joseph, Miller Andrew, Clark Jeremy et al., 'SoK: Research Perspectives and Challenges for Bitcoin and Cryptocurrencies' (2015) Proceedings of the IEEE Symposium on Security and Privacy, 104, 108.

Brousseau Eric, Marzouki Meryem, and Méadel Cécile, *Governance, Regulation and Powers on the Internet* (Cambridge University Press 2012).

Buntinx J. P., 'Bitcoin Core Members Discuss Blockchain Consensus at Chinese Event' (*TheMerkle.com*, 11 December 2016) https://themerkle.com/bitcoin-core-members-discuss-blockchain-consensus-at-chinese-event/, accessed on 11 January 2019.

Buntinx J. P., 'Jihan Wu Wants to Accelerate the Bitcoin Unlimited Hard Fork Regardless of Community Sentiment' (*News BTC*, 19 March 2017) http://www.newsbtc.com/2017/03/19/

jihan-wu-wants-accelerate-bitcoin-unlimited-hard-fork-regardless-community-sentiment/, accessed on 11 January 2019.

Buntinx J. P., 'What is a Bitcoin Replay Attack?' (*TheMerkle*, 22 March 2017).

Buntinx J. P., 'Cryptocurrency ICO Education—the Basics' (*TheMerkle*, 6 June 2017) https://themerkle.com/cryptocurrency-ico-education-the-basics/, accessed on 11 January 2019.

Buterin Vitalik, 'Bitcoin Network Shaken by Blockchain Fork' (*Bitcoin Magazine*, 12 March, 2013) https://bitcoinmagazine.com/articles/bitcoin-network-shaken-by-blockchain-fork-1363144448, accessed on 11 January 2019.

Buterin Vitalik 'A Next Generation Smart Contract and Decentralized Application Platform' (2014) Ethereum White Paper.

Buterin Vitalik, 'Hard Fork Completed' (*EthereumBlog.org*, 20 July 2016) https://blog.ethereum.org/2016/07/20/hard-fork-completed/, accessed on 11 January 2019.

Byrne David, *Complexity Theory and the Social Sciences* (Routledge 1998).

Cheah Eng-Tuck and Fry John, 'Speculative Bubbles in Bitcoin Markets? An Empirical Investigation into the Fundamental Value of Bitcoin' (2015) 130 *Economics Letters*, 32.

Cheah Eng-Tuck and Fry John, 'Negative Bubbles and Shocks in Cryptocurrency Markets' (2016) 47 *International Review of Financial Analysis*, 343.

Clarke Thomas and Branson Douglas, 'Introduction: Corporate Governance—and Emergent Discipline?' in *The SAGE Handbook of Corporate Governance*, edited by Thomas Clarke and Douglas Branson (SAGE 2012).

CoinMarketCap, 'Bitcoin Gold [Futures]', https://coinmarketcap.com/currencies/bitcoin-gold/, accessed on 11 January 2019.

CoinMarketCap, 'Cryptocurrency Market Capitalizations', https://coinmarketcap.com/, accessed on 11 January 2019.

Committee on the Financial Aspects of Corporate Governance, *Report* (Gee 1992).

Craven David, Piercy Nigel, Shipp Shannon, 'New Organizational Forms for Competing in Highly Dynamic Environments: The Network Paradigm' (1996) 7 *British Journal of Management*, 203.

CoinMarketCap, 'Top 100 Cryptocurrency Exchanges by Trade Volume', <https://coinmarketcap.com/rankings/exchanges/>, accessed on 11 January 2019.

Davies Paul, 'Enlightened Shareholder Value and the New Responsibilities of Directors' (2005) Lecture at University of Melbourne Law School, http://law.unimelb.edu.au/__data/assets/pdf_file/0014/1710014/94-Enlightened_Shareholder_Value_and_the_New_Responsibilities_of_Directors1.pdf, accessed on 11 January 2019.

De Filippi Primavera and Loveluck Benjamin, 'The Invisible Politics of Bitcoin: Governance Crisis of a Decentralised Infrastructure' (2016) 5(3) *Internet Policy Review*, 1.

Deschapel Ariel, 'Why Segwit2x Is Doomed to Fail' (*CoinDesk.com*, 6 November 2017) under "Scheduled Chaos", https://www.coindesk.com/opinion-segwit2x-doomed-fail/, accessed on 11 January 2019.

Dwyer Gerald, 'The Economics of Bitcoin and Similar Private Digital Currencies' (2015) 17 *Journal of Financial Stability*, 81.

Eisenberg Melvin, 'The Duty of Good Faith in Corporate Law' (2006) 31 *Delaware Journal of Corporate Law*, 1.

Fama Eugene and Jensen Michael, 'Separation of Ownership and Control' (1983) 26 *The Journal of Law and Economics*, 301.

Financial Reporting Council, UK Corporate Governance Code ('CGC') (2016), [5], https://www.frc.org.uk/Our-Work/Codes-Standards/Corporate-governance/UK-Corporate-Governance-Code.aspx, accessed on 11 January 2019.

Garcia David, Tessone Claudia, Mavrodiev Pavlin, and Perony Nicolas, 'The Digital Traces of Bubbles: Feedback Cycles between Socio-Economic Signals in the Bitcoin Economy' (2014) 11 *Journal of the Royal Society Interface*, 20140623.

Geist Michael, 'Fair.com? An Examination of the Allegations of Systemic Unfairness in the ICANN UDRP' (2002) 27 *Brooklyn Journal of International Law*, 903.

Gervais Arthur, Karame Ghassen, Capkun Vedran, and Capkun Srdjan, 'Is Bitcoin a Decentralized Currency?' (2014) 12(3) *IEEE Security & Privacy*, 54.

GitHub, https://github.com/bitcoin/bips/blob/master/README.mediawiki, accessed on 11 January 2019.

Grundmann Stefan, *European Company Law* (2nd edn, Intersentia 2012).

Hacker Philipp, 'Nudge 2.0: The Future of Behavioral Law and Economics, in Europe and Beyond' (2016) 24 *ERPL*, 297.

Hacker Philipp and Thomale Chris, 'Crypto-Securities Regulation: ICOs, Token Sales and Cryptocurrencies under EU Financial Law' (2018) 15 *European Company and Financial Law Review* 645, https://papers.ssrn.com/sol3/papers.cfm?abstract_id=3075820, accessed on 11 January 2019.

Hamermesh Lawrence, 'Twenty Years after Smith v. Van Gorkom: An Essay on the Limits of Civil Liability of Corporate Directors and the Role of Shareholder Inspection Rights' (2006) 45 *Washburn Law Journal*, 283.

Harvey David and Read Michael, 'The Evolution of Dissipative Social Systems' (1994) 17 *Journal of Social and Evolutionary Systems*, 371.

Hertig Alyssa, 'Bitcoin Cash: Why It's Forking the Blockchain and What That Means' (*CoinDesk.com*, 26 July 2017) https://www.coindesk.com/coindesk-explainer-bitcoin-cash-forking-blockchain/, accessed on 11 January 2019.

Hertig Alyssa, 'Bitcoin Gold: What to Know About the Blockchain's Next Split' (*CoinDesk.com*, 23 October 2017) https://www.coindesk.com/bitcoin-gold-know-blockchains-next-split/, accessed on 11 January 2019.

Hertig Alyssa, '2x Called Off: Bitcoin Hard Fork Suspended for Lack of Consensus' (*CoinDesk.com*, 8 November 2017) https://www.coindesk.com/2x-called-off-bitcoin-hard-fork-suspended-lack-consensus/, accessed on 11 January 2019.

Hertzog Eyal, Benartzi Guy, Benartzi Galia, 'Bancor Protocol' (2017) White Paper.

Hirschman Albert, *Exit, Voice, and Loyalty: Responses to Decline in Firms, Organizations, and States* (Harvard University Press 1970).

Hochstein Marc, 'Tezos Founders on ICO Controversy: "This Will Blow Over"' (*CoinDesk.com*, 25 October 2017) https://www.coindesk.com/tezos-founders-ico-controversy-will-blow/ , accessed on 11 January 2019.

Hofmann Jeanette, Katzenbach Christian, and Goliatz Kirsten, 'Between Coordination and Regulation: Finding the Governance in Internet Governance' (2016) *New Media and Society*, 1.

Hommes Cars, *Behavioral Rationality and Heterogeneous Expectations in Complex Economic Systems* (Cambridge University Press 2013).

Hope Jarred, Volosovskyi Chris, Hutchinson Ricardo et al., 'The Status Network' (2017), White Paper.

Hsieh David, 'Chaos and Nonlinear Dynamics: Application to Financial Markets' (1991) 46 *Journal of Finance*, 1839.

Hsieh Ying-Ying, Vergne Jean-Philippe, and Wang Sha, 'The Internal and External Governance of Blockchain-Based Organizations: Evidence from Cryptocurrencies' in *Bitcoin and Beyond: Blockchains and Global Governance*, edited by M. Campbell-Verduyn (Routledge 2017), 48.

Kauffman Stuart, *At Home in the Universe. The Search for Laws of Self-Organization and Complexity* (Oxford University Press 1995).

Keirns Garrett, 'Bitcoin Unlimited Nodes Recover after Second Bug Exploit' (*CoinDesk.com*, 23 March 2017) http://www.coindesk.com/bitcoin-unlimited-releases-bug-patch-as-exploit-brings-down-nodes/, accessed on 11 January 2019.

Koppell Jonathan, 'Pathologies of Accountability: ICANN and the Challenge of "Multiple Accountabilities Disorder"' (2005) 65 *Public Administration Review*, 94.

LeBaron Blake, 'Agent-Based Computational Finance' in *Handbook of Computational Economics*, edited by Leigh Tesfatsion and Kenneth L. Judd (Volume 2, North-Holland 2006).

Levy David, 'Chaos Theory and Strategy: Theory, Application, and Managerial Implications' (1994) 15 *Strategic Management Journal*, 167.

Leyens Patrick, 'Selbstbindungen an untergesetzliche Verhaltensregeln' (2015) 215 *AcP* 611.

Leyens Patrick, 'Comply or Explain' (2016) *ZEuP*, 388.

Luu Loi, Velner Yaron, Teutsch Jason, and Saxena Prateek, 'Smartpool: Practical Decentralized Pooled Mining' (2017) USENIX Security Symposium.

Macey Jonathan, 'An Economic Analysis of the Various Rationales for Making Shareholders the Exclusive Beneficiaries of Corporate Fiduciary Duties' (1991) 21 *Stetson Law Review*, 23.

Manesh Mohsen, 'What Is the Practical Importance of Default Rules under Delaware LLC and LP Law?' (2012) *Harvard Business Law Review Online*, 121.

Mann Maximilian, 'Die Decentralized Autonomous Organization—ein neuer Gesellschaftstyp?' (2017) 26 *NZG*, 1014.

Manne Henry, 'Mergers and the Market for Corporate Control' (1965) 73 *Journal of Political Economy*, 110.

Max Moeller, 'Ethereum Competitors: Guide to the Alternative Smart Contract Platforms' (*Blockonomi.com*, 26 February 2018) https://blockonomi.com/ethereum-competitors/, accessed on 11 January 2019.

Moloney Niamh, *EU Securities and Financial Markets Regulation* (Oxford University Press 2014).

Nakamoto Satoshi, 'Bitcoin: A Peer-to-Peer Electronic Cash System' (31 October 2008) https://bitcoin.org/bitcoin.pdf, accessed on 11 January 2019.

Narayanan Arvind, 'Analyzing the 2013 Bitcoin Fork: Centralized Decision-Making Saved the Day' (26 July 2015) https://freedom-to-tinker.com/blog/randomwalker/analyzing-the-2013-bitcoin-fork-centralized-decision-making-saved-the-day/, accessed on 11 January 2019.

Narayanan Arvind, Bonneau Joseph, Felten Edward, Miller Andrew, and Goldfelder Steven, *Bitcoin and Cryptocurrency Technologies. A Comprehensive Introduction* (Princeton University Press 2016).

Nian Lam Pak and Lee David Kuo Chuen, 'Introduction to Bitcoin' in *Handbook of Digital Currency* (edited by David Lee Kuo Chuen (Elsevier 2015).

Nyman Linus and Lindman Juho, 'Code Forking, Governance, and Sustainability in Open Source Software' (2013) 3 *Technology Innovation Management Review*, 7.

O'Leary Rachel, 'Parity Says 'No Intention' to Split Ethereum over Fund Recovery' (*CoinDesk.com*, 26 April 2018) https://www.coindesk.com/parity-says-no-intention-to-split-ethereum-over-fund-recovery/, accessed on 11 January 2019.

Paech Philipp, 'The Governance of Blockchain Financial Networks' (2017) 80(6) *Modern Law Review*, 1073.

Parker Luke, 'Ethereum Hard Fork Results in Two Surviving Cryptocurrencies, Both Are Now Trading' (*BraveNewCoin.com*, 26 July 2016) https://bravenewcoin.com/news/ethereum-hard-fork-results-in-two-surviving-cryptocurrencies-both-are-now-trading/, accessed on 11 January 2019.

Peters Edgar, *Fractal Market Analysis. Applying Chaos Theory to Investment and Economics* (Wiley 1994).

Protocol Labs, 'Filecoin: A Decentralized Storage Network' (2017) Updated White Paper.

Quintenz Brian, 'Keynote Address by Commissioner Brian Quintenz before the DC Blockchain Summit' (2018) https://www.cftc.gov/PressRoom/SpeechesTestimony/opaquintenz8, accessed on 11 January 2019.

Reddit, 'Critical Update RE: DAO Vulnerability' (2016) https://www.reddit.com/r/ethereum/comments/4oiqj7/critical_update_re_dao_vulnerability, accessed on 11 January 2019.

Rizzo Pete, 'Making Sense of Bitcoin's Divisive Block Size Debate' (*CoinDesk.com*, 19 January 2016) http://www.coindesk.com/making-sense-block-size-debate-bitcoin/, accessed on 11 January 2019.

Rizzo Pete, 'Understanding Segwit2x: Why Bitcoin's Next Fork Might Not Mean Free Money' (*CoinDesk.com*, 1 November 2017) https://www.coindesk.com/understanding-segwit2x-bitcoins-next-fork-might-different/, accessed on 11 January 2019.

Rizzo Pete and Hertig Alyssa, 'Relief and Disbelief: Bitcoin Reacts to Sudden '2x' Suspension' (*CoinDesk.com*, 8 November 2017) https://www.coindesk.com/relief-disbelief-bitcoin-reacts-sudden-2x-suspension/, accessed on 11 January 2019.

Rohr Jonathan and Wright Aaron, 'Blockchain-Based Token Sales, Initial Coin Offerings, and the Democratization of Public Capital Markets' (forthcoming) 70 *Hastings Law Journal*, https://papers.ssrn.com/sol3/papers.cfm?abstract_id=3048104.

Shin Laura, 'Will This Battle for the Soul of Bitcoin Destroy It?' (*Forbes.com*, 23 October 2017) https://www.forbes.com/sites/laurashin/2017/10/23/will-this-battle-for-the-soul-of-bitcoin-destroy-it/#3f4e323d3c0, accessed on 11 January 2019.

Siegel David, 'Understanding the DAO Attack' (*Coindesk.com*, 25 June 2016) http://www.coindesk.com/understanding-dao-hack-journalists/, accessed on 11 January 2019.

Strevens Michael, *Bigger than Chaos. Understanding Complexity through Probability* (Harvard University Press 2003).

Tapscott Don and Tapscott Alex, *Blockchain Revolution* (Penguin 2016).

Tapscott Don and Tapscott Alex, 'Realizing the Potential of Blockchain' (2017), World Economic Forum White Paper.

Thiétart R. and Forgues B., 'Chaos Theory and Organization' (1995) 6 *Organization Science*, 19.

Tricker R. (Bob), *Corporate Governance* (2nd edn, Oxford University Press 2012).

Tricker R. (Bob), 'The Evolution of Corporate Governance' in *The SAGE Handbook of Corporate Governance*, edited by Thomas Clarke and Douglas Branson (SAGE, 2012).

Turnbull Shann, *A New Way to Govern: Organizations and Society after Enron* (New Economics Foundation Pocketbook 2002).

Turnbull Shann, 'The Limitations of Corporate Governance Best Practices' in *The SAGE Handbook of Corporate Governance*, edited by Thomas Clarke and Douglas Branson (SAGE, 2012).

US Securities Exchange Commission ('SEC'), 'Report of Investigation Pursuant to Section 21(a) of the Securities Exchange Act of 1934: The DAO' (25 July 2017) Release No. 81207.

Velasco Julian, 'Taking Shareholder Rights Seriously' (2007) 41 *UC Davis Law Review*, 605.

Walch Angela, 'The Bitcoin Blockchain as Financial Market Infrastructure: A Consideration of Operational Risk' (2015) 18 *New York University Journal of Legislation and Public Policy*, 837.

Walch Angela, 'Call Blockchain Developers What They Are: Fiduciaries' (9 August 2016) *American Banker*, htps://www.americanbanker.com/opinion/call-blockchain-developers-what-they-are-fiduciaries.

Waldrop Mitchell, *Complexity. The Emerging Science at the Edge of Order and Chaos* (Simon & Schuster 1992).

Wilke Jeffrey, 'To Fork or Not to Fork' (*EthereumBlog.org*, 15 July 2016) https://blog.ethereum.org/2016/07/15/to-fork-or-not-to-fork/, accessed on 11 January 2019.

Wirdum Aaron van, 'Segregated Witness, Part 1: How a Clever Hack Could Significantly Increase Bitcoin's Potential' (*BitcoinMagazine.com*, 19 December 2015) https://bitcoinmagazine.com/articles/segregated-witness-part-how-a-clever-hack-could-significantly-increase-bitcoin-s-potential-1450553618/, accessed on 11 January 2019.

Witte Jan, 'The Blockchain: A Gentle Introduction' (2016) Working Paper, https://ssrn.com/abstract=2887567, accessed on 11 January 2019.

Wong Joon Ian and Klar Ian, 'Everything You Need to Know About The Ethereum "Hard Fork"' (*Quartz*, 18 July 2016) http://qz.com/730004/everything-you-need-to-know-about-the-ethereum-hard-fork/, accessed on 11 January 2019.

World Economic Forum, 'Realizing the Potential of Blockchain' (2017), White Paper.

Yellen Janet, Letter to Congressman Mick Mulvany (2015) 8, https://de.scribd.com/document/283714666/Janet-Yellen-Response-to-US-Representative-Mick-Mulvaney-on-Bitcoin, accessed on 11 January 2019.

Yermack David, 'Is Bitcoin a Real Currency: An Economic Appraisal' in *Handbook of Digital Currency*, edited by David Lee Kuo Chuen (Elsevier 2015).

Yermack David, 'Corporate Governance and Blockchains' (2017) 21 *Review of Finance*, 7.

Zattoni Alessandro and Cuomo Francesca, 'Why Adopt Codes of Good Governance? A Comparison of Institutional and Efficiency Perspectives' (2008) 16 *Corporate Governance: An International Review*, 1.

Zetzsche Dirk, Buckley Ross, and Arner Douglas, 'The Distributed Liability of Distributed Ledgers: Legal Risks of Blockchain' (forthcoming), *University of Illinois Law Review*, https://papers.ssrn.com/sol3/papers.cfm?abstract_id=3018214, accessed on 11 January 2019.

PART III

BLOCKCHAIN AND THE FUTURE OF BANKING, FINANCE, INSURANCE, AND SECURITIES REGULATION

8

Banking in a Digital Fiat Currency Regime

Rohan Grey

I. Introduction

In recent years, policy-makers around the world have begun to experiment with new forms of central bank-issued digital currency technology.[1] At the same time, there has been growing scholarly and political interest in the direct public provisioning of digital payments and basic banking services to both retail and wholesale non-bank customers, either through the expansion of central bank services to non-bank actors,[2] or the creation of new public or postal banking institutions.[3]

Together, these developments point towards a possible future in which both retail and wholesale transactions are settled directly via a universally accessible, public digital payments network, without recourse to the current bank depository system.[4] Such a digital fiat currency ('DFC') regime could significantly increase payment efficiency and access to payments services amongst the unbanked and underbanked,[5] while improving transactional privacy by preserving the possibility of decentralized, anonymous, cash-like digital payments.[6]

Currently, most discussions of DFC proposals have yet to fully grapple with the implications of widespread retail deposit flight upon banking-sector dynamics or macroprudential

---

[1] See, e.g., Max Seddon and Martin Arnold, 'Putin Considers "Cryptoruble" as Moscow Seeks to Evade Sanctions' (*FinancialTimes.com*, 1 January 2018) https://www.ft.com/content/54d026d8-e4cc-11e7-97e2-916d4fbac0da; Lynsey Chutel, 'West Africa Now Has Its Own Digital Currency' (*Quartz.com*, 27 December 2016) https://qz.com/872876/fintech-senegal-is-launched-the-ecfa-digital-currency/; Riksbank Sveriges, The Riksbank's E-Krona Project (*Sveriges Riksbank*, September 2017) https://www.riksbank.se/globalassets/media/rapporter/e-krona/2017/rapport_ekrona_uppdaterad_170920_eng.pdf; Will Knight, 'China's Central Bank Has Begun Cautiously Testing a Digital Currency' (2017) *MIT Technology Review*, https://www.technologyreview.com/s/608088/chinas-central-bank-has-begun-cautiously-testing-a-digital-currency/; Ben Schiller, 'Ecuador is the World's First Country with a Digital Cash System' (*FastCompany.com*, 10 August 2015) https://www.fastcompany.com/3049536/ecuador-is-the-worlds-first-country-with-a-public-digital-cash-system.

[2] See, e.g., Morgan Ricks, John Crawford, and Lev Menand, 'A Public Option for Bank Accounts (or Central Banking for All)' (2018) Vanderbilt Law Research Paper, 18–33, https://papers.ssrn.com/sol3/papers.cfm?abstract_id=3192162; Thurvald Grung Moe, 'Shadow Banking: Policy Challenges for Central Banks' (2014) Levy Economics Institute Working Paper No. 802, http://citeseerx.ist.psu.edu/viewdoc/download?doi=10.1.1.434.3922&rep=rep1&type=pdf.

[3] A. P. Joyce, 'Progressive Groups are Launching a Movement to Create a Public Bank in New York City' (*Mic.com*, 6 June 2018) https://mic.com/articles/189687/progressive-groups-are-launching-a-movement-to-create-a-public-bank-in-new-york-city#.hqKRq1Plo; Daniel Marans, 'Kristen Gillibrand Unveils a Public Option for Banking' (*HuffPost.com*, 25 April 2018) https://www.huffingtonpost.com/entry/kirsten-gillibrand-postal-banking-bill_us_5ae07f9fe4b07be4d4c6feae; Mehrsa Baradaran, 'It's Time for Postal Banking' (2014) 127 *Harvard Law Review*, 165; Heather Morton, 'Many States See the Potential of Public Banking' (*NYTimes.com*, 1 October 2013) https://www.nytimes.com/roomfordebate/2013/10/01/should-states-operate-public-banks/many-states-see-the-potential-of-public-banking.

[4] See, e.g., Jonathan Dharmapalan and Rohan Grey, 'The Macroeconomic Policy Implications of Digital Fiat Currency' (*eCurrency.net*, 2017) https://www.ecurrency.net/static/resources/201802/TheMacroeconomicImplicationsOfDigitalFiatCurrencyEVersion.pdf.

[5] See, e.g., Jonathan Dharmapalan and Carolyn Hall McMahon, 'Central Bank Issued Digital Currency and Its Impact on Financial Inclusion' (*eCurrency.net*, 2016) https://www.ecurrency.net/static/resources/201802/TheCaseForDigitalLegalTender-ImpactOnFinancialInclusion.pdf.

[6] See, e.g., David Clarke, 'The Future of Cash: Protecting Access to Payments in the Digital Age' (*PositiveMoney.org*, 25 March 2018) http://positivemoney.org/wp-content/uploads/2018/03/Positive-Money-Future-of-Cash.pdf.

regulation more broadly.[7] Instead, most policy-makers identify the risk of a run from deposits towards DFC as unequivocally negative outcome.[8] Indeed, some proposals even include limits on DFC functionality intended to reduce the risk of deposit flight occurring.[9]

This chapter takes a different approach. Rather than attempting to minimize the disruptive impact of DFC technology, it embraces the possibility of widespread consumer flight out of bank deposits and into the DFC payments network, on the basis that such a shift would improve the safety and functioning of the financial system.[10] From this view, the critical question is not how to preserve the banking system as it currently exists, but rather how to preserve the socially valuable functions of banking, while jettisoning those aspects that have been rendered obsolete or inferior compared to modern alternatives, such as a dedicated public payments network.

In particular, I argue that the core social responsibility of the banking system is not to maintain a monopoly over payments processing but to conduct credit analysis and collateral evaluation in ways that promote the capital development of the economy.[11] By accepting a borrower's IOU, or a pledge of collateral of a certain quality, in exchange for its own, more liquid and publicly supported deposit liabilities, banks engage in a form of credit laundering.[12] That is to say, they effectively transform illiquid promissory notes or collateral assets into demand deposits with greater 'moneyness'[13] by virtue of their underwriting and validation practices. Bank deposits, in turn, are backstopped by the central bank and the political authority of the backing monetary sovereign through deposit insurance, discount window access, lender of last resort support and a general commitment to maintain at-par convertibility between fiat currency and bank deposits. Thus, as Hockett and Omarova have argued, the act of commercial bank lending resembles a franchised exercise of sovereign monetary power in which a bank generates new purchasing power, backed by the sovereign, and gives it to a borrower, in exchange for a commitment to repay a specified amount in the future.[14]

---

[7] A notable exception is Ricks et al. (n 2), whose analysis and arguments closely resemble those articulated in this chapter.

[8] See, e.g., Bank of International Settlements ('BIS'), 'Central Bank Digital Currencies' (2018) Bank of International Settlements, Committee on Payments and Market Infrastructures Report No. 174, 16, https://www.bis.org/cpmi/publ/d174.pdf: 'Arguably, the most significant and plausible financial stability risk of a general purpose CBDC is that it can facilitate a flight away from private financial institutions and markets towards the central bank.'

[9] See, e.g., John Barrdear and Michael Kumhof, 'The Macroeconomics of Central Bank Issued Digital Currencies' (2016), Bank of England Staff Working Paper No. 605, 15, https://papers.ssrn.com/sol3/papers.cfm?abstract_id=2811208, who propose quantitative restrictions on the supply of central bank digital currency.

[10] As shadow banking scholar Zoltan Poszar has argued, the existence of deposit insurance caps on individual accounts renders the retail banking system unsuitable for the large institutional cash pools held by money managers. This, in turn, has contributed to the structural undersupply of safe assets relative to investor demand prior to 2008, which fuelled the growth of shadow banking. Zoltan Poszar, 'Can Shadow Banking Be Addressed without the Balance Sheet of the Sovereign?' (*Vox.org*, 16 November 2011) https://voxeu.org/article/shadow-banking-what-do.

[11] The term 'capital development' was used by Hyman Minsky to refer to 'a broad measure of investment that goes beyond privately owned capital equipment ... to include technology, human capital, and public infrastructure'. Mariana Mazzucato and L. Wray, 'Financing the Capital Development of the Economy: A Keynes-Schumpeter-Minsky Synthesis' (2015) Levy Economics Institute Working Paper No. 837, 2, http://www.levyinstitute.org/pubs/wp_837.pdf.

[12] Hyman Minsky described this as the 'acceptance' function of banking. See, e.g., *Stabilizing an Unstable Economy* (McGraw-Hill 2008 [1986]), 256: 'the fundamental banking activity is accepting, that is, guaranteeing that some party is credit worthy. A bank, by accepting a debt instrument, agrees to make specific payments if the debtor will not or can not. Such an accepted or endorsed note can then be sold in the open market.'

[13] See, e.g., J. P. Koning, 'Why Moneyness?' (*Moneyness*, 4 December 2012) http://jpkoning.blogspot.com/2012/12/why-moneyness.html: 'when it comes to monetary analysis, you can divide the world up two ways. The standard way is to draw a line between all those things in an economy that are "money" and all those things which are not ... The second way to classify the world is to ... ask the following sorts of questions: in what way are all of these things money-like? How does the element of moneyness inhere in every valuable object? To what degree is some item more liquid than another?'

[14] Robert Hockett and Saule Omarova, 'The Finance Franchise' (2017) 102 *Cornell Law Review*, 1143.

In this sense, commercial banking is, at least, in part, a form of delegated public policy-making,[15] whereby financial authorities establish regulatory standards and guidelines for the banking system, which, in turn, determines the kinds of profitable lending activities banks are permitted to engage in as franchisees of the monetary sovereign. Crucially, however, banks do not require a monopoly over the payments system or even any control over consumer payment accounts whatsoever in order to fulfil this social function. With the correct technical, accounting, and legal framework, it is possible to preserve the core underwriting and collateral evaluation functions of contemporary banking, even while allowing—and encouraging—deposit outflow as part of a broader shift towards a DFC-centred universal payments system.[16]

The remainder of this chapter proceeds as follows. Section II explores the legal, economic, and operational dynamics of modern commercial banking. Section III introduces a conceptual framework for evaluating the relevant features of a DFC-centred monetary regime. Section IV outlines one legal and accounting approach to preserving core features of modern banking under a DFC regime, while section V considers potential challenges and objections to such an approach. Section VI concludes by recommending further research into the macroprudential implications of digital fiat currency technology.

II. Modern Commercial Banking

In order to understand the relationship between digital fiat currency technology and the banking system, it is important to first clarify what is meant by modern commercial banking. Contrary to popular understanding, commercial banks do not simply act as intermediaries between borrowers and savers by lending out existing depositor funds, anchored by a 'fractional reserve'.[17] Instead, commercial bank lending involves the creation of new purchasing power, *ex nihilo*, through banks' acceptance of borrowers' loans, or other adequate collateral, in exchange for newly created demand deposits.[18] This process, in which loans make deposits, rather than the other way around, has been described as 'fountain pen' money, as bankers effectively create new monetary instruments with the stroke of a pen by approving new loans.[19]

From a balance sheet perspective, the act of 'acceptance' of a borrower's loan involves four simultaneous entries, consisting of two pairs of identical entries on the two actors' respective balance sheets:

1. The borrower records its new loan as a liability on its balance sheet;

2. the bank records the borrower's new loan as an asset on its balance sheet;

3. the borrower records the bank's new demand deposit balance as an asset on its balance sheet; and

4. the bank records its new demand deposit balance as a liability on its balance sheet.

---

[15] ibid., 1215.

[16] See, e.g., Dharmapalan and Grey (n 4). Note that this proposal is distinct from the traditional 'Chicago Plan' proposals, in that it proposes the separation of banks and payments institutions, rather than the complete elimination of banking itself. For more on the Chicago Plan and its limits, see Jan Kregel, 'Minsky and the Narrow Banking Proposal' (2012) Levy Economics Institute Public Policy Brief No. 125, http://www.levyinstitute.org/pubs/ppb_125.pdf.

[17] See, e.g., Michael McLeay, Amar Radia, and Thomas Ryland, 'Money Creation in the Modern Economy' (2014) Bank of England Quarterly Bulletin, Q1, https://www.bankofengland.co.uk/-/media/boe/files/quarterly-bulletin/2014/money-creation-in-the-modern-economy.pdf; Paul Sheard, 'Repeat After Me: Banks Cannot and Do Not "Lend Out" Reserves' (2013), Standard & Poor's RatingsDirect, https://www.kreditopferhilfe.net/docs/S_and_P__Repeat_After_Me_8_14_13.pdf.

[18] Banks only need to obtain reserves to settle interbank payments and transfers on behalf of customers to another bank or the government, or to satisfy minimum reserve requirements.

[19] McLeay et al. (n 17), 16.

Thus, the end result is that the borrower's balance sheet has both an asset (deposits) and liability (loan), and the bank has both an asset (loan) and liability (deposits).

In addition to accepting actors' unsecured IOUs, banks may also choose to accept certain kinds of real or financial assets as collateral for a secured loan, on the understanding that in the event of borrower default, the bank is granted rights over the pledged collateral. In these situations, banks are responsible for evaluating not only the creditworthiness of the borrower, but also the value of the underlying collateral. Thus, contemporary banking involves making decisions about the creditworthiness of actors and the value of collateral assets, often in combination.[20]

In addition to determining whether a borrower and/or pledged collateral is adequate to warrant extending a loan, banks also have to ensure that the loans they acquire are consistent with their regulatory requirements regarding capital adequacy, leverage, and liquidity coverage ratios.[21] Crucially, however, such requirements do not require the accumulation of passive, liquid settlement balances prior to extending a new loan.[22] Indeed, it is possible for a new loan to satisfy its own capital requirements, i.e. if the lending bank charges an origination fee that it then records as retained earnings.[23] Thus, the overriding limit on bank lending activity is not availability of loanable funds but the perceived profitability of the loan relative to the cost of the liabilities required to fund it.[24]

Funding costs include not only the rate of interest paid on the newly created deposits, but also the cost of securing any additional liquidity necessary to satisfy daily settlement needs and reserve requirements, if they exist. In a floating fiat currency regime, settlement liquidity is not restricted in quantity but is made available upon demand to the market, at a price consistent with the central bank's prevailing overnight rate target.[25] In such contexts, central banks must provide settlement reserves on demand to the banking sector, at whatever quantity they require, or else risk serious disruption to the payments system and loss of control over interest rate policy.[26]

The most simple and straightforward way for banks to acquire additional funding is to either sell assets or borrow the funds directly from the central bank at the prevailing discount rate, either on an unsecured basis or in exchange for pledging adequate collateral. By contrast, in countries with established interbank markets, and/or deep capital markets, banks have historically sought funding from banks and/or other financial institutions[27] first and only relied on the central bank as a last resort.[28] This is due, in part, to the perceived stigma

---

[20] Indeed, collateral-driven financial dynamics are a dominant driver of both commercial and shadow banking activity in the modern economy. See Daniela Gabor and Jakob Vestergaard, 'Toward a Theory of Shadow Money' (2016) The Institute for New Economic Thinking, https://www.ineteconomics.org/uploads/papers/Towards_Theory_Shadow_Money_GV_INET.pdf; Annalise Riles, *Collateral Knowledge: Legal Reasoning in the Global Financial Markets* (University of Chicago Press 2011).

[21] In addition, banks have additional non-financial regulatory requirements, such as Know-Your-Customer ('KYC') and Anti-Money Laundering ('AML'), that must be satisfied before extending a loan.

[22] Sheard (n 17).

[23] John Carney, 'Basics of Banking: Loans Create a Lot More than Deposits' (*CNBC.com*, 26 February 2018) https://www.cnbc.com/id/100497710, explains this process.

[24] In this context, 'funding liabilities' refers to the deposits issued to the borrower at the point of extension of the loan, which typically pay interest, and thus represent an interest-earning liability of the issuing bank. For an extended treatment of this issue, see Basil Moore, *Horizontalists and Verticalists: The Macroeconomics of Credit Money* (Cambridge University Press 1988).

[25] Scott Fullwiler, 'Modern Central Bank Operations—the General Principles' in *Advances in Endogenous Money Analysis*, edited by Louis-Philippe Rochon and Sergio Rossi (Edward Elgar 2017), 6.

[26] Scott Fullwiler, 'Setting Interest Rates in the Modern Era' (2006) 28(3) *Journal of Post Keynesian Economics*, 514: 'because the Fed must accommodate overnight and (even larger) intraday demands for reserve balances to achieve its target ... the Fed's commitment to its target is always being "tested"'.

[27] In recent decades, the share of overall bank funding sourced directly from capital market lenders, as opposed to depositors, has increased dramatically. See, e.g., Adam Tooze, *Crashed: How a Decade of Financial Crises Changed the World* (Viking 2018), 111–12 (noting that prior to the 2008 crisis, less than 20% of Northern Rock's funding came from deposits).

[28] Since the implementation of quantitative easing following the global financial crisis, many banking systems around the world have been awash in excess settlement balances, causing the interbank lending market

of using the discount window,[29] and, in part, to the discount rate often being intentionally set above the prevailing market rate as part of an interest rate corridor system of monetary policy implementation.[30]

In addition, banks also seek to attract retail and wholesale depositors, who represent a relatively cheap and stable source of funds compared to the central bank or discount window.[31] For example, in an environment where the prevailing cost of overnight reserves is 2% but the average rate paid out to depositors is 1%, it may be cheaper to attract new depositors or poach existing depositors from other banks than to borrow reserves directly from the central bank or overnight money market. Unfortunately, this practice has given the impression that banks need to acquire deposits in order to then 'lend them out', when, in fact, deposits represent a liability of the bank and, thus, can never be 'borrowed' by the bank itself.[32]

Each of these approaches to obtaining additional liquidity (central bank discount window lending, interbank market borrowing, and deposit seeking) have different balance sheet dynamics and exert different effects on the broader financial system. Nevertheless, they represent equally viable sources of additional funding liquidity, even as their relative attractiveness depends on prevailing regulatory, market, and interest rate conditions.

Indeed, it is possible to imagine a context in which a bank continues to lend in the absence of both interbank lending *and* additional depositor funding. In such a system, bank settlement liquidity is obtained exclusively via direct overdrafts from the central bank on either a secured or unsecured basis.[33] As long as other regulatory requirements are satisfied, banks are free to continue making loans they perceive to be profitable relative to the prevailing overdraft interest rate.

Thus, it is clear that contemporary banks do not require customer deposits, or other forms of idle funds, in order to extend new loans.[34] Furthermore, the fact that central banks are required to defensively accommodate the banking system's demand for additional reserves in order to maintain control over its target interest rate,[35] as well as the existence of other banking system supports such as deposit insurance, clearly establishes that bank lending is not a purely private endeavour.[36] Rather, it represents a form of indirect government sponsorship of private activity undertaken by a privileged class of chartered, limited liability depository institutions.[37] Thus, as Hockett and Omarova argue, banks are best thought of today as licensed franchisees of the monetary sovereign, responsible for allocating the full faith and credit of the monetary sovereign in accordance with collateral and prudential regulatory standards intended to promote economic development and the capital formation of the economy.[38] Banks may exercise discretion in choosing which loans and forms of collateral

---

to largely dry up. See, e.g., Stephen Cecchetti and Kermit Schoenholtz, 'Bank Financing: The Disappearance of Interbank Lending' (2018) Money & Banking, https://www.moneyandbanking.com/commentary/2018/3/4/bank-financing-the-disappearance-of-interbank-lending.

[29] See, e.g., Mark Carlson and Jonathan Rose, 'Stigma and the Discount Window' (2017) Federal Reserve System —FEDS Notes, https://www.federalreserve.gov/econres/notes/feds-notes/stigma-and-the-discount-window-20171219.htm.

[30] See, e.g., George Kahn, 'Monetary Policy under a Corridor Operating Framework' (2010) Federal Reserve Bank of Kansas City Economic Review (Q4), https://www.kansascityfed.org/publicat/econrev/pdf/10q4Kahn.pdf.

[31] See, e.g., Ellen Brown, "Why Do Banks Want Our Deposits? Hint: It's Not to Make Loans' (*Web of Debt*, 27 October 2014) https://ellenbrown.com/2014/10/26/why-do-banks-want-our-deposits-hint-its-not-to-make-loans/.

[32] See Sheard (n 17).

[33] Ultimately, all settlement liquidity, including that which banks seek via interbank loans and depositor funding, originates from the central bank. Thus, of the three sources of liquidity identified above, it makes most sense to focus primarily on central bank's balance sheet.

[34] McLeay et al. (n 17).   [35] Fullwiler, 'Setting Interest Rates' (n 26).

[36] Hockett and Omarova, 'The Finance Franchise' (n 14).

[37] See, e.g., Robert Hockett and Saule Omarova, 'Special, Vestigial, or Visionary? What Bank Regulation Tells Us About the Corporation—and Vice Versa' (2015) 39 *Seattle Law Review*, 453: '[r]ediscovering and reaffirming [the] painfully derived historical understanding of banks' public–private franchise nature should once again be at the top of our policy agenda'.

[38] Hockett and Omarova, 'The Finance Franchise' (n 14).

to 'accept', but their decisions are bounded and guided by the legal requirements of their banking charters, deposit insurance schemes, and the prevailing macroprudential regulatory framework.[39]

III. Imagining Digital Fiat Currency

There are many varying proposals to extend the range of financial services and products offered directly by the public sector. Many of these proposals share similar policy goals and operational outcomes but differ in the legal or institutional form by which they seek to achieve them. For example, proposals to introduce postal/public bank and central bank retail accounts share many similarities in terms of their impact on consumer behaviour and their ability to provide a public option in contrast to private banks but they have vastly different implications for intra-government legal and accounting practices.

For the purposes of this chapter, a DFC regime is defined as a monetary regime with a universally accessible and interoperable payments network, managed by the government, which settles and stores balances in digital fiat currency units that are legal tender[40] and are readily convertible at par with other forms of government currency. Such a regime could be implemented via universal retail central bank or public/postal bank deposit accounts[41] and/ or a decentralized e-wallet network in which wallet-holders exchange DFC balances without intermediaries via an open, secure transaction protocol, similar to certain kinds of mobile money transactions today.[42]

Under such a regime, individuals could manage their own accounts or wallets, or, alternatively, could authorize payments intermediaries to make transactions from their wallet on their behalf.[43] Intermediaries could even host or manage accounts or wallets on their clients' behalf, similar to commercial email hosts or lawyers' escrow accounts. Unlike with commercial banking, however, the individual would retain direct ownership over the DFC balance in question, rather than exchanging it for a generalized deposit liability against the intermediary.[44]

In addition to expanding the availability of basic consumer banking services, a DFC regime could significantly improve the stability of the broader financial system by providing large, institutional investors with access to safe, cash-like accounts not subject to deposit

---

[39] See, e.g., the guidelines issued by the Federal Reserve regarding what collateral they would accept in discount window lending. Federal Reserve Discount Window, 'Pledging Collateral' (2018) https://www.frbdiscountwindow. org/RightNavPages/Pledging-Collateral.aspx.

[40] The critical aspect of legal tender status that gives an instrument a high degree of moneyness is acceptability in payment of taxes. Acceptability for payment of private debts is an additional benefit to an IOU's 'moneyness', but not a necessary one.

[41] See, e.g., Ricks et al. (n 2); Baradaran (n 3).   [42] See Dharmapalan and Grey (n 4).

[43] Such a set-up would allow for competition and choice in consumer-facing, API-layer applications, whilst preserving the standardization and integrity of the back-end accounting database.

[44] The relevant legal principle is that of 'bailment', which predates the origins of transferable deposit law in the sixteenth century. According to legal-monetary historian Benjamin Geva, there were originally two different kinds of bailment rights relevant to monetary custodianship: the first concerned bailment with respect to a sum of money, which gave rise to a rightwhile; the second concerned bailment over a particular 'bag' or 'box' that contained money. Benjamin Geva, 'Bank Money: The Rise, Fall, and Metamorphosis of the "Transferable Deposit"' in *Money in the Western Legal Tradition*, edited by David Fox and Wolfgang Ernst (Oxford University Press 2015), 361. The former, known as a 'right of debt', ultimately developed into the modern depository obligation, while the latter, also known as a 'right of detinue', remained focused on chattel property. ibid., 362. In the context of government-managed accounts, the right of debt would likely suffice, whereas for individual wallets, a right of detinue would be necessary to prevent mixing between the individual wallet holder's funds and the intermediary's funds. See Richard Werner, 'How Do Banks Create Money, and Why Can Other Firms Not Do the Same? An Explanation for the Co-existence of Lending and Deposit-Taking' (2014) 36 *International Review of Financial Analysis*, 71, arguing that contemporary banks' unique money-creation powers derive in part from the relaxing for banks of standard Client Money Rules, which prevent the mixing of client and personal funds.

insurance caps.[45] This, in turn, would reduce demand for private 'near-monies' and treasury securities to serve as alternative forms of 'wholesale money'.[46]

A DFC regime could also potentially simplify monetary and fiscal policy operations by facilitating direct monetary finance of fiscal spending (while monetary policy is maintained entirely through central bank balance sheet operations).[47] Under such a system, monetary policymakers could pay interest directly on DFC accounts[48] and/or issue central bank securities and other instruments to maintain a government securities market and a maturity yield curve if they so desired.[49] This would also eliminate the need for banks and other financial intermediaries to serve as primary dealers in treasury auctions, thereby further reducing entanglement between public financial operations and the banking system.[50]

IV. Commercial Bank Lending under a DFC Regime

As discussed in section II, commercial bank lending is best understood as the franchised extension of sovereign monetary power to a limited class of licensed financial institutions. These institutions are empowered to extend the full faith and credit of the sovereign to borrowers, in accordance with public lending standards, in pursuit of profit and the capital development of the economy. Furthermore, while commercial bank loan-making occurs primarily via accounting operations conducted on the bank's balance sheet, the socially valuable aspects of credit and collateral analysis take place off the balance sheet. Thus, they can be maintained even under a different monetary regime with different accounting practices.

In the context of a DFC regime, the fundamental design question is how to accommodate large-scale deposit flight away from the banking system and into the DFC system without undermining bank lending activity. Or, to put it another way, the challenge is how to create a banking system that does not include any bank deposits.

From an accounting perspective, the solution to this problem is remarkably simple. Commercial banks could be authorized to extend DFC overdrafts directly to successful loan applicants who are creditworthy and/or whose proffered collateral meets prudential regulatory standards. Such overdrafts could be obtained from the government (or central bank) via a secure loan, collateralized by the newly created loan asset.[51] These DFC overdrafts would,

---

[45] Currently, in the United States, deposit insurance is capped at $250,000 per account, thereby limiting its functional use for large, institutional cash-pool investors.

[46] According to Poszar (n 10), the undersupply of safe, government-guaranteed instruments, in the form of either insured bank deposits or government-guaranteed cash/securities played a large role in the growth of shadow banking activity prior to the global financial crisis.

[47] For example, the treasury could announce that all future fiscal spending would be implemented through the direct injection of DFC balances, which would be offset by the simultaneous issuance of new central bank securities at auction. From the market's perspective, the end result of this process would be functionally similar to the Treasury conducting a securities auction, and the central bank engaging in open market operations ('OMOs') in order to sterilize any imbalances in reserve levels caused by the auction (or subsequent fiscal spending). See, e.g., Scott Fullwiler, 'Treasury Debt Operations: An Analysis Integrating Social Fabric Matrix and Social Accounting Matrix Methodologies' (2011), Social Science Research Network Working Paper, https://papers.ssrn.com/sol3/papers.cfm?abstract_id=1825303.

[48] It could be possible, for example, to conduct monetary policy via paying interest directly on excess DFC balances, similar to the practice of paying interest on excess reserves. See Scott Fullwiler, 'Paying Interest on Reserve Balances: It's More Significant Than You Think' (2004), Social Science Research Network Working Paper, https://papers.ssrn.com/sol3/papers.cfm?abstract_id=1723589.

[49] For more on the central bank securities and their capacity to serve as a substitute for treasury securities in money market operations, see Simon Gray and Runchana Pongsaparn, 'Issuance of Central Bank Securities: International Experiences and Guidelines' (2015), International Monetary Fund Working Paper No. 15-106, https://www.imf.org/external/pubs/ft/wp/2015/wp15106.pdf.

[50] Of course, this disentanglement process would likely require structural changes to existing public budgeting and accounting practices.

[51] It would also be possible to achieve a similar result via extending unsecured loans; however, for reasons discussed below, such an approach would be less desirable from a macroprudential regulatory perspective, as it would limit the ability of regulators to inspect bank assets and would permit banks to continue to sell, lend, and pledge their assets in the secondary lending markets, rather than holding them to maturity.

in turn, be recorded as a liability of the lending bank, and an asset of the government (or central bank).[52]

Hence, the four-entry accounting record of a bank loan described in section II would be replaced with a six-entry process, reflecting the government's new role as explicit central counterparty to the transaction:

1. The borrower records its new loan as a liability on its balance sheet;

2. the bank records the borrower's new loan as an asset on its balance sheet;

3. the borrower records its new DFC balance as an asset on its balance sheet;

4. the government (central bank) records the new DFC balance as a liability on its balance sheet;

5. the bank records its DFC overdraft as a liability on its balance sheet; and

6. the government (central bank) records the bank's DFC overdraft as an asset on its balance sheet.

For the borrower, the end result is functionally identical to under the current process of obtaining a loan, except that they end up holding DFC balances as an asset, rather than demand deposits.[53] Given that DFC balances would not have deposit insurance caps and would be more interoperable across payments media than deposits, this represents an improvement in security and flexibility for the borrower.

For the lending bank, however, the accounting treatment is somewhat similar but the legal and financial dynamics are very different. In particular, the bank's balance sheet features a new loan asset, and a new DFC overdraft liability (instead of a deposit liability) and its profits are still determined by the spread between the risk-adjusted return on the loan, and the prevailing interest rate paid on the DFC overdraft. However, because the bank pledges the new loan asset as collateral to secure the DFC overdraft, it retains the right to any income earned on the asset but is unable to securitize, sell, or repledge the loan in the secondary market. Furthermore, the bank must maintain a DFC overdraft equivalent to the full value of the loan, in contrast to the current system, whereby it must only seek reserve balances to satisfy settlement and minimum reserve requirements. Thus, a DFC system restricts secondary market trading, forcing banks to effectively hold loans to maturity, while simultaneously replacing depositor funding risk with central bank-determined interest rate risk.[54]

For the government, the regulatory and accounting treatment of bank lending is also vastly different under a DFC regime, along with most other aspects of macroeconomic policy. First, providing automatic DFC overdrafts for the full value of loans at the point they are made effectively transforms the discount window from a liquidity provider of last resort into a lender of first resort for the banking system.[55] This, in turn, eliminates the need for interbank lending markets and significantly reduces the risk of liquidity crises and contagion

---

[52] In many respects, this set-up resembles the US financial system in the postbellum era. At that time, national banks pledged government securities to the treasury in exchange for national bank notes, which circulated as legal tender currency. However, because government securities were in limited supply, demand for bank notes outstripped capacity, encouraging the rise of new forms of shadow 'near monies'. By contrast, under the approach proposed here, intermediaries would be permitted to submit a wider range of collateral in exchange for DFC balances, thereby reducing the pressure to provide alternative monies. See Nathan Tankus, 'Receivability for Public Dues: The Unrecognized Glue of the Antebellum Monetary System' (2019), Institute for Sustainable Prosperity Working Paper (unpublished); Howard Bodenhorn, *A History of Banking in Antebellum America: Financial Markets and Economic Development in an Era of Nation-Building* (Cambridge University Press 2000).

[53] Another way of viewing this transaction is as a quasi-fiscal operation, in which the lender, acting as a public spending franchisee, makes a payment of new DFC dollars to the borrower, and later 'taxes' back an amount equivalent to the total repayment amount of the loan.

[54] As discussed in section II, this would not be an issue in terms of bank lending rates, provided the policy rate was kept sufficiently low.

[55] See Ricks et al. (n 2).

in the event of bank failure. Second, providing safe, liquid DFC funds directly to borrowers, and insulating them from direct exposure to their lending bank, effectively eliminates the need for deposit insurance, while significantly reducing the likelihood of commercial banks becoming 'too big to fail'. Third, requiring banks to pledge their entire loan book as collateral in exchange for DFC overdrafts increases financial market transparency and makes it easier for regulators and auditors to inspect the quality of loans and experiment with different risk models used for evaluating loans and collateral.[56] Fourth, making explicit the fiscal/monetary aspect of bank lending allows policy-makers and the public to directly compare the social value of additional lending compared to additional public spending and to compare the broader effects of banking activity on the macroeconomy.

Therefore, it is clearly possible to preserve, and even strengthen, basic commercial banking services under a DFC regime, albeit in ways that potentially alter and transform the existing financial system and underlying power dynamics between customers, banks, and public authorities.[57]

V. Criticisms and Concerns

One potential objection to this approach is that it would drastically expand the government's presence in lending markets and expose it to potential financial losses in the event of bank failure. While this is accurate, there is nothing intrinsically harmful or undesirable about a large government balance sheet expansion accompanied by a parallel contraction in the combined balance sheet of the banking system. Indeed, such a shift would significantly reduce the implicit public subsidies granted to the banking system as well as the economic and regulatory costs of maintaining deposit insurance and other forms of banking support. Furthermore, eliminating interbank lending and keeping customers' funds ringfenced away from banks' balance sheets will reduce the fragility and interconnectedness of the banking system, thereby minimizing the systemic costs of individual bank failure.

Another objection is that requiring banks to borrow DFC balances equivalent to the full value of their loan books is significantly more costly than requiring them to borrow reserves for interbank settlement and other liquidity-related needs. However, this concern is easily addressed. Simply by reducing the interest rate charged on DFC overdrafts until the effective cost of funds is similar or equivalent to what it would be under a traditional banking system. Alternatively, it would be entirely feasible to establish a permanent zero interest rate on DFC overdrafts to lending institutions and instead regulate overall bank lending rates through qualitative credit controls and adjustments to bank lending fees and tax rates.

A third concern is that such a system would place an excessive administrative burden on the government, both in terms of liquidity provisioning and loan/collateral review and inspection. While it is undoubtedly true that transitioning to a DFC regime would require a large-scale restructuring of existing public financial regulatory practices as well as a carefully managed transitional period, the end result would be a much more coherent financial architecture and macroprudential framework, which, in turn, would simplify regulatory enforcement and reduce administrative overhead. Thus, any additional administrative costs of DFC system regulation would likely be offset by the reduced costs of banking system regulation as well as the improved efficiency of the underlying payments and banking system.

A fourth concern is that a DFC-based system would peel back the 'monetary veil' of how public finance and banking actually work, thereby causing a general market panic

---

[56] In this sense, a DFC-based banking system has the potential to improve capital risk weighting practices and refigure the debate over future modifications to the Basel Accords.

[57] The implications of a DFC system for shadow banking and the financial system more general are equally important questions; however, it is beyond the scope of this chapter to attempt to address them here.

and collapse in the value of currency and the financial system more broadly.[58] While this is possible, it is far more likely that a DFC regime would do exactly the opposite. It would serve as a teaching moment to educate the populace about how money and banking actually work and, in doing, so open up new spaces for debate and political action in ways that improve the financial system.

VI. Conclusion

DFC technologies today are still in their infancy, with a wide range of models and permutations vying for viability and dominance. As central bankers and the broader public begin to consider more seriously proposals for new, large-scale public payments and banking infrastructure reform, the second- and third-order economic and regulatory implications of DFC technologies are likely to receive increasing attention and scrutiny.

For advocates of expanded public payments and banking services, it is critical to develop a clear and comprehensive vision of the interaction between DFC technologies and the broader financial system, including banking activities, in order to address theoretical and practical concerns and objections in the planning stage. This chapter offers only a brief glimpse of such a vision. Further research is necessary to address more granular questions relating to: (i) loan approval and discount window operations; (ii) collateral adequacy and loan evaluation standards; (iii) bank balance sheet reporting requirements; and (iv) the implications of DFC technology for shadow banking and collateral-based capital market activity.

Overall, DFC technology, if properly designed and implemented, could revolutionize the payments system, and with it the financial system and economy more broadly. Just as importantly, it has the potential to spark a new public discussion around money, banking, and the future of the financial system.

VII. Bibliography

Bank of International Settlements ('BIS'), 'Central Bank Digital Currencies' (2018) Bank of International Settlements, Committee on Payments and Market Infrastructures Report No. 174, 16, https://www.bis.org/cpmi/publ/d174.pdf, accessed on 12 January 2019.

Baradaran Mehrsa, 'It's Time for Postal Banking' (2014) 127 *Harvard Law Review*, 165.

Barrdear John and Kumhof Michael, 'The Macroeconomics of Central Bank Issued Digital Currencies' (2016) Bank of England Staff Working Paper No. 605, 15, https://papers.ssrn.com/sol3/papers.cfm?abstract_id=2811208, accessed on 12 January 2019.

Bodenhorn Howard, *A History of Banking in Antebellum America: Financial Markets and Economic Development in an Era of Nation-Building* (Cambridge University Press 2000).

Brown Ellen, 'Why Do Banks Want Our Deposits? Hint: It's Not to Make Loans' (*Web of Debt*, 27 October 2014) https://ellenbrown.com/2014/10/26/why-do-banks-want-our-deposits-hint-its-not-to-make-loans/, accessed on 12 January 2019.

Buchanan Neil, 'If You're Explaining, Everyone's Losing (Platinum Coin Edition)' (*Dorf on Law*, 11 January 2013) http://www.dorfonlaw.org/2013/01/if-youre-explaining-everyones-losing.html, accessed on 12 January 2019.

---

[58] See, e.g., Neil Buchanan, 'If You're Explaining, Everyone's Losing (Platinum Coin Edition)' (*Dorf on Law*, 11 January 2013) http://www.dorfonlaw.org/2013/01/if-youre-explaining-everyones-losing.html: 'If the [trillion-dollar platinum coin is] merely an accounting fiction ... then why should anyone care? We should care, because looking "undignified" is not merely a matter of rustling the hoop skirts of nervous Nellies. Even business columnists at top newspapers like *The New York Times* make a big deal of the Fed "creating money out of thin air," ... We are ... talking about pulling back the curtain on the entirely ephemeral nature of money and finance itself. That will affect not just Wall Street traders, but everyone in the world. A monetary system simply cannot work if people do not collectively take a leap of faith.... If the delusion starts to fall apart, then there are very real, very negative effects.'

Carlson Mark and Rose Jonathan, 'Stigma and the Discount Window' (2017), Federal Reserve System—FEDS Notes, https://www.federalreserve.gov/econres/notes/feds-notes/stigma-and-the-discount-window-20171219.htm, accessed on 12 January 2019.

Carney John, 'Basics of Banking: Loans Create a Lot More than Deposits' (*CNBC.com*, 26 February 2018) https://www.cnbc.com/id/100497710, accessed on 12 January 2019.

Cecchetti Stephen and Schoenholtz Kermit, 'Bank Financing: The Disappearance of Interbank Lending' (2018) *Money & Banking*, March 5, https://www.moneyandbanking.com/commentary/2018/3/4/bank-financing-the-disappearance-of-interbank-lending>, accessed on 12 January 2019.

Chutel Lynsey, 'West Africa Now Has Its Own Digital Currency' (*Quartz.com*, 27 December 2016) https://qz.com/872876/fintech-senegal-is-launched-the-ecfa-digital-currency/, accessed on 12 January 2019.

Clarke David, 'The Future of Cash: Protecting Access to Payments in the Digital Age (*PositiveMoney.org*, 25 March 2018) http://positivemoney.org/wp-content/uploads/2018/03/Positive-Money-Future-of-Cash.pdf, accessed on 12 January 2019.

Dharmapalan Jonathan and Grey Rohan, 'The Macroeconomic Policy Implications of Digital Fiat Currency' (*eCurrency.net*, 2017) https://www.ecurrency.net/static/resources/201802/TheMacroeconomicImplicationsOfDigitalFiatCurrencyEVersion.pdf, accessed on 12 January 2019.

Dharmapalan Jonathan and Hall McMahon Carolyn, 'Central Bank Issued Digital Currency and Its Impact on Financial Inclusion' (*eCurrency.net*, 2016) https://www.ecurrency.net/static/resources/201802/TheCaseForDigitalLegalTender-ImpactOnFinancialInclusion.pdf, accessed on 12 January 2019.

Federal Reserve Discount Window, 'Pledging Collateral' (2018) https://www.frbdiscountwindow.org/RightNavPages/Pledging-Collateral.aspx, accessed on 12 January 2019.

Fullwiler Scott, 'Paying Interest on Reserve Balances: It's More Significant than You Think' (2004) Social Science Research Network Working Paper, https://papers.ssrn.com/sol3/papers.cfm?abstract_id=1723589, accessed on 12 January 2019.

Fullwiler Scott, 'Setting Interest Rates in the Modern Era' (2006) 28(3) *Journal of Post Keynesian Economics*, 496.

Fullwiler Scott, 'Treasury Debt Operations: An Analysis Integrating Social Fabric Matrix and Social Accounting Matrix Methodologies' (2011) Social Science Research Network Working Paper, https://papers.ssrn.com/sol3/papers.cfm?abstract_id=1825303, accessed on 12 January 2019.

Fullwiler Scott, 'Modern Central Bank Operations—The General Principles' in *Advances in Endogenous Money Analysis*, edited by Louis-Philippe Rochon and Sergio Rossi (Edward Elgar 2017).

Gabor Daniela and Vestergaard Jakob, 'Toward a Theory of Shadow Money' (2016) *The Institute for New Economic Thinking*, https://www.ineteconomics.org/uploads/papers/Towards_Theory_Shadow_Money_GV_INET.pdf, accessed on 12 January 2019.

Geva Benjamin, 'Bank Money: The Rise, Fall, and Metamorphosis of the "Transferable Deposit"' in *Money in the Western Legal Tradition*, edited by David Fox and Wolfgang Ernst (Oxford University Press 2015).

Gray Simon and Pongsaparn Runchana, 'Issuance of Central Bank Securities: International Experiences and Guidelines' (2015) International Monetary Fund Working Paper No. 15-106, https://www.imf.org/external/pubs/ft/wp/2015/wp15106.pdf, accessed on 12 January 2019.

Hockett Robert and Omarova Saule, 'Special, Vestigial, or Visionary? What Bank Regulation Tells Us about the Corporation—and Vice Versa' (2015) 39 *Seattle Law Review*, 453.

Hockett Robert and Omarova Saule, 'The Finance Franchise' (2017) 102 *Cornell Law Review*, 1143.

Joyce A. P., 'Progressive Groups are Launching a Movement to Create a Public Bank in New York City' (*Mic.com*, 6 June 2018) https://mic.com/articles/189687/progressive-groups-are-launching-a-movement-to-create-a-public-bank-in-new-york-city#.hqKRq1PIo, accessed on 12 January 2019.

Kahn George, 'Monetary Policy under a Corridor Operating Framework' (2010), Federal Reserve Bank of Kansas City Economic Review (Q4) 5, https://www.kansascityfed.org/publicat/econrev/pdf/10q4Kahn.pdf, accessed on 12 January 2019.

Knight Will, 'China's Central Bank Has Begun Cautiously Testing a Digital Currency' (2017) *MIT Technology Review*, https://www.technologyreview.com/s/608088/chinas-central-bank-has-begun-cautiously-testing-a-digital-currency/, accessed on 12 January 2019.

Koning J. P., 'Why Moneyness?' (*Moneyness*, 4 December 2012) http://jpkoning.blogspot.com/2012/12/why-moneyness.html, accessed on 12 January 2019.

Kregel Jan, 'Minsky and the Narrow Banking Proposal' (2012) Levy Economics Institute Public Policy Brief No. 125, http://www.levyinstitute.org/pubs/ppb_125.pdf, accessed on 12 January 2019.

Marans Daniel, 'Kristen Gillibrand Unveils a Public Option for Banking' (*HuffPost.com*, 25 April 2018) https://www.huffingtonpost.com/entry/kirsten-gillibrand-postal-banking-bill_us_5ae07f9fe4b07be4d4c6feae, accessed on 12 January 2019.

Mazzucato Mariana and Wray L., 'Financing the Capital Development of the Economy: A Keynes–Schumpeter-Minsky Synthesis' (2015) Levy Economics Institute Working Paper No. 837, 2, http://www.levyinstitute.org/pubs/wp_837.pdf, accessed on 12 January 2019.

McLeay Michael, Radia Amar, and Ryland Thomas, 'Money Creation in the Modern Economy' (2014) Bank of England Quarterly Bulletin, Q1, https://www.bankofengland.co.uk/-/media/boe/files/quarterly-bulletin/2014/money-creation-in-the-modern-economy.pdf, accessed on 12 January 2019.

Minsky Hyman, *Stabilizing an Unstable Economy* (McGraw-Hill 2008 [1986]).

Moe Thurvald Grung, 'Shadow Banking: Policy Challenges for Central Banks' (2014) Levy Economics Institute Working Paper No. 802, http://citeseerx.ist.psu.edu/viewdoc/download?doi=10.1.1.434.3922&rep=rep1&type=pdf, accessed on 12 January 2019.

Moore Basil, *Horizontalists and Verticalists: The Macroeconomics of Credit Money* (Cambridge University Press 1988).

Morton Heather, 'Many States See the Potential of Public Banking' (*NYTimes.com*, 1 October 2013) https://www.nytimes.com/roomfordebate/2013/10/01/should-states-operate-public-banks/many-states-see-the-potential-of-public-banking, accessed on 12 January 2019.

Poszar Zoltan, 'Can Shadow Banking Be Addressed without the Balance Sheet of the Sovereign?' (*Vox.org*, 16 November 2011) https://voxeu.org/article/shadow-banking-what-do, accessed on 12 January 2019.

Ricks Morgan, Crawford John, and Menand Lev, 'A Public Option for Bank Accounts (Or Central Banking For All)' (2018) Vanderbilt Law Research Paper, 18, https://papers.ssrn.com/sol3/papers.cfm?abstract_id=3192162, accessed on 12 January 2019.

Riles Annalise, *Collateral Knowledge: Legal Reasoning in the Global Financial Markets* (University of Chicago Press 2011).

Schiller Ben, 'Ecuador is the World's First Country with a Digital Cash System' (*FastCompany.com*, 10 August 2015) https://www.fastcompany.com/3049536/ecuador-is-the-worlds-first-country-with-a-public-digital-cash-system, accessed on 12 January 2019.

Seddon Max and Arnold Martin, 'Putin Considers "Cryptoruble" as Moscow Seeks to Evade Sanctions' (*FinancialTimes.com*, 1 January 2018) https://www.ft.com/content/54d026d8-e4cc-11e7-97e2-916d4fbac0da, accessed on 12 January 2019.

Sheard Paul, 'Repeat after Me: Banks Cannot and Do Not "Lend Out" Reserves' (2013) Standard & Poor's RatingsDirect, https://www.kreditopferhilfe.net/docs/S_and_P__Repeat_After_Me_8_14_13.pdf, accessed on 12 January 2019.

Sveriges Riksbank, The Riksbank's E-Krona Project (*Sveriges Riksbank*, September 2017) https://www.riksbank.se/globalassets/media/rapporter/e-krona/2017/rapport_ekrona_uppdaterad_170920_eng.pdf, accessed on 12 January 2019.

Tankus Nathan, 'Receivability for Public Dues: The Unrecognized Glue of the Antebellum Monetary System' (2019), Institute for Sustainable Prosperity Working Paper (unpublished).

Tooze Adam, *Crashed: How a Decade of Financial Crises Changed the World* (Viking 2018).

Werner Richard, 'How Do Banks Create Money, and Why Can Other Firms Not Do the Same? An Explanation for the Co-existence of Lending and Deposit-Taking' (2014) 36 *International Review of Financial Analysis*, 71.

9

Regulating the Shadow Payment System

Bitcoin, Mobile Money, and Beyond

Jonathan Greenacre

I. Introduction

On 28 February 2014, Mt Gox, a cryptocurrency exchange, entered into bankruptcy proceedings in Japan. It appears that users of Mt Gox will receive little, if any, of the $500 million worth of bitcoins within this exchange. The failure of Mt Gox was notable because, up until that point, it was a cornerstone of the Bitcoin ecosystem. Furthermore, its failure triggered a legislative response. On 3 July 2016, the Japanese Government imposed new *ex ante* legal requirements designed to protect users' funds in services like Mt Gox.

What received less immediate attention is that Mt Gox is just one service within a global 'shadow payment system'. This system includes a growing number of firms, cryptocurrency exchanges, which provide payment services outside the scope of standard banking regulation. Relevant actors include Bitcoin, PayPal, Alipay in China, and phone companies providing mobile money services in Africa.

Members of the public store funds in the shadow payment system. The collapse of Mt Gox raises an important question: what legal tools can protect users' funds from bankruptcy-related risks in digital currency exchanges?

Answering this question is more complicated than it may at first appear. This is because traditionally banks provide payment systems. Micro-prudential regulation addresses risks banks can create through their intermediation, payment, and other functions. What tools can be used when non-bank actors provide payments? There is very little scholarship on this point. Furthermore, the pace of technological change in the shadow payment system is creating a set of rapidly evolving terms which do not appear to easily fit into traditional legal and regulatory categories.

This chapter leaves behind the traditional bank-based regulatory paradigm. In its place, it uses a framework, based on the functional approach to regulation, to identify risks to users' funds, the range of tools available to address them, and their effectiveness. The chapter uses the framework as a base to make three main claims.

First, risks to users' funds emerge from insolvency of the actor in the shadow payment system which actually receives users' funds. In such a situation, legal rules which underpin bankruptcy regimes in most countries, expose users' funds to two risks. One is *loss of value*, which means the potential write-down of funds when users are characterized as unsecured creditors. The other is *illiquidity*, meaning users face a delay in converting or transferring funds during bankruptcy proceedings. Furthermore, these insights apply across actors in the shadow payment system so long as they are subject to the same essential bankruptcy regimes. This point applies regardless of the title of the service, such as 'PayPal' in developed countries and 'mobile money' in Africa.

Second, there is little information about legal tools which can address risks in shadow payment systems and the benefits and costs of choosing between them. This is, at least, partly because the shadow payment system and scholarship into its operation is relatively new when compared to the bank-based payment system. In particular, there is little guidance concerning the benefits and costs of using *ex post* legal tools, such as deposit insurance,

Regulating the Shadow Payment System: Bitcoin, Mobile Money, and Beyond. Jonathan Greenacre. © Jonathan Greenacre 2019. Published 2019 by Oxford University Press.

lender of last resort, and accelerated bankruptcy regimes to protect funds within the shadow payment system. This is because, amongst other potential reasons, the policy community is yet to determine a socially desirable role for the shadow payment system. Is it an investment asset, alternative retail funds transfer system, vital payment infrastructure on which the economy relies, much like the bank-based payment system, or something else? Additional research on the benefits and costs of different roles for the shadow payment system within an economy could help guide the majority of legal regimes.

Third, and the main claim of this chapter, is that mobile money can provide insights into legal tools, their effectiveness and their benefits and costs, including in relation to *ex post* regulation. This is because over the past ten years, this shadow payment service has grown rapidly in Africa. In response, many countries have implemented increasingly sophisticated legal and regulatory regimes, which are designed to protect users' funds. The key insight from these legal developments is that *ex ante* tools, including the type introduced in Japan, appear to have limited effectiveness in addressing loss of value and illiquidity risks. As a result, many African countries are developing complementary *ex post* regulation. A similar package of *ex ante* and *ex post* tools may be required to comprehensively address risks to users' funds in the shadow payment system in Japan and other developed countries.

The chapter uses mobile money in Malawi as a case study for developing this point, drawing upon the author's fieldwork in Africa. This fieldwork was conducted from August to October 2017 in partnership with Oxford University and the United Nations Capital Development Fund.

The chapter proceeds as follows. Section II argues that the rise of the shadow payment system requires a rethink of the regulation of payment systems. Section III explains how a functional approach can serve as a starting point for this rethink and identifying risks to users' funds, legal tools which can address them, and the benefits and costs of choosing between them. Section IV applies the functional framework to mobile money, particularly mobile money in Malawi. It focuses on two sets of *ex ante* tools: one is a combination of structural separation, storing funds in trusts, and auditing; the other is portfolio restrictions, involving the storing of users' funds in one or more liquid assets.

II. The Rise of the Shadow Payment System

Mt Gox was a cryptocurrency exchange based in Japan. Launched in July 2010, by 2014 Mt Gox was the world's largest Bitcoin exchange. It handled an estimated 70% of all Bitcoin transactions. These transactions came to a halt on 28 February 2014, when Mt Gox filed for bankruptcy. It cited the loss of 850,000 bitcoins estimated at a value of around $US500 million. At the time of writing, legal proceedings were still underway, and it is unclear what portion, if any, of these funds will be returned to users of Mt Gox.[1]

In 2014, the Japanese Government began a series of legal and regulatory reviews in order to address, amongst other issues, legal tools which can be used to protect users' funds in digital currency exchanges like Mt Gox. On 3 July 2016, the Japanese Government amended the Payment Systems Act by imposing new *ex ante* legal requirements designed to protect users' funds stored in digital currency exchanges and providers. In particular, a service provider must segregate virtual currencies and cash belonging to the service provider and users, disclose to users that virtual currencies are not legal tender, and ensure that segregated funds are audited.[2]

---

[1] For a full discussion of the Mt Gox case, see Mai Ishikawa, 'Designing Virtual Currency Regulation in Japan: Lessons from the Mt Gox Case' (2017) 3 *Journal of Financial Regulation*.
[2] Malawi National Payment Systems Act, 2016, § 63-10.

The risks to users' funds and potential legal tools to address them matter far beyond Mt Gox and Japan. This is partly because other Bitcoin-related platforms have begun to fail, causing the potential loss of users' funds. For example, Moore and Christin examined the record of forty Bitcoin exchanges. They found that eighteen had closed, and usually users' balances were 'wiped out'.[3] Other studies have begun to identify fraud and hacking in Bitcoin, with resulting loss of funds.[4]

The significance of Mt Gox and Japan's legislative amendments go further still. This is because Mt Gox is just one of a vibrant and growing global 'shadow payment system'. In this system, non-bank firms, cryptocurrency exchanges, and other actors provide equivalent payment functions as banks except that they do so outside the scope of bank regulation. In particular, actors in the shadow payment system do not have access to the prudential regulatory tools at the disposal of banks, which include deposit guarantee schemes, lender of last resort, and special bankruptcy regimes. This point was made clear when Mt Gox declared bankruptcy; unlike the collapse of a bank, users' funds were not insured by the Japanese Government.

A number of actors in the shadow payment system now provide a significant portion of payments in many economies without any explicit *ex post* government support. For example, in December 2017, Bitcoin had a market capitalization on $335 billion.[5] It is accepted by over 100,000 retailers, including Expedia, Dell, Microsoft, PayPal, and Amazon. As of 31 December 2016, PayPal had approximately 197 million active accounts supporting payments in over 100 currencies. The total volume of payments processed through PayPal in 2016 was approximately $USD 354 billion, roughly $USD 11,225 every second.[6]

Shadow payment systems are poised to underpin an ever-greater proportion of payment infrastructure in many economies. In a 2016 Report, the World Economic Forum claimed that Blockchain technology 'should be viewed as one of [the] technologies that will form the foundation of next generation financial services infrastructure'. In a news release issued with the Report, Giancarlo Bruno, head of financial services industries at the World Economic Forum, said that 'Blockchain will become the beating heart of [the finance industry]'.[7]

The shadow payment system has also grown rapidly in developing countries. Traditionally, banks have found it unprofitable to serve the majority of the population in these countries.[8] The spread of mobile phone technology has radically changed this picture. In Africa, this growth has been particularly rapid in relation to mobile phone subscriptions. Phone companies have taken advantage of this growth to provide payment services, normally labelled 'mobile money'. Launched in Kenya in 2007, mobile money has grown significantly; there are over 500 million mobile money accounts in ninety-three countries, overwhelmingly located in Africa.[9] Zoona, legally classified as a 'payments provider', has also grown quickly in Africa. Launched in 2009, Zoona has spread across Zambia, Malawi, and Mozambique and in 2017, processed $US 200 million in transactions.[10]

---

[3] See discussion in Tyler Moore and Nicolas Christin, 'Beware the Middleman: Empirical Analysis of Bitcoin Exchange Risk' in *Financial Cryptography and Data Security*, edited by A. R. Sadeghi (Springer-Verlag Berlin and Heidelberg 2013).

[4] ibid.

[5] Note, however, how challenging it is to get an accurate picture of the market capitalization of Bitcoin. See Joe Tambini, 'Bitcoin Price News' (29 January 2018) https://www.express.co.uk/finance/city/911501/bitcoin-price-news-why-btc-going-down-crashing-today-cryptocurrency.

[6] See these figures in Daniel Awrey and Kristin van Zwieten, 'The Shadow Payment System' (2017) 43 *Journal of Corporate Law*, 775.

[7] Angela Walch, 'The Path of the Blockchain Lexicon' (2017) *Regulation of Banking and Financial Law*, 713.

[8] For a description of the challenges this causes such communities, see also Daryl Collins, Jonathan Morduch, Stuart Rutherford, and Orlando Ruthven, *Portfolios of the Poor: How the World's Live on $2 a Day* (Princeton University Press 2009).

[9] GSM Association, 'State of Industry' (2015) Report, 9 and 13.

[10] See discussion in The Economist, 'Zoona' (2016). For a more detailed description of these and similar new payment services, see: Jonathan Greenacre, 'The Roadmap Approach to Regulating Digital Financial Services' (2015) 1(2) *Journal of Financial Regulation*, 298.

Shadow payment services have also emerged in Asia. For example, in 2004, Alibaba Group, an e-commerce company, launched Alipay in China. By 2017, this payment service operated in 110 countries and processed $US 1.7 trillion in payments.[11]

This chapter examines the legal protection of users' funds stored within the shadow payment system. The chapter asks what legal tools can protect users' funds from loss? This is not a simple task because financial regulatory literature tends to focus on non-payment financial functions and products, such as derivatives and structured finance.[12] More fundamentally, payments scholarship, regulation, and international standards usually assume that a bank, not a non-bank firm, currency or exchange provides payment services to the public.[13] This is because such scholarship has emerged from developed countries where an overwhelming majority of the population have bank deposits and have traditionally used the bank-based payment system.[14]

The assumption of the bank-based payment system, thus, informs regulatory frameworks. In the bank-based business model, a bank takes and invests deposits in longer-term investments *and* performs payments. Regulation responds to these functions by primarily targeting a bank's intermediation function which, by extension, *also* protects the stability of the payment system. This assumption means there is very little scholarship on legal tools which protect users' funds stored in the shadow payment system. Much research in this field tends to take the form of reports which list a range of risks in shadow payment systems, such as mobile money, but neither pull the material together into a framework nor explore legal solutions to them.[15]

The pace of technological change in the shadow payment system compounds the challenge of determining appropriate legal tools for this sector. Many services are stimulating a rapidly evolving terminology and lexicon which does not appear to easily fit into traditional legal and regulatory categories. For example, Angela Walch explains that 'blockchain technology' is variously labelled 'the blockchain', 'blockchain', 'distributed ledger technology', 'shared ledger technology', 'consensus ledger', 'mutual distributed ledger', and 'distributed database'.[16] She also identifies complex and different terminology used for ownership structures and descriptions of digital currencies.[17]

There is similar confusion about appropriate terminology for other services in the shadow payment system. For example, 'mobile money' in Africa is variously described as 'branchless banking', 'mobile money', 'digital financial services', 'person-to-person-payments', 'cash-in', 'cash-out', 'savings', 'mobile banking', and more.[18]

This chapter provides a framework, outlined in section III, through which to identify the functions of the shadow payment system, risks to users' funds and their source, and

---

[11] Better than Cash Alliance, 'State of Industry' (2017).   [12] Awrey and van Zwieten (n 6).

[13] See, e.g., Bruce Summers (ed), 'Banking and the Payment System' in *The Payment System: Design, Management and Supervision* (International Monetary Fund 1994), 427; Marvin Goodfriend states 'it is thus the banking system, with the central bank at its head, which serves as the backbone of the cashless payment system', Marvin Goodfriend, 'Money, Banking and Payment System Policy' in *The US Payments System: Efficiency Risk and the Role of the Federal Reserve*, edited by David Humphrey (Kluwer International 1990), 1.

[14] Estimated at around 80–90%. See, e.g., Lords Select Committee, 'Financial Exclusion Committee' (*Parliament. uk*, 2016) https://www.parliament.uk/financial-exclusion.

[15] USAid, 'Mobile Financial Services Risk Matrix' (*GSMA.com*) https://www.gsma.com/mobilefordevelopment/programme/mobile-money/usaid-releases-mobile-financial-services-risk-matrix; Janine Aron, ' "Leapfrogging": A Survey of the Nature and Economic Implications of Mobile Money' (2017) CSAE Working Paper Series 2017-2, Centre for the Study of African Economies, University of Oxford; Timothy Lyman, Mark Pickens, and David Porteus, 'Regulation Transformation Branchless Banking' (2008) Consultative Group to Assist the Poor, Focus Note No. 43.

[16] Walch (n 7).

[17] These include 'public blockchains', 'permissionless blockchains', 'open blockchains', private blockchains', 'permissioned blockchains', 'closed blockchains', and descriptions of currencies, such as 'virtual currencies', 'digital currencies', 'central bank digital currencies', 'cryptocurrencies', 'tokens', 'protocol tokens', 'app coins', 'alt-coins', and meta-coins: see Walch (n 7).

[18] See Lyman et al. (n 15).

potential legal tools. In doing so, it aims to contribute to discussions about how to regulate this rapidly evolving component of many economies.

III. A Functional Framework

This chapter uses a functional framework to begin building clarity on legal tools which can protect users' funds stored in the shadow payment system. This approach involves focusing on the risks of the *function* being performed, regardless of the legal classification of the actor providing it.[19] This approach can be used to identify the payment *functions* performed in the shadow payment system, *risks* to users' funds which arise in the performance of payment functions, and the range of potential legal *tools* which can respond to these risks.

This section applies each component of a functional approach to Mt Gox, PayPal in the United States, and mobile money in Malawi. It combines conceptual foundations in this field developed by Awrey and van Zwieten and results from the author's fieldwork in Africa, focusing on mobile money services provided by two phone companies in Malawi: Airtel Malawi (Airtel) and Telekom Networks Malawi (TNM) (collectively, 'Malawi's mobile money firms'), which provide 'Airtel Money' and 'TNM Mpamba', respectively.[20] The analysis also involves examining the surrounding regulation of these mobile money services in Malawi, which comprises the Banking Act (2010), Insolvency Act (2016), Mobile Payment Guidelines (2011), National Payment System Act (2016), and Trustees Act (1968).

Doing so provides a range of insights into legal tools which can protect users' funds in the shadow payment system. These insights can be applied across the shadow payment system, regardless of the title of the service. This is because each service performs the same functions and is subject to similar bankruptcy regimes.[21]

A. Functions

Awrey and van Zwieten identify the functions of the shadow payment system, focusing on Bitcoin, PayPal, and M-Pesa in Kenya.[22] M-Pesa is the world's first mobile money system, launched by Safaricom, a Vodafone subsidiary, in 2007. Each are payment systems because they transfer funds from debtors (payors) to creditors (payees) in satisfaction of financial obligations.[23] Furthermore, each provide three payment functions. One is *custodial storage*, which is the acceptance of users' funds and their protection from misappropriation and destruction in the period preceding their use to make a payment. The next is *transactional storage*, the safe and secure transfer of stored funds to third parties. The final function is *liquidity*, the ability to return or transfer these funds on demand.[24] These are the same functions as found in the bank-based payment system.

---

[19] Robert Merton and Zvi Bodie, 'A Conceptual Framework for Analyzing the Financial Environment' in *The Global Financial System: A Functional Perspective*, edited by Dwight Crane, Kenneth Froot, Andre Perold et al. (Harvard Business School 1995).

[20] Awrey and van Zwieten (n 6). Money was launched in 2012: Airtel, 'Airtel Money Launches in Malawi' (*AfricaAirtel.com*) http://www.africa.airtel.com/wps/wcm/connect/africarevamp/malawi/home/personal/airtel-money. TNM Mpamba was launched in 2013: Gregory Gondwe, 'TNM Launches Mobile Money' (*BizTechAfrica.com*) http://www.biztechafrica.com/article/tnm-launches-mobile-banking/5928/.

[21] Note that limited literature which mentions the regulation of these new shadow payment system, often alludes to the functional approach. For example, Walch (n 7), proposes that 'it may be helpful to focus on the function and activities performed by a party, rather than what they call themselves'.

[22] This list is not intended to be exhaustive. There will be other components of the shadow payment system which require additional research.

[23] Bruce Summers, 'The Payment System in a Market Economy' in *The Payment System: Design, Management and Supervision* (International Monetary Fund 1994), 1; Andrew Haldane, Stephen Millard, and Victoria Saporta, *The Future of Payment Systems* (Routledge, 2007), 2, cited in Awrey and van Zwieten (n 6), 8.

[24] Awrey and van Zwieten (n 6).

Each of Mt Gox, PayPal, and Malawi's mobile money firms use different technology and institutional arrangements to provide their relevant services. What matters is that collectively each actor uses these arrangements to provide the *same* payment functions.

Mt Gox serves as a useful starting point. In August 2015, during the ongoing legal proceedings into the bankruptcy of the cryptocurrency exchange, the Tokyo District Court found that in transferring bitcoin to Mt Gox for an exchange, a prospective seller actually transfers an asset.[25] This means that the seller is no longer the owner of bitcoin; her funds enter and are 'stored' within the exchange (custodial storage).[26] The prospective seller then transfers bitcoin to the buyer in exchange for funds (transactional storage). In theory, a user can redeem her bitcoin (liquidity), although potentially at a discount, as the resulting bankruptcy proceedings made clear, and as discussed below.

In PayPal, a user can transfer funds from her bank account or credit card. Such funds can then be stored within the PayPal system (custodial storage). A user can transfer funds to other accounts (transactional storage), including to make purchases (liquidity).

Malawi's mobile money firms provide the same payment functions as the two other shadow payment services discussed above. A user deposits cash with an agent in exchange for 'e–money'. These agents are corner stores, petrol stations, and other types of retail outlets which operate on behalf of the mobile money firms. Her funds are stored within the M-Pesa system through mechanisms discussed in section IV below (custodial storage).[27] A user can transfer some of the funds in her account to others, including to pay a bill, purchase goods, or simply as a present (transactional storage). A user can also redeem any remaining e–money in her account for cash at any time (liquidity).[28] To do so, she transfers an amount of e-money to an agent in exchange for an equivalent value of cash.

B. Risks

The funds received from users of Mt Gox, PayPal, and Malawi's mobile money firms are exposed to the same bankruptcy-related risks. These risks emerge from three interlinking components. One is that users of the shadow payment system will be classified as unsecured creditors in such proceedings unless there is legal authority to the contrary. A second is insolvency of whichever actor actually receives such funds. These are Mt Gox, PayPal, or in the case of M-Pesa, M-Pesa Holding Company. When this actor becomes insolvent it will usually enter bankruptcy proceedings. A third are provisions which apply across most bankruptcy regimes, including those which apply to each of Mt Gox, PayPal, and Malawi's mobile money firms. Users' funds are subject to *loss of value risk*, which means the potential write-down of these funds. This arises because most bankruptcy regimes contain a substantive rule that unsecured creditors, which will include users of the shadow payment system, share in any subsequent distribution of the debtor's assets on a *pro rata* basis. In other words, users are likely to only receive a portion of the original value of funds deposited into the shadow payment system. This is because users receive whatever is remaining after secured creditors, bondholders, and other entities have been repaid.[29]

Bankruptcy also exposes users' funds to *illiquidity risk*. This means that users face a delay in converting their funds back into cash (liquidity) or transferring them to others (transactional storage). It arises due to a procedural rule suspending enforcement action against assets held by the debtor while bankruptcy proceedings take place. Put simply, users of shadow

---

[25] Ishikawa (n 1).   [26] ibid.
[27] Airtel, Terms and Conditions, Clause 7, FAQs, http://www.africa.airtel.com; Airtel, 'Airtel Money', TNM: Terms and Conditions, Clause 2 and Email Confirmation from TNM, http://www.africa.airtel.com/; Airtel, 'What is Mpama?, FAQs, http://www.africa.airtel.com/.
[28] See n 28.   [29] The precise ranking will depend on provisions in a country's bankruptcy regime.

payment systems cannot recover their funds during bankruptcy proceedings. Instead, they must wait for such proceedings to finish, which may take a non-trivial amount of time.[30]

These risks can intersect. Users requiring liquidity may liquidate their claims at a significant discount to their nominal value, thereby causing loss of value.

Users' funds in Mt Gox, PayPal, and Malawi's mobile money firms are exposed to the same loss of value and illiquidity risks. This is because users in each scheme are unsecured creditors. The decision of the Tokyo District Court, discussed in section III.A, confirms that users of Mt Gox are unsecured creditors. PayPal's US user terms and conditions state that users are unsecured creditors and their funds are not insured by the government.[31]

Similarly, Malawi's mobile money firms will be subject to Malawi's corporate bankruptcy law.[32] Customers are likely to be unsecured creditors of the relevant mobile money firm.[33] Furthermore, Malawi's corporate bankruptcy regime, namely the Insolvency Act, *does* contain the substantive and procedural rules discussed above.[34]

C. Legal tools

Our understanding of legal tools which address loss of value and liquidity risks are limited in two ways. First, little is known about which legal tools are *available* to address risks to users' funds in shadow payment systems, at least in developed countries. This is due to the relatively short history of the shadow payment system when compared to the bank-based payment system. Angela Walch's proposal that blockchain developers be classified as fiduciaries is a useful starting point and warrants further explanation.[35] The new *ex ante* legal requirements for actors providing digital currency exchanges in Japan, focusing on asset segregation and auditing, may also form part of a catalogue of available legal tools.[36]

Awrey and van Zwieten expand our understanding by exploring a range of *ex ante* legal strategies which, in theory, can protect users' funds in the event of institutional distress and/ or bankruptcy of actors within the shadow payment system.[37] These include portfolio restrictions, third-party insurance, outsourcing the storage of users' funds to deposit-taking banks, using trusts to ring-fence users' funds and structural separation. These scholars expressly state that actors within the shadow payment system may use other legal tools which can be added to this list.[38] Moving forward, they propose that additional empirical study take place, involving uncovering actual tools used within the shadow payment system.

Second, and perhaps most fundamentally, there has been little discussion about the *benefits and costs* of choosing between the tools. The relative desirability of different legal tools will depend, in part, on their effectiveness. This desirability will also depend on how a policy-maker conceptualizes the shadow payment system. Should the shadow payment system be conceptualized as an investment choice, alternative retail transfer system, vital infrastructure on which the economy relies, much like the bank-based payment systems, or something else?

---

[30] Awrey and van Zwieten (n 6).

[31] See the full text: 'if you do hold a Balance, that Balance represents an unsecured claim against PayPal and is not insured by the FDIC ... PayPal will not voluntarily make Balances available to its creditors in the event of bankruptcy': PayPal Holdings Inc., Annual Report (Form 10K) for Period Ending 31 December 2016 (2016) https:// investor.paypal-corp.comcited in Awrey and van Zwieten (n 6).

[32] This is because the mobile money firms are regulated by the Payment System Act and so, like other firms subject to this legislation, are subject to the Insolvency Act § 27.

[33] The Payment Systems Act and Insolvency Act are silent on the ranking of customers of the mobile money firms. For this reason, and as a matter of general law, these customers are likely to be legally classified as unsecured creditors of the relevant mobile money firm: Awrey and van Zwieten (n 6), note 2 at 10–11.

[34] The substantive provision is contained in the Insolvency Act, sections 297 and 298. The procedural provision is contained in the Insolvency Act, section 158(C).

[35] Walch (n 7).   [36] Malawi National Payment Systems Act, 2016 § 63-10.

[37] Awrey and van Zwieten (n 6).   [38] ibid.

Decisions about the role of the shadow payment system may inform which legal rules are deemed appropriate. For example, if the shadow payment system is considered as an investment choice, a policy-maker may simply impose traditional investor protection rules on firms within it. These tend to focus on disclosure, licensing requirements, custodial requirements, and other measures to control conflicts of interest and enhance competence.[39] Alternatively, conceptualization of the shadow payment system as a retail transfer system may justify less stringent regulation. Usually, regulation of retail payment systems focuses on competition issues with private contract deemed sufficient for the remaining rules on how it operates.[40]

Finally, should a policy-maker view the shadow payment system as providing vital infrastructure, *ex post* regulatory tools, such as deposit insurance, lender of last resort, and accelerated bankruptcy regimes may be considered appropriate. This is due to externalities, namely the extensive cost to society should the shadow payment system collapse.

On this conceptualization, the shadow payment system would be considered as important to society as the traditional, bank-based payment system. It would mean the state should essentially backstop the operation of the shadow payment system, much as it does for banks. This approach may seem radical, but should the shadow payment continue to underpin a greater portion of payments in an economy, it may be deemed appropriate in some jurisdictions.

To this author's knowledge, there has been no substantive discussion on the benefits and costs of different roles for the shadow payment system. Any references tend to be made in passing. For example, when discussing Mt Gox, Mai Ishikawa mentioned that the rise of Mt Gox and other digital currency exchanges questioned 'the role of banks and other financial institutions in fund transfers'.[41] Mai Ishikawa also suggests that the new regulations in Japan resemble those imposed on funds transfer providers. However, this point was not developed.

This chapter does not seek to determine a socially desirable role for the shadow payment system in a given jurisdiction. This approach would be unwise given the rapidly evolving nature of this system. Furthermore, such a role is likely to depend upon a range of domestic considerations. Instead, section IV uses mobile money in Malawi as a case study to widen the range of known legal tools which can protect users' funds and study their effectiveness. This section also explores how different views on the role of the shadow payment system within an economy can inform the design of its regulation.

IV. Application to Malawi

This section applies the functional framework discussed in section III to mobile money. The material below draws upon the author's fieldwork conducted from August to October 2017 in partnership with Oxford University and the United Nations Capital Development Fund. The fieldwork focused on working with the Reserve Bank of Malawi to better understand risks to users' funds in mobile money schemes and legal tools used to address them in Malawi.

Mobile money is a useful case study because a range of material exists on its operation. The service emerged over ten years ago and has become a well-established industry; there are over 500 million mobile money accounts in ninety-three countries, overwhelmingly located in Africa.[42] The growth of mobile money has prompted the emergence of a large amount of information about the operation, institutional arrangements, and regulation of the service.

---

[39] See John Armour, Dan Awrey, Paul Davies et al., *The Principles of Financial Regulation* (Oxford University Press 2016), Ch 1.
[40] ibid.   [41] Ishikawa (n 1), 126.   [42] GSM Association (n 9).

A key insight from mobile money is that *ex ante* tools of the type recently introduced in Japan may have limited effectiveness in addressing loss-of-value and illiquidity risks. As a result, many African countries are developing complementary *ex post* regulation. M-Pesa in Kenya serves as a useful example. Initially, the Central Bank of Kenya issued a 'letter of no objection' to Safaricom.[43] The firm was required to implement 'adequate' protection of users' funds but was free to determine what measures would be appropriate.[44]

Over time, regulation moved from the relatively 'light-touch' requirements in the letter of no objection to more substantive regulation. For example, in 2013, the Central Bank of Kenya ('CBK') passed the Regulation for Designation of a Payment System and E-Money Regulations. This Regulation contained a series of *ex ante* regulatory tools designed to protect users' funds, which will be explored below.

In 2014, the CBK passed the National Payment Systems Regulations ('NPS Regulations'). These contained more onerous *ex ante* regulatory requirements for M-Pesa and other phone companies providing mobile money. The NPS Regulations also included an accelerated bankruptcy regime for shadow payment firms, including Safaricom. In 2016, the CBK began plans to design pass-through deposit insurance for shadow payment schemes.

Other countries have followed the CBK's legislative history. For example, many countries, including Fiji, Papua New Guinea, Samoa, Uganda, and Tanzania issued letters of no objection to phone companies wishing to launch mobile money services.[45] Many of these other countries have also followed the CBK's steps and implemented more substantive rules for mobile money. For example, Malawi issued the Mobile Money Guidelines 2013, Tanzania has passed the E-Money Regulations 2015 and Payment Systems Licensing and Approval Regulations 2015, and Ghana passed the Guidelines for E-Money Issuers in Ghana in 2015.

Other countries have moved still further and implemented *ex post* tools. For example, on 18 January 2016, the Nigeria Deposit Insurance Corporation announced that pass-through deposit insurance would be extended to mobile money.[46]

There is less information as to why many of these countries gradually buttressed *ex ante* with *ex post* tools. However, it appears that, at least, part of the reason is that these *ex ante* tools, including the type recently introduced in Japan, cannot, in themselves, fully address loss-of-value and illiquidity risks to users' funds. The discussion below explores this point, focusing on mobile money in Malawi.

Malawi's regulatory framework aims to address loss-of-value and illiquidity risks by requiring a mobile money firm to take three key steps: (i) maintain a trust account with a bank whose usage shall be restricted to facilitating mobile payment transactions;[47] (ii) reflect all monetary values relating to transactions in the mobile payment service in the trust account at the bank;[48] and (iii) ensure that the balance in the trust account shall, at all times, be equal to the total outstanding (unclaimed) balance of all holders of e-money in the service ('e-float').[49]

---

[43] Alliance for Financial Inclusion ('AFI'), 'Enabling Mobile Money Transfer: The Central Bank of Kenya's Treatment of M-Pesa' (2010) http://www.afi-global.org/sites/default/files/publications/afi_casestudy_mpesa_en.pdf >.

[44] ibid.

[45] This approached was used by the Central Bank of Uganda, see Stephen Staschen, 'Mobile Money Moves Forward in Uganda Despite Legal Hurdles' (*CGAP.com*, 9 March 2015) http://www.cgap.org/blog/mobile-money-moves-forward-uganda-despite-legal-hurdles; the Central Bank of Tanzania, see Simone di Castri and Lara Gidvani, 'Enabling Mobile Money Policies in Tanzania' (*GSMA.com*, February 2014) 2, http://www.gsma.com/mobilefordevelopment/wp-content/uploads/2014/03/Tanzania-Enabling-Mobile-Money-Policies.pdf; and the Central Bank of Kenya, see (xlii).

[46] See announcement in Babajide Komolafe, 'NDIC Issues Deposit Insurance Guidelines for Mobile Money' (*Vanguard.com*, 18 January 2016) http://www.vanguardngr.com/2016/01/ndic-issues-deposit-insurance-guidelines-for-mobile-money/.

[47] Malawi Mobile Payment Guidelines, 2011, cl 8.7.   [48] ibid., cl 8.9.   [49] ibid., cl 8.10.

This provision can be divided into three key tools, each of which are designed to address loss-of-value and illiquidity risks. The discussion below analyses each tool. First, a mobile money firm must store all customers' funds in a *trust* account. The amount in the trust account must match the e-float.

Second, as part of the obligation to maintain an equivalent amount of funds in the trust account and e-float, a mobile money firm can only make use of trust assets for mobile payment transactions. This is a form of *structural separation* aiming to separate payment functions from other business activities.[50] This is because the relevant mobile money firm cannot use customers' funds, which are trust assets, to fund its other, non-payment services. For example, Airtel or TNM could not use customers' funds for their mobile phone related services.

If implemented effectively this structure can protect users' funds from institutional distress or bankruptcy of the phone company because, while the phone company takes legal title to users' funds, users retain beneficial ownership.[51] Effectively implemented, storing funds in trust achieves the same purpose as the rules recently introduced in Japan's amended Payment Systems Act; the segregation of assets of the shadow payment firm from users' funds. This means funds are ring-fenced in the event of insolvency. This is because users' funds usually stored in a trust will not form part of the company's estate and so will not be available for other creditors.[52] In such circumstances, users' funds will retain their full value during corporate bankruptcy proceedings. In turn, this means the full value of these funds will be available for users at the conclusion of those proceedings.

Structural separation and trusts face a range of potential limitations. These have not been sufficiently researched and require additional examination. In particular, if effectively implemented, a combination of structural separation and trusts can address loss-of-value risk. However, they cannot, in and of themselves, address illiquidity risk. This is due to the potentially slow speed at which users' funds (trust assets) will be distributed to users (as beneficiaries). Put alternatively, a valid trust may ensure that users obtain *full value* of their funds (which addresses loss-of-value risk); however, the protracted nature of bankruptcy proceedings mean they face a considerable *delay* in obtaining them. The existence of a valid trust may require users to wait even longer to receive their funds. This is because the bankruptcy practitioner must confirm the existence of a valid trust along with the identity and entitlements of beneficiaries.[53] Such delays may be particularly considerable in mobile money in Malawi. There is no public information available to forecast how long Malawi's corporate bankruptcy would take to complete. The World Bank's 2016 'Doing Business Study of Sub-Saharan Africa', which contained a component of corporate bankruptcy, may provide initial guidance on this point.[54] This study estimates that the average length of a corporate bankruptcy process in Sub-Saharan Africa is approximately *3 years*.[55] To the extent that Malawi's corporate bankruptcy regime mirrors those of other countries in Sub-Saharan Africa, if at all, this means mobile money users are likely to face a significant delay before they receive

---

[50] Awrey and van Zwieten (n 6), 52.

[51] This is central to the operation of a trust, as follows. A trust is a legal relationship, in which legal title in property is given to a 'trustee'. The trustee holds the property (the 'trust property' or 'trust assets') on behalf of a third person—the 'beneficiary', who holds beneficial interest in the property. Frederic Maitland, *Equity: A Course of Lectures* (Oxford University Press 1969), 44; David Hayton, Paul Matthews, and Charles Mitchell, *Law Relating to Trusts and Trustees* (17th edn, LewisNexis 2007), 2; *Re Marshall's Will Trusts* [1945] Ch 217, 219. Properly constituted, a declaration of trust is a means by which a trust can be established. It involves a person (who becomes the trustee) declaring that it holds property on trust for the beneficiary. Glanville Williams, 'The Three Certainties' (1940) 4(1) *Modern Law Review*, 20; *Stapelton v Stapleton* (1844) 60 ER 328.

[52] Jonathan Greenacre and Ross Buckley, 'Using Trusts to Protect Mobile Money Customers' (2014) *Springer Journal of Legal Studies*, 59.

[53] Awrey and van Zwieten (n 6), 52.

[54] See World Bank, 'Doing Business Survey —Resolving Insolvency Methodology', http://www.doingbusiness. org/methodology/resolving-insolvency#time, cited in Awrey and van Zwieten (n 6), 37.

[55] This is measured by reference to the time between default and the distribution to a senior secured creditor in full or partial satisfaction of their claim: Awrey and van Zwieten (n 6), 37.

their funds. In turn, this means payments are likely to be disrupted for an extended period of time.

Users of shadow payment systems in developed countries may also face a delay in receiving their funds in the event of insolvency. This point will apply even if the asset segregation rules of the type introduced in Japan are implemented effectively. The extended insolvency proceedings in *Lehman Brothers International (Europe)* are a pertinent example of the delays that can arise in the process of working out the extent of beneficiaries' claim over trust funds.[56] More recently, the Mt Gox insolvency proceedings have taken, at the time of writing, almost four years, and are not yet complete.

Third, customers' funds, which are trust assets, must be stored in a *bank deposit*. Assuming a mobile money firm complies with this obligation, the amount of funds in the deposit represents the total value of trust assets. By storing funds in a bank, mobile money schemes in Malawi should always have sufficient liquidity to enable users to convert their e-money back into cash. Crucially, this availability comes from prudential regulation and supervision of Malawi's banks. In particular, a set of micro-prudential tools, namely deposit guarantee schemes, lender of last resort facilities, and special bankruptcy regime for failing banks, enable banks to continue performing their economic functions during times of institutional distress.[57] Effectively designed and enforced, such rules can help guarantee the availability of customers' funds. However, in Malawi, banks can only access lender of last resort and special bankruptcy regimes.[58] Deposit insurance is yet to be established. Without it, Malawian banks are still exposed to depositor runs, which can result in liquidity and potentially solvency problems. This may then mean that customers' funds stored in non-bank payment systems are not, in fact, guaranteed while stored in a bank.

Recognizing these limitations, some countries have required shadow payment firms to store users' funds across banks. This approach is used for mobile money in Afghanistan and Namibia and Uganda.[59] However, like other *ex ante* and *ex post* legal tools used in the shadow payment system, the effectiveness of this approach is unclear and requires additional research. In theory, diversification across banks reduces the exposure of users' funds to loss from the one bank. However, the operation of this regulatory tool is uncertain. It is unclear how losses would be shared amongst users in the event that one of the relevant banks fail. In particular, it is not clear whether the funds in the failed bank are specifically associated with particular users or shared proportionally among them all.

The perceived shortcomings in *ex ante* regulation has meant that, in recent years, increasingly mobile money regulators are moving towards *ex post* regulation. In particular, this involves extending pass-through deposit insurance to mobile money. In this scheme, the deposit insurance provider acknowledges that the shadow payment firm's bank account can be characterized as a number of smaller accounts for the purposes of deposit insurance. This means that each users' account (namely the amount of cash each user holds with a shadow payment firm) receives the full protection of the country's deposit insurance scheme.

As discussed above, in 2016, Nigeria extended pass-through deposit insurance to mobile money.[60] Other countries have also sought to do so. As of November 2016, Tanzania, Kenya, Uganda, and Zimbabwe were planning to implement pass-through deposit insurance but were unsure about the form it should take.[61] However, a range of legal and operational issues

---

[56] See a discussion on this case in Paul Greenwood and Robert Miles, 'In the Matter of Lehman Brothers International (Europe) (In Administration)' (2013) 19(7), *Trusts and Trustees*, 787–93.

[57] Awrey and van Zwieten (n 6), 4 and 48.

[58] Reserve Bank Act § 4(g) 1964; Insolvency Act (Section 3) 2016; Banking Act (Part IV) 1989.

[59] See United Nations Conference on Trade and Development ('UNCTAD'), 'Mobile Money for Business Development in the East African Community' (2012) Discussion, 27–28, http://unctad.org/en/PublicationsLibrary/dtlstict2012d2_en.pdf.

[60] Komolafe (n 46).

[61] Khalid Moh'd, 'Opening Speech' (1 September 2016) Africa Regional Committee Conference; Gift Chirozva, 'Presentation 1. Zimbabwe' (1 September 2016) IADI Africa Regional Committee Conference.

around this tool remain unclear. For example, in Nigeria, policy-makers have expressed concern over a potential lack of ability of the Nigerian Deposit Insurance Corporation to effectively implement pass-through deposit insurance. Lack of awareness amongst the population has also been highlighted, suggesting that pass-through deposit insurance may not build public confidence in mobile money.[62]

Collectively, then, this analysis outlines that *ex ante and ex post* tools appear to be required to address loss-of-value and illiquidity risks for mobile money. It may appear that this analysis should apply in a narrow way to mobile money in Malawi, alone. However, given its functional nature, this analysis can apply to other services in the shadow payment system. This is because each of them performs the same payment functions. For example, in 2014, Zoona Transactions International Limited (Zoona) launched its Zoona product in Malawi. This service provides the same functions: custodial storage (entry and protection of funds);[63] transactional storage (transferal of funds to other users for payment purposes);[64] and liquidity (transfer or convert funds into more liquid asset on demand). [65] This service is subject to the same functions and, by virtue of being subject to the same insolvency regime as mobile money firms in Malawi, faces the same insolvency-related risks to customers' funds.

Other services, such as Bitcoin currency exchanges and Paypal, perform the same payment functions as mobile money and Zoona.[66] By providing equivalent functions, users' funds are exposed to the same risks of loss of value and illiquidity, regardless of the title of the service or the firm providing it. This point applies so long as the insolvency regime in question contains the substantive and procedural rules discussed above, causing loss of value and illiquidity, respectively.[67] In turn, this similarity in risk profile means legal tools can, in theory, be applied across different services in the shadow payment system.

Institutional differences between countries may be significant and mitigate against directly transplanting regulatory and legal lesson from one jurisdiction to another.[68] However, the discussion above demonstrates the value in, at least, understanding the functions of these services. Services providing comparable functions and subject to equivalent insolvency regimes put customers' funds to the same basic loss-of-value and illiquidity risks. Policy-makers can then research different tools which, at least in theory, can address these risks, regardless of whether the service operates in Malawi or the United States.

V. Conclusion

The growth of Bitcoin, PayPal, M-Pesa, AliPay, and other services suggest that this shadow payment system will process an ever-greater proportion of transactions in the economy. This chapter has used a functional framework to identify risks to users' funds in the shadow payment system, the range of tools available to address them, and their potential effectiveness.

Using a framework as a base, the chapter has explained that users' funds are exposed to loss-of-value and illiquidity risks. These emerge from insolvency of the actor in the shadow payment system which receives users' funds and substantive and procedural bankruptcy rules, respectively. It is relatively straightforward to identify risks to users' funds stored in the shadow payment system. However, identifying tools and evaluating their effectiveness in addressing these risks is more challenging. This is partly because little is known about them. Furthermore, there is a lack of discussion on the desirability of using these tools, particularly

---

[62] Kingsley Nwaigwe, 'Presentation 3. Deposit Insurance and Mobile Money in Africa' (1 September 2016) IADI Africa Regional Committee Conference.
[63] Zoona Ltd, Terms and Conditions, General Clause 1; Clause 6 of Zoona Sunga.
[64] ibid., Clauses 1 and 5, and Addendum to Terms and Conditions. 　　[65] ibid., Clauses 1 and 5.
[66] Awrey and van Zwieten (n 6). 　　[67] ibid.
[68] See Richard Posner, 'Law and Economics in Common-Law, Civil-Law, and Developing Nations' (2004) 17(1) *Ratio Juris*, 42, 66–79.

those that are *ex post* in nature. This is because policy-makers are yet to determine a socially desirable role for the shadow payment system.

Research should aim to identify additional legal rules used in the shadow payment system. Furthermore, policy-makers and scholars should explore the benefits and costs of different roles for the shadow payment system in an economy. This is because such rules can motivate different rules. Until then, the ten-year history of mobile money and its surrounding legal and regulatory frameworks suggests that *ex ante* tools of the type recently introduced in Japan appear to have limited effectiveness in addressing loss-of-value and illiquidity risks. A package of *ex ante* and *ex post* tools may be required to comprehensively address risks to users' funds in the shadow payment system in Japan and other developed countries. Doing so can support the growth of strong, stable shadow payment systems.

VI. Bibliography

Airtel, 'Airtel Money', TNM: Terms and Conditions, Clause 2 and Email Confirmation from TNM, http://www.africa.airtel.com/, accessed on 13 January 2019.

Airtel, 'Airtel Money Launches in Malawi' (*AfricaAirtel.com*) http://www.africa.airtel.com/wps/wcm/connect/africarevamp/malawi/home/personal/airtel-money, accessed on 13 January 2019.

Airtel, Terms and Conditions, Clause 7, FAQs, http://www.africa.airtel.com/, accessed on 13 January 2019.

Airtel, 'What is Mpama?', FAQs, http://www.africa.airtel.com/, accessed on 13 January 2019.

Alliance for Financial Inclusion ('AFI'), 'Enabling Mobile Money Transfer: The Central Bank of Kenya's Treatment of M-Pesa' (2010) http://www.afi-global.org/sites/default/files/publications/afi_casestudy_mpesa_en.pdf, accessed on 13 January 2019.

Armour John, Awrey Dan, Davies Paul et al., *The Principles of Financial Regulation* (Oxford University Press 2016).

Aron Janine, '"Leapfrogging": A Survey of the Nature and Economic Implications of Mobile Money' (2017) CSAE Working Paper Series 2017-2, Centre for the Study of African Economies, University of Oxford.

Awrey Daniel and Van Zwieten Kristin, 'The Shadow Payment System' (2018) 43(4) *Journal of Corporation Law*, 775.

Better than Cash Alliance, 'State of Industry' (2017) Report.

Castri Simone di and Gidvani Lara, 'Enabling Mobile Money Policies in Tanzania' (*GSMA.com*, February 2014) 2, http://www.gsma.com/mobilefordevelopment/wp-content/uploads/2014/03/Tanzania-Enabling-Mobile-Money-Policies.pdf, accessed on 13 January 2019.

Chirozva Gift, 'Presentation 1. Zimbabwe' (1 September 2016), IADI Africa Regional Committee Conference.

Collins Daryl, Morduch Jonathan, Rutherford Stuart, and Ruthven Orlando, *Portfolios of the Poor: How the World's Live on $2 a Day* (Princeton University Press 2009).

Goodfriend Marvin, 'Money, Banking and Payment System Policy' in *The US Payments System: Efficiency Risk and the Role of the Federal Reserve*, edited by David Humphrey (Kluwer International 1990).

Gondwe Gregory, 'TNM Launches Mobile Money' (*BizTechAfrica.com*) http://www.biztechafrica.com/article/tnm-launches-mobile-banking/5928/, accessed on 13 January 2019.

Greenacre Jonathan, 'The Roadmap Approach to Regulating Digital Financial Services' (2015) 1(2) *Journal of Financial Regulation*, 298.

Greenacre Jonathan and Buckley Ross, 'Using Trusts to Protect Mobile Money Customers' (2014) *Springer Journal of Legal Studies*, 59.

Greenwood Paul and Miles Robert, 'In the Matter of Lehman Brothers International (Europe) (In Administration)' (2013) 19(7) *Trusts and Trustees*, 787.

GSM Association, 'State of Industry' (2015) Report.

Haldane Andrew, Millard Stephen, and Saporta Victoria, *The Future of Payment Systems* (Routledge 2007).

Hayton David, Matthews Paul, and Mitchell Charles, *Law Relating to Trusts and Trustees* (17th edn, LewisNexis 2007).

Information Telecommunications Union, 'Digital Financial Services' (2015) Focus Group, https://itunews.itu.int/en/6027-ITUFocus-Group-on-Digital-Financial-Services.note.aspx, accessed on 13 January 2019.

Ishikawa Mai, 'Designing Virtual Currency Regulation in Japan: Lessons from the Mt Gox Case' (2017) 3 *Journal of Financial Regulation*, 125.

Komolafe Babajide, '*NDIC Issues Deposit Insurance Guidelines for Mobile Money*' (*Vanguard.com*, 18 January 2016) http://www.vanguardngr.com/2016/01/ndic-issues-deposit-insurance-guidelines-for-mobile-money/, accessed on 13 January 2019.

Lords Select Committee, 'Financial Exclusion Committee' (*Parliament.uk*, 2016) https://www.parliament.uk/financial-exclusion, accessed on 13 January 2019.

Lyman Timothy, Pickens Mark, and Porteus David, 'Regulation Transformation Branchless Banking' (2008) Consultative Group to Assist the Poor, Focus Note No. 43.

Maitland Frederic, *Equity: A Course of Lectures* (Oxford University Press 1969).

Merton Robert and Bodie Zvi, 'A Conceptual Framework for Analyzing the Financial Environment' in *The Global Financial System: A Functional Perspective*, edited by Dwight Crane, Kenneth Froot, Andre Perold et al. (Harvard Business School 1995).

Moh'd Khalid, 'Opening Speech' (1 September 2016), IADI Africa Regional Committee Conference.

Moore Tyler and Christin Nicolas, 'Beware the Middleman: Empirical Analysis of Bitcoin Exchange Risk' in *Financial Cryptography and Data Security*, edited by A. R. Sadeghi (Springer-Verlag Berlin and Heidelberg 2013).

Nwaigwe Kingsley, 'Presentation 3. Deposit Insurance and Mobile Money in Africa' (1 September 2016), IADI Africa Regional Committee Conference.

PayPal Holdings Inc., Annual Report (Form 10K) for Period Ending 31 December 2016 (2016) https://investor.paypal-corp.com, accessed on 13 January 2019.

Posner Richard, 'Law and Economics in Common-Law, Civil-Law, and Developing Nations' (2004) 17(1) *Journal of Financial Regulation*, 42.

Staschen Stephen, 'Mobile Money Moves Forward in Uganda Despite Legal Hurdles' (*CGAP.com*, 9 March 2015) http://www.cgap.org/blog/mobile-money-moves-forward-uganda-despite-legal-hurdles, accessed on 13 January 2019.

Summers Bruce (ed), 'Banking and the Payment System' in *The Payment System: Design, Management and Supervision* (International Monetary Fund 1994).

Summers Bruce, 'The Payment System in a Market Economy' in *The Payment System: Design, Management and Supervision* (International Monetary Fund 1994).

Tambini Joe, 'Bitcoin Price News'(29 January 2018) https://www.express.co.uk/finance/city/911501/bitcoin-price-news-why-btc-going-down-crashing-today-cryptocurrency, accessed on 13 January 2019.

The Economist, 'Zoona' (2016).

United Nations Conference on Trade and Development ('UNCTAD'), 'Mobile Money for Business Development in the East African Community' (2012) Discussion, 27–28, http://unctad.org/en/PublicationsLibrary/dtlstict2012d2_en.pdf, accessed on 13 January 2019.

USAid, 'Mobile Financial Services Risk Matrix' (*GSMA.com*) https://www.gsma.com/mobilefordevelopment/programme/mobile-money/usaid-releases-mobile-financial-services-risk-matrix.

Walch Angela, 'The Path of the Blockchain Lexicon' (2017) 36 *Rev Banking & Fin L*, 713.

Williams Glanville, 'The Three Certainties' (1940) 4(1) *Modern Law Review*, 20.

World Bank, 'Doing Business Survey —Resolving Insolvency Methodology', http://www.doingbusiness.org/methodology/resolving-insolvency#time, accessed on 13 January 2019.

World Bank, 'Mobile Phone Subscriptions' (2013).

10

Blockchain-Based Insurance

Michael Abramowicz

I. Introduction

Insurance is a mechanism for pooling risk. Insurance companies are integral to various aspects of risk pooling: they draft, price, and sell policies, and they handle claims. But are insurance companies necessary for the functioning of insurance? This chapter argues that they are not, and, moreover, that the blockchain could potentially disrupt the insurance industry.[1] With a cryptocurrency supporting smart contracts, insureds could pool their resources by digitally agreeing that their cryptocurrency funds will be governed by a protocol. The smart contract would specify the insurable interest—perhaps a particular piece of property or a life—as well as the insurance term, providing a link to documents providing more information. If an insured later claimed a loss, the insurance claim would be resolved pursuant to protocols specified in the smart contract. These protocols ultimately would determine how all the pooled resources would be allocated among the various contributors to the pool (or their beneficiaries) and investors.

The obstacles to blockchain-based insurance are many but the objections may be grouped crudely into two: first, that insurance companies perform many functions beyond risk pooling and claim resolution; and second, that a blockchain with smart contracts would not be able to perform these functions as effectively. Insurance companies are indeed complex entities. Much of the complexity, however, results from the need to function in a complex legal environment. Insurance companies must comply with detailed legal regimes governing insurance—not to mention other areas of law, such as antitrust and employment. An insurance company must be prepared to defend denials of claims in court, and litigation is expensive. Moreover, an insurer must draft contracts with due attention to the possibility of eventual adjudication, recognizing the legal principle that ambiguities in insurance policies will be resolved against the insurer,[2] as well as the practical reality that juries do not much like insurance companies.[3]

It is precisely the cost of this legal complexity that creates the possibility for industry disruption. It would not be easy for the government to regulate insurance purchased via a smart contract embedded in a cryptocurrency. The fundamental problem is that if there is no insurer, the traditional target of regulation is missing. Thus, a government intent on preserving traditional forms of regulation of insurance, including the adjudicative process, would need to target individuals or businesses purchasing insurance on the blockchain, rather than insurers. If the government is not willing to do so, blockchain-based insurance will have a competitive advantage over traditionally provided insurance, namely that it does not need to follow the law. This advantage may exist where regulation prevents insurance from being priced at an actuarially fair rate, for example, because of cross-subsidies or because the

---

[1] This chapter builds on a prior work exploring the possibility of cryptocurrency-based insurance. See Michael Abramowicz, 'Cryptoinsurance' (2015) 50 *Wake Forest Law Review*, 671.

[2] See n 39 and accompanying text.

[3] For convincing empirical evidence that juries are more likely to find liability when defendants are insured, see Alan Calnan, 'The Insurance Exclusionary Rule Revisited: Are Reports of Its Demise Exaggerated?' (1991) 52 *Ohio State Law Journal*, 1203–04. See also Valuerie Hans, 'The Illusions and Realities of Jurors' Treatment of Corporate Defendants' (1998) 48 *DePaul Law Review*, 327.

Blockchain-Based Insurance. Michael Abramowicz. © Michael Abramowicz 2019. Published 2019 by Oxford University Press.

law requires certain types of coverage that insureds might otherwise prefer not to purchase.[4] More subtly, blockchain-based insurance may avoid the necessity, and thus the expense of traditional adjudication or arbitration.

This observation leads naturally to the second objection, that the blockchain is incapable of substituting itself for the functions that insurance companies perform. Indeed, it strengthens that objection, because for blockchain-based insurance to be successful, the blockchain will need to substitute itself not only for insurance companies but also for the legal system that gives policy-holders the confidence that their claims will be paid. Blockchain-based insurance does not seem possible today. Smart contracts are in their infancy and contemporaneous experiments have shown a susceptibility to hacking.[5] Moreover, cryptocurrencies themselves are highly speculative,[6] and the last thing that one looking to limit risk would want is to have one's own risk cushion invested in a volatile asset. These problems might, however, be overcome with time. Smart contracts will improve with technological development and formal proofs verifying their properties.[7] Nascent cryptocurrencies include mechanisms making it possible to hold assets denominated in dollars or other traditional currencies.[8] Even if such stability is impossible in a traditional cryptocurrency, if a single country were to adopt a cryptocurrency as its national currency, that currency's fiat status could establish sufficient stability for smart contracts.

Even with a hypothetically functioning and stable cryptocurrency with smart contract capabilities, mimicking the functions of insurance companies and the legal system will not be straightforward.[9] Perhaps the simplest design would be to create a 'pure fund', where all pooled resources will be returned to insureds in proportion to their realized losses. But even this approach requires a mechanism to measure those losses and to do so without courts. A pool of contracts could specify an arbitrator with the power to determine losses.[10] The arbitrator might be paid by a party filing a claim, with payment proportionate to the claim made. If there is concern that an arbitrator might have a conflict of interest (perhaps the arbitrator has surreptitiously contributed to the pool), a variety of mechanisms could be used to limit the power of any one cryptocurrency owner. For example, an appellate system could be based on relatively simple voting rules,[11] or a truly peer-to-peer system could be used to generate decentralized decisions.[12] Individuals would have incentives to develop reputations as fair arbitrators, since that would make them more likely to be selected for future insurance pools and thus to earn arbitral fees.

Existing insurance, of course, is more sophisticated than this, not merely redistributing premiums to insureds but also providing for the possibility that total claims might be in excess of premiums. Yet many types of insurance, covering many insureds with losses unlikely

---

[4] See section III.A.3.

[5] See Stan Schroeder, 'Not Again: Hackers Steal $32 Million Worth of Ethereum (*Mashable.com*, 20 July 2017) https://mashable.com/2017/07/20/ethereum-hackers-theft-32-million/?europe=true.

[6] There is considerable recent debate about whether Bitcoin is overvalued. See Tyler Cowen, 'Is Bitcoin Just a Bubble?' (*MarginalRevolution.com*, 30 November 2017) http://marginalrevolution.com/marginalrevolution/2017/11/bitcoin-just-bubble.html.

[7] See, e.g., GitHub, https://github.com/pirapira/ethereum-formal-verification-overview.

[8] See, e.g., BitShares, https://bitshares.org.

[9] An existing foray by a major insurer, AXA, into blockchain-based insurance only strengthens this point. AXA offers a product called 'fizzy', which allows for insurance against delayed flights. For this product, a source of truth (databases of flight delays) exists that allows adjudication to be automatic. The more general problem is for insurance to be provided on the blockchain when some judgement will be needed as to whether an insurable loss has occurred.

[10] See, e.g., Don Tapscott and Alex Tapscott, *Blockchain Revolution* (Penguin 2016), 104.

[11] See, e.g., Vitalik Buterin, 'Decentralized Court' (*Reddit.com*, 16 April 2016) https://www.reddit.com/r/ethereum/comments/4gigyd/decentralized_court/, proposing a 'decentralized court' 'by which a user could ask a question, expressed in the form of English text, and have a decentralized mechanism ... determine the answer, and then send a callback and a log to the user who asked the question'.

[12] See *infra* para accompanying n 31.

to be highly correlated, could work reasonably well with such a simple scheme. Moreover, it is possible to imagine blockchain-based insurance that would also allow for pay-outs to be greater or less than insureds' contributions. Investors might contribute to the pool as well, performing a function similar to buyers of catastrophe bonds.[13] Then, the smart contract protocol would need to specify a process for determining what percentage of the total pool would be awarded to insureds based on their claims. If the level of losses were unexpectedly high, then the investors might not recover all of the funds they invested; if they were lower or the same as expected, then investors would recover their funds, plus some portion of the funds provided by the insureds. A more elaborate design might allow for reinsurance.

Whether or not the pay-outs are guaranteed to equal the contributions to the pool, an insured would be hesitant to contribute to a pool as described so far, if the insured expected other insureds to be of higher risk. If pay-outs are simply proportional to losses, then the pool will be beset by adverse selection,[14] with only those insureds with the highest risk willing to join the pool. Lower-risk parties will either forego insurance altogether or will opt for traditional insurance, where an insurance company adjusts premia based on the risk of each insured. Meanwhile, moral hazard would likely rear its ugly head if the rules of the insurance pool did not ban highly risky activities.[15] The twin dangers of adverse selection and moral hazard, it might seem, would doom blockchain-based insurance by preventing it from performing perhaps the most important function of an insurance company: underwriting.

There are, however, at least two possible means of making pay-outs proportional to risk. The first approach is to change the arbitrator's assignment. Instead of measuring only the loss amount, the arbitrator would seek to estimate *ex post* the *ex ante* distribution of various possible loss levels. This would make it possible to determine the portion of the premium allocated to the loss level realized and the *ex ante* probability of that loss. The insured would then be credited with that portion of the premium multiplied by the *ex ante* probability. High-risk insureds would thus receive lower pay-outs. One can view this system as an *ex post* alternative to underwriting. Meanwhile, some insureds might exclude coverage for high-risk activities or find other means of committing to being low risk (such as installing fire protection devices), thus lowering moral hazard. This is a form of self-underwriting. The reward for doing so is that if a still-covered loss occurs, the arbitrator will conclude that the losses were lower probability and thus the pay-outs were higher. A challenge with this approach is that it may sometimes be challenging to measure *ex ante* risk *ex post*. But perfection is not needed for such insurance to serve a risk-reducing function, and insureds who need greater assurance can always break their *ex ante* payments down into categories for which more risk data is generally available. It might seem more troublesome that there might be systematic errors in making such hindsight valuations. Any systematic errors, however, will affect all insureds making claims on the fund and will thus cancel out.

The second approach for considering insureds' various risk profiles would be for blockchain-based insurance to develop a system of underwriting, thus making it more akin to existing forms of insurance. This system might piggy-back on existing insurance contracts or alternative form contracts might be developed. Either way, a decentralized system of assessing the risk of a potential insured would be needed. For example, some third parties might specialize in certifying insureds for a fee. Investors would then take into account the reputation of these third parties in determining whether to cover some portion of the risk for an insured. The arrangement would thus be similar to that provided by Lloyds of

[13] See Lawrence Cunningham, 'Securitizing Audit Failure Risk: An Alternative to Caps on Damages' (2007) 49 *William and Mary Law Review*, 764–66, describing the market for such bonds.

[14] See George Akerlof, 'The Market for "Lemons": Quality Uncertainty and the Market Mechanism' (1970) 84 *Quarterly Journal of Economics*, 488, providing the canonical explanation of the problem.

[15] See generally 44 AM. JUR. 2D Insurance § 1198.

London.[16] Algorithmically, this is not much more complex to implement than the approach above. It insists on taking risk into account *ex ante* rather than *ex post*, thus providing greater predictability but at larger transactions costs. The principal challenge with this approach is that it could take longer to develop as investors would only gradually be able to learn which third parties' evaluations to trust.

If blockchain-based insurance can gain a foothold in the market despite the value instability of existing cryptocurrencies, one virtue of the blockchain is that information on transactions would be publicly available. A critical function of modern insurance companies is to provide actuarial expertise, largely based on proprietary data. If the blockchain makes publicly available all contracts, along with third-party certifications and *ex post* adjudications, then the relevant data will be shared. Data, of course, must be analysed. Possibly, such analysis will take the form of open-source code. Alternatively, market participants, such as certifiers and investors, may independently analyse the data, therefrom obtaining a competitive advantage to the extent that their trade secret models are more accurate than their competitors'. Either way, potential insureds would be in a much better position to evaluate potential insurance contracts. The large expenditures of insurance companies on advertising, much of it largely uninformative, likely reflect the difficulty that modern-day consumers have in evaluating potential insurers. With blockchain insurance, there are no insurance companies but there might be other market participants the credibility of whom is at issue. Open data might allow for the creation of metrics to inform questions such as how commonly arbitrators are overturned on appeal and how much reinsurance counterparties have. Of course, some potential insureds will not want their contracts to be publicly available, but in a world in which property values are either published or generally estimable, many insureds may not be bothered by the loss of privacy.[17]

Prognosticating future market developments is always risky and I do not mean to imply that blockchain-based insurance will necessarily upend the insurance industry as conventionally understood, or even that it will earn substantial market share. Indeed, this chapter will identify significant obstacles to such insurance, and although these obstacles could be overcome, it is difficult to guess whether that might happen in the next decade, or even in the next fifty years. Even once the obstacles have been removed, private ordering can take a long time. There are strong network benefits to existing insurance, and blockchain-based insurance would, for the most part, need to be built from the ground up. Finally, even if blockchain-based insurance is developed, it is not clear what precise form such insurance would take—for example, whether the total amount of premiums to be returned to insureds will be set in advance.

The purpose of this chapter is not to resolve such questions, but rather to simply sketch out some ways that blockchain-based insurance might work—to establish a proof of concept rather than a prediction. This sketch, much of which has already been accomplished in this introduction, is needed to support the chapter's observations about how the law might affect blockchain-based insurance. As suggested above, existing regulation of insurance carriers may boost blockchain-based insurance because some forms of blockchain-based insurance may be beyond the reach of regulators, in much the same way as municipal regulation of taxi drivers allegedly helped ride-sharing services such as Uber.[18] On the other hand, this perspective may underestimate the willingness of lawmakers to regulate blockchain-based

---

[16] See generally Alan S. Gutterman, 'Business Transactions Solutions' § 231:62 (August 2018 update) https://www.westlaw.com/Document/I350570b33d2811e0b13e817f061d3d9b/View/FullText.html?transitionType=Default&contextData=(sc.Default)&VR=3.0&RS=cblt1.0 (discussing the Lloyds of London marketplace).

[17] It also might be possible to develop smart contracts that protect privacy, while still providing relevant data in aggregate. See Ahmed Kosba, Andrew Miller, Elaine Shi et al., 'Hawk: The Blockchain Model of Cryptography and Privacy-Preserving Smart Contracts', 2016 IEEE Symposium on Security and Privacy (SP), 839.

[18] See, e.g., Katherine O'Connor, 'Along for the Ride: Regulating Transportation Network Companies' (2016) 51 *Tulsa Law Review*, 582.

insurance, for example, by targeting purchasers, or to provide advantages like tax deductibility to providers of traditional insurance. Meanwhile, a foreign legal system could significantly boost the prospects of blockchain-based insurance by creating a fiat cryptocurrency; Venezuela has done this with its Petro coin, but in principle this could occur in a country with a stable economy. Alternatively, a government could boost cryptocurrency-based insurance by creating a regulatory framework making it possible for premiums to be invested in real assets during the life of insurance contracts.

The chapter continues as follows. Section II describes how blockchain-based insurance might work, first identifying a limited role for the blockchain with traditional insurers and then expanding on this introduction's sketch of how the blockchain might facilitate insurance disintermediation—that is, the pooling of risk without insurance companies as conventionally conceived. Section III then documents how the legal system can make insurance expensive, thus providing a market opportunity for a new, unregulated product, and identifies legal obstacles to blockchain-based insurance.

II. How Blockchain-Based Insurance Would Work

McKinsey & Co.'s report, entitled 'Blockchain-in-Insurance—Opportunity or Threat?',[19] limits its discussion of the 'threat' to a single sentence. 'As an innovative technology, blockchain presents a threat for incumbents in the form of innovative business models and/or cost advantages.'[20] The report does not elaborate on what these 'innovative business models' might be, focusing instead on potential benefits of the blockchain to incumbent insurance policies. An Ernst & Young report on blockchain-based insurance takes a similar approach.[21] Perhaps the assumption is that incumbent insurance companies will be as well positioned to take advantage of the opportunities offered by the blockchain in insurance as upstarts. These 'opportunities', however, signal the possibility for broader disruptions than the reports acknowledge.

A. With traditional insurers

The McKinsey report suggests that the blockchain may provide a mechanism for customers to provide data to insurance, and other, companies without being subject to endless entry and verification screens. The report describes technology as allowing a 'customer [to] grant a company access to identity data when necessary for a contract closure'.[22] While this may seem relatively trivial, the report is correct to highlight it because the easier it is for customers to share their information, the more likely customers will compare different companies' insurance products. But even if insurance companies can obtain customer information more easily, a significant explanation for customer loyalty lies in the difficulty of comparing insurance products. We will see below, however, that a public blockchain may make it easier for customers to determine which insurance product is likely to provide it with the best risk protection.[23]

The McKinsey report specifically identifies 'smart contracts on top of a blockchain' as offering various benefits, such as 'automation of claims handling' and as providing 'a reliable and transparent payout mechanism for the customer'.[24] But barring rare instances of cheques lost in the mail, customers already know when insurance companies make pay-outs to them

---

[19] McKinsey & Co., 'Blockchain in Insurance—Opportunity or Threat?' (2016) https://www.mckinsey.com/industries/financial-services/our-insights/blockchain-in-insurance-opportunity-or-threat.

[20] ibid., 7.

[21] Ernst & Young, 'Blockchain in Insurance: Applications and Pursuing a Path to Adoption' (2017) https://webforms.ey.com/Publication/vwLUAssets/EY-blockchain-in-insurance/$FILE/EY-blockchain-in-insurance.pdf.

[22] ibid., 3.   [23] See section II.B.3.   [24] See McKinsey & Co. (n 19), 4.

and the use of permissioned blockchains will not guarantee faster delivery to the customer. The report notes that 'a smart contract can ensure that the claim is only paid out if the car is repaired in a garage preferred and pre-defined by the insurer',[25] but insurance companies can easily enforce such restrictions absent smart contracts. The greater potential for smart contracts is that they might provide greater assurance to the customer that the insurance company will make appropriate payments when claims arise. But this will occur only if smart contracts change the process for resolving claims in a fundamental way, for example, by allowing a third-party arbitrator to determine whether to honour claims.

The report also notes that the blockchain might reduce fraudulent transactions, by allowing for validation of documents, such as customer medical reports, and 'detect[ing] patterns of fraudulent behavior related to a specific identity'.[26] But as the report notes, such benefits require 'intensive cooperation between insurers, manufacturers, customers, and other parties'.[27] Insurance companies might not have sufficient incentive to share data, particularly if their data provides them a competitive advantage. But competitors relying solely on the blockchain would need to be transparent almost by necessity. If the transparency of blockchain-based insurance deters customers from engaging in fraud (perhaps those customers will continue to work with traditional insurers), blockchain-based insurance might gain a significant advantage over those insurers. Meanwhile, the report notes that reinsurance may be more feasible if insurance transactions are represented on the blockchain,[28] but this too suggests that a form of competition featuring transparency may have some long-term advantages over existing proprietary competition.

B. Without traditional insurers

Neither the McKinsey nor the Ernst & Young report considers the possibility that smart contracts might facilitate the development of an unregulated form of insurance. The legal system has long played a critical role in the insurance market. It is possible to imagine a world in which companies, like telecommunications providers, could furnish services even if the contracts they entered into with customers were not legally enforceable,[29] as customers would recognize the reputational incentives that such providers would have to furnish services. But this seems far less plausible in the insurance context. Though relatively few insureds end up in coverage litigation with their insurance companies, the possibility of such litigation has a substantial disciplining effect. It assures customers that insurance companies will not simply walk off with their premiums if they determine that the funds being held for consumers exceed the present discounted value of profits from honest insurance provision. Smart contracts, however, provide an alternative form of guarantee to customers that no one will breach their promise and walk off with their funds. They can thus serve as an alternative to the legal system, in terms of both regulation and adjudication.

Indeed, with the pure insurance pool model, insureds need not trust one another so long as the smart contract provides assurance that total pay-outs will be equal to premiums. There is no party that has the ability with such an arrangement to take the premiums and run, assuming that the smart contracts cannot be exploited by hackers. It is this advantage that makes this type of blockchain-based insurance coverage more likely to develop initially rather than a full-blown substitute for the existing insurance system. But

---

[25] ibid.   [26] ibid., 5.   [27] ibid., 5.

[28] ibid., 6. Similarly, the Ernst & Young report (n 21), 4, notes that 'P&C insurers seeking clearer visibility into their reinsurance contracts and risk exposures may gain it through blockchain.'

[29] For an argument that contracts sometimes can be self-enforcing, see Alan Schwartz and Robert Scott, 'Contract Theory and the Limits of Contract Law' (2003) 113 *Yale Law Journal*, 541. Given that consumers generally do not read contracts, the mandated disclosure of contract terms may produce relatively little consumer benefit. See, e.g., Omri-Ben Shahar and Carl Schneider, *More Than You Wanted to Know: The Failure of Mandated Disclosure* (Princeton University Press 2014).

a pooling approach has its own challenges, as insureds must still be convinced that other contributors to the pool will not have some inherent advantage over them in claiming the funds *ex post*. Insureds must thus have some ability to trust an arbitrator, but we will see that careful design can limit the power of any single arbitrator and thus facilitate a pooling arrangement. Trustworthy adjudication will be even more important if the total size of pay-outs is not guaranteed to be equal to the total premiums, especially if a substitute for *ex ante* underwriting is used.

1. Pooling through smart contracts

The smart contract insurance pool is straightforward in design. A smart contract would be produced as a form of open-source software code. To purchase insurance, an individual or entity would digitally sign the smart contract. The smart contract would include virtual blanks for two important pieces of information. The first is the amount of cryptocurrency being contributed to the contract (which might be constrained by the smart contract to being within some range, to avoid both frivolously low coverage amounts and coverage amounts so high as to increase risk to other members of the pool). The smart contract might be considered incomplete until this money is paid, or the contract could be designed so that a specific premium is required, with the contract ceasing to be operational if a premium payment is not later made. The second type of information concerns the insurable interest. The simplest form this might take is a hash code uniquely identifying a document created by the insured, and made publicly available, that provides information about the interest insured. Insureds might fill out open-source forms that solicit relevant questions about the insurable interest. Critically, placing the hash on a reliable blockchain using a suitably robust protocol such as proof of work makes it virtually impossible to change the document after its initial creation.

The smart contract would be governed by its code but claim arbitrators would be expected to make their decisions according to the contract terms applying to all insureds using that smart contract. The code for the smart contract might include a hash of a document containing such terms. (Again, the smart contract code itself could produce a hash, thus ensuring that the terms cannot be tampered with.) These terms might be designed to combat obvious forms of adverse selection. For example, the terms might provide that no coverage will be available if it turns out that the insured failed to disclose certain types of information, such as pre-existing conditions in a health insurance contract. Or, a fire insurance policy might combat moral hazard by barring coverage if it turned out that the insured failed properly to maintain smoke detectors. Meanwhile, individual insureds might add their own coverage restrictions to the contract. By eliminating coverage for some scenarios, the insured effectively allocates more of the premium to coverage in other scenarios, thus increasing pay-outs in those cases.

Specific exclusions, however, are not essential, so long as claim pay-outs are based on *ex post* estimates of *ex ante* risk. What is essential is that the contract specify, both with code and with instructions, how claims should be handled. A simple arrangement would work as follows. An insured with a claim will specify the maximum amount of the claim. To discourage frivolous and excess claims, the insured must pay some percentage of this amount (perhaps 5%), but no less than a specified minimum, to fund the claim arbitrator. The arbitrator's role will then be to determine how much of the claim to allow. The arbitrator would do this by retrospectively allocating the premium across different types and levels of losses. That is, the arbitrator would estimate the *ex ante* probability of every type of loss and level of loss within that type and would then allocate the premium across these types and levels in the way that *ex ante* would most reduce risk. That should allow the arbitrator to determine what portion of the premium should be attributed to a loss of the type and level experienced. Then, the arbitrator would determine the type and level of loss actually experienced, multiply by the amount of the premium allocated to this loss, and divide this by the *ex ante* probability of the loss. The lesser of this number and the claim sought can be defined as the 'verified claim'.

Consider the following basic example. Suppose that an insured purchases car insurance and specifies no further exclusions. The arbitrator might determine that there was a 1% chance of a $10,000 loss and a 2% chance of a $5,000 loss. The optimal *ex ante* insurance premium would then have been $200 (0.01*$10,000 + 0.02*$5,000). If the insured, in fact, purchased $200 in insurance, then this insurance would be allocated evenly between the two contingencies as this would provide optimal insurance. If the insured only purchased $100 in insurance then that $100 would be allocated entirely to insurance against the chance of the higher loss, as this can be shown to minimize the variance of loss. For a $150 premium, $100 would be allocated against the $10,000 risk and $50 would be allocated against the $5,000 risk. Of course, in reality there might be many more levels of loss, as well as possibly losses of different types (say, vehicle damage and rental costs while the vehicle is being fixed). Still, so long as the arbitrator can estimate the *ex ante* probabilities of these events—and, in time, the transparency of the blockchain should improve an arbitrator's accuracy in doing so—it should be straightforward to determine the optimal insurance allocation.

Smart contracts would be paid out all at once, at the conclusion of the policy period. (An insured would be able to sell the right to a smart contract payment at an earlier time.) Particularly with early smart contracts, this should also facilitate making *ex ante* assessments as the arbitrator would, at least, be able to look at data associated with all contracts and claims. If verified claims exceed the total premiums, then an insured with a verified claim would receive the verified amount multiplied by the quotient of total premiums divided by total verified claims. The smart contract, however, also must address the contingency in which verified claims are less than total premiums. One possibility is to pay extra on claims. This may be an appropriate approach if there is a concern that arbitrators may pay too little on claims. Another possibility is to refund the remaining amount to all insureds in an amount proportional to their contributions. Mutual insurance companies often take a similar approach, paying dividends to insureds when claim pay-outs are sufficiently low.[30] This approach avoids providing a windfall to those who have verified claims and it is essential, at least, if there are no verified claims.

All of this should be straightforward to implement in a smart contract, once a smart contract platform is suitably developed. Calculating pay-outs is a matter of arithmetic that can easily be implemented in a computer algorithm. The hard work is done by the arbitrators. The most important function of a smart contract is to provide a suitable mechanism for selection of an arbitrator. A smart contract might just select the arbitrator in advance. This can technically be implemented by including in the smart contract the public key of the arbitrator, who would then use the corresponding private key to confirm particular awards. The public–private key pair might be owned by an entity or by an individual. Indeed, this might well be the entity that constructs and markets the particular smart contract. So long as this entity is sufficiently trustworthy, insureds should be willing to participate.

There are two possible concerns about such an arrangement. First, particularly if the goal is to avoid legal regulation, it might be desirable for the arbitrator to be anonymous. This concern may be overstated, however, particularly since the arbitrator could be based in a 'friendly' jurisdiction like the Cayman Islands, reviewing evidence submitted electronically. Second, and more seriously, there is a danger that the arbitrator might engage in fraud, for example, by adding one or more spurious insurance contracts to the pool and then filing false claims that are then given higher verified values. Over time, such a scheme is likely to

---

[30] See, e.g., Investopedia, https://www.investopedia.com/terms/a/annual-dividend.asp.

be uncovered. At least, it would be apparent that verified claims for smart contracts resolved by the arbitrator tended to be high and this should lead individuals seeking the best deal to contract with other insurance pool providers. In the long run, arbitrators might develop sufficient reputations to make it more profitable to arbitrate honestly than to submit false claims. Assuming self-dealing can be avoided, at least in the long term, arbitrators should prove more trustworthy than traditional insurance companies, who have an inherent conflict of interest.

A slightly more complex arrangement would allow for the smart contract provider to designate a pool of arbitrators, with the arbitrator for any particular claim selected at random from the pool. A further improvement is to allow one arbitrator's judgment to be challenged by an appeal to a second arbitrator. The insured might be allowed a rehearing if the insured were willing to pay the required arbitral fee again or perhaps only if the insured were willing to pay some higher fee. Meanwhile, a third party might be allowed to pay the same amount to challenge an initial arbitrator's ruling as being too large. The right to be that third party might be auctioned to the third party willing to pay the most (but no less than the arbitral fee) for the right to receive any decline in the size of the verified claim. Any auction proceeds in excess of the arbitral fee could be added to the premium pool and thus distributed among verified claimants. Further refinements could be made. For example, if an appeal results in a sufficiently different valuation, the initial arbitrator might forfeit the arbitral fee, or even be required to forfeit a bond. The point here is not to determine the optimal contract, something that could be worked out with time, but simply to indicate that relatively simple systems for choosing and incentivizing arbitrators and creating a form of appellate adjudication could be devised.

Perhaps the most ambitious approach to arbitration would be one that I have discussed in earlier papers: the use of peer-to-peer adjudication.[31] I will not repeat a full description of peer-to-peer adjudication here, but its most important characteristic is that no arbitrator need be selected. Instead, anyone would be able to offer a suggested resolution of the claim. A participant in the resolution process, however, would be given economic incentives to announce a resolution as close as possible to any resolution that a *subsequent* participant in the process might provide. A participant who announces a valuation closer to the later valuation than the prior valuation will earn currency, while a participant who pushes the valuation in one direction only to have the valuation pushed back in the opposite direction will generally lose currency. Because a participant will not know who might participate later, the incentive of each participant is to seek out the 'focal' resolution to the question of how large the verified claim should be. The provisions of the smart contract concerning how claims should be resolved are likely to determine what participants in this market believe is focal.

2. Underwriting, investment, and reinsurance

Just as one might develop much more complex mechanisms for resolving claims than the one specified here, so too might one develop more complex insurance schemes, including insurance schemes where total pay-outs do not necessarily equal total premiums paid. One means of accomplishing this would be for the smart contract sponsor to commit funds to the pool (or to find outside investors willing to commit funds). Instead of the insureds receiving a refund if total premiums are in excess of verified claims, the smart contract provider would receive the difference but the provider could lose some or all of the funds if verified claims exceed premiums. This approach magnifies the importance of insureds' trust in the arbitration process. Insureds may have more faith in that process if the arbitrators' responsibility is

---

[31] See Michael Abramowicz, 'Cryptocurrency-Based Law' (2016) 58 *Arizona Law Review*, 359; see also Abramowicz, 'Cryptoinsurance' (n 1), applying peer-to-peer adjudication to the insurance context.

less open-ended than making *ex post* assessments of *ex ante* probabilities. Hence, it is likely that once the market moves away from the pool model, there will be a concomitant tendency for insurance contracts to become more rule-bound.

An approach of this sort will be essential in any insurance context in which losses are likely to be highly correlated, for example, property insurance that includes protection against hazards like hurricanes or earthquakes. A pool approach might still be viable for insurance of that sort, but the risks would need to be diversified. Smart contract sponsors, for example, might seek out smart contract holders from many different locations in order to minimize the risk that total claims will greatly exceed total premiums. But if the adjudicative process were some day to become sufficiently trusted, then there is no reason that blockchain-based insurance cannot protect against highly correlated losses in much the same way as regular insurance. It is also possible to imagine hybrid approaches. For example, the smart contract provider might place aside funds to be added to the pool only in the event of some specific contingency, for example a hurricane with damages in a particular region exceeding some threshold. The smart contract provider might even raise such funds from third parties looking for high returns, thus creating an investment vehicle similar to catastrophe bonds.[32] With this contingent financing, insureds might still face some risk that losses might be unexpectedly high as a result of a statistical blip but would receive assurance that sufficient funds would be available in the event of an identifiable catastrophe.

Another means of protecting insureds in the event of high losses would be for some form of blockchain-based reinsurance to emerge. This could be implemented in smart contracts as well and provide a means for risk pooling to occur beyond the limits of any particular smart contract. For example, a smart contract sponsor might provide that some portion of premiums for the smart contract will be placed aside, with the aggregate invested into a reinsurance smart contract. That smart contract might itself take the form of an insurance pool with pay-outs made to the smart contracts in the pool with the most unexpectedly high losses. Of course, just as the insurance industry features tiers of reinsurance, so too could smart insurance contracts on the blockchain.

It might also be possible for blockchain-based insurance to increase its credibility by piggybacking off existing legal regimes. For example, a smart contract sponsor based in the Cayman Islands might wish to use certain real assets as security for smart contracts in the event that claims are sufficiently high. Meanwhile, the smart contract might provide for adjudication in a traditional court or arbitral body to determine whether those real assets must be sold so that the proceeds can be added to a smart insurance pool. One defect of the smart contract arrangements described so far is that assets such as premiums are tied up in the smart currency during the contract period, rather than invested, as would occur with typical insurance arrangements. But if a single jurisdiction credibly commits to enforcing contracts related to blockchain-based insurance, regardless of whether those contracts accord with the insurance law of other jurisdictions, then that provides a nexus between the cryptocurrency and the broader financial world. Different jurisdictions might perform different roles—supporting a fiat cryptocurrency, performing adjudication, recognizing the possibility that a smart contract may be a beneficial owner of real assets,[33] and enforcing judgments accordingly—but a single jurisdiction might determine that it could benefit by serving as a virtual host for smart contracts, in much the same way as Delaware has profited from its domination in corporate law charters.

---

[32] See Cunningham (n 13), discussing catastrophe bonds.
[33] See Abramowicz, 'Cryptocurrency-Based Law' (n 31), 413, discussing the possibility that a cryptocurrency could own property.

3. Consumer information

Blockchain-based insurance is non-existent, and even if it emerges, it will initially be unfamiliar. Most insurance customers will, at first, be more comfortable sticking with established players. Yet the radical transparency of such insurance makes it plausible that consumers might learn that smart contracts are trustworthy, and more than that, consumers might be able to determine which smart contracts are most appropriate for their particular circumstances. The defining differences between smart contracts will be the code governing them and the instructions for arbitrators. Media companies like *Consumer Reports* or the *Wall Street Journal* might review such documents and rate these contracts. Over time, more sophisticated ratings might be developed based on the results of adjudications for different smart contracts.

It is also possible that further smart contracts might be developed to provide guidance to consumers. For example, third parties might contract with insureds to rate insureds' likely customer satisfaction with different smart contract providers. The third parties might be compensated based on the degree to which their assessments proved accurate, with the compensation formulas depending on the third parties' performance across many smart contracts and thus not dependent solely on the vagaries of any single customer's experience. Such third parties would in effect serve a role of insurance brokers but unlike traditional insurance brokers, they would only be paid to the extent that they provided useful information to consumers about their likely satisfaction. This would give the third parties some incentive to determine which smart contracts might be most appropriate for which customers. In principle, it may be possible for similar institutions to evolve with traditional insurance but it is much more straightforward in a world in which customers can simply be required to assess their satisfaction *ex post* and these values can automatically determine brokers' success.

III. The Law's Role in Blockchain-Based Insurance

Sections I and II have described how blockchain-based insurance might work, but that still leaves the fundamental question of whether blockchain-based insurance has any inherent competitive advantage over ordinary insurance. The blockchain may well be an overhyped technology. At its core, a blockchain has no technical advantages over an ordinary database and, indeed, the challenges of scaling blockchain technology may mean that blockchains will often be inferior to databases.[34] If the blockchain is to serve a significant role in the insurance market, it is likely to be not because the technology is revolutionary as a database technology but because a cryptocurrency armed with smart contract capabilities can escape legal regulation. Indeed, the goal of escaping regulation may well be a principal motivating factor in some other smart contract projects, such as augur.net, a decentralized prediction market that can be used for sports gambling.

This section addresses two questions. To what extent does legal regulation create expenses for traditional insurance carriers that blockchain-based insurance would not need to bear? And, to what extent could legal regulators successfully defend the project of insurance regulation by blocking unregulated blockchain-based insurance? This section does not address the broader question of whether blockchain-based insurance on the whole would improve social welfare. There are significant benefits to many existing forms of insurance regulation, for example in protecting consumers from fraud. Just as some investors lost money in insecure Bitcoin-based banks, there is a danger that investors might lose money as a result of poorly designed blockchain-based insurance contracts. The ultimate question, not addressed

---

[34] See Preethi Kasireddy, 'Blockchains Don't Scale. Not Today, at Least, but There's Hope' (*Hackernoon.com*, 23 August 2017) https://hackernoon.com/blockchains-dont-scale-not-today-at-least-but-there-s-hope-2cb43946551a.

here, is whether the transparency of the blockchain and smart contracts could lead to a form of private ordering that is equally or more effective in providing value to insureds.

A. The expense of law

1. Compliance

Smart contract providers might not need to employ lawyers to ensure compliance with state, national, and international insurance regulation. The potential savings from direct compliance activities, however, may be small. A recent survey of property and casualty insurers determined that the insurers' average corporate and regulatory compliance expenses amounted to 0.19% of premiums.[35] By itself, this is not a sufficiently large amount of money to make a compelling case for smart contracts. It is quite small relative to expenses overall. In the first half of 2016, the expense ratio for property-and-casualty insurers in the United States was 27.7%.[36] Of course, without insurance companies, other expenses contributing to this ratio would also be eliminated. Once the smart contract exists, all that is needed are willing insureds, arbitrators, and, if applicable, investors who provide a cushion in the event of high claims. To be sure, arbitrators will demand compensation. But this suggests that the most relevant savings are not directly from compliance activities but from other sources, such as reduced marketing expenses, reduced costs associated with processing claims, and reduced inefficiencies resulting from legal compliance that forces insurers to adopt inefficient contracts.

2. Adjudication

There is no inherent guarantee that claims processing will be cheaper with smart contracts than with traditional blockchain-based insurance. Indeed, a strong argument against the insurance pool is that every insurance claim will result in some form of adjudication as the arbitrator will need to determine *ex ante* probabilities of losses and thus allocate premia, in addition to determining whether the claimed loss occurred. Yet much of this work will likely not be repeated from one arbitration to another. Furthermore, if there is some form of appellate review, arbitrators will have some incentive to explain their decisions and an arbitrator will likely start by looking at similar past decisions to determine how to allocate *ex ante* probabilities. The types of information relevant to determining whether a loss occurred—photographs, statements from witnesses, and so forth—are likely to be relatively standardized. So too are the types of information likely to be relevant to assessing *ex ante* probabilities, particularly information that shows the level of care that the defendant was exercising. Just as precedent is valuable in traditional adjudication, so too might it be used even in an informal system of adjudication on the blockchain.[37]

Inevitably, there will be some claims that require arbitrators to exercise judgement in certain respects, but the informality of the arbitration process should allow arbitrators to focus specifically on these aspects of claims. Part of the expense of the legal system owes

---

[35] See Property Casualty Insurers, 'Regulatory Compliance', http://www.pciaa.net/industry-issues/erm-emerging-risks/news/emerging-risks-regulatory-compliance.

[36] National Association of Insurance Commissioners, '2016 Mid-Year Property and Casuality Insurance Industry' (2016), Centre for Insurance Policy and Research Report.

[37] For a sceptical view on adjudication for smart contracts, see Jeremy Sklaroff, 'Comment, Smart Contracts and the Cost of Inflexibility' (2017) 166 *University of Pennsylvania Law Review*, 300–02. Sklaroff argues that with adjudication by smart contracts, parties 'cannot cite precedent to incorporate previous decisions, and may not even know what those previous decisions were'. But adjudicative opinions could be made public, and adjudicators (who wish to avoid being overturned on appeal) will have incentives to make their arguments clear and to give appropriate weight to arguments made in the past. A full analysis of smart contract-based adjudication is a project for future development.

to its formality, as well as to regulations requiring law degrees and bar admissions for law-yers. Of course, there are benefits to such formality, and the ultimate question in assessing blockchain-based insurance is whether a sufficiently strong adjudication system can be de-signed without these formal processes. Perhaps the arbitration process, as described above, will not be sufficient, but a virtue of private ordering is that aspects of the system that prove problematic can be improved upon without requiring revolutions in civil procedure. For example, if a perception develops that there is too much fraud, then smart contracts might provide for benefits to whistleblowers who identify such fraud.

Similarly, if the adjudicative process is too open-ended, the system can rely more on underwriting. Yet, there are strong reasons to believe that a system of smart contracts will rely more on standards than on rules. This may seem counterintuitive; it might seem that a mechanical system like a smart contract necessarily will require unambiguous rules. But that is impossible. Any contract that relies not just on code but also on human language to refer to events in the real world, as any insurance contract must, will necessarily require the exer-cise of judgement. We might tolerate a greater degree of subjectivity with smart contracts so long as arbitrators have incentives to make decisions as other arbitrators would, rather than according to their whim or political preference, and the appellate process can provide such incentives.

One reason that insurance contracts are relatively rule-like is that rules provide protec-tion against legal decision maker biases. Sometimes, these biases may be essentially random, with some judges biased in favour of insurance companies and some biased in favour of insureds. But most bias will be of the latter type. This is true for two reasons. First, the doc-trine of *contra proferentum* provides that ambiguous policy provisions will be interpreted against the insurance company.[38] Second, juries may have a natural bias to favour insureds, especially when the insureds are individuals. Collectively, these two pressures will push in-surance companies in the direction of using clear rules, rather than relying on standards. Rules are inevitably over-inclusive and under-inclusive and this may lead the companies to adopt inefficient contracts, relative to those they would adopt in a world in which they did not expect bias in adjudication.

Of course, it is possible that arbitrators may have their own biases but individual monetary incentives seem likely to go a long way towards providing fairness incentives. Moreover, with an insurance pool, if arbitrators are systematically biased, that will have little effect. If, for example, every insured receives a valuation 20% higher than it should be, then all claimants will still receive the same amount of money as if this did not occur, since pay-outs are pro-portional to verified claims. Some bias might still inhere in the initial question of whether a covered loss occurred at all, and fraudulent or generous claims will come at the expense of other policy-holders making claims. But if the problem is serious, providers of smart contracts might choose different arbitrators who they are confident will not permit weakly supported claims too easily.

3. Regulation

Perhaps the greatest market opportunities for unregulated insurance will arise where regu-lations cause market distortions. For example, laws may prevent insurers from taking into account applicants' genetic data in pricing coverage.[39] Should widespread whole genome testing become available, these laws threaten to create adverse selection problems, as indi-viduals with greater susceptibility to health problems may be most likely to purchase health

---

[38] See, 5 L. Toxic Torts § 31:65 (2017) https://legalsolutions.thomsonreuters.com/law-products/Treatises/Law-of-Toxic-Torts-Environmental-Law-Series/p/100027815.

[39] See, e.g., Massachusetts General Laws Ann. 175 § 1081 (2006).

and life insurance.[40] If this occurs, there will be a market opportunity to sell unregulated insurance to individuals lucky enough to have genes that make them lower risk. As discussed below, there may be challenges to offering unregulated blockchain insurance, but assuming that such insurance can exist, the market would be able to avoid regulations that cross-subsidize those with less healthy genes. My argument here is positive not normative; there are strong arguments for preventing genetic discrimination,[41] and perhaps even stronger ones for preventing race discrimination in insurance.[42] The point is simply that if the law prevents efficient contracting between insureds and insurers, that provides a competitive advantage to blockchain-based insurers that avoid regulation.

Other forms of regulation may similarly create market opportunities. Consider, for example, rate regulation. If rate regulation has the effect of cartelizing the industry and raising prices, unregulated insurers may be able to undercut existing prices. If, however, rate regulation tends to lower prices,[43] that can lead to supply shortages,[44] and blockchain-based insurance may fill the void by offering coverage. Meanwhile, coverage mandates can create opportunities for blockchain-based insurers. If all health insurance purchasers must provide maternity coverage,[45] then individuals who are confident that they will not need such coverage may purchase cheaper insurance. Similarly, some states provide that policies shall be incontestable after a certain period of time, meaning that false statements can no longer invalidate the policy.[46] If this is inefficient, either because it means that honest policy-holders are cross-subsidizing fraudsters or because it forces insurance companies to spend funds in excessive *ex ante* monitoring of insureds, there may again be a market opportunity for unregulated insurance.

The question, of course, is how great the market opportunities are. Insureds presumably already could purchase offshore insurance and submit claims over websites, yet such markets have not materialized as significant competitors to traditionally provided insurance. This may, however, be in part because insureds might not fully trust offshore insurers, a problem that smart contracts may address. Meanwhile, if smart contract-based insurance is administratively cheaper than traditional insurance, that provides further market opportunities.

B. Legal challenges

1. Legality

While legal regulation of insurance may create market opportunities for unregulated insurance, the possibility that lawmakers will seek to regulate unregulated insurance creates an obvious obstacle. The challenge is that if insurance is sold entirely through a cryptocurrency, it may be difficult to regulate. The government, however, may still have several possible approaches to blocking unregulated insurance.

First, the government might seek to regulate purchasers of insurance directly. Such regulation could be quite effective, particularly because the most obvious implementations of

---

[40] See, e.g., Chetan Gulati, 'Genetic Antidiscrimination Laws in Health Insurance: A Misguided Solution' (2001) 4 *Quinnipiac Health Law Journal*, 149.

[41] See Sonia Suter, 'The Allure and Peril of Genetics Exceptionalism: Do We Need Special Genetics Legislation?' (2001) 79 *Washington University Law Quarterly*, 669, noting that issues may be similar to those involved in medical discrimination.

[42] See, e.g., Jill Gaulding, 'Race, Sex, and Genetic Discrimination in Insurance: What's Fair?' (1995) 80 *Cornell Law Review*, 1646.

[43] Rate regulation may lower prices in the short term but raise them in the long term. See Angelo Borselli, 'Insurance Rates Regulation in Comparison with Open Competition' (2011) 18 *Connecticut Insurance Law Journal*, 109.

[44] See, e.g., Paul Joskow, 'Cartels, Competition and Regulation in the Property-Liability Insurance Industry' (2017) 4 *Bell Journal of Economics and Management Science*, 375.

[45] See, e.g., 42 U.S.C. § 2000e(k) (2012).   [46] See, e.g., California Insurance Code § 10206 (2017).

blockchain-based insurance require that insurance policies be stored transparently on the blockchain. The question is whether governments are willing to target consumers of insurance, rather than producers. If the government did decide to target consumers, the question then becomes whether such insurance might continue to exist without requiring consumers to identify themselves. Plausibly, information could be stored in encrypted form, but, at least, the arbitrator will need to be able to read an unencrypted version of the policy in determining whether to pay out claims. Conceivably, the government could pose as arbitrators to perform a sting operation against those filing insurance claims. Even less extreme action, however, could undermine aspects of the use case for blockchain by making it less transparent.

Second, the government might seek to ban the underlying cryptocurrency. China has aggressively cracked down on Bitcoin,[47] illustrating that a regulatory ban is at least possible. But such a crackdown is far easier in a country in which the internet is pervasively regulated. It seems unlikely that the United States or European countries would enact internet filtering to prevent consumers from contacting insurance sites. More plausibly, the government might regulate financial exchange transactions into and out of a cryptocurrency. Blockchain-based insurance could be considerably hampered if it were impossible to use a credit card or a bank account to purchase (or receive the sale proceeds of) cryptocurrency.[48] It will be difficult, however, for government officials to eradicate black markets, which might also be used for other troubling uses of cryptocurrency, such as paying extortion demands from ransomware developers. The question is whether government regulation adds enough hassle to cryptocurrency transactions to make blockchain-based insurance infeasible. At this point, the government has shown little interest in banning Bitcoin or Ethereum and it may be impractical for the government to add regulatory controls once the public depends on these cryptocurrencies.

2. Legal requirements

The legal system, however, may be able to thwart the development of particular blockchain-based insurance markets by requiring individuals to purchase legally regulated insurance. For example, drivers are generally required to purchase automobile insurance[49] and unregulated blockchain-based insurance presumably would not qualify. That does not necessarily entirely eliminate the possibility of blockchain-based insurance for additional coverage above and beyond that provided by insurance companies, such as for optional collision coverage. Meanwhile, to the extent that the law provides tax breaks for insurance, thus subsidizing legally recognized insurance, blockchain-based insurance will be at a considerable disadvantage. For example, life insurance proceeds are generally excludable from gross income under the Internal Revenue Code.[50] Any uncertainty about whether such income would be excludable would likely doom that form of blockchain-based insurance, at least, unless beneficiaries of such policies evade their tax liabilities, for example, by disguising their receipt of life insurance proceeds.

3. Legal support for blockchain-based insurance

It is not inevitable that the legal system will treat blockchain-based insurance disadvantageously. Existing insurance companies have rents to protect and can thus be expected to

---

[47] See Chen Jia, 'Crackdown Signals End of Illegal Exchanges' (*ChinaDaily.com*, 19 September 2017) 13, http://www.chinadaily.com.cn/business/2017-09/19/content_32183847.htm.

[48] 31 U.S.C. §§ 5361–5367 (2006): Unlawful Internet Gambling Enforcement Act of 2006, Pub. L. No. 109-347, tit. VIII, 120 Stat. 1952.

[49] See, e.g., Code of Virginia, Ann. § 46.2-439 (2017).

[50] See 26 U.S.C. International Revenue Code ('IRC') § 101.

lobby to cement their existing advantages and disadvantage blockchain-based insurance. But such efforts are not always successful. Taxicab companies, for example, have been mostly ineffective in countering ride-sharing services such as Uber, which have greatly reduced the value of medallion licenses.[51] Blockchain-based insurance could follow a similar path, in which customers purchase policies when their legal status remains uncertain but then provide pressure on legislators to allow such insurance.

If for these or other reasons, a legislature wanted to promote blockchain-based insurance, how might it do so? First, the law might explicitly allow such insurance and provide that blockchain-based insurance contracts are unenforceable in court. This would ensure continued evolution and competition in the design of arbitral mechanisms. Second, the law might allow for courts to be used to enforce promises that cannot be enforced by smart contracts alone, such as promises to use property recognized by the traditional legal system as security for blockchain-based insurance contracts. Third, if some degree of regulation is to be retained, these regulations should be tailored to blockchain-based insurance, recognizing that there may be no insurance company associated with any particular smart contract to regulate. Thus, regulation should directly affect insureds, for example, by providing penalties should insureds release types of information that should be irrelevant to insurance pricing, such as genetic information. Fourth, and most radically, a legislature might create a fiat cryptocurrency, denominated in the same currency unit as the main currency. A legal commitment that the government will exchange cryptocurrency units for dollars or other internationally recognized currency would reduce the risk associated with the volatility of the cryptocurrency itself. This could facilitate blockchain-based insurance not only in that country but also elsewhere. The absence of these forms of support could make it much more challenging for blockchain-based insurance to emerge.

IV. Conclusion

The sceptical perspective on blockchain-based insurance is that the blockchain merely facilitates transactions that easily can be performed without the blockchain and, indeed, that were performed at relatively low transactions costs without the internet. The bullish case for blockchain-based insurance highlights the possibility that such insurance could exist largely separate from the legal system, freeing it both of burdens associated with regulation by the administrative state and the expense associated with traditional adjudication in courts. This would require development of software code and accompanying contracts that insureds will trust, and such trust would likely come only with time. In the long run, however, it is plausible that more informal adjudicative structures could be cheaper and thus allow for more efficient, cheaper insurance contracts. Blockchain-based insurance also might be more transparent and trustworthy than traditional insurance, perhaps making it easier for consumers to determine which insurance is most appropriate for their needs. The legal system poses challenges for blockchain-based insurance as well. There is the danger that the legal system might effectively ban such insurance and the possibility that even if blockchain-based insurance avoids regulation, the absence of the legal system will cause inefficiencies, for example, by preventing the effective investment of premiums. Finally, if blockchain-based insurance does prosper, that might provide economic efficiency but at the expense of other goals of the legal system, such as ensuring that certain factors not be taken into account in insurance pricing.

---

[51] See BizJournals, 'Uber's Heavy Impact on Taxi Industry is Plainly Seen in the (Falling) Numbers)' (2015) *New York Business Journal*, https://www.bizjournals.com/newyork/news/2015/01/08/ubers-heavy-impact-on-taxi-industry-is-plainly.html.

V. Bibliography

5 L. Toxic Torts § 31:65 (2017) https://legalsolutions.thomsonreuters.com/law-products/Treatises/Law-of-Toxic-Torts-Environmental-Law-Series/p/100027815, accessed on 14 January 2019.

Abramowicz Michael, 'Cryptoinsurance' (2015) 50 *Wake Forest Law Review* 671.

Abramowicz Michael, 'Cryptocurrency-Based Law' (2016) 58 *Arizona Law Review* 359.

Akerlof George, 'The Market for "Lemons": Quality Uncertainty and the Market Mechanism' (1970) 84 *Quarterly Journal of Economics* 488.

BitShares, https://bitshares.org, accessed on 14 January 2019.

BizJournals, 'Uber's Heavy Impact on Taxi Industry is Plainly Seen in the (Falling) Numbers)' (2015) *New York Business Journal*, https://www.bizjournals.com/newyork/news/2015/01/08/ubers-heavy-impact-on-taxi-industry-is-plainly.html, accessed on 14 January 2019.

Borselli Angelo, 'Insurance Rates Regulation in Comparison with Open Competition' (2011) 18 *Connecticut Insurance Law Journal*.

Buterin Vitalik, 'Decentralized Court' (*Reddit.com*, 16 April 2016) https://www.reddit.com/r/ethereum/comments/4gigyd/decentralized_court/, accessed on 14 January 2019.

Calnan Alan, 'The Insurance Exclusionary Rule Revisited: Are Reports of Its Demise Exaggerated?' (1991) 52 *Ohio State Law Journal* 1177.

Cowen Tyler, 'Is Bitcoin Just a Bubble?' (*MarginalRevolution.com*, 30 November 2017) http://marginalrevolution.com/marginalrevolution/2017/11/bitcoin-just-bubble.html., accessed on 14 January 2019.

Cunningham Lawrence, 'Securitizing Audit Failure Risk: An Alternative to Caps on Damages' (2007) 49 *William and Mary Law Review* 711.

Ernst & Young, 'Blockchain in Insurance: Applications and Pursuing a Path to Adoption (2017) https://webforms.ey.com/Publication/vwLUAssets/EY-blockhain-in-insurance/$FILE/EY-blockhain-in-insurance.pdf, accessed on 14 January 2019.

Gaulding Jill, 'Race, Sex, and Genetic Discrimination in Insurance: What's Fair?' (1995) 80 *Cornell Law Review* 1646.

GitHub, https://github.com/pirapira/ethereum-formal-verification-overview, accessed 14 January 2019.

Gulati Chetan, 'Genetic Antidiscrimination Laws in Health Insurance: A Misguided Solution' (2001) 4 *Quinnipiac Health Law Journal* 149.

Gutterman Alan S., 'Business Transactions Solutions' § 231:62 (August 2018 update) https://www.westlaw.com/Document/I350570b33d2811e0b13e817f061d3d9b/View/FullText.html?transitionType=Default&contextData=(sc.Default)&VR=3.0&RS=cblt1.0, accessed on 14 January 2019.

Hans Valerie, 'The Illusions and Realities of Jurors' Treatment of Corporate Defendants' (1998) 48 *DePaul Law Review* 3227.

Investopedia, https://www.investopedia.com/terms/a/annual-dividend.asp., accessed on 14 January 2019.

Jia Chen, 'Crackdown Signals End of Illegal Exchanges' (*ChinaDaily.com*, 19 September 2017) 13, http://www.chinadaily.com.cn/business/2017-09/19/content_32183847.htm, accessed on 14 January 2019.

Joskow Paul, 'Cartels, Competition and Regulation in the Property-Liability Insurance Industry' (2017) 4 *Bell Journal of Economics and Management Science* 375.

Kasireddy Preethi, 'Blockchains Don't Scale. Not Today, at Least, but There's Hope' (*Hackernoon.com*, 23 August 2017) https://hackernoon.com/blockchains-dont-scale-not-today-at-least-but-there-s-hope-2cb43946551a, accessed on 14 January 2019.

Kosba Ahmed, Miller Andrew, Shi Elaine et al., 'Hawk: The Blockchain Model of Cryptography and Privacy-Preserving Smart Contracts', 2016 IEEE Symposium on Security and Privacy (SP).

McKinsey & Co., 'Blockchain in Insurance—Opportunity or Threat?' (2016) https://www.mckinsey.com/industries/financial-services/our-insights/blockchain-in-insurance-opportunity-or-threat, accessed on 14 January 2019.

National Association of Insurance Commissioners, '2016 Mid-Year Property and Causality Insurance Industry' (2016) Centre for Insurance Policy and Research Report.

O'Connor Katherine, 'Along for the Ride: Regulating Transportation Network Companies' (2016) 51 *Tulsa Law Review* 582.

Property Casualty Insurers, 'Regulatory Compliance', http://www.pciaa.net/industry-issues/erm-emerging-risks/news/emerging-risks-regulatory-compliance, accessed on 14 January 2019.

Schroeder Stan, 'Not Again: Hackers Steal $32 Million Worth of Ethereum' (*Mashable.com*, 20 July 2017) https://mashable.com/2017/07/20/ethereum-hackers-theft-32-million/?europe=true, accessed on 14 January 2019.

Schwartz Alan and Scott Robert, 'Contract Theory and the Limits of Contract Law' (2003) 113 *Yale Law Journal* 541.

Shahar Omri-Ben and Schneider Carl, *More Than You Wanted to Know: The Failure of Mandated Disclosure* (Princeton University Press 2014).

Sklaroff Jeremy, 'Comment, Smart Contracts and the Cost of Inflexibility' (2017) 166 *University of Pennsylvania Law Review* 263.

Suter Sonia, 'The Allure and Peril of Genetics Exceptionalism: Do We Need Special Genetics Legislation?' (2001) 79 *Washington University Law Quarterly* 669.

Tapscott Don and Tapscott Alex, *Blockchain Revolution* (Penguin 2016).

11

Blockchain, Securities Markets, and Central Banking

Alexandros L. Seretakis

I. Introduction

On 15 September 2008 Lehman Brothers filed for bankruptcy, unleashing the most severe economic crisis since the Great Depression.[1] The bankruptcy of Lehman Brothers was followed by the dry-up of liquidity in financial markets and the simultaneous distress of multiple, systemically important, financial institutions. In their quest to avert an economic calamity, governments and central banks around the world decided to massively intervene in financial markets and expend vast sums of taxpayer money in order to bail out failing financial institutions and stabilize the financial system.[2] Shortly after Lehman's bankruptcy, in November 2008, Satoshi Nakamoto, whose real identity remains unknown, driven in part by anger over the financial crisis, published a proposal for a peer-to-peer electronic cash system.[3] The proposal formed the basis for the launch, in January 2009, of Bitcoin, the world's first decentralized digital currency. Despite the initial enthusiasm surrounding Bitcoin and its potential to bypass the banking system and displace sovereign fiat currencies, the cryptocurrency has witnessed limited success due to its high volatility, its increasing use to facilitate criminal activities, and its vulnerability to hacking attacks and thefts.[4] Numerous market participants have forcefully expressed their scepticism regarding Bitcoin. For instance, Jamie Dimon, CEO of J. P. Morgan Chase, recently dubbed Bitcoin a fraud and predicted that it will blow up.[5]

While the hype around Bitcoin is already starting to fade, financial industry participants, regulators, and central bankers have turned their attention to Bitcoin's underlying technology, the blockchain, and its variants, collectively referred to as 'distributed ledger technologies'. Distributed ledger technologies have been touted as a panacea for resolving the inefficiencies of the current system for trading financial assets. For instance, in a rare case of industry-wide cooperation, over eighty of the world's most prominent financial institutions and regulators have formed a consortium led by financial technology company R3.[6] The aim of the consortium is the development of commercial applications of distributed ledger technologies for the financial industry and the promotion of industry-wide standards. Beyond that, central banks in both developed and developing countries are examining

---

[1] For an excellent account of the financial crisis, see Andrew Sorkin, *Too Big to Fail* (Penguin 2010); Gary Gordon and Andrew Metrick, 'Securitized Banking and the Run on Repo' (2012) 104 *Journal of Financial Economics*, 425.

[2] Mohamed El-Erian, *The Only Game in Town: Central Banks, Instability and Avoiding the Next Collapse* (Random House 2016); Ben Bernanke, *The Courage to Act: A Memoir of a Crisis and Its Aftermath* (Norton 2015).

[3] Satoshi Nakamoto, 'Bitcoin: A Peer-to-Peer Electronic Cash System' (*Bitcoin.org*, 2008) http://bitcoin.org/bitcoin.pdf [https://perma.cc/GXZ8-6 SDR].

[4] David Yermack, 'Is Bitcoin a Real Currency?' in *The Handbook of Digital Currency*, edited by David Kuo Chuen Lee (Elsevier 2015).

[5] Emily Glazer, 'J. P. Morgan's Jamie Dimon May Hate Bitcoin, but He Loves Blockchain' (*WallStreetJournal. com*, 16 October 2017) https://www.wsj.com/articles/j-p-morgans-james-dimon-may-hate-bitcoin-but-he-loves-blockchain-1508146203.

[6] Jemima Kelly, 'Blockchain Platform Developed by Banks to be Open-Source' (*Reuters.com*, 20 October 2016) http://uk.reuters.com/article/us-banks-blockchain-r3-exclusive-idUKKCN12K17E.

potential applications of distributed ledger technology in order to more effectively carry out their tasks. Andy Haldane, Chief Economist of the Bank of England, was the first central banker to publicly acknowledge the central role that the technology can play in supporting the future issuance of central bank digital currency.[7]

Nonetheless, the widespread adoption of the technology faces considerable legal hurdles, including the numerous new regulations imposed on financial markets and market participants in the aftermath of the financial crisis. In a recent speech, Abigail Johnson, CEO of Fidelity Investments, cited regulatory issues as a major obstacle to broader adoption of distributed ledger technology.[8] The aim of this chapter is to disentangle the myths from the realities of the so-called distributed ledger technology or blockchain revolution and discuss how the legal regime can act both as an impediment and as a catalyst to the widespread adoption of the technology.

Section I offers an introduction to distributed ledger technologies and seeks to demystify them. Section II examines the potential application of distributed ledger technologies to securities markets and central banking. Finally, section III discusses the role of law in the development of distributed ledger technology and its widespread adoption. On the one hand, numerous legal hurdles hinder the adoption of the technology. On the other hand, tweaks in the legal rules can act as a catalyst for its application. The Delaware Blockchain Initiative and the French Government's initiative to authorize the use of distributed ledger technology for the issuance and transfer of mini-bonds and unlisted securities serve as examples of changes to the regulatory regime, which can act as a catalyst for the application of distributed ledger technology to securities markets.

II. Demystifying Distributed Ledger Technologies

The term 'distributed ledger' essentially refers to a database, which is shared across a network. Distributed ledgers can be used to transfer, store, and maintain ownership records of digital assets or digital representations of assets. Distributed ledger technology allows users, who do not necessarily trust each other, to share the responsibility of database management without recourse to a central validation authority.[9] The technology was first used for the transfer of Bitcoin and other digital currencies. The transfer process and recordkeeping of assets is supported by certain innovative elements of distributed ledger technology.[10] Peer-to-peer networking and distributed data storage allow for the sharing of a single ledger across participants in the network, with participants having a shared history of transactions. Another innovative feature of the technology is the extensive use of cryptography to securely transmit and store assets and validly initiate a transaction. Moreover, consensus algorithms are utilized for the confirmation and addition of transactions to the ledger.

The most famous variant of distributed ledger technology is the blockchain, the technology underlying Bitcoin and other digital currencies. The blockchain records transactions in a sequential archive. All individual transactions are stored in blocks, which are attached to each other in chronological sequence using cryptographic techniques (hashing), thus

---

[7] Andrew Haldane, 'How Low Can You Go?' (18 September 2015) Speech given at the Portadown Chamber of Commerce Northern Ireland, http://www.bankofengland.co.uk/publications/Pages/speeches/2015/840.aspx.

[8] Sarah Krouse, 'Bitcoin's Unlikely Evangelist: Fidelity CEO Abigail Johnson' (*WallStreetJournal.com*, 23 May 2017) https://www.wsj.com/articles/fidelity-ceo-bringing-blockchain-to-the-masses-harder-than-it-seemed-1495548000.

[9] Andrea Pinna and Wiebe Ruttenberg, 'Distributed Ledger Technologies in Securities Post-Trading: Revolution or Evolution?' (2016) European Central Bank ('ECB') Occasional Paper No. 172, 6, https://www.ecb.europa.eu/pub/pdf/scpops/ecbop172.en.pdf.

[10] Lael Brainard, 'The Use of Distributed Ledger Technologies in Payment, Clearing and Settlement' (14 April 2016) Speech at the Institute of International Finance Blockchain Roundtable, Washington D.C., https://www.federalreserve.gov/newsevents/speech/brainard20160414a.htm.

creating a long chain.[11] The chain forms a record of transactions. Another variant of distributed ledger technology are consensus ledgers. In contrast to blockchain technology, which groups and chains transactions, only the balance of accounts of participants is updated in validation rounds by users. Finally, synchronized bilateral ledgers allow counterparties to update the information that pertains to their reciprocal activity and display that information to a broader range of users.

Depending on who can access the ledger and become a member of the network, distributed ledger technologies are divided into *restricted* and *unrestricted* systems.[12] In an unrestricted system, any unknown entity can access the database and play any role, such as proposing updates to the ledger and contributing to the validation of transactions. The blockchain is an example of an unrestricted system. Any entity can access the network and contribute to the validation of transactions through a process called mining. Participants on the network, known as 'miners', add new records by solving complex cryptographical problems. The participant who first solves the problem and inserts new records on the ledger is rewarded with bitcoins. Users are identified solely by a cryptographic public key, which is not necessarily linked to their real identity.

In contrast, in restricted systems, membership in the network is limited. Only identified entities can participate in the network. One can further distinguish between restricted egalitarian and tiered systems. On the one hand, in restricted egalitarian systems, the identified entities which participate in the network can assume any role, such as contributing to the validation of transactions. On the other hand, restricted tiered systems impose restrictions not only on which entities can become members of the network, but also on the roles that these entities can assume once they have joined the network. For instance, only certain authorized entities may be allowed to validate transactions.

Smart contracts are another technology that can be combined with and leverage the potential of distributed ledger technology. Pursuant to Szabo, a smart contract can be defined as 'a computerized protocol that executes the terms of a contract'.[13] In essence, the terms of the contracts are written in computer language. Smart contracts seek to assure the fulfilment of the promises of a party to a contract. Their promise lies in their potential to drastically reduce the costs of verification, mediation, and enforcement.[14] It should be noted that the concept of smart contracts predates the current digital revolution. An example of a smart contract is the vending machine. In the context of a distributed ledger, smart contracts can be used to transpose the contractual obligations of parties to a transaction into the ledger and transfer assets pursuant to contractual terms via automated procedures when specified events occur either inside or outside the ledger.[15]

Distributed ledger technologies offer numerous advantages over proprietary ledgers. Most notably, a distributed ledger network dispenses with the necessity of relying on a

---

[11] For an excellent technical analysis of blockchain technology, see David Yermack, 'Corporate Governance and Blockchains' (2017) 21 *Review of Finance*, 7.

[12] Bank of International Settlements ('BIS') Committee on Payments and Market Infrastructures, 'Distributed Ledger Technologies in Payment, Clearing and Settlement: An Analytical Framework' (2017), 7–9; European Central Bank ('ECB'), 'Distributed Ledger Technology' (2016) https://www.ecb.europa.eu/pub/annual/special-features/2016/html/index.en.html.

[13] Nick Szabo, 'A Formal Language for Analyzing Contracts' (2002), Nick Szabo's Essays, Papers, and Concise Tutorials. Numerous other authors have offered alternative definitions of smart contracts. See, e.g., Max Raskin, 'The Law and Legality of Smart Contracts' (2017) 1 *Georgetown Law Review*, 309–10: 'a smart contract is an agreement whose execution is automated. This automated execution is often effected through a computer running code that has translated legal prose into an executable program. This program has control over the physical and digital objects needed to effect execution'; Christopher Clack, Vikram A. Bakshi, and Lee Braine, 'Smart Contract Templates: Foundations, Design Landscape and Research Directions' (2016), Unpublished manuscript, 2, http://arxiv.org/pdf/1608.00771v2.pdf [https://perma.cc/8Z5P-QRM9]: 'a smart contract is an agreement whose execution is both automatable and enforceable. Automatable by computer, although some parts may require human input and control. Enforceable by either legal enforcement of rights and obligations or tamper-proof execution.'

[14] Raskin (n 13), 320.   [15] Pinna and Ruttenberg (n 9), 18.

central validation authority. Instead of relying on a single authoritative 'golden' ledger, multiple copies of the ledger are spread across a network of users, with each user having its own copy. As a result, the network is resilient against the failure of a single network node or a cyberattack. In addition, tampering with the ledger becomes prohibitively difficult, since users are able to observe changes to the data recorded on the ledger. Furthermore, distributed ledger technology guarantees transaction permanence and immutability by making retroactive editing of the ledger extremely onerous. Moreover, distributed ledgers provide a solution to the double-spending problem, common in other digital cash schemes.

Furthermore, distributed ledger technologies can be applied to the transfer and storage of a wide array of financial assets. As a result, market participants can leverage the potential of the technology at various stages of the trading cycle across numerous asset classes. Finally, distributed ledger technologies combined with smart contracts can lead to the creation of a new form of organization called the decentralized autonomous organization.[16] These organizations operate pursuant to rules and procedures specified in smart contracts. An example of a decentralized organization was the decentralized autonomous organization ('DAO'), a venture capital fund governed by its investors and operating on Ethereum, Bitcoin blockchain's main rival blockchain platform. The DAO, which had managed to raise more than $150 million worth in cryptocurrency, was attacked by hackers, who were able to siphon off more than $50 million.[17]

III. Distributed Ledger Technologies, Securities Markets, and Central Banking

The potential of distributed ledger technologies has not gone unnoticed by market participants and policy-makers in both the developed and the developing world. Numerous financial centres are engaging in a race to the top, seeking to position themselves at the forefront of the distributed ledger revolution.[18] The world's largest financial institutions, including household names such as Morgan Stanley, Goldman Sachs, and Bank of China, are forming consortia or bankrolling projects, in order to develop applications of the technology in the financial sector.[19] Furthermore, central banks of the world's major economies, namely the Federal Reserve, the European Central Bank, the Bank of Japan, the Reserve Bank of India, and the Bank of England are exploring the possibility of using the technology in market infrastructures operated by central banks and are even exploring the possibility of issuing digital base money.[20] Finally, financial supervisory and regulatory authorities, such as the Financial Conduct Authority in the UK (hereafter 'FCA') and the European Securities Market Authority (hereafter 'ESMA') are examining the risks posed and the opportunities offered by distributed ledger technology and are considering the implications of the use of the technology for the existing regulatory framework.

---

[16] For an overview of the concept of decentralized organizations, see Aaron Wright and Primavera De Filippi, 'Decentralized Blockchain Technology and the Rise of Lex Cryptographia' (2015) SSRN Working Paper, 15 https://papers.ssrn.com/sol3/papers.cfm?abstract_id=2580664.

[17] Nathaniel Popper, 'A Hacking of More than 50 Million Dashes Hopes in the World of Virtual Currency' (*NYTimes.com*, 17 June 2016) https://www.nytimes.com/2016/06/18/business/dealbook/hacker-may-have-removed-more-than-50-million-from-experimental-cybercurrency-project.html?_r=0.

[18] Nikhil Lohade, 'Dubai Aims to Be a City Built on Blockchain' (*WallStreetJournal.com*, 24 April 2017) https://www.wsj.com/articles/dubai-aims-to-be-a-city-built-on-blockchain-1493086080.

[19] Telis Demos, 'Banks Test Blockchain Network to Share Trade Data; (*WallStreetJournal.com*, 20 September 2016) https://www.wsj.com/articles/banks-test-blockchain-network-to-share-trade-data-147437989.

[20] Bank of Japan, 'ECB and the Bank of Japan Launch a Joint Research Project on Distributed Ledger Technology' (2016) News release, Payment and Settlement Systems Department Bank of Japan, https://www.boj.or.jp/en/announcements/release_2016/rel161207a.htm/; Jon Sindreu, 'The Central Bankers' Bold New Idea Print Bitcoin' (*WallStreetJournal.com*, 19 July 2016) https://www.wsj.com/articles/the-central-bankers-bold-new-idea-print-bitcoins-1468936751.

A. Distributed ledger technologies and securities markets

Exploitation of the distributed ledger technology in securities markets is still in its infancy. Financial markets participants and supervisory and regulatory authorities are carefully examining the potential benefits and risks of the technology and the implications that its adoption would entail for the financial system. Proponents of the technology claim that it can streamline complex financial processes and save costs. The technology has the potential to radically alter the role played by financial intermediaries in trading, clearing, and settlement.[21] In its most extreme scenario, distributed ledger technology could completely change the current market structure, allowing financial market participants to directly transact with each other and exchange assets and funds instantaneously without the involvement of financial intermediaries.[22] The promise of the technology is such that over eighty of the world's largest financial institutions, in a rare case of industry-wide cooperation, decided to form a consortium led by R3, a FinTech company.[23] The efforts of the consortium have resulted in the creation of an open-source distributed ledger platform, named 'Corda', which is designed to record financial events and execute smart contracts.

The issuance and trading of securities on a distributed ledger could result in greater transparency and faster clearing and settlement. The issuance of securities on a distributed ledger platform may facilitate the recording and tracking of ownership of the securities.[24] For instance, shareholders of a company would have a complete view of the record of ownership of the securities and would be able to instantaneously identify changes in ownership. The implications for securities markets and corporate governance would be profound.[25] Shareholders would be able to observe the trades of managers in real time. As a result, managers would be more closely monitored by outside shareholders. Furthermore, managers' ability to engage in insider trading would be severely curtailed. Moreover, managers would be prevented from backdating financial instruments, such as stock option awards and stock option exercises, since entries on certain distributed ledger platforms, such as blockchain platforms, are time-stamped and cannot be changed retroactively.[26] Numerous financial institutions are already experimenting with the use of the technology for securities issuance. Nasdaq's blockchain platform, called 'Linq', is designed for private companies issuing debt and stock.[27] Furthermore, in December 2016, online retailer Overstock completed the issuance of digital securities on a proprietary blockchain platform.[28]

Moreover, distributed ledger technology can radically alter the current clearing and settlement cycle. The technology can lead to the reduction of costs and the shortening of the time required for clearing and settling securities transactions. According to proponents of distributed ledger technology, the application of the technology in securities markets could result in faster clearing and settlement of transactions.[29] In theory, clearing and settlement could be combined in a single step and become (almost) instantaneous. Generally, securities trades require three business days for settlement in the United States and two business days

---

[21] Brainard (n 10).   [22] ibid.

[23] Paul Vigna, 'Blockchain Firm R3 Raises 107 Million' (*WallStreetJournal.com*, 23 May 2017) https://www.wsj.com/articles/blockchain-firm-r3-raises-107-million-1495548641.

[24] Yermack, 'Corporate Governance and Blockchains' (n 11), 15–16.   [25] ibid.

[26] For an analysis of the practice of backdating by managers, see Jesse Fried, 'Option Backdating and Its Implication' (2008) 65 *Washington & Lee Law Review*, 853; David Cicero, 'The Manipulation of Executive Stock Option Exercise Strategies: Information Timing and Backdating' (2009) 64 *Journal of Finance*, 26–27.

[27] Paul Vigna, 'Nasdaq Blockchain-Based Securities Platform Records First Transaction' (*WallStreetJournal.com*, 30 December 2015) https://blogs.wsj.com/moneybeat/2015/12/30/nasdaqs-blockchain-based-securities-platform-records-first-transaction/#_=_.

[28] Michael Del Castillo, 'Overstock Raises 10.9 Million in First Blockchain Stock Issuance' (*Coindesk.com*, 15 December 2016) http://www.coindesk.com/overstock-first-blockchain-stock-issuance/.

[29] European Securities and Markets Authority ('ESMA'), 'The Distributed Ledger Technology Applied to Financial Markets' (2016) Discussion Paper 2016/773, 10.

in Europe. Numerous intermediaries are involved before settlement occurs and ownership moves formally from seller to buyer.[30]

The adoption of distributed ledger technology has the potential to dispense with a number of intermediaries and make the reconciliation process more efficient. Since all participants in the distributed ledger network would have access to copies of a single authoritative ledger, the need for reconciling duplicative, and at times conflicting, records would be eliminated. Shorter settlement cycles would mitigate counterparty risk, since each party would be exposed for a shorter time period to the default risk of its counterparty. Distributed ledger technology could even eliminate counterparty risk and remove the need for clearing if settlement becomes instantaneous. However, it should be noted that the elimination of counterparty risk is only possible in case of cash spot transactions. In contrast to spot transactions where a single settlement extinguishes the obligations of the parties to the transactions, term transactions, most notably derivatives, create obligations throughout the life of the contract. In the case of derivative transactions, there is a need to reduce counterparty risk throughout the life of the contract. Consequently, distributed ledger technology is unlikely to lead to an elimination of counterparty risk, with clearing retaining its importance for derivative transactions. What is more, faster settlement would lower the amount of collateral posted for hedging counterparty risk. Finally, the reduction in costs and the compression of the settlement cycle could result in an increase in liquidity.

Smart contracts have numerous applications in the field of corporate finance and securities markets. Their use has the potential to reduce costs and improve the efficiency of post-trade processes. Smart contracts allow for the automatic execution of transactions to take place in the ledger based upon simple events, such as the passage of time, specific corporate actions, or market events.[31] As a result, numerous transactions, including the payment of coupons or dividends, the transfer of collateral in case of default, the issuance of margin calls and the exchange of margin for derivatives, netting, and the exercise of options embedded in derivatives can become fully automated.[32]

Distributed ledger technologies can also greatly facilitate the collection and sharing of data for supervisory purposes. Regulators can be granted special access to the distributed ledger platform in order to retrieve data from the platform, such as the exposures or the transactions made by a financial institution. Hence, regulators will have direct and immediate access to valuable information, which will allow them to monitor the build-up of systemic risk in the financial system. Nonetheless, granting access to regulators is not without its risks. As ESMA notes, direct access may entail reputational risks for regulators, since it might result in a sharing of responsibility between regulated institutions and regulators.[33] Moreover, the ability of distributed ledger platforms to process transactions 24/7 has the potential to promote the globalization of securities markets.

Nonetheless, it should be stressed that the widespread adoption of the technology and the radical transformation of securities markets as envisioned by its utopian proponents faces considerable obstacles. For instance, shorter settlement cycles will reduce, or even eliminate netting. In addition, a shift to near real-time settlement will lead to profound changes in business processes, with parties to a transaction having to hold securities or cash prior

---

[30] For an overview of the current state of equity post-trade processes, see World Economic Forum, 'Future of Financial Infrastructure: An Ambitious Look at How Blockchain Can Reshape Financial Services' (2016) Report, 121–23.

[31] Pinna and Ruttenberg (n 9), 18.

[32] Yermack, 'Corporate Governance and Blockchains' (n 11), 33; Oliver Wyman, 'Blockchain in Capital Markets: The Prize and the Journey' (2016), 10–11.

[33] European Securities and Markets Authority ('ESMA'), 'The Distributed Ledger Technology Applied to Securities Markets' (2017) Report ESMA50-1121423917-285.

to trade.[34] Moreover, the challenge of replacing existing legacy systems and changing incumbent business processes should not be underestimated. The adoption of the technology hinges on a careful analysis of, on the one hand, the benefits of the technology in terms of cost reduction and improvements in efficiency and, on the other hand, the cost of investment in the technology and operational changes.[35]

Furthermore, since it is highly unlikely that only a single distributed ledger arrangement will be deployed in financial markets, interoperability across different distributed ledger arrangements will be a crucial factor in determining the extent of the application of the technology. Under the most plausible scenario, certain legacy systems will continue to exist. Consequently, market participants seeking to adopt the technology must also ensure the interoperability between distributed ledger arrangements and legacy systems (see Chapter 1 by Tasca and Piselli in this volume). Finally, significant doubts remain on whether distributed ledger technology can be scalable to high-volume markets, such as the US stock market.

With regard to what the future may look like, one can discern three alternative scenarios concerning the adoption of the technology: (i) individual financial market participants apply the technology in order to improve internal efficiency without a major impact on the financial ecosystem; (ii) a group of core market players embrace a shared distributed ledger, thereby making some other players redundant; or (iii) a peer-to-peer world exists without financial intermediaries, where issuers and investors are able to transact directly on the ledger.[36] Real-world applications of the technology predominantly revolve around the first and second scenarios.[37]

B. Distributed ledger technologies and central banking

The advent of Bitcoin spurred discussions regarding the potential of cryptocurrencies to become viable competitors to fiat money. Bitcoin and imitator digital currencies were designed in order to bypass the modern central banking system. Proponents of Bitcoin touted the currency's algorithmic growth rate and deterministic supply, which make it immune to manipulation by central banks or any other government authority. Nevertheless, Bitcoin has not managed to establish itself as a viable alternative to central bank fiat money, with the total value of all bitcoins in circulation standing at approximately 110 billion US dollars,[38] a fraction of the approximately 1.5 trillion of dollars in circulation.[39] Thus, the attention of central bankers has turned to distributed ledger technology. The interest of central banks in distributed ledger technology stems from their role in defining and implementing monetary policy, promoting financial stability, supervising financial institutions, issuing physical currency, overseeing payment systems, and operating financial market infrastructures for the settlement of payments and securities.[40]

---

[34] Michael Mainelli and Alistair Milne, 'The Impact and Potential of Blockchain on the Securities Transaction Lifecycle' (2015) Swift Institute Working Paper No. 2015-007, 28, https://papers.ssrn.com/sol3/papers.cfm?abstract_id=2777404.

[35] David Mills, Kathy Wang, and Brendan Malone et al., 'Distributed Ledger Technology in Payments, Clearing and Settlement' (2016) Federal Reserve Board, Finance and Economics Discussion Series No. 2016-095, 22, https://papers.ssrn.com/sol3/papers.cfm?abstract_id=2881204.

[36] Yves Mersch, 'Distributed Ledger Technology: Role and Relevance of the ECB' (6 December 2016) Speech at 22nd Handelsblatt Annual Conference Banken-Technologie, https://www.ecb.europa.eu/press/key/date/2016/html/sp161206.en.html.

[37] ibid.

[38] Steven Russolillo and Eun-Young Jeong, 'Bitcoin Falls Below $6,000, Plummeting 70% From December High' (*WallStreetJournal.com*, 16 October 2017) https://www.wsj.com/articles/bitcoin-falls-below-6-000-plummeting-70-from-december-high-1517907009.

[39] Board of Governors of the Federal Reserve System, 'Currency in Circulation, Value', https://www.federalreserve.gov/paymentsystems/coin_currcirvalue.htm.

[40] Bank of International Settlements ('BIS') Committee on Payments and Market Infrastructures, 'Digital Currencies' (2015), 13.

Central banks in developed and developing economies are examining the potential of using the technology in market infrastructures operated by central banks and are even exploring the possibility of issuing central bank-issued digital currency. For instance, the European Central Bank and the Bank of Japan have launched a joint research programme, called 'Stella', into the possible use of distributed ledger technology for market infrastructures,[41] while the Bank of England is undertaking a multi-year research programme into the implications of a central bank-issued digital currency and has recently launched a FinTech accelerator seeking to harness innovations for central banking.[42]

In fulfilling their tasks as operators and overseers of payment systems and other financial market infrastructures and as catalysts for financial market development and integration, central banks are responsible for the safe and efficient functioning of financial market infrastructures. The safe and efficient functioning of financial market infrastructures is of the utmost importance for maintaining price stability, conducting monetary policy, and safeguarding financial stability. Numerous central banks around the world are operators of financial market infrastructures, with the most prominent example being the European Central Bank ('ECB').

In its quest to promote financial market integration, the European Central Bank has developed two significant innovations in the field of payment and settlement systems: TARGET2 and TARGET2-Securities. TARGET2 is the real-time gross settlement system for the euro, while TARGET2-Securities is a single pan-European platform for securities settlement in central bank money. Central banks, including the European Central Bank, have openly acknowledged that they are examining the possibility of moving the market infrastructure operated by them on a distributed ledger platform. Despite the promise of distributed ledger technology in terms of cost reduction, speed, and efficiency, central bank officials have determined that distributed ledger technology is not yet ready for mass adoption and is not capable of meeting central banks' safety and efficiency standards.[43] Moreover, the first findings of the Stella project led to the conclusion that distributed ledger technology is not a solution for large-scale payment services, such as TARGET2.[44]

The use of distributed ledger technology as a platform on which central banks might launch a digital currency has become by far the most hotly debated topic among central bankers.[45] It should be noted that central bank digital currency already exists in the form of deposits at the central bank held by commercial banks.[46] The recent discussion revolves around whether non-bank institutions, including households, should be allowed to directly open accounts at the central bank instead of depositing their funds at a traditional banking institution. Due to the enormous complexity and volume of required recordkeeping and customer support, central banks have traditionally shied away from allowing the public to open accounts and deposit funds.[47] Digital technologies, most notably distributed ledger

[41] Bank of Japan, 'ECB and the Bank of Japan' (n 20).

[42] Mark Carney, Governor of the Bank of England (12 April 2017) Speech at International FinTech Conference 2017, Old Billingsgate: Building the Infrastructure to Realize Fintech Potential, London, https://www.bis.org/review/r170424d.htm.

[43] Mersch, 'Distributed Ledger Technology' (n 36).

[44] Bank of Japan, 'Project Stella: The ECB and the Bank of Japan Release Joint Report on Distributed Ledger Technology' (2018), News release, Payment and Settlement Systems Department Bank of Japan, https://www.boj.or.jp/en/announcements/release_2018/data/rel180327a2.pdf.

[45] In a recent study, researchers at the Bank of England found that the issuance of central bank digital currency could, under certain conditions, permanently increase GDP by as much as 3% due to reductions in real interest rates, monetary transaction costs, and discretionary taxes. See John Barrdear and Michael Kumhof, 'The Macroeconomics of Central Bank Issued Digital Currencies' (2016) Bank of England, Staff Working Paper No. 605, http://www.bankofengland.co.uk/research/Pages/workingpapers/2016/swp605.aspx.

[46] Yves Mersch, 'Digital Base Money: An Assessment from the ECB's Perspective' (16 January 2017) Speech at the Farewell Ceremony [of the] Deputy Governor of Finlands Bank, Helsinki, https://www.ecb.europa.eu/press/key/date/2017/html/sp170116.en.html.

[47] Robin Winkler, 'Fedcoin: How Banks Can Survive Blockchains' (2015) 6 *Deutsche Bank Research House Konzept*, 6–7.

technology, might prove a solution to this problem. Central banks could operate their own distributed ledger platform on which they would issue digital currency. Depositors at the central bank would transfer digital currency over the ledger to other accountholders. The distributed ledger platform operated by the central bank would differ from distributed ledger technologies that do not rely on a trusted third party, such as blockchain. The central bank would assume the role of a trusted gatekeeper, adding and modifying entries.

According to proponents of allowing the public to deposit funds at the central banks, a central bank-issued digital currency would eliminate the shortcomings of fractional reserve banking. The central bank would not be subject to bank runs, and the government could end the explicit and implicit guarantees offered to the banking system, such as deposit insurance, lender of last resort facilities, and bailouts.[48] Furthermore, a central bank-issued digital currency would greatly simplify the conduct of monetary policy. The central bank could bypass the banking system as a transmission channel of monetary policy and directly manipulate accountholder balances. As Andy Haldane has noted, a digital currency could solve the lower bound problem, allowing the central bank to reduce interest rates on deposits at below zero in order to spur consumption and investment.[49]

Moreover, on a macroeconomic level, the government would be able to implement its desired economic policy in a more precise manner. For instance, it could directly credit funds to citizens of an underdeveloped geographic region that it wishes to support. Nevertheless, a major drawback of the issuance of central bank digital currency is that it would drain deposits from banks, a major source of their funding. In response, banks might severely reduce their lending activities, leading to adverse consequences for the real economy.[50]

IV. The Role of Regulation

Despite the promise offered by distributed ledger technology, considerable regulatory obstacles create uncertainty regarding its widespread adoption in financial markets. The widespread adoption of distributed ledger technology depends on its ability to comply with the existing regulatory framework, including the numerous new regulations imposed on financial markets and market participants in the aftermath of the financial crisis. The existing regulatory framework is largely built upon the current financial market architecture, which is comprised of a network of financial institutions performing distinct functions and regulated and overseen by different supervisors. As a result, the development and widespread adoption of distributed ledger technology hinges on changes to the existing regulatory regime. The regulatory regime can thus serve as a catalyst for the further development and application of the technology in financial markets. Two notable examples are the Delaware Blockchain Initiative, which is a comprehensive programme to provide an enabling regulatory and legal environment for the development of distributed ledger technology, and the initiatives of the French Government to spur the application of distributed ledger technology in the issuance and trading of mini-bonds and unlisted securities.

A. Regulation as an impediment to the evolution of distributed ledger technologies

Financial markets and financial market participants are subject to stringent regulation, which is premised upon the need to protect investors, safeguard financial stability, and promote

---

[48] Max Raskin and David Yermack, 'Digital Currencies, Decentralized Ledgers, And the Future of Central Banking' (2016) National Bureau of Economic Research Working Paper No. 22238, 12, http://www.nber.org/papers/w22238.
[49] Haldane (n 7).   [50] Raskin and Yermack (n 48), 13.

transparent and fair financial markets.[51] Indeed, the Global Financial Crisis and the flaws exposed in the previous regulatory framework led to a radical overhaul and strengthening of financial market regulation. Apart from the regulatory framework applicable to financial markets and their participants, distributed ledger technologies are also subject to numerous other regulations, such as the regulatory framework governing data protection.

The promise of distributed ledgers lies in their ability to create a record of information that is updated and shared by participants. The reliability of the record as the source of the underlying obligations and the enforceability of these obligations must therefore be guaranteed. Thus, the legal basis for these records is of utmost importance for the widespread adoption of distributed ledger technology. Where the legal regime cannot assure the reliability of the records, existing laws must be changed to accommodate recordkeeping on a distributed ledger. Furthermore, uncertainty from a legal point of view remains in relation to the ownership rights and obligations associated with digital representation of assets and digital assets, such as digital shares or bonds.[52] The legal validity of financial instruments issued on a distributed ledger must be assured regulators and supervisors.

Furthermore, significant uncertainty remains regarding the legal nature of smart contracts. Smart contracts can be considered as either an enforceable contractual agreement or just tools that execute a contractual agreement.[53] In order for smart contracts to be considered as enforceable contractual agreements, they must abide by the basic principles of contract law, including the rules regarding contract formation, amendment, and termination. Some aspects of smart contracts are, currently, in contradiction with contract law doctrines. For instance, the automatic execution of smart contracts contravenes the doctrine of amendment of contracts due to changed circumstances.[54] Moreover, commentators have questioned the ability of the current technology to accurately encode the terms of a complex, natural language contract.[55] Significant challenges may also arise with regard to their enforceability. There may be no central administering authority to settle disputes between the parties, forcing them to resort to courts. Nonetheless, in numerous cases, such as in cases of operational defects resulting in non-performance of the smart contract, there may be no obvious defendant against whom legal action may be brought.[56]

Taking into account that distributed ledger technologies are, at the moment, primarily explored for post-trading activities, such as clearing, settlement, and securities servicing, the technologies are further subject to the numerous regulations governing these activities. For instance, regulations adopted in the aftermath of the Global Financial Crisis, require the clearing of derivative transactions through central counterparties ('CCP').[57] As a result, a distributed ledger network created in order to clear derivatives would still need to comply with these requirements, namely that a central counterparty would be needed.

In addition, an important concept in financial markets is settlement finality. Settlement finality is a legally defined moment and refers to the point at which an order becomes irrevocable in relation to counterparties and when those parties have discharged their contractual

---

[51] John Armour, Dan Awrey, Paul Davies et al., *Principles of Financial Regulation* (Oxford University Press 2016), 51–80.

[52] Mills et al. (n 35), 28.

[53] See also R3 and Norton Rose, 'Can Smart Contract Be Legally Binding Contracts?' (2016), 13, discussing the spectrum of possibilities of what a smart contract could be. At the one end of the spectrum, contract school of thought considers that the code constitutes the entirety of the terms of a contract and a running programme referring to that code is a complete contract undergoing performance. On the other end of the spectrum, smart contracts could simply be the digitized performance of business logic. See also Chapter 17 by Brownsword in this volume on smart contracts.

[54] Mills et al. (n 35), 29.   [55] R3 and Norton Rose (n 53), 13–14.

[56] R3 and Norton Rose (n 53), 18.

[57] Julia Allen, 'Derivatives Clearinghouses and Systemic Risk: A Bankruptcy and Dodd–Frank Analysis' (2012) 64 *Stanford Law Review*, 1079; Richard Squire, 'Clearing Houses as Liquidity Partitioning' (2014) 99 *Cornell Law Review*, 857.

obligations.[58] The definition and timing of finality is crucial for the parties to a transaction and the intermediaries involved in the process when updating their ledger to settle the transaction and ascertain ownership rights concerning the assets involved in the transaction. Nonetheless, certain distributed ledger arrangements utilize consensus methods, which are probabilistic. Multiple participants are allowed to contribute to the updating of the ledger through the consensus process, whereby participants agree on the status of the ledger. The likelihood that a transaction will be reversed is reduced the longer the participants consider the transaction settled. Thus, a clear and transparent moment of finality does not exist. Furthermore, settlement finality is complicated in cases where the transaction has two legs, namely delivery of an asset versus payment, and the two legs do not occur on the same ledger. As a result, there may be a need to introduce a new legal concept of finality for distributed ledger arrangements in order to define when settlement takes place.[59]

Moreover, market participants are obliged to comply with stringent anti-money laundering, counter-terrorist financing and know-your-customer rules. In restricted systems, participants can be held accountable for their illegal activity in the ledger. In contrast, unrestricted systems do not provide the tools for allocating accountability. Thus, their operators may be held responsible for illegal activity in the ledger. Finally, data protection issues loom large (see also the introductory chapter by Hacker, Lianos, Dimitropoulos, and Eich in this volume). More specifically, sharing a ledger among users of a network poses data privacy risks.[60] In financial markets, the identity of parties to a transaction is not usually public except when regulations require disclosure. In addition, in the case of distributed ledgers with immutable records, the right to be forgotten under European data protection law is technically excluded, or at least rendered difficult to implement.[61] Nevertheless, it should be noted that developers are currently working on a number of technical solutions, which seek to ensure blockchain's compliance with data protection requirements.[62]

B. Regulation as a catalyst to the evolution of distributed ledger technologies

The state of Delaware in the United States is the preferred state of incorporation for the overwhelming majority of US companies. Delaware's competitive advantages include an adaptive and business-friendly legal framework, a highly specialized judiciary in resolving corporate law disputes, and responsiveness to the needs of its corporations.[63] As a result, Delaware corporate law serves as the foundation of American corporate finance. The Delaware Blockchain Initiative, launched by the state's Governor, seeks to promote the adoption of distributed ledger technology in the private and public sectors. In the framework of this Initiative, the Governor asked the Delaware State Bar Association's Corporation Law

---

[58] Andrea Pinna, 'Distributed Ledger Technologies in Financial Markets? An Introduction and Some Point of Interest for Legal Analysis' (2017) ESCB Legal Conference, 128, https://www.ecb.europa.eu/pub/pdf/other/escblegalconference2016_201702.en.pdf.

[59] ibid., 129.

[60] Dirk Zetzsche, Ross Buckley, and Douglas Arner, 'The Distributed Liability of Distributed Ledgers: Legal Risks of Blockchain' (2017), University of Luxembourg Law School, Law Working Paper Series No. 2017-007, 14–15, https://papers.ssrn.com/sol3/papers.cfm?abstract_id=3018214.

[61] Financial Conduct Authority ('FCA'), 'Distributed Ledger Technology' (2017), Discussion Paper 17/3, 26; Regulation (EU) 2016/679 of the European Parliament and of the Council (27 April 2016) on the Protection of Natural Persons with regard to the Processing of Personal Data and on the Free Movement of Such Data, and repealing Directive 95/46/EC (General Data Protection Regulation) [2016] OJ L119/1, Art. 17.

[62] Michele Fink, 'Blockchains and Data Protection in the European Union' (2017), Max Planck Institute for Innovation and Competition, Research Paper No. 18-01, 23–26, https://papers.ssrn.com/sol3/papers.cfm?abstract_id=3080322.

[63] More than half of all US publicly traded companies and 64% of Fortune 500 companies are incorporated in Delaware. See Christopher Wink, '64% of Fortune 500 Firms Are Delaware Incorporations: Here's Why' (*Technically Delaware*, 23 September 2014) https://technical.ly/delaware/2014/09/23/why-delaware-incorporation.

Council to examine whether changes should be made to the Delaware General Corporation Law to expressly authorize tracking of share issuances and transfers on a distributed ledger.

In March 2017, the Council released a set of proposed amendments to the Delaware General Corporation Law allowing corporations incorporated in Delaware to authorize and issue so-called 'Distributed Ledger Shares' that could be authorized, issued, transferred, and/or redeemed on a distributed ledger.[64] The Delaware Governor officially signed the 'Blockchain Amendments' into law on 21 July 2017. The newly enacted legislation seeks to put Delaware at the forefront of the FinTech revolution by modernizing its corporate law and allowing corporations established in the Delaware to reap the benefits of blockchain technology.

Delaware corporations are required to maintain a stock ledger, which lists the names and addresses of the corporation's record owners, and to register the issuance and transfer of shares on the ledger. Stock ledgers are usually maintained by the corporate secretary or the corporation's transfer agent and are maintained and updated by individuals. Any transfer of record ownership must be notified to the corporation or its transfer agent, who must record the transfer on the corporation's stock ledger in order for the transferee to become the record owner of the transferred share. Pursuant to the amendments, corporations are allowed to use distributed ledgers to create and administer corporate records, including the stock ledger, without the involvement of any intermediary. Furthermore, amendments to the Delaware General Corporation Law enable corporations to give notices through the use of distributed ledger technology. Thus, the amendments pave the way for the electronic transmission of investor communication using a distributed ledger.[65]

Other initiatives seeking to promote the application of distributed ledger technology via changes to the legal framework are the initiatives of the French Government to authorize the use of distributed ledger technology for the issuance and the recording of transfers of financial instruments termed 'mini-bonds' and unlisted securities. Mini-bonds are obligations to reimburse, issued by companies to investors, in exchange for a loan.[66] The term of the loan is generally between one and five years. At the end of the term, investors receive the principal amount and interest at a rate fixed at the beginning of the loan. Mini-bonds, which have been traditionally issued by small and medium-sized enterprises (SMEs), are particularly attractive for crowdfunding. They are used to circumvent regulatory requirements, which allow only physical persons to lend via crowdfunding platforms and which limit the amount of the loan to 2,000 euros for each project.[67]

As part of the French Government's initiative, a Government Order was adopted, which explicitly permits the issuance and transfer of mini-bonds on a blockchain platform under certain conditions. The registration of the transfer of mini-bonds on the blockchain will be considered as a transfer of ownership title.[68] Most notably, the Government Order gives a legal definition of blockchain, defining it as a 'shared electronic recording system allowing for authentication'.[69] Following the initiative of the French Government, the Securities Division

---

[64] Andrea Tinianow, 'Delaware Blockchain Initiative: Transforming the Foundational Infrastructure of Corporate Finance' (Harvard Law School on Corporate Governance and Financial Regulation, 16 March 2017) https://corpgov.law.harvard.edu/2017/03/16/delaware-blockchain-initiative-transforming-the-foundational-infrastructure-of-corporate-finance/; Cooley, 'Newly Released Delaware Corporate Law Amendments Would Permit Blockchain Shares' (2017).

[65] Matthew O'Toole and Michael Reilly, 'The First Block in the Chain: Proposed Amendments to the DGCL Pave the Way for Distributed Ledgers and Beyond' (Harvard Law School on Corporate Governance and Financial Regulation, 16 March 2017) https://corpgov.law.harvard.edu/2017/03/16/the-first-block-in-the-chain-proposed-amendments-to-the-dgcl-pave-the-way-for-distributed-ledgers-and-beyond/.

[66] Dominique Legeais, 'La Blockchain: Ordonnance Relative aux Minibons' (2016) 4 *Revue Trimestrielle de Droit Commercial*, 831.

[67] ibid.   [68] Ordonnance No. 2016-520 (28 April 2016) relative aux bons des caisse, Art 2, Sec 2.

[69] ibid.

of BNP Paribas announced that it was expanding its blockchain platform for private stocks to help private companies issue mini-bonds via crowdfunding platforms.[70]

In its quest to become a pioneer in blockchain technology, France has also adopted a government order, which authorizes the use of blockchain technology for the issuance and transfer of unlisted securities.[71] The reform covers securities that are not admitted to the operations of central depository or traded through a securities settlement system, including negotiable debt securities, units or shares of collective investment undertakings, unlisted equity securities issued by joint stock companies, and debt securities that are not traded on trading platforms.[72] Under French law, these securities must be registered in a securities account opened in the name of the owner. The Government Order provides that the registration of the abovementioned securities in a blockchain will have the same legal effect as the entry in a securities account.[73] As a result, issuers have the option of using blockchain technology for the issuance and transfer of unlisted securities.

V. Conclusion

This chapter has sought to disentangle the myths from the realities of the so-called distributed ledger technology or blockchain revolution and to discuss how the legal regime can act both as an impediment and a catalyst to the widespread adoption of the technology. Despite the hype surrounding distributed ledger technology, regulatory obstacles can act as an impediment to the widespread adoption of the technology in financial markets. Nonetheless, as experimentation with the technology continues and its potential benefits for financial markets are revealed, policy-makers are starting to foster the development of the technology. The Delaware Blockchain Initiative and the French Government's initiatives to authorize the issuance and transfer of mini-bonds and unlisted securities are examples of changes to the regulatory regime, which can act as a catalyst for the application of distributed ledger technology to securities markets.

VI. Bibliography

Allen Julia, 'Derivatives Clearinghouses and Systemic Risk: A Bankruptcy and Dodd–Frank Analysis' (2012) 64 *Stanford Law Review* 1079.

Armour John, Awrey Dan, Davies Paul et al., *Principles of Financial Regulation* (Oxford University Press 2016).

Bank of International Settlements ('BIS') Committee on Payments and Market Infrastructures, 'Digital Currencies' (2015).

Bank of International Settlements ('BIS') Committee on Payments and Market Infrastructures, 'Distributed Ledger Technologies in Payment, Clearing and Settlement: An Analytical Framework' (2017).

Bank of Japan, 'ECB and the Bank of Japan Launch a Joint Research Project on Distributed Ledger Technology' (2016) News release, Payment and Settlement Systems Department Bank of Japan, https://www.boj.or.jp/en/announcements/release_2016/rel161207a.htm/, accessed on 14 January 2019.

---

[70] BNP Paribas, 'BNP Paribas Securities Services Expands its Blockchain Platform for Private Stocks' (2016) Press release, https://group.bnpparibas/en/press-release/bnp-paribas-securities-services-expands-blockchain-platform-private-stocks.

[71] Ordonnance No. 2017-1674 (8 December 2017) relative à l'utilisation d'un dispositif d'enregistrement électronique partagé pour la représentation et la transmission de titres financiers. See also Sam Schechner and Patricia Kowsmann, 'France Allows Use of Blockchain to Trade Some Traditional Securities' (*WallStreetJournal.com*, 8 December 2017) https://www.wsj.com/articles/france-allows-use-of-blockchain-to-trade-some-traditional-securities-1512761292.

[72] DavisPolk & Wardwell, 'France Revolutionizes the Representation and Transmission of Unlisted Securities by allowing the Use of Blockchain Technology' (2017).

[73] ibid.

Bank of Japan, 'Project Stella: The ECB and the Bank of Japan Release Joint Report on Distributed Ledger Technology' (2018) News release, Payment and Settlement Systems Department Bank of Japan, https://www.boj.or.jp/en/announcements/release_2018/data/rel180327a2.pdf, accessed on 14 January 2019.

Barrdear John and Kumhof Michael, 'The Macroeconomics of Central Bank Issued Digital Currencies' (2016) Bank of England, Staff Working Paper No. 605, http://www.bankofengland.co.uk/research/Pages/workingpapers/2016/swp605.aspx, accessed on 14 January 2019.

Bernanke Ben, *The Courage to Act: A Memoir of a Crisis and Its Aftermath* (Norton 2015).

BNP Paribas, 'BNP Paribas Securities Services Expands Its Blockchain Platform for Private Stocks' (2016), Press release, https://group.bnpparibas/en/press-release/bnp-paribas-securities-services-expands-blockchain-platform-private-stocks, accessed on 14 January 2019.

Board of Governors of the Federal Reserve System, 'Currency in Circulation, Value', https://www.federalreserve.gov/paymentsystems/coin_currcircvalue.htm, accessed on 14 January 2019.

Brainard Lael, 'The Use of Distributed Ledger Technologies in Payment, Clearing and Settlement' (Speech at the Institute of International Finance Blockchain Roundtable, Washington, D.C., 14 April 2016) https://www.federalreserve.gov/newsevents/speech/brainard20160414a.htm, accessed on 14 January 2019.

Carney Mark, 'Building the Infrastructure to Realize FinTech Potential' (Speech at International FinTech Conference 2017, 12 April 2017) https://www.bis.org/review/r170424d.htm, accessed on 14 January 2019.

Castillo Michael Del, 'Overstock Raises 10.9 Million in First Blockchain Stock Issuance' (*Coindesk.com*, 15 December 2016) http://www.coindesk.com/overstock-first-blockchain-stock-issuance/, accessed on 14 January 2019.

Cicero David, 'The Manipulation of Executive Stock Option Exercise Strategies: Information Timing and Backdating' (2009) 64 *Journal of Finance*.

Clack Christopher, Bakshi Vikram A., and Braine Lee, 'Smart Contract Templates: Foundations, Design Landscape and Research Directions' (2016) Unpublished manuscript, 2, http://arxiv.org/pdf/1608.00771v2.pdf [https://perma.cc/8Z5P-QRM9], accessed on 14 January 2019.

Cooley, 'Newly Released Delaware Corporate Law Amendments Would Permit Blockchain Shares' (2017).

DavisPolk & Wardwell, 'France Revolutionizes the Representation and Transmission of Unlisted Securities by Allowing the Use of Blockchain Technology' (2017).

Demos Telis, 'Banks Test Blockchain Network to Share Trade Data' (*WallStreetJournal.com*, 20 September 2016) https://www.wsj.com/articles/banks-test-blockchain-network-to-share-trade-data-147437989, accessed on 14 January 2019.

El-Erian Mohamed, *The Only Game in Town: Central Banks, Instability and Avoiding the Next Collapse* (Random House 2016).

European Central Bank ('ECB'), 'Distributed Ledger Technology' (2016) https://www.ecb.europa.eu/pub/annual/special-features/2016/html/index.en.html, accessed on 14 January 2019.

European Securities and Markets Authority ('ESMA'), 'The Distributed Ledger Technology Applied to Financial Markets' (2016) Discussion Paper 2016/773.

European Securities and Markets Authority ('ESMA'), 'The Distributed Ledger Technology Applied to Securities Markets' (2017) Report ESMA50-1121423017-285.

Financial Conduct Authority ('FCA'), 'Distributed Ledger Technology' (2017) Discussion Paper 17/3.

Fink Michele, 'Blockchains and Data Protection in the European Union' (2017), Max Planck Institute for Innovation and Competition, Research Paper No. 18-01, 23-26, https://papers.ssrn.com/sol3/papers.cfm?abstract_id=3080322.

Fried Jesse, 'Option Backdating and Its Implication' (2008) 65 *Washington & Lee Law Review* 853.

Glazer Emily, 'J. P. Morgan's Jamie Dimon May Hate Bitcoin, but He Loves Blockchain' (*WallStreetJournal.com*, 16 October 2017) https://www.wsj.com/articles/j-p-morgans-james-dimon-may-hate-bitcoin-but-he-loves-blockchain-1508146203, accessed on 14 January 2019.

Gordon Gary and Metrick Andrew, 'Securitized Banking and the Run on Repo' (2012) 104 *Journal of Financial Economics* 425.

Haldane Andrew, 'How Low Can You Go?' (18 September 2015), Speech given at the Portadown Chamber of Commerce Northern Ireland, http://www.bankofengland.co.uk/publications/Pages/speeches/2015/840.aspx, accessed on 14 January 2019.

Kelly Jemima, 'Blockchain Platform Developed by Banks to be Open-Source' (*Reuters. com*, 20 October 2016) http://uk.reuters.com/article/us-banks-blockchain-r3-exclusive-idUKKCN12K17E, accessed on 14 January 2019.

Krouse Sarah, 'Bitcoin's Unlikely Evangelist: Fidelity CEO Abigail Johnson' (*WallStreetJournal.com*, 23 May 2017) https://www.wsj.com/articles/fidelity-ceo-bringing-blockchain-to-the-masses-harder-than-it-seemed-1495548000, accessed on 14 January 2019.

Legeais Dominique, 'La Blockchain: Ordonnance Relative aux Minibons' (2016) 4 *Revue Trimestrielle de Droit Commercial*.

Lohade Nikhil, 'Dubai Aims to Be a City Built on Blockchain' (*WallStreetJournal.com*, 24 April 2017) https://www.wsj.com/articles/dubai-aims-to-be-a-city-built-on-blockchain-1493086080, accessed on 14 January 2019.

Mainelli Michael and Milne Alistair, 'The Impact and Potential of Blockchain on the Securities Transaction Lifecycle' (2015) Swift Institute Working Paper No. 2015-007, 28, https://papers.ssrn.com/sol3/papers.cfm?abstract_id=2777404, accessed on 14 January 2019.

Mersch Yves, 'Distributed Ledger Technology: Role and Relevance of the ECB' (6 December 2016) Speech at 22nd Handelsblatt Annual Conference Banken-Technologie, https://www.ecb.europa.eu/press/key/date/2016/html/sp161206.en.html, accessed on 14 January 2019.

Mersch Yves, 'Digital Base Money: An Assessment from the ECB's Perspective' (16 January 2017) Speech at the Farewell Ceremony [of the] Deputy Governor of Finlands Bank, Helsinki, https://www.ecb.europa.eu/press/key/date/2017/html/sp170116.en.html, accessed on 14 January 2019.

Mills David, Wang Kathy, Malone Brendan et al., 'Distributed Ledger Technology in Payments, Clearing and Settlement' (2016) Federal Reserve Board, Finance and Economics Discussion Series No. 2016-095, 22, https://papers.ssrn.com/sol3/papers.cfm?abstract_id=2881204, accessed on 14 January 2019.

Nakamoto Satoshi, 'Bitcoin: A Peer-to-Peer Electronic Cash System' (*Bitcoin.org*, 2008), http://bitcoin.org/bitcoin.pdf [https://perma.cc/GXZ8-6SDR], accessed on 14 January 2019.

O'Toole Matthew and Reilly Michael, 'The First Block in the Chain: Proposed Amendments to the DGCL Pave the Way for Distributed Ledgers and Beyond' (16 March 2017) Harvard Law School on Corporate Governance and Financial Regulation, https://corpgov.law.harvard.edu/2017/03/16/the-first-block-in-the-chain-proposed-amendments-to-the-dgcl-pave-the-way-for-distributed-ledgers-and-beyond/, accessed on 14 January 2019.

Pinna Andrea, 'Distributed Ledger Technologies in Financial Markets? An Introduction and Some Point of Interest for Legal Analysis' (2017) ESCB Legal Conference, 128, https://www.ecb.europa.eu/pub/pdf/other/escblegalconference2016_201702.en.pdf, accessed on 14 January 2019.

Pinna Andrea and Ruttenberg Wiebe, 'Distributed Ledger Technologies in Securities Post-Trading: Revolution or Evolution?' (2016) European Central Bank ('ECB') Occasional Paper No. 172, 6, https://www.ecb.europa.eu/pub/pdf/scpops/ecbop172.en.pdf, accessed on 14 January 2019.

Popper Nathaniel, 'A Hacking of More than 50 Million Dashes Hopes in the World of Virtual Currency' (*NYTimes.com*, 17 June 2016) https://www.nytimes.com/2016/06/18/business/dealbook/hacker-may-have-removed-more-than-50-million-from-experimental-cybercurrency-project.html?_r=0, accessed on 14 January 2019.

R3 and Norton Rose, 'Can Smart Contract be Legally Binding Contracts?' (Norton Rose Fulbright 2016).

Raskin Max, 'The Law and Legality of Smart Contracts' (2017) 1 *Georgetown Law Review* 304.

Raskin Max and Yermack David, 'Digital Currencies, Decentralized Ledgers, and the Future of Central Banking' (2016) National Bureau of Economic Research Working Paper No. 22238, 12 http://www.nber.org/papers/w22238, accessed on 14 January 2019.

Russolillo Steven and Jeong Eun-Young, 'Bitcoin Falls Below $6,000, Plummeting 70% from December High' (*WallStreetJournal.com*, 16 October 2017) https://www.wsj.com/articles/bitcoin-falls-below-6-000-plummeting-70-from-december-high-1517907009, accessed 14 January 2019.

Schechner Sam and Kowsmann Patricia, 'France Allows Use of Blockchain to Trade Some Traditional Securities' (*WallsStreetJournal.com*, 8 December 2017) https://www.wsj.com/articles/france-allows-use-of-blockchain-to-trade-some-traditional-securities-1512761292, accessed on 14 January 2019.

Sindreu Jon, 'The Central Bankers' Bold New Idea Print Bitcoin' (*WallStreetJournal.com*, 19 July 2016) https://www.wsj.com/articles/the-central-bankers-bold-new-idea-print-bitcoins-1468936751, accessed on 14 January 2019.

Squire Richard, 'Clearing Houses as Liquidity Partitioning' (2014) 99 *Cornell Law Review* 857.

Sorkin Andrew, *Too Big to Fail* (Penguin 2010).

Szabo Nick, 'A Formal Language for Analyzing Contracts' (2002) Nick Szabo's Essays, Papers, and Concise Tutorials.

Tinianow Andrea, 'Delaware Blockchain Initiative: Transforming the Foundational Infrastructure of Corporate Finance' (16 March 2017) Harvard Law School on Corporate Governance and Financial Regulation, https://corpgov.law.harvard.edu/2017/03/16/delaware-blockchain-initiative-transforming-the-foundational-infrastructure-of-corporate-finance/, accessed on 14 January 2019.

Vigna Paul, 'Nasdaq Blockchain-Based Securities Platform Records First Transaction' (*WallStreetJournal.com*, 30 December 2015) https://blogs.wsj.com/moneybeat/2015/12/30/nasdaqs-blockchain-based-securities-platform-records-first-transaction/#_=_, accessed on 14 January 2019.

Vigna Paul, 'Blockchain Firm R3 Raises 107 Million' (*WallStreetJournal.com*, 23 May 2017) https://www.wsj.com/articles/blockchain-firm-r3-raises-107-million-1495548641, accessed on 14 January 2019.

Wink Christopher, '64% of Fortune 500 Firms Are Delaware Incorporations: Here's Why' (*Technically Delaware*, 23 September 2014) https://technical.ly/delaware/2014/09/23/why-delaware-incorporation, accessed 14 January 2019.

Winkler Robin, 'Fedcoin: How Banks Can Survive Blockchains' (2015) 6 *Deutsche Bank Research House Konzept* 6.

World Economic Forum, 'Future of Financial Infrastructure: An Ambitious Look at How Blockchain Can Reshape Financial Services' (2016) Report.

Wright Aaron and De Filippi Primavera, 'Decentralized Blockchain Technology and the Rise of Lex Cryptographia' (2015) SSRN Working Paper, 15, https://papers.ssrn.com/sol3/papers.cfm?abstract_id=2580664, accessed on 14 January 2019.

Wyman Oliver, 'Blockchain in Capital Markets: The Prize and the Journey' (Euroclear 2016).

Yermack David, 'Is Bitcoin a Real Currency' in *The Handbook of Digital Currency*, edited by David Kuo Chuen Lee (Elsevier 2015).

Yermack David, 'Corporate Governance and Blockchains' (2017) 21 *Review of Finance* 7.

Zetzsche Dirk, Buckley Ross, and Arner Douglas, 'The Distributed Liability of Distributed Ledgers: Legal Risks of Blockchain' (2017) University of Luxembourg Law School, Law Working Paper Series No. 2017-007, 14–15, https://papers.ssrn.com/sol3/papers.cfm?abstract_id=3018214, accessed on 14 January 2019.

12

The Crypto-Security

Initial Coin Offerings and EU Securities Regulation

Philipp Hacker and Chris Thomale

I. Introduction

In recent stages of its development, blockchain technology has been employed by smart investment vehicles, allowing the planning and then automatic execution of investing and divesting decisions as well as managing the distribution of profits. Used in this way, the blockchain is hardly more than an investment and asset management machine. More importantly, however, the blockchain also can be used in order to code and, hence, to represent virtually any entitlement in the form of derivative tokens.[1] These tokens embody cryptographically secured bundles of rights.[2] Having raised around $5 billion in 2017 and even more in 2018,[3] offerings of such tokens could fall under a variety of regulatory regimes. The traditional legal sphere of 'things' being divided into different fields by the nature of the paradigmatic object each field is dealing with (chattel, land, IP, etc.), the law needs to identify if and when a token should get equated with, or treated analogously to, which paradigmatic object. In this chapter, we focus on securities; it is one of the paradigmatic objects of corporate and capital markets law. The key question we want to address is this: when do blockchain-based tokens qualify as a security in this functional sense? Or, taking a regulator's point of view: when, if at all, *should* securities regulations apply to blockchain-based investments?

For practical reasons, we focus on capital market disclosure obligations. At the initialization stage, this notably raises the question whether the issuing of tokens, such as during initial coin offerings ('ICOs', also called 'token sales'), triggers prospectus obligations. Later, one may also ask whether there is a duty incumbent upon the issuer of certain tokens to continuously disclose inside information about himself. We start with an initial assessment of existing European Union (EU) law on the matter (section II), after which the US Securities regulation is briefly looked at (section III) in order to allow for some comparative observations and proposals for legal reform (section IV).

---

[1] Konstantinos Christidis and Michael Devetsikiotis, 'Blockchains and Smart Contracts for the Internet of Things' (2016) 4 *IEEE Access*, 2295; Alex Mizrahi, 'A Blockchain-Based Property Ownership Recording System' (2015) http://chromaway.com/papers/A-blockchain-based-property-registry.pdf; David Johnson, Joel Dietze, Ron Gross et al., 'The Value of AppCoins' (*GitHub.com*, 10 June, 2014) https://github.com/DavidJohnstonCEO/TheValueofAppCoins.

[2] cf. the definition in Monetary Authority of Singapore, 'MAS Clarifies Regulatory Position on the Offer of Digital Tokens in Singapore' (1 August, 2017) http://www.mas.gov.sg/News-and-Publications/Media-Releases/2017/MAS-clarifies-regulatory-position-on-the-offer-of-digital-tokens-in-Singapore.aspx, para.[2] provides the definition.

[3] CoinDesk, 'State of Blockchain Q4' (*CoinDesk.com*, 2017) https://www.coindesk.com/research/state-blockchain-q4-2017/, 101; CoinSchedule, 'Cryptocurrency ICO Stats 2018' (*CoinSchedule.com*, 2018) https://www.coinschedule.com/stats.html?year=2018.

II. EU Capital Markets Law: Blockchain Tokens as 'Transferable Securities'

In the EU, until today, there is no comprehensive Capital Markets Code, EU Securities and Exchange Act, or the like to be found. One can only speculate as to why exactly this is still the case. Many obstacles will be due to the persisting intergovernmental structure of the EU, driving EU policy-makers to small, phenomenon-oriented steps rather than fundamental systematic legislative projects. Be that as it may, recently, a certain constitutionalization of EU capital markets law has taken place. On the top of this pyramid structure, we find the MiFID II-Directive,[4] containing key definitions and structural decisions ubiquitously binding upon the Member States, albeit non-self-executory, but dependent on implementing legislation in the various Member States. The MiFID II-Directive sets the stage for two main legislative acts concerned with capital market disclosure obligations: the Prospectus Regulation (PrR)[5] and the Market Abuse Regulation (MAR).[6]

A. General extent of capital market disclosure obligations

1. Prospectus disclosure

Before securities can be offered to the public on the primary market or be traded on a regulated secondary market, the issuer has to draw up a 'prospectus', which, after official approval, has to be published. The prospectus is supposed to contain all the information necessary for an informed investment decision, presented in an accurate and transparent way. Its principal function is to level out information asymmetries between the issuer and investors.[7] Form and contents of such prospectus are regulated on the EU level.[8] EU Member States, within a certain frame of reference,[9] are free to draft their own criminal and administrative sanctions as well as private liability rules with regard to misrepresentations and determination of liability. The latter indeterminacy is particularly regrettable, for it means that in every case where issuers are taking liability risks— which includes handling them, for example via insurance—of publishing no prospectus or an insufficient one, they need to evaluate both the EU PrR itself *and* the applicable Member State civil liability rules. The latter presupposes that there is such a thing as a designated Member State law applicable to the prospectus liability of every given offer of securities. However, it is still an open debate as to how far the connecting factor of that choice of law rule may be prescribed by EU law. According to some authors, the law applicable to prospectus liability is supposed to coincide with the *lex societatis*, i.e. the corporate law applicable to the issuers' internal matters according to its place of incorporation or statutory seat.[10] However, this proposal does not seem to be in conformity with the express, far-reaching indifference of PrR towards the place of incorporation. It seems odd to assume that the market-oriented approach adopted by the PrR should fail precisely on one of the most topical questions of prospectus law.[11] There seems more

---

[4] Directive 2014/65/EU (15 May 2014) on Markets in Financial Instruments ('MiFID II').

[5] Regulation (EU) 2017/1129 (14 June 2017) on the Prospectus to be Published when Securities are Offered to the Public or Admitted to Trading on a Regulated Market ('PrR'), applicable for its largest part from 21 July 2019 on; see (8).

[6] Regulation (EU) 596/2014 (16 April 2014) on Market Abuse ('MAR').   [7] PrR (n 5), Recital 3.

[8] For cases post 21 July 2019, see PrR (n 5). Until then, subject to Art. 49 PrR (n 5), the Directive 2003/71/EC (4 November 2003) on the Prospectus to be Published when Securities are Offered to the Public or Admitted to Trading ('PrD') and its implementing Member State legislation applies.

[9] PrR (n 5), Arts 11 and 38 et seq.

[10] Wolf-Georg Ringe and Alexander Hellgardt, 'The International Dimension of Issuer Liability—Liability and Choice of Law from a Transatlantic Perspective' (2001) 31 *Oxford Journal of Legal Studies*, 45 et seq.

[11] See also Philipp Hacker and Chris Thomale, 'Crypto-Securities Regulation: ICOs, Token Sales and Cryptocurrencies under EU Financial Law' (2018) 15 *ECFR*, 645.

reason to suppose that the *lex mercatus* applies,[12] a solution which also finds authority in EU choice of law regulation.[13] Therefore, by choosing to offer securities in a given Member State, an issuer also subjects itself to that Member State's rules of prospectus liability. Selling tokens in various Member States at the same time will hence allow an equivalent number of liability laws to apply to one single offer of tokens. Despite the growing convergence of EU prospectus liability laws in some questions,[14] this multiplicity in itself asks for legislative reform, of which more later on.

2. Continuous disclosure

In the attempt to ensure market integrity and hence minimize insider trading and other forms of market manipulation, the EU has put in place the MAR. It lays down certain prohibitions, such as market manipulation, insider trading, and managers' transactions. Furthermore, it subjects issuers to continuous, ad hoc disclosure of inside information in order to pro-actively prevent insider trading based on that information. Article 17 (1) MAR reads: 'an issuer shall inform the public as soon as possible of inside information which directly concerns that issuer'. Such obligation, however, is only incumbent upon an issuer if he trades or intends to trade his financial instrument on a regulated market, a multilateral trading facility ('MTF'), or an organized trading facility ('OTF') within the meaning of Article 4(1) points 21–23 MiFID II-Directive.[15] Leaving aside the question whether current cryptocurrency exchanges such as coinone, Kraken, or HitBTC already qualify as being a multilateral trading facility or not,[16] sooner or later, token sales will likely seek access to MTFs or OTFs in order to attract more capital. When that time comes, issuers, just as in the case of prospectus liability, will face very vague sanctioning regimes. While administrative sanctions[17] and criminal sanctions[18] have at least been given express consideration by the EU legislator, not even the vague minimum civil liability rule contained in Article 11 PrR is offered here. Following the *lex mercatus* approach outlined in section II.A.1 above, it will be upon the Member State's capital markets and torts law applicable at the place of the regulated market, multilateral trading facility, or organized trading facility, to determine the availability and extent of civil liability for wrongful disclosure. This is important, because Member State solutions vary from extensive quasi-strict liability to complete exemption.[19] However, the multiplicity problem identified for prospectus liability will be somewhat limited here, as by choosing one single trading venue, the issuer effectively can also choose the one liability regime applicable in that given Member State.

---

[12] Stefan Grundmann, 'Deutsches Anlegerschutzrecht in internationalen Sachverhalten' (1990) 54 *RabelsZ*, 305.

[13] See Regulation (EC) No. 864/2007 (11 July 2007) Art. 4(3) on the law applicable to non-contractual obligations. The basic principle is that the default connecting factor for the choice of tort law, which is the *locus damni*, can be trumped by a closer connection with a different legal order. For reasons of efficiency and legal certainty, the law of the market is such a legal order, see Ringe and Hellgardt (n 10), 45. Similar recent examples of such closer connections are treated in Chris Thomale, 'Harmonization over Maximization: European Choice of Law Solutions to Aviation Accidents' (2015) 3 *The Aviation and Space Journal*, 2–10; Chris Thomale and Leonhard Hübner, 'Zivilgerichtliche Durchsetzung transnationaler Unternehmensverantwortung' (2017) *Juristenzeitung*, 382–97.

[14] Klaus Hopt and Hans-Christoph Voigt, *Prospekt- und Kapitalmarktinformationshaftung* (Mohr Siebeck 2005), 44 et seq.

[15] See MAR (n 6), Arts 2(1) and 3(1)[6]–[8].   [16] See Hacker and Thomale (n 11), 665.

[17] See MAR (n 6), Arts 30 et seq.

[18] Directive 2014/57/EU (16 April 2014) on Criminal Sanctions for Market Abuse ('CSMA').

[19] For a recent comprehensive study, see Chris Thomale, *Der gespaltene Emittent—Ad-hoc-Publizität, Schadenersatz und Wissenszurechnung* (Mohr Siebeck 2018).

B. Material scope: transferable security

The PrR, according to its Article 1(1), only applies to securities, the meaning of which is clarified in Article 2(a) as referring to the concept of 'transferable securities' defined in Article 4(1) point 44 MiFID II-Directive. In a similar manner, Articles 2(1) and 3(1) point 1 MAR refer to 'financial instruments' within the meaning of Article 4(1) point 15 MiFID II-Directive, which, according to its Annex I, Section C first and foremost also comprises 'transferable securities'. Hence, for the material scope of European capital market disclosure obligations, the definition in Article 4 (1) point 44 MiFID II-Directive of transferable securities is key. Under this provision:

> 'transferable securities' means those classes of securities which are negotiable on the capital market, with the exception of instruments of payment, such as: (a) shares in companies and other securities equivalent to shares in companies, partnerships, or other entities, and depositary receipts in respect of shares; (b) bonds or other forms of securitised debt, including depositary receipts in respect of such securities; (c) any other securities giving the right to acquire or sell any such transferable securities or giving rise to a cash settlement determined by reference to transferable securities, currencies, interest rates or yields, commodities, or other indices or measures.

1. Negotiability

According to this definition, the one common characteristic of all transferable securities is to be 'negotiable on the capital market'. While this will necessarily imply formal transferability, this criterion is generally understood to go beyond that. It is a key characteristic of securities traditionally deemed to fall outside capital markets regulation, such as equity shares in close corporations, to still be assignable, albeit under certain delaying conditions such as writing or notary requirements.[20] The European Commission has expressed the view that '[i]f the securities in question are of a kind that is capable of being traded on a regulated market or MTF [multilateral trading facility], this will be a conclusive indication that they are transferable securities'.[21] This will be the case with most blockchain tokens, but even if not, the Commission expresses a sufficient, but by no means a necessary, condition in order to be considered a transferable security. So, if indeed capital markets are to be understood broadly such as to 'include all contexts where buying and selling interest in securities meet',[22] there is little doubt that tokens, typically and almost inevitably, will fulfil the condition of negotiability.

2. Standardization

Both the condition of negotiability and the reference to '*classes* of securities' point to the fact that in order to be considered transferable securities, securities have to share certain generic characteristics which render them mutually interchangeable. As we have shown elsewhere in more detail,[23] this can be the case, notwithstanding the fact that tokens can come in different shapes and groups. Again, a brief look at the diversity of equity shares immediately reveals that the mere fact that a given set of tokens, as a class, should be individually structured and

---

[20] See, for a detailed analysis, Hacker and Thomale (n 11), 664–66; on German law, see Chris Thomale, 'Minderheitenschutz gegen Delisting—die MACROTRON-Rechtsprechung zwischen Eigentumsgewähr und richterlicher Rechtsfortbildung' (2013) *ZGR*, 711.

[21] See, 'Your Questions on MiFID [Directive 2014/65/EU (15 May 2014) Markets in Financial Instruments]' (2008), Question 115.

[22] ibid.   [23] Hacker and Thomale (n 11), 666–69.

defined does not jeopardize their negotiable and, even more broadly speaking, marketable character.

3. Type-related characteristics

Despite the innocently open formula used in Article 4(1) point 44 MiFID II-Directive, introducing its list with 'such as', the catch-all character of lit. a) ('securities equivalent to shares'), lit. b) ('... or other forms'), and lit. c) ('any other securities ...') points to the fact that the legislator considered this list to be, at least thematically, exhaustive. This means, figuratively speaking, that the list is open horizontally, but not vertically. So, for example, while there is room for legal argument as to which securities, while being no share in companies, may still be equated with such shares, Article 4 (1) point 44 does not allow for an unwritten lit. d), i.e. an entirely new category of transferable securities. Furthermore, the question whether a security falls into the category of equity (lit. a) or non-equity (lit. b) securities[24] has an important bearing on the details of the issuer's disclosure obligation, for example the availability of a base prospectus to issuers of non-equity securities according to Article 8 PrR.[25] Likewise, Member State legislation as well as future (reformed) EU law might want to draw similar or even further-reaching distinctions. Hence, it would seem that one cannot simply gloss over the characteristics of the three types of transferable securities sketched out in Article 4 (1) point 44 MiFID II-Directive, but rather has to treat that list as a binding taxonomy, a list of pigeonholes into which a given security either falls or does not, *tertium non datur*. In the sections to follow, we will thus analyse what these characteristics are, as well as if and under which conditions they are fulfilled by a given token. In this endeavour, as we have explained in greater detail elsewhere, it will be crucial to distinguish between three archetypes of tokens: investment, utility, and currency tokens.[26] Investment tokens promise some future cash flow; utility tokens in body the right of access to some blockchain-based platform; and currency tokens function as a means of payment for external goods or services.

C. Shares et al.: the equity security

In Article 4 (1) point 44 lit. a) MiFID II-Directive, the economic paradigm is equity. This means that 'shares' and 'securities equivalent to shares', from an economic point of view, simply circumscribe what famously has been called the ultimate claim principle: 'Equity investors are paid last, after debt investors, employees and other investors with (relatively) "fixed" claims. These equity investors have the "residual" claim in the sense that they get only what is left over—but they get all of what is left over.'[27]

It is from this purely functional and economic perspective that the tricolon 'companies, partnerships or other entities' needs to be assessed. The legislator indeed does not mean to stipulate any further necessary condition so to exert any specific properties with regard to the entity to which an equity investment refers. Notably, an equity security within the meaning of Article 4 (1) point 44 lit. a) MiFID II-Directive does not presuppose any fully fledged legal personality of the entity. This is important when it comes to blockchain-based vehicles such as the infamous decentralized autonomous organization ('DAO').[28] The qualification

---

[24] Securities of lit. c) may be equity or non-equity securities; see PrR (n 5), Art. 2(b) and (c).
[25] See PrR (n 5), Art. 2(a)–(c).   [26] Hacker and Thomale (n 11), 652 et seq.
[27] Frank Easterbrook and Daniel Fischel, *The Economic Structure of Corporate Law* (Harvard University Press 1991), 11; Frank Knight, *Risk Uncertainty and Profit* (Houghton Mifflin Company 1921), 271, 280, 306 et seq.
[28] For further details, see Christoph Jentzsch, 'Decentralized Autonomous Organization to Automate Governance' (2016) https://download.slock.it/public/DAO/WhitePaper.pdf; Andrew Hinkes, 'The Law of The DAO' (*CoinDesk.com*, 19 May 2016) http://www.coindesk.com/the-law-of-the-dao/; Stephen Palley, 'How to Sue a Decentralized Autonomous Organization' (*CoinDesk.com*, 20 March 2016) https://www.coindesk.com/how-to-sue-a-decentralized-autonomous-organization/; Maximilian Mann, 'Die Decentralized Autonomous

of the DAO token as a transferable equity security cannot be challenged based on the fact that the DAO was not a valid entity, as it was only based on a network of smart contracts. To the contrary: the DAO not only finally attaches meaning to what 'other entities' besides corporations and partnerships may be envisaged by Article 4 (1) point 44 lit. a), but actually subscribes to one of the leading theories of general corporate law, the nexus-of-contracts approach. Starting off as an economic deconstruction of reified legal personality, dissolving corporations into the various contractual relationships constituting them, this theory has, as of late, moved towards a nexus-*for*-contracts perspective.[29] That is, the corporation is being reduced to a point of reference, a node for contracts, bestowing, for example, ways to assign bundles of contracts at comparatively low costs. So, in a way, purely contract-based vehicles like the DAO do not even represent an off-beat to traditional views of legal subjectivity, but might play a leading voice in revitalizing the debate, fuelling contractual approaches to corporate and legal personality in general.[30]

Leaving aside the problem of legal subjectivity, the real challenge to the taxonomy of an equity security is mezzanine capital, i.e. intermediate solutions between equity and debt. In other words: when exactly is a security 'equivalent' to a share in terms of being an equity rather than a debt investment? If one had not already given up on a clear demarcation line between the two, one would have to do so in the light of blockchain tokens that can be structured so idiosyncratically that any middle ground between or outside the equity–debt divide can and will be covered. Having said that, there are straightforward cases, especially when tokens are investment tokens, i.e. represent entitlements to receive dividends or other distributions of residual profits and when they convey voting rights or other ultimate decision and governance rights (see also section II.F.2 for the question of utility tokens). It is at least in these cases that blockchain tokens should be deemed equity securities within the meaning of Article 4 (1) point 44 lit. a) MiFID II-Directive.

D. Bonds et al.: the debt security

The second category of instruments explicitly mentioned in Article 4 (1) point 44 MiFID II-Directive, in its lit. b), are debt securities. Epitomized by bonds, they comprise every type of 'securitised debt'. This broad definition is problematic insofar as, on a literal reading, every claim that is sufficiently negotiable could be understood as a debt security, even transferable, marketable subscriptions to the zoo. Generally speaking, any obligation may constitute a debt, irrespective of whether the obligation consists in the omission to paint one's living room wall in green, in the granting of access to an event or a platform, or in the repayment of a sum of money.[31] To be 'securitised', the debt need not even be incorporated in an official document; rather, it is sufficient that it is transferable and negotiable.[32] Subscription rights with respect to shares, for example, are generally considered debt securities.[33]

This is particularly important in the context of tokens, as debt securities could potentially cover utility tokens. As explained in greater detail in section II.F.2., these tokens embody non-financial claims to use a product or platform, for example, a messaging service.[34] They

Organization—ein neuer Gesellschaftstyp?' (2017) *NZG*, 1017; Dirk Zetzsche, Ross Buckley, and Douglas Arner, 'The Distributed Liability of Distributed Ledgers: Legal Risks of Blockchain' (forthcoming) *University of Illinois*, 36 et seq., https://papers.ssrn.com/sol3/papers.cfm?abstract_id=3018214.

[29] For details, see Chris Thomale, *Kapital als Verantwortung—Kritik der institutionellen Haftungsbeschränkung, Band I: Trennungsprinzip und nexus of contracts* (Mohr Siebeck 2018).

[30] See also Chapter 2 by Rohr and Wright in this volume.

[31] Andreas Fuchs, *Wertpapierhandelsgesetz Kommentar* (2nd edn, Beck 2016), § 2 [27].

[32] ibid., § 2 [28].   [33] ibid., § 2 [28].

[34] Jarrad Hope, Roman Volosovskyi, Chris Hutchinson et al., 'The Status Network' (2017), White Paper, https://status.im/whitepaper.pdf.

constitute the vast majority of tokens launched so far.[35] The obligation to grant access to a product, such as a blockchain-based service or platform, may qualify as a debt, and if tokens are easily tradable on exchanges, they could therefore constitute debt securities.

However, there are good reasons to restrict debts in the sense of Article 4 (1) point 44 lit. b) MiFID II-Directive to monetary claims.[36] First, bonds, the archetypical debt securities mentioned prominently in the provision, grant monetary claims (fixed income).[37] Second, other claims that qualify as debt securities often occupy a middle ground between membership rights (equity securities) and monetary rights, such as 'Genussscheine' under German law;[38] however, utility tokens typically grant consumption, not equity-like membership rights. Third, Article 4 (1) point 44 lit. c) MiFID II-Directive, the third category of securities, also chiefly adds derivatives leading to 'cash settlements', reinforcing the focus of EU securities regulation on financial, not consumptive claims.[39] Finally, this aligns debt with equity instruments (lit. a), the central characteristic of which is also to confer financial claims against the issuer.[40] The mere fact that utility tokens offer a claim against the issuer to provide (access to) a product should not therefore qualify them as debt securities. We shall later address the separate and delicate question of whether investment components of utility tokens, such as their profitable tradability on cryptocurrency exchanges, may turn them into securities (see section II.F.2.).

E. Options and other derivatives

The third category of instruments listed in Article 4 (1) point 44 MiFID II-Directive, in its lit. c), comprises options[41] and certain other derivatives that reference indices or measures. Options include put and call options;[42] the category comprises physically settled (leading to an actual transfer of a security) and merely cash-settled derivatives (e.g. index or basket options).[43] With respect to the treatment of tokens, they do not contribute any significant expansion of the previous categories. First, if the option consists in the right to transfer a security (physical settlement), it presupposes the existence of a security. Therefore, if a token constitutes a security, a put or call option concerning that token also qualifies as a security, but this does not add any insight as to whether the original token is a security or not. Second, if the token imitates an index or basket derivative, by granting a right to a cash settlement with reference to an index or measure, it undoubtedly constitutes a security. However, these

---

[35] Saman Adhami, Giancarlo Giudici, and Stefano Martinazzi, 'Why Do Businesses Go Crypto? An Empirical Analysis of Initial Coin Offerings' (forthcoming), *Journal of Economics and Business*, 17, https://ssrn.com/abstract=3046209, 68% embody the right to access a platform service.

[36] Same result, without arguments, in Paul Nelson, *Capital Markets Law and Compliance. The Implications of MiFID* (Cambridge University Press 2008), 67.

[37] Sunil Parameswaran, *Fundamentals of Financial Instruments. An Introduction to Stocks, Bonds, Foreign Exchange, and Derivatives* (Wiley 2011), 167.

[38] Fuchs (n 31), § 2 [28].

[39] Niamh Moloney, *EU Securities and Financial Markets Regulation* (Oxford University Press 2014), 345 with n. 154; Jonathan Herbst, 'Revision of the Investment Services Directive' (2003) 11 *Journal of Financial Regulation and Compliance*, 214.

[40] Lars Klöhn, Nicolas Parhofer, and Daniel Resas, 'Initial Coin Offerings' (2018) *ZBB*, 102.

[41] In fact, options generally also constitute debt securities, but are treated separately by the MiFID regime due to their derivative character; see Commission Directive 2006/73/EC (10 August 2006) Art. 38(a) implementing Directive 2004/39/EC of the European Parliament and of the Council as regards Organisational Requirements and Operating Conditions for Investment Firms and Defined Terms for the Purposes of that Directive, OJ 2006 L 241/26.

[42] See Jürgen Vandenbroucke, '(Non)Complexity through the Eyes of MiFID' (2014) 37(3) *European Journal of Law and Economics*, 481; Nelson (n 36), 71 et seq.

[43] Cf. Jonathan Marsh, 'UK Legal and Regulatory Developments: HM Treasury's Consultation on the UK Implementation of MiFID—Proposed Changes to the Scope of Regulated Activities' (2006) 11 *Derivatives Use, Trading & Regulation*, 389.

cases will be rare, and promoters will usually be aware of the fact that such structured instruments lead to the applicability of securities regulation.[44]

Only derivatives in this restricted list (lit. c) fall under the definition of a (transferable) security. However, other derivatives may fall under the wider definition of a financial instrument according to Article 4(1) point 15 of the MiFID II-Directive in conjunction with Section C of Annex I of that Directive. Financial instruments are subject to the MiFID regime (Art. 1(1) in conjunction with Art. 4(1) point 2 of the MiFID II-Directive) and the MAR (Art. 2(1) in conjunction with Art. 3(1) point 1 MAR) but not to prospectus regulation, which only applies to transferable securities (Art. 1(1) in conjunction with Art. 2(a) PrR). If a utility token embodies a right that can only be exercised at a future point in time, because either the digital environment for the token is yet to be built at the time of the ICO or the token itself is delivered significantly later than the contribution is made (prefinancing), one could argue that it resembles an atypical derivative in the form of a future or forward contract.[45] There are, however, three reasons speaking against such a classification.

First, future or forward contracts[46] are concluded on one specific day but only oblige the parties to exchange performance and counter-performance *at some later point in time* (commitment contract). In this, they serve hedging or speculation purposes.[47] However, in typical token contributions, the contribution (whether it be in cryptocurrency or fiat currency) is made at the time of the conclusion of the token contract and only the delivery of the asset is deferred. This also distinguishes such contracts from options, which give a right to sell or buy but do not constitute a firm commitment to the exchange itself (as typically in tokens, even if delivery is deferred).[48]

Second, the derivatives included in Section C of Annex I of the MiFID II-Directive (= financial instruments) also include 'any other derivative contracts' (points 4–7 and 10). However, those are usually either cash settled or require a physical delivery (points 4–7). As mentioned above, tokens are typically not cash settled. However, typical utility tokens do not include a right to a physical delivery (e.g. like that of a commodity). Rather, they function as a type of access right. The exception would be if the token *itself* remains so it needs to be 'physically', i.e., electronically, delivered via the blockchain. However, even deferred delivery of tokens would need to 'have the characteristics of other derivative financial instruments' (Section C of Annex I, point 10).

Third, importantly, such a high-level similarity between typical derivative financial instruments and tokens is lacking in two cases, one in which the delivery of the token itself is deferred, and one in which only the functionality of the token is deferred. The value of typical derivatives directly relates to, but is distinct from, the value of the underlying component.[49] The underlying component, if one wanted to understand a (contract for a) utility token as an atypical forward contract, would have to be the development of the functional components of the token (or the token itself). However, this ultimately seems unconvincing. It is economically trivial that the value of any right will depend on parameters that influence the supply and demand of that right. Therefore, in order to distinguish derivatives from any other tradable rights of changeable value, the value of derivatives must be defined in a direct

---

[44] For the qualification of cryptocurrency derivatives, whose underlying is a token, as financial instruments within the meaning of MiFID II, see AMF, 'Analysis of the Legal Qualification of Cryptocurrency Derivatives' (2018) http://amf-france.org/en_US/Reglementation/Dossiers-thematiques/Marches/Produits-derives/Analyse-sur-la-qualification-juridique-des-produits-d-riv-s-sur-crypto-monnaies.

[45] Swiss Financial Market Supervisory Authority ('FINMA'), 'Guidelines for Enquiries regarding the Regulatory Framework for Initial Coin Offerings' (2018), 8. Swiss securities regulation differs, however, from EU securities regulation.

[46] The main difference between them is that futures are standardized and traded on exchanges, Parameswaran (n 37), 283 et seq., 325.

[47] Alan Rechtschaffen, *Capital Markets, Derivatives and the Law* (2nd edn, Oxford University Press 2014), 148; Investopedia, 'Futures' (3 August 2016) https://www.investopedia.com/terms/f/futures.asp.

[48] Parameswaran (n 37), 343.   [49] Rechtschaffen (n 47), 51; Parameswaran (n 37), 16.

and precise (*quasi-*) mathematical relationship to the underlying.[50] This is not typically the case for tokens, even if the exercise of the right or the delivery of the token is deferred. If you buy and pay for a car today and that car is bound to be delivered in three months, this does not turn the contract of sale into a derivative. The reason is that the default (counter-party credit) risk, which distinguishes forward and future contracts,[51] is much reduced if the counter-performance is made on the spot. Hence, token sales lack the general shifting of investment risks inherent in derivatives.[52] Of course, risks for the contributing party remain, but as we shall see, these are better addressed by consumer law than securities regulation (see section II.F.2.). Having said that, there are, of course, genuine futures (deferred per-formance *and* counter-performance) with tokens as underlyings,[53] and these will typically be derivatives in the sense of point 10 of Section C of Annex I.[54] However, once again, this is not the structure of a typical utility token sale.

F. Exceptions: instruments of payment and utility claims

As mentioned in section II.B.3, tokens come in three different archetypes:[55] investment, cur-rency, and utility. Investment tokens typically constitute equity securities as they grant rights to participate in future cash flows (see section II.C). The big question for EU securities regu-lation, however, is whether currency and utility tokens are exempt from the definition of a security. As we shall see, this is more straightforward for currency tokens, but more complex for utility tokens.

1. Instruments of payment: currency tokens

Article 4 (1) point 44 MiFID II-Directive explicit exempts payment instruments from the definition of a security. In the traditional sense, this comprises all liquid forms of payment, such as cash and cheques.[56] The Court of Justice of the European Union (CJEU) updated this concept in the *Hedqvist* decision by qualifying Bitcoin as a 'contractual means of payment'.[57] This offers a first indication that currency tokens, i.e. tokens primarily designed to enable payments (for goods outside of the token ecosystem), must be considered to be instruments of payment. This qualification is of practical relevance, as a recent study showed that 20% of tokens exhibit payment features.[58] However, the *Hedqvist* decision does not entirely settle the matter since it was handed down in relation to the field of VAT rules. The concept of a se-curity, in Article 135(1)(f) VAT Directive,[59] is narrower than the one in MiFID II. The former does not include, for example, 'shares in other entities' or 'other forms of securitised debt'.

Nonetheless, currency tokens should be considered more similar to payment instruments than to equity or debt securities. While they are less liquid than traditional payment instru-ments, like cash or cheques,[60] the risks they exhibit (such as identity verification, double spending, delayed transfer of value, etc.) are not typically covered in securities regulation. Rather, such operational, credit, and liquidity risks for users of currency tokens are found

---

[50] See Ali Hirsa and Salih Neftci, *An Introduction to the Mathematics of Financial Derivatives* (Elsevier 2014); Parameswaran (n 37), 326 and 384.

[51] Parameswaran (n 37), 285; Rechtschaffen (n 47), 156.

[52] On risk shifting as the defining purpose of derivatives, see Rechtschaffen (n 47), 148.

[53] See, e.g., Rakesh Sharma, 'Bitcoin Futures on CBOE vs. CME: What's the Difference?' (*Investopedia*, 12 December 2017) https://www.investopedia.com/news/bitcoin-futures-cboe-vs-cme-whats-difference/.

[54] See AMF (n 44).   [55] Hacker and Thomale (n 11), 652 et seq.

[56] Heinz-Dieter Assmann, *Wertpapierhandelsgesetz Kommentar* (6th edn, Otto Schmidt 2012), § 2 [12]; see also BT-Drucks, 'Proposal for a Law Transposing MiFID by the German Government' (12 January 2007) 16/4028, 54.

[57] Case C-264/14, *Hedqvist*, EU:C:2015:718, [42].   [58] Adhami et al. (n 35), 17.

[59] Directive 2006/112/EC (28 November 2006) on the Common System of Value Added Tax, OJ 2006 L 347/1.

[60] See, Prableen Bajpai, 'Liquidity of Bitcoins' (*Investopedia.com*, 8 January 2018) http://www.investopedia.com/articles/investing/112914-liquidity-bitcoins.asp.

in payment services regulation,[61] which is the natural place for the regulation of payment instruments and arguably the reason they are exempted from securities regulation. The European Central Bank ('ECB') shares this view,[62] as does the German BaFin[63] and, since January 2019, ESMA.[64] This perception has been further endorsed by recent legislation in Japan, where cryptocurrencies are not regulated as legal tender but as a means of payment akin to prepaid payment instruments.[65]

2. Instruments of consumption: utility tokens

The theoretically most intriguing and practically most important question is the treatment of so-called 'utility tokens'. These tokens embody a bundle of rights that give access to some product via a decentralized application conferring a certain utility on the user due to its functionality. One example would be filecoin, a token that confers the right to use computer storage space on other computers in the network in exchange for filecoin.[66]

As to the question of to what extent utility tokens qualify as securities under EU law, the answer to this question will likely determine the fate of the ICO market in the EU. Unfortunately, there is no explicit exemption of 'instruments of consumption' from EU securities regulation. The decision by the SEC to qualify utility tokens as general securities under US securities regulation has considerably chilled the US ICO market.

The pure utility component of such tokens—i.e. the mere access to some functional product—testifies to a consumption aspect that is devoid of the investment risks addressed by securities regulation. However, in addition to this consumptive use, utility tokens can often be traded on secondary markets, such as cryptocurrency exchanges. They can therefore be sold for profit and the prospect of such profit is a major force in the purchase decisions of many of the buyers of such tokens. This investment component, in turn, could trigger the applicability of EU securities regulation. However, many consumption goods (e.g. cars) can be bought and resold for profit on organized primary and secondary (second-hand) markets, without being considered securities. Therefore, under EU law, utility tokens will qualify as securities if they are comparable, in terms of their main features, to one of the established categories of securities.

Most importantly, one could argue that utility tokens raise certain risks that are similar to those inherent in stocks. The US Supreme Court, in its *Landreth* decision, established five criteria that helpfully list the distinguishing characteristics of stocks: the right to dividends, voting rights, negotiability, the possibility to be pledged as collateral, and the possibility to appreciate in value.[67] Negotiability, as mentioned earlier, is a necessary prerequisite for issued units to be considered securities and, therefore, must be fulfilled in all circumstances. Out of the remaining four criteria, only the right to dividends (i.e. future cash flows) and the possibility to appreciate in value speak directly to the investment component of stocks, determining the return on investment. It seems clear that a token would qualify as a security if it simultaneously offers these two ways of financial gain; such tokens constitute the archetype of investment tokens. For example, the DAO promised future cash flows derived from the return on the investment of collected crypto-funds into other (crypto) projects *and* a possible appreciation in value from trading on secondary markets. Utility tokens, however,

---

[61] European Central Bank ('ECB'), 'Virtual Currency Schemes' (2012), 17.

[62] ibid., 40; European Central Bank ('ECB'), 'Virtual Currency Schemes—a Further Analysis' (2015), 27.

[63] Jens Münzer, 'Bitcoin. Aufsichtsrechtliche Bewertung und Risiken für Nutzer' (2014) *BaFin Journal*, 27.

[64] ESMA, 'Advice. Initial Coin Offerings and Crypto-Assets', Report (9 January 2019), 5.

[65] Mai Ishikawa, 'Designing Virtual Currency Regulation in Japan: Lessons from the Mt Gox Case' (2017) 3 *Journal of Financial Regulation*, 128; Garrett Keirns, 'Japan's Bitcoin Law Goes into Effect Tomorrow' (*CoinDesk. com*, 31 March 2017) https://www.coindesk.com/japan-bitcoin-law-effect-tomorrow/.

[66] Protocol Labs, 'Filecoin: A Decentralized Storage Network' (2017), Updated White Paper, https://filecoin.io/.

[67] *Landreth Timber Co. v. Landreth*, 471 U.S. 681, 686 (1985).

lack the right to dividends or more generally the right to future cash flows derived from the ongoing project; they do, however, typically present an opportunity to speculate on an appreciation in value.

Could this be enough for them to qualify as securities under EU law? Functionally speaking, securities regulation, including prospectus obligations, should be triggered if an instrument raises information asymmetries with respect to financial (as opposed to product functionality) risks that can be remedied by a prospectus (and not better by consumer law disclosures). This opens three possible perspectives on utility tokens. It could be sufficient, (i) for the typical investor to *subjectively* expect any profits; (ii) for the structure and promotion of the token to *objectively* highlight return on investment via an appreciation in value; or (iii) to offer the possibility of both an appreciation in value and future cash flows, in order to qualify as a security.

Under the subjective (first) approach, one may affirm the applicability of securities regulation if the motive of the typical investor is to derive profit via speculation of an appreciation of value. In this case it is the expectation of profits, not the consumption aspect, that dives the individual's decision. However, to make this the basis of the comparability with stocks seems misguided for three reasons. On the one hand, this criterion fails to distinguish between utility tokens and collectors' items (e.g. vintage cars) that are also often bought in order to profit from an appreciation of value, but these clearly do not constitute securities. One could argue that collectors' items typically do not come in the form of negotiable rights, but physical goods, and that their value does not depend on the ongoing efforts of the original manufacturer. However, it remains that subjective profit-seeking does not always necessitate securities regulation-type rules. On the other hand, a purely subjective position would introduce excessive legal uncertainty as it would be highly difficult to ascertain the motives of the typical investor. Importantly, it is also not warranted by EU law, which attempts to objectively define categories of instruments that qualify as securities.

The second option is to qualify as securities those utility tokens for which return on investment via the appreciation in value constitutes an objectively key component of the structure, environment, and 'business case' of the token. This would particularly apply to cases in which the promoters highlight the possibility to profit from rising token values on secondary markets in the promotional materials and take active steps to ensure, both technically and commercially, the tradability of the tokens on those secondary markets. This is precisely the position the SEC has adopted in the United States. In its *Munchee Token* Decision, it noted that the mere possibility of the tokens to appreciate in value was enough to bring them under the US concept of a 'security' if the promoters, in the promotional materials, raised significant expectations of profit derived from the efforts of the promoters to improve the underlying functionality of the token environment.[68] This decision has probably been more important for the development of the ICO market in the United States than the (more discussed) DAO Report. The latter has shown that *any utility token*, at least if resale options exist in the way touted by the promoters, may qualify as a security under US law. Unsurprisingly, the US token market has struggled as a consequence,[69] with promoters trying to make good faith efforts to prevent US citizens from buying their tokens via geo-blocking or know-your-customer ('KYC') rules in order to evade US securities regulation.[70] Under EU law, it is not impossible to argue that a token structure and promotion that focuses on appreciation of value makes the token similar to a stock. After all, there are many stocks

---

[68] US Securities and Exchange Commission ('SEC'), *In the Matter of Munchee Inc.*, Order (11 December 2017, 8 et seq.

[69] Brady Dale, 'ICOs Iced: A 12-Month Freeze on US Token Trading May Just Be Beginning' (*CoinDesk.com*, 19 March 2018) https://www.coindesk.com/icos-iced-12-month-freeze-us-token-trading-just-beginning/.

[70] EOS, 'Frequently Asked Questions' Question No. 17, https://eos.io/faq.html; Dom Raider, 'ICO' (2017) White Paper, 2.

or shares in partnerships where return on investment is mainly driven by appreciation in value, not by dividends. This is particularly the case with shares in start-ups and technology companies (such as Alphabet, Facebook, and Amazon), where profit is often directly invested into product improvement and not distributed as dividends.[71] One could even contemplate that the stocks of a company that explicitly excluded the right to dividends for a certain time period, or even indefinitely, would still qualify as securities.

However, important differences between such stocks and utility tokens remain. First, even if dividends are not paid (de facto or de iure), shareholders remain the ultimate claimants of any residual profit in the case of liquidation or sale of the company. This is not the case with token-holders. They do not hold an equity position in the company founding the blockchain-based organization (often a Ltd, GmbH, S.a.r.l., or the like). Therefore, this company, and its promoters/founders, may amass a fortune from which the token-holders can never benefit. The blockchain-based organization itself, i.e. the community of token-holders, does not, in the case of utility tokens, typically accumulate (crypto) assets that would be distributed to token-holders in the event of the liquidation of that organization. Therefore, the *only* way for token-holders to achieve a return on investment with utility tokens is by reselling tokens on secondary markets following an appreciation in their value. While we do not want to exclude that there may be extreme cases in which the other stock criteria (voting rights, use as collateral, negotiability, etc.) and the appreciation in value dominate the token structure so that it can be declared sufficiently similar to traditional shares, the mere possibility to appreciate in value, even if advertised, does not seem to objectively qualify utility tokens as 'shares in other entities'. Second, because the only way for investors in utility tokens to achieve a return on investment is by reselling the token on a secondary market, the typical investment risks addressed by a prospectus are not present in utility tokens. A prospectus would describe, inter alia, the financial situation of the issuer;[72] however, this is usually a company separate from the blockchain-based organization, a company in which the token-holders do not have a stake. There may or may not be a strong link between the evolution of the financial position of this company and the evolution of the token value. The token value (and hence the 'investment risk' in utility tokens) is entirely driven by supply and demand on cryptocurrency exchanges.[73] Often, if the project delivers significant utility this will positively affect the value of tokens on secondary exchanges.[74] Conversely, if there is a deficiency in the underlying product (e.g. the allocation of storage space in the case of filecoin), this will negatively impact token value. However, such issues concerning the functionality of the product are precisely those addressed by consumer law. In fact, European consumer law not only provides remedies for product deficiencies, but also mandates the disclosure of such, particularly in electronically concluded, long-distance contracts, such as that involved in any typical token purchase.[75] For utility tokens, it makes sense to ensure, possibly via a tailored disclosure rule for utility tokens, that these disclosures contain the necessary information for users, and particularly for blockchain technology specialists, to assess the likelihood that the product will function properly and that the relevant collected funds are used adequately. While it is true that the mandatory content of the securities prospectus is openly worded ('necessary information' for an informed investment decision[76]), adaptable to different types

---

[71] Timothy Green, 'This Is the Best Tech Dividend Stock' (*The Motley Fool.com*, 29 November 2017) https://www.fool.com/investing/2017/11/29/this-is-the-best-tech-dividend-stock.aspx.

[72] See PrR (n 5), Art. 6(1)(a).

[73] See Crypto Gurus Admin, '3 Reasons Why Hdac Is the Worst ICO of 2017' (*CryptoGurus.com*, 11 December 2017) http://cryptogurus.com/reviews/hdac-review/; Klöhn et al. (n 40), 94 et seq.

[74] Jonathan Rohr and Aaron Wright, 'Blockchain-Based Token Sales, Initial Coin Offerings, and the Democratization of Public Capital Markets' (forthcoming) 70 *Hastings Law Journal*, 30.

[75] Article 6 of Directive 2011/83/EU (25 October 2011) on Consumer Rights, OJ 2011 L 304/64.

[76] See PrR (n 5), Art. 6(1)(1)(a).

of issuers[77] and could, thus, potentially accommodate many of the important features of utility tokens, these questions are still best dealt with by consumer law; not by securities regulation. The investment risk, in the case of utility tokens, seems more closely related to consumption and product functionality risks than to the financial risks that securities regulation and the prospectus typically address.

Therefore, we suggest that the third option of dealing with utility tokens only delivering the possibility of appreciation in value, but not future cash flows, is preferable. Utility tokens are not sufficiently comparable to stocks in order to qualify as an equity security. This view has now also been endorsed by ESMA.[78]

Several reasons can be put forward in its support. As has recently been suggested, the economics of such utility tokens are entirely different from those of instruments promising future cash flows.[79] Hence, only if both typical revenue roads for return on investment—i.e. future cash flows and appreciation in value—are present does the need for registering and publishing a prospectus arise. A recent empirical study found that 26% of tokens embody such profit rights.[80] The description of the financial situation of the issuer only makes sense if the investor has a residual claim in the issuer's assets. If, as is typical for utility tokens, the financial risk is closely associated with the functionality of the product, i.e. its utility value,[81] then the disclosure of product attributes, as mandated by a (potentially updated crypto) consumer law, is the appropriate way of addressing information asymmetries. As mentioned above, this may be different in the exceptional case where all the other four stock criteria (negotiability, voting rights, use as collateral, appreciation in value) completely dominate the token structure, and thus eclipse the lack of future cash flows. However, this will be quite rare. As we have seen (sections II.D–E.), utility tokens will also typically not resemble securitized debt as they do not give rise to financial claims but to platform access and product use. Also, they typically lack the structure of options or derivatives; they present no occasion for a deferred cash settlement.

This implies that, other than in the United States (see section III), utility tokens under EU law do not typically qualify as securities, even if they can be traded on secondary markets. Rather, deficiencies and information asymmetries need to be, and to a certain extent already are, addressed by consumer law. This, in turn, highlights the comparative advantage of the EU vis-à-vis the US legal system when it comes to the accommodation of ICOs and token markets. Utility tokens may, in this reading, be distributed without having to comply with EU securities regulation. As a matter of precaution, however, promoters should still refrain from touting resale possibilities in promotional materials.

G. Hybrid tokens

The key question of Article 4 (1) point 44 MiFID II-Directive, as of any taxonomy, is how to deal with intermediate cases. Such cases inevitably arise in the blockchain world. When it comes to hybrids between the exempted instruments of payment and utility claims with equity, debt, or derivative securities, the answer seems straightforward. If, in a given

---

[77] See ibid.; Art. 3 of Regulation (EC) No. 809/2004, 29 April 2004 implementing Directive 2003/71/EC of the European Parliament and of the Council as regards information contained in prospectuses as well as the format, incorporation by reference and publication of such prospectuses and dissemination of advertisements, last amended by Commission Delegated Regulation (EU) No. 759/2013 of 30 April 2013 amending Regulation (EC) No. 809/2004 as regards the disclosure requirements for convertible and exchangeable debt securities, OJ 2013 L 213/1; Moloney (n 39), 106 et seq.

[78] ESMA (n 64) 20, para 86 (discussing Filecoin).

[79] See Chris Burniske and Jack Tatar, *Cryptoassets* (McGraw-Hill 2017), Chs 8 and 12; Chris Burniske, 'Cryptoasset Valuations' (*Medium.com*, 24 September 2017) https://medium.com/@cburniske/cryptoasset-valuations-ac83479ffca7.

[80] Adhami et al. (n 35), 17.   [81] Burniske and Tatar (n 79), Ch. 12.

token, one of the components that feature in the latter category is present, in a significant way, the whole token will have to be qualified as a transferable security. If this were not so, the consequence of such would invite evasive strategies such as pimping a given token with fig-leaf utility components in order to exempt it from investor protection and allow straight-up scams.

It seems less clear how to deal with hybrid tokens between equity, debt, and derivative securities such as mezzanine investment tokens. One easy conceptual way out would be to shift all hybrid cases into the broader category of financial instruments within the meaning of Article 4 (1) point 15 MiFID II-Directive. However, this would engender two disadvantages that cannot be permitted. First, the additional items contained in Annex I, Section C MiFID II-Directive beyond transferable securities do not really catch such hybrid cases. Second, there is no reason to assume that solely due its hybrid nature a given token would trigger the need of market abuse protection by MAR, whilst exempting it from prospectus transparency according to PrR (which is precisely one of the main differences between financial instruments and securities in terms of their legal consequences). Therefore, such hybrids need to be dealt with inside the taxonomy of Art. 4 (1) point 44 MiFID II-Directive. In the absence of any clear alternative, a preponderance-of-character approach needs to be adopted. In the case of tokens that are not exempted from Article 4 (1) point 44, a global assessment of each token's individual economic structure needs be undertaken to determine whether its preponderant character is of an equity, debt, or derivative nature. The order is set by point 44. First, the preponderant equity character needs to be investigated. If such investigation is answered in the negative, the assessment moves on to consider debt, and then derivative.

III. US Securities Regulation

A. General extent of capital market disclosure obligations

1. Prospectus disclosure

In the United States, there is a statutory prohibition on issuing unregistered securities, according to Sec. 5 Securities Act 1933. The registration process requires the provision of a prospectus, the details of which are laid down in Rules 420 et seq. to that Act. This is not the place to get into the details; suffice to say that the obligation to create a prospectus is germane to US Securities Regulation, as is a cascade of criminal, administrative, and civil sanctions, if this duty is not being complied with.[82]

2. Continuous disclosure

According to Sec. 13 (1) Securities Exchange Act 1934 in connection with sec. 409 Sarbanes–Oxley Act 2002, issuers are generally obliged to disclose, in real time, any material information in addition to their periodic disclosure obligations. Once again, whilst criminal and administrative sanctions are available, civil liability for wrongful disclosure is somewhat more complicated. Generally speaking, wrongful real-time disclosure leads to civil liability only if such disclosure has been used in order to deliberately manipulate the market.[83]

B. Material scope: security as defined by the *Howey* test

The material scope of US Securities Regulation is essentially defined by its definition of 'security'. Section 2 (a) (1) of the Securities Act 1933 lists a very long series of instruments that

---

[82] See, e.g. Stephen Choi and AC Pritchard, *Securities Regulation* (Foundation Press 2012), Chs 8 and 13.
[83] For details and comparative observations, see Thomale, *Der gespaltene Emittent* (n 19).

are considered to be securities, notably, the 'investment contract'. The meaning of 'investment contract' has famously been fleshed out by the Supreme Court in the *Howey* case.[84] According to this decision and subsequent case law, an investment contract consists of four elements that need to be fulfilled (*Howey* test): (i) investment of money; into (ii) a common enterprise; with (iii) the reasonable expectation of profits; derived (iv) from the entrepreneurial or managerial efforts of others.[85] This test seeks to distil the essential economic components of investment activities and flexibly applies to all 'schemes devised by those who seek the use of the money of others on the promise of profits'.[86] Indeed, whenever profits are expected from the significant efforts of others, a principal–agent conflict and, hence, information asymmetry arises between investors and promoters concerning the intention and capacity of the promoters to deliver on their promises. Therefore, it is precisely in these situations that, at least from a classical economic perspective, a prospectus containing detailed information about the investment project as well as continuous disclosure about ad hoc developments makes sense.[87]

The applicability of this *Howey* concept of an investment contract was assessed by the SEC in its investigative report of July 2017 on DAO tokens.[88] The SEC concluded that they did constitute investment contracts and, by extension, securities. First, the SEC noted that it was immaterial that consideration for the tokens was not given in dollars but in a cryptocurrency ether.[89] Since ethers were a valuable contribution to the issuer, buyers did 'invest money'. In stating this, the SEC confirmed previous case law which had held that Bitcoin investments equally count as investment of money.[90] Second, the SEC, albeit implicitly, considered the DAO vehicle as a common enterprise.[91] Third, it held that, pursuant to the promotional materials and issuer communications, investors had a reasonable expectation of profits,[92] with profits including 'dividends, other periodic payments, or', importantly, 'the increased value of the investment'.[93] Fourth, the SEC concluded that these profits were expected not only from the interplay of market forces but from the substantial efforts of the DAO promoters.[94] The voting and proposal rights conferred on investors were not enough to refute this conclusion.[95] Under US case law, it suffices that the promoters make significant efforts, 'those essential managerial efforts which affect the failure or success of the enterprise'.[96] Since investors were not even on equal footing with the DAO promoters concerning the maintenance, curation, and daily as well as strategic operation of the DAO, the SEC considered the last criterion of the *Howey* test to be fulfilled as well.[97] The agency came to the same conclusion in a complaint in securities fraud investigations against the initiators of the REcoin, Diamond,[98] and AriseBank,[99] as well as in a recent Order against a token for a restaurant rating system (Munchee).[100]

---

[84] *SEC v. W. J. Howey Co.*, 328 U.S. 293 (1946); see also chapter 13 in this volume.

[85] *SEC v. Edwards*, 540 U.S. 389, 393 (2004); *United Housing Found., Inc. v. Forman*, 421 U.S. 837, 852–53 (1975); see *SEC v. W. J. Howey Co.* (n 81), 301.

[86] See *SEC v. W. J. Howey Co.* (n 81), 299.

[87] Cf. Stefan Grundmann, *European Company Law* (2nd edn, Intersentia 2012), § 20 [2]-[5].

[88] US Securities and Exchange Commission ('SEC'), 'Report of Investigation Pursuant to Section 21(a) of the securities Exchange Act of 1934; The DAO' (25 July 2017) Release No. 81207.

[89] See SEC, 'Report of Investigation' (n 88), 11.

[90] *SEC v. Shavers*, No. 4:13-CV-416, 2014 WL 4652121, at *1 (E.D. Tex. 18 September 2014).

[91] See SEC, 'Report of Investigation' (n 86), 11; see also the more detailed discussion in Jeffrey Alberts and Bertrand Fry, 'Is Bitcoin a Security?', (2015) 21 *Boston University Journal of Science and Technology Law*, 15–20; more nuanced perspective in Rohr and Wright (n 74), 28–30.

[92] See SEC, 'Report of Investigation' (n 88), 11 et seq.   [93] See *SEC v. Edwards* (n 85), 394.

[94] See SEC, 'Report of Investigation' (n 88), 12 et seq.

[95] See ibid., 13; for a critique, see Rohr and Wright (n 74), 38.

[96] *SEC v. Glenn W. Turner Enters., Inc.*, 474 F.2d 476, 482 (9th Cir. 1973).

[97] See SEC, 'Report of Investigation' (n 88), 13–15.

[98] *SEC v. Recoin Group Foundation*, LLC, Complaint (29 September 2017), 16.

[99] *SEC v. AriseBank* et al., Complaint (25 January 2018), 7.

[100] See SEC, *In the Matter of Munchee Inc.* (n 68), 8.

The latter decision, which was discussed above (section II.F.2), shows that under US law even utility tokens are not necessarily exempt from securities regulation, particularly if the promoters raise profit expectations. In fact, as the SEC Chairman Jay Clayton famously said: 'every ICO I've seen is a security'.[101] Furthermore, the ex-Commodities Futures Trading Commission (CFTC) Chairman Gary Gensler recently noted that, in his opinion, ether, and even more so ripple coins (XRP), could constitute securities under US law.[102] Such claims will be tested in court as initiators of ICOs are increasingly the subject of class action law suits alleging violations of US securities regulation.[103]

IV. Comparative Observations and Recommendations

The US and the EU solutions to capital market disclosure to some extent mirror the usual divide between common law and civil law systems in terms of conceptual flexibility. Where the EU tries to design an architecture built around a firm taxonomy of 'transferable security', the United States works with a vast series of legislative concepts, the elements of which get developed by the Supreme Court as well as the SEC administrative practice in a way and at a pace that is not equalled by the CJEU, ESMA, and Member State financial authorities. To a certain extent, these structural deficiencies of EU capital markets law may be rooted in the remaining intergovernmentalist residues left in the European Treaties. To another extent, however, it is inherent upon the EU to change and catch up with the degree of coherence and flexibility that US law has reached. Blockchain and other phenomena of modern legal tech are but messengers reminding the EU that the project of a Capital Markets Union, although already commenced, does not go far enough. In the long run, ESMA has to be installed as the central body of capital markets oversight, thereby replacing the current multitude of national bodies and incoherent administrative practices inherent in such. Civil liability for wrongful capital market disclosure—i.e. the availability and conditions of it—needs to be regulated uniformly throughout the EU.

When it comes to the substance, however, it seems rather questionable whether the US solution is entirely desirable. The *Howey* test, for example, does not seem all that elementary when applying it to more complicated tokens and, notably, does not play that easily into the division-of-labour paradigm implicit in its fourth condition. Thus, it seems legitimate to push for autonomous regulation of blockchain technology inside EU capital markets law. The real question is if the status quo really requires that much legislative reform in order to embrace blockchain tokens as securities, do their characteristics warrant such qualification? As we have shown, it is not impossible to subsume tokens under the current Article 4 (1) point 44 MiFID II-Directive. Admittedly, hybrid tokens in particular are and will be pushing the boundaries of the taxonomy contained therein, but they will do so with any new possible regulation. Thus, perhaps it comes down to how to work with the definition of transferable securities. Just like the SEC stressed in the DAO Report, it is crucial to put substance over form and look at the blockchain from a strictly economic and teleological point of view.

Such a perspective, however, reveals that, at least for EU law, utility tokens will not typically represent securities. While they do give rise to information asymmetries, these do not

[101] Stan Higgins, 'SEC Chief Clayton: 'Every ICO I've Seen Is a Security' (2018).

[102] Annaliese Milano, 'Everything Ex-CFTC Chair Gary Gensler Said about Cryptos Being Securities' (*CoinDesk.com*, 24 April 2017) https://www.coindesk.com/ex-cftc-chair-gary-gensler-on-tokens-securities-and-the-sec/; for comments, see Rakesh Sharma, 'ICO Tokens Are Securities: Former CFTC Chief' (*Investopedia.com*, 24 April 2018) https://www.investopedia.com/news/ico-tokens-are-securities-former-cftc-chief/.

[103] See Richard Levin, 'Cryptocurrency Class Action Lawsuits: A New Frontier' (*BraveCoin*, 17 March 2018) https://bravenewcoin.com/insights/cryptocurrency-class-action-lawsuits-a-new-frontier; Romain Dambre, 'Initial Coin Offerings and U.S. Securities Regulation: Challenges and Perspectives' (2018) *Revue internationale des services financiers*, 13.

usually relate to investment but to product development and functionality risks that are better addressed by consumer law than by securities regulation. The functionality of, and hence the demand for, utility tokens will primarily drive their value on secondary markets. Those purchasing utility tokens may lose money if the tokens do not deliver on their promised functional potential, but that is the same for every other kind of good or service. Under EU law, consumer disclosures, remedies for non-conformity of sold products and, to a large extent, pre-contractual liability attached to non-disclosure of essential information are potentially promising bases for the regulation of utility tokens. While the necessary adaptations of EU consumer law to utility tokens transcend the scope of this chapter,[104] it generally addresses both the information asymmetry and non-conformity of products vis-à-vis the promotional materials, whilst not mandating the registration of a prospectus prior to an ICO. European Union consumer law is therefore well positioned to tackle the core challenges of ICO markets without foreclosing innovation.

US law differs in two key aspects from this analysis. First, it contains a catch-all category of securities ('investment contracts') that does not exist under EU law. Second, consumer law and, in particular, pre-contractual liability are typically weaker under US law than under EU law.[105] Hence, it is understandable, from a comparative perspective, that both legal regimes arrive at different conclusions when it comes to the treatment of typical utility tokens. Since the regulatory burden of consumer law vis-à-vis securities regulation is typically lighter, however, this amounts to a comparative advantage of EU law for token ecosystems. Nevertheless, absent clear regulatory guidance and court decisions, significant legal uncertainty remains. This is certainly good news for lawyers, but less so for developers, users, and innovation generally.

V. Bibliography

Adhami Saman, Giudici Giancarlo, and Martinazzi Stefano, 'Why Do Businesses Go Crypto? An Empirical Analysis of Initial Coin Offerings' (forthcoming), *Journal of Economics and Business*, https://ssrn.com/abstract=3046209, accessed on 14 January 2019.

Alberts Jeffrey and Fry Bertrand, 'Is Bitcoin a Security?' (2015) 21 *Boston University Journal of Science and Technology Law*, 1.

AMF, 'Analysis of the Legal Qualification of Cryptocurrency Derivatives' (2018) http://amf-france.org/en_US/Reglementation/Dossiers-thematiques/Marches/Produits-derives/Analyse-sur-la-qualification-juridique-des-produits-d-riv-s-sur-crypto-monnaies, accessed on 14 January 2019.

Assmann Heinz-Dieter, *Wertpapierhandelsgesetz Kommentar* (6th edn, Otto Schmidt 2012).

Bajpai Prableen, 'Liquidity of Bitcoins' (*Investopedia.com*, 8 January 2018) http://www.investopedia.com/articles/investing/112914/liquidity-bitcoins.asp , accessed on 14 January 2019.

Burniske Chris, 'Cryptoasset Valuations' (*Medium.com*, 24 September 2017) https://medium.com/@cburniske/cryptoasset-valuations-ac83479ffca7, accessed on 14 January 2019.

Burniske Chris and Tatar Jack, *Cryptoassets* (McGraw-Hill 2017).

Choi Stephen and AC Pritchard, *Securities Regulation* (Foundation Press 2012).

Christidis Konstantinos and Devetsikiotis Michael, 'Blockchains and Smart Contracts for the Internet of Things' (2016) 4 *IEEE Access*, 2295.

CoinDesk, 'State of Blockchain Q4' (*CoinDesk.com*, 2017) https://www.coindesk.com/research/state-blockchain-q4-2017/, accessed on 14 January 2019.

CoinSchedule, 'Cryptocurrency ICO Stats 2018' (*CoinSchedule.com*, 2018) https://www.coinschedule.com/stats.html?year=2018, accessed on 14 January 2019.

Crypto Gurus Admin, '3 Reasons Why Hdac Is the Worst ICO of 2017' (*CryptoGurus.com*, 11 December 2017) http://cryptogurus.com/reviews/hdac-review/, accessed on 14 January 2019.

---

[104] Proposals for tailored disclosure rules can be found in Hacker and Thomale (n 11), 692 et seq.

[105] cf. § 205 cmt. c of the Restatement (Second) of Contracts (for US law) 1981 as well as Sections II—3:101 and 102 of the Draft Common Frame of Reference (for EU law).

Dale Brady, 'ICOs Iced: A 12-Month Freeze on US Token Trading May Just Be Beginning' (*CoinDesk.com*, 19 March 2018) https://www.coindesk.com/icos-iced-12-month-freeze-us-token-trading-just-beginning/, accessed on 14 January 2019.

Dambre Romain, 'Initial Coin Offerings and U.S. Securities Regulation: Challenges and Perspectives' (2018) 1 *Revue internationale des services financiers*, 9.

BT-Drucks, 'Proposal for a Law Transposing MiFID by the German Government' (12 January 2007), 16/4028.

Easterbrook Frank and Fischel Daniel, *The Economic Structure of Corporate Law* (Harvard University Press 1991).

EOS, 'Frequently Asked Questions', Question No. 17, https://eos.io/faq.html, accessed on 14 January 2019.

ESMA, 'Advice. Initial Coin Offerings and Crypto-Assets'. Report (19 January 2019).

European Central Bank ('ECB'), 'Virtual Currency Schemes' (2012).

European Central Bank ('ECB'), 'Virtual Currency Schemes—a Further Analysis' (2015).

European Commission, 'Your Questions on MiFID [Directive 2014/65/EU (15 May 2014) Markets in Financial Instruments]' (2008).

Fuchs Andreas, *Wertpapierhandelsgesetz Kommentar* (2nd edn, Beck 2016).

Green Timothy, 'This Is the Best Tech Dividend Stock' (*The Motley Fool.com*, 29 November 2017) https://www.fool.com/investing/2017/11/29/this-is-the-best-tech-dividend-stock.aspx, accessed on 14 January 2019.

Grundmann Stefan, 'Deutsches Anlegerschutzrecht in internationalen Sachverhalten' (1990) 54 *RabelsZ*, 305.

Grundmann Stefan, *European Company Law* (2nd edn, Intersentia 2012).

Hacker Philipp and Thomale Chris, 'Crypto-Securities Regulation: ICOs, Token Sales and Cryptocurrencies under EU Financial Law' (2018) 15 ECFR, 645.

Herbst Jonathan, 'Revision of the Investment Services Directive' (2003) 11 *Journal of Financial Regulation and Compliance*, 214.

Higgins Stan, 'SEC Chief Clayton: "Every ICO I've Seen Is a Security"' (*CoinDesk*, 7 February 2018) https://www.coindesk.com/sec-chief-clayton-every-ico-ive-seen-security, accessed 16 February 2019.

Hinkes Andrew, 'The Law of The DAO' (*CoinDesk.com*, 19 May 2016) http://www.coindesk.com/the-law-of-the-dao/, accessed on 14 January 2019.

Hirsa Ali and Neftci Salih, *An Introduction to the Mathematics of Financial Derivatives* (Elsevier 2014).

Hope Jarrad, Volosovskyi Roman, Hutchinson Chris et al., 'The Status Network' (2017), White Paper.

Hopt Klaus and Voigt Hans-Christoph, *Prospekt- und Kapitalmarktinformationshaftung* (Mohr Siebeck 2005).

Investopedia, 'Futures' (3 August 2016) https://www.investopedia.com/terms/f/futures.asp, accessed on 14 January 2019.

Ishikawa Mai, 'Designing Virtual Currency Regulation in Japan: Lessons from the Mt Gox Case' (2017) 3 *Journal of Financial Regulation*, 128.

Jentzsch Christoph, 'Decentralized Autonomous Organization to Automate Governance' (2016) https://download.slock.it/public/DAO/WhitePaper.pdf, accessed on 14 January 2019.

Johnson David, Dietze Joel, Gross Ron et al., 'The Value of AppCoins' (*GitHub.com*, 10 June, 2014) https://github.com/DavidJohnstonCEO/TheValueofAppCoins, accessed on 15 January 2019.

Keirns Garrett, 'Japan's Bitcoin Law Goes into Effect Tomorrow' (*CoinDesk.com*, 31 March 2017) https://www.coindesk.com/japan-bitcoin-law-effect-tomorrow/, accessed on 14 January 2019.

Klöhn Lars, Parhofer Nicolas, and Resas Daniel, 'Initial Coin Offerings (ICOs): Economics and Regulation' (2018) ZBB, 102.

Knight Frank, *Risk Uncertainty and Profit* (Houghton Mifflin Company 1921).

Landreth Timber Co. v. Landreth, 471 U.S. 681, 686 (1985).

Levin Richard, 'Cryptocurrency Class Action Lawsuits: A New Frontier' (*BraveNewCoin*, 17 March 2018) https://bravenewcoin.com/insights/cryptocurrency-class-action-lawsuits-a-new-frontier, accessed on 16 February 2019.

Mann Maximilian, 'Die Decentralized Autonomous Organization – ein neuer Gesellschaftstyp?' (2017) *NZG*, 1017.

Marsh Jonathan, 'UK Legal and Regulatory Developments: HM Treasury's Consultation on the UK Implementation of MiFID—Proposed Changes to the Scope of Regulated Activities' (2006) 11 *Derivatives Use, Trading & Regulation*, 389.

Milano Annaliese, 'Everything Ex-CFTC Chair Gary Gensler Said about Cryptos Being Securities' (*CoinDesk.com*, 24 April 2017) https://www.coindesk.com/ex-cftc-chair-gary-gensler-on-tokens-securities-and-the-sec/, accessed on 14 January 2019.

Mizrahi Alex, 'A Blockchain-Based Property Ownership Recording System' (2015) https://chromaway.com/papers/A-blockchain-based-property-registry.pdf, accessed on 15 January 2019.

Moloney Niamh, *EU Securities and Financial Markets Regulation* (Oxford University Press 2014).

Monetary Authority of Singapore, 'MAS Clarifies Regulatory Position on the Offer of Digital Tokens in Singapore' (2017) http://www.mas.gov.sg/News-and-Publications/Media-Releases/2017/MAS-clarifies-regulatory-position-on-the-offer-of-digital-tokens-in-Singapore.aspx, accessed on 14 January 2019.

Münzer Jens, 'Bitcoin. Aufsichtsrechtliche Bewertung und Risiken für Nutzer' (2014) *BaFin Journal*, 27.

Nelson Paul, *Capital Markets Law and Compliance. The Implications of MiFID* (Cambridge University Press 2008).

Palley Stephen, 'How to Sue a Decentralized Autonomous Organization' (*CoinDesk.com*, 20 March 2016) https://www.coindesk.com/how-to-sue-a-decentralized-autonomous-organization/, accessed on 14 January 2019.

Parameswaran Sunil, *Fundamentals of Financial Instruments. An Introduction to Stocks, Bonds, Foreign Exchange, and Derivatives* (Wiley 2011).

Protocol Labs, 'Filecoin: A Decentralized Storage Network' (2017) Updated White Paper, https://filecoin.io/, accessed on 14 January 2019.

Raider Dom, 'ICO' (2017) White Paper.

Rechtschaffen Alan, *Capital Markets, Derivatives and the Law* (2nd edn, Oxford University Press 2014).

Ringe Wolf-Georg and Hellgardt Alexander, 'The International Dimension of Issuer Liability—Liability and Choice of Law from a Transatlantic Perspective' (2001) 31 *Oxford Journal of Legal Studies*, 45.

Rohr Jonathan and Wright Aaron, 'Blockchain-Based Token Sales, Initial Coin Offerings, and the Democratization of Public Capital Markets' (forthcoming) 70 *Hastings Law Journal*, https://papers.ssrn.com/sol3/papers.cfm?abstract_id=3048104.

Sharma Rakesh, 'Bitcoin Futures on CBOE vs. CME: What's the Difference?' (*Investopedia*, 12 December 2017) https://www.investopedia.com/news/bitcoin-futures-cboe-vs-cme-whats-difference/, accessed on 14 January 2019.

Sharma Rakesh, 'ICO Tokens Are Securities: Former CFTC Chief' (*Investopedia.com*, 24 April 2018) https://www.investopedia.com/news/ico-tokens-are-securities-former-cftc-chief/, accessed on 14 January 2019.

Swiss Financial Market Supervisory Authority ('FINMA'), 'Guidelines for Enquiries regarding the Regulatory Framework for Initial Coin Offerings' (2018).

Thomale Chris, 'Minderheitenschutz gegen Delisting—die MACROTRON-Rechtsprechung zwischen Eigentumsgewähr und richterlicher Rechtsfortbildung' (2013) *ZGR*, 711.

Thomale Chris, 'Harmonization over Maximization: European Choice of Law Solutions to Aviation Accidents' (2015) 3 *The Aviation and Space Journal*, 2.

Thomale Chris, *Der gespaltene Emittent—Ad-hoc-Publizität, Schadenersatz und Wissenszurechnung* (Mohr Siebeck 2018).

Thomale Chris, *Kapital als Verantwortung—Kritik der institutionellen Haftungsbeschränkung, Band I: Trennungsprinzip und nexus of contracts* (Mohr Siebeck 2018).

Thomale Chris and Hübner Leonhard, 'Zivilgerichtliche Durchsetzung transnationaler Unternehmensverantwortung' (2017) *Juristenzeitung*, 382.

United Housing Found., Inc. v. Forman, 421 U.S. 837, 852–53 (1975).

US Securities and Exchange Commission ('SEC'), 'Report of Investigation Pursuant to Section 21(a) of the Securities Exchange Act of 1934: The DAO' (25 July 2017) Release No. 81207 ('SEC Report').

US Securities and Exchange Commission ('SEC'), *In the Matter of Munchee Inc.*, Order (11 December 2017).

Vandenbroucke Jürgen, '(Non-)Complexity through the Eyes of MiFID' (2014) 37(3) *European Journal of Law and Economics*, 481.

Zetzsche Dirk, Buckley Ross, and Arner Douglas, 'The Distributed Liability of Distributed Ledgers: Legal Risks of Blockchain' (forthcoming) *University of Illinois*, https://papers.ssrn.com/sol3/papers.cfm?abstract_id=3018214 , accessed on 14 January 2019.

13

Regulation of Blockchain Token Sales in the United States

Houman B. Shadab

I. Introduction

Federal law in the United States requires that all offers and sales of securities be registered with the Securities and Exchange Commission ('SEC') and subjects the sellers to compliance with Federal securities law requirements, including those with respect to mandatory disclosure and prohibitions on fraud, insider trading, and market manipulation. A primary goal of US securities law is for investors to receive sufficient disclosures about investments to enable them to make informed investment decisions. Compliance with registration and disclosure requirements is not required if the offering is made pursuant to an offering exemption, such as in a private offering limited to wealthy investors that possess sufficient wealth and sophistication such that they are able to fend for themselves.[1]

A threshold question in determining whether a transaction is a regulated transaction involves determining whether the transaction is a securities transaction or a commercial transaction involving non-financial goods or services. Commercial transactions do not fall under the definition of a 'security' and are not generally subject to securities law. Under US law, a 'security' is defined broadly and includes notes, stocks, bonds, interests in any profit-sharing agreement, options or other derivatives on securities, and investment contracts.[2] The definition of 'investment contract' has been subject to significant judicial scrutiny as the SEC and companies often argue in court over whether a particular transaction meets the definition of an 'investment contract'. In 1946, the modern approach for defining an 'investment contract' was articulated by the United States Supreme Court in *SEC v. W. J. Howey Co.*[3] The Supreme Court defined the now well-known 'Howey test', which holds that a transaction is a securities transaction if it involves all four of the following elements: (i) an investment of money; (ii) in a common enterprise; (iii) with the expectation of profits; (iv) resulting solely from the managerial efforts of a promoter or third party.

In *Howey*, the Court found that transactions consisting in the sale of land coupled with a lease of the land from the purchaser to share in profits from cultivating the land 'clearly involved' regulated investment contracts.[4] In the years following the Court's decision, the *Howey* test has been applied to numerous other transactions in hundreds of distinct federal and state court opinions. Courts have found the following transactions to constitute regulated securities transactions: earthworm farm interests;[5] a seat on the New York Stock Exchange;[6] and virtual shares in a fantasy investment game.[7] On the other hand, based on the *Howey* test, courts have found the following transactions *not* to be regulated securities transactions: selling memberships/subscriptions to use a pre-existing service due to lacking

---

[1] See *SEC v. Ralston Purina Co.*, 346 U.S. 119 (1053).   [2] 15 United States Code Section 77b(a)(1).
[3] *SEC v. W. J. Howey Co.*, 328 U.S. 293 (1946).   [4] *SEC v. W.J. Howey Co.*, 328 U.S. 293, 299 (1946).
[5] *Smith v. Gross*, 604 F. 2d 639 (Court of Appeals, 9th Cir. 1979).
[6] *Wey v. New York Stock Exchange, Inc.* (NY: Supreme Court 2007).
[7] *SEC v. Sg Ltd.*, 265 F. 3d 42 (Court of Appeals, 1st Cir. 2001).

the expectation of profits element;[8] buying access to discretionary trading accounts in commodity futures due to the lack of the 'common enterprise' element;[9] purchasing shares in housing cooperatives or condominiums due to lacking the expectation of profits element;[10] and buying partnership interests due to lacking the sole reliance on the managerial efforts of others element.[11] Generally, US courts are less likely to find that a transaction is a securities transaction if it closely resembles commercial contracts that are obviously not securities.[12]

II. Whether Tokens Qualify as Regulated Investment Contracts

A key principle underlying the determination of whether a transaction constitutes a regulated securities transaction is that the substance of the financial and governance aspects of the transaction are relevant; not the form, medium, or description surrounding a transaction. Accordingly, despite the fact that token sales may use digital, automated transactions and do not involve any form of officially recognized government currency, token sales nonetheless qualify as regulated securities transactions if the elements of the *Howey* test are satisfied in substance. By contrast, token sales that do not fulfil the *Howey* test would be viewed by the SEC as sales of software services or products that operate using tokens not subject to the SEC's jurisdiction. Such non-investment tokens are often referred to as 'utility tokens'. Aaron Wright and Jonathan Rohr note that utility tokens 'grant holders the right to access, use, and enjoy a given technology or participate in an online organization ... [including] provid[ing] holders with governance rights, such as the right to vote on how the online service should be updated or evolve'.[13]

As early as July 2013, and then again in May 2014, the US SEC effectively implied that cryptocurrencies and related investments may qualify as securities in issuing official Investor Alerts, stating that securities investments must generally be registered.[14] On 25 July 2017, the SEC clarified its approach in its landmark 'Report of Investigation Pursuant to Section 21(a) of the Securities Exchange Act of 1934: The DAO' and its accompanying Investor Bulletin.[15] In the report, the SEC applied the *Howey* test to the unincorporated decentralized autonomous organization ('DAO') and concluded that its tokens qualified as regulated securities because their offering and sale met each of the four elements of the test. As noted in the report,

> [t]he DAO was created [...] with the objective of operating as a for-profit entity that would create and hold a corpus of assets through the sale of DAO tokens to investors, these assets would then be used to fund 'projects'. The holders of DAO tokens stood to share in the anticipated earnings from these projects as a return on their investment in DAO tokens. In addition, DAO token holders could monetize their investments in DAO tokens by re-selling DAO tokens on a number of web-based platforms [...] that supported secondary trading in DAO tokens.[16]

---

[8] *All Seasons Resorts v. Abrams*, 68 NY 2d 81 (NY: Court of Appeals 1986).

[9] *Curran v. Merrill Lynch, Pierce, Fenner and Smith, Inc.*, 622 F. 2d 216 (Court of Appeals, 6th Cir. 1980).

[10] *United Housing Found., Inc. v. Forman*, 421 U.S. 837 (1975).

[11] *SEC v. Shields* (Dist. Court, D. Colorado 2012).   [12] *Reves v. Ernst & Young*, 494 U.S. 56 (1990).

[13] Jonathan Rohr and Aaron Wright, 'Blockchain-Based Token Sales, Initial Coin Offerings, and the Democratization of Public Capital Markets' (forthcoming) *Hastings Law Journal*, https://ssrn.com/abstract=3048104, 22.

[14] US Securities and Exchange Commission, 'Investor Alert: Ponzi Schemes Using Virtual Currencies', (*Investor.gov*, 25 July 2014) https://www.investor.gov/additional-resources/news-alerts/alerts-bulletins/investor-alert-ponzi-schemes-using-virtual; US Securities and Exchange Commission, 'Investor Alert: Bitcoin and Other Virtual Currency-Related Investments' (*Investor.gov*, 7 May 2014) https://www.investor.gov/additional-resources/news-alerts-bulletins/investor-alert-bitcoin-other-virtual-currency.

[15] US Securities and Exchange Commission, 'Report of Investigation Pursuant to Section 21(a) of the Securities Exchange Act of 1934: The DAO' (25 July 2017) Release No. 81207, https://www.sec.gov/litigation/investreport/34-81207.pdf; US Securities and Exchange Commission, 'Investor Bulletin: Initial Coin Offerings' (*Investor.gov*, 25 July 2014) https://www.investor.gov/additional-resources/news-alerts/alerts-bulletins/investor-bulletin-initial-coin-offerings.

[16] US Securities and Exchange Commission, 'Report' (n 15).

On 25 September 2017, the SEC announced the creation of a Cyber Unit to focus on cyber-related misconduct involving token sales that violate Federal securities laws. Soon thereafter, the SEC began to bring enforcement actions against unregistered tokens sales that involved fraud. From September 2017 to July 2018, the SEC brought enforcement actions against seven separate issuers and reportedly issued subpoenas and requests for information from parties that may have reached into the hundreds.[17]

III. The Simple Agreement for Future Tokens

On 2 October 2017, Protocol Labs and the law firm Cooley published the white paper, 'The SAFT Project: Toward a Compliant Token Sale Framework'.[18] The SAFT ('simple agreement for future tokens') white paper describes an approach to issuing tokens that purports to be compliant with US securities law. A typical SAFT transaction consists of four steps:

Step 1: Developers publish their white paper, incorporate a Delaware corporation called Developers Inc., and secure commitments from accredited investors.

Step 2: Developers enter into a SAFT with the accredited investors, relying on the exemption set forth in Rule 506(c) of Regulation D of the Securities Act, and the accredited investors transfer funds in the amount of $15 million to Developers Inc. The SAFT offers investors a discount on the final token sale and is a security, so the developers file a Form D with the SEC disclosing the sale.

Step 3: Developers Inc. uses the proceeds to develop the network into a product that provides genuine utility to its users.

Step 4: Developers Inc. launches the network and delivers the tokens to the investors. The investors (and potentially Developers Inc.) begin sales of the token to the public, either directly or through exchanges.[19]

According to the SAFT white paper, the SAFT itself is a securities transaction, hence the observation that it would likely rely on the well-known Rule 506 private offering exemption under Regulation D. If the token project is successful, tokens will be created and sold to the public. Importantly, the token sales *fail* the *Howey* test because, according to the SAFT white paper, such tokens qualify as commercially functional utility tokens and not regulated investment contracts. As described in the white paper,

> the token must be genuinely useful such that they are actually used on a functional network. This means that any future agreement to purchase the tokens and indeed the tokens themselves should fail the Howey test and fall outside the definition of a security. […] [T]he tokens themselves are not, and never were, securities.[20]

The SAFT white paper's key argument is that utility tokens fail the *Howey* test because they are sold in one of either two types of transactions that do not meet the test's requirement. First, purchasers may be buying the tokens only for their commercially valuable, functional properties (such as the ability to access a distributed network and distributed file storage), no different than any other commercial sale of software. Second, even if purchasers *are* seeking to resell the tokens for a financial gain such that the 'expectation of profits' element of the *Howey* test is satisfied, the 'efforts of others' element of the *Howey* test would not be satisfied

---

[17] See Marc Hochstein and Bailey Reutzel, 'SEC ICO Probe Underway, but Stories Conflict on Size of Sweep', (*CoinDesk.com*, 1 March 2018) https://www.coindesk.com/sec-ico-probe-underway-stories-conflict-extent-sweep/.

[18] Juan Batiz-Benet, Jesse Clayburgh, and Marco Santori, 'The SAFT Project: Toward a Compliant Token Sale Framework' (2 October 2017) https://www.cooley.com/~/media/cooley/pdf/reprints/saft-project-whitepaper.ashx.

[19] ibid.   [20] ibid., 9.

due to the market price of the tokens being reliant primarily on a wide variety of factors *other than* those of the promoters of the network that issued the token such that the 'managerial efforts' element would not be satisfied.[21] As the white paper argues:

> the secondary market price of a decentralized token system is driven exclusively by supply and demand. Supply and demand can be due to a variety of factors. One of those factors could be the efforts of the development team creating the token's functionality; but once that functionality is created, any 'essential' efforts have by definition already been applied. It would be difficult to argue that any improvement on an already-functional token is an 'essential' managerial effort [...]. Furthermore, the market effect of a mere improvement on an already functional utility token is likely dwarfed by the multitude of other factors that act on it.[22]

The SAFT white paper's reliance on cases to support the proposition that functional tokens fail the *Howey* test due to the 'managerial efforts' element not being present may be problematic. As noted in a Cardozo Blockchain research report, many of the cases relied upon by the SAFT white paper may be distinguishable on the grounds that '[u]nlike physical commodities—such as gold, silver, or sugar—utility tokens are not homogenous and carry with them various rights, features, and obligations'[23] such that merely being a utility token does not deem its sale a commercial transaction. The SAFT white paper does note, however, that utility tokens may still pass the *Howey* test and qualify as regulated in at least three circumstances.[24] First, the token seller may sell to purchasers unable to successfully use the token, thereby leaving such purchasers with no motive or activity with respect to the tokens other than financial speculation. Second, the token seller may make such large promises with respect to future network functionality that even functional tokens will still rely predominantly on the sellers' efforts to become fully functional as promised. Third, a token seller's control over the supply of tokens may result in the seller's 'efforts' in the form of reducing their supply being the predominant factor impacting the token's price, as opposed to market factors outside of their control.

Ultimately, the SAFT approach fell out of favour due to sales of utility tokens to the public nonetheless being viewed as securities (notwithstanding any non-financial, utilitarian character) and hence the white paper's analysis about failure of the *Howey* test's 'efforts of others' prong for utility tokens.

Indeed, in December 2017, SEC Chairman Jay Clayton explained what the Commission believes to be the troublesome aspects of ICOs and also that most seem to qualify as securities transactions.

> [M]any token offerings appear [...] analogous to interests in a yet-to-be-built publishing house with the authors, books and distribution networks all to come. It is especially troubling when the promoters of these offerings emphasize the secondary market trading potential of these tokens. Prospective purchasers are being sold on the potential for tokens to increase in value—with the ability to lock in those increases by reselling the tokens on a secondary market—or to otherwise profit from the tokens based on the efforts of others. These are key hallmarks of a security and a securities offering [...]. By and large, the structures of ICOs that I have seen promoted involve the offer and sale of securities and directly implicate the securities registration requirements and other investor protection provisions of our federal securities laws.[25]

Clayton's remarks suggest that token sales to the public that may have relied on a SAFT framework nonetheless qualified as regulated securities transactions because of the token

---

[21] ibid., 9.   [22] ibid., 9–10.

[23] Cardozo Blockchain Project, 'Not So Fast—Risks Related to the Use of a "SAFT" for Token Sales' (21 November 2017), Research Report #1, 7, https://cardozo.yu.edu/sites/default/files/Cardozo%20Blockchain%20 Project%20-%20Not%20So%20Fast%20-%20SAFT%20Response_final.pdf.

[24] Batiz-Benet et al. (n 18), 20.

[25] Jay Clayton, 'Statement on Cryptocurrencies and Initial Coin Offerings' (11 December 2017), Speech.

sellers cultivating an expectation of profits on others' efforts and the tokens being sold before they were actually functional. Clayton's observations are also consistent with the Cardozo Blockchain research paper's argument that relying on a SAFT promotes the expectation of profits not just for SAFT holders but for subsequent token purchasers.[26] Indeed, the SEC's 11 December 2017 action against Munchee to stop the sale of its tokens purporting to offer significant functionality suggests that in practice the sale of utility tokens is often accompanied by elements that satisfy the *Howey* test so as not to prevent the applicability of securities laws.[27]

IV. Intertemporal Classification and Decentralized Token Networks

Implicit in the SAFT white paper's approach and analysis is that a sale of the same tokens may qualify as a regulated securities transaction based upon the functionality of the tokens at the time of their sale. In principle, the sale of non-functional tokens is a regulated 'investment contract' transaction due to meeting all four elements of the *Howey* test. Likewise, if a distributed network is operational and its tokens are fully functional commercial products bought solely for consumptive purposes, then their sale would likely not classify as an investment contract. Accordingly, sales of the same tokens would have a different regulatory classification *over time* based on the surrounding circumstances.

This potential for an intertemporal transformation in the regulatory treatment of the sale of the same underlying tokens was addressed in a widely discussed 14 June 2018 speech by William Hinman, Director of the SEC's Division of Corporation Finance that covered a wide range of issues surrounding the question of the circumstances under which token sales qualify as securities.[28] Director Hinman made the following points. First, the regulatory jurisdiction issue involves not a digital token per se, but the surrounding transactional circumstances. Second, a token that was originally sold in the form of securities may be later sold in a manner that does not constitute an offering of a security if either the relevant centrally managed enterprise no longer exists (the network is 'sufficiently decentralized' in Hinman's language) or if the digital asset is sold as a utility token—only to purchase a good or service available through the network on which it was created. Third, the application of mandatory disclosure regimes to decentralized token networks is less meaningful due to the difficulty in identifying a single promoter entity to regulate and the lack of value in such disclosures. Specifically, Director Hinman noted that while the original sale of Ethereum tokens may have been securities transactions, given the current decentralized state of Ethereum network, 'current offers and sales of Ether are not securities transactions'. Finally, Hinman suggested the following general factors and economic substance of transactions are significant in determining whether a token sale qualifies as a securities transaction (Table 13.1).

Hinman's analysis is broadly consistent with the SAFT white paper's analysis that sales of pre-functional tokens may qualify as securities transactions and, later, when the tokens are functional and sold as useful commodities on a distributed network, no longer qualify as a securities transaction. Hinman's approach, however, emphasizes the decentralized nature of the network as undermining the *Howey* test's managerial efforts element. By contrast, the SAFT approach emphasizes the impact of market factors other than those of the managers as undermining the managerial efforts element.

---

[26] Cardozo Blockchain Project (n 23), 5.

[27] SEC Order, *In the Matter of Munchee, Inc.*, Order instituting Cease-and desist Proceedings Pursuant to Section 8a of the Securities Act of 1933, Making Findings, and Imposing a Cease-and-desist Order (11 December 2017).

[28] William Hinman, 'Digital Asset Transactions: When Howey Met Gary (Plastic)' (14 June 2018) Speech.

Table 13.1 General factors significant in determining whether a token sale qualifies as a securities transaction

General facts and circumstances	Economic substance of token sale
Is there a person or group that has sponsored or promoted the creation and sale of the digital asset, the efforts of whom play a significant role in the development and maintenance of the asset and its potential increase in value?	Is token creation commensurate with meeting the needs of users or, rather, with feeding speculation?
Has this person or group retained a stake or other interest in the digital asset such that it would be motivated to expend efforts to cause an increase in value in the digital asset?	Are independent actors setting the price or is the promoter supporting the secondary market for the asset or otherwise influencing trading?
Would purchasers reasonably believe such efforts will be undertaken and may result in a return on their investment in the digital asset?	Is it clear that the primary motivation for purchasing the digital asset is for personal use or consumption, as compared to investment?
Has the promoter raised an amount of funds in excess of what may be needed to establish a functional network, and, if so, has it indicated how those funds may be used to support the value of the tokens or to increase the value of the enterprise?	Have purchasers made representations as to their consumptive—as opposed to their investment—intent?
Does the promoter continue to expend funds from proceeds or operations to enhance the functionality and/or value of the system within which the tokens operate?	Are the tokens available in increments that correlate with a consumptive versus investment intent?
Are purchasers 'investing' (i.e. seeking a return)? In that regard, is the instrument marketed and sold to the general public instead of to potential users of the network for a price that reasonably correlates with the market value of the good or service in the network?	Are the tokens distributed in ways to meet users' needs? For example, can the tokens be held or transferred only in amounts that correspond to a purchaser's expected use?
Does the application of the Securities Act protections make sense?	Are there built-in incentives that compel using the tokens promptly on the network, such as having the tokens degrade in value over time, or can the tokens be held for extended periods for investment?
Is there a person or entity upon whom others are relying that plays a key role in the profit making of the enterprise such that disclosure of their activities and plans would be important to investors?	Is the asset marketed and distributed to potential users or the general public?
Do informational asymmetries exist between the promoters and potential purchasers/investors in the digital asset?	Are the assets dispersed across a diverse user base or concentrated in the hands of a few that can exert influence over the application?
Do persons or entities other than the promoter exercise governance rights or meaningful influence?	Is the application fully functioning or in its early stages of development?

Two important aspects of Hinman's analysis will likely prove to be highly significant. First, Hinman's suggestion that the regulatory classification of a transaction involving the same underlying asset may change over time from being a securities transaction to *not* being a securities transaction is a novel principle under securities regulation. Typically, if the sale of a financial asset is deemed to be a securities offering when the asset is initially issued, all subsequent sales of the same asset will also be deemed to be securities transactions. Sales of stocks, bonds, and investment contracts on secondary markets are always securities transactions. However, given that the characteristics of digital tokens can change due to being based on and operating through an underlying software-driven network, it is possible that the functionality of the token and its surrounding transactional characteristics indeed would change over time from being investment related (and hence SEC regulated) to being non-financial and solely commercial or technological. As with Ethereum, agreements to sell tokens may constitute regulated investment contracts but then later change to agreements to sell (distributed) software applications not subject to securities regulation. The newfound ability of transactions in the same asset to morph from securities to non-securities transactions is due to the fact that the same digital asset may change in functionality over time.

Second, Hinman's suggestion that the *reason why* the sale of token may no longer qualify as regulated is due to its network being 'sufficiently decentralized' is vague enough such that it will likely require to be clarified by the SEC before offering the market sufficient legal certainty. Specifically, Hinman stated that '[i]f the network on which the token or coin is to function is sufficiently decentralized—where purchasers would no longer reasonably expect a person or group to carry out essential managerial or entrepreneurial efforts—the assets may not represent an investment contract'. A fundamental problem is that Hinman's speech does not clarify the meaning of being sufficiently decentralized in this context, or even give factors that should be weighed in assessing whether a network is sufficiently decentralized. Indeed, the extent to which a distributed ledger is decentralized is a subject of debate within technology governance. For example, Ethereum cofounder Vitalik Buterin distinguishes between architectural decentralization regarding how many computers make up a network, political decentralization regarding the entities that control the network, and logical decentralization regarding diverse data structures and interfaces.[29] In comparing the relative decentralization of the Bitcoin and Ethereum networks, computer science researchers note that Ethereum nodes are more geographically dispersed and a lower percentage reside in data centres.[30] Commentators also often focus on the concentration level of a network's hash rate as indicative of the relative decentralization of a network's validators (or nodes). It is unclear how the SEC will assess decentralization among different types of distributed networks.

V. Conclusion

Token sales in the United States are treated no differently under securities laws than any other business transaction. If the economic substance of a token sale is such that they constitute securities transactions, they are subject to securities law requirements. Given that it is typically difficult to separate the non-financial, utilitarian aspects of tokens from their investment-like nature, and the surrounding regulatory uncertainty, well-advised token sales are generally sold pursuant to an offering exemption sought to ensure regulatory compliance. To reduce regulatory uncertainty with respect to whether token sale transactions are subject to securities regulation, the SEC could adopt a regulation specifically tailored for digital assets that may have both functional and financial characteristics at the same time— or that change over time—similar to the SEC's 1998 regulation specifically targeted to clarify application of securities laws to technology-driven, alternative trading systems.[31] Another approach, as suggested by Wright and Rohr, would be for the US Congress and the SEC to create a Securities Act registration safe harbour for exchanges that list tokens and create an exemption from registration for tokens that do qualify as securities to strike a proper balance between innovation and investor protection.[32]

---

[29] Vitalik Buterin, 'The Meaning of Decentralization' (*Medium*, 6 February 2017) https://medium.com/@VitalikButerin/the-meaning-of-decentralization-a0c92b76a274.

[30] Adem Efe Gencer, Soumya Basu, Ittay Eyal, Robbert van Renesse, and Emin Gün Sirer, 'Decentralization in Bitcoin and Ethereum' (15 January 2018) https://arxiv.org/abs/1801.03998.

[31] See Romain Dambre, 'Initial Coin Offerings and U.S. Securities Regulation: Challenges and Perspectives' (2018) 1 *Int'l J. Fin. Serv.*, 9, 13.

[32] Rohr and Wright (n 13), 90–91.

VI. Bibliography

Batiz-Benet Juan, Clayburgh Jesse, and Santori Marco, 'The SAFT Project: Toward a Compliant Token Sale Framework' (2 October 2017) https://www.cooley.com/~/media/cooley/pdf/reprints/saft-project-whitepaper.ashx, accessed on 15 January 2019.

Buterin Vitalik, 'The Meaning of Decentralization' (*Medium*, 6 February 2017) https://medium.com/@VitalikButerin/the-meaning-of-decentralization-a0c92b76a274, accessed on 15 January 2019.

Cardozo Blockchain Project, 'Not So Fast—Risks Related to the Use of a "SAFT" for Token Sales' (21 November 2017) Research Report #1, https://cardozo.yu.edu/sites/default/files/Cardozo%20Blockchain%20Project%20-%20Not%20So%20Fast%20-%20SAFT%20Response_final.pdf, accessed on 15 January 2019.

Clayton Jay, 'Statement on Cryptocurrencies and Initial Coin Offerings' (11 December 2017) Speech.

Dambre Romain, 'Initial Coin Offerings and U.S. Securities Regulation: Challenges and Perspectives' (2018) 1 *Int'l J. Fin. Serv.*, 9.

Gencer Adem Efe, Basu Soumya, Eyal Ittay, van Renesse Robbert, and Sirer Emin Gün, 'Decentralization in Bitcoin and Ethereum' (15 January 2018) https://arxiv.org/abs/1801.03998, accessed on 15 January 2019.

Hinman William, 'Digital Asset Transactions: When Howey Met Gary (Plastic)' (14 June 2018) Speech at the Yahoo Finance All Markets Summit, Crypto.

Hochstein Marc and Reutzel Bailey, 'SEC ICO Probe Underway, but Stories Conflict on Size of Sweep' (*CoinDesk.com*, 1 March 2018) https://www.coindesk.com/sec-ico-probe-underway-stories-conflict-extent-sweep/, accessed on 15 January 2019.

PriceWaterhouseCoopers, 'Initial Coin Offerings: A Strategic Perspective' (June 2018) 1, https://cryptovalley.swiss/wp-content/uploads/20180628_PwC-S-CVA-ICO-Report_EN.pdf, accessed 17 February 2019.

Rohr Jonathan and Wright Aaron, 'Blockchain-Based Token Sales, Initial Coin Offerings, and the Democratization of Public Capital Markets' (forthcoming) *Hastings Law Journal*, https://ssrn.com/abstract=3048104, accessed on 15 January 2019.

SEC Order, *In the Matter of Munchee, Inc.*, Order instituting Cease-and-desist Proceedings pursuant to Section 8a of the Securities Act of 1933, Making Findings, and Imposing a Cease-and-desist Order (11 December 2017).

US Securities and Exchange Commission, 'Investor Alert: Ponzi Schemes Using Virtual Currencies' (*Investor.gov*, 23 July 2013) https://www.investor.gov/additional-resources/news-alerts/alerts-bulletins/investor-alert-ponzi-schemes-using-virtual, accessed on 15 January 2019.

US Securities and Exchange Commission, 'Investor Alert: Bitcoin and Other Virtual Currency-Related Investments' (*Investor.gov*, 7 May 2014) https://www.investor.gov/additional-resources/news-alerts/alerts-bulletins/investor-alert-bitcoin-other-virtual-currency, accessed on 15 January 2019.

US Securities and Exchange Commission, 'Investor Bulletin: Initial Coin Offerings' (*Investor.gov*, 25 July 2014) https://www.investor.gov/additional-resources/news-alerts/alerts-bulletins/investor-bulletin-initial-coin-offerings, accessed on 15 January 2019.

US Securities and Exchange Commission, 'Report of Investigation Pursuant to Section 21(a) of the Securities Exchange Act of 1934: The DAO' (25 July 2017) Release No. 81207, https://www.sec.gov/litigation/investreport/34-81207.pdf, accessed on 15 January 2019.

PART IV

BEYOND FINANCE: BLOCKCHAIN AS A LEGAL AND REGULATORY CHALLENGE

14

Blockchain and Payment Systems

A Tale about Re-Intermediation

Agnieszka Janczuk-Gorywoda*

I. Introduction

Bitcoin—the first virtual currency based on blockchain technology[1]—was born out of an anarcho-libertarian dream to create a monetary system that would be completely independent of the state and established financial institutions.[2] The dream to enable free and unconstraint human exchanges: a silent revolution that would wash away the J. P. Morgans of the world and much more. 'Blockchainiacs' would fantasize of an 'alternate universe, [where] the blockchain devours banks and credit cards, and smashes the concept of authoritarian ownership of people via workdays, cubicles, and 6-month reviews'.[3] This has been the dream of 'trustless trust', which would develop quickly and effortlessly among peer strangers, allowing them to cooperate on various dimensions without the need for the mighty intermediary organizations.

Today, there is no doubt that blockchain technology will transform payments, the financial industry, and many other areas. However, this contribution argues that with regard to payments, this transformation will be far from the libertarian ideal mentioned above. Rather, blockchain (1) will enable the rise of new powerful intermediaries and (2) it will be embraced by established payment services providers, who will use blockchain to modernize their services.[4] As a result, decentralized virtual currencies like Bitcoin will remain on the periphery of the mainstream payments landscape.

Blockchain has focused too narrowly on providing a technological solution to the issue of scarcity and solving the double-spending problem. Yet, problems involved in monetary and payment systems are broader. In particular, payment systems provide for a broad range of mechanisms supporting circulation of money which, for the scale and complexity of a modern economy must be backed by the state. Money is a hybrid public–private institution and it seems naïve to think that technology alone could render the role of state institutions in monetary and payment systems obsolete.

* I am grateful to Georgios Dimitropoulos and participants in a 2018 conference 'Blockchain, Public Trust, Law and Governance' at the Groningen University for comments on this chapter. All errors remain mine.

[1] In fact, Blockchain is one type of distributed ledger technology and it is this broader technology, not necessarily limited to blockchain, that will underlie the transformation. For the sake of simplicity, this contribution focuses on blockchain.

[2] See Aaron Wright and Primavera De Filippi, 'Decentralized Blockchain Technology and the Rise of *Lex Cryptographia*' (25 July 2017) https://papers.ssrn.com/sol3/papers.cfm?abstract_id=2580664.

[3] Daily Hodl Staff, 'The New Freedom: Bitcoin, Blockchainiacs, and the Alternate Universe' (*DailyHodl*, 16 November 2017) https://dailyhodl.com/2017/11/16/the-new-freedom-bitcoin-blockchainiacs-and-the-alternate-universe/.

[4] In a similar vein, Georgios Dimitropoulos argues that intermediary intervention can only be expected to rise as the proportion of virtual currencies in the global economy increases; see Chapter 6 by Georgios Dimitropoulos in this volume, 46. Stefan Eich, on the other hand, argues that neither the generation of bitcoins nor the confirmation of Bitcoin payments is truly decentralized. Instead, its mining and the processing of payments tends to be heavily centralized, with a small number of extremely large miners operating in an oligopolistic structure that strikingly resembles that of the global banking system; see Chapter 4 by Stefan Eich in this volume, 21.

Blockchain and Payment Systems: A Tale about Re-Intermediation. Agnieszka Janczuk-Gorywoda. © Agnieszka Janczuk-Gorywoda 2019. Published 2019 by Oxford University Press.

This chapter is structured as follows. Section II provides a brief overview of blockchain technology and its ideological foundations. Section III illuminates money as a hybrid public–private system and explains the role of a payment system in supporting the operation of money. Section IV argues that decentralized virtual currencies are not competitive enough to displace traditional providers of national payment services. Section V, in turn, argues that decentralized virtual currencies are not properly structured to expand in the area of international payments without reliance on intermediaries. Section VI concludes.

II. A Blockchain Primer, Once Again

A. Bitcoin's ideology and dream

Bitcoin was the first and so far the most successful virtual currency scheme based on blockchain technology.[5] Virtual currency is best described as 'a digital representation of value, not issued by a central bank, credit institution or e-money institution, which in some circumstances can be used as an alternative to money'.[6] A virtual currency scheme is a protocol underlying the creation of virtual currency and the inherent mechanisms ensuring that it can be transferred (i.e. commercially exchanged).

Bitcoin emerged from the 2007–2009 Global Financial Crisis, when trust in financial markets plunged. It was born out of the desire to eliminate the need for trusted third parties, to eliminate financial institutions and, beyond that, the state and its legal and administrative system, in order to create a government-independent, censorship-resistant, anonymous monetary and payment system.[7] Hopes have been high. First, Bitcoin has been expected to sweep away potent financial institutions by democratizing money and finance and, in turn, redistributing wealth and achieving greater social justice. Second, Bitcoin, according to its 'ideologists', shall also reduce governmental control over the economy and over individuals, thereby resulting in a freer society.[8] In particular, by being censorship-resistant, Bitcoin is to allow transactions to be made freely, without any attempts at controlling or censoring them.

All the abovementioned expectations rest almost entirely on the fundamental and revolutionary feature of Bitcoin and more broadly blockchain: its ability to 'govern without government';[9] its ability to remove the need for central intermediaries to coordinate individual activities.

'Decentralization' is said to destabilize existing power structures by removing a control point.[10] Bitcoin, in particular, has challenged one of the main prerogatives of the state—that of money issuance and regulation—and questioned the need for the existing financial institutions. It has been argued that as a decentralized platform for financial transactions, Bitcoin sets a limit on the power of central banks and other financial institutions to define the terms and conditions, and to control the execution of financial transactions. In addition, by enabling people to coordinate their activity without relying on a centralized third party

---

[5] In 2015, Bitcoin accounted for more than 80% of the market capitalization of around 500 known decentralized virtual currency schemes; see European Central Bank ('ECB'), 'Virtual Currency Schemes—a Further Analysis' (February 2015), 6.

[6] ibid., 4.

[7] As explicitly stated by Satoshi Nakamoto in various blog posts and forums, Bitcoin aimed to eliminate corruption from the realm of currency issuance and exchange; Primavera De Filippi and Benjamin Loveluck, 'The Invisible Politics of Bitcoin: Governance Crisis of a Decentralised Infrastructure' (2016) 5(3) *Internet Policy Review*, 4.

[8] Primavera De Filippi, 'Bitcoin: A Regulatory Nightmare to a Libertarian Dream' (2014) 3(2) *Internet Policy Review*.

[9] De Filippi and Loveluck (n 7), 3. The other fundamental feature, from this perspective, is pseudonymity of transactions.

[10] ibid., 15.

or trusted authority, Bitcoin and blockchain have been expected to promote individual free-doms and emancipation.[11]

B. Distributed ledger and intermediaries

The key role of intermediaries in financial markets is to maintain a reliable record of all trans-actions and holdings.[12] It is only thanks to such reliable records that market participants can trust that facts have been logged accurately and nobody has tampered with the data.[13] The essence of the revolution brought by blockchain is that instead of a single record kept by a central intermediary, each participant in the system (a 'node') maintains a complete record of all past transactions made within that system and all nodes are constantly updated with information on the new transactions. Blockchain is 'an Internet-based database'—typically called a 'ledger'—'to store entitlements, of which identical copies of equal constitutive value are held by every network participant. The database enables each participant to trade these entitlements by instructing the database software, which, accordingly, will then autono-mously and irreversibly effect the relevant changes to the network participants' holdings'.[14]

A distributed ledger on its own is not enough to function without intermediaries. Two additional features are necessary. First, there must be a way of approving valid changes in the ledger; and, second, there must be a way of securing accuracy of the ledger and preventing unauthorized changes. The latter is achieved through the organization of the data (informa-tion about transactions and entitlements) into blocks that are cryptographically locked and chained together in an append-only mode that cannot be changed.

Regarding the mode of approving changes, there is a fundamental difference between cen-tralized and decentralized virtual currency schemes.[15] The original idea of Bitcoin is based on a decentralized consensus mechanism whereby all participants in the network can par-ticipate in the validation of transactions. A new transaction will be appended to the end of the blockchain only after computers on the network reach consensus as to its validity. Each new transaction is recorded into a block with a limited capacity. Once the block is full, nodes simultaneously perform some work (hence, 'Proof of Work')—cryptographic puzzles that are hard to solve but the correct solution of which is easy to verify. These mathematical op-erations are unrelated to the Bitcoin transactions but are indispensable to the operation of the system as they force the verifying nodes to expend processing power which would be wasted if they included any fraudulent or invalid transactions. The first node that succeeds in solving the 'Proof of Work' problem sends it to the network. Other nodes can quickly and cheaply verify the accuracy of the transactions and the solution, and when 51% of the pro-cessing power of the network votes to approve the block, it is irreversibly appended to the Blockchain.[16] Accordingly, the Proof of Work protocol is dependent on the high processing power threshold to prevent both hacking and the establishment of central control.[17]

By contrast, in a centralized scheme, coins are issued and redeemed by a single in-stitution (or a group of institutions) at its choice.[18] Centralized schemes solve many

---

[11] ibid.
[12] See Philipp Paech, 'The Governance of Blockchain Financial Networks' (2017) 80(6) *Modern Law Review*, 1078.
[13] See Wright and De Filippi (n 2), 5.   [14] Paech (n 12), 1074.
[15] Actually, governance of virtual currency schemes includes three components: (i) the issuance and redeemability of the virtual currency; (ii) mechanisms to implement and enforce internal rules on the use and cir-culation of the currency; and (iii) the payment and settlement process. Each area of operation may be managed by a trusted central (and private) party or in a decentralized manner among participants. See International Monetary Fund (IMF), 'Virtual Currencies and Beyond: Initial Considerations' (January 2016), IMF Discussion Note, 9, http://www.imf.org/external/pubs/ft/sdn/2016/sdn1603.pdf.
[16] See Saifedean Ammous, *The Bitcoin Standard: The Decentralized Alternative to Central Banking* (Wiley 2018), 172.
[17] ibid., 220–21.   [18] See ECB, 'Virtual Currency Schemes' (n 5), 11.

governance problems created by decentralized schemes, including problems discussed in this contribution.[19]

However, centralized schemes depart from the fundamental dogma underlying the introduction of Bitcoin, i.e. that there should be no intermediaries and no controlling authority. After all, a central entity managing the scheme is just a different type of intermediary. And there is nothing preventing governments or mainstream financial institutions from forming their own centralized schemes capable of issuing digital currencies. In fact, both central banks and major international banks have started experimenting with blockchain technology.[20]

III. Money and Payment Systems

A. Bitcoin as money

A lot has been written about whether Bitcoin and other virtual currencies can be considered money.[21] From a legal perspective, money is identified with official currency to which national monetary law has conferred the status of legal tender.[22] Furthermore, contemporary currency is 'fiat money', that is, it is currency because a state has declared it to be legal tender but is neither backed by a physical commodity nor has any intrinsic value.

Of course, no national law has conferred the status of legal tender to Bitcoin or any other virtual currency. However, more needs to be said here. Bitcoin as an asset is unique in that, although it is not backed by any central bank or government, it is also not anchored to any specific official currency or other tradable asset. Instead, like fiat currencies, Bitcoin is self-anchored.[23] The dollar is a dollar; the bitcoin is a bitcoin. Bitcoin is a network protocol that prescribes rules by which network nodes ('traders') acquire and exchange units of Bitcoin ('bitcoins'). It is defined without regard to anything outside the network protocol.[24] It is a mathematical creature governed by its own inferential consistency and hinging on cryptographic algorithms to create new units.[25]

Yet Bitcoin has been intended to be used as means of payment and calls its self-created units ('bitcoins') money. This intention has proven quite successful because Bitcoin is indeed used as a means of payments that is slowly spreading beyond a narrow group of tech geeks or criminals willing to escape the official economy. Increasingly, mainstream retailers and service providers have accepted Bitcoin.[26]

Notwithstanding all the volatility of the Bitcoin's value, it is remarkable that a private entity which is completely anonymous,[27] has managed to create a self-anchored asset which is used as a means of exchange. Bitcoin is even more remote than fiat money from anything having utility value. The value of fiat currencies is backed by the creditworthiness of the issuing central bank and the government. The value of privately issued money has been supported by the private issuer's credibility and commodity reserves. Even centralized virtual currency schemes rely on the backing of the private issuer's credibility. By contrast, the value

---

[19] See, e.g., Benjamin Geva, 'Banking in the Digital Age: Who is Afraid of Payment Disintermediation?' (2018) European Banking Institute Working Paper No. 23/2018, 35.

[20] See, e.g., James Chapman, Rodney Garratt, Scott Hendry et al., 'Project Jasper: Are Distributed Wholesale Payment Systems Feasible Yet?' (*BankofCanada.ca*, June 2017) www.bankofcanada.ca/wp-content/uploads/2017/05/fsr-june-2017-chapman.pdf.

[21] See Chapter 6 by Dimitropoulos in this volume, and the references therein.

[22] See Noah Vardi, 'Bit by Bit: Assessing the Legal Nature of Virtual Currencies' in *Bitcoin and Mobile Payments: Constructing a European Union Framework*, edited by Gabriella Gimigliano (Palgrave Macmillan 2016), 59.

[23] Gideon Samid, *Tethered Money: Managing Digital Currency Transactions* (Academic Press 2015), 14.

[24] ibid., 109.   [25] ibid., 14.

[26] Such as, e.g., Expedia, Microsoft, Newegg; see 99 Bitcoins, https://99bitcoins.com/who-accepts-bitcoins-payment-companies-stores-take-bitcoins/.

[27] In reality, Satoshi Nakamoto, the legendary creator of Bitcoin, could be a pseudonym used by the state; however, given his full anonymity it is entirely irrelevant.

of Bitcoin and other decentralized currencies receives no backing from any source. Bitcoins derive value solely from the expectation that others will also value and use them.[28] No wonder so many got fascinated with the question as to whether Bitcoin constitutes 'money'.

B. Money as a hybrid public–private institution

Two major theories have dominated the discussion concerning the concept of 'money'. On the one hand, the 'state theory' of money asserts that money is whatever the state as a sovereign declares it to be.[29] It is the state, and only the state, that has the monopoly power to designate money. On the other hand, 'social theory' of money claims that money is whatever society accepts as money.[30] Nobody, be it the state or any other entity, has the power to impose on society a 'money' that the society does not want to accept. In other words, money is conceptualized either as a public or private phenomenon.

Without entering into this debate, modern money exhibits features that make it fair to say that it is a hybrid public–private concept.[31] On the one hand, the state has exclusive power to determine what forms of money constitute legal tender and to fix its nominal value by law.[32] The status of legal tender implicates that—unless consensually agreed otherwise by parties—it must be accepted at nominal value to discharge monetary debts within the territory of the issuing state.[33] Refusal to accept legal tender as means of discharging debts results in negative legal consequences for the refusing creditor. What is more, modern legal tender constitutes fiat currency: it does not have any intrinsic value and it functions as money solely because it has been declared by the state to be legal tender. Its value, which is its purchasing power, is backed by the creditworthiness of the issuing central bank, the government, and its taxing power, as well as the value—the gross domestic product (GDP)—of the respective economy.

Having said that, except for designating money in which taxes have to be paid, the power of the state to impose the use of legal tender on society is limited, especially in market economies based on individual freedoms.[34] If nothing else, as an expression of the contractual freedom, parties can always agree to settle debts by other means. Moreover, at the end of the day, fiat currency is only a credit against the issuing central bank. Hence, its public acceptance depends on the society's trust that that central bank, and the respective government, will retain its value over time. If people have no trust in the official currency, they will refrain from exchanging it as means of payment among themselves. The rise of black markets or alternative currencies whenever a national currency experiences significant devaluation testify to this.[35]

---

[28] IMF (n 15), 9. As argued by Hossein Nabilou and André Prüm, a crucial source of Bitcoin's value is that it is information-insensitive. That means that nobody can gain any advantage by acquiring superior information about the level of Bitcoin's safety from bankruptcy. As a result, adverse selection problem does not arise and a liquid market in Bitcoin can be formed. See Hossein Nabilou and André Prüm, 'Ignorance, Debt and Cryptocurrencies: The Old and the New in the Law and Economics of Concurrent Currencies' (30 August 2018) https://papers.ssrn.com/sol3/papers.cfm?abstract_id=3121918.

[29] *Locus classicus* is Georg Friedrich Knapp, *Staatliche Theorie des Geldes* (4th edn, Duncker & Humblot 1923), translated by H. M. Lucas and J. Bonar, *The State Theory of Money* (Macmillan 1924). Also, the more recent Charles Proctor, *Mann on the Legal Aspect of Money* (7th edn, Oxford University Press 2012).

[30] Arthur Nussbaum, *Money in the Law: National and International* (The Foundation Press 1950).

[31] Christine Desan has argued that money has always depended on public–private cooperation, whereby the state provides a public institution consisting in common standards, universality, and scale whilst the society accepts specific money to be exchanged between its members; Christine Desan, *Making Money: Coin, Currency, and the Coming of Capitalism* (Oxford University Press 2014).

[32] Rosa Maria Lastra, *International Financial and Monetary Law* (2nd edn, Oxford University Press 2015) 16.

[33] Proctor (n 29), 68.

[34] Short of total surveillance, such capacity is not absolute even in authoritarian states.

[35] Most recently, Venezuela has experienced hyperinflation spiralling towards a surreal level of one million per cent, prompting Venezuelans to abandon bolívares whenever possible; see, e.g., Rachelle Krygier, 'In Socialist Venezuela, The U.S. Dollar Becomes King' (*The Washington Post*, 2 August 2018) https://www.washingtonpost.

Then again, modern money is mostly issued by private entities. Notably, it functions predominantly as scriptural money,[36] that is, money created by commercial banks as records on their books.[37] Scriptural money is essentially a debt against the issuing private bank. Yet, it is denominated in, and redeemable to, fiat money on demand.

Scriptural money is essential for the functioning of an economy of the current complexity and scale. It enables fast, cheap, and widespread circulation of the monetary value. It also allows for relatively smooth adaptations of the monetary aggregate to the needs of the economy without full dependence on the state and its administrative apparatus. Instead, commercial banks are largely independent in deciding on either expansion or contraction of the money aggregate. However, scriptural money is not anchored in any physical commodity but in official currency which, as discussed above, is fiat money.

More generally, the state cannot prevent society from resorting to alternative money. Anybody can always issue an IOU. In different types of relationships different types of IOUs may be used to discharge monetary obligations. Certain IOUs can become so broadly accepted without significant discount as to start performing a monetary function. Of course, the lack of state recognition implies that such money would be imperfect. Most importantly, in times of stress the value of such money can fade quickly, leaving its holders empty-handed.

Then again, scriptural money can function as universal medium of exchange and store of value due to its fundamental links to the state. First, scriptural money is denominated in, and redeemable to, fiat currency on demand. These features support scriptural money with the credibility of the state and its central bank. Furthermore, as discussed in more detail in section III.C, for its acceptance and circulation scriptural money requires institutions and a legal framework backed by the state. In other words, private entities are not capable of creating universally accepted money without the involvement of the state.

To sum up, modern money is a hybrid public–private institution: it operates through both private and state mechanisms. State designates legal tender, establishes the general monetary legal framework, and promises to intervene if needed to prevent a crisis and secure financial stability or safeguard some other public policy goal. The majority of money in circulation, however, is issued by private entities, which enables the operation of market forces and personal freedoms in the selection and pricing of particular money. Then again, private money requires an institutional and legal framework to support it,[38] which, for the scale and complexity of a modern economy, must be backed by the state.

C. Institutional dimension of payment systems

A payment system constitutes a crucial component of the institutional and legal framework enabling the functioning of money. It is an institutional set-up for transferring value and ensuring the circulation of money. Money does not travel from place to place on its own; it requires an entire institutional structure. Even simple cash transactions require legal rules specifying when monetary obligations are discharged with finality, as well as enforcement institutions. As will be explained below, transfers of scriptural money—for instance bank transfers—require a more complex set of rules, including a prudential regime concerning

com/world/in-socialist-venezuela-the-us-dollar-becomes-king/2018/08/01/7af16482-9442-11e8-818b-e9b7348cd87d_story.html?noredirect=on&utm_term=.0ad0c304b191.

[36] In developed countries, notes and coins (i.e. currency in circulation) accounts for no more than approximately 10% of the money supply; see Claus D. Zimmermann, *A Contemporary Concept of Monetary Sovereignty* (Oxford University Press 2013), 17.

[37] In reality, the notion of scriptural money encompasses a broader range of financial instruments, notably Eurocurrencies and credit derivatives; however, for the sake of simplicity of exposition they are not mentioned here. See, e.g., ibid., 17–18.

[38] Antonio Sáinz De Vicuña, 'An Institutional Theory of Money' in *International Monetary and Financial Law: The Global Crisis*, edited by Mario Giovanoli and Diego Devos (Oxford University Press 2010).

payment institutions, the mechanisms and rules governing clearing and settlement, the mechanisms and rules warranting liquidity of payment intermediaries, also in times of financial stress, rules ensuring finality of payments, the assigning of liability for erroneous and fraudulent payments, and so on and so forth.

Understanding the relationship between money and a payment system is crucial for appreciating what is necessary to establish a successful money. It is the payment system that enables the functioning of scriptural money. Money is an essentially hierarchical phenomenon.[39] The concept of hierarchy highlights that people accept different types of assets with different readiness. Different levels of acceptance of various types of assets translates into their different price, different liquidity, and so forth. What people accept as money is dependent on the money's ability to be transferred to third parties at any time and without the loss of value. This is what is conventionally referred to as medium of exchange and store of value functions of money. Both are ultimately a matter of degree and depending on aspects such as risk appetite, patience, or a point in time,[40] different parties can accept various classes of assets 'as money'; that is, to redeem outstanding obligations.

As discussed above, there is nothing inherent in the modern money itself—whether issued by public or private bodies—that could be considered as embodying anything of value. That value is derived solely from the fact that the society uses specific money which, in turn, depends on the full faith and credit of the government and central bank behind official currency on the one hand, and credibility of the issuer of private money on the other. Consequently, public acceptance and use of money depends on the trust (i) that its issuer is capable of—and that it will—maintain the money's value over time; (ii) that the money will be available even in times of financial stress; (iii) that the money is capable of discharging monetary obligations; and (iv) that the money's functionality and convenience of use is reliable. These aspects, in turn, hinge on the institutional and legal framework supporting money, including the payment system.

There are many institutional and legal arrangements that ensure the functioning of money and payments, and this contribution cannot discuss them all. With the advent of fiat money all eyes turned to the central banks and their institutional set-up. This is because central banks have been tasked with ensuring, over time, the stability of the value of money ('price stability'). Volatility of the value of money would not only have negative consequences for the economy, but would also diminish public acceptance of money. People would simply switch to alternative, more stable, money.

However, many other arrangements are also crucial. Clearing and settlement systems enable efficient circulation of money across the many banks and other payment services providers and hence secure liquidity in the system.

Prudential regulation of banks together with deposit insurance and emergency liquidity assistance for banks promise that depositors will not loose their money. This is necessary because scriptural money is issued by private entities, which inevitably have lower credibility than a central bank. A central bank will always meet its nominal obligation to pay its own currency.[41] With fiat money, there is nothing constraining a central bank from issuing

---

[39] Perry Mehrling, *The New Lombard Street: How the Fed Became the Dealer of Last Resort* (Princeton University Press 2010).

[40] Importantly, the hierarchy fluctuates at all times, and at almost all timescales, expanding and contracting sequentially. As it expands, the hierarchy flattens and IOUs ever farther down the hierarchy are accepted as means of payment. But then the system contracts, and the hierarchy becomes steep again. At this moment, 'flight to quality' begins. Within the business cycle contraction means that economic agents increasingly refuse to accept IOUs at the lower levels of the hierarchy, demanding higher-level money instead. Cash becomes king and a financial crisis knocks on the door. See Perry Mehrling, 'The Inherent Hierarchy of Money' in *Social Fairness and Economics: Economic Essays in the Spirit of Duncan Foley*, edited by Lance Taylor, Armon Rezai, and Thomas Michl (Routledge 2013).

[41] Of course, a national currency may be subject to devaluation vis-à-vis other currencies, resulting (in an open economy) in a loss of purchasing power.

additional currency if needed. However, by holding scriptural money people are no longer a creditor of a central bank but of a commercial bank instead. In contrast to central banks, commercial banks are prone to insolvency, which implicates credit risks to deposit holders. A claim against a particular issuer can function as money only if the issuer can promise to its creditors that they will not loose money.

Therefore, institutional solutions decreasing the risk of bankruptcy and, should a bank become insolvent, guaranteeing that depositors would not lose their money, are essential in providing the security that money can be safely deposited in commercial banks. These institutions include prudential regulation and supervisory regime for banks and other payment services providers, compulsory deposit guarantee schemes, and emergency liquidity assistance from central banks. These institutions are essential in enabling the public acceptance of commercial banks' money because they render claims on commercial banks information-insensitive.[42] That means that nobody could gain any advantage by acquiring superior information about the level of Bitcoin's safety from bankruptcy. As a result, adverse selection problem does not arise and a liquid market in Bitcoin can be formed.

Finally, payments law serves multiple purposes: it specifies when payments are made; it governs rights and obligations of the parties participating in payments transactions; it protects users against fraud; and it assigns liabilities. Traditionally, the core of payments law revolved around three fundamental issues: (i) the allocation of loss resulting from fraud, forgery, and error; (ii) the determination of when payments are completed so that the underlying liability is discharged; and (iii) the determination of when payments can be reversed.[43]

Liability rules lie at the heart of payments law because they distribute losses when a payment transaction is disrupted. However, they are important not only because of their distributional consequences but also because of the incentives they create.[44] The greater a party's liability for losses, the greater incentive it will have to take care to avoid such losses. Finally, liability rules also have implications for the parties' perception of the safety of a payment system. A party that has to bear the losses more often than not may develop a perception of a dysfunctional system. If this is a user of the payment services, he or she might become discouraged from using it.

D. Bitcoin as a payment system

Bitcoin as a payment system has been less exciting than Bitcoin as money.[45] However, as a self-anchored currency Bitcoin has created its own closed universe in which bitcoins are stored and exchanged; in other words, it has created its own payment system. What is more, virtual currencies have emerged that are pegged against—and sometimes also backed by reserves of—some official currency.[46] The aim of such 'stablecoins' is not to create alternative money, but rather to explore the opportunities offered by blockchain technology to create payment systems.

---

[42] Nabilou and Prüm (n 28).

[43] Ronald Mann, 'Making Sense of Payments Policy in the Information Age' (2005) 93 *Georgetown Law Journal*, 638.

[44] Adam Levitin, 'Private Disordering: Payment Card Fraud Liability Rules' (2011) 5 *Brooklyn Journal of Corporate, Financial & Commercial Law*, 3.

[45] But a lot has been written on that topic as well; see, e.g., Iris H.-Y. Chiu, 'A New Era of Fintech Payment Innovations? A Perspective from the Institutions and Regulation of Payment Systems' (2017) 9(2) *Law, Innovation and Technology*; Geva (n 19), and references therein.

[46] For instance, in May 2018 Goldman Sachs-backed (GS.N) cryptocurrency start-up Circle launched Circle USD Coin (USDC), a Blockchain-based cryptocurrency pegged to and fully backed by reserves of US dollars (stablecoin); see Sean Neville and Jeremy Allaire, 'Circle Announces USD Coin, Bitmain Partnership, and New Strategic Financing' (*Blog.Circle.com*, 15 May 2018) https://blog.circle.com/2018/05/15/circle-announces-usd-coin-bitmain-partnership-and-new-strategic-financing/.

However, Bitcoin functions mostly outside the official legal and institutional framework supporting traditional forms of money. This has been the desire of its creator and most faithful adherents and indeed policy-makers, regulators, and courts are not sure how to approach it. The blockchain revolution consists in an attempt to replace the legal and administrative framework with technology. Sections IV and V argue that this will not be entirely successful and will have profound consequences for the (un-)feasibility of the disintegration model.

IV. Virtual Currencies for Domestic Payments

The casual portrait of virtual currency transactions is that they offer many advantages in comparison to traditional payments. They are supposed to offer anonymity to their users, be safer, cheaper, and quicker than traditional payments. Yet, this section argues that virtual currencies are safer, cheaper, and faster only in comparison to international payment services, not when compared to domestic payments. At the same time, traditional domestic payments offer many advantages over virtual currencies, such as stability of value, legal certainty, consumer protection, and their ability to be employed within and by well-known business models. What is more, traditional providers of payment services have started experimenting with blockchain and it is possible that they will use blockchain to outcompete virtual currency schemes. Accordingly, it is not likely that decentralized virtual currencies will displace existing payment services providers for domestic transactions.

A. Settlement time and use costs

Virtual currencies involve a relatively short time for the verification and settlement of the payment transaction, which is not linked to the geographical location of the parties.[47] However, the truly short validation and settlement time (instantaneous) can only be obtained for centralized schemes, whilst in decentralized schemes it typically takes an hour. This is still significantly shorter than many traditional transnational payments, which can take days to go through the correspondent banking channel. However, it is significantly slower than domestic payments, which are frequently settled instantaneously. Accordingly, settlement times for virtual currencies are less attractive than for traditional domestic payment methods.

The cost of using virtual currencies is also believed to be low. There are no account-holding fees if one stores virtual coins privately and the transaction fees for a single transaction have either been absent or low.[48] Yet, due to the high volatility of their value, the final costs related to the use of virtual currencies are higher than it initially appears.

High value volatility largely decreases virtual currencies' ability to function as a unit of account or as a store of value. This in turn undermines the efficiency, including cost-efficiency, of virtual currency schemes. First, no prices are likely to be set in any virtual currency. Instead, to obtain the actual price, in say Bitcoin, a conversion from the price set in another currency will always have to be made. Second, because of the high volatility, few people will hoard virtual currencies over time. As a result, in order to make a transaction in Bitcoin a payer would have to purchase bitcoins directly prior to the transaction whilst the payee would have to sell them directly afterwards. These conversions take additional time and involve additional costs—something that is not, but should be, taken into account when calculating Bitcoin's efficiency and cost.

---

[47] With much shorter times for centralized than decentralized networks; see ECB, 'Virtual Currency Schemes' (n 5), 18.
[48] ibid., 19.

B. Protection against fraud

Protection against fraud is very relevant in practice because payments fraud is a multi-billion-pound problem. The exact numbers are difficult to obtain as currently official statistics only cover card transactions. Yet, even if we look only at card fraud, the most recent European Central Bank report estimated its total value in the Single Euro Payments Area to be €1.44 billion in 2013.[49] This resulted from 11.29 million fraudulent transactions.

First, blockchain transactions are believed to be safe, offering a high level of protection against fraud. In particular, blockchain transactions are pseudonymous,[50] as a result of which no personal or sensitive payment data is needed for making a payment. This strengthens both the level of privacy protection of the transacting parties and the security of the transaction; once the transaction is verified, no transaction information can be reused to conduct a fraudulent payment.[51]

However, the promise of safety has to be weighed against the cash-like attribute of virtual currencies and the risks resulting from it. Virtual coins are essentially sequences of bits which need to be stored somewhere. An 'owner' can choose either to store it at a professional exchange or privately at some electronic data storage device. The obvious disadvantage of the latter solution is that loss or damage to the device is equal to the loss of virtual coins. Professional virtual currency exchanges seem to be more secure. These are companies that hold virtual currencies and are willing to buy and sell them at a specified exchange rate.[52] Yet, these entities are not regulated in any way and there have already been some spectacular exchange failures.[53] Hence, whilst the transactions themselves present a much lower risk of fraud, storage of digital currencies is more risky than for traditional money. A solution to this problem would be to develop a regulatory and supervisory system for entities storing (i.e. accepting deposits of) virtual currencies, however, this would obviously depart from the disintermediation ideal.

Second, anonymity and the irreversibility of transactions means that an erroneous transaction, which is simply sent to the wrong payee, can never be reimbursed. This is, however, less of a competitive disadvantage than initially thought because many national laws also do not provide for reimbursement of erroneous payments made by traditional means. In particular, the Payments Services Directive ('PSD')[54] in the European Union has introduced a principle that the recipient of a bank transfer is to be identified solely by means of an international bank account number ('IBAN').[55] The risk of providing a wrong IBAN rests entirely with the payer. The PSD has forced many EU Member States to change their national laws, which previously offered higher levels of protection to payers.[56]

---

[49] European Central Bank ('ECB'), 'The Fourth Report on Card Fraud' (*ECB. Europa.eu*, July 2015) https://www.ecb.europa.eu/pub/pdf/other/4th_card_fraud_report.en.pdf.

[50] In contrast to frequently held beliefs, blockchain transactions are not anonymous. Beyond that, even in consideration of the pseudonymous nature of the blockchain, it is already possible to trace back certain transactions to a particular identity, or even just to infer the identity of the person associated with a particular address by means of big data analysis over the blockchain (so-called blockchain analytics); see Wright and De Filippi (n 2), 53. In fact, Wright and De Filippi argue that without appropriate legal safeguards the development of blockchain technology could lead to increased surveillance; ibid., 53.

[51] ECB, 'Virtual Currency Schemes' (n 5), 18.

[52] Andres Guadamuz and Chris Marsden, 'Blockchains and Bitcoin: Regulatory Responses to Cryptocurrencies' (2015) 20 (12) *First Monday*.

[53] ibid.

[54] Directive 2007/64/EC of the European Parliament and of the Council (13 November 2007) on Payment Services in the Internal Market amending Directives 97/7/EC, 2002/65/EC, 2005/60/EC, and 2006/48/EC, and repealing Directive 97/5/EC, OJ [2007] L 319/1) PSD I has been repealed by Directive 2015/2366 of the European Parliament and of the Council (25 November 2015) on Payment Services in the Internal Market (PSD II), amending Directives 2002/65/EC, 2009/110/EC, and 2013/36/EU and Regulation (EU) No. 1093/2010, and repealing Directive 2007/64/EC, OJ [2015] L 337/35.

[55] Article 74 PSD and now Art. 88 of the PSD II.

[56] See, e.g., judgment of the Austrian Oberste Gerichtshof of 23 October 2010, 2Ob224/13z, JBl 2015,48.

All in all, virtual currencies are not more efficient than domestic payments. Perhaps the only real advantages of virtual currencies are pseudonymity and the high security of transactions. However, it is possible that traditional payment services providers will adopt blockchain in order to offer these qualities to their users.[57] At the same time, traditional payments providers can offer their users stability of value, legal certainty, consumer protection, and well-known business models. On its own, legal certainty problems could likely discourage regulated companies and (possibly all) users contemplating transfers of larger sums from using virtual currencies.[58] Further, customers of traditional payment services providers can make payments in official currency directly from their bank accounts. For domestic payments this implies no conversion costs. History has shown that the most efficient way to provide transaction services is for the provider to hold the customers' accounts.[59] Accordingly, the traditional banking model in which payment services are offered by entities which also accept and hold the customers' deposits has historically prevailed over stand-alone payments services. Some commentators predict that efficiency is bound either to turn payment institutions like PayPal into banks or for banks to take over payment institutions, either directly or as subsidiaries, so as to eliminate the unnecessary layer of intermediation.[60] The same can be largely expected for virtual currencies. Hence, it is unlikely that virtual currencies would be able to displace traditional payments intermediaries for domestic payments.

V. Cross-Border Trade with Bitcoin?

Even sceptics admit that virtual currencies have exposed and challenged the inefficiencies of cross-border retail payments.[61] The latter are disproportionally expensive, can take a long time to be processed, and are most unfavourable to the most disadvantaged groups. International remittances—that is, transfers from migrant workers coming from developing countries sending some of their income back home to support their families—are a case in point.

Even if Bitcoin is much slower, less transparent, and more expensive than domestic retail payments, in comparison to cross-border payments, it offers a cheaper and faster way to pay for overseas goods bought online or to send money home to a different country, thereby supporting financial inclusion and development. Accordingly, cross-border payments seem to be just the right niche for Bitcoin to flourish. Nonetheless, this section argues that Bitcoin and other decentralized virtual currencies are less well suited for cross-border retail payments than it appears. As a result, it is not likely that they could become major payment providers for cross-border transactions.

A. International remittances

Despite their clear advantages in terms of cost and efficiency, virtual currencies are not well suited for international remittances. Technical knowledge and the infrastructure necessary to use virtual currencies constitutes a considerable barrier.[62] In particular, most receivers of international remittances lack internet access and the knowledge necessary to open and operate a virtual currency account, as well as to convert virtual coins into the local currency.

---

[57] See, e.g., Neville and Allaire (n 46).   [58] See Chiu (n 45), 229.
[59] Richard Carnell, Jonathan Macey, and Geoffrey Miller, 'Banks: Fundamental Concepts' (2016) NYU Law and Economics Research Paper No. 16-37, 20.
[60] Geva (n 19), 23.
[61] See, e.g., Benoît Cœuré and Jacqueline Loh, 'Bitcoin Not the Answer to a Cashless Society' (*Ft.com*, 13 March 2018) https://www.ft.com/content/31abc532-25d0-11e8-b27e-cc62a39d57a0. Benoît Cœuré is a member of the Executive Board of the ECB and is the Chair of the Bank for International Settlements Committee on Payments and Market Infrastructures; Jacqueline Loh is the Chair of the BIS Markets Committee.
[62] See ECB, 'Virtual Currency Schemes' (n 5).

In consequence, in developing countries virtual currencies are expanding in cooperation with intermediaries, which help their customers overcome these barriers. For instance, the leading South-East Asia's blockchain payments platform, Coins, is a digital wallet provider enabling payments in Bitcoin and other virtual currencies. What is more, it operates in partnership with mobile operators and traditional banks.[63]

B. The problem of trust: delivery versus payment

It is also not clear that virtual currencies represent a more attractive alternative for cross-border payments for online purchases. Difficulties and risks related to transactions between parties from distant locations are not limited to technical problems of how to send payments, ship goods, or deliver services.

There is also the problem of trust. In long-distance transactions, the performance of reciprocal contractual obligations cannot be simultaneous and is inevitably deferred: one party pays immediately and the other promises to subsequently deliver the goods, or vice versa. Even if both parties perform their obligation at the same moment, it will take some time before the goods and payment are actually delivered. This time deferral creates the risk that one of the parties will not keep their promise or that their performance will deviate from the agreed contract terms. Such a risk can be reduced, and thus the benefits of transacting increased, through effective enforcement institutions.[64]

In local exchanges, dense social networks and lower information costs enable the effective punishment of the breaching party through mechanisms such as social ostracism, and thus significantly reduce incentives to renege on promises. Local legal institutions complement the picture and further ensure the enforcement of contracts.

In long-distance or transnational trade, the parties are 'strangers' to one another. They do not know one another's characteristics, social networks are absent, and the local legal systems lose their traction. The global marketplace is a sphere of lawlessness.[65] Lawlessness in this context does not suggest that there is no state-made law applicable in the global sphere, but rather that at the transnational level there is no clearly identifiable set of rules to be applied to cross-border transactions.[66] As a result, there is a risk that contracts will not be enforced and that property rights will not be secure. Moreover, long-distance trade involves a number of additional risks. Those concerning payments involve: (i) the risk of loss in transit; (ii) the risk of loss in currency exchange; (iii) the risk that the money will be received only with substantial delay; (iv) the risk of receiving a lower amount than agreed; and/or (v) the risk that payment will not be executed at all.

In such circumstances, transactions are only possible if alternative mechanisms of ensuring performance are in place. The situation of lawlessness induces participants in global trade to design governance mechanisms to support credible commitments. In some instances, this lacuna has been filled by payments rules created by private parties enabling cross-border payments, for example PayPal.[67] Virtual currency schemes, however, do not provide such rules. This issue will be explored in the next section.

---

[63] Tanya Mariano, 'How Bitcoin is Disrupting Southeast Asia's Remittance Industry. For the Region's Migrant Workers, an Alternative to Traditional Channels' (22 August 2016) http://inc-asean.com/editor-picks/bitcoin-disrupting-southeast-asias-remittance-industry.

[64] See Douglas North, 'Institutions' (1991) 5 *The Journal of Economic Perspectives*, 97.

[65] Avinas Dixit, *Lawlessness and Economics: Alternative Modes of Governance* (Princeton University Press 2007).

[66] Gralf-Peter Calliess, 'Transnational Civil Regimes: Economic Globalisation and the Evolution of Commercial Law' in *Contractual Certainty in International Trade: Empirical Studies and Theoretical Debates on Institutional Support for Global Economic Exchanges*, edited by Volkmar Gessner (Hart 2009), 226.

[67] See Agnieszka Janczuk-Gorywoda, 'Online Platforms as Providers of Transnational Payments Law' (2016) 24(2) *European Review of Private Law*, 223.

C. Escrow accounts and ... intermediaries

A crucial factor is certainty that payment for delivery of goods or services will be made and, as a corollary, that payment will only be executed when the delivery of goods or services complies with the terms of the contract. With the development of smart contracts, it is technically possible to record contractual terms into blockchain transactions and to autonomously enforce them.[68] Hence it is possible, for instance, to record in a particular blockchain transaction a term providing for a refund right in case of non-delivery or faulty delivery of goods by the seller. Moreover, it could be possible to impose such a term for all transactions in a particular virtual currency scheme by programming it into the overall scheme protocol. Yet, there still remains a question of how to notify and verify non-delivery or faulty delivery in a decentralized scheme.

The Bitcoin community has found a solution to the problem of deferred performance. It consists in the implementation of 'escrow transactions'. An escrow transaction can be implemented using multi-signature addresses requiring a specified number of people, for instance two, to sign to redeem coins.[69]

Suppose that Alice wants to buy online some goods from Bob and pay in bitcoins. However, as explained above, Alice does not want to pay until after she has received the goods and Bob does not want to send the goods until Alice has paid. With a multigeniture transaction, Alice can send bitcoins to an escrow account held between her, Bob and a third-party, Judy, specifying that these bitcoins shall be redeemed either to Bob or Alice if any two out of the three sign.[70] At this point Bob can feel safe to send the goods. If the goods arrive and Alice is satisfied with the delivery, she and Bob sign the transaction, thereby redeeming the bitcoins from the escrow account to Bob. If the goods do not arrive or for any other reason Alice is unhappy with the delivery, she can refuse to sign the transaction redeeming the bitcoins to Bob. Now Bob can agree with Alice (for instance, because he recognizes that the goods were damaged) and sign a counter-transaction redeeming the bitcoins from the escrow account back to Alice. However, Bob could equally think that Alice is dishonest and therefore refuse to sign. This is when Judy, the third-party arbitrator, comes into play. Judy has to decide which of the two parties is right. If she decides for Alice, Judy and Alice will both sign a transaction which redeems the bitcoins from the escrow account to Alice. If Judy decides for Bob, they both will sign and Bob will receive the bitcoins.

This form of private dispute mechanism has been used for an increased proportion of blockchain transactions.[71] Pietro Ortolani rightly argues that in light of the limited value of a significant proportion of current Bitcoin transactions, this dispute mechanism is much more accessible to the transacting parties than court litigation, which would be disproportionately costly.[72] Just as more traditional payment intermediaries are the first and often the last point of reference for disputes concerning payments, Bitcoin has devised a solution for situations where the legal system would be of little help anyway. Yet, this solution came at an ideological cost to the original dogma of Bitcoin.

For the escrow account mechanism to work both Alice and Bob must trust Judy. Because they are from distant locations, they are not likely to find somebody they both trust in their respective communities. Judy needs to be a party with some established reputation recognized by both Alice and Bob. In other words, they need a reputable transnational intermediary.

Furthermore, while we can imagine that a different intermediary is appointed each time, in practice, specialized intermediaries would likely emerge. Specialized intermediaries could

---

[68] See Eliza Mik, 'Smart Contracts: Terminology, Technical Limitations and Real-World Complexity' (2017) 9 *Law, Innovation and Technology*, 269.

[69] Arvind Narayanan, Joseph Bonneau, Edward Felten et al., *Bitcoin and Cryptocurrency Technologies: A Comprehensive Introduction* (Princeton University Press, 2016), 60.

[70] ibid., 60–61. [71] See Chapter 16 by Ortolani in this volume, section III.B. [72] ibid.

acquire skills and resources to become more effective and efficient. In addition, if they repeatedly serve as intermediaries for specific people or companies, they could acquire knowledge about them, leading to less costly and more accurate decision making. Alternatively, information concerning parties' past behaviour related to Bitcoin or other payments could be stored and retrieved from some data repositories. In any case, centralized intermediaries are bound to arise.

To conclude, decentralized virtual currencies are not a suitable solution for cross-border retail payments without the involvement of any intermediaries. The development of the virtual currencies market confirms this proposal. Notably, so far, most people rely on intermediaries when using virtual currencies.[73]

VI. Conclusion

Blockchain was born out of a desire to establish a monetary and payment system free of intermediaries, in particular, to be free of the involvement of established financial institutions and independent of governments. While the motives of current virtual currency users may deviate widely from the original ideal, the appeal of 'no intermediaries' concept remains strong.

It is hard to predict how exactly blockchain will impact upon payment systems and whether new forms of intermediation, represented by centralized virtual currency schemes, will replace those intermediated through banks. This contribution has argued, however, that blockchain will not lead to the development of major decentralized payment systems. In contrast, (1) it will enable the rise of new powerful intermediaries and (2) it will be embraced by existing payment services providers in order to modernize their services and stabilize their position. This is because, first, other than offering pseudonymity, blockchain is not competitive enough in relation to domestic payment services, and second, the current fully decentralized blockchain solution does not solve the problem of the lack of trust between the parties entering into transnational transactions.

In order to expand beyond its original constituency, Bitcoin had to become surrounded by an entire ecosystem of intermediaries, such as exchanges, wallets, or payment processors.[74] In the extreme, some envisage scenarios where blockchain would enable central banks or other governmental agencies to completely displace banks and other payment service providers and instead fully monopolize the issuance of money and provision of transaction services.[75] This would make blockchain realize the ultimate nightmare scenario of its founders.

In a more optimistic scenario, virtual currencies claim to be just like cash and it is possible that they will retain a position similar to cash when it comes to the volume of transactions. Cash is used for a very high number of transactions—which is impossible to measure—but these are for very limited, petty amounts. Average daily payments in cash as against non-cash is below 10% of total amounts.[76] It seems likely that virtual currencies will also only be used for small transactions.

Blockchain has focused too narrowly on providing a technological solution to the issue of scarcity and solving the double-spending problem. Yet, problems involved in monetary and payment systems are broader. In particular, payment systems provide for a broad range of mechanisms supporting circulation of money which, for the scale and complexity of a modern economy must be backed by the state. Money is a hybrid public–private institution and it seems naïve to think that technology alone could render the role of state institutions

---

[73] See Chapter 6 by Dimitropoulos in this volume, section IV.B.2. Dimitropoulos argues that intermediary intervention can only be expected to rise as the proportion of virtual currencies in the global economy increases.

[74] Gene Neyer and Benjamin Geva, 'Blockchain and Payment Systems: What are the Benefits and Costs?' (2017) 11(3) *Journal of Payments Strategy and Systems*, 216.

[75] For a discussion see Geva (n 19), 24.   [76] Zimmermann (n 36), 17.

in monetary and payment systems obsolete. This contribution has highlighted the role of law and institutions in generating users' acceptance of a certain form of money and payment services.

VII. Bibliography

99 Bitcoins, https://99bitcoins.com/who-accepts-bitcoins-payment-companies-stores-take-bitcoins/, accessed 15 January 2019.

Ammous Saifedean, *The Bitcoin Standard: The Decentralized Alternative to Central Banking* (Wiley 2018).

Calliess Gralf-Peter, 'Transnational Civil Regimes: Economic Globalisation and the Evolution of Commercial Law' in *Contractual Certainty in International Trade: Empirical Studies and Theoretical Debates on Institutional Support for Global Economic Exchanges*, edited by Volkmar Gessner (Hart 2009).

Carnell Richard, Macey Jonathan, and Miller Geoffrey, 'Banks: Fundamental Concepts' (2016) NYU Law and Economics Research Paper No. 16-37.

Chapman James, Garratt Rodney, Hendry Scott et al., 'Project Jasper: Are Distributed Wholesale Payment Systems Feasible Yet?' (*BankofCanada.ca*, June 2017) www.bankofcanada.ca/wp-content/uploads/2017/05/fsr-june-2017-chapman.pdf, accessed on 15 January 2019.

Chiu Iris H.-Y., 'A New Era of Fintech Payment Innovations? A Perspective from the Institutions and Regulation of Payment Systems' (2017) 9(2) *Law, Innovation and Technology*, 190.

Cœuré Benoît and Loh Jacqueline, 'Bitcoin Not the Answer to a Cashless Society' (*Ft.com*, 13 March 2018) https://www.ft.com/content/31abc532-25d0-11e8-b27e-cc62a39d57a0, accessed on 15 January 2019.

Daily Hodl Staff, 'The New Freedom: Bitcoin, Blockchainiacs, and the Alternate Universe' (*DailyHodl*, 16 November 2017) https://dailyhodl.com/2017/11/16/the-new-freedom-bitcoin-blockchainiacs-and-the-alternate-universe/, accessed on 15 January 2019.

De Filippi Primavera, 'Bitcoin: A Regulatory Nightmare to a Libertarian Dream' (2014) 3(2) *Internet Policy Review*.

De Filippi Primavera and Loveluck Benjamin, 'The Invisible Politics of Bitcoin: Governance Crisis of a Decentralised Infrastructure' (2016) 5(3) *Internet Policy Review*.

Desan Christine, *Making Money: Coin, Currency, and the Coming of Capitalism* (Oxford University Press 2014).

De Vicuña Antonio Sáinz, 'An Institutional Theory of Money' in *International Monetary and Financial Law: The Global Crisis*, edited by Mario Giovanoli and Diego Devos (Oxford University Press 2010).

Dixit Avinas, *Lawlessness and Economics: Alternative Modes of Governance* (Princeton University Press 2007).

European Central Bank ('ECB'), 'Virtual Currency Schemes—a Further Analysis' (*ECB. Europa. eu*, February 2015) https://www.ecb.europa.eu/pub/pdf/other/virtualcurrencyschemesen.pdf, accessed on 15 January 2019.

European Central Bank ('ECB'), 'The Fourth Report on Card Fraud' (*ECB. Europa.eu*, July 2015) https://www.ecb.europa.eu/pub/pdf/other/4th_card_fraud_report.en.pdf, accessed on 15 January 2019.

Geva Benjamin, 'Banking in the Digital Age: Who is Afraid of Payment Disintermediation?' (2018) European Banking Institute Working Paper No 23/2018.

Guadamuz Andres and Marsden Chris, 'Blockchains and Bitcoin: Regulatory Responses to Cryptocurrencies' (2015) 20(12) *First Monday*.

International Monetary Fund (IMF), 'Virtual Currencies and Beyond: Initial Considerations' (IMF Discussion Note, January 2016) http://www.imf.org/external/pubs/ft/sdn/2016/sdn1603.pdf, accessed on 15 January 2019.

Janczuk-Gorywoda Agnieszka, 'Online Platforms as Providers of Transnational Payments Law' (2016) 24(2) *European Review of Private Law*, 223.

Knapp Georg Friedrich, *Staatlich Theorie des Geldes* (4th edn, Duncker & Humblot 1923), translated by H. M. Lucas and J. Bonar, *The State Theory of Money* (Macmillan 1924).

Krygier Rachelle, 'In Socialist Venezuela, The U.S. Dollar Becomes King' (The Washington Post, 2 August 2018) https://www.washingtonpost.com/world/in-socialist-venezuela-the-us-dollar-becomes-king/2018/08/01/7af16482-9442-11e8-818b-e9b7348cd87d_story.html?noredirect=on&utm_term=.0ad0c304b191, accessed on 15 January 2019.

Lastra Rosa Maria, *International Financial and Monetary Law* (2nd edn, Oxford University Press 2015).

Levitin Adam, 'Private Disordering: Payment Card Fraud Liability Rules' (2011) 5 *Brooklyn Journal of Corporate, Financial & Commercial Law*, 1.

Mann Ronald, 'Making Sense of Payments Policy in the Information Age' (2005) 93 *Georgetown Law Journal*, 633.

Mariano Tanya, 'How Bitcoin is Disrupting Southeast Asia's Remittance Industry. For the Region's Migrant Workers, an Alternative to Traditional Channels' (22 August 2016) http://inc-asean.com/editor-picks/bitcoin-disrupting-southeast-asias-remittance-industry, accessed on 15 January 2019.

Mehrling Perry, *The New Lombard Street: How the Fed Became the Dealer of Last Resort* (Princeton University Press 2010).

Mehrling Perry, 'The Inherent Hierarchy of Money' in *Social Fairness and Economics: Economic Essays in the Spirit of Duncan Foley*, edited by Lance Taylor, Armon Rezai, and Thomas Michl (Routledge 2013).

Mik Eliza, 'Smart Contracts: Terminology, Technical Limitations and Real-World Complexity' (2017) 9 *Law, Innovation and Technology*, 269.

Nabilou Hossein and Prüm André, 'Ignorance, Debt and Cryptocurrencies: The Old and the New in the Law and Economics of Concurrent Currencies' (30 August 2018) https://papers.ssrn.com/sol3/papers.cfm?abstract_id=3121918, accessed on 15 January 2019.

Narayanan Arvind, Bonneau Joseph, Felten Edward et al., *Bitcoin and Cryptocurrency Technologies: A Comprehensive Introduction* (Princeton University Press 2016).

Neville Sean and Allaire Jeremy, 'Circle Announces USD Coin, Bitmain Partnership, and New Strategic Financing' (*Blog.Circle.com*, 15 May 2018) https://blog.circle.com/2018/05/15/circle-announces-usd-coin-bitmain-partnership-and-new-strategic-financing/, accessed on 15 January 2019.

Neyer Gene and Geva Benjamin, 'Blockchain and Payment Systems: What are the Benefits and Costs?' (2017) 11(3) *Journal of Payments Strategy and Systems*, 215.

North Douglas, 'Institutions' (1991) 5 *The Journal of Economic Perspectives*, 97.

Nussbaum Arthur, *Money in the Law: National and International* (The Foundation Press 1950).

Paech Philipp, 'The Governance of Blockchain Financial Networks' (2017) 80(6) *Modern Law Review*, 1073.

Proctor Charles, *Mann on the Legal Aspect of Money* (7th edn, Oxford University Press 2012).

Samid Gideon, *Tethered Money: Managing Digital Currency Transactions* (Academic Press 2015).

Vardi Noah, 'Bit by Bit: Assessing the Legal Nature of Virtual Currencies' in *Bitcoin and Mobile Payments: Constructing a European Union Framework*, edited by Gabriella Gimigliano (Palgrave Macmillan 2016).

Wright Aaron and De Filippi Primavera, 'Decentralized Blockchain Technology and The Rise of *Lex Cryptographia*' (25 July 2017) https://papers.ssrn.com/sol3/papers.cfm?abstract_id=2580664, accessed on 15 January 2019.

Zimmermann Claus D., *A Contemporary Concept of Monetary Sovereignty* (Oxford University Press 2013).

15

Conflicts of Laws and Codes

Defining the Boundaries of Digital Jurisdictions

Florian Möslein

I. The Nature of 'Digital Jurisdictions'

In order to analyse the relationship between law and code, it is important to understand the nature of the relevant technological code. While some examples may help to illustrate the similarities between legal and blockchain-based rules, the equation of code and law (and of law and Code) is debatable at best. Rather, these two different regulatory systems operate separately to each other, thereby raising questions about their mutual relationship and the resolution of potential conflict between them.

A. Smart contracts

Blockchain and distributed ledger technologies are increasingly regarded as regulatory technologies.[1] Their core regulatory devices are so-called smart contracts, i.e. self-executing agreements that are usually written in code in the blockchain. When coining this term in the 1990s, Nick Szabo defined a smart contract as:

> a computerized transaction protocol that executes the terms of a contract. The general objectives of smart contract design are to satisfy common contractual conditions (such as payment terms, liens, confidentiality, and even enforcement), minimize exceptions both malicious and accidental and minimize the need for trusted intermediaries. Related economic goals include lowering fraud loss, arbitration and enforcement costs and other transactions costs.[2]

As smart contracts are automatable by computers and enforceable via tamper-proof execution of software codes, they can perform tasks that have traditionally been assigned to the realm of law. They not only define the rules and penalties around an agreement but also automatically enforce those obligations. The design of smart contracts, therefore, allows for the digital codification of entire legal institutions and also helps to ensure the automatic enforcement of respective rights and duties.[3]

Such devices are applied, for instance, with respect to loan contracts. In the case of payment defaults, smart contracts can automatically block the keys that are required to enter the respective apartment so that a tenant no longer has access to it. Similarly, rented or leased cars can be blocked in the case of payment defaults. In fact, such starter interrupt

---

[1] See, e.g., Primavera de Filippi and Samer Hassan, 'Blockchain Technology as a Regulatory Technology: From Code Is Law to Law Is Code' (2016) *First Monday*, 21, http://firstmonday.org/ojs/index.php/fm/article/view/7113/5657.

[2] Nick Szabo, 'Smart Contracts' (1994) http://www.fon.hum.uva.nl/rob/Courses/InformationInSpeech/CDROM/Literature/LOTwinterschool2006/szabo.best.vwh.net/smart.contracts.html; see also Szabo's 'Formalizing and Securing Relationships on Public Networks' (1997) *First Monday*, 2, http://firstmonday.org/ojs/index.php/fm/article/view/548/469-publisher=First.

[3] For more details, see Primavera de Filippi and Aaron Wright, *Blockchain and the Law: The Rule of Code* (Harvard University Press 2018), 74 et seq.; Carlos Tur Faúndez, *Smart Contracts—Análisis jurídico* (Reus Editorial 2018), 51–71; see also Don Tapscott and Alex Tapscott, *Blockchain Revolution* (Penguin 2016), 101–03.

devices are already very common in the United States.[4] Conversely, smart contracts can also be applied for the benefit of consumers by automatically enforcing their rights (instead of their duties). For example, these consumer-friendly smart contracts are becoming increasingly widespread in the insurance industry, with blockchain-based insurance policies providing for pay-outs that are automatically triggered once predetermined parameters are met. For instance, flight-delay decentralized applications provide for such automated payments whenever flight delays or cancellations arise. Both Etherisc, a small German start-up, and AXA, the French multinational insurance company, are already marketing insurance policies of the kind described.[5] The feasibility of respective automatization depends on the unambiguous nature of the triggering event. While it is relatively easy to decide upon the justification of insurance pay-outs in the case of flight delays or compensation, the evaluation process needs to be differentiated for other, more complex, types of insurance; it is all the more difficult to convert those insurances into a form of smart contract.[6]

Smart contracts do not necessarily require blockchain technology as they can also be based on more traditional technologies. For instance, automated locks on credit cards are similarly triggered whenever suspicious activities arise, but they are usually based on more traditional telecommunication and computer technologies. Similarly, typical vending machines only deliver the desired goods once payment is made. Even though their technological basis consists of simple mechanics, these devices also define the rules and penalties around an agreement, as well as automatically enforcing those obligations, much like blockchain-based smart contracts.[7]

B. Blockchain-based regulation

Blockchain technology, however, allows for more sophisticated rules and enforcement mechanisms to be implemented. Moreover, it provides for a decentralized, technological environment with a built-in settlement system.[8] These features widen the scope for the application of smart contracts and explain the regulatory character of blockchain and distributed ledger technologies.[9] They also allow for the development of entire regulatory infrastructures in the blockchain, grandiosely designated as 'digital jurisdictions'.

More specifically, the Aragon Project, which promises to develop such jurisdictions, has convinced thousands of blockchain users. It raised capital worth more than 24 million US dollars in less than fifteen minutes.[10] Its developers seek to establish a regulatory environment in the blockchain that is business-friendly, similar to the real-world jurisdiction of Delaware.[11] They created an Ethereum platform, which allows users to set up decentralized autonomous organizations ('DAOs'), i.e. entities similar to corporations but based on distributed ledger technologies.[12] The Aragon network is equipped with a binding 'constitution', which provides a variety of ready-made regulations, statutes, and contracts that

---

[4] Michael Corkery and Jessica Silver-Greenberg, 'Miss a Payment? Good Luck Moving that Car' (*NYTimes.com*, 24 September 2014) https://dealbook.nytimes.com/2014/09/24/miss-a-payment-good-luck-moving-that-car/.

[5] For more information, see Etherisc, https://etherisc.com; AXA, https://fizzy.axa.

[6] For further applications in the insurance industry, see Tapscott and Tapscott (n 3), 159.

[7] Melanie Swan, *Blockchain: Blueprint for a New Economy* (O'Reilly 2015), 16.

[8] Tapscott and Tapscott (n 3), 102.   [9] See n 1.

[10] Richard Kastelein, 'Aragon Smashes ICO Record Pulling in $25 million in 15 Minutes' (*BlockchainNews*, 18 May 2017) http://www.the-blockchain.com/2017/05/18/aragon-smashes-ico-record-pulling-25-million-15-minutes/.

[11] Luis Cuende and Jorge Izquierdo, 'Aragon Network: A Decentralized Platform for Value Exchange' (20 April 2017) https://www.chainwhy.com/upload/default/20180705/49f3850f2702ec6bc0f57780b22feab2.pdf, accessed 16 February 2019., 20: 'Looking for a real-world metaphor, the best one would be what Delaware is today for companies, investors and entrepreneurs.'

[12] For more details on such entities see, e.g., Usman Chohan, 'The Decentralized Autonomous Organization and Governance Issues' (4 December 2017) Working Paper, https://ssrn.com/abstract=3082055.

can be chosen as internal rules for the DAOs established on that network.[13] While the respective rights and obligations are encrypted as smart contracts, the Aragon network goes even further towards creating a quasi-jurisdictional infrastructure. Based on the insight that not all future disputes can be solved by the implementation of objective, but schematic, rules in the blockchain, Aragon's developers designed an arbitration system similar to a real-world judicial system. It consists of three different instances of courts. These courts are composed of randomly selected, human Aragon users, incentivized by token payments (or penalties, if decisions are either not made or overturned) and supported by prediction marketplaces.[14]

C. Code vs law

With the evolution of such digital jurisdictions, the famous equation, 'Code Is Law', coined by Lawrence Lessig in the late 1990s,[15] takes on an entirely new significance. Lessig was referring to the architecture of the internet and its potential to impose certain regulatory effects on internet users: by embedding certain value principles, that architecture sets the terms on which the internet can be used and thereby defines what is possible in that space.[16] Due to smart contracts based on blockchain technology and their self-executing nature, the two components of that equation seem to converge even further. In a recent paper, Primavera de Filippi and Samer Hassan reversed the equation, claiming that 'Law Is Code', i.e. that law itself can be codified and defined as technological code. 'As a result of these technological advances, the lines between what constitutes a legal or technological rule becomes more blurred since smart contracts can be used as both a support and as a replacement to legal contracts.'[17]

But, can law, or at least private law, effectively be substituted in its entirety by the blockchain? The functional similarities of code and law, and of digital and legal jurisdictions, may indeed seem increasingly striking due to the advances in blockchain technology. The actual concern, however, should be that, in substance, both sets of rules are by no means necessarily congruent as they may well lead to different substantive results. Conflicts arise whenever technologically codified rules differ from the applicable legal rules or whenever both sets of rules, even if their substance agrees in principle, are applied in different ways. In both cases, the two aforementioned equations are misleading: instead of 'Code Is Law' or 'Law Is Code', the accurate identifier would rather be 'Code vs. Law'.[18]

What happens then whenever code and law conflict with each other? How can situations be handled 'when code isn't law'?[19] Can parties still count on legal enforcement if such conflicts arise? While blockchain technologies increasingly provide for alternative, digital mechanisms of contract enforcement, their relation to the legal sphere remains largely unclear. The challenge consists in identifying the boundaries of those digital jurisdictions and in developing some new sort of conflict of laws principles or, rather, principles for conflicts between laws and codes.

---

[13] cf. Aleksandra Lisicka, 'First Jurisdiction on the Blockchain' (*newtech.law*, 9 October 2017) https://newtech.law/en/first-jurisdiction-the-blockchain/.

[14] Cuende and Izquierdo (n 11), 26–32.

[15] Lawrence Lessig, 'Code is Law: On Liberty in Cyberspace' (2000) *Harvard Law Magazine*, 1, https://harvardmagazine.com/2000/01/code-is-law.html; see also Lawrence Lessig, *Code and the Laws of Cyberspace* (Basic Books 1999).

[16] Lawrence Lessig, ''The Code in Law, and the Law in Code' (2000) pcForum Lecture Transcript, https://cyber.harvard.edu/works/lessig/pcforum.pdf.

[17] De Filippi and Hassan (n 1), 2.

[18] See also Graham Greenleaf, 'An Endnote on Regulating Cyberspace: Architecture vs Law?' (1988) 21(2) *University of New South Wales Law Journal*, 593.

[19] Tim Wu, 'When Code Isn't Law' (2003) *Virginia Law Review*, 103.

II. Recognition of Codes

Such principles for conflict between laws and codes can be elaborated on two conceptually different levels. On the one hand, the question arises as to whether those technological codes require legal recognition, and, if so, in what way such recognition should take place. On the other hand, even if the law does recognize technological codes, it may well override their substance. Similar to public policy provisions in traditional conflicts of laws, the law can, and often will, subject the substance of technological codes to some sort of legal scrutiny (cf. section III).

A. The requirement of recognition

Both the discourse among blockchain enthusiasts and the online presence of various platforms seem to suggest that smart contracts, blockchain-based regulation, and digital jurisdictions are able to operate entirely independent of legal jurisdictions.[20] The Aragon network, for instance, advertises itself as offering 'an online decentralized court system that is not bound by traditional artificial barriers such as national jurisdictions'.[21] Such announcements are reminiscent of the early days of the internet, with its promise to liberate us from governments, borders, and even our physical selves.[22] That promise of a borderless world, however, has turned out to be nothing but an illusion.[23] In a similar vein, even the most sophisticated blockchain-based digital jurisdictions cannot and do not operate within a legal vacuum; as the law also applies within blockchain environments, legal jurisdictions will also play a role within digital jurisdictions.

The fundamental reason for the applicability of law relates to the state monopoly concerning the legitimate use of force, also known as the monopoly on violence ('staatliches Gewaltmonopol'). Ever since the era of Thomas Hobbes and Jean Bodin,[24] the modern conception of the state has been built on the idea that the state alone has the right to use or authorize the use of physical force. This idea is widely regarded as a defining characteristic of the modern state.[25] Accordingly, Max Weber once defined the state as a 'human community that (successfully) claims the monopoly on the legitimate use of physical force within a given territory'.[26] However, with respect to smart contracts based on blockchain technology, it would be going too far to interpret that idea as a strict prohibition of self-executing technological arrangements, even though self-execution, by definition, involves some degree of physical force. Rather, smart contracts are a new variety of pre-emptive self-help.[27] Self-help remedies are not outright illegal.[28] Moreover, in many other instances, legal systems allow

---

[20] See, e.g., Marcella Atzori, 'Blockchain Technology and Decentralized Governance: Is the State Still Necessary?' (13 June 2016) Working Paper, https://papers.ssrn.com/sol3/papers.cfm?abstract_id=2709713.

[21] cf. Aragon One AG, 'A Digital Jurisdiction', https://aragon.one/.

[22] See, e.g., John Barlow, 'A Declaration of Independence of Cyberspace' (1996) https://www.eff.org/cyberspace-independence.

[23] Jack Goldsmith and Tim Wu, *Who Controls the Internet? Illusions of a Borderless World* (Oxford University Press 2008); see also Tim Wu, 'Cyberspace Sovereignty?—the Internet and the International System' (1997) 10 *Harvard Journal of Law & Technology*, 647.

[24] Thomas Hobbes, *Leviathan* (Penguin 1985) [first published in 1651]; Jean Bodin, *Les Six livres de la République* (Scientia 1977) [first published in 1576].

[25] See, e.g., Detlef Merten, *Rechtsstaat und Gewaltmonopol* (Mohr, 1978).

[26] Max Weber, 'Politics as a Vocation' in *From Max Weber: Essays in Sociology*, edited by H. H. Gerth and C. Wright Mills (Routledge 1948), 77–78.

[27] In this sense, see Max Raskin, 'The Law and Legality of Smart Contracts' (2017) 1 *Georgetown Law Technology Review*, 333–40; see also Catherine Sharey, 'Trespass Torts and Self-Help for an Electronic Age' (2008) 44 *Tulsa Law Review*, 677.

[28] See Douglas Brandon, Melinda Lee-Cooper, Jeremy H. Greshin et al., 'Self-Help: Extrajudicial Rights, Privileges and Remedies in Contemporary American Society' (1984) 37 *Vanderbilt Law Review*, 850, which defines self-help remedies as 'legally permissible conduct that individuals undertake, absent the compulsion of law and without the assistance of a government official in efforts to prevent or remedy a civil wrong'.

individuals to implement their rights without resorting to state authorities, at least under certain conditions. Most private laws regard certain forms of self-help remedies as legitimate,[29] with the doctrine of self-help codified, for example, in Article 229 of the German Civil Code.[30]

Conversely, the state monopoly on violence requires the law to authorize self-help. Ultimately, the state needs to maintain the ultimate competence to decide whether self-help is legitimate or not.[31] In turn, it is the law that can (and must) decide upon whether blockchain-based, self-executing rules are legally enforceable or not. As a consequence, even if smart contracts are self-executing in the sense that they are technically enforceable, they are not necessarily legally enforceable. On the contrary, such rules are embedded in national jurisdictions, and it is a question of law as to whether their self-executing character is legitimate or not.[32] More specifically, the key problem is 'What happens when the outcomes of the smart contract diverge from the outcomes that the law demands?'[33] Imagine, for instance, an insurance holder who is not satisfied with the blockchain-based denial of a pay-out, or a DAO shareholder who is not satisfied with an Aragon network's jurisdiction judgment. These parties must have access to legal jurisdictions so that the legality of the respective blockchain-based decisions can effectively be scrutinized. Only if the law is in a position to suspend or conversely recognize technology-based self-execution will the state be able to maintain its monopoly on power.

B. Legal recognition

If smart contracts require legal recognition, this can be achieved by two different regulatory alternatives. Both approaches have their specific advantages and inconveniences and it is for the legislator of the relevant jurisdiction to choose between the two.

On the one hand, the legislator can enact explicit provisions that are specifically tailored to blockchain-based smart contracts. For instance, Arizona has recently introduced a Bill giving legal status to such contracts by stating that 'a signature that is secured through blockchain technology is considered to be in an electronic form and to be an electronic signature.'[34] Moreover, this law states that a contract 'may not be denied legal effect, validity or enforceability solely because that contract contains a smart contract term.'[35] The lawmaker in Florida recently introduced a very similar bill,[36] with other state laws in the United States expected to follow suit in the very near future.[37] Some European jurisdictions are starting to explore similar legal avenues. For example, lawmakers in Monaco recently approved a bill that creates a legal foundation for smart contracts by stating that they 'constituent des actes juridiques et produisent des effets de droit', and by adding that 'l'inscription d'un acte juridique dans une blockchain (chaine de blocs) est présumée constituer une copie fidèle, opposable et durable de l'original, portant une date certaine.'[38]

---

[29] For a comparative overview, see Cătălin Stănescu, *Self-Help, Private Debt Collection and the Concomitant Risks: A Comparative Law Analysis* (Springer 2015), 51–95.

[30] For an extensive discussion, see Michael Beurskens, *Privatrechtliche Selbsthilfe: Rechte, Pflichten und Verantwortlichkeit bei digitalen Zugangsbeschränkungs—und Selbstdurchsetzungsbefugnissen* (Mohr Siebeck 2017).

[31] In a similar vein, see Richard Epstein, 'The Theory and Practice of Self-Help' (2005) 1 *Journal of Law, Economics & Policy*, 26: 'what the law should do is to supply a second legal remedy that offers the complete relief (or at least more complete relief) that the self-help remedy could not supply'.

[32] Raskin (n 27), 340.   [33] ibid., 328.

[34] Arizona Bill HB 2417/2017, Provision 44-7061 A, https://legiscan.com/AZ/text/HB2417/id/1497439.

[35] ibid.   [36] Florida House Bill 1357/2018, https://legiscan.com/FL/text/H1357/2018.

[37] More precisely, the states of Delaware, Vermont, Nevada, Hawaii, New Hampshire, and Illinois have all sought, or are seeking to, pass legislation to recognize the use of smart contracts and blockchain technology; cf. Paul Catchlove, 'Smart Contracts: A New Era of Contract Use' (23 December 2017) Research Paper, 2, https://papers.ssrn.com/sol3/papers.cfm?abstract_id=3090226.

[38] cf. *Text Consolidé de la Loi Relative à la Blockchain* (14 December 2017) Articles 2 and 6, http://www.conseil-national.mc/index.php/textes-et-lois/propositions-de-loi/item/600-237-proposition-de-loi-relative-a-la-blockchain.

French legislators have also introduced blockchain-specific legislation, albeit with a stronger focus on financial instruments.[39] While interested parties demand similar provisions in other European countries, such as Germany,[40] the political and regulatory strategies remain comparatively vague to date. The recent German coalition agreement, for example, simply promises the development of comprehensive blockchain technology and states its commitment to an appropriate regulatory framework at both the European and the international level.[41]

C. Judicial recognition

The alternative regulatory strategy would be to refrain from introducing explicit provisions that are specifically tailored to blockchain-based smart contracts. In such a scenario, the question of recognition is left to the judiciary, as the courts would then have to examine the legal status of smart contracts on a case-by-case basis, in accordance with generally applicable rules. More specifically, such judicial recognition requires courts to assess whether or not the smart contract in question constitutes an effective, legally binding agreement between parties or whether a specific rule codified in blockchain technology is an authentic reproduction of a mandatory legal provision. To be legally enforceable, contracts must meet a number of conditions imposed by law, such as multiple parties, the capacity of the parties, mutual assent, and consideration. The judiciary, therefore, has to consider whether a specific smart contract meets those general contract law conditions of contract formation— such as offer and acceptance, for instance—in order for it to also qualify as a contract in the legal sense.[42] While this approach does not give rise to fundamental qualification problems, smart contracts have some specific features that need to be taken into account. For instance, as opposed to traditional contracts, acceptance comes through performance, since there is no smart contract unless the programme initiates the execution.[43] Furthermore, formal requirements of contract formation can pose problems under certain contract laws, namely, whether or not specific contracts should be in writing.[44] While such difficulties do not seem insurmountable, they can only be regularly resolved using the instruments of general contract law.

The more fundamental question for the legislator concerns which of these two regulatory strategies to apply. The second approach may raise concerns of legal certainty. Depending on the outcome of the case-by-case assessment, every single smart contract will either be legally or not legally enforceable.[45] Moreover, this assessment could well give rise to practical difficulties for judges who have to examine blockchain-based codes in each and every single case as a precondition for their legal qualification. On the other hand, the second approach

---

[39] For more details, see Stéphane Blemus, 'Law and Blockchain: A Legal Perspective on Regulatory Trends Worldwide' (2017) 4 *Revue Trimestrielle de Droit Financier*, 1 and 11 et seq.

[40] Bundesverband Blockchain e.V., Chancen und Herausforderungen einer neuen digitalen Infrastruktur für Deutschland, Version 1.1 (2017) 32 et seq., https://bundesblock.de/wp-content/uploads/2017/10/bundesblock_positionspapier_v1.1.pdf.

[41] Koalitionsvertrag zwischen CDU, CSU und SPD (14 March 2018) Coalition Agreement, 70 et seq., https://www.bundesregierung.de/Content/DE/StatischeSeiten/Breg/koalitionsvertrag-inhaltsverzeichnis.html.

[42] For more extensive discussion, see Martin Heckelmann, 'Zulässigkeit und Handhabung von Smart Contracts' (2018) *Neue Juristische Wochenschrift*, 504–07 (with respect to German law); Raskin (n 27), 322–26 (with respect to US law); Rolf Weber, 'Blockchain als rechtliche Herausforderung' (2017) *Jusletter IT*, 8 et seq., https://www.bratschi.ch/fileadmin/daten/dokumente/publikation/2017/05/Blockchain_als_rechtliche_Herausforderung_-_Rolf_H._Weber_-_jusletter-18.05.2017.pdf (with respect to Swiss law).

[43] Raskin (n 27), 322.   [44] Weber, R. (n 42), 9.

[45] Some uncertainty, however, will also remain regarding the first approach, at least until the courts begin to adjudicate the treatment of smart contracts on the basis of such special regimes, cf. Stuart Levi, Gregory Fernicola, and Eytan Fisch, *The Rise of Blockchains and Regulatory Scrutiny* (9 March 2018) Harvard Law School Forum on Corporate Governance and Financial Regulation, https://corpgov.law.harvard.edu/2018/03/09/the-rise-of-blockchains-and-regulatory-scrutiny/.

adheres to the general principles of contract law, thereby safeguarding the consistency of contract law as well as the effectiveness of contractual consent. Since no special legal regime applies, contract formation is treated equally, regardless of the technological means through which it is realized.[46] With a view to future innovations, this regulatory characteristic should not be underestimated.

III. Code Override

In any event, the recognition of technological codes does not necessarily imply that the law accepts their regulatory content to its full extent. The law does not simply accept the outcome of these rules, as it may well override their substance. Similar to public policy provisions—the 'ordre public'—in traditional conflicts of laws,[47] the law can subject the substance of technological codes to legal scrutiny. In fact, it will quite regularly do so, albeit by different regulatory approaches.

A. Public policy exceptions ('*ordre public*')

In deciding traditional conflicts of laws questions, courts sometimes decide that 'the foreign law ordinarily applicable will not be applied in this case because to do so would violate our public policy'.[48] Accordingly, the recognition of foreign laws and the operation of the choice of law rules are subject to a public policy exception. The main function of this exception is 'to protect the fundamental values of the forum state against unacceptable results which may derive either from the application of foreign law or from the recognition of foreign judgments'.[49] Despite all the differences in relation to traditional conflicts of laws, similar exceptions will apply when rules for conflicts of laws and codes evolve. For even if state law recognizes blockchain-based rules in principle, it cannot simply accept *carte blanche* all outcomes of self-executing smart contracts and blindly adopt all value principles that are embedded in the blockchain. When these outcomes diverge from the outcomes that the law demands,[50] the legal system needs to be able to claim precedence over the relevant code in order to safeguard the state's monopoly on power. In order to uphold fundamental legal values, some sort of 'code override' must be possible.[51]

Starter interrupt devices may serve as an example, concerning not only the operation of smart contracts but also the need to scrutinize their impact by law.[52] By enabling the blocking of rented or leased vehicles in the case of payment defaults, these devices significantly reduce the cost of locating and then repossessing those cars; indeed, they have already been installed in more than two million automobiles in the United States alone.[53] From a

---

[46] In a similar vein, with regard to contract formation via the Internet, see: *Nguyen v. Barnes & Noble, Inc.*, 763 F.3d 1171, 1175 (9th Cir. 2014), which states that internet commerce may have presented novel situations, but has not 'fundamentally changed the principles of contract', including 'mutual manifestation of assent'.

[47] cf., for instance: Farshad Ghodoosi, *International Dispute Resolution and the Public Policy Exception* (Routledge 2017); Mathias Weller, *Ordre-public-Kontrolle internationaler Gerichtsstandsvereinbarungen im autonomen Zuständigkeitsrecht*, (Mohr Siebeck 2005), 219 et seq.

[48] Monrad Paulsen and Michael Sovern, '"Public Policy" in the Conflict of Laws' (1956) 56 *Columbia Law Review*, 969.

[49] Burkhard Hess and Thomas Pfeiffer, *Interpretation of the Public Policy Exception as referred to in EU Instruments of Private International and Procedural Law* (2011) Study requested by the European Parliament's Committee on Legal Affairs, 27, http://www.europarl.europa.eu/RegData/etudes/STUD/2011/453189/IPOL-JURI_ET(2011)453189_EN.pdf; see also Martin Gebauer, 'Ordre public' in *Max Planck Encyclopedia of Public International Law*, edited by Rüdiger Wolfrum (Oxford University Press 2007) http://opil.ouplaw.com/home/EPIL.

[50] See Arizona Bill (n 34).

[51] The wording is borrowed from the International Tax Law debate on 'treaty override'; see, e.g., Reuven Avi-Yonah and Haiyan Xu, 'A Global Treaty Override? The New OECD Multilateral Tax Instrument and Its Limits' (13 April 2017) University of Michigan Public Law Research Paper No. 542, https://ssrn.com/abstract=2934858.

[52] Raskin (n 27), 330 ('archetypical example').   [53] Corkery and Silver-Greenberg (n 4).

legal perspective, their use is seen as admissible under US law due to the secured parties' right to take possession after default, as provided for in Paragraph 9-609 of the Uniform Commercial Code, a self-help provision that most states have adopted in their contract laws.[54] After default, the rule allows a secured creditor to either 'take possession of the collateral' or to 'render equipment unusable' without judicial process as long as the creditor proceeds 'without breach of peace'. Even if phrased in very general words, that rule allows for the specific use of starter interrupt devices, thereby recognizing this form of technology-based self-help.[55] However, concurrently, it also stipulates a public policy limitation in order to protect fundamental legal values. By providing for the fact that creditors need to proceed without breaching peace, the provision sets a legal standard that aims at protecting debtors from abusive self-help. Since its meaning has been shaped by jurisprudence on a case-by-case basis, it can presumably be applied to new technological forms of self-help as well, such as starter interrupt devices.[56]

In fact, many cases could be imagined, or have indeed been reported, where such devices produce outcomes that seem to contradict fundamentals legal values. For example, imagine starter interrupt devices blocking cars (i) while they are currently running; (ii) that are generally needed by debtors for transportation to work; or (iii) that are urgently needed in a specific situation, say, for medical reasons, in order to get a patient to an emergency room.[57] Since the automatic blocking of a car triggers harsh consequences in all three situations, either by causing accidents, by making earnings impossible, or by putting human lives at risk, the legitimacy of the blocking needs to be critically examined, especially if the payment has only been overdue for a very short period of time. Some of these concerns can be addressed by technical safeguards as the devices can be designed so that they do not block cars while they are currently being driven or creditors can be given a certain number of one-off codes to manually override the devices so that they effectively enjoy a period of grace.[58] In fact, such modifications are increasingly incorporated into the best-practice guidelines of the industry.[59] Technical safeguards, however, cannot entirely replace legal value judgements, at least when the respective conflict is of a situational nature (as in the third example above). But, how can the law claim precedence over technological code in order to safeguard public policy considerations? By what means can it override that code?

B. Legal override

Again, the lawmaker can choose between two different regulatory strategies. According to the well-known distinction between bright-line rules and flexible standards,[60] the choice at this level is also between explicit provisions that are specifically tailored to blockchain-based smart contracts and the application of more general legal standards. That choice has much

---

[54] Kwesi Atta-Krah, 'Preventing a Boom from Turning Bust: Regulators Should Turn Their Attention to Starter Interrupt Devices Before the Subprime Auto Lending Bubble Bursts' (2016) 101 *Iowa Law Review*, 1201–08.

[55] In a similar vein, but more generally, see Craig Dolly, 'The Electronic Self-Help Provisions of UCITA: A Virtual Repo Man?' (1999) 33 *John Marshall Law Review*, 671–86.

[56] Raskin (n 27), 332 and 338 et seq.; in general, on the provision's interpretation, see: Ryan MacRobert, 'Defining "Breach of Peace" in Self-Help Repossessions' (2012) 87 *Washington Law Review*, 571–78.

[57] Corkery and Silver-Greenberg (n 4); see also Raskin (n 27), 330 et seq.

[58] Raskin (n 27), 330 et seq.

[59] For more details, see Eric Johnson and Corinne Kirkendall, 'Starter Interrupt and GPS Devices: Best Practices' (*PassTimeGPS.com*, 14 January 2016) https://passtimegps.com/starter-interrupt-and-gps-devices-best-practices/.

[60] For more details, see Ronald Dworkin, 'The Model of Rules'(1967) 35 *University of Chicago Law Review*, 22–29; H. L. A. Hart, *The Concept of Law*, (3rd edn, Oxford University Press 2012), 130–35; Mark Kelman, *A Guide to Critical Legal Studies* (Harvard University Press 1990), 15–63; Pierre Schlag, 'Rules and Standards' (1985) 33 *UCLA Law Review*, 379.

to do with regulatory competences, given that the relevant public policy decision is made by the legislator in the first case, and by the judiciary in the second.[61]

To take the example of starter interrupt devices further, lawmakers could introduce specific legal rules in order to handle conflicts that arise out of the use of various smart contracts. In fact, a number of state legislators are considering such provisions or have already introduced them. In Nevada, for instance, a new piece of legislation provides for a number of requirements for the use of starter interrupt devices, inter alia, written consumer disclosure, at least forty-eight hours' actual notice of disablement, the provision of two twenty-four-hour overrides in the event of emergency, the prohibition of charges for the installation or use of starter interrupt technology, restrictions on device data collection, and the length of data retention and the use of certified device installers.[62] New Jersey and California have also enacted specific rules concerning motor vehicle payment assurance devices, providing for similar requirements.[63]

C. Judicial override

Otherwise, the use of starter interrupt devices in particular, and smart contracts in general, is subject to conventional legal standards. Those standards have a wider scope of application but are less precise with respect to the requirements that they prescribe. As with other forms of self-help, starter interrupt devices are subject to the prerequisite that creditors need to proceed without any breach of peace. As has been shown, this general standard is shaped by jurisprudence on a case-by-case basis.[64] Therefore, it is difficult to evaluate whether it implies the same or at least similar requirements, given that the more explicit rules have been enacted, for example, in Nevada. Another question that cannot be answered simply is whether the general standard applies only in the absence of more specific rules. In accordance with legal methodology and the principle *lex specialis derogat legi generali*, more specific rules usually prevail over more general ones but the interpretation of the rules in question may result in different outcomes.[65] Lawmakers should ideally clarify their priorities if and when they introduce specific rules that overlap with more general standards.

Apart from the breach of peace condition, according to Paragraph 9-609 of the Uniform Commercial Code, a number of other general legal standards can conceivably be applied to smart contracts and open up the possibility of a judicial override of their substantive content, i.e. blockchain-based rules. For instance, the general restrictions on self-help apply in accordance with national law. They usually require that, if the aid of governmental authorities cannot be obtained promptly, the party is threatened with a permanent loss of his or her legal rights and that the self-help remedy is proportionate and not excessive.[66] Applying

---

[61] On these and further divisions of competence implications more generally (and with respect to EU law), see: Anne Röthel and Florian Möslein, 'Concretisation of General Clauses' in *European Legal Methodology*, edited by Karl Riesenhuber (Intersentia 2017), 265–72.

[62] Senate Bill No. 350, Act Relating to Trade Regulations; Prohibiting Certain Persons from Installing, Requiring to Be Installed or Using certain Technology Devices in a Motor Vehicle in Certain Circumstances; Providing a Penalty; and Providing Other Matters Properly Relating Thereto, introduced 20 March 2017, https://www.leg.state. nv.us/App/NELIS/REL/79th2017/Bill/5377/Overview.

[63] New Jersey Assembly Bill No. 756, An Act Concerning Motor Vehicle Payment Assurance Devices, approved 22 March 2017, https://legiscan.com/NJ/text/A756/id/1368292; California Assembly Bill No. 265, An Act to Amend Section 2983.37 of the Civil Code, Relating to Consumer Protection, approved 12 August 2015, https:// leginfo.legislature.ca.gov/faces/billNavClient.xhtml?bill_id=201520160AB265.

[64] See Corkery and Silver-Greenberg (n 4); Raskin (n 27), 330 et seq.

[65] For a jurisprudential discussion on this principle, see, e.g., Silvia Zorzetto, 'The Lex Specialis Principle and Its Uses in Legal Argumentation. An Analytical Inquiry' (2013) 3 *Eunomía Revista en Cultura de Legalidad*, 61; cf. also Nancie Prud'homme, 'Lex Specalis: Oversimplifying a More Complex and Multifaceted Relationship?' (2007) 40 *Israel Law Review*, 355.

[66] Arwed Blomeyer, 'Types of Relief Available (Judicial Remedies)' in *International Encyclopaedia of Comparative Law, Vol. XVI: Civil Procedure*, edited by Mauro Capelletti (Mohr/Martinus Nijhoff1982), 4; see also n 29.

these general rules to self-executing, blockchain-based rules would considerably limit their scope. Moreover, standard contract terms are usually subject to restrictions, which may also be applied to smart contracts. For instance, Article 3, Paragraph 1, of the European Unfair Terms Directive provides that a standard term is 'regarded as unfair if, contrary to the requirements of good faith, it causes a significant imbalance in the parties' rights and obligations arising under the contract, to the detriment of the consumer'. In addition, the same Directive provides for various transparency requirements.[67] However, whether blockchain-based rules in smart contracts qualify as standard terms is debatable. Some argue that smart contracts are not drafted by one party in advance for a multitude of contracts but are usually provided by third parties, namely, platform providers, and only taken advantage of by the contracting parties themselves. Moreover, smart contracts are regarded as more flexible and adaptable than typical standard contracts.[68] Despite these concerns, smart contracts are not usually individually negotiated. That said, where this is the case, it would seem more persuasive to submit them to the good-faith requirement of the Unfair Terms Directive.[69] Another, potentially competing general legal standard for smart contracts stems from the (draft) Directive on Contracts for the Supply of Digital Content. In Article 6, Paragraph 2, this Directive provides that, in the absence of any contractual stipulation, the digital content 'shall be fit for the purposes for which digital content of the same description would normally be used including its functionality, interoperability and other performance features such as accessibility, continuity and security'.[70] The provision potentially subjects blockchain-based rules to a general fitness control, to be measured against the best market practices; however, the conditions to which and under which it effectively applies to smart contracts is open to debate. Likewise, additional standards of general contract law could be applied to such contracts, for example, in the context of good faith and unlawful interference. Moreover, smart contracts, as well as digital jurisdictions in general, need to comply with data protection laws and also potentially with regulations on legal services.[71] To sum up, a whole set of different and competing general standards opens up the possibility for judicial override in response to public policy concerns.

IV. Conflicts of Laws and Codes vs Conflict of Laws

From all that has been said, it can be summarized that legal jurisdictions must, can, and will need to develop rules on conflicts of laws and codes in order to define the boundaries of digital jurisdictions, which are based on blockchain-based rules. Two different levels of such rules have been differentiated, namely, rules of recognition and rules subjecting the substance of blockchain-based rules to legal scrutiny. At both levels, it has emerged that either the lawmaker can intervene and introduce new, specific rules or the judiciary can develop rules on the basis of existing and more general legal standards. Whenever existing general laws can be applied in order to recognize or override smart contracts, the need for additional, specific legal rules is not self-evident, especially given that general laws are more

---

[67] In general (and with respect to similar rules in common European sales law), see, e.g., Florian Möslein, 'Kontrolle vorformulierter Vertragsklauseln' in *Ein einheitliches europäisches Kaufrecht?*, edited by Martin Schmidt-Kessel (Sellier 2012), 255.

[68] In this vein, see, for instance: Heckelmann (n 42), 507.

[69] See also Markus Kaulartz and Jörn Heckmann, 'Smart Contracts—Anwendungen der Blockchain-Technologie' (2016) *Computer und Recht*, 622; Joachim Schrey and Thomas Thalhofer, 'Rechtliche Aspekte der Blockchain' (2017) *Neue Juristische Wochenschrift*, 1436.

[70] On this provision in general, see, e.g., Paula Giliker, 'Regulating Contracts for the Supply of Digital Content: The EU and UK Response' in *EU Internet Law: Regulation and Enforcement*, edited by Tatiana-Eleni Synodinou, Philippe Jougleux, Christiana Markou, and Thalia Prastitou (Springer 2017), 110 et seq.

[71] For more details, see: Markus Kaulartz, 'Rechtliche Grenzen bei der Gestaltung von Smart Contracts' in *Smart World—Smart Law? Weltweite Netze mit regionaler Regulierung*, edited by Jürgen Taeger (Oldenburger Verlag für Wirtschaft, Informatik und Recht 2016), 1032–34.

flexible and less technology-specific. While this is certainly true with respect to substantive law, one should add that difficulties in enforcement could require additional, albeit procedural, rules. As a consequence of the self-executing nature of smart contracts, the burden of enforcement shifts to the other party. Moreover, the anonymity and non-traceability of certain blockchain transactions will often become a practical obstacle to obtaining legal remedies. Such effects would indeed seem to justify new procedural rules that facilitate the legal enforcement of the substantive rules discussed.

Since all these questions have been considered under the heading 'conflicts of laws and codes', one should not conclude without three clarifications, all of them with respect to the relationship with traditional conflict of laws rules. First, the wording of this analogy falls short of its true content. Since questions of enforcement are also implicated, the conflict is not only a conflict of legal norms but also a conflict of jurisdictions.[72] Second, the analogy is ambiguous because the two different varieties of conflict rules do not replace each other. The existence of rules on conflicts of laws and codes does not make the traditional rules on conflict of laws redundant. On the contrary, the applicability of one or other national law is an upstream question. It needs to be decided before one can apply rules on conflicts between laws and codes. Finally, and most fundamentally, this analogy is also deficient because both sets of conflicts are only to some limited extent comparable. From a functional perspective, conflicts between legal jurisdictions, and between legal and digital jurisdictions, have many similarities. Due to the regulatory character of each of these subsystems, rules can collide; hence, the need for rules to solve such conflicts is clear. Despite this similarity, one should not forget the fundamental difference between the two different conflicts. While legal jurisdictions conflict on an equal level, legal and digital jurisdictions differ with respect to their respective binding force: only the former are based on the state monopoly of the legitimate use of force. As opposed to conflicts of laws, conflicts of laws and codes are not 'among equals'. Instead, legal jurisdictions will always prevail over digital jurisdictions, at least, as long as nation states exist (and technical difficulties of enforcement can be overcome).

V. Bibliography

Aragon One AG, 'A Digital Jurisdiction', https://aragon.one/, accessed on 15 January 2019.

Arizona Bill HB 2417/2017, Provision 44-7061 A, https://legiscan.com/AZ/text/HB2417/id/1497439, accessed on 15 January 2019.

Atta-Krah Kwesi, 'Preventing a Boom from Turning Bust: Regulators Should Turn Their Attention to Starter Interrupt Devices before the Subprime Auto Lending Bubble Bursts' (2016) 101 *Iowa Law Review*, 1187.

Atzori Marcella, 'Blockchain Technology and Decentralized Governance: Is the State Still Necessary?' (13 June 2016), Working Paper, https://papers.ssrn.com/sol3/papers.cfm?abstract_id=2709713 , accessed on 15 January 2019.

Avi-Yonah Reuven and Xu Haiyan, 'A Global Treaty Override? The New OECD Multilateral Tax Instrument and Its Limits' (13 April 2017) University of Michigan Public Law Research Paper No. 542, https://ssrn.com/abstract=2934858, accessed on 15 January 2019.

AXA, https://fizzy.axa/, accessed on 15 January 2019.

Barlow John, 'A Declaration of Independence of Cyberspace' (1996) https://www.eff.org/cyberspace-independence, accessed on 15 January 2019.

Beurskens Michael, *Privatrechtliche Selbsthilfe: Rechte, Pflichten und Verantwortlichkeit bei digitalen Zugangsbeschränkungs —und Selbstdurchsetzungsbefugnissen* (Mohr Siebeck 2017).

Blemus Stéphane, 'Law and Blockchain: A Legal Perspective on Regulatory Trends Worldwide' (2017) 4 *Revue Trimestrielle de Droit Financier*, 34.

---

[72] For more extensive discussion on this distinction, see, e.g. Gabrielle Marceau, 'Conflicts of Norms and Conflicts of Jurisdictions' (2001) 35 *Journal of World Trade*, 1081.

Blomeyer Arwed, 'Types of Relief Available (Judicial Remedies)' in *International Encyclopaedia of Comparative Law, Vol. XVI: Civil Procedure*, edited by Mauro Capelletti (Mohr/Martinus Nijhoff 1982).

Bodin Jean, *Les Six livres de la République* (Scientia 1977) [first published in 1576].

Brandon Douglas, Lee-Cooper Melinda, Greshin Jeremy H. et al., 'Self-Help: Extrajudicial Rights, Privileges and Remedies in Contemporary American Society' (1984) 37 *Vanderbilt Law Review*.

Bundesverband Blockchain e.V., Chancen und Herausforderungen einer neuen digitalen Infrastruktur für Deutschland, Version 1.1 (2017) 32 et seq., https://bundesblock.de/wp-content/uploads/2017/10/bundesblock_positionspapier_v1.1.pdf, accessed on 15 January 2019.

California Assembly Bill No. 265, An Act to Amend Section 2983.37 of the Civil Code, Relating to Consumer Protection, approved 12 August 2015, https://leginfo.legislature.ca.gov/faces/billNavClient.xhtml?bill_id=201520160AB265, accessed on 15 January 2019.

Catchlove Paul, 'Smart Contracts: A New Era of Contract Use' (23 December 2017) Research Paper, 2, https://papers.ssrn.com/sol3/papers.cfm?abstract_id=3090226, accessed on 15 January 2019.

Chohan Usman, 'The Decentralized Autonomous Organization and Governance Issues' (4 December 2017) Working Paper, https://ssrn.com/abstract=3082055, accessed on 15 January 2019.

Corkery Michael and Silver-Greenberg Jessica, 'Miss a Payment? Good Luck Moving that Car' (*NYTimes.com*, 24 September 2014) https://dealbook.nytimes.com/2014/09/24/miss-a-payment-good-luck-moving-that-car/, accessed on 15 January 2019.

Cuende Luis and Izquierdo Jorge, 'Aragon Network: A Decentralized Platform for Value Exchange', White Paper, 19 (20 April 2017) https://www.chainwhy.com/upload/default/20180705/49f3850f2702ec6bc0f57780b22feab2.pdf, accessed 16 February 2019.

De Filippi Primavera and Hassan Samer, 'Blockchain Technology as a Regulatory Technology: From Code Is Law to Law Is Code' (2016) *First Monday*, 21, http://firstmonday.org/ojs/index.php/fm/article/view/7113/5657, accessed on 15 January 2019.

De Filippi Primavera and Wright Aaron, *Blockchain and the Law: The Rule of Code* (Harvard University Press 2018).

Dolly Craig, 'The Electronic Self-Help Provisions of UCITA: A Virtual Repo Man?' (1999) 33 *John Marshall Law Review*, 663.

Dworkin Ronald, 'The Model of Rules' (1967) 35 *University of Chicago Law Review*, 14.

Epstein Richard, 'The Theory and Practice of Self-Help' (2005) 1 *Journal of Law, Economics & Policy*, 1.

Etherisc, https://etherisc.com/, accessed on 15 January 2019.

Faúndez Carlos Tur, *Smart Contracts—Análisis jurídico* (Reus Editorial 2018).

Florida House Bill 1357/2018, https://legiscan.com/FL/text/H1357/2018, accessed on 15 January 2019.

Gebauer Martin, 'Ordre public' in *Max Planck Encyclopedia of Public International Law*, edited by Rüdiger Wolfrum (Oxford University Press 2007) http://opil.ouplaw.com/home/EPIL, accessed on 15 January 2019.

Giliker Paula, 'Regulating Contracts for the Supply of Digital Content: The EU and UK Response' in *EU Internet Law: Regulation and Enforcement*, edited by Tatiana-Eleni Synodinou, Philippe Jougleux, Christiana Markou, and Thalia Prastitou (Springer 2017).

Ghodoosi Farshad, *International Dispute Resolution and the Public Policy Exception* (Routledge 2017).

Goldsmith Jack and Wu Tim, *Who Controls the Internet? Illusions of a Borderless World* (Oxford University Press 2008).

Greenleaf Graham, 'An Endnote on Regulating Cyberspace: Architecture vs Law?' (1988) 21(2) *University of New South Wales Law Journal*, 593.

Hart H. L. A., *The Concept of Law* (3rd edn, Oxford University Press 2012).

Heckelmann Martin, 'Zulässigkeit und Handhabung von Smart Contracts' (2018) *Neue Juristische Wochenschrift*, 504.

Hess Burkhard and Pfeiffer Thomas, *Interpretation of the Public Policy Exception as referred to in EU Instruments of Private International and Procedural Law* (2011) 27, Study requested by the European Parliament's Committee on Legal Affairs, http://www.europarl.europa.eu/RegData/etudes/STUD/2011/453189/IPOL-JURI_ET(2011)453189_EN.pdf, accessed on 15 January 2019.

Hobbes Thomas, *Leviathan* (Penguin 1985) [first published in 1651].

Johnson Eric and Kirkendall Corinne, 'Starter Interrupt and GPS Devices: Best Practices' (*PassTimeGPS.com*, 14 January 2016) https://passtimegps.com/starter-interrupt-and-gps-devices-best-practices/, accessed on 15 January 2019.

Kastelein Richard, 'Aragon Smashes ICO Record Pulling in $25 million in 15 Minutes' (*BlockchainNews*, 18 May 2017) http://www.the-blockchain.com/2017/05/18/aragon-smashes-ico-record-pulling-25-million-15-minutes/, accessed on 15 January 2019.

Kaulartz Markus, 'Rechtliche Grenzen bei der Gestaltung von Smart Contracts' in *Smart World—Smart Law? Weltweite Netze mit regionaler Regulierung*, edited by Jürgen Taeger (Oldenburger Verlag für Wirtschaft, Informatik und Recht, 2016).

Kaulartz Markus and Heckmann Jörn, 'Smart Contracts—Anwendungen der Blockchain-Technologie' (2016) *Computer und Recht*, 1431.

Kelman Mark, *A Guide to Critical Legal Studies* (Harvard University Press, 1990).

Koalitionsvertrag zwischen CDU, CSU und SPD (14 March 2018) Coalition Agreement, 70 et seq., https://www.bundesregierung.de/Content/DE/StatischeSeiten/Breg/koalitionsvertrag-inhaltsverzeichnis.html, accessed on 15 January 2019.

Lessig Lawrence, *Code and Other Laws of Cyberspace* (Basic Books 1999).

Lessig Lawrence, 'Code is Law: On Liberty in Cyberspace' (2000) *Harvard Magazine*, https://harvardmagazine.com/2000/01/code-is-law-html, accessed on 15 January 2019.

Lessig Lawrence, 'The Code in Law, and the Law in Code' (2000) pcForum Lecture Transcript, https://cyber.harvard.edu/works/lessig/pcforum.pdf, accessed on 15 January 2019.

Lessig Lawrence, 'Code is Law: On Liberty in Cyberspace' (2000) *Harvard Magazine*, 1, https://harvardmagazine.com/2000/01/code-is-law-html, accessed on 16 February 2019.

Levi Stuart, Fernicola Gregory, and Fisch Eytan, *The Rise of Blockchains and Regulatory Scrutiny* (9 March 2018) Harvard Law School Forum on Corporate Governance and Financial Regulation, https://corpgov.law.harvard.edu/2018/03/09/the-rise-of-blockchains-and-regulatory-scrutiny/, accessed on 15 January 2019.

Lisicka Aleksandra, 'First Jurisdiction on the Blockchain' (*newtech.law*, 9 October 2017) https://newtech.law/en/first-jurisdiction-the-blockchain/, accessed on 15 January 2019.

MacRobert Ryan, 'Defining "Breach of Peace" in Self-Help Repossessions' (2012) 87 *Washington Law Review*, 569.

Marceau Gabrielle, 'Conflicts of Norms and Conflicts of Jurisdictions' (2001) 35 *Journal of World Trade*, 1081.

Merten Detlef, *Rechtsstaat und Gewaltmonopol* (Mohr 1978).

Möslein Florian, 'Kontrolle vorformulierter Vertragsklauseln' in *Ein einheitliches europäisches Kaufrecht?*, edited by Martin Schmidt-Kessel (Sellier, 2012).

New Jersey Assembly Bill No. 756, An Act Concerning Motor Vehicle Payment Assurance Devices, approved 22 March 2017, https://legiscan.com/NJ/text/A756/id/1368292, accessed 15 January 2019.

Paulsen Monrad and Sovern Michael, '"Public Policy" in the Conflict of Laws' (1956) 56 *Columbia Law Review*, 969.

Prud'homme Nancie, 'Lex Specalis: Oversimplifying a More Complex and Multifaceted Relationship?' (2007) 40 *Israel Law Review*, 355.

Raskin Max, 'The Law and Legality of Smart Contracts' (2017) 1 *Georgetown Law Technology Review*, 304.

Reidenberg Joel, 'Lex Informatica: The Formulation of Information Policy Rules through Technology' (1998) 76 *Texas Law Review*, 553.

Röthel Anne and Möslein Florian, 'Concretisation of General Clauses' in *European Legal Methodology*, edited by Karl Riesenhuber (Intersentia 2017).

Schlag Pierre, 'Rules and Standards' (1985) 33 *UCLA Law Review*.

Schrey Joachim and Thalhofer Thomas, 'Rechtliche Aspekte der Blockchain' (2017) *Neue Juristische Wochenschrift*, 1431.

Senate Bill No. 350, Act Relating to Trade Regulations; Prohibiting Certain Persons from Installing, Requiring to Be Installed or Using Certain Technology Devices in a Motor Vehicle in Certain Circumstances; Providing a Penalty; and Providing Other Matters Properly Relating Thereto, introduced 20 March 2017, https://www.leg.state.nv.us/App/NELIS/REL/79th2017/Bill/5377/Overview, accessed on 15 January 2019.

Sharey Catherine, 'Trespass Torts and Self-Help for an Electronic Age' (2008) 44 *Tulsa Law Review*, 677.

Swan Melanie, *Blockchain: Blueprint for a New Economy*, (O'Reilly 2015).

Stănescu Cătălin, *Self-Help, Private Debt Collection and the Concomitant Risks: A Comparative Law Analysis* (Springer 2015).

Szabo Nick, 'Smart Contracts' (1994) http://www.fon.hum.uva.nl/rob/Courses/InformationInSpeech/CDROM/Literature/LOTwinterschool2006/szabo.best.vwh.net/smart.contracts.html, accessed on 15 January 2019.

Szabo Nick, 'Formalizing and Securing Relationships on Public Networks' (1997) *First Monday*, 2, http://firstmonday.org/ojs/index.php/fm/article/view/548/469-publisher=First, accessed on 15 January 2019.

Tapscott Don and Tapscott Alex, *Blockchain Revolution* (Penguin 2016).

Text Consolidé de la Loi Relative à la Blockchain (14 December 2017) Articles 2 and 6, http://www.conseil-national.mc/index.php/textes-et-lois/propositions-de-loi/item/600-237-proposition-de-loi-relative-a-la-blockchain, accessed on 15 January 2019.

Weber Max, 'Politics as a Vocation' in *From Max Weber: Essays in Sociology*, edited by H. H. Gerth and C. Wright Mills (Routledge 1948).

Weber Rolf, 'Blockchain als rechtliche Herausforderung' (2017) *Jusletter IT*, 1.

Weller Mathias, *Ordre-public-Kontrolle internationaler Gerichtsstandsvereinbarungen im autonomen Zuständigkeitsrecht*, (Mohr Siebeck 2005).

Wu Tim, 'Cyberspace Sovereignty?—the Internet and the International System' (1997) 10 *Harvard Journal of Law & Technology*, 647.

Wu Tim, 'When Code Isn't Law' (2003) 89(4) *Virginia Law Review*, 103.

Zorzetto Silvia, 'The Lex Specialis Principle and its Uses in Legal Argumentation. An Analytical Inquiry' (2013) 3 *Eunomía Revista en Cultura de Legalidad*, 61.

16

The Judicialization of the Blockchain

Pietro Ortolani

I. Introduction

Since 2009, the emergence of Bitcoin and other cryptographically secure digital currencies has served as a proof of concept, demonstrating the innovating and potentially disruptive impact of blockchain technologies[1] on a wide range of social relations. While a wealth of legal scholarship has scrutinized the legal status of digital currencies and their consequences from the point of view of financial regulation,[2] one aspect of the phenomenon is, to date, still understudied: the effects of blockchains on dispute resolution. Blockchain technologies have the potential to disrupt the way justice is administered and legal conflicts are settled: as a growing range of human interactions are channelled through distributed ledgers and smart contracts, a new demand for dispute resolution arises and new methods to meet such demand are devised. The main argument of this chapter is that blockchain technologies structurally tend towards judicialization: the unprecedented potential for contract automation, brought about by decentralized technological architectures, triggers the creation of internal systems of private adjudication. Hence, by developing its own judicial mechanisms, blockchain technologies challenge the traditional, state-centric notions of jurisdiction and enforcement and prompt us to re-conceptualize our notion of justice under conditions of technology-induced self-sufficiency.

This chapter proceeds in three section. Section II sets the scene by locating the emergence of blockchains within the broader debate concerning the relationship between national and transnational law. Such a contextualization is crucial, in order to develop a reliable understanding of the impact of this set of technologies on the state's capacity to preserve its central role in the administration of justice through a system of courts. Against this background, section III investigates the effect of blockchain judicialization on the notion of jurisdiction, with specific reference to civil justice. Relying on empirical data, this section argues that the growth of blockchain technologies has given rise to a proliferation of private arbitral systems, thus potentially disrupting the traditional centrality of the state in the administration

---

[1] For the sake of simplicity, this chapter generally refers to 'blockchain technologies' and 'blockchain(s)' as synonyms.

[2] Rhys Bollen, 'The Legal Status of Online Currencies—Are Bitcoins the Future?' (22 February 2016) https://papers.ssrn.com/sol3/papers.cfm?abstract_id=2736021; Max Raskin, 'The Law and Legality of Smart Contracts' (2016) 1(2) *Georgetown Law Technology Review*, 305; Lawrence Trautman, 'Is Disruptive Blockchain Technology the Future of Financial Services?' (2016) 69 *Consumer Finance Law Quarterly*, 232; Larissa Lee, 'New Kids on the Blockchain: How Bitcoin's Technology Could Reinvent the Stock Market' (2016) 12(2) *Hastings Business Law Journal*, 81; Lawrence Trautman, 'Virtual Currencies; Bitcoin and What Now after Liberty Reserve, Silk Road, and Mt. Gox?' (2014) 20(4) *Richmond Journal of Law and Technology*, 1; Nicholas Plassaras, 'Regulating Digital Currencies: Bringing Bitcoin within the Reach of the IMF' (2013) 14(1) *Chicago Journal of International Law*, 377; Omri Marian, 'Are Cryptocurrencies "Super" Tax Havens?' (2013) 112 *Michigan Law Review First Impressions*, 38; Jerry Brito, Houman Shadab, and Andrea Castillo, 'Bitcoin Financial Regulation: Securities, Derivatives, Prediction Markets, and Gambling' (2014) 16 *Columbia Science & Technology Law Review*, 144; Reuben Grinberg, 'Bitcoin: An Innovative Alternative Digital Currency' (2012) 4(1) *Hastings Science & Technology Law Journal*, 159; Nikolei Kaplanov, 'Nerdy Money: Bitcoin, the Private Digital Currency, and the Case Against Its Regulation' (22 July 2012) Temple University Legal Studies Research Paper, https://papers.ssrn.com/sol3/papers.cfm?abstract_id=2115203.

of justice. Finally, section IV considers the emergence of self-enforcing smart contracts and their consequences for the traditional view whereby the state maintains a monopoly over the use of force.

II. Placing Digital Currencies in the Context of the Nationalism/Transnationalism Tension

A. Nationalism and transnationalism as two conceptual placeholders

Before scrutinizing the structural tendency of blockchains to morph into self-sufficient judicial systems, it is necessary to locate the emergence of the technology within the broader debate concerning the relationship between national and transnational law. Such a contextualization is crucial in order to develop a reliable understanding of the impact of cryptocurrencies and other distributed ledger technologies on national systems of civil justice. One of the main focuses of this chapter is the inverse relationship between the diffusion of blockchains, on the one hand, and the state's capacity to maintain its central role in the administration of justice through a system of courts, on the other. In light of this, any discussion of the phenomenon would lose a good deal of its explanatory power if it failed to connect to the general discussion concerning the potential conflict between state authority and transnational normative orderings.

The dialectics between nationalism and transnationalism constitute perhaps the defining tension of our times. At the end of the twentieth century, transnationalism seemed to be bound to transform the world and our intellectual representations thereof. The dramatic rise of international capital flows, in both trade and investment, apparently anticipated a future where multinational corporations would operate freely, developing regulatory frameworks of their own and conversely escaping the constraints of state-made law.[3] Along similar lines, the ease of long-distance communication, made possible by digital technology, was deemed to prefigure the advent of a global village, a post-national self-regulated space where physical location, language, or law could no longer hinder human interaction.[4] Twenty years on, the reality we face is significantly more complex than we had imagined. To be sure, the forecasts prompted by economic and digital globalization were not entirely inaccurate or delusional: multinational corporations have indeed impacted on the way states (succeed or fail to) regulate economic activities and the internet has undoubtedly transformed the way we communicate and interact in all aspects of our life. However, on the other hand, national legal systems have not been entirely taken over either by multinational corporations[5] or by the internet. To date, states still embody the cluster of ideological and institutional premises around which we build our conceptions of power.

Although the phenomena at hand are incredibly multifaceted and difficult to define in their exact contours, it makes sense to use the notions of nationalism and transnationalism

---

[3] Susan Strange, *The Retreat of the State: The Diffusion of Power in the World Economy* (Cambridge University Press 1996).

[4] Paul Virilio, *La Bombe Informatique* (Galilée 1998), 17, theorizes the end of space, paraphrasing Francis Fukuyama's end of history. The representation itself of the internet as a space, a 'cyberspace', is a remnant of the forward-looking, trans-nationalist intellectual mood underlying the rise of communication technologies in the 1990s: Caroline Bassett and Chris Wilbert, 'Where You Want to Go Today (Like it or Not): Leisure Practices in Cyberspace' in *Leisure/Tourism Geographies: Practices and Geographical Knowledge*, edited by David Crouch (Routledge 1999), 181; Dan Nguyen and Jon Alexander, 'The Coming of Cyberspacetime and the End of the Polity' in *Cultures of Internet: Virtual Spaces, Real Histories, Living Bodies*, edited by Rob Shields (SAGE 1996), 99.

[5] With specific respect to multinational corporations, it is interesting to note that the 2007–2008 crisis triggered a significant decrease in the outflow of foreign direct investment from developed economies. This data point, considered together with the declining return on equity, has led some commentators to wonder whether the age of the global company is coming to an end: The Economist, 'The Retreat of the Global Company' (*Economist.com*, 28 January 2017) https://www.economist.com/briefing/2017/01/28/the-retreat-of-the-global-company.

as two conceptual placeholders, i.e. useful simplifications labelling two composite group-ings of mutually exclusive normative standpoints. In a nutshell, nationalism designates the points of view of those who maintain that the central position of the state as a system of governance should be protected against attempts at its erosion brought by those forces and phenomena we conventionally file under 'globalization'. By contrast, transnationalists argue that the Westphalian conception of the world as a juxtaposition of self-contained national states was a historical contingency and, partially, an illusion, the untenability of which is in-creasingly demonstrated by the growing level of global interconnectedness in different forms (economic, technological, etc.). In other words, according to the transnationalist point of view, the age of the law as an exclusive product of the state has largely come to an end and new and more efficient regulatory standards are being and should be developed across na-tional borders.[6]

Sub-sections II.A and II.B sketch a basic summary of the debate, addressing first nation-alism and then transnationalism. Against this background, it is possible to gain a new under-standing of the emergence of blockchain technologies and its consequences.

B. Nationalism: one standpoint, multiple reasons for action

It is easy—perhaps too easy—to suggest that nationalism is the driving ideological force be-hind many recent political developments, such as the rejection of international law as a con-straint on the regulatory discretion of states, the increasing scepticism vis-à-vis international jurisdictions, and the appeal of narratives placing national interests before international and/ or humanitarian considerations. Such an equation would ultimately result in a banalization of the reasons for action of those whose normative standpoints we have grouped under the label of 'nationalism'. There are, in fact, many compelling reasons why one could argue that the position of the state as a monopolistic or quasi-monopolistic administrator of power should be safeguarded. By way of example, in the Brexit referendum debates, the 'Leave' campaign was supported not only by xenophobic and right-wing political parties, but also by critics of neoliberalism.[7]

One of the most interesting arguments in favour of a state-centric vision of public life has been put forth by Jedediah Purdy, inter alia in his recent paper 'Wealth and Democracy'.[8] Discussing the pressing issue of growing inequality, Purdy provides a fascinating account of the fundamental transformation that the state has undergone over the past forty years. According to this conceptualization, in the decades immediately following World War II, states were able to regulate economic activities effectively, thanks to strong controls on

---

[6] Needless to say, these two conceptual placeholders are just one of the ways in which the globalization de-bate can be recast and de-complexified. The economist Dani Rodrik, for instance, has developed a conceptual model based on the trilateral interaction among deep economic integration, democratic politics, and the national sovereignty: Dani Rodrik, *The Globalization Paradox. Democracy and the Future of the World Economy* (Norton 2011), 200–01. Even from this point of view, however, the tension between nationalism and transnationalism con-tinues to carry significant explanatory power: the rejection of transnationalism, currently observable in different polities, can to a large extent be explained in light of the difficulties of exporting the mechanisms of democratic politics outside of the architecture of the nation-state. And conversely, the call of transnationalists for more global regulation is often backed by the hope for a future where deep economic integration can be coupled with authen-tically democratic politics. For a debate concerning Rodrik's theses, see Rosa Maria Lastra, 'The Globalization Paradox: Review of Dani Rodrik, The Globalization Paradox: Democracy and the Future of the World Economy' (2013) 11(3) *International Journal of Constitutional Law*, 809; Rob Howse, 'Further Considerations on Dani Rodrik, *The Globalization Paradox*' (2013) 11(3) *International Journal of Constitutional Law*, 813; Dani Rodrik, 'The Globalization Paradox: A Response to Rosa Lastra and Robert Howse' (2013) 11(3) *International Journal of Constitutional Law*, 816.

[7] Susan Watkins, 'Casting Off?' (2016) 100 *New Left Review*, 5; AAlan Johnson, 'Why Brexit is Best for Britain: The Left-Wing Case' (*NYTimes.com*, 28 March 2017) https://www.nytimes.com/2017/03/28/opinion/why-brexit-is-best-for-britain-the-left-wing-case.html.

[8] Jedediah Purdy, 'Wealth and Democracy' in *Nomos LVIII—Wealth*, edited by Jack Knight and Melissa Schwartzberg (New York University Press 2017), 235.

international capital flows. By contrast, with the advent of globalization, economic life has ceased being a 'plastic object of regulation' and has emerged, instead, as a cluster of agents of political power.[9] Against this background, Purdy advocates a renewed widespread political engagement, based on the postulate of the primacy of politics over economic activities. Although not necessarily confined within national boundaries, Purdy's call for a democratic resurgence is strongly linked to the institutional framework of the state, as 'sovereignty remains almost exclusively a phenomenon on the national scale'.[10] More explicitly, Purdy argues, in another of his writings, that 'getting beyond the nation-state is an illusion, at least for now. Democratic politics requires collective action and the state is the uniquely effective vehicle of that action'.[11]

To sum up, the current legal and political debate is characterized by an articulate plurality of points of view identifying the centrality of the state (and, therefore, of national law) as a shared normative postulate. Beyond this important commonality, however, the 'nationalist camp' is undoubtedly fragmented: the same standpoint can in principle be justified by different, and even opposite reasons for action, ranging from isolationism, to the rejection of the Hayekian neoliberalism allegedly embedded in supranational governance, to the simple observation that the state is in any case still the best vehicle for democratic expression.

C. Transnationalism between Utopia and pragmatism

Transnationalism relies on a basic observation: reality cannot be entirely encompassed within the boundaries of any given state. Law's claim to authority covers an enormously complex mass of events and interactions, which in many cases occur across national borders. For this reason, transnationalists argue that any attempt to draw a sharp distinction between the public and the private sphere is destined to fail: in order to adequately understand (and shape) the regulatory framework for a globalized reality, it is necessary to bridge the gap between public and private international law, and enlarge the perspective to consider non-state-made normative regimes as well.[12] In the transnationalist representation of the law, states are not monopolists: they do play an important role as regulators but they coexist (and potentially compete) with other orderings whose prominence has been enhanced by global interconnectedness.[13]

One of the most evident characteristics of transnationalism is its historical approach: transnational lawyers commonly depict the monopoly of the state over the production of law as a chronologically limited contingency, conversely rejecting the idea of state-centrism as a structural necessity. Law—so the transnationalist argument goes—existed before the Westphalian representation of the world as a juxtaposition of self-contained national legal system, and will still exist once the untenability of such a representation is definitively demonstrated. To a certain extent, thus, transnationalism is nothing new; in fact, it can be largely understood as a re-emergence on a worldwide scale of the same legal pluralism that characterized the western world before the advent of the nation-state.[14]

Although transnational lawyers share the intention to look at law beyond the paradigm of state authority, the 'camp' is far from homogeneous. The positions of different transnational lawyers, in particular, could be arrayed on a spectrum ranging from utopia to pragmatism. On the one hand, some transnational lawyers qualify the prospect of transnational regulation in overtly enthusiastic terms, 'achieving the dream'[15] of breaking free of the constraints

---

[9] ibid., 239.   [10] ibid., 256.   [11] Jedediah Purdy, 'The Bars on the Cage' (2017) *The Nation*.

[12] Philip Jessup, *Transnational Law* (Yale University Press 1956).

[13] Thomas Schultz, *Transnational Legality: Stateless Law and International Arbitration* (Oxford University Press 2014).

[14] Paolo Grossi, *L'ordine Giuridico Medievale* (7th edn, Laterza 2006).

[15] Julian Lew, 'Achieving the Dream: Autonomous Arbitration' (2006) 22(2) *Arbitration International*, 179. For a reply, see Ralf Michaels, 'Dreaming Law without a State: Scholarship on Autonomous International Arbitration as Utopian Literature' (2013) 1(1) *London Review of International Law*, 35.

and the inadequacies of state-made law. On the other hand, other observers stick to a rather pragmatic approach, whereby if a growing amount of law is being produced outside of the state, legal studies and legal research must necessarily follow suit and adapt, or be condemned, to marginality.

Therefore, just like nationalists, transnational lawyers are united by a basic standpoint but are moved by different reasons for action. One of the most instructive points of view, in this respect, is that of Ralf Michaels.[16] Despite being an advocate of transnationalism, Michaels honestly acknowledges that the development of a conception of law divorced from the paradigm of state authority presents three significant obstacles: elitism, the lack of democratic accountability, and the absence of symbolic power. A brief overview of the hurdles identified by Michaels is useful in order to lay the groundwork for the discussion of the impact of blockchain technologies on national systems of justice.[17]

First, transnational law should overcome its current elitism. So far, according to Michaels, transnational law has been theorized and practiced by a small pool of sophisticated lawyers who have not taken into adequate consideration the effects of globalization on the weaker and less privileged members of western societies. In brief, transnational lawyers typically fail to observe that the internationalization of capital flows and communications can harm not only developing countries, but also the increasingly impoverished lower layers of societies which, when observed as a whole, may be seen as privileged. Needless to say, these dynamics can trigger a disenfranchisement of large sectors of the population and the outright rejection of any form of law that is not made by the state.

Second, Michaels acknowledges that the infrastructure of democratic decision making has been largely developed in the context of nation-states. Transnational law, admittedly, has not devised anything comparable to national democratic accountability so far.[18] According to Michaels, however, this observation does not provide enough ground to argue that law cannot exist beyond national borders; instead of cultivating an unrealistic 'nostalgia of the nation-state', lawyers should embrace transnationalism and develop forms of democratic expression and accountability adequate for our interconnected reality.[19]

Third, transnational law has so far been developed pursuant to a problem-based approach whereby specific regulatory solutions are devised to meet a particular demand. By way of example, international arbitration has emerged as a neutral forum for the resolution of cross-border commercial disputes which, for different reasons, could not be satisfactorily resolved before state courts. Along similar lines, the Internet Corporation for Assigned Names and Numbers (ICANN) Uniform Domain-Name Dispute-Resolution Policy ('UDRP') has been

---

[16] Ralf Michaels, 'Globalization and Law: Law Beyond the State' in *Law and Social Theory*, edited by Reza Banakar and Max Travers (2nd edn, Hart 2013), 287.

[17] The arguments summarized below are set forth in Ralf Michaels, 'Does Brexit Spell the Death of Transnational Law?' (2016) 17 *German Law Review*, 51 (Brexit Special Supplement).

[18] For instance, the limitations of transnational multistakeholderism as a mode of democratic deliberative governance of the internet have been scrutinized by Enrico Calandro, Alison Gillwald, and Nicolo Zingales, 'Mapping Multistakeholderism in Internet Governance: Implications for Africa' (28 March 2014) Research ICT Africa, https://papers.ssrn.com/sol3/papers.cfm?abstract_id=2338999.

[19] In the 1990s, the geographical transformations challenging the distinction between city and suburb triggered a strand of scholarship arguing for a detachment of democratic decision making from a strict territorial approach. The rationale behind this argument is that territoriality's justifiability as a criterion for the grounding of political rights is inversely related to the ease of mobility through space: see Richard Ford, 'Beyond Borders: A Partial Response to Richard Briffault' (1996) 48(5) *Stanford Law Review*, 1173. Such argument builds on the idea that the city/suburb dichotomy has lost a good deal of its significance and explanatory purchase over time, with the emergence of different modes of human/space coordination. Already by 1987, Robert Fishman was using the notion of 'technoburb' to argue that, for Americans, the centre of life is not defined by the boundaries between inner cities and suburbs, but by 'the locations they can conveniently reach in their cars', i.e. through technology: Robert Fishman, *Bourgeois Utopias: The Rise and Fall of Suburbia* (Basic Books 1987), 185. Along the same lines one could argue that, since today's technology allows us to reach increasingly vast portions of reality on a worldwide basis, it is inadequate to structure democratic expression after a territorial model which is almost entirely based on the ideal of the nation-state.

devised to regulate certain aspects of the ownership of domain names, in an immaterial global field where state-made property rules were structurally unable to resolve the problem. Because of this pragmatism, transnational lawyers have often disregarded the importance of law's symbolic power; beyond the circle of sophisticated specialists, the general public's support for the law is a function of the law's ability of creating a positive and understandable image of itself.[20]

D. The optical illusion of blockchains

Sub-sections II.B and II.C have set the stage by providing a broad-stroke portrait of two opposite intellectual moods: nationalism and transnationalism. At a first glance, both points of view seem to offer attractive arguments in favour or against the use of decentralized, trustless digital technologies, such as Ethereum or Bitcoin. On the one hand, if we were to embrace the nationalist standpoint, we would be tempted to conclude that these technologies are dangerous, as they weaken the control of democratic states over economic activities and they potentially endanger the role of state law as an effective regulator of private behaviours in the public interest. On the other hand, if we adopt the transnationalist point of view, we could argue that the blockchain is a positive step towards the development of a more egalitarian, post-geographic[21] society, where cooperation replaces the coercion and the inadequacy of the state.[22]

Put in these terms, the blockchain is a fascinating, but irresolvable, conundrum. Do decentralized technologies weaken national democratic accountability in favour of an opaque technocracy?[23] Or do they pave the way towards a more sustainable economic model, where interaction takes place on a peer-to-peer basis without the need to empower and trust centralized financial, legal, and political authorities? Or, maybe, can we even argue that they do *both things at the same time*? Albeit superficially interesting, this point of view proves unable to further our understanding of the phenomenon beyond subjective petitions of principle.

The reason why this conundrum is impossible to solve is that it is, to a large extent, an optical illusion: when we observe the phenomenon of digital currencies and other blockchain technologies, we tend to superimpose two dimensions which should remain distinct. On the one hand, Bitcoin and other cryptocurrencies have been developed by communities that share, to a certain extent, specific ideologies and reasons for action.[24] From this first point of view, it would be correct to argue that digital currencies were born as a transnationalizing experiment, undertaken by libertarian cryptographists and economists as a result of the growing dissatisfaction with national financial institutions. On the other hand, however, we must also consider the blockchain as a technological infrastructure. The infrastructure is structurally independent from the ideologies that gave rise to it and can still survive when

---

[20] Michaels makes the example of the European Union, whose image he describes as 'that of a cold regulator of bananas' (Michaels, 'Does Brexit Spell the Death' (n 17), 61).

[21] On the influence of legal pluralism on human notions of space, see Franz von Benda-Beckmann and Keebet von Benda-Beckmann, 'Places that Come and Go: A Legal Anthropologist Perspective on the Temporalities of Space in Plural Legal Orders' in Irus Braverman, Nicholas Blomley, David Delaney, and Alexandre Kedar, *The Expanding Spaces of Law—A Timely Legal Geography* (Stanford University Press 2014), 30.

[22] On the political consequences of decentralization, see Aaron Wright and Primavera De Filippi, 'Decentralized Blockchain Technology and the Rise of *Lex Cryptographia*' (25 July 2017) https://papers.ssrn.com/sol3/papers.cfm?abstract_id=2580664.

[23] It is incidentally interesting to note that, in its most extreme form, the defence of democracy against technocracy may result in the Luddite rejection of all technical innovations threatening the disruption of the status quo within which the nation-state gained its central position in the governance of society. The danger of this posture, substantially isolating technology from all other aspects of reality, has been highlighted by Gilbert Simondon, *Du mode d'existence des objets techniques* (Aubier 1958).

[24] For an overview of these ideologies, see Marcella Atzori, 'Blockchain Technology and Decentralized Governance: Is the State Still Necessary?' (13 June 2016) https://papers.ssrn.com/sol3/papers.cfm?abstract_id=2709713.

such ideologies no longer exist. One's judgement of the technological tools (such as smart contracts or distributed ledgers) should not be biased by the acceptance (or refusal) of the contingent reasons for action animating those who built such tools. By way of comparison, the internet was initially developed (as ARPANET) to meet the needs of military command and control; yet it can hardly be argued that by using today's internet one necessarily endorses militarism. Once released, technology lives its own life, independent from the ideologies of its developers. On the one hand, a group of anarchic hacktivists may develop a piece of software that, in practice, has no discernible impact on the solidity of the institutions of the state. On the other hand, a commercial company lawfully operating for profit may end up developing a technology which challenges the functioning of national democratic institutions.[25] Hence, if we want to locate blockchain technologies within the nationalism/transnationalism debate, the ideologies of the creators should not be the focus.

An additional, related reason to de-couple technologies from ideologies is that there is a positive relationship between the diffusion of the technologies and the dilution of the underlying ideologies. As long as blockchains are used by a relatively close-knit community of enthusiasts, a certain degree of ideological homogeneity may be preserved; by contrast, when the technology percolates to the general public, its user base becomes unlikely to share a recognizable set of ideological standpoints. To further blur the boundaries, technologies are sometimes embraced by social groups that have little in common with the user profiles that the developers originally had in mind. For instance, SMS was originally created for business, but it was widely embraced by teenagers in the 2000s. The risks of blurring technology with ideology are particularly clear if we consider that several national central banks are currently exploring the possibility of adopting blockchain-based solutions to develop state-sponsored digital currencies.[26] Obviously, one could hardly imagine that the purpose of such initiatives is the systematic weakening of state authority in favour of boundless transnationalism. In light of this, it is reasonable to imagine a future where blockchains will be a widespread reality but that their ties with a specific ideology or conception of the role of the state in the governance of society will be increasingly indiscernible.

The need to de-couple technology from ideology does not mean that we should abstain from locating blockchain technologies within the debate between nationalists and transnationalists. To the contrary, understanding the impact of these technologies on the state and its institutions (i.e. on what Lawrence Lessig would call the state's 'architectures of control')[27] is crucial in order to assess their impact. However, in doing so, we must disregard ideologies, and focus on the structural characters of the technologies instead. What is the impact of blockchains when observed without any ideological pre-judgement? What happens, for instance, when the circulation of money is not overseen by a centralized institution but recorded on a distributed ledger? Or when contractual agreements are encoded in the form of software script? How do these changes affect our (economic, political, legal) reality? These questions can help us solve the conundrum because they elucidate how the existing architectures of control evolve as a result of the diffusion of a given technology, irrespective of the original ideological underpinnings of the latter. In a nutshell, we should analyse the real-life consequences of innovation, irrespective of the motives of the innovators.

---

[25] With respect to dispute resolution, the marginalization of state courts is already visible in the relations among online platforms offering matchmaking services, small businesses operating online, and consumers. Business-to-consumer disputes are routinely dealt with by the platform, which effectively operates like an adjudicator in this type of case: see Ethan Katsh and Orna Rabinovich-Einy, *Digital Justice: Technology and the Internet of Disputes* (Oxford University Press 2017), 57–80; Rory van Loo, 'The Corporation as a Courthouse' (2016) 33 *Yale Journal on Regulation*, 547.

[26] For an overview of different national regulatory approaches, see Mai Ishikawa, 'Designing Virtual Currency Regulation in Japan: Lessons from the Mt Gox Case' (2017) 3(1) *Journal of Financial Regulation*, 125; Alexander Loke, 'Virtual Currency Regulation in Singapore' (2015) 1(2) *Journal of Financial Regulation*, 290; and Chapter 6 by Dimitropoulos in this volume.

[27] Lawrence Lessig, *Code: And Other Laws of Cyberspace, Verson 2.0* (2nd edn, Basic Books 2006), 38, 282.

Apart from avoiding bias, this methodological starting point is attractive because it allows us to observe the phenomenon of blockchain technologies from a more comprehensive and reliable perspective. The effects of the diffusion of these technologies are not limited to finance but they encompass a wide range of other systems. Law is undoubtedly one of them. Sections III and IV address the effects of blockchains on law, with specific reference to courts, dispute resolution, and the administration of justice. This is a particularly promising field of analysis, as courts are widely regarded as a fundamental part of the institutional architecture of the state through which democratically enacted laws are translated into practical reality. By observing how blockchain technologies affect the functioning of justice, we can determine whether the state is likely to retain its central position in the making and enforcement of the law, in the (not-so-distant) future. The remainder of this chapter aims to contribute to this debate by answering two main questions. Section III investigates whether the diffusion of blockchains is likely to marginalize state court litigation as a technology for law enforcement and dispute resolution. Subsequently, section IV scrutinizes the effect of blockchains on the state's monopoly over the use of force at the stage where a decision has been issued and must be enforced.

III. The Effects of Blockchain Technologies on State Jurisdiction

A. A brief glimpse into the history of jurisdiction: from service to sovereignty

The administration of justice is typically considered as a fundamental power of the state. In fact, we are so used to the idea of jurisdiction as an expression of sovereignty over a defined territory, that we often use the word 'jurisdiction' as a synonym for 'state'. Historically, however, this equation is not to be taken for granted: in the middle ages, the administration of justice (*jus dicere*) was much less an exertion of public power than it was a private service. Hence, a brief overview of the historical evolution of the concept of jurisdiction can offer a useful background against which it will be possible to understand the current impact of blockchain technologies on the administration of justice.

One could half-jokingly argue that in the beginning there was nothing but arbitration. The image of jurisdiction depicted by legal history, starting from the dissolution of the Roman Empire, is much closer to our current conception of arbitration than to any contemporary notion of state justice. Of course, disputes have always arisen, and they have often (albeit not always)[28] been resolved by relying on some kind of normative system. What is striking about medieval justice, however, is its detachment from the notion of sovereignty: around the twelfth century, adjudicating disputes was not so much the expression of a power but a service provided to the litigants. Judging was mainly conceived by the medieval mind as a professional activity, much like our contemporary perception of arbitration.[29] In this period, multiple jurisdictions overlapped, as power was distributed among a diverse multitude of institutional architectures (the church, the city-states, the guilds, etc.), none of which had a monopoly over the use of force. While a thorough reconstruction of the evolution of the notion of jurisdiction would clearly exceed the scope of our current analysis, we can touch upon two specific characters of medieval justice: the impossibility to distinguish between appeals and actions for liability against the judge; and the detachment of the rules of procedure from the paradigm of sovereign power. These two aspects can help us understand that the

---

[28] On the diversity of mechanisms deployed by different cultures to resolve disputes, see Oscar Chase, *Law, Culture and Ritual: Disputing Systems in Cross-Cultural Context* (New York University Press 2005).

[29] The private service nature of the contractual arrangements underlying arbitration has been scrutinized by the UK Supreme Court in *Jivraj v. Hashwani* [2011] UKSC 40.

close ties between the administration of justice and the idea of sovereignty are a historical contingency, not a structural necessity.

Between the eleventh and thirteenth centuries, in Italian communes, adjudicative functions were typically performed by professional jurists. These adjudicators were not governmental officials drawing their authority from political power but professional service-providers. They were neither tenured nor were they embedded in the constitutional architecture of the city-state: most of the time, in fact, they were foreigners coming from a different city so to avoid risks of partiality arising out of intra-communal relations. Their jurisdictional authority did not derive from political power but from their intellectual status of learned lawyers.[30] For this reason, the medieval legal doctrine did not draw an exact distinction between appeals brought against a judgment, on the one hand, and an action for liability brought against the judge, on the other hand. In practical terms, attacking the judgment amounted to attacking the judge, i.e. complaining about the defective nature of the decision-making service he/she had provided. The judge's liability was not disciplinary but professional; issuing a wrong judgment was essentially seen as a failure to discharge the obligation to adjudicate enshrined in the service contract.[31]

An additional confirmation of the service-like conception of jurisdiction in the Middle Ages is the different conception of procedural law during this historical phase. From our contemporary viewpoint, procedure is inextricably linked with the idea of power. Procedural rules determine 'who gets to do what', striking a delicate balance among different actors and interests.[32] By contrast, for medieval jurists, procedural law was not linked to the paradigm of sovereign power and it was possible for different and unrelated judicial authorities to apply the same set of procedural rules. Between the twelfth and fifteenth centuries, the rules of procedure applied by different adjudicative authorities were typically set forth in the *ordines judiciarii*.[33] The *ordines judiciarii* were not procedural statutes enacted by a sovereign authority but professional handbooks for the conduct of proceedings; they could be used in a wide range of different *fora*[34] as they were not deemed to be laws allocating public powers but technical guidelines for the effective provision of private adjudicative services.

The medieval conception of jurisdiction is the result of a complex interaction among multiple factors, both political and technological. From the first point of view, the notion of jurisdiction as an expression of sovereignty presupposes the existence of a strong state, exerting monopolistic or quasi-monopolistic authority over a defined territory. Given the chaotic overlap of different authorities existing before the rise of the nation-state, it is unsurprising that medieval jurists failed to understand jurisdiction as a fundamental component of public power. From the second point of view, as noted by Richard Ford, the conception of territorially based jurisdiction presupposes the existence of a refined cartographic technology. Cartography is a powerful and relatively recent cognitive tool for the definition of power allowing the observers to visualize exact boundaries and, hence, conceive of territory as

---

[30] Alessandro Giuliani and Nicola Picardi, 'La responsabilità del giudice: problemi storici e metodologici' in *L'educazione giuridica—III: La responsabilità del giudice*, edited by Alessandro Giuliani and Nicola Picardi (Università degli Studi di Perugia 1978), 3, 22; Ugo Nicolini, *Il principio di legalità nella democrazia italiana* (CEDAM 1955), 367.

[31] Nicola Picardi, *La giurisdizione all'alba del terzo millennio* (Giuffrè 2007), 31.

[32] It is this conception that Mirjan Damaška relies on, when he argues that procedural law is the reflection of a given approach to the relations between the individual and the state: Mirjan Damaška, *The Faces of Justice and State Authority: A Comparative Approach to the Legal Process* (Yale University Press 1986). Furthermore, it is because of this close link between procedure and power that states allow their courts to apply foreign law to the merits of the dispute, but do not typically allow for any derogation to the *lex fori* on procedural matters.

[33] A. M. Stickler, 'Ordines Judiciarii' in *L'Educazione Giuridica: VI—Modelli storici della procedura continentale*, edited by Alessandro Giuliani and Nicola Picardi (Volume 2, Edizioni Scientifiche Italiane 1994), 3.

[34] It should incidentally be noted that a similar phenomenon is currently happening with respect to the UNCITRAL Arbitration Rules, which are equally applied by international commercial and investment arbitral tribunals.

an abstract blank entity to be governed through a uniform and indiscriminate exertion of sovereignty.[35] For this reason, in some regions of the world, power was not organized on a territorial basis until colonialism.[36]

The conception of jurisdiction changed dramatically when the state established itself as the primary set of infrastructures for the exertion of power. Starting from the sixteenth and seventeenth centuries, one of the key steps towards the establishment of centralized nation-states was the creation of a hierarchically structured system of courts, organized and supervised by the sovereign. While in feudal times judicial decision making drew its legitimacy from the quality of the reasoning put forth by professional jurists, in this state-centric context the administration of justice found a new justification in its being an expression of sovereign power. Louis XIV's *ordonnance civile* of 1667 was a pivotal event—with this act the French sovereign aimed, for the first time, to systematically subject all judges to the same set of sovereignly enacted rules, specifying that all non-conforming decisions would be regarded as null and void.[37] The same mindset can also be observed in the works of the political theorists of that period. When describing the concept of *Republique*, in 1576, Jean Bodin no longer refers to the medieval idea of *iurisdictio*, but relies instead on the concept of *puissance souveraine* (sovereign power).[38] In 1672, Samuel Pufendorf theorized jurisdiction not as a self-standing power but as one of the components of sovereignty through which the sovereign's legislative decisions are translated into practical reality.[39]

The intellectual process of embedding of jurisdiction within the broader concept of national sovereignty had its climax in the Age of Enlightenment. Most prominently, Montesquieu conceptualized the resolution of disputes as one of the fundamental powers of the state, together with its executive and legislative powers.[40] It is also interesting to notice that in the *Encyclopedie*, edited by Diderot and D'Alembert, 'judge' was defined as a 'magistrate constituted by the sovereign, to render justice in his name to those who are subject to him'.[41] According to this conception, the idea of judge was directly dependent on the notion of sovereign power and the administration of justice derived its legitimacy from the circumstance that the adjudicator operated not in his/her own name but as a mouthpiece of the sovereign's legislative will. While the medieval mind conceived of jurisdiction as a professional service delivered on a peer-to-peer basis, the illuminist notion was based on an inextricable link between the resolution of disputes and the hierarchical exertion of power. In other words, the judge became an agent of the state, imposing sovereign power on its behalf over a defined territory.

This notion of jurisdiction acted as a potent vehicle for the establishment and progressive reinforcement of the state as a monopolistic administrator of justice. On top of this, currency acted as an additional catalyst of state-centrism. For a long time, in many national systems, it was settled law that courts could not render judgments denominated in a foreign currency.[42] This scenario amounts to a powerful feedback loop, in which courts are created *by the state*, to apply the laws enacted *by the state*, through procedures devised *by the state*, issuing judgments denominated in the currency issued *by the state*. It is therefore

---

[35] Richard Ford, 'Law's Territory (A History of Jurisdiction)' (1999) 97(4) *Michigan Law Review*, 843; Dan Svantesson, *Solving the Internet Jurisdiction Puzzle* (Oxford University Press 2017), 14.

[36] Ford, 'Law's Territory' (n 35), 868–72.   [37] Picardi (n 31), 128–36.

[38] Jean Bodin, *Les six livres de la republique* (Jacques du Puys, 1576), 1.

[39] Samuel Pufendorf, *De jure naturae et gentium libri octo* (Londini Scanorum, 1672), 906–19.

[40] Charles Montesquieu, *De l'esprit des lois* (Barillot 1748) book XI, ch. VI.

[41] Louis de Jaucourt, 'Juge (Droit moral)' in *Encyclopédie ou dictionnaire raisonné des sciences, des arts et des métiers* (Faulche 1765) vol 9, 5.

[42] *Bagshaw v. Playn* (1594) Cro Eliz 536, 78 ER 783 (KB); *Rastell v. Draper* (1605) 1 Cro Jac 88, 80 ER 55 (KB); *Ward v. Kidswin* (1625) Latch 77, 82 ER 283 (KB); *Manners v. Peason & Son* [1898] 1 Ch. 581; *Madeleine Vionnet et Cie. v. Wills* [1939] 4 All E.R. 136; *Re United Railways of Havana and Regla Warehouses Ltd* [1961] AC 1007 (HL) 1044. See Otto Kahn-Freund, 'Foreign Money Debts—Conversion into Sterling' (1940) 3(3) *Modern Law Review*, 229, describing the rule as 'fundamental'.

unsurprising that, to date, we still largely regard jurisdiction as a sovereign power. On the one hand, it must be noted that the monopoly of the state over the administration of justice has been notably relaxed over the past four decades, as demonstrated by the diffusion of arbitration as a mechanism for the resolution of a wide range of civil and commercial disputes[43] and the abandonment of the prohibition against judgments denominated in foreign currencies.[44] On the other hand, however, the importance of this cultural heritage on the currently prevailing notion of jurisdiction can hardly be overstated; the hierarchical, state-centric idea of the judge as an agent of sovereign power still informs our mentality when we think about a system of justice.

We can draw one important lesson from this very brief glimpse into the history of the notion of jurisdiction: there is a complex relationship between the exertion of power and the development of a self-sufficient infrastructure for the administration of justice, the former being both a prerequisite for, and a driver of, the latter. From the first point of view, having control over the use of force is a necessary condition for the establishment of a system of justice. In the absence of the systematic ability to ensure compliance through coercion, the nation-state would not have been able to develop an architecture of courts resolving disputes with a reliable degree of finality. From the second point of view, the establishment of monopolistic sovereignty triggers judicialization. Becoming the sole repository of power encouraged the nation-state to supplant the chaotic overlap of jurisdictions characterizing the Middle Ages and replace it with a single, hierarchically organized court structure. In a nutshell, the history of jurisdiction and sovereignty demonstrates a clear correlation between seizure of power and judicialization. In transposing this lesson to our current reality, one fundamental question arises: if blockchain technologies enable the autonomous and decentralized management of a growing range of assets and resources, without the need to rely on the support of the state, do they also trigger the development of a transnational system of adjudication, and the corresponding marginalization of state courts?

B. Blockchain technologies as an exogenous shock and the reaction of state justice

The emergence of blockchain technologies is an exogenous shock for national systems of justice, from multiple points of view. First of all, technologies like Bitcoin and Ethereum allow private parties to denominate a transaction in a currency which not only is not the one of the state where the litigation takes place but does not belong to any state at all. Furthermore, at a deeper level, blockchain technologies allow for an unprecedented degree of automation. Through smart contracts, private parties can devise mechanisms whereby disputes arising out of or in connection with an agreement are resolved by private adjudicators through self-enforcing decisions, the enactment of which does not depend on state-controlled recognition and enforcement procedures.[45] What is the effect of this shock on the administration of justice?

In order to answer the question, we can test diverging hypotheses against the available data, using Bitcoin as a case study. The rise in the number of transactions verified on the blockchain suggests that Bitcoin is currently used in a wide range of economic interactions. This trend must structurally generate a certain demand for dispute resolution. As the volume

---

[43] Alec Stone Sweet and Florian Grisel, *The Evolution of International Arbitration: Judicialization, Governance, Legitimacy* (Oxford University Press 2017), 35–79.

[44] *Miliangos v. George Frank (Textiles) Ltd* [1976] AC 443 (HL); see Vaughan Black, *Foreign Currency Claims in the Conflict of Laws* (Hart 2010).

[45] For a description of the technical mechanisms through which self-enforcement is attained, see Pietro Ortolani, 'Self-Enforcing Online Dispute Resolution: Lessons from Bitcoin' (2016) 36 *Oxford Journal of Legal Studies*, 595; Pietro Ortolani, 'The Three Challenges of Stateless Justice' (2016) 7 *Journal of International Dispute Settlement*, 596.

Table 16.1 Number of US court cases mentioning 'Bitcoin' per year

Year	Bitcoin transactions (total)	US court cases mentioning Bitcoin	US criminal cases mentioning Bitcoin	US civil cases mentioning Bitcoin	US court cases arising out of a transaction denominated in bitcoin
2009	32.687	0	0	0	0
2010	217,320	0	0	0	0
2011	2,118,551	0	0	0	0
2012	10,566,336	1	0	1	0
2013	30,152,682	1	0	1	0
2014	55,462,897	8	3	5	2
2015	100,960,169	13	3	9	1
2016	183,614,465	18	6	9	3
2017	287,815,664	20	8	8	1
2018 (1 May)	313,493,494	4	1	3	2

of transactions increases, some of them are likely to give rise to disputes, and hence, to trigger the need for adjudication and contract enforcement. Given these basic premises, then, it is possible to measure the effect of digital currencies on national systems of justice by testing how often Bitcoin transactions 'end up in court', i.e. how frequently disputes arising out of or in connection with contracts denominated in Bitcoin are settled by state courts. In this respect, it is possible to formulate two mutually exclusive hypotheses. On the one hand, if one were to assume that national systems of justice are able to absorb the shock of blockchain technologies and preserve their central governance role, it would be logical to speculate that the increase in the number of transactions denominated in Bitcoin should be mirrored by an increase in the number of related disputes being resolved by state courts. On the other hand, if one were to assume that the diffusion of digital currencies leads to a marginalization of state justice, inter alia because users typically rely on internal, self-enforcing arbitral mechanisms, it could be contended that Bitcoin-related transactions exist but they do not end up before state courts. The available data corroborates the second hypothesis.

As Table 16.1 illustrates, the amount of transactions verified on the blockchain has increased dramatically between 2009 and 2018. This increase, however, has not been mirrored by any booming expansion of Bitcoin-related court cases. With respect to the United States, Bitcoin was mentioned in a court case for the first time in 2012, and despite a timid increase over the years, the number of Bitcoin-related court decisions is still rather limited. Furthermore, not all of these cases deal with the enforcement of obligations arising out of contracts denominated in Bitcoin. Many of them are criminal cases, or civil cases where Bitcoin is mentioned incidentally but does not constitute the very subject matter of the litigation. Excluding these cases, to date, US courts have only dealt with nine cases arising out of a transaction denominated in Bitcoin.[46] In other jurisdictions, Bitcoin-related cases are even less frequent.

---

[46] The *Tezos* class action, the most prominent example of this type of litigation, is dealt with in further detail below (n 49); *Leidel v. Coinbase, Inc.*, No. 17-12728, 2018 WL 1905954 (11th Cir. 23 April 2018); *Commodity Futures Trading Comm'n v. McDonnell*, 287 F. Supp. 3d 213, 218 (E.D.N.Y. 2018); *Gordon v. Dailey*, 2016 U.S. Dist. LEXIS 80205 (D.N.J. 20 June 2016); *Leidel v. Project Investors, Inc.*, 2016 U.S. Dist. LEXIS 150009 (S.D. Fla. 26 October 2016); *Greene v. Mizuho Bank, Ltd*, 206 F. Supp. 3d 1362, 1368 (N.D. Ill. 26 August 2016); *Morici*

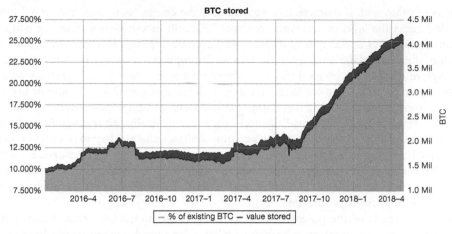

Fig. 16.1 Percentage of existing Bitcoin stored in 'pay-to-script-hash' addresses
Source: P2SH.info

What happens to Bitcoin cases, then? If the parties who conclude a transaction denominated in Bitcoin do not routinely use the dispute resolution services of state courts, how are their cases resolved? The answer to these questions is twofold. First, it is necessary to consider the dispute resolution potential of smart contracts and the corresponding marginalization of national justice systems. Second, however, it is also necessary to place these findings in context, taking into consideration the framework of incentives within which dispute resolution decisions concerning small claims are made.

From the first point of view, a useful starting point is the observation that the Bitcoin protocol can be used to devise transactions more complex than a simple transfer of funds between two wallets. This potential can be exploited in many different ways, especially through the development of smart contracts, which can to a certain extent translate a given contractual arrangement into code. As already mentioned, one possible cluster of such arrangements concerns dispute resolution. By using multi-signature transactions, for example, users can ensure that, in the case of a dispute, a third party will act as an adjudicator and decide upon the final destination of the coins stored in this type of address. Blockchain analysis demonstrates that 'pay-to-script-hash', which is routinely relied on to implement multi-signature transactions, is used for a significant portion of the existing coins, currently amounting to over 24% (Fig. 16.1).[47] In light of this, it is reasonable to conclude that Bitcoin users are devising private, largely informal mechanisms of private adjudication that enforce transactions denominated in Bitcoin more often than court litigation does.

From the second point of view, it is crucial to provide some context for the above findings in order to obtain a reliable picture of the phenomenon at hand. While there are strong reasons to believe that private adjudication based on digital currencies is an existing and growing reality, this does not necessarily entail that the further diffusion of Bitcoin would lead to a radical marginalization of state systems of justice. In particular, it should be taken into account that a significant proportion of current Bitcoin transactions are relatively

---

v. Hashfast Techs. LLC, 2015 U.S. Dist. LEXIS 107449 (N.D. Cal. 14 August 2015); *Hussein v. Coinabul, LLC*, 2014 U.S. Dist. LEXIS 175333 (N.D. Ill. 19 December 2014); *SEC v. Shavers*, 2014 U.S. Dist. LEXIS 130781 (E.D. Tex. 18 September 2014). Several of these cases concern the 'Bitcoin mining industry': in these litigations, the plaintiffs bought mining equipment and claimed that the seller did not respect the terms of the contract because the machines either did not have the promised computational power, or they were delivered late, when they were already obsolete due to the increased difficulty per block.

[47] P2SH Statistics, https://p2sh.info/dashboard/db/p2sh-statistics?orgId=1.

limited in value, and, if characterized according to the categories of state law, would probably fall under the label of 'consumer contracts'. Plaintiff inactivity is a recurring issue for
disputes arising out of this type of transaction. Given the typically low value in dispute, the
lodging of a court claim is likely to be seen as disproportionately costly. Furthermore, in
this type of dispute, it may be difficult to identify the respondent (often operating behind
pseudonyms on online marketplaces), let alone enforce a judgment against him or her. For
these reasons, it is not entirely surprising that transactions denominated in bitcoin do not
currently result in frequent court litigation—they may be dealt with through informal adjudicative mechanisms based on multi-signature transactions, or they may simply remain
unresolved. However, the average low value of bitcoin transactions is, of course, a contingent phenomenon. If digital currencies were to establish themselves in the future as a usual
means for the conclusion of high-value transactions, the costs of court litigation may no
longer be seen as disproportionate.

A good example of the potential for future, high-value blockchain-related litigation is
the phenomenon of initial coin offerings ('ICOs'). Despite the many unanswered questions surrounding their regulatory framework (see Chapter 12 by Hacker and Thomale and
Chapter 13 by Shadab in this volume), ICOs are currently widely used by start-up companies
as a technique to attract venture capital.[48] There are multiple ways in which this phenomenon may trigger a need for dispute resolution. For instance, depending on the details of
the operation, the issuance of tokens may be regarded as securities fraud, opening the way
for legal action on the part of the token-holders. Furthermore, the company issuing the
tokens may fail to complete the development steps promised during the offering phase, on
which the value of the tokens hinges. In principle, many of the possible litigation scenarios
arising out of ICOs may be dealt with through blockchain-based arbitral systems. It could be
possible, for example, to link the release of a certain percentage of the funds raised through
the ICO to pre-determined development milestones, the achievement of which may be as-
certained by the token-holders through voting mechanisms. However, when (i) the value
in dispute is significant; (ii) the defendant can be clearly identified; and (iii) enforcement is
feasible, court litigation is still likely to come across as a reliable and attractive alternative,
as recently demonstrated by the *Tezos* class action. On 25 October 2017, a plaintiff filed a
proposed class action against multiple defendants, concerning the ICO for tokens related to
the *Tezos* blockchain project.[49] While it remains to be seen how the case will eventually be

---

[48] Iris Barsan, 'Legal Challenges of Initial Coin Offerings (ICO)' (2017) 3 *Revue Trimestrielle de Droit
Financier*, 54; Jonathan Rohr and Aaron Wright, 'Blockchain-Based Token Sales, Initial Coin Offerings, and
the Democratization of Public Capital Markets' (2017) Cardozo Legal Studies Research Paper No. 527; Saman
Adhami, Giancarlo Giudici, and Stefano Martinazzi, 'Why Do Businesses Go Crypto? An Empirical Analysis of
Initial Coin Offerings' (2017) https://papers.ssrn.com/sol3/papers.cfm?abstract_id=3046209; Jin Enyi and Ngoc
Le, 'The Legal Nature of Cryptocurrencies in the US and the Applicable Rules' (2017) https://papers.ssrn.com/
sol3/papers.cfm?abstract_id=2995784&download=yes; John Conley, 'Blockchain and the Economics of Crypto-
Tokens and Initial Coin Offerings' (2017) Vanderbilt University Department of Economics Working Paper,
VUECON-17-00008; Michael Bacina and Sina Kassra, 'Technology: Unlocking Cryptocurrency Token Sales'
(2017) 37 *Law Society of New South Wales Journal*, 79; Sviatoslav Rosov, 'Beyond Bitcoin: Crypto-Currencies Are
Only the Beginning' (2015) 26(1) *CFA Institute Magazine*, 37.

[49] *Baker v. Dynamic Ledger Sols, Inc.*, No. 17-CV-06850-RS, 2018 WL 656012 (N.D. Cal. 1 February 2018);
MacDonald v. Dynamic Ledger Sols, Inc., No. 17-CV-07095-RS, 2017 WL 6513439 (N.D. Cal. 20 December 2017);
Okusko v. Dynamic Ledger Solutions, Inc. et al., Case No. 17-cv-6829; *GGCC, LLC v. Dynamic Ledger Sols*, Inc.,
No. 17-CV-06779-RS, 2018 WL 1388488 (N.D. Cal. 16 March 2018). John Wagster and Courtney Rogers Perrin,
'It Begins: The First ICO-Related Securities Litigation Has Been Filed—and There are Lessons in It for Those
Hoping to File Their Own ICO' (*FrostBrownTodd.com*, 15 November 2017) http://www.fbtbankingresource.
com/it-begins-the-first-ico-related-securities-litigation-filed#page=1; Artificial Lawyer, 'Former Clifford Chance
Lawyer Brings Landmark Blockchain ICO Class Action' (6 November 2017) https://www.artificiallawyer.com/
2017/11/06/former-clifford-chance-lawyer-brings-landmark-blockchain-ico-class-action/. Other ICOs have also
recently given rise to court litigation: see, e.g., *Rensel v. Centra Tech Inc., et al.*, 17-cv-24500-JLK (S.D. Fla.); *Hodges,
et al. v. Monkey Calital, LLC, et al.*, 17-81370 (S.D. Fla.); *Balestra v. ATBCOIN, LLC, et al.*, 17-10001 (S.D.N.Y.);
Stormsmedia, LLC v. Giva Watt, Inc., et al., 17-00438 (E.D.Wash.); *Davy, et al. v. Paragon Coin, Inc., et al.*, 18-00671
(N.D.Cal.).

resolved, the circumstance that ICO-related securities cases are currently being filed before state courts suggests that blockchain technologies have not entirely marginalized national systems of justice. Rather, what seems to be emerging at the moment is a pragmatic division of labour. While self-enforcing arbitral systems based on smart contracts are being used to resolve a multitude of unrelated small claims that could not realistically be brought before national courts, traditional litigation avenues are starting to be used for economically significant and legally complex cases. In the specific case of ICOs, a large number of subscribers may seek redress for the same type of harm, for example arising out of the violation of securities law or the devaluation of the tokens, thus triggering a class action or other collective redress mechanisms. Given the amount of venture capital that has recently been raised through ICOs, the latter phenomenon may be a non-negligible portion of the future reality of blockchain-related dispute resolution.

To sum up, the diffusion of blockchain technologies is currently triggering the development of private systems of arbitration, often relying on smart contracts. This trend, though, should not be understood exclusively as a symptom of the progressive marginalization of state justice. On the one hand, online dispute resolution based on blockchain technologies seems to be a growing reality, meeting a demand of adjudication that cannot be satisfied by state courts due to the excessive costs of litigation. On the other hand, however, traditional avenues of court litigation could become more attractive for users were blockchain technologies to become relevant on a wide scale for high-value transactions. In light of this, claims that blockchains are radically disrupting the way justice is administered by courts are excessive. Nonetheless, there is an additional aspect of blockchain-based adjudication the disruptive potential of which has been so far understudied: 'self-enforcement'. Section IV scrutinizes this problem in detail.

IV. Self-Enforcement and the End of State Monopoly over the Use of Force

While it is substantially inaccurate (and in any event too early) to claim that blockchain technologies have entirely disrupted the centrality of the state in the administration of justice, one particular aspect of these technologies is likely to have a profound impact on the way national systems of justice function and, more specifically, on the enforcement of dispute resolution decisions.

Every dispute resolution mechanism structurally faces the problem of non-compliance. What happens if, once a dispute has been resolved, a party does not act in accordance with the outcome of the procedure? What happens if, for instance, a party that has been ordered to pay a certain amount of money refuses to do so? In order to survive, every system of justice must find a structural solution to this problem. If losing parties were left free to systematically ignore judgments, the system from which those judgments originate would cease to exist as such. In these scenarios, compliance must be ensured through coercion, i.e. by forcing the party to do what he/she has been ordered to do. In order to obtain the coercive enforcement of a decision, it is generally necessary to rely on the assistance of the state, which maintains a monopoly over the use of force.[50] This holds true not only for judgments issued by a state court, but also for arbitral awards. While private parties are left free to opt out of state court litigation by submitting to arbitration, they are always required to apply for state-controlled enforcement procedures whenever they need to obtain the coercive execution of the final outcome. Furthermore, the same state monopoly can be observed when a judgment or arbitral award must be executed in a foreign national system. The interested

---

[50] Max Weber, 'Politics as a Vocation' in *The Vocation Lectures*, edited by David Owen and Tracy B Strong (Hackett 2004), 33.

party must apply for recognition and enforcement before the competent authorities of the state where the execution is sought and it is up to the state to decide whether and to what extent force will be used. The rationale underlying these limitations is to avoid any situation in which the party prevailing in a litigation may privately make use of force in order to protect his or her rights.

Smart contracts have the potential to disrupt this state of affairs by opening the unprecedented possibility of self-enforcement. In the example of multi-signature transactions described in section III, the outcome of the dispute resolution procedure is enforced privately without relying on the coercive apparatus of the state. In fact, it even becomes difficult to distinguish the issuance of a decision from its enforcement, as the adjudicator resolves the case by determining the final destination of a disputed sum of money. In this new scenario, non-compliance is made structurally impossible as software script enables the adjudicator to coercively allocate the disputed assets to the prevailing party. As different industries adopt blockchain technologies, this form of private enforcement may permeate a growing number of aspects of our social and economic life, ranging from financial markets to real estate.[51] In addition, the development of the Internet of Things ('IoT') may act as an additional catalyst for enabling private enforcement. Let us scrutinize two particularly relevant effects of this unprecedented development on the role of the state as an administrator of justice.

A. Limitation of the possibility of state scrutiny

The first, evident consequence of self-enforcement through technology is the isolation of arbitral systems from the control of the state. Traditionally, even when private parties escape the adjudicative jurisdiction of state courts by using arbitration, the state maintains a certain control, mainly through setting aside and recognition and enforcement procedures. More specifically, setting- aside procedures enable the courts of a given state to annul arbitral awards rendered by tribunals seated in that state, under specific conditions.[52] Recognition and enforcement procedures, instead, are the mechanisms through which state courts decide whether an arbitral award should coercively be executed, as long as no grounds for refusal occur.[53] Both of these procedures are tools through which state courts can prevent an arbitral award from producing effects. For this reason, they play a key role in striking a balance between private autonomy and public control. Notably, these tools may be unavailable if private adjudication arises out of a self-enforcing smart contract. This largely informal dispute resolution procedure may not even be regarded as a type of arbitration from the point of view of state law and, thus, no setting-aside procedures may be available.[54] However, most importantly, smart contracts allow parties to obtain enforcement without requesting the support of the state. The decisions issued by the private adjudicators may never end up before national courts, thereby remaining immune from any type of state scrutiny.

This development can potentially marginalize the role of the state and its courts, even in a scenario where court litigation is not rendered completely obsolete. On the one hand,

---

[51] Philipp Paech, 'The Governance of Blockchain Financial Networks' (2017) 80(6) *Modern Law Review*, 1073.

[52] For a comparative analysis of the grounds for annulment of arbitral awards see, e.g., Gary Born, *International Commercial Arbitration* (2nd edn, Kluwer 2014), 3163–393.

[53] ibid., 3394–731.

[54] For an example of the typical scope of application of national arbitration statutes, see Articles 1 and 2 of the UNCITRAL Model Law on International Commercial Arbitration. Applying this standard, private adjudication based on smart contracts would probably not be qualified as arbitration. To be sure, even in the absence of setting aside procedures, state courts would theoretically still have the power to 'undo' the solution imposed by the private adjudicators, e.g. by ordering the party who has prevailed in the private procedure to pay a certain sum of money to the losing one, hence modifying the allocation of resources envisaged in the dispute resolution procedure based on smart contracts. In order for this to happen, however, the dispute would need to be brought before a state court; as illustrated above, this is unlikely to happen when the value in dispute does not justify the costs and complexity of court litigation.

private adjudication may not wipe out state courts entirely. As explained in section III, the current trend seems to suggest a division of labour, with blockchain-based arbitral systems being used to deal with small claims and traditional court litigation still being deployed when the amount in dispute is sufficiently high. On the other hand, however, even within this scenario, the state may partially lose its centrality, inasmuch as its courts are deprived of all forms of control over that portion of cases which are resolved privately through smart contracts. The landscape of dispute resolution may hence be partitioned off into two distinct regions: one where state courts continue to administer justice, and one where blockchains trigger an unprecedented form of state-less, transnational judicialization.

B. A paradigm shift: from balancing to automation

The second consequence is a paradigm shift concerning the structure of enforcement mechanisms. The traditional, state-controlled enforcement instruments and the new, private self-enforcement devices respond to two different, and not necessarily compatible, logics: balancing and automation. In order to elucidate this point, it is useful to consider some practical examples.

State laws governing the enforcement of judgments and awards aim to balance different needs. Let us consider, for example, the case of a debtor failing to pay the sum of money ordered in a judgment. In many jurisdictions, the creditor can pursue several enforcement strategies, such as the attachment of the debtor's earnings. In this case, the competent court will typically order the debtor's employer to start making deductions from the debtor's salary to satisfy the creditor.[55] This possibility to order a deduction, however, is not unlimited. The law typically requires that a certain rate of the earnings be preserved to ensure that the debtor maintains a minimum level of subsistence.[56] Obviously, the rationale underlying this rule is the need to balance the creditor's right to obtain the money with the debtor's basic needs and fundamental rights. According to a similar logic, a landlord seeking to evict a tenant cannot obtain this result overnight; this is so even when there exist legitimate grounds justifying the eviction. National legal systems typically require that the tenant be given a minimum notice in order to balance the landlord's right to regain possession of the house with the tenant's need to find an alternative solution for his or her accommodation.[57] In a nutshell, the enforcement procedures set forth by state law require a certain amount of time not only because instantaneous coercion is not practically feasible but also because they function according to criteria of balancing between different rights and needs.[58]

Blockchain technologies have the potential to impact upon this state of affairs dramatically. In the example of the attachment of earnings, smart contracts may make it possible to operate an automatic deduction on the salary and the debtor may be able to recover his/her money privately, without the need to rely on state-mediated procedures imposing a protected earnings rate. In the case of eviction, the use of smart door locks managed through blockchain technologies may immediately make it impossible for the tenant to access the house once the landlord triggers the eviction through software script. The logic of private enforcement is one of automation, rather than balancing. Blockchain technologies can enable private parties to autonomously obtain what the state would traditionally not allow. While an incalculable multitude of white papers extol the virtues of blockchain technologies,

---

[55] An example of such procedures is the attachment of earnings, in England and Wales, regulated by the Attachment of Earnings Act 1971. For a comparative overview, see Carel van Lynden, *Enforcement of Judgments, Awards and Deeds in Commercial Matters* (Thomson Reuters 2013).

[56] See, e.g., Attachment of Earnings Act 1971, Section 6(5)(b).

[57] In England and Wales, for instance, Section 21(1)(b) of the Housing Act 1988, requires that the landlord give the tenant not less than two months' notice before a court makes an order for possession of the house.

[58] Konstantinos Kerameus, 'Enforcement Proceedings' in *International Encyclopedia of Comparative Law: Civil Procedure*, edited by Mauro Cappelletti (Volume 16, Mohr Siebeck 1987), 10–19.

stressing the significant gains in terms of efficiency and reliability, the time has come to acknowledge that there may be another, darker side of the automation medal (or, perhaps more appropriately, coin): the potential violation of fundamental rights.

As automation permeates different aspects of our lives, the need for balancing will become more evident. While current attempts to operationalize blockchains and smart contracts focus on what these technologies can do, the unanswered question that is likely to gain prominence in the near future is whether they should be allowed to do everything they technically can. Who should answer this question, and potentially constrain automation in order to protect fundamental rights? In principle, states could regulate smart contracts, restricting private autonomy and prohibiting certain enforcement practices because of their unfairness.[59] Such prohibitions, however, would face the risk of unevenness in regulation and compliance. From the first point of view, in the absence of any multilateral understanding, different states would be likely to adopt different approaches as to how smart contracts should be regulated. As a result, the same smart contract could be subject to different rules, thus resulting in uneven levels of protection of parties engaging in the same type of transaction and increasing compliance costs.[60] From the second point of view, national law may be difficult to translate into practice because certain types of smart contract are unlikely to be subject to court scrutiny. As described above, one of the effects of blockchain technologies is the creation of a new division of labour between state courts and private arbitral systems based on self-enforcing smart contracts. While the former are unlikely to be entirely disrupted, the latter are better positioned to resolve certain high-volume, low-value disputes.[61] In light of this, even if state law prohibited certain smart contract practices, such prohibition would likely be applied unevenly, with certain categories of transactions falling outside of the shadow of state law.

A possible complement to state-made law would be the adoption of standards at the transnational level. Rather than leaving private autonomy entirely free to express itself through code, the industry itself should embrace the logic of balancing and should transnationally set some limits to the degree of automation attainable through blockchains and smart contracts. Similarly to what happened in the over-the-counter derivatives market, where the International Swaps and Derivatives Association ('ISDA') has promoted contractual standardization in order to manage risk and preserve the industry's reputation,[62] blockchain developers stand to gain a lot from the transnational regulation of smart contracts. The end-users would perceive this new set of technologies as more reliable if their functioning were governed by some widely shared principles, instead of being seen as a quasi-anarchic space of libertarian experimentation. Blockchain technologies would come across as the backbone of a new, solid regime of regulation and contract-making, rather than as a potentially disruptive, ungovernable force. By adopting the same logic of balancing that has for a long time informed the national laws regulating enforcement, instead of discarding it as outdated, blockchain technologies would attain the legitimacy they need to move beyond the utopian realm of white papers.

---

[59] The limitation of private autonomy is a well-known regulatory approach in scenarios where there is a significant unbalance in the power of the contracting parties: see, e.g., in the European Union, Council Directive 93/13/EEC (5 April 1993) on unfair terms in consumer contracts, OJ L 95 (21 April 1993), 29–34.

[60] The same smart contract may be subject to different substantive laws, depending on the applicable conflict-of-laws rules. Hence, a business operating across national borders would have to take into account all of the potentially applicable laws, so as to ensure that the adopted smart contract does not run counter to any of them.

[61] The expression 'high-volume, low-value' is adopted inter alia by the UNCITRAL Working Group III, to designate the type of electronic transaction suitable for online dispute resolution: see UNCITRAL Working Group III, 'Report of Working Group III (Online Dispute Resolution) on the Work of its 33rd Session (New York 29 February–4 March 2016) UN Doc A/CN.9/868, 2.

[62] John Biggins, '"Targeted Touchdown" and "Partial Liftoff": Post-Crisis Dispute Resolution in the OTC Derivatives Markets and the Challenge for ISDA' (2012) 13(12) *German Law Journal*, 1297.

V. Conclusion

This chapter has analysed the impact of blockchain technologies on the administration of justice and on the central role traditionally played by the state in this context. In order to do so, it has sought to de-couple technology from ideology in order to prioritize a sound understanding of the phenomenon over the a priori rejection or endorsement thereof.

After having located the theme within the nationalism/transnationalism debate, the chapter has considered the claim that blockchain technologies are rendering state courts obsolete as they allow private parties to devise largely self-sufficient arbitral systems. Historical analysis demonstrates the existence of a correlation between the seizure of power and the development of a system of justice. In light of this, the question arises whether blockchain technologies tend towards judicialization as they permeate different types of social and economic interaction. The available empirical evidence offers some support for such a claim. To date, the rise in the volume of Bitcoin transactions has not been mirrored by a comparable size in the number of disputes arising out of contracts denominated in bitcoin being dealt with by state courts. Nonetheless, it must also be noted that mechanisms of private adjudication based on smart contracts seem to be mainly suitable for small claims, while state court litigation is likely to maintain a certain degree of attractiveness in the future for complex, high-value disputes (such as the ones arising in connection with ICOs). In light of this, claims that blockchain technologies have already marginalized state courts may be inaccurate and are, in any event, premature.

Nevertheless, the diffusion of blockchain technologies and smart contracts already has a visible impact on one of the fundamental features through which the centrality of the state in the administration of justice is articulated: the monopoly over the use of force, at the stage where dispute resolution decisions are coercively enforced. Smart contracts allow for an unprecedented degree of automation, thus (potentially) factually disrupting the monopoly of the state over coercion. As a result, the state may be increasingly unable to exercise an effective scrutiny over certain types of transactions, and the balancing rationale traditionally underlying enforcement procedures may be substituted by automation. In light of this, this chapter has argued that automatic enforcement should be limited in order to avoid the violation of fundamental rights. This result may be attained through regulation at the national level and through transnational standard-setting.

VI. Bibliography

Adhami Saman, Giudici Giancarlo, and Martinazzi Stefano, 'Why do Businesses Go Crypto? An Empirical Analysis of Initial Coin Offerings' (2017) https://papers.ssrn.com/sol3/papers.cfm?abstract_id=3046209 , accessed on 16 January 2019.

Artificial Lawyer, 'Former Clifford Chance Lawyer Brings Landmark Blockchain ICO Class Action' (6 November 2017) https://www.artificiallawyer.com/2017/11/06/former-clifford-chance-lawyer-brings-landmark-blockchain-ico-class-action/, accessed on 16 January 2019.

Atzori Marcella, 'Blockchain Technology and Decentralized Governance: Is the State Still Necessary?' (13 June 2016) https://papers.ssrn.com/sol3/papers.cfm?abstract_id=2709713, accessed on 16 January 2019.

Bacina Michael and Kassra Sina, 'Technology: Unlocking Cryptocurrency Token Sales' (2017) 37 *Law Society of New South Wales Journal* 79-81.

Barsan Iris, 'Legal Challenges of Initial Coin Offerings (ICO)' (2017) 3 *Revue Trimestrielle de Droit Financier*, 54.

Bassett Caroline and Wilbert Chris, 'Where You Want to Go Today (Like it or Not): Leisure Practices in Cyberspace' in *Leisure/Tourism Geographies: Practices and Geographical Knowledge*, edited by David Crouch (Routledge 1999).

Biggins John, '"Targeted Touchdown" and "Partial Liftoff": Post-Crisis Dispute Resolution in the OTC Derivatives Markets and the Challenge for ISDA' (2012) 13(12) *German Law Journal*, 1297.

Black Vaughan, *Foreign Currency Claims in the Conflict of Laws* (Hart 2010).

Bodin Jean, *Les six livres de la republique* (Jacques du Puys 1576).

Bollen Rhys, 'The Legal Status of Online Currencies—are Bitcoins the Future?' (22 February 2016) https://papers.ssrn.com/sol3/papers.cfm?abstract_id=2736021, accessed on 16 January 2019.

Born Gary, *International Commercial Arbitration* (2nd edn, Kluwer 2014).

Brito Jerry, Shadab Houman, and Castillo Andrea, 'Bitcoin Financial Regulation: Securities, Derivatives, Prediction Markets, and Gambling' (2014) 16 *Columbia Science & Technology Law Review*, 144.

Calandro Enrico, Gillwald Alison, and Zingales Nicolo, 'Mapping Multistakeholderism in Internet Governance: Implications for Africa' (12 October 2013) Research ICT Africa, https://papers.ssrn.com/sol3/papers.cfm?abstract_id=2338999, accessed 16 January 2019.

Chase Oscar, *Law, Culture and Ritual: Disputing Systems in Cross-Cultural Context* (New York University Press 2005).

Commodity Futures Trading Comm'n v. McDonnell, 287 F. Supp. 3d 213, 218 (E.D.N.Y. 2018).

Conley John, 'Blockchain and the Economics of Crypto-Tokens and Initial Coin Offerings' (2017) Vanderbilt University Department of Economics Working Paper, VUECON-17-00008.

Damaška Mirjan, *The Faces of Justice and State Authority: A Comparative Approach to the Legal Process* (Yale University Press 1986).

Enyi Jin and Le Ngoc, 'The Legal Nature of Cryptocurrencies in the US and the Applicable Rules' (2017) https://papers.ssrn.com/sol3/papers.cfm?abstract_id=2995784, accessed on 16 January 2019.

Fishman Robert, *Bourgeois Utopias: The Rise and Fall of Suburbia* (Basic Books 1987).

Ford Richard, 'Beyond Borders: A Partial Response to Richard Briffault' (1996) 48(5) *Stanford Law Review*, 1173.

Ford Richard, 'Law's Territory (A History of Jurisdiction)' (1999) 97(4) *Michigan Law Review*, 843.

Giuliani Alessandro and Picardi Nicola, 'La responsabilità del giudice: problemi storici e metodologici' in *L'educazione giuridica—III: La responsabilità del giudice*, edited by Alessandro Giuliani and Nicola Picardi (Università degli Studi di Perugia 1978).

Grinberg Reuben, 'Bitcoin: An Innovative Alternative Digital Currency' (2012) 4(1) *Hastings Science & Technology Law Journal*, 159.

Grossi Paolo, *L'ordine Giuridico Medievale* (7th edn, Laterza 2006).

Howse Rob, 'Further Considerations on Dani Rodrik, *The Globalization Paradox*' (2013) 11(3) *International Journal of Constitutional Law*, 813.

Ishikawa Mai, 'Designing Virtual Currency Regulation in Japan: Lessons from the Mt Gox Case' (2017) 3(1) *Journal of Financial Regulation*, 125.

Jaucourt Louis de, 'Juge (Droit moral)' in *Encyclopédie ou dictionnaire raisonne des sciences, des arts et des métiers* (Faulche 1765).

Jessup Philip, *Transnational Law* (Yale University Press 1956).

Johnson Alan, 'Why Brexit is Best for Britain: The Left-Wing Case' (*NYTimes.com*, 28 March 2017) https://www.nytimes.com/2017/03/28/opinion/why-brexit-is-best-for-britain-the-left-wing-case.html, accessed on 16 January 2019.

Kahn-Freund Otto, 'Foreign Money Debts—Conversion into Sterling' (1940) 3(3) *Modern Law Review*, 228.

Kaplanov Nikolei, 'Nerdy Money: Bitcoin, the Private Digital Currency, and the Case Against Its Regulation' (22 July 2012) Temple University Legal Studies Research Paper, https://papers.ssrn.com/sol3/papers.cfm?abstract_id=2115203, accessed on 16 January 2019.

Katsh Ethan and Rabinovich-Einy Orna, *Digital Justice: Technology and the Internet of Disputes* (Oxford University Press 2017).

Kerameus Konstantinos, 'Enforcement Proceedings' in *International Encyclopedia of Comparative Law: Civil Procedure*, edited by Mauro Cappelletti (Volume 16, Mohr Siebeck 1987).

Lastra Rosa Maria, 'The Globalization Paradox: Review of Dani Rodrik, The Globalization Paradox: Democracy and the Future of the World Economy' (2013) 11(3) *International Journal of Constitutional Law*, 809.

Lee Larissa, 'New Kids on the Blockchain: How Bitcoin's Technology Could Reinvent the Stock Market' (2016) 12(2) *Hastings Business Law Journal*, 81.

Lessig Lawrence, *Code: And Other Laws of Cyberspace, Verson 2.0* (2nd edn, Basic Books 2006).

Lew Julian, 'Achieving the Dream: Autonomous Arbitration' (2006) 22(2) *Arbitration International* 179-204.

Loke Alexander, 'Virtual Currency Regulation in Singapore' (2015) 1(2) *Journal of Financial Regulation*, 290.

Marian Omri, 'Are Cryptocurrencies "Super" Tax Havens?' (2013) 112 *Michigan Law Review First Impressions*, 38.

Michaels Ralf, 'Dreaming Law without a State: Scholarship on Autonomous International Arbitration as Utopian Literature' (2013) 1(1) *London Review of International Law*, 35.

Michaels Ralf, 'Globalization and Law: Law Beyond the State' in *Law and Social Theory*, edited by Reza Banakar and Max Travers (2nd edn, Hart 2013).

Michaels Ralf, 'Does Brexit Spell the Death of Transnational Law?' (2016) 17 *German Law Review* (Brexit Special Supplement), 51.

Montesquieu Charles-Louis de Secondat, *De l'esprit des lois* (Barillot 1748).

Nguyen Dan and Alexander Jon, 'The Coming of Cyberspacetime and the End of the Polity' in *Cultures of Internet: Virtual Spaces, Real Histories, Living Bodies*, edited by Rob Shields (SAGE 1996).

Nicolini Ugo, *Il principio di legalità nella democrazia italiana* (CEDAM 1955).

Ortolani Pietro, 'Self-Enforcing Online Dispute Resolution: Lessons from Bitcoin' (2016) 36 *Oxford Journal of Legal Studies*, 595.

Ortolani Pietro, 'The Three Challenges of Stateless Justice' (2016) 7 *Journal of International Dispute Settlement*, 596.

P2SH Statistics, https://p2sh.info/dashboard/db/p2sh-statistics?orgId=1, accessed on 16 January 2019.

Paech Philipp, 'The Governance of Blockchain Financial Networks' (2017) 80(6) *Modern Law Review*, 1073.

Picardi Nicola, *La giurisdizione all'alba del terzo millennio* (Giuffrè 2007).

Plassaras Nicholas, 'Regulating Digital Currencies: Bringing Bitcoin within the Reach of the IMF' (2013) 14(1) *Chicago Journal of International Law*, 377.

Pufendorf Samuel, *De jure naturae et gentium libri octo* (Londini Scanorum 1672).

Purdy Jedediah, 'The Bars on the Cage' (2017) *The Nation*.

Purdy Jedediah, 'Wealth and Democracy' in *Nomos LVIII—Wealth,* edited by Jack Knight and Melissa Schwartzberg (New York University Press 2017).

Raskin Max, 'The Law and Legality of Smart Contracts' (2016) 1(2) *Georgetown Law Technology Review*, 305.

Rodrik Dani, *The Globalization Paradox. Democracy and the Future of the World Economy* (Norton 2011).

Rodrik Dani, 'The Globalization Paradox: A Response to Rosa Lastra and Robert Howse' (2013) 11(3) *International Journal of Constitutional Law*, 816.

Rohr Jonathan and Wright Aaron, 'Blockchain-Based Token Sales, Initial Coin Offerings, and the Democratization of Public Capital Markets' (2017) Cardozo Legal Studies Research Paper No. 527.

Rosov Sviatoslav, 'Beyond Bitcoin: Crypto-Currencies Are Only the Beginning' (2015) 26(1) *CFA Institute Magazine*, 37.

Schultz Thomas, *Transnational Legality: Stateless Law and International Arbitration* (Oxford University Press 2014).

Simondon Gilbert, *Du mode d'existence des Objets Techniques* (Aubier 1958).

Stickler A. M., 'Ordines Judiciarii' in *L'Educazione Giuridica: VI—Modelli storici della procedura continentale*, edited by Alessandro Giuliani and Nicola Picardi (Volume 2, Edizioni Scientifiche Italiane 1994).

Strange Susan, *The Retreat of the State: The Diffusion of Power in the World Economy* (Cambridge University Press 1996).

Svantesson Dan, *Solving the Internet Jurisdiction Puzzle* (Oxford University Press 2017).

Sweet Alec Stone and Grisel Florian, *The Evolution of International Arbitration: Judicialization, Governance, Legitimacy* (Oxford University Press 2017).

The Economist, 'The Retreat of the Global Company' (*Economist.com*, 28 January 2017) https://www.economist.com/briefing/2017/01/28/the-retreat-of-the-global-company, accessed on 16 January 2019.

Trautman Lawrence, 'Virtual Currencies; Bitcoin and What Now after Liberty Reserve, Silk Road, and Mt. Gox?' (2014) 20(4) *Richmond Journal of Law and Technology*, 1.

Trautman Lawrence, 'Is Disruptive Blockchain Technology the Future of Financial Services?' (2016) 69 *Consumer Finance Law Quarterly*, 232.

UNCITRAL Working Group III, Report of Working Group III (Online Dispute Resolution) on the Work of its 33rd Session (New York, 29 February–4 March 2016) UN Doc A/CN.9/868.

van Loo Rory, 'The Corporation as a Courthouse' (2016) 33 *Yale Journal on Regulation*, 547.

van Lynden Carel, *Enforcement of Judgments, Awards and Deeds in Commercial Matters* (Thomson Reuters 2013).

Virilio Paul, *La Bombe Informatique* (Galilée 1998).

von Benda-Beckmann Franz and von Benda-Beckmann Keebet, 'Places that Come and Go: A Legal Anthropologist Perspective on the Temporalities of Space in Plural Legal Orders' in Irus Braverman, Nicholas Blomley, David Delaney, and Alexandre Kedar, *The Expanding Spaces of Law—A Timely Legal Geography* (Stanford University Press 2014).

Wagster John and Rogers Perrin Courtney, 'It Begins: The First ICO-Related Securities Litigation Has Been Filed—and There Are Lessons in It for Those Hoping to File Their Own ICO' (*FrostBrownTodd.com*, 15 November 2017) http://www.fbtbankingresource.com/it-begins-the-first-ico-related-securities-litigation-filed#page=1, accessed on 16 January 2019.

Watkins Susan, 'Casting Off?' (2016) 100 *New Left Review*, 5.

Weber Max, 'Politics as a Vocation' in *The Vocation Lectures*, edited by David Owen and Tracy B Strong (Hackett 2004).

Wright Aaron and De Filippi Primavera, 'Decentralized Blockchain Technology and the Rise of *Lex Cryptographia*' (25 July 2017) https://papers.ssrn.com/sol3/papers.cfm?abstract_id=2580664, accessed on 16 January 2019.

17

Smart Contracts

Coding the Transaction, Decoding the Legal Debates

Roger Brownsword

I. Introduction

This chapter considers how lawyers will engage with so-called 'smart contracts',[1] with a world in which contracts are self-enforcing and where commerce is largely conducted by means of a 'conversation conducted entirely among machines'.[2] In such a world, is there any role for the law of contract? Is this, as some suppose, the end of contracts?[3]

For my purposes, we can treat these as questions that are technology-neutral. What we are interested in is simply the use of smart machines (whether or not involving blockchain technologies) that take humans out of the transactional loop, leaving it to the technology to form, perform, and enforce contracts.

How, then, should we expect lawyers to engage with smart contracts? Broadly speaking, my expectation is that there will be two principal conversations: one conversation will be between 'coherentists' asking how smart contracts fit with existing legal frameworks for contracts; the other will be between 'regulatory-instrumentalists', where the focus will be on assessing and managing the risks associated with the use of the new technologies with a view to ensuring that the regulatory environment is fit for purpose. In the former conversation, there will be both 'transactionalist' and 'relationalist' voices; in the latter conversation, there will be both 'rule-based' and 'technocratic' voices. We can also expect that, while coherentist voices will be loudest in the courts, regulatory-instrumentalist voices will be the loudest in legislative and policy-making arenas.

The chapter is in four parts. First, the general contrast between 'coherentist' and 'regulatory-instrumentalist' approaches is sketched. Second, transactionalist and relationalist variants of coherentism are elaborated. Third, rule-based and technocratic variants of regulatory-instrumentalism are elaborated. Finally, with a view to decoding the relevant debates, these four forms of engagement are applied to the use of smart contracts in consumer transactions, commercial transactions, and peer-to-peer transactions, respectively.

---

[1] Commonly defined as 'a set of promises, specified in digital form, including protocols within which the parties perform on these promises'. See The Chamber of Digital Commerce, 'Smart Contracts: 12 Use Cases for Business and Beyond: A Technology, Legal and Regulatory Introduction—Foreword by Nick Szabo' (2017) http://www.digitalchamber.org/smartcontracts.html, 8. Whether or not such 'smart contracts' are strictly speaking 'contracts' is, of course, one of many questions raised by new transactional technologies: see, further n 32 and, for an excellent discussion, Eliza Mik, 'Smart Contracts: Terminology, Technical Limitations and Real-World Complexity' (2017) 9 *Law Innovation and Technology*, 269. For an extraordinarily helpful mapping of the way in which an ever-changing world of digital instruments and digital objects relates to the European law of contract, see Stefan Grundmann and Philipp Hacker, 'The Digital Dimension as a Challenge to European Contract Law—The Architecture' in *European Contract Law in the Digital Age*, edited by Stefan Grundmann (Intersentia 2018), 3.

[2] W. Brian Arthur, 'The Second Economy' (2011) *McKinsey Quarterly*, quoted in Nicholas Carr, *The Glass Cage* (Vintage 2015), 197.

[3] See Shoshana Zuboff, 'Big Other: Surveillance Capitalism and the Prospects of an Information Civilization' (2015) 30 *Journal of Information Technology*, 75, 85–86.

II. The Contrast between Coherentist and Regulatory-Instrumentalist Approaches

In this part of the chapter, the contrast between the two dominant ways in which lawyers are likely to engage with new transactional technologies is outlined. We can start with a sketch of coherentism, which is a traditional legal approach, before contrasting it with regulatory-instrumentalism.

A. Coherentism

Coherentism is defined by three characteristics. First, for coherentists, what matters above all is the integrity and internal consistency of legal doctrine—in the case at hand, the internal consistency of the law of contract. This is viewed as desirable in and of itself. Second, coherentists are not concerned with the fitness of the law for its regulatory purpose. Third, coherentists approach new transactional technologies by asking how they fit within existing legal categories (and then try hard to fit them in). Coherentism is, thus, the natural language of litigators and judges, who seek to apply the law in a principled way.[4]

However, according to Edward Rubin, the days of coherentism are numbered. Rubin claims we live in the age of modern administrative states where the law is used 'as a means of implementing the policies that [each particular state] adopts. The rules that are declared, and the statutes that enact them, have no necessary relationship with one another; they are all individual and separate acts of will.'[5] In the modern administrative state, the 'standard for judging the value of law is not whether it is coherent but rather whether it is effective, that is, effective in establishing and implementing the policy goals of the modern state'.[6]

In contrast to such modern regulatory thinking, coherentism presupposes a world of, at most, leisurely change. It is not geared to respond to a world of rapidly emerging and highly disruptive technologies. When they are called on to respond to new technological developments, coherentists tend to try to classify the new phenomena within existing legal categories. For example, a nice coherentist question might be whether, with humans out of the transactional loop, automated and autonomous performance systems could be treated *relative to recognized legal concepts and categories* (such as the limited liability company) as having their own legal personality.[7] Similarly, when the technologies that support e-commerce appeared, the coherentist response was to treat on-line transactions as if they were off-line transactions, copying across the principles of the traditional law of contract to the emerging world of on-line contracts.[8]

---

[4] For a somewhat similar view, presented as a 'legalistic approach' to emerging technologies, see Nicolas Petit, 'Law and Regulation of Artificial Intelligence and Robots: Conceptual Framework and Normative Implications' (14 March 2017) https://papers.ssrn.com/sol3/papers.cfm?abstract_id=2931339.

[5] Edward Rubin, 'From Coherence to Effectiveness' in *Rethinking Legal Scholarship*, edited by Rob van Gestel, Hans-W. Micklitz, and Edward Rubin (Cambridge University Press 2017), 311.

[6] ibid., 328.

[7] Compare with Shawn Bayern, Thomas Burri, Thomas Grant et al., 'Company Law and Autonomous Systems: A Blueprint for Lawyers, Entrepreneurs, and Regulators' (2017) 9 *Hastings Science and Technology Law Journal*, 135, where company structures that are provided for in US, German, Swiss, and UK law are reviewed to see whether they might plausibly act as a host for autonomous systems that provide a service such as file storage, file retrieval, and meta-data management.

[8] For discussion, see Roger Brownsword, 'The E-Commerce Directive, Consumer Transactions and the Digital Single Market: Questions of Regulatory Fitness, Regulatory Disconnection and Rule Redirection' in *European Contract Law in the Digital Age*, edited by Stefan Grundmann (Intersentia 2018), 165.

B. Regulatory instrumentalism

In contrast with coherentism, regulatory-instrumentalism is defined by the following three features. First, it is not concerned with the internal consistency of legal doctrine. Second, it is entirely focused on whether the law is instrumentally effective in serving specified regulatory purposes. Regulatory-instrumentalists do not ask whether the law is coherent but whether it works. Third, regulatory instrumentalism has no reservation about enacting new bespoke laws if this is an effective and efficient response to a question raised by new transactional technologies. Regulatory-instrumentalism is, thus, the natural language of legislators and policy-makers.

From the industrial revolution onwards—at any rate, in the common law world—the direction of travel in criminal law, torts, and contracts has been away from coherentism and towards regulatory-instrumentalism. While intentionality and fault were set aside in the regulatory parts of criminal law and torts, classical transactionalist ideas of consent and agreement were marginalized, being replaced in the *mainstream* of contract law by 'objective' tests and standards set by reasonable business practice. As Morton Horwitz puts it, there was a dawning sense that 'all law was a reflection of collective determination, and, thus, inherently regulatory and coercive'.[9]

What we see across these developments is a pattern of disruption to legal doctrines that were organically expressed in smaller-scale non-industrialized communities. Here, the legal rules presuppose very straightforward ideas about holding to account those who engage intentionally in injurious or dishonest acts, about expecting others to act with reasonable care, and about holding others to their word. Once new technologies disrupt these ideas, we see the move to strict or absolute criminal liability without proof of intent, to tortious liability without proof of fault, and to contractual liability (or limitation of liability) without proof of actual intent, agreement, or consent. Even if the development in contract is less clear at this stage, in both criminal law and torts we can see the early signs of a risk-management approach to liability. Moreover, we also see the early signs of doctrinal bifurcation, with some parts of criminal law, tort law, and contract law resting on traditional principles (and representing, so to speak, 'real' crime, tort, and contract) while others deviate from these principles—often holding enterprises to account more readily but also sometimes easing the burden on business for the sake of beneficial innovation[10]—in order to strike a more acceptable balance of the benefits and risks that technological development brings with it.

Against this background, recall the case of *Thornton v. Shoe Lane Parking*,[11] where the claimant was injured at the defendants' car park through the negligence of one of their employees. Interestingly, this was half way to a smart contract because there was no human in attendance at the entrance to the car park. To this extent, the contract was automated. At the point at which the charges were displayed, there was a barrier that controlled entry and a machine that issued a ticket (referring to the terms and conditions for parking) to the claimant. The question of contract law was whether the defendants could rely on those terms and conditions in response to a claim for negligence. In the Court of Appeal's reasoning (in favour of the claimant) there are several signs of coherentism—for example, in the attempt made (by Lord Denning MR) to analyse the somewhat unusual facts into the traditional slots of offer and acceptance, and in the court's focus on a transactional basis for the risks assumed by the customer. (In other words, the central question for the court was whether

---

[9] Morton J. Horwitz, *The Transformation of American Law 1870–1960* (Oxford University Press 1992), 50.
[10] For example, in the United States, the interests of the farming community were subordinated to the greater good promised by the development of the railroad network: see Morton J. Horwitz, *The Transformation of American Law 1780–1860* (Cambridge, Mass.: Harvard University Press 1977).
[11] *Thornton v. Shoe Lane Parking* [1971] 2 QB 163.

Mr Thornton could be reasonably treated as having agreed to the terms in general, or the particular term on which the defendants relied.) Six years later, the Unfair Contract Terms Act ('UCTA') 1977 introduced a legislative response to the problem of unfair contract terms. Taking a regulatory-instrumentalist approach, UCTA does not focus on whether there is consent to the terms and conditions. Rather, reliance on terms such as the exclusionary terms at issue in *Thornton* is simply disallowed.

Imagine that, at some future time, a case like *Thornton* repeats itself, save only that Mr Thornton is a passenger in an autonomous vehicle. In this future scenario, the transaction is fully automated. At the entrance to the car park, humans are completely out of the contractual loop. What we now have are smart machines transacting on behalf of 'interested' or 'connected' human parties. What I am suggesting, thus far, is that lawyers might engage with such a smart contract in a coherentist and transactionalist way, or in a regulatory-instrumentalist way. If the former, lawyers will probably look for the interested or connected party's authorization or ratification (as in agency). If, however, our approach is of a regulatory-instrumentalist kind, we will simply decide on the acceptable terms and conditions for this kind of fully automated transaction.

However, as we move into section III of the chapter, we will see that this is too simple: within each form or approach, there are variants.

III. Two Coherentist Variants: Transactionalist and Relationalist

Thus far, I have presented coherentism as an approach that lawyers might adopt when they engage with new technologies. To be clear, it should be emphasized that coherentism is not just an approach that *contract* lawyers might adopt: criminal lawyers, tort lawyers, property lawyers—in fact, all lawyers—can, and often do, take such an approach. However, where we are focusing on coherentism and *contract lawyers*, we can detect both a transactionalist and a relationalist variant.

A. Transactionalism

In an uncompromising form, transactionalism will treat a deal between A and B as the legitimate source of the parties' rights and obligations *inter se* only if A and B each truly agreed to the deal. The parties must have 'subjectively' intended to signal their agreement and 'subjectively' understood the terms of the deal in the same way. There must have been a consensus *ad idem*. However, such a thoroughgoing commitment to subjectivism threatens to jeopardize both reliance on, and the utility of, contracts. Not surprisingly, then, following the industrial revolution, in the common law of contract there was a shift from a 'subjective' (purely transactional) model to an 'objective' approach.

In the United States, against the background of an 'increasingly national corporate economy', the goal of standardization of commercial transactions began to overwhelm the desire to conceive of contract law as expressing the subjective desires of individuals'.[12] In English law, in addition to the general shift to an objective approach, there was a particularly significant shift to a reasonable notice model in relation to the incorporation of the terms and conditions on which carriers (of both goods and persons) purported to contract. In the jurisprudence, this latter shift is symbolized by Mellish LJ's direction to the jury in *Parker v. South Eastern Railway Co.*,[13] where the legal test was said to be not so much whether a

---

[12] Horwitz, *The Transformation of American Law* (n 9), 37. At 48–49, Horwitz notes a parallel transformation in relation to both corporate forms and agency.

[13] *Parker v. South Eastern Railway Co.* (1877) 2 C.P.D. 416; and, see, Stephen Waddams, *Principle and Policy in Contract Law* (Cambridge University Press 2011), 39.

customer actually was aware of the terms and had agreed to them but whether the company had given reasonable notice.

Stated shortly, the transactionalist response to smart contracts will be to deny that an automated transaction with humans out of the loop can, of itself, give rise to rights and obligations between humans and to look for an upstream master transaction that is the source of such rights and obligations. If such a master transaction can be identified, then its terms and conditions will bind the parties and they will be taken to have agreed to the downstream automated transaction to the extent that this is in line with the objective test.

B. Relationalism

Relationalists might be prepared to accept that the deal between A and B is the basis of their contractual obligations but they will want to emphasize that they are referring not to the 'paper deal' but to the 'real deal'.[14] They will be much more comfortable saying that contractual rights and obligations are based on the dealing(s) between the parties, the context in which they have dealt, and the reasonable expectations that they have in that setting.[15] For relationalists, the paper deal is not irrelevant and neither are the rules of the law of contract, but the paper terms and conditions are just one part of the picture and the rules of contract law have to be treated as defaults.

Traditionally, the English *commercial law* of contract has had the reputation for taking a robustly individualistic (even adversarial) view of transactions—recall, for example, Lord Ackner's hostile remarks about good faith in negotiation in *Walford v. Miles*[16]—coupled with a literal approach to the interpretation and application of the paper deal. Critics have objected to both aspects of this approach. First, the rugged individualism that is inscribed in the law seems to be out of kilter with much business practice, where the parties relate to one another in a far more cooperative way and in a spirit of compromise and common purpose.[17] Second, literal interpretation can sometimes defeat the obvious purpose of the provisions and generate outcomes that make no commercial sense. Although this traditional reputation is probably well deserved, for much of the past twenty years, the Supreme Court (led by Lords Hoffmann and Steyn) has embraced a much more 'contextual' approach.[18] Most recently, however, the Court has drawn back somewhat (notably, in *Marks and Spencer plc v. BNP Paribas Services Trust Company (Jersey) Limited*[19] (on implied terms); and, *Arnold v. Britton*[20] and *Wood v. Capita Insurance Services Ltd*[21] (on interpretation)), reacting against expansive implication and interpretation of terms, particularly in carefully drafted commercial contracts. While this development will delight 'minimalists'[22] and trouble 'contextualists',[23] it leaves all coherentists with many questions, as the

---

[14] See, Stewart Macaulay, 'The Real and the Paper Deal: Empirical Pictures of Relationships, Complexity and the Urge for Transparent Simple Rules' (2003) 66 *Modern Law Review*, 44.

[15] Seminally, see Johan Steyn, 'Contract Law: Fulfilling the Reasonable Expectations of Honest Men' (1997) 113 *Law Quarterly Review*, 433.

[16] *Walford v. Miles* [1992] 1 All ER 453, 460–61.

[17] Compare Stewart Macaulay, 'Crime and Custom in Business Society' (1995) 22 *Journal of Law and Society*, 248; and 'Non-Contractual Relations in Business' (1963) 28 *American Sociological Review*, 55.

[18] See Roger Brownsword, 'The Law of Contract: Doctrinal Impulses, External Pressures, Future Directions' (2014) 31 *Journal of Contract Law*, 73. The root cases on interpretation are *Mannai Investments Co. Ltd v. Eagle Star Life Assurance Co. Ltd* [1997] 3 All ER 352 and *Investors Compensation Scheme Ltd v. West Bromwich Building Society* [1998] 1 All ER 98; on implied terms, the root is *AG of Belize v. Belize Telecom Ltd* [2009] UKPC 10; and on defaults it is *Transfield Shipping Inc. v. Mercator Shipping Inc.* [2008] UKHL 48.

[19] *Marks and Spencer plc v. BNP Paribas Services Trust Company (Jersey) Limited* [2015] UKSC 72.

[20] *Arnold v. Britton* [2015] UKSC 36.   [21] *Wood v. Capita Insurance Services Ltd* [2017] UKSC 24.

[22] For 'minimalism', see Jonathan Morgan, *Contract Law Minimalism* (Cambridge University Press 2013), who advocates a clear and minimal set of hard-edged rules.

[23] For 'contextualism', see Catherine Mitchell, *Contract Law and Contract Practice* (Hart 2013).

balance between the paper deal and the context is left unclear. However, that is another story.[24]

We should not misunderstand 'relationalism'. Relationalists do not claim that business contractors deal in a 'law-free' zone. Far from it, many business people are guided by their own self-governing norms of the trading community. To be sure, there is much more that might be said about this but the immediate question is what relationalists are likely to say about smart contracts and how they might engage with the new transactional technologies.

One thing that they might say is that we should not assume that all business communities will embrace smart contracts. Some business people might resist the very idea of being put out of the loop and they will want to retain practices that reinforce their sense of the relational nature of their rights and obligations.[25] Unless the state has an interest in compelling the use of smart contracts, there seems to be no problem. Even so, what will relationalists make of those business contractors who do use smart contracts?

Relationalists are much more flexible in their thinking than transactionalists. They understand that deals are done in many different ways and they have no desire to force the facts to fit into traditional doctrinal templates or straitjackets. One size does not fit all. Moreover, as we have said, relationalists will not focus exclusively on the paper deal; they will take a much broader view of the transactional setting. Taking this broader view, relationalists will neither puzzle over the fact that humans are not in the loop at the time of the deal nor will they be concerned that the deal is executed in a fraction of a second. Assuming that connected or interested human parties can still be identified, the question for relationalists will be whether the law runs with the grain of their reasonable expectations. Provided that it does, then all is well.

So far so good but, of course, a view will need to be taken about the parties' reasonable expectations and this is problematic unless the reference point for reasonableness has been stabilized.[26] If the expectations are rooted in 'club rules' for the use of the relevant technologies (amongst club members, this is the way that deals will be done) or in some originating 'contract', then this might be a clear case; if the practice of the club members or the parties deviates from the paper rules, relationalists will be guided by the context and the real deal. However, if there are concerns about the reality of agreement around the anchoring contract, then there might be some convergence as between relationalists and transactionalists, particularly in support of the interests of vulnerable parties.

IV. Two Regulatory-Instrumentalist Variants: Rule-Based and Technocratic

There are two phases to the technological disruption of the law. In the first phase, we realize that we need *different* rules to serve our collective purposes. In the second phase, we realize that we do not always need to rely on *rules* to serve our regulatory purposes. In both phases, the legal mind-set becomes more regulatory-instrumental. However, whereas, in the first phase, we are still thinking about using rules to achieve our regulatory purposes, in the second phase we begin to see the possibility of employing technological tools (rather than rules) to achieve the desired regulatory effects. Stated starkly, in the second phase, we begin to see that, by using appropriate technological tools, we can either reduce or eliminate the

---

[24] See Roger Brownsword, 'After Brexit: Regulatory Instrumentalism, Coherentism, and the English Law of Contract' (2018) 34 *Journal of Contract Law* 139.

[25] Compare the excellent discussion in Karen Levy, 'Book-Smart, Not Street-Smart: Blockchain-Based Smart Contracts and The Social Workings of Law' (2017) 3 *Engaging Science, Technology, and Society*, 1.

[26] See, e.g., Roger Brownsword, 'After *Investors*: Interpretation, Expectation and the Implicit Dimension of the "New Contextualism"' in *The Implicit Dimensions of Contract*, edited by David Campbell, Hugh Collins, and John Wightman (Hart 2003), 103.

possibility that there will be non-compliance or, in the case of transactions, breaches of contract.

Having already said quite a bit about the variant of regulatory-instrumentalism that is focused on using rules as the regulatory modality, about the kind of changes made to the traditional rules in criminal law, torts, and contracts, and about the development of a risk management mentality, we do not need to repeat this. In this phase, the legal and regulatory enterprise, as Lon Fuller famously put it, continues to be one of 'subjecting human conduct to the governance of *rules*'.[27] However, in this part of the chapter, we can concentrate on introducing the technocratic variant, which is encouraged during the second phase of the technological disruption of the law.

With a risk management approach well established, regulators now find that they have the option of responding by employing various technological instruments either in support of, or in place of, rules. In the criminal justice system, technological instruments (such as CCTV surveillance and DNA profiling) *support* the rules (and their enforcement) by discouraging offending and by aiding the detection and identification of offenders. Similarly, in consumer contracts, technological instruments (such as smart machines that can rapidly scan documents) might assist both consumers and agencies charged with consumer protection responsibilities to spot potentially unfair terms and conditions;[28] and there is the much-debated example of digital force being employed to immobilize a vehicle where the purchaser fails to make a payment that is due. However, the technological tools might be more than assistive; they might wholly replace the prior rules. For example, in the criminal justice system, measures of technological management might automatically disable persons who attempt to drive while under the influence of drink or drugs, or even immobilize the vehicle. Similarly, digital rights management (for the sake of protecting intellectual property rights) can be achieved through product design rather than (less effectively) by contractual stipulation. In principle, technological management might be applied to the design of products, places, and people, and increasingly, with automation, the design means that humans, who once were the targets of the legal rules, are no longer in the loop.

Two things are characteristic of technological management. First, unlike rules, when technological management is employed the focus of the regulatory intervention is on the practical (not the paper) options of regulatees.[29] Second, whereas legal rules back their prescriptions with *ex post* penal, compensatory, or restorative measures, the focus of technological management is entirely *ex ante*, aiming to anticipate and prevent wrongdoing rather than punish or compensate after the event. As Lee Bygrave puts it in the context of the design of information systems and the protection of both intellectual property rights and privacy, the assumption is that, by embedding norms in the architecture, there is 'the promise of a significantly increased *ex ante* application of the norms and a corresponding reduction in relying on their application *ex post facto*'.[30]

This evolution in regulatory thinking is not surprising. Having recognized the limited fitness of traditional legal rules, and having taken a more regulatory approach, the next step surely is to think not just in terms of risk assessment and risk management but also to be

---

[27] Lon Fuller, *The Morality of Law* (rev. edn, Yale University Press 1969).

[28] For just such an application of new technological tools to the regulation of unfair terms in consumer contracts, see Hans-W. Micklitz, Przemyslaw Palka, and Yannis Panagis, 'The Empire Strikes Back: Digital Control of Unfair Terms of Online Services' (2017) 40 *Journal of Consumer Policy*, 367. Similarly, but with machine learning applied to flag up provisions in on-line privacy policies that are problematic relative to the GDPR, see Giuseppe Contissa, Koen Docter, Francesca Logioia et al., 'Claudette Meets GDPR: Automating the Evaluation of Privacy Policies Using Artificial Intelligence' (25 July 2018) http://ssrn.com/abstract=3208596.

[29] See, e.g., Roger Brownsword, 'Whither the Law and the Law Books: From Prescription to Possibility' (2012) 39 *Journal of Law and Society*, 296; and 'Law, Liberty and Technology' in *The Oxford Handbook of Law, Regulation and Technology*, edited by Roger Brownsword, Eloise Scotford, and Karen Yeung (Oxford University Press 2017), 41.

[30] Lee Bygrave, 'Hardwiring Privacy' in *The Oxford Handbook of Law, Regulation and Technology*, edited by Roger Brownsword, Eloise Scotford, and Karen Yeung (Oxford University Press 2017), 755.

mindful of the technological instruments that increasingly become available for use by regulators.[31] Once the conversation becomes more technocratic, the only things that will slow down the take up of technological management are the pace of technological innovation and resistance by regulatees.

V. Decoding the Legal Debates

What can we expect coherentists and regulatory-instrumentalists to say about smart contracts? In general, whereas coherentists will focus on the fit between smart contracts and the law of contract (typified by the question of whether smart contracts fit the specification for standard 'fiat' contracts that are recognized and enforced by the courts),[32] regulatory-instrumentalists will focus on whether the law is fit for whatever desired purposes are to be served by smart contracts.

Let us suppose that the relevant conversations focus on smart contracts that are used in: (i) business-to-consumer transactions; (ii) business-to-business (commercial) transactions; and (iii) private peer-to-peer transactions.

A. Consumer transactions

The first thing to say about consumer transactions is that the discourse is currently dominated by regulatory-instrumental thinking.[33] On the one hand, a high level (or at any rate, an acceptable level) of consumer protection is sought so that consumers are confident and ready to spend their money. On the other hand, regulators do not want to stifle innovation that might encourage economic growth and greater prosperity.[34] Accordingly, it seems unlikely that we will hear many coherentist voices in debates about the automation of consumer transactions or consumer smart contracts, although there might be a renewed interest in a transactionalist bottom line, as we will explain shortly.

Much of the regulatory-instrumentalist discourse will focus on finding an acceptable balance between the interests of those who supply into the consumer market and the interests of consumers themselves. On the supplier side, we can expect smart contracts to be directed at ensuring that payment is made.[35] Generally, this is unproblematic, but there might

---

[31] Compare Article 25 (data protection by design and by default) of the General Data Protection Regulation (GDPR), Regulation (EU) 2016/679. In this context, note Philipp Hacker, 'Teaching Fairness to Artificial Intelligence: Existing and Novel Strategies against Algorithmic Discrimination in EU Law' (2018) 55 *Common Market Law Review*, 1143. Here, in response to the perceived lack of regulatory fitness of EU anti-discrimination law relative to the operation of algorithmic decisions, an approach that draws on the enforcement tools introduced by the GDPR (such as data protection impact assessments (DPIAs)) together with bias-detecting and bias-minimizing tools developed by computer scientists is proposed. Similarly, it has been argued that the best response to concerns about unfairness in algorithms is to be found in the computer scientists' toolkits; see Joshua A. Kroll, Joanna Huey, Solon Barocas et al., 'Accountable Algorithms' (2017) 165 *University of Pennsylvania Law Review* 633.

[32] This is not a question that I will take up here. Suffice it to say that, where smart contracts are simply used as a tool to give effect to part of a standard fiat contract, there is no difficulty; and, where smart contracts are invisibly embedded in the practice of supply and consumption, the coherentist question is probably the wrong one to be asking. For elaboration, see Roger Brownsword, 'Regulatory Fitness: Fintech, Funny Money and Smart Contracts' (2019) *European Business Organization Law Review*, 1-23 DOI 10.1007/s40804-019-00134-2; and, compare Primavera De Filippi and Aaron Wright, *Blockchain and the Law* (Harvard University Press 2018), 74 et seq.

[33] See Brownsword, 'After Brexit' (n 24).

[34] Compare European Commission, 'Digital Contracts for Europe—Unleashing the Potential of e-Commerce', Communication from the Commission to the European Parliament, the Council and the European Economic and Social Committee, COM (2015) 633 final; European Commission, 'Report on the Fitness Check of EU Consumer and Marketing Law', SWD (2017) 209 final; and European Commission, 'A New Deal for Consumers', Communication from the Commission to the European Parliament, the Council and the European Economic and Social Committee, COM (2018) 183 final.

[35] See, e.g., the features of the Amazon Go store: Mark Harris, 'Amazon Go Day One of a Retail Revolution?' (*The Guardian*, 23 January 2018), 31.

need to be some restriction on applications that are judged to be unacceptable. For example, recalling the case of a consumer-debtor who fails to make payment on time, some might argue that any use of technological instruments (such as disabling the use of a product or service) should be 'proportionate' (see also Chapter 16 by Ortolani in this volume).

On the consumer side, unfair terms (on black lists and grey lists) will continue to be regulated. As we have already said, legislative provisions going back nearly fifty years that in effect black-list certain terms have taken out transactionalism; and, with legislative grey lists, such as that in Directive 93/13/EEC on unfair terms in consumer contracts, the reasonableness of a term will not depend—at any rate, not for the most part—on transactional considerations. If a smart machine that procures to the consumer's needs fails to spot a black-listed term, the legislative protection will still be in place. If the goods or services supplied fall below the regulatory requirements for fitness and quality, consumers will need a simple and straight-forward remedy, albeit with a human back in the loop. If there is a malfunction, such as too many orders being placed or a pricing error, the regulatory regime might cap the consumer's liability. If the technologies are to be used, consumers need to have confidence in them.

This leaves the transactionalist bottom line. Let us suppose that consumers have a choice of automated service providers, each provider offering a package of terms and conditions. Some of these packages will be relatively narrow and specialized, others will be far broader. Within these broader packages, defaults will be set for supplying needs that are widely regarded as basic, repeat, and routine. However, there will be goods and services that some individuals will choose to treat as routine while others will want to treat them as non-routine (meaning that they will be ordered only as and when they are specifically requested). Perhaps, there will be some goods and services which will never be ordered without the specific request of the consumer. So, contract is the basis on which consumers sign up to a particular package and, within the package, specific authorization is sometimes required for non-routine purchases. The critical point is that transactionalists will insist that, insofar as the package contract is concerned, the ideal-typical contractual conditions must be satisfied; or, as Margaret Radin says, 'if the future of contract makes it ever more clear that the only point of choice is whether or not to buy the product-plus-terms, we could focus our attention on making that choice really a choice'.[36]

That said, as the balance changes between fully automated and non-automated consumption, there will probably be defaults and nudges towards automated packages. This might well be viewed as acceptable when it is reasonable to assume that this is what most consumers want. In time, consumers who want to consume in the old-fashioned way might find that this is no longer a practical option. In time, the justification for what is, in effect, imposed automation is not that it rests on consensually agreed packages but that it serves the general welfare. Instead of transactionalism, the justification is utility, based on an acceptable distribution of benefit and risk. Instead of a last-stand coherentist approach, we revert to regulatory-instrumentalist thinking.

Once we are thinking in a regulatory-instrumentalist way, might there be some interest in a technocratic approach? Even if the content of the rules is aligned with regulatory objectives, there are reasons for thinking that a rule-based approach to consumer protection, such as that in the Consumer Rights Act 2015, is relatively ineffective in practice. The problem is that neither consumers nor suppliers are fully aware of their legal rights and responsibilities; for top-of-the-market suppliers, brand and reputation is far more important than legal compliance (so they may over-comply); for bottom-of-the-market suppliers, they can get away with non-compliance; protective agencies are under-resourced; litigation is too expensive

---

[36] Margaret Radin, 'Humans, Computers, and Binding Commitments' (2000) 75 *Indiana Law Journal*, 1161. If the choice is simply too complex for consumers, the alternative is to leave it to regulators to black-list some terms, to require other terms to be set aside for separate explicit agreement, and to require other terms to be conspicuously displayed.

and repeat players are advantaged, and so on. If a technological fix can be applied to greater effect, without negative side-effects, it might appeal to the state.

A technocratic approach might also appeal to those who are actually dealing in the consumer marketplace. On the one side, suppliers might be attracted by technological measures that protect their economic interests. For example, they might be attracted by technological platforms that guarantee payment; or by technologies, such as those that allow for the disabling of the benefit of the contract. However, as we have already suggested, the state is unlikely to stand by and allow suppliers to engage in technological self-help where this has unacceptable negative effects for consumers. On the other side, consumer associations might be attracted by some assistive technologies that can improve the position of their members.[37]

B. Commercial transactions

As with consumer transactions, we should expect the dominant discourse in response to smart (commercial) contracts to be regulatory-instrumental. The leading questions will be about identifying and managing the risks. However, there might be some echoes of coherentism.

First, where big businesses agree their own club rules for the use of automated transactions, this might be to the significant disadvantage of smaller business contractors. If so, there might be pressure from coherentist transactionalists to take a harder look at the validity of the latter's supposed consent.

Second, although, as we have said, relationalists will not worry too much about how smart contracts fit with a transactional template, they might well return (like coherentists) to the originating agreement, which they will regard as important for their assessment of the parties' reasonable expectations.

That said, much of the discourse will be concerned in a typically regulatory-instrumentalist way with assessing and managing the risks. Assuming that a community sees benefits (such as reducing court enforcement costs or designing in compensatory arrangements that are a workaround relative to restrictions in the law of contract [such as third-party claims]) in entrusting transactions to smart technologies, the conventional wisdom will be that regulators need to assess whatever risks there might be and put in place acceptable measures of risk management.

Of course, the risks will vary from one kind of contract to another. We can place some transactions, such as the one-off exchange between contractors, at one end of the spectrum of duration and complexity and other transactions, such as major construction contracts, at the opposite end. Once smart machines run the simple exchange at one end of the relational spectrum, they will take over relatively simple formation and performance functions—executing payments is the paradigmatic example. At the other end of the spectrum, there will be a range of in-contract decisions to be made, for example, involving variation, renegotiation, exercises of discretion, serving notices, and so on. Here, the problem is not that the technologies are unlikely to be up to the task but that some contractors might be reluctant to yield such decisions to the machines or, at any rate, they might want to retain control.

In general, there are at least five kinds of risks that might be anticipated as follows. First, there might be a malfunction in the technology. This means that the regulatory framework must provide for the correction of the malfunction (e.g. completion of performance or setting aside a transaction that should not have been formed). The required corrective measures might include rescission or rectification of transactions on which the malfunction has impacted (which, if smart contracts run on blockchain, could be somewhat problematic) as well as arrangements for compensation and insurance. Second, the integrity of the

---

[37] Compare n 28.

technology might be compromised by unauthorized third-party acts. Acts of this kind will need to be covered by the criminal law or tort law or both, and there will need to be provision for the adjustment of losses so occasioned. Third, the way that the technology functions (not malfunctions) might mean that some decisions are made that do not align with the preferences or interests of the human who is relevantly connected to the transaction. This suggests that regulators might need to find ways of bringing humans back into the loop for critical decisions, capping the financial loss that can be generated by the machine, or putting humans in control (just like principals) of the terms and conditions of the machine's authorization. Fourth, as the famous flash crash of 6 May 2010 reminds us, fully automated algorithmic trading can involve systemic risks to whole markets and not just to individual contractors.[38] This implies that the regulatory framework needs to make provision for human oversight of markets along with powers to intervene and to suspend trading and transactions.[39] Finally, although the technologies seem to comply with general legal requirements, the fact that they have 'black-box' elements might seem unduly risky[40]—particularly, for example, if there is a concern that they might be operating in unlawful discriminatory ways.[41] This implies that regulators either have to grant a degree of immunity to these technologies (reflecting how far the risk of unlawful practice can be tolerated) or introduce measures to constrain such practices.[42]

If the state is content largely to leave commercial contractors to self-regulate, then the adoption of smart contracts is likely to be at the initiative of business contractors themselves. Coherentists, as we have suggested, might question whether parties who sign up for the club rules do so on a free and informed basis as required by transactionalism; but they might also want to query the use of smart contracts where they code in some arrangement that would not be enforced by the law of contract (as in, say, third-party claims in networks).[43]

On the face of it, though, provided that the effect achieved by technological means is not incompatible with some prohibition or rule of public policy, but simply would not be enforced if presented to a court as a matter of contract law, there is surely no problem. If, however, coherentists see a problem here, we are likely to find a tension between the coherentist and regulatory-instrumentalist approaches, with the latter prevailing eventually.

C. Peer-to-peer transactions

Following in the footsteps of eBay, we find a burgeoning 'sharing economy' with online platforms (such as Uber and Airbnb) facilitating peer-to-peer consumer service provision, whether for taxis or accommodation, etc.[44] In practice, the operation and growth of these

---

[38] See Frank Pasquale and Glyn Cashwell, 'Four Futures of Legal Automation' (2015) 63 *UCLA Review Discourse*, 38–39.

[39] Compare Philip Paech, 'The Governance of Blockchain Financial Networks' (2017) LSE Law, Society and Economy Working Papers 16/2017, 18.

[40] Generally, see Frank Pasquale, *The Black Box Society* (Cambridge, Mass: Harvard University Press 2015).

[41] See, e.g., Cathy O'Neil, *Weapons of Math Destruction* (London: Allen Lane 2016).

[42] For advocacy of technocratic measures, see, e.g., Hacker (n 31) and Kroll et al. (n 31).

[43] On networks, see, e.g., Roger Brownsword, 'Network Contracts Revisited' in *Networks: Legal Issues of Multilateral Contracts*, edited by Marc Amstutz and Gunther Teubner (Hart, 2009), 31; 'Contracts in a Networked World' in *Commercial Contract Law: Transatlantic Perspectives*, edited by Larry di Matteo, Qi Zhou, Severine Saintier, and Keith Rowley (Cambridge University Press 2012), 116; 'Contracts with Network Effects: Is the Time Now Right?' in *The Organizational Contract: From Exchange to Long-Term Network Cooperation in European Contract Law*, edited by Stefan Grundmann, Fabrizio Cafaggi, and Giuseppe Vettori (Ashgate 2013), 137; and 'Smart Transactional Technologies, Legal Disruption, and the Case of Network Contracts' (Cambridge University Press forthcoming). Specifically, on smart contracts and networks, see Florian Idelberger, 'Connected Contracts Reloaded—Smart Contracts as Contractual Networks' in *European Contract Law in the Digital Age*, edited by Stefan Grundmann (Intersentia 2018), 205.

[44] See, e.g., Vanessa Mak, 'Regulating Contract Platforms, the Case of Airbnb' in *European Contract Law in the Digital Age*, edited by Stefan Grundmann (Intersentia 2018), 87.

networks is provoking at least three kinds of concern:[45] (i) about the compliance responsibilities of the platform providers;[46] (ii) about the status of service providers;[47] and (iii) about
the adequacy and application of the law of contract. Pending the resolution of such questions, the Commission has taken a conspicuously regulatory-instrumentalist approach by
emphasizing that the 'EU should proactively support the innovation, competitiveness and
growth opportunities offered by [the sharing economy]' while, at the same time, ensuring
'fair working conditions and adequate and sustainable consumer and social protection.'[48]

If smart contracts are introduced into the gig economy, the dominant discourse is likely to
be of a regulatory-instrumentalist kind but, if particular disputes arise in the courts, where
claimants are pleading a breach of contract, there will be a coherentist strand to the debates.
Although this is largely uncharted territory, the coherentist view might be that claims have
to be assessed as if these were arrangements between private parties (needing to displace the
presumption that they do not intend to create legal relations and without the protections that
consumers have when they deal with business contractors), and that the platform providers
have no responsibility to either of the peer-to-peer parties beyond those explicitly written
into the particular contracts. If this generates results that are out of line with the background
policy thinking in relation to the cultivation of this economy, there might well be some
regulatory-instrumentalist intervention and it might be technologically assisted.[49]

This leaves the possibility that the platform providers themselves might wish to engineer
into the transaction some effects that might be problematic if pursued as a matter of contract
law. As with self-regulating use of smart contracts by the business community, initiatives of
this kind will have to be cross-checked for their lawfulness. However, I take it that, other
things being equal, the fact that the courts applying the law of contract would not assist
party A, say, to recover compensation from third-party C, will not be an effective objection
to the employment of smart contract technologies that ensure precisely that A does receive
compensation from C.[50]

VI. Concluding Remarks

By way of a conclusion, we can return to the questions that we posed at the beginning
of the chapter. How will lawyers engage with smart contracts? What kinds of things are
contract lawyers likely to say? Do smart contracts signify the end of contracts, the end of
transactionalism, and the end of contract law?

---

[45] See, e.g., Larry Di Matteo, 'Regulation of Share Economy: A Consistently Changing Environment' in *Digital
Revolution: Challenges for Contract Law in Practice*, edited by Reiner Schulze and Dirk Staudenmayer (Nomos
2016), 89–109.
[46] See the Judgment of the Court of Justice of the European Union in Case C-434/15, *Asociación Profesional
Élite Taxi v. Uber Systems Spain SL* (December 20, 2017), where Uber is treated as providing transport, rather than
information society services and, thus, is subject to the local licensing regulations for taxi services.
[47] See, e.g., Duncan Robinson and Madhumita Murgia, 'European Court Takes up the Question: What is Uber?'
(*FT.com*, 28 November 2016), https://www.ft.com/content/f2774c9a-b566-11e6-ba85-95d1533d9a62.
[48] European Commission, 'A European Agenda for the Collaborative Economy', Communication from the
Commission to the European Parliament, the Council, the European Economic and Social Committee and the
Committee of the Regions, COM (2016) 356 final, 16.
[49] According to Mak (n 44), 97, the main concern in the host–guest relationship in Airbnb settings 'is not
related to the terms of the contract but rather to the potential lack of financial recourse for a guest who suffers
damage in the host's rental space'. If this concern crystallizes, a regulatory-instrumentalist response will surely be
required. Compare Grundmann and Hacker (n 1), 22–26.
[50] Of course, in some legal regimes, it might be possible for A to receive compensation from third-party C by
relying on an action in tort or restitution. My point is simply that I assume that it will be no objection to a smart
contract that it has the effect of transferring a compensatory sum from C to A in circumstances where a court
would not order such a transfer if A brought an action in contract against C. Moreover, other things being equal,
I assume this to be so irrespective of whether A might have an alternative cause of action against C and irrespective
of the local judicial view about reliance on tort or restitution to get around restrictions in contract law.

In relation to the first couple of questions, we can expect lawyers to relate to smart contracts either as coherentists or as regulatory-instrumentalists. In courtrooms and in litigation settings, lawyers are likely to reason like coherentists. As coherentists, they will ask how the new transactional phenomena fit with existing thinking in contract law. That will produce both transactionalist and relationalist responses. In both variants, coherentists might be able to go further than we might expect in forcing the facts of smart contracts to fit into the existing paradigm, but the relationalist variant has more flexibility and should experience less strain. Away from courtrooms or in settings that are more obviously policy-orientated, lawyers are likely to reason like regulatory-instrumentalists. From a state perspective, the use of smart contracts in the consumer marketplace is likely to be one of the hot spots for regulatory debate and, possibly, the sharing economy will give rise to some questions about an acceptable balance of interests. From the perspective of self-regulating businesses, the use of smart contracts might raise both coherentist and regulatory-instrumentalist voices in defence of smaller business parties and coherentists might question how far it is permissible, even if it is technically possible, to use smart contracts in ways that do not mirror traditional contracts and contract law.[51]

In relation to the latter questions, we need to 'get real' about transactionalism. Ideal-typical transactionalism was left behind in the nineteenth century. That said, if the accept-ability of smart contracts is seen to hinge on anchoring agreements or the like, particularly in the consumer marketplace, then there might be a revival of transactionalist thinking. As for concerns about the end of contract, we again need to get real. Contract qua transactionalism is not to be found in the consumer marketplace and, in the business community, contract is, at least, as much about relational dealing as it is about transactionalism. However, there might be pockets of business dealing where transactionalism, and contract in this sense, survives, smart contracts notwithstanding. What will not survive in a world of automated transactions, where humans are taken out of the loop, is face-to-face dealing of the kind evoked by the traditional idea of contracts and haggling in a market place. Arguably, as we have said, something like this needs to survive in relation to the anchoring agreement or signing up to the club rules. However, just as autonomous vehicles signify the end of cars as we have known them, smart contracts signify the end of contracts as we have known them. Moreover, once humans are out of the loop, rules of law that previously guided the conduct of humans (whether drivers or transactors) are redundant. To this extent, this does signal the end of the law of contract.

This leaves many questions unanswered. For example, automation is fine but can a community afford to lose the skill of contracting? It is one thing to map the different ways in which lawyers are likely to relate to smart contracts, but how should they relate? Should we, as Holmes apparently thought, follow the regulatory-instrumentalist path (because coherentism does not necessarily address the right questions)?[52] Even if transactions are largely automated, are there not still *Rule of Law* concerns implying that there will be some limits on the permitted characteristics of smart contracts?[53] If so, will the law of contract come

---

[51] Compare Aaron Wright and Primavera De Filippi, 'Decentralized Blockchain Technology and the Rise of *Lex Cryptographia*' (25 July 2017) https://papers.ssrn.com/sol3/papers.cfm?abstract_id=2580664, 26. Here, having raised the question of what is legally binding versus technically binding, and having noted that there might be some divergence between what the law of contract will enforce or invalidate and what smart contracts, operating within their own closed technological framework, will enforce or invalidate, the authors conclude that while 'implementing basic contractual safeguards and consumer protection provisions into smart contracts is theoretically possible, it may prove difficult given the formalized and deterministic character of code'. However, beyond the question of technical possibility, there is the question of how the state manages the conflict between the law of consumer contracts and the actual operation of smart contracts. In other words, is there an implicit requirement that the latter should be congruent with the former?

[52] See David Rosenberg, 'The Path Not Taken' (1997) 110 *Harvard Law Review*, 1044.

[53] See Roger Brownsword, 'Technological Management and the Rule of Law' (2016) 8 *Law, Innovation and Technology*, 100.

in through the back door? And, if so, will it be a coherentist or regulatory-instrumentalist mind-set that we find coming in? To which, no doubt, the smart answer is that we will simply have to wait and see.

VII. Bibliography

Arthur W. Brian, 'The Second Economy' (2011) *McKinsey Quarterly*, https://www.mckinsey.com/business-functions/strategy-and-corporate-finance/our-insights/the-second-economy, accessed on 16 February 2019.

Bayern Shawn, Burri Thomas, Grant Thomas et al., 'Company Law and Autonomous Systems: A Blueprint for Lawyers, Entrepreneurs, and Regulators' (2017) 9 *Hastings Science and Technology Law Journal*, 135.

Brownsword Roger, 'After *Investors*: Interpretation, Expectation and the Implicit Dimension of the "New Contextualism"' in *The Implicit Dimensions of Contract*, edited by David Campbell, Hugh Collins, and John Wightman (Hart 2003).

Brownsword Roger, 'Network Contracts Revisited' in *Networks: Legal Issues of Multilateral Contracts*, edited by Marc Amstutz and Gunther Teubner (Hart 2009).

Brownsword Roger, 'Contracts in a Networked World' in *Commercial Contract Law: Transatlantic Perspectives*, edited by Larry di Matteo, Qi Zhou, Severine Saintier, and Keith Rowley (Cambridge University Press 2012).

Brownsword Roger, 'Whither the Law and the Law Books: From Prescription to Possibility' (2012) 39 *Journal of Law and Society*, 296.

Brownsword Roger, 'Contracts with Network Effects: Is the Time Now Right?' in *The Organizational Contract: From Exchange to Long-Term Network Cooperation in European Contract Law*, edited by Stefan Grundmann, Fabrizio Cafaggi, and Giuseppe Vettori (Ashgate 2013).

Brownsword Roger, 'The Law of Contract: Doctrinal Impulses, External Pressures, Future Directions' (2014) 31 *Journal of Contract Law*, 73.

Brownsword Roger, 'Technological Management and the Rule of Law' (2016) 8 *Law, Innovation and Technology*, 100.

Brownsword Roger, 'Law, Liberty and Technology' in *The Oxford Handbook of Law, Regulation and Technology*, edited by Roger Brownsword, Eloise Scotford, and Karen Yeung (Oxford University Press 2017).

Brownsword Roger, 'After Brexit: Regulatory Instrumentalism, Coherentism, and the English Law of Contract' (2018) 34 *Journal of Contract Law*, 139.

Brownsword Roger, 'The E-Commerce Directive, Consumer Transactions and the Digital Single Market: Questions of Regulatory Fitness, Regulatory Disconnection and Rule Redirection' in *European Contract Law in the Digital Age*, edited by Stefan Grundmann (Intersentia 2018).

Brownsword Roger, 'Regulatory Fitness: Fintech, Funny Money and Smart Contracts' (2019) *European Business Organization Law Review*, 1-23 DOI 10.1007/s40804-019-00134-2.

Brownsword Roger, 'Smart Transactional Technologies, Legal Disruption, and the Case of Network Contracts' (Cambridge University Press forthcoming).

Bygrave Lee, 'Hardwiring Privacy' in *The Oxford Handbook of Law, Regulation and Technology*, edited by Roger Brownsword, Eloise Scotford, and Karen Yeung (Oxford University Press 2017).

Carr Nicholas, *The Glass Cage* (Vintage 2015).

Case C-434/15, *Asociación Profesional Élite Taxi v. Uber Systems Spain SL* (20 December 2017) Judgment of the CJEU.

Contissa Giuseppe, Docter Koen, Lagioia Francesca et al., 'Claudette Meets GDPR: Automating the Evaluation of Privacy Policies Using Artificial Intelligence' (25 July 2018) https://ssrn.com/abstract=3208596, accessed on 16 January 2019.

De Filippi Primavera and Wright Aaron, *Blockchain and the Law* (Harvard University Press 2018).

Di Matteo Larry, 'Regulation of Share Economy: A Consistently Changing Environment' in *Digital Revolution: Challenges for Contract Law in Practice*, edited by Reiner Schulze and Dirk Staudenmayer (Nomos 2016).

European Commission, 'Digital Contracts for Europe—Unleashing the Potential of e-Commerce', Communication from the Commission to the European Parliament, the Council and the European Economic and Social Committee, COM (2015) 633 final.

European Commission, 'A European Agenda for the Collaborative Economy', Communication from the Commission to the European Parliament, the Council and the European Economic and Social Committee, COM (2016) 356 final.

European Commission, 'Report on the Fitness Check of EU Consumer and Marketing Law', SWD (2017) 209 final.

European Commission, 'A New Deal for Consumers', Communication from the Commission to the European Parliament, the Council and the European Economic and Social Committee, COM (2018) 183 final.

Fuller Lon, *The Morality of Law* (rev. edn, Yale University Press, 1969).

Grundmann Stefan and Hacker Philipp, 'The Digital Dimension as a Challenge to European Contract Law—The Architecture' in *European Contract Law in the Digital Age*, edited by Stefan Grundmann (Intersentia 2018).

Hacker Philipp, 'Teaching Fairness to Artificial Intelligence: Existing and Novel Strategies against Algorithmic Discrimination in EU Law' (2018) 55 *Common Market Law Review*, 1143.

Harris Mark, 'Amazon Go Day One of a Retail Revolution?' (*The Guardian*, 23 January 2018).

Horwitz Morton, *The Transformation of American Law 1780–1860* (Harvard University Press 1977).

Horwitz Morton, *The Transformation of American Law 1870–1960* (Oxford University Press 1992).

Idelberger Florian, 'Connected Contracts Reloaded—Smart Contracts as Contractual Networks' in *European Contract Law in the Digital Age*, edited by Stefan Grundmann (Intersentia 2018).

Kroll Joshua A., Huey Joanna, Barocas Solon et al., 'Accountable Algorithms' (2017) 165 *University of Pennsylvania Law Review*, 633.

Levy Karen, 'Book-Smart, Not Street-Smart: Blockchain-Based Smart Contracts and the Social Workings of Law' (2017) 3 *Engaging Science, Technology, and Society*, 1.

Macaulay Stewart, 'Non-Contractual Relations in Business' (1963) 28 *American Sociological Review*, 55.

Macaulay Stewart, 'Crime and Custom in Business Society' (1995) 22 *Journal of Law and Society*, 248.

Macaulay Stewart, 'The Real and the Paper Deal: Empirical Pictures of Relationships, Complexity and the Urge for Transparent Simple Rules' (2003) 66 *Modern Law Review*, 44.

Mak Vanessa, 'Regulating Contract Platforms, the Case of Airbnb' in *European Contract Law in the Digital Age*, edited by Stefan Grundmann (Intersentia 2018).

Micklitz Hans-W, Palka Przemyslaw, and Panagis Yannis, 'The Empire Strikes Back: Digital Control of Unfair Terms of Online Services' (2017) 40 *Journal of Consumer Policy*, 367.

Mik Eliza, 'Smart Contracts: Terminology, Technical Limitations and Real-World Complexity' (2017) 9 *Law Innovation and Technology*, 269.

Mitchell Catherine, *Contract Law and Contract Practice* (Hart 2013).

Morgan Jonathan, *Contract Law Minimalism* (Cambridge University Press 2013).

O'Neil Cathy, *Weapons of Math Destruction* (Allen Lane 2016).

Paech Phillip, 'The Governance of Blockchain Financial Networks' (2017) LSE Law, Society and Economy Working Papers 16/2017.

Pasquale Frank and Cashwell Glyn, 'Four Futures of Legal Automation' (2015) 63 *UCLA Review Discourse*, 26.

Pasquale Frank, *The Black Box Society* (Harvard University Press 2015).

Petit Nicolas, 'Law and Regulation of Artificial Intelligence and Robots: Conceptual Framework and Normative Implications' (14 March 2017) https://papers.ssrn.com/sol3/papers.cfm?abstract_id=2931339, accessed on 16 January 2019.

Radin Margaret, 'Humans, Computers, and Binding Commitments' (2000) 75 *Indiana Law Journal*, 1125.

Robinson Duncan and Murgia Madhumita, 'European Court Takes Up the Question: What is Uber?' (*FT.com*, 28 November 2016) https://www.ft.com/content/f2774c9a-b566-11e6-ba85-95d1533d9a62, accessed on 16 January 2019.

Rosenberg David, 'The Path Not Taken' (1997) 110 *Harvard Law Review*, 1044.

Rubin Edward, 'From Coherence to Effectiveness' in *Rethinking Legal Scholarship*, edited by Rob van Gestel, Hans-W Micklitz, and Edward Rubin (Cambridge University Press 2017).

Steyn Johan, 'Contract Law: Fulfilling the Reasonable Expectations of Honest Men' (1997) 113 *Law Quarterly Review*, 433.

The Chamber of Digital Commerce, 'Smart Contracts: 12 Use Cases for Business and Beyond: A Technology, Legal and Regulatory Introduction—Foreword by Nick Szabo', www.digitalchamber.org/smartcontracts.html, accessed on 16 January 2019.

Waddams Stephen, *Principle and Policy in Contract Law* (Cambridge University Press 2011).

Wright Aaron and De Filippi Primavera, 'Decentralized Blockchain Technology and the Rise of *Lex Cryptographia*' (25 July 2017) https://papers.ssrn.com/sol3/papers.cfm?abstract_id=2580664, accessed on 16 January 2019.

Zuboff Shoshana, 'Big Other: Surveillance Capitalism and the Prospects of an Information Civilization' (2015) 30 *Journal of Information Technology*, 75.

PART V

CONNECTING THE DOTS: COMPETITIVE ADVANTAGE AND REGULATION IN THE ERA OF BLOCKCHAIN

18

Blockchain Competition

Gaining Competitive Advantage in the Digital Economy—Competition Law Implications

Ioannis Lianos*

I. Introduction

Far from its depiction as a well-defined and linear techno-social phenomenon that developed incrementally over the past three decades following a consistent masterplan, the internet of today has been transformed beyond recognition from its original version. The initial conditions under which it developed were characterized by its distributed technological structure, which relied on an interconnected system of thousands of individual networks enabling people to connect directly with each other through desktop computers.[1] In this system, people were able to create and use new peer-to-peer services without needing to seek permission from any third party.[2] The internet dream was depicted as 'decentralized', 'democratic', and profoundly inspired by the 'hacker ethic' of freedom.[3] This anarchic or libertarian—depending on whom you ask—vision of the internet welcomed the lack of a centre and underpinned a preference for this being a space of atomistic competition where no private or public actor would be able to own or control the medium and its content.

In reality, its technological foundations favoured a distributed, and not decentralized as such, structure of control.[4] Despite the emphasis put on decentralization, a few tens of networks providing international connectivity spanning countries and continents occupy central positions in the global internet topology; these constituting, from a technical perspective,

* The author would like to thank Dr Yannis Stamelakos for useful discussions and some research work and drafting undertaken that was very helpful for completing sections II.B and III.A of this study, Igor Nikolic for helpful research assistance on the intellectual property law issues discussed in this study, and Meg Cochrane for outstanding editing.

[1] Note, however, that ARPANET, the first network to implement the protocol suite Transmission Control Protocol/Internet Protocol (TCP/IP), which became the technical foundation of the internet was administered by a single organization through centralized control.

[2] Yochai Benkler, 'Degrees of Freedom, Dimensions of Power' (2016) 145(1) *Daedalus*, 19 writes that during this first period 'the Internet was not only a technical system but also an innovative organizational system; an institutional system pervaded by commons; a competitive market with low barriers to entry; and, finally, a zeitgeist, cultural habit of mind, or ideology, perhaps best captured by the saying from computer scientist and early architect of the Internet, David Clark: "We reject: kings, presidents and voting. We believe in: rough consensus and running code".'

[3] Jennifer Grannick, 'The End of the Internet Dream?' (*Wired*.com, 17 August 2015) https://www.wired.com/2015/08/the-end-of-the-internet-dream/.

[4] Ashwin Matthew, 'The Myth of the Decentralised Internet' (2016) 5(3) *Internet Policy Review*, https://policyreview.info/node/425/pdf, noting that the Border Gateway Protocol ('BGP'), the technology that enables the interconnection of separate networks to form the global internet relies on three elements: (i) the packet switched networks that break up communications into individual packets of data; (ii) the routing protocols: each of these packets traverses multiple independently administered networks, each of them taking different paths to their eventual destination, at which point they are reassembled, the route being determined by a number of routing protocols which are variations of the BGP, which forms the common routing protocol; and (iii) the topology of these interconnected networks, which is a complex graph 'consisting of over 55,000 individual networks'.

distributed points of control.[5] However, even if technology was not exactly decentralized, the ethos of this first-generation internet was profoundly marked by the decentralization narrative. Benkler, one of the leading legal commentators on internet-related issues, notes how the basic end-to-end design principle characterizing the web and the generality of the protocol made it quite difficult to identify the nature of parties to a communication; it offered 'no control points through which an entity could exclude or constrain another discrete entity attempting to use it'.[6]

This portrayal of the internet, however, soon became antiquated, as the shift to proprietary, controlled devices, software, and networks in the early 2000s led to the emergence of a number of intermediaries and additional points of control, in both technical and economic senses. This led to the accumulation of power by a limited set of influential players that re-shaped the internet's architecture, thereby countering the initial decentralization dynamic. Of course, this re-shaping was not the inevitable consequence of the techno-social structures of the internet, which, as mentioned, were biased towards decentralization, but was entirely due to the strategies (and thus the agency) of a few players, which soon came to control the vast amounts of information generated by internet use.[7] App store centres constitute the first type of these new points of control, as internet access through smartphones, rather than browsers, gained traction, enabling 'the majority of Internet-mediated practice' to be undertaken 'with devices that are either narrowly customizable appliances or controlled on the app store model'.[8] The move to wireless cellular networks and cable broadband offered further possibilities of identification of internet users and usage and the development of strategies of monetization of internet access, now controlled by a limited number of players, in comparison to the old copper network.[9] The rise of Cloud computing, which emerged in order to provide co-location services for data storage and computation, is controlled by a few firms. Resources (including control over data) move away from end-users, towards centralized systems that possess huge processing power and storage capacities.[10] The shift towards the Internet of Things ('IoT') will further revolutionize the medium as it makes possible, for the first time, an 'unconscious' use of the internet and offers a new point of control, to the extent that most of the internet use will occur through smart devices taking action on their own without direct human intervention. Indeed, those that control these devices will control the majority of internet *use*, not just internet access.

Of course, 'centralization and decentralization, in and of themselves, are neither good nor bad'.[11] It all depends on the governance system that the various entities put in place and the possibility of all 'stakeholders', particularly internet users, for them to participate in it and for their interests to be considered. There is no guarantee that a decentralized system will be better than a centralized one, but it is likely that a decentralized system will be more inclusive of all those whose interests are affected by internet use. The developments of the past decade and the more recent rise of the cloud computing model indicate a growing trend towards centralization, which, in conjunction with the development of Big Data, behavioural

---

[5] ibid.   [6] Benkler (n 2), 20.

[7] This process and strategies are well described in Tim Wu, *The Master Switch: The Rise and Fall of Information Empires* (First Vintage Book 2011) and in Tim Wu, *The Attention Merchants: The Epic Scramble to Get Inside Our Heads* (Penguin 2016).

[8] Benkler (n 2), 21.   [9] ibid.

[10] Primavera de Filippi and Smari McCarthy, 'Cloud Computing: Centralization and Data Sovereignty' (2012) 3(2) *European Journal for Law and Technology*, http://ejlt.org/article/view/101/234, observe that '(c)loud services, whether they're infrastructural, platform-based, or software as a service, present a fiction of decentralization to the user in the form of network effects, while the service is increasingly operated by large companies that leverage their position to limit interoperability. Because of their dominant position, large service providers can exert a degree of subjugation never conceived of by smaller and more local services, and a degree of control that would be impossible in a peer-to-peer network.'

[11] Benkler (n 2), 19: 'to imagine either that all centralized power is good and all decentralized power is criminal and mob-like, or that all decentralized power is participatory and expressive and all centralized power is extractive and authoritarian is wildly ahistorical'.

profiling, and online manipulation, let us contemplate a future where a small number of digital platforms will hold immense power that is expanding in all sectors of the digital economy, but also beyond, in politics and culture. This has led some legal scholars to plead for specific regulation and law for the platform economy, in order to introduce some form of democratic control and accountability.[12]

This rather gloomy prediction for our shared internet future may be avoided if blockchain or distributed ledger technology ('DLT') were to deliver on its promises. Blockchain is set to become the 'Internet of value'[13] that will complement the current internet architecture, albeit on very different principles. Blockchain is a technology that facilitates the value exchanges in a secure and decentralized manner, without the need for an intermediary. Its main components are a distributed ledger recording all transactions or assets that are part of its domain, an encryption protecting this ledger from tampering, and the distributed storage of all data through the sharing of excess drive and network capacity on PCs and in data centres. The essence of the 'blockchain dream' is that the decentralization and disintermediation it enables will challenge the current centralized architecture of the internet and will accomplish the expectations of the original internet dream for a borderless and radically democratic space. As Lana Swartz writes, 'the blockchain is meaningful as an inventory of desire ... (i)t is an engine of alterity: an opportunity to imagine a different world and imagine the mechanics of how that different world might be run'.[14]

Blockchain is often opposed to the centralized paradigm of digital platforms that dominate different segments of the digital economy, often reducing consumer choice and privacy. The entities controlling these digital platforms now constitute the largest companies in the world.[15] An essential component of the blockchain dream is that it would finally fulfil the aspiration of a competitive space for the internet, where peer-to-peer exchange without intermediaries would provide immense opportunities to establish alternative communities of economic, social, and political exchange, whilst also resolving the difficulty of combining this with the respect of privacy and digital autonomy.

Protecting consumers' privacy and promoting a competitive market are certainly important ingredients of the blockchain narrative. However, that which really stands out is the perception that DLT may profoundly alter the economic and social structures of our societies, bringing 'disruptive innovation' to all the economic areas in which it would be implemented.[16] DLT has the potential to apply in different economic (and non-economic) digital sectors. It could also be considered as a general purpose technology ('GPT'),[17] to the extent that it satisfies the three conditions usually required for such qualification:[18]

- *Pervasiveness*—DLT should be capable of infiltrating most economic sectors, to the extent that 'they can be used as inputs in a wide range of downstream sectors'.[19] This is

---

[12] See Julie Cohen, 'Law for the Platform Economy' (2017) 51 *U.C. Davis School of Law Review*, 133.

[13] See McKinsey&Company, 'Getting Serious about Blockchain' (*mckinsey.com*, May 2017) https://www.mckinsey.com/industries/high-tech/our-insights/getting-serious-about-blockchain.

[14] Lana Swartz, 'Blockchain Dreams: Imagining Techno-Economic Alternatives after Bitcoin' in *Another Economy is Possible: Culture and Economy in a Time of Crisis*, edited by Manel Castells (Polity Press 2017), 83.

[15] The five largest companies in the world are tech platforms: see Alex Wilhelm, 'Big Tech Goes Five for Five' (*techcrunch.com*, October 2017) https://techcrunch.com/2017/11/06/big-tech-goes-five-for-five/.

[16] There are countless articles in the popular press and in legal and other specialized academic journals referring to the 'disruptive' potential of the blockchain. A search engine search with the words 'blockchain' and 'disruptive innovation' may provide an illustration of this point.

[17] For a similar characterization, see Sinclair Davidson, Primavera De Filippi, and Jason Potts, 'Blockchains and the Economic Institutions of Capitalism' (2018) 14(4) *Journal of Institutional Economics*, 639; Ethan Kane, 'Is Blockchain a General Purpose Technology?' (11 March 2017) https://ssrn.com/abstract=2932585.

[18] Timothy Bresnahan and Manuel Trajtenberg, 'General Purpose Technologies: Engines of Growth?' (1995) 65(1) *Journal of Econometrics*, 83–108; Boyan Jovanovic and Peter Rousseau, 'General Purpose Technologies' in *Handbook of Economic Growth*, edited by Philippe Aghion and Steven Durlauf (Volume 1, Elsevier 2005), 1181.

[19] Boyan Jovanovic and Peter Rousseau, 'General Purpose Technologies' in *Handbook of Economic Growth*, edited by Philippe Aghion and Steven Durlauf (Volume 1, Elsevier 2005), 1181.

certainly the case for blockchain, which although it was first used in cryptocurrencies and FinTech, its implementation has recently expanded to a variety of sectors of the digital economy.

- *Improvement*—the GPT should improve over time and, hence, should keep lowering the costs of its users, leading to increased economies of scale. Blockchain also satisfies this criterion as the blockchain functionalities have improved so as to not only store information of all kinds protected by a cryptographic token, but also to serve as a decentralized platform allowing programmable transactions of assets between a decentralized peer-to-peer network that allows the implementation of any computable function effectuated through smart contracts, that is, in-built executable code.[20]

- *Innovation spawning* (or 'innovation complementarities')—the GPT should make it easier to invent and produce new products or processes. In particular, the development of the IoT, smart property and artificial intelligence provides the possibility to automate, through blockchains (and smart contracts), a number of activities that were previously undertaken by humans acting as intermediaries. This may give rise to the unbundling of various economic activities as the focus shifts to micro-transactions, which may be executed automatically, not only through some decentralized application, but also, in future, through some form of decentralized autonomous organization and algorithmic entities.[21] This could eventually reduce the labour costs involved in the organization of economic activity, in view of the great degree of scalability enabled by artificial intelligence, thus, enabling the development of blockchains for various activities currently organized through centralized platforms.

The explosion of public attention and academic commentary on blockchain that followed the rise of the value of cryptocurrencies in 2016 and 2017 has so far largely focused on the way financial regulation has grappled with this technology and how it engaged with the risks and opportunities its implementation may bring. Financial regulation was one of the first fields of law to collide with the new social reality, to be more precise, the frenzy of cryptocurrencies, initial coin offerings ('ICOs'), and other crypto-assets that took hold of a global public opinion witnessing the meteoric rise of the value of Bitcoin during the same period. What is particularly significant is that regulatory action strived to respond to the exciting narrative of 'disruptive innovation' put forward by blockchain evangelists, in all possible forms, while still trying to cope with the 'parochial' concerns of consumer and investment protection, and the natural cynicism of the lawyer, who sees control, accountability, and governance as the crucial elements to think about when regulating a new technology. Although some more recent work has engaged with the more general theme of the interaction between blockchain and the law,[22] that which has been less explored is the implications of DLT, from both a competition policy and law perspective.

This is a crucial issue. More than the technological innovation brought by DLT, the return to a more competitive and decentralized internet that will break the hold on it by few digital platforms and the organizational innovations that will consequently emerge constitute the principal elements underlying the appeal of the 'blockchain dream' to policy-makers and the public opinion. The relatively few works that have engaged so far with blockchain from a competition law and policy perspective provide useful insights on some of the economics of

---

[20] Roman Alyoshkin, 'Blockchain 2.0. The Purpose of Blockchain' (3 October 2017) https://medium.com/polys-blog/blockchain-2-0-the-purpose-of-blockchain-e84e5a95cdd9.

[21] The possibility of legal entities without human controllers is examined in detail by Lynn Lopucki, 'Algorithmic Entities' (2018) 95 *Washington University Law Review*, 887.

[22] See, Primavera De Filippi and Aaron Wright, *Blockchain and the Law* (Harvard University Press 2018).

DLT and lessons for competition law enforcement.[23] However, a comprehensive study that will not only reflect on the welfare economics of DLT or the implementation of competition law to some blockchain-related conduct, but will attempt to understand the new competition dynamics unleashed by the blockchain revolution is still lacking. Furthermore, understanding how DLT may impact upon competitive advantage is crucial if one is to design a competition law enforcement that will not only be reactive but also proactive and will fully engage with both the protection of consumers (and other stakeholders) and also the promotion of innovation.

This chapter aims to fill this gap. Section II engages initially with the broader perception of blockchain as an antagonistic narrative to that of platforms for the digital economy. The study provides a critical analysis of the decentralization and disintermediation potential of the blockchain and how this perception of DLT may ignore the emergence of blockchain intermediaries and some potential points of control. Section III engages with a discussion of the fundamentals of blockchain competition by exploring the various strategies for acquiring competitive advantage and how these determine the incentives of the various blockchain actors. Two broad categories of competitive advantage are discussed: conventional strategic competitive advantage and 'architectural advantage', the latter of which is less explored in competition law and policy literature. Various economic actors use DLT and the different dimensions of competitive advantage it confers on them in order to enhance their power, i.e. their ability to shape the actions of other actors forming part of their environment. Hence, the discussion over the various forms of competitive advantage is directly linked in Section IV with the social and economic implications of a more expansive use of this new GPT in other areas of economic activity. Science and technology studies literature instructs us that the direction of technological change is profoundly shaped by the interests and positioning of the social forces that promote the use of the new technology, of those who, in the disruptive potential of a new technological paradigm, see the opportunity to re-position themselves more centrally by being able to shape competition.[24] It is no different with blockchain. Following the analysis of the various forms of blockchain competition on product and financial markets, Section V of this chapter reaches some preliminary conclusions as to how DLT transforms the competitive game in the digital economy, from one that centres on a 'winner-takes-all' dynamic with the development of digital platforms to one that focuses on 'co-opetition' in ecosystems. Section VI draws lessons from this broader competition analysis for competition law enforcement. It provides an in-depth discussion of the various forms of DLT-related conduct that may raise competition concerns, as well as reflecting on the broader implications of blockchain competition for existing competition law doctrines, methodologies, and tools.

---

[23] See, inter alia, the work of Christian Catalini and Joshua Gans, 'Some Simple Economics of the Blockchain' (2017), Rotman School of Management Working Paper No. 2874598, MIT Sloan Research Paper No. 5191-16; Christian Catalini and Catherine Tucker, 'Antitrust and Costless Verification: An Optimistic and a Pessimistic View of the Implications of Blockchain Technology' (2018), MIT Sloan Research Paper No. 5523-18; Peder Østbye, 'The Adequacy of Competition Policy for Cryptocurrency Markets' (28 August 2017) https://ssrn.com/abstract=3025732; Jesús Fernández-Villaverde and Daniel Sanches, 'Can Currency Competition Work?' (2016) National Bureau of Economic Research No. w22157; Thibault Schrepel, 'Is Blockchain the Death of Antitrust Law? The Blockchain Antitrust Paradox' (6 October 2018) https://ssrn.com/abstract=3193576; Brad Finney, 'Blockchain and Antitrust: New Tech Meets Old Regs' (2018) 19 *Transactions: The Tennessee Journal of Business Law*, 709; Rory Van Loo, 'Making Innovation More Competitive: The Case of Fintech' (2018) 65 *UCLA Law Review*, 232.

[24] On this fundamental insight, see Giovanni Dosi, 'Technological Paradigms and Technological Trajectories' (1982) 11 *Research Policy*, 147, noting how the development of a technology is contextual to the history of the industrial structures associated with that technology, where the emergence of a new paradigm is often related to new 'Schumpeterian' companies, while its establishment denotes a process of 'oligopolistic stabilization'; Brian Arthur, 'Competing Technologies, Increasing Returns, and Lock-In by Historical Events' (1989) 99(394) *The Economic Journal*, 116, examining competition between two increasing returns technologies and what determines equilibrium selection.

II. Blockchain and Digital Platforms as Alternative Organizational Narratives in the Digital Economy

Decentralization and disintermediation constitute the two most cited benefits of blockchain technology and to a large extent they explain the reason for which DLT is often considered as an important challenge to the power of digital platforms and intermediaries dominating the digital economy. However, the question emerges as to whether this narrative is factually justified. Section A focuses on the basic components of the decentralization and disintermediation story, whilst section B presents an alternative account.

A. The promise of decentralization and disintermediation

The internet era gave rise to online intermediaries and digital platforms controlling and orchestrating value-generating ecosystems that not only offered products and online services, but also provided the infrastructure and tools on which other platform businesses can be built. In contrast, blockchain technology has been widely perceived as promising a decentralized and largely disintermediated model of organization of the digital economy that would dispense with intermediaries and, consequently, the risk of monopolistic bottlenecks. While in the digital platform model only the centralized online platform collects information about past transactions, blockchain offers a distributed decentralized ledger, which keeps a complete record of all past transactions on the network. This enables all participants to have access to information about past transactions and, thus, ensures that no participant to the network enjoys a position of superior bargaining power due to informational asymmetries. This equality is furthered by the transparency of the process: each new transaction is broadcast to the entire network and each participant has the power to determine its authenticity. This breaks with the centralized data silos model of the platform economy, where only some actors have access to this information, as all interactions between the network participants happen through them, thus, enabling them to accumulate data, which, in turn, can help them to increase their bargaining power and to erect barriers to entry.

Of course, blockchain is not a monolith. There exist various types of blockchain, some of which are closer to the centralized ledger model of digital platforms. It is customary to distinguish 'private' or 'federated' blockchains from 'public' blockchains.

A private blockchain is controlled by a centralized entity, like an intranet. Only the entity controlling the blockchain has the possibility to approve participants, to read and/or write new blocks, and to validate the transactions. The entity also benefits from information concerning the identity of the participants. As with digital platforms, users are free to leave a platform in the case that competitive alternatives exist. However, it should be noted that contrary to digital platforms, each participant maintains a replica in sync of the ledger of digitally signed transactions, thus, guaranteeing the immutability of the blockchain. Private blockchains are transparent and can be read in real time by a regulator.

Federated blockchains are private blockchains managed by a consortium of multiple organizations. As with private blockchains, the participants are identified and pre-approved by the entity that manages the blockchain. The consensus process is controlled by a pre-selected set of nodes. R3 constitutes an example of an open-source and federated distributed ledger controlled by a consortium of more than forty financial companies and an ecosystem of more than 200 companies. R3 was put in place in 2015. Its aim was to develop apps for finance and commerce capable of running on its blockchain platform, Corda. The objective was to replace complex legacy systems that could not handle complex transactions and suffered from interoperating difficulties. Private or federated blockchains are usually permissioned, although one cannot exclude the possibility of a 'permission-less', private or federated blockchain (e.g. a Byzantine agreement).[25]

Public blockchains are closer to the decentralized model and are characterized by free entry: anyone may contribute to it by adding a block, execute the consensus protocol, and/or maintain the shared ledger. Public blockchain protocols are open source. In principle, anyone can download the protocol and validate transactions. In this context, the blockchain is considered to be 'permission-less' (e.g. Bitcoin). There is also the possibility that, although in principle open to any participant, the participant should satisfy some conditions. The imposition of such would qualify the public blockchain as 'permissioned'. For instance, anyone can develop a decentralized application ('DApp') on Ethereum *so long as* they purchase some Ether (the native token of this blockchain). The network provides an incentive system in order to encourage more participants to join. This is done with either the release of native tokens or the payment of commission fees to miners and other developers for each transaction added to the chain. Due to its openness and the risk of double-spending, public blockchains need an identity management system. This system enables the participants to the blockchain to achieve consensus. Each node in the network must solve a complex, resource-intensive cryptographic problem ('proof of work') or other mechanisms of pre-approval (e.g. 'proof of stake', etc.) for a new block to be added to the blockchain.

The use of blockchain technology offers numerous advantages, in comparison to interacting across different networks. First, it facilitates the organization of micro-transactions. There is no need for a centralized network intermediating all transactions, nor for administration costs to be incurred for each additional transaction. Blockchain may enable direct transactions to take place between the various nodes of a network, without being necessary for these to be administered from the centre of the network. This greatly reduces transaction costs. Consequently, micro-transactions that were too expensive to organize in the context of a centralized network because their value was lower than the administration costs are now, due to the much lower administrative costs of DLT, economically rational. Blockchain can thus charge lower fees than that which platforms usually charge.

Second, all transactions that run through blockchain benefit from in-built network neutrality, to the extent that the only criterion for processing a transaction is whether the appropriate fee has been paid. Contrary to platforms, it is not technically possible for an entity to either control the traffic in the blockchain network or differentiate the way in which various transactions will be executed in terms of speed, quality, etc. In comparison to neutrality arising from the structure of a blockchain network, for digital platforms neutrality obligations are usually mandated by law.[26]

Third, once a transaction is 'mined' into a block, after a certain period of time it is nearly impossible to reverse it because it would mean that you would have to re-mine the block and all the other blocks added on top of that; this computationally intensive operation would incur high costs that would likely be disproportionate to the value of reversing the original transaction. Transactions in blockchain thus become irreversible, and this reduces the risk of manipulation of the data by an operator, a risk that is very much present with regard to digital platforms.

Fourth, everybody can check the public ledger and verify whether the transaction took place or not, the identity of the sender, and the locations between which the value was

---

[25] A 'Byzantine agreement' or 'Byzantine fault tolerance' exists where participants to the blockchain, which are known and who possess a public key, agree on a concerted strategy to sign with their public key, validating a block as it passes through their node. Once a predefined number of participants sign the block, this is deemed valid and added to the chain.

[26] See, e.g., the 2017, Google Search (Shopping) competition law Case AT.39740 in the EU, regarding search neutrality, or the Proposal for a Regulation of the European Parliament and of the Council on Promoting Fairness and Transparency for Business Users of Online Intermediation Services, 2018/0112 (COD), imposing neutrality requirements in the way digital platforms treat other websites and other businesses with regard to ranking, etc.

transferred. The transparency of the blockchain offers significant advantages to platforms when organizing a network of transactions, as transparency generates institutions-based trust, without that being based on the power of control exercised by an intermediary, as is the case in platform-based networks. This also has profound implications as to the ability of each participant to this network to feel as though they are in control. One of the main features of blockchain-based applications is that users have absolute ownership of their assets (e.g. money, data, etc.) without the need for any kind of custodian (e.g. banks, online intermediaries, etc.). Thus, once someone generates a private key, no other person can claim the assets, confiscate them, or deny access to them.

Fifth, blockchain leads to a reduction of economies of scale and network effects. These well-known features of digital platforms, to a large extent, explain the higher levels of economic concentration in the platform economy. New technologies require important investments and fixed costs for their development, which often lead to network effects (i.e. the use of a product or service by any user increases the product's value for other—potentially all—users). Indeed, the value of the product to one user is positively affected when another user joins and enlarges the network (i.e. 'positive network externalities'). For instance, an additional user of a search engine may increase the quality of search provided by this search engine because the search engine, with its increased stock of queries can, through the data stemming user's expressed preferences, seek to better tailor the results displayed to the user. In turn, this process has the capacity to benefit all users. This 'positive feedback loop' mechanism explains the reason for these markets being so tippy and being characterized as 'winner-takes-most' competition. For instance, there might be fierce competition to conquer a market share advantage over rivals, with regard to the specific technology or standard applying in the industry, as the market may switch almost completely to the winner ('competition for the market').[27] Quite often, these products or services constitute a package of complementary products and technologies, which form a system competing with other systems ('systems competition').[28] The value of the product does not always depend directly on the number of adopters but on the adoption of some complementary products that are bundled or packaged with the first product (think about a book reader and the content of the book).

Network effects lead to collective switching costs and lock-in effects, which reduce competition and may entrench the dominant position of the winner for a significant period of time. Firms are quite imaginative in their business models, sometimes distributing the product for free on one side of the market, thereby inducing more users to join the network and, thus, increasing the value of the product for other users situated on the other, paying side of the market, with this (multi- or two-sided market) platform facilitating the interaction between these two different customer groups. Firms may also use various business practices, such as penetration pricing, where they charge low prices (even below their costs) to gain market share, or strategic bundling of their products in order to gain a foothold in another market prior to expanding its market share in this latter market. In these latter markets, it is possible that firms may incur losses for a significant period of time in order to invest in acquiring market share (either through natural growth or by buying out actual or potential competitors) or in order to constitute one-stop-shop solutions or essential platforms for various groups of customers. Competition between firms takes on unexpected

---

[27] Usual examples include the videotape format war between VHS and Sony's BETAMAX, or the competition between Windows and Intel from one side and Apple from the other for the microcomputer market. For an analysis of competition in open and closed systems see Competition and Markets Authority (UK) and Autorité de la Concurrence (France), 'The Economics of Open and Closed Systems' (2014) Report.

[28] Michael Katz and Carl Shapiro, 'Systems Competition and Network Effects' (1994) 8(2) *Journal of Economic Perspectives*, 93.

forms, such as competing for consumers' attention (or eyeballs), eventually profiling them, and using algorithms in order to predict and possibly manipulate their behaviour.[29]

Blockchain leads to lower network costs, 'both in the phase of bootstrapping a new platform and in the phase of operating it'.[30] With regard to the advancing of a new platform, it is unclear if the development of a blockchain requires lower fixed costs than setting up a traditional centralized platform. Blockchains rely on a number of miners running a cryptographic programme in order to verify the authenticity of the transactions in the decentralized ledger. The first generation of blockchains ('blockchain 1.0') relied on the proof-of-work ('PoW') concept. It required the use of the highest number of central processing units (CPUs) to validate a block. Miners had to go through more computational work in order to prove that a transaction hash is legitimate: the more computers used, the stronger the authenticity of the ledger becomes ('one CPU, one vote').[31] Miners running the cryptographic programme start from the final hash of the current block hashed with the previous block searching for the answer to this mathematical puzzle (the 'proof string'). Once a miner discovers the correct proof string, this is broadcast to the rest of the network of other miners active on the system who will verify if all the transactions are valid and that the proof string broadcasted has, in fact, solved the puzzle. The number of verifications a string receives counts as votes, leading the block with the highest number of verifications to win and, thus, to be officially added to the chain. The reward is released as soon as a new block is added to the chain. This can either consist on a coinbase reward (a native token that compensates the miners) or, in view of the diminishing returns of the coinbase reward, a fee (e.g. a percentage of the transaction). PoW thus relies on competition between network participants (i.e. 'miners') on who will be the first one to validate the transaction.

PoW enables trustless consensus to develop by deterring attacks to the blockchain. This is done by raising the costs of an attack, as a successful attack requires a lot of computational power and a lot of time to do the necessary calculations. Miners perform a lot of calculations in order to generate blocks and maintain the security of the chain. Their role is to ensure the legitimacy of a transaction by avoiding any double-spending. The asymmetry of computational power required by those requesting the addition of a new block in the blockchain, in comparison to the rest of the network, means that, on average, a higher number of calculations needs to be performed each time in order to create a new block. Hence, the more the blockchain grows, the more hash and computational power algorithms are needed in order to generate consensus. The difficulty of the hash depends on the number of users, the network load, and the current computational power used. The algorithm rewards the first miner that has completed this extra computational work and has solved this increasingly difficult mathematical problem, thereby enabling the creation of this additional block or the release of the commission fee.

This computational work involves the consumption of a lot of electricity power and the use of computer hardware only focused on maintaining the operation and security of the blockchain. In addition to these variable costs, blockchain involves high fixed costs concerning storage. Contrary to platforms that may store information on the cloud, by paying a monthly fee for cloud storage, blockchain 1.0 projects require the storage of data indefinitely and, hence, must opt for paying upfront the storage costs. This, in turn, increases fixed costs, which could be considered as a barrier to entry for newcomers. The shift from centralized

---

[29] Frank Pasquale, *The Black Box Society—The Secret Algorithms that Control Money and Information* (Harvard University Press, 2015).

[30] Catalini and Gans (n 23), 12.

[31] Satoshi Nakamoto, 'Bitcoin: A Peer-to-Peer Electronic Cash System' (2008) https://bitcoin.org/bitcoin.pdf, 3, explains that '(i)f the majority were based on one-IP-address-one-vote, it could be subverted by anyone able to allocate many IPs. Proof-of-work is essentially one-CPU-one-vote. The majority decision is represented by the longest chain, which has the greatest proof-of-work effort invested in it.'

to decentralized cloud computing, with data being maintained on both public and private clouds, may, nevertheless, reduce the costs of storage and the significance of this entry barrier. The PoW model is also risky as it may be subject to the '51% attack'. This may occur if a miner or pool of miners have attained 51% of the computing power, thereby providing them with the ability to re-write the entire blockchain. Although this could easily be observed by other participants of the network and could result in the value of the native token of the blockchain collapsing, the attackers may have more to win than to lose, as they many not own any of these native tokens. The risk of centralization is particularly high when the mining activity is concentrated among a limited number of entities or pools, as is the case for Bitcoin mining, because of the costs engendered by the PoW approach.

The high costs of the PoW concept led the second-generation ('blockchain 2.0') projects (based on Ethereum) to switch to the proof-of-stake ('PoS') approach, which requires far less computational power and, thus, far less electricity for the creation of cryptographic proof. In contrast to the PoW system, which takes into account the amount of CPU devoted to the system, in a PoS system it is not the amount of computational power one is willing to spend in order to confirm the legitimacy of the block that counts for the payment of the reward. Rather the creators of a new block are chosen in a deterministic way that depends on the 'stakes' they hold. The weight to their vote is proportional to the ownership stake they hold. For instance, a miner holding 2% of the total bitcoins may have the possibility to mine 1% of the blocks. In PoS, miners are mostly rewarded with transaction fees. The system is preserved from double-spending and attacks by the fact that a cyber-attack, for instance, by someone holding 51% of the computational power of the network may affect the value of the specific digital asset held, with the result that it would make it disadvantageous to attack the network. The majority stake owner is therefore incentivized to maintain a secure network. This system drastically reduces the costs linked to the use of computational power (e.g. energy costs). However, such a system may risk being exposed to the potential for a miner, or a group of miners, to monopolize it, to impose conditions on the rest of the network, which could involve the adoption of exploitative practices or leveraging practices in related markets. Hence, although the PoS approach is more secure than the PoW approach with regard to the risk of a 51% attack, given the importance of the stakes of the miners in preserving the value of the blockchain's assets, one cannot categorically exclude the possibility of abuse.

The incentives of the developers also differ between digital platforms and blockchain. Platforms rely on the indirect network effects they generate to incentivize developers to write applications for their (dominant) platform, as higher consumer use of a platform makes the platform more valuable for producers (this is called 'cross-side network effects'). Blockchain relies on an incentive system based on the venture capital model, whereby early contributors earn tokens for providing the resources (capital and time) needed for the operations of the platform.[32] Developers are attracted by the prospect of potential future profits generated by the appreciation in value of the native token, once the ICO is completed. Following the initial process of development of the blockchain, miners are initially compensated with native tokens; later they are compensated with the payment of transaction fees.

An important difference between the traditional centralized platform model and the blockchain is that users of the latter are less anchored to the specific platform because of the risk of losing the data it contains. This may harm the users to the extent that the harvesting of data contributes to higher performance, as, for instance, search results become more personalized and irrelevant advertising is excluded. An important feature of blockchain is that information is distributed in a decentralized ledger and it is possible for anyone (in the case of public blockchain), or for a number of participants (in the case of a permissioned blockchain) to have access to it, particularly if they decide to switch to a different platform or

---

[32] Catalini and Gans (n 23), 12.

blockchain 'fork'. Contrary to centralized platforms, where users are averse to switching, the replicability of data makes it easier for blockchain to switch to competing forks and abandon the older version of the blockchain.[33] This also has important implications for indirect network effects, as blockchain developers (writing apps) and blockchain operators (e.g. miners) also have fewer reasons to be anchored to a specific platform. It is in their interest to be among the first to contribute to a fork because if such were to attract a considerable number of existing users, in particular at the initial stages of its development, rewards (for mining) may be very high. Hence, contrary to centralized platforms which, due to indirect network effects have the capacity to dissuade competing platforms from entering into the market, by denying them access to an efficient scale (of developers and contributors, etc.), or to maintain a competitive advantage over their competitors, in the case that there is entry, thereby leading to a gap between the fee charged by the incumbent and the fee charged by the entrant, these indirect network externalities are much lower for blockchain.[34]

Sixth, the form that competition may take is different for blockchains than for centralized platforms. As indicated above, competition among platforms mostly takes the form of 'competition for the market', as network effects often lead to 'winner-takes-most' competition, with only one platform controlling, or being the significant player, for a relevant market or, more broadly, a value chain. Thus, markets marked by platform competition are concentrated, sometimes to such an extent that the second or third player in the market may not offer a viable competitive alternative to the established platform, with the result that inter-platform competition remains weak and there is significant inequality in the distribution of market shares among (horizontal) competitors. At the same time, the centralized platform forms a 'bottleneck' with the power to determine the allocation of the surplus generated by the value chain between the various contributors, and, in particular, to keep the overwhelming part of this surplus thereby accumulating significant profits for itself. In view of the (reported) low levels of users switching to competing platforms, platform operators can be confident that the reduction of vertical competition between the different segments of the value chain, with regard to the allocation of the total surplus value generated by the value chain, will not lead to a significant number of applications developers deserting their platform. Hence, value chains dominated by digital platforms are also marked by a very unequal distribution of profits between the relevant established platform and other participants in the ecosystem. Users are also unable to identify how much value they add to the platform's operations, as the history of transactions is not public and this information is only collected and stored by the platform or online intermediary.

In contrast, blockchain enables various forms of competition to intensify. First, due to the reduced significance of direct and indirect network effects, inter-platform competition is more intense. Both users and app developers may switch more easily to competing platforms. If a platform economy is characterized by 'winner-takes-most' competition or 'competition for the market', blockchain reverts the focus to 'competition in the market', as lower entry costs and the reduced significance of network effects have the potential to lead to less concentrated, more contestable markets. Quite significantly, horizontal competition is not only limited between the blockchain and other competing platforms but may also consist in competition from a 'fork' blockchain (i.e. the blockchain with a different set of rules), should the developers and users of a blockchain decide to migrate to the new one because of their dislike of the former system's existing rules or blockchain governance. In this case, the information in the blockchain will be replicated, thereby levelling the playing field between the 'old' and the 'fork' blockchain. At the same time, through their private key, users maintain

---

[33] Joseph Abadi and Markus Brunnermeier, 'Blockchain Economics' (1 May 2018) https://scholar.princeton.edu/sites/default/files/markus/files/blockchain_paper_v2c.pdf.

[34] ibid., 3.

information about their contribution to the value of the blockchain. The fact that this information is not controlled by a centralized ledger makes it possible to devise ways to compensate users for the value they add. Thus, vertical competition is more intensive and the surplus generated by the value chain more fairly distributed among the various contributors.

B. The new blockchain intermediaries and centralization dynamics

Despite the various advantages of blockchain in comparison to centralized platforms and the dominant decentralization narrative, the choice of a decentralized distributed ledger does not dispense of any risk of intermediation and centralization.

I will first focus on intermediaries. As it is rightly noted by Arruñada, '[…] blockchain applications require the intervention of between parties' intermediaries to write the code, run the system, and store data'.[35] There are different types of intermediaries.[36]

Oracles serve as links between the blockchain and external 'off blockchain' events that may trigger the enforcement of smart contracts when these external conditions reach the level specified in the contract. Oracles bring data from an outside source onto the blockchain. There is a number of companies specializing in connecting web applications programming interfaces ('APIs), which allow software to interact with another piece of software), or any other data sources, thus, enabling the implementation of smart contracts and the interaction of the blockchain with the context external to it. In view of the relative failure of a decentralized and distributed Oracles network, such as Orisi for cryptocurrency contracts in which a large number of players operated as blockchain oracles reporting data from the outside,[37] more centralized oracles solutions were developed, either by trusting the companies controlling the data sources or by involving third parties that developed authentication and verification procedures for external data sources—a distributed but not a decentralized oracle system). Oracles may even be algorithmic entities operating on the basis of sensors or other trusted data-feeds generated by devices (in the IoT environment), Big Data harvested from the internet, or other trusted web application programming interfaces ('APIs'), thus, establishing a reliable connection between these APIs and the DApps. Therefore, their main function is to connect the blockchain to the real world. They may also serve as reliable sources of information about the external world when engaged in online dispute resolution systems.[38]

Curators perform a variety of technical functions, such as contributing to the selection of proposals coming from the contractors and/or preventing 51% attacks that could undermine the integrity of the blockchain.[39] This form of architecture was selected for the decentralized autonomous organisation ('DAO') launched in 2016, with twelve curators, most of them respected and trusted Ethereum programmers, who were able to whitelist proposals (i.e. add contractor addresses to the DAO whitelist), by checking the identity of people submitting them (making sure that the code of the proposal actually originates from the contractor, thus, confirming that the proposal comes from an identified entity or person). These curators were also able to freeze the DAO activities in case of attack.[40] The nature of this

---

[35] Benito Arruñada, 'Blockchain's Struggle to Deliver Impersonal Exchange' (2018) 19 *Minnesota Journal of Law, Science and Technology*, 65.

[36] ibid.

[37] See GitHub, Orisi White Paper (29 November 2014) https://github.com/orisi/wiki/wiki/Orisi-White-Paper.

[38] For instance, Jurico is a decentralized blockchain-based dispute resolution platform designed to help resolve smart contract-related disputes by allowing users to open disputes and then oracles to vote on who won the dispute, with the most votes making the decision; see Oliver Dale, 'JUR ICO: Decentralised Dispute Resolution Platform' (*Blockonomi.com*, 11 July 2018) https://blockonomi.com/jur-ico/.

[39] ibid.

[40] See Stephen Tual, 'On DAO Contractors and Curators' (*blog.slock.it*, 10 April 2016) https://blog.slock.it/on-contractors-and-curators-2fb9238b2553.

intermediary role involves curators being appointed by the token holders (most likely in the form of a 'multisig' contract) but potentially being fired by them at will. This control structure avoids the risk of centralization.

For its operation, blockchain also requires the presence of a number of intermediaries, whose function is either to keep the blockchain operational, in principle by validating the transactions/blocs, or to enable transactions between different blockchains, thus, ensuring that the native tokens of one blockchain may be exchanged with those of another.

The first operation is performed by *miners*. 'Mining', in blockchain terminology, is the procedure that aggregates pending transactions in a block and by making a vast amount of cryptographic calculations ('hash functions') produces a valid outcome that satisfies a list of strict, predefined conditions encoded in software. The block is appended to the head of the blockchain and the procedure starts all over again. The miner is rewarded for the processing power spent to produce the block with either a newly generated coin or by a transaction fee. The Bitcoin architecture is a deflationary policy designed and implemented on a protocol level, with the quantity of bitcoins minted per block being reduced by 50% every four years ('halving period'). Initially, the block reward was fifty BTC, then twenty-five, and in July 2016, it was reduced to 12.5. The aim is to ensure that the number of bitcoins in existence will not exceed 21 million and the last satoshis (i.e. the smallest denomination, one hundred millionth of a bitcoin) will have been mined by the year 2140.

During the first years of the network, a simple desktop computer could be used to mine bitcoins, which is compatible with Satoshi's vision of 'one CPU, one vote'. However, as it became more popular and its price appreciated, the attention bitcoins received led to the development of more efficient hashing hardware, thereby excluding from the market normal miners who were previously mining Bitcoin using their consumer grade hardware, such as computer processing units ('CPUs') and graphic processing units ('GPUs'). GPUs, and then field-programmable gate array ('FPGA') devices, were used by sophisticated users for mining. Nowadays this can only be done by powerful specialized hardware that performs several billions of hash operations per second: application-specific integrated circuits ('ASICs'). These ASIC devices, with chips developed for the purpose of mining specific algorithms, were developed by a small number of top Chinese companies. This has made Bitcoin mining unprofitable for individuals and has led to the creation of big mining facilities, the so-called *mining farms*. Usually, these farms are built in places that provide cheap electricity, preferably combined with a cold environment for facilitating the dissipation of the excessive heat produced by the mining equipment. Most of them are located in China (60% of the total hashpower) due to the cheap coal-based electricity, as well as the abundance of hydro-electric facilities, while most other locations are based on far north countries such as Canada, Sweden, and Iceland. These facilities earn important revenues but they need to sell a big portion of the bitcoins produced in order to pay the bills and re-invest in hardware equipment since this becomes obsolete rather quickly. Mining pools enable the aggregation of various miners that want to invest in mining equipment but do not have a high enough hash-rate. The miners involved form big groups. They combine their computational power and share the resulting profits between them according to each individual's contribution. At the moment, there are many pools with different economic models but most of them take a portion of the profits as a fee. Other cryptocurrencies, such as Bitcoin Gold ('BTG') have adopted ASIC-resistant algorithms to avoid the problem of mining centralization by big players and to instill trust in normal miners that they can use their average hardware for mining. This has led to a huge demand in GPUs. The stock of big manufacturers, like NVIDIA, have been emptied, whilst the prices of GPUs have rapidly increased. This may, in itself, lead to some degree of centralization as fewer miners will be able to afford them and reach the minimum efficient scale.

Digital wallets and *digital exchanges* enable the exchange of native tokens of different blockchains, which, in turn, enables the development of blockchain-based digital marketplaces.

Digital wallets can be both software and hardware. The *hardware* wallets provide strong, banking-grade security. The keys that manage the funds are generated by the hardware whilst the transactions are signed internally and then broadcasted. Hence, there is no online exposure of the keys. This provides a lot more safety and reduces the potential for hacking as no connection to the internet is required. There are three main hardware wallet providers: Ledger, which provides wallets for the average user ('Ledger Nano S/Blue') as well as security solutions ('Ledger Vault') for customers that demand higher guarantees (e.g. banks and hedge funds), Trezor, and KeepKey.

Software wallets, on the contrary, do not require the purchase of any specialized device. They can run on a smartphone or desktop. They are less secure than the hardware ones because the attack vector is larger, mostly because these devices require access to the internet and in order to be fully secure the underlying software platform needs to be secure, which is never the case; for example a vulnerability in the Android OS can give full access to the wallet app and a potential hacker can steal the relevant funds. Most software wallets are open-source projects, the development of which was initially dependent on user donations. Consequently, many of the wallets that have been very popular in previous years have stopped being used due to halts in development. Since all of them are free to download and install, the common business model and, hence, the main source of revenue, is based on fees charged for additional services and support. Recently, driven by the ICO explosion, most of them have found another way to profit. They advertise and promote their service and support efforts, usually through the so called 'airdrops' (free token delivery to the wallet users). Some of the most popular wallets are Electrum, Green Address, Coinomi, Bitcoin.info, Jaxx, BitGo, and Mycellium. An interesting development in this area is the idea of a hybrid approach that integrates a fully operational exchange into the wallet. Wallet providers could take advantage of their user base and provide a user-friendly way for their users to buy and trade cryptocurrencies at the same time whilst they, as the providers, receive the fees charged for the services offered. One of the first attempts of this is Eidoo, a multicurrency wallet that aims to provide the service of a decentralized exchange. It is of great interest to note here that companies from the traditional FinTech world are starting to consider this route as well. Revolut, a digital banking solution offering peer-to-peer payment options, pre-paid cards, and multi-currency accounts and exchange, a few months ago announced the launch of a crypto-exchange offering their users the possibility of buying, storing, and trading certain cryptocurrencies.

Exchanges that act as intermediaries between the people that want to trade blockchain-based cryptocurrencies have thus far constituted the most profitable business model that has emerged in the blockchain space. The market, in contrast to regulated ones (e.g. stock exchanges) operates 24/7 and the volatility of the prices is huge. The exchanges offer a variety of trading products such as margin trading, with up to 100x leverage on occasions. At this moment, since mining cryptocurrencies is either too expensive, due to investment in specialized hardware and power consumption, or can only be done by tech-savvy individuals, the exchanges are the only way for regular people to obtain cryptocurrencies. In order to do so, they have to go through know-your-customer ('KYC') and anti-money laundering ('AML') procedures; thus, the anonymity that the blockchain offers is lost to a certain extent. However, the exchanges introduce a big risk in the whole ecosystem because they represent a single point of failure in a system where everything is supposed to be decentralized and the need for third-party custodians or intermediaries eliminated. When you buy or deposit cryptocurrencies in an exchange, you do not really own them (you do not possess the private keys), but you own IOUs instead. Additionally, exchanges are the target of constant attacks from hackers and if one gets hacked, then all its users may lose their assets, something that would not have otherwise happened since the assets on the blockchain are secured by strong cryptographic guarantees. Almost all existing exchanges have had a hacking incident, with the biggest event being the final collapse of Mt Gox in 2014, which was responsible for almost

70% of the whole Bitcoin trading volume at this time and, thus, led to a 67% price crash. Finally, being an entity, the operations of an exchange can be easily regulated or even halted by governments, which represents a contradiction to the nature of Bitcoin and blockchain technology. A recent example of such are the bans announced by China and South Korea which, once again, led to a price crash in all cryptocurrencies. This is something that is actually being addressed by using the same technology, i.e. blockchain, in order to build decentralized exchanges. In that way, the user can be sure that, if it is not impossible, it would be extremely hard for a single government or jurisdiction to control it or seize the funds.

Turning now to decentralization, this constitutes the '*raison d'être*' of the blockchain.[41] However, the exact meaning of the concept is debated. Vitalik Buterin, the creator of Ethereum, distinguishes between three types of decentralization:

- '*Architectural (de)centralization*—how many physical computers is a system made up of? How many of those computers can it tolerate breaking down at any single time?
- *Political (de)centralization*—how many individuals or organizations ultimately control the computers that the system is made up of?
- *Logical (de)centralization*—does the interface and data structures that the system presents and maintains look more like a single monolithic object, or an amorphous swarm? One simple heuristic is: if you cut the system in half, including both providers and users, will both halves continue to fully operate as independent units?.[42]

He argues that 'blockchains are politically decentralized (no one controls them) and architecturally decentralized (no infrastructural central point of failure) but they are logically centralized (there is one commonly agreed state and the system *behaves* like a single computer)'.[43] The idea that the blockchain is logically centralized may seem like it is not considering the possibility of a fork (the fork constituting a separate blockchain that operates as an independent unit).

As previously explained, from a political perspective, there are various possibilities through which a blockchain ecosystem may become centralized if we follow Buterin's typology. Mining constitutes the first centralization lever. Miners provide consensus for the blockchain. They enable it to function by verifying transactions, pool correct information into the transaction block, perform proof-of-work processes in order to authenticate the transaction, and broadcast the results to the network of miners, who accept it as the new end of the blockchain. Everything operates through a democratic consensus under the 'one CPU/GPU, one vote' mechanism. However, it is possible that some miners (mining farms or pools) end up controlling enough computational power to produce proof of work at a faster pace than all the other miners of the network, thereby lengthening the chain at a faster rate than all other users. If the computation power of these mining pools or firms exceeds that of the rest of the network, it is likely that some miners will be able to add new blocks to the chain and effectively act as gatekeepers, picking the transactions they want to include in a new forked chain. This suppresses competition between miners to validate transactions, the competition between whom is supposed to make it impossible to predict which specific miner will solve the cryptographic puzzle. It may also generate a double-spend problem, leading to a duplication of the blockchain. The possibility of a 51% attack that would enable some malevolent actors to re-write the blockchain's history is particularly high if mining becomes centralized among some large players. As explained above, because of the high costs of mining and the development of ASICs, industrial mining and mining pools that allow

---

[41] Vitaliak Buterin, 'The Meaning of Decentralisation' (*medium.com*, 6 February 2017) https://medium.com/@VitalikButerin/the-meaning-of-decentralization-a0c92b76a274.
[42] ibid.   [43] ibid.

group of miners to collectively solve the proof of work and split the reward between them, with most of the mining activity being concentrated among a limited number of mining pools, the resulting market structure would be oligopolistic.[44]

The shift from a PoW to a PoS approach limits the risk of the 51% attack. If the consensus is formed on the basis of votes representing the ownership stakes of a miner, the miner's incentive is to ensure the transactions. or else the future performance of the native token may be affected, which could potentially undermine the system and lead to a loss of its value, thereby inflicting losses to the miner. Hence, in a PoS approach, the miners do not have incentives to cheat on the system. However, PoS has its own issues as PoS limits the possibility of 'competition on the merits' for the verification of transactions, to the extent that it is not the fastest miner to verify the transaction that is rewarded but the actor that has the highest stakes, with these actors being offered considerable leeway to shape the evolution of the blockchain in a way that is proportional to their stake in the platform (in terms of their control of assets, such as storage and computational power, labour, or capital dedicated to it). This could lead to some form of plutocratic governance. However, in contrast to the world of digital platforms, lock-in effects in blockchain are quite limited, as those that disagree with the strategy of the core developers may fork the chain and launch a separate, backwards-compatible platform, which responds more closely to their preferences.

Blockchain intermediaries and other suppliers of resources may also constitute another possible centralization lever to the extent that they can use their control over key inputs to shape competition on the marketplace in their favour. This, for instance, may be the case of an oracle that controls access to essential external data sources for the operation of specific smart contracts, exchanges, or digital wallets that have become indispensable, for instance because of network effects, or because they gain critical mass by leveraging their dominant position from another network, external to the blockchain. An example would be a blockchain teaming up, on an exclusive basis, with a digital platform whose consolidation of a digital sector has resulted in it controlling some indispensable asset, such as storage on the cloud.[45]

Although the crowdsourcing model for the funding of blockchain applications may preserve us from the problem of the same group of venture capitalists and institutional investors controlling or influencing it, one may not exclude the possibility that a core team of developers controls or influences competing blockchain applications. The small community of blockchain experts, some of whom have thousands of followers and exercise an undeniable influence over the actors' perceptions of the evolution of the industry, provide some stakeholders with the power to frame the ongoing conversation/agenda about the future of the blockchain. Due to the important weight of its futurity dimension, this power may be easily converted to economic rents. I will explore this potential, when examining the need to move beyond the strict confines of market power, as this is understood in competition law, in order to assess the power dynamics in a blockchain.

---

[44] For an extensive discussion of the market structure of Bitcoin mining, see June Ma, Joshua Gans, and Rabee Tourky, 'Market Structure in Bitcoin Mining' (2018) Rotman School of Management Working Paper No. 3103104.

[45] See Andrew Bartels, Dave Bartoletti, John Rymer, Matthew Guorini, and Robert Valdovinos, 'The Coming Consolidation of Cloud' (2017) Forrester Report, noting that the three areas of greatest consolidation are currently in the base-level computing and storage known as infrastructure as a service ('IaaS'), desktop applications delivered via the cloud, and customer relationship management. The report notes that the three largest providers in those markets already collectively hold 70% or more of subscription revenues, with little chance that their market share declines. Amazon Web Services ('AWS') dominates the public cloud market, followed by Microsoft Azure and Google Cloud Platform.

III. Blockchain Competition: Traditional Strategic Competitive Advantage

Blockchain technology has already been applied in various industries and will continue to be in the near future. Although the technology is quite new and has not yet permeated the entire economy, in this section the purpose is to understand the various ways firms implementing this technology have attempted to gain strategic competitive advantage both vis-a-vis competing technologies and within the blockchain competitive space. The underlying assumption is that, as with traditional industrial capitalism, economic actors operating in the digital or 'informational' capitalist system compete for rents ('capital') by using different resources at their disposal, including technology assets. They strive to direct their entrepreneurial activity and disposable capital to industries that provide them the highest rate of return. Usually, their strategy is to take advantage of the industry structure in a way that enables them to constitute 'bottlenecks', i.e. activities where scarcity and the potential for control offer superior opportunities for profit or, in other words, to gain strategic competitive advantage. Although this is not the only form of competitive advantage that may generate power, it is still the one on which competition law enforcement usually focuses. In view of the idiosyncratic method of the funding of DLT projects through ICOs, this strategic competitive advantage may take different forms than is usually the case in traditional digital platform competition.

A. The emergence of blockchain-powered industries

Some authors distinguish between three categories of blockchain technology with increasing degrees of complexity.[46] The first applications of blockchain (Blockchain 1.0) concerned digital currencies which, for the first time, involved the use of a public ledger system to validate transactions. The next step (Blockchain 2.0) was to move the use of this technology from digital currencies to broader economic sectors. This step enabled the implementation of smart contracts and related applications. The final stage (Blockchain 3.0) will concern the complete diffusion of blockchain technology throughout economy and society. Blockchain technology is already utilized in various areas of economic activity.[47] Starting with the remittance industry and then expanding into various subsectors of the financial industry (including insurance), this merger of technologies and financial capabilities, which has given rise to the term 'FinTech', has since expanded into diverse areas ranging from gambling to content distribution, decentralized marketplaces, management, and decentralized autonomous organizations, to the IoT or to the Internet of Services ('IoS').

1. The remittance industry

One of the first ambitions of cryptocurrencies and blockchain technology was to completely disrupt the remittance industry. Blockchain technology was considered the perfect candidate for substituting the traditional error-prone, costly system that took a few days to produce a settlement. A number of companies offer end-to-end blockchain-powered remittance services.[48] In 2004, Santander became one of the first banks to merge blockchain to

---

[46] Kane (n 17).
[47] For a complete survey, see Deloitte, 'Global Survey: Breaking Blockchain Open' (2018) https://www2.deloitte.com/us/en/pages/consulting/articles/innovation-blockchain-survey.html.
[48] For instance, Align Commerce and Bitspark.

a payments app, thereby enabling customers to make international payments twenty-four hours a day, whilst clearing would occur the next day. Additionally, there are quite a few services that offer to users the possibility to pay with cryptocurrencies while they absorb all the risk of price volatility. BitPay, for example, is a global bitcoin payment service provider, that entered into collaboration with many companies such as Microsoft, TigerDirect, and Warner Bros. and processes more than $1 million per day. Other companies, such as Cryptopay, Xapo, and Wirex, provide Bitcoin debit cards.

2. *FinTech*

FinTech is certainly the acronym that most people are familiar with when they are asked to provide the example of an industry where blockchain technology has led to significant changes in the industry landscape. The term was coined to describe the intersection between finance and technology. It may refer to technical innovation being applied in a traditional financial services context or to innovative financial services offerings which disrupt the existing financial services market. It is one of the most exciting and dynamic segments of the financial services marketplace. Global investment in FinTech ventures has increased considerably over the past few years. There have also been a few global alternative finance entrants, digital platforms such as PayPal, Apple, Facebook, and Amazon, which have changed the digital finance ecosystem beyond recognition. Some use data in a way that is customer facing. They use data to segment customer populations, identify opportunities for new products and services, and to optimize pricing. Others use data to help manage risk. They use data to spot outlier transactions that may indicate fraud or cybersecurity breach, or to validate credit-worthiness decisions. It will be interesting to see how blockchain-based FinTech will interact with these digital platforms that are also entering into this industry.

3. *Insurance*

Blockchain technology can also be used to implement various insurance policies. This is done usually with the use of a smart contract. The assets can be kept in an escrow account until the triggering condition is satisfied and then the prearranged action takes place. This eliminates counterparty risk, intermediaries, and costly delays. For example, a flight delay insurance policy may be easily implemented using a smart contract, and there are some pilot projects already.[49]

4. *Gambling*

Another promising application is gambling on the blockchain and this was actually the first 'killer app' built on Bitcoin (Shatoshi Dice). In this case, the blockchain solves the most important thing missing in online gambling today: *provable fairness*. The current status is that an auditing authority certifies the algorithms (mainly the random number generation algorithm, the 'RNG') being used by the gambling company, but the client can never be sure about what is actually running at the time when they are playing. However, this could be easily tackled by the blockchain. Its public ledger could be used to prove that the code running is the audited one.[50]

---

[49] See https://fdd.etherisc.com/.
[50] See, e.g., Funfair Technologies, 'Blockchain Solutions for Gaming' (*funfair.io*) https://funfair.io/; EtherFlip, (*etherflip.co*) http://www.etherflip.co/; Winsome, (*blog.winsome.io*) https://blog.winsome.io.

5. *Digital content*

Since the blockchain is a decentralized, permission-less system, everybody and anybody can release any kind of digital media content (music, video, blog) and be paid in its native token or any other cryptocurrency. With the new advances in payment channel technology such as the 'lightning network', which introduces the concept of micro-transactions, blockchain will be able to scale to thousands or even millions of transactions per second ('TPS'). Anybody interested will have access to that content and pay per second, per word, per byte, etc. (the concept of 'micropayments'). This could be a revolutionary development in the digital media sector, creating a new on-demand, real-time context and eradicating the monopoly of the big players, as well as the classic model of subscriptions and omnipresent advertisements.[51]

6. *Management and decentralized autonomous organizations (DAOs)*

The concept of decentralized applications is not a new concept introduced by blockchain technology, but the recent advances and the hype surrounding it has brought it back to prominence. Peer-to-peer systems existed in the past. Napster, an example of a peer-to-peer music file-sharing system, was the start of the traditional music industry decline and the transition to the digital age. Decentralized protocols like 'BitTorrent' have always been used by people to exchange digital content, but the infrastructure to build and develop truly decentralized apps emerged with the creation of the blockchain. However, a concept that is not yet widespread despite it being considered by many the holy grail of blockchain technology is the decentralized autonomous organization ('DAO'). Vitalik Buterin, the inventor and co-creator of Ethereum, defines it as follows: 'an entity that lives on the internet and exists autonomously but also heavily relies on hiring individuals to perform certain tasks that the automaton itself cannot do.[52] The main characteristic of a DAO is that it processes an internal capital or property that has some value and can use it as an incentive mechanism for motivating and putting in action certain activities. In a few words, a DAO aims to automate and set in stone the rules that will manage and govern the organization through software. The rules that would run the organization are formalized in software code, then the tokens that represent ownership are distributed through a token sale, and finally people can vote on how to allocate resources or on whether a new project should be approved or rejected.

This could provide the foundation for the development of ambitious projects that could potentially threaten and disrupt the monopoly of big established players. For example, there could be a truly decentralized transportation system, using a similar business model to the one of Uber, but running on the blockchain and controlled entirely by a DAO. People could register and participate as employees or clients, or in extreme cases it could use the available funds and allocate resources (cars, buses, helicopters, etc.) in order to build its own. In a (not so) futuristic scenario, if this were to be combined with the self-driving vehicle technology currently being developed, it could create a truly automated corporation, leaving humans completely out of the equation. Another example could be a decentralized version of the Airbnb hospitality service. The DAO, in a similar fashion as outlined in the previous case, could allocate resources and operate autonomously. The potential benefits of that could be numerous and of great value. The costs of administration would be significantly reduced, thereby making the service less expensive whilst providing more competitive prices for

---

[51] For instance, Steemit, (*steemit.com*) https://steemit.com/, is a blogging and social networking platform where users are free to post, comment, and generally interact with the platform, and they get rewarded in STEEM tokens, which are pegged to the US dollar.

[52] See Vitaliak Buterin, 'DAOs, DACs, DAs and More: An Incomplete Terminology Guide' (*blog.ethereum.org*, 6 May 2014) https://blog.ethereum.org/2014/05/06/daos-dacs-das-and-more-an-incomplete-terminology-guide/.

low-end management services. The lack of an intermediary taking an arbitrary commission would increase the profits of the people offering their properties, and it would increase trust whilst reducing, or completely eliminating, the risks of human-run corporations, such as fund embezzlement, opaque processes, and various other scandals taking place in such environments.

7. The Internet of Things/Internet of Services

The transition from smartphones to the IoT where millions of devices will get direct internet connectivity including thermostats, refrigerators, cars, etc. will increase the means through which companies may gain access to valuable consumer data. One of the possible uses of blockchain technology and associated cryptocurrencies is that it could become the backbone of the machine-payable web, i.e. machines communicating, sharing processing power, and exchanging value with each other, and the base layer connecting the different industries. IOTA[53] is the first cryptocurrency designed to power the IoT revolution. It enables the secure sharing of resources between smart devices with zero transaction fees. IOTA has also been used as the underlying ledger for transferring information during the production process in Industry 4.0 projects, while also leading to a tamper-proof audit trail.

8. Decentralized marketplaces

Elements of DLT have also been implemented in online decentralized marketplaces. For instance, OpenBazaar, a decentralized marketplace, much like eBay or Amazon, operates independently of any intermediary operator. The platform relies on blockchain technology to ensure that buyers and sellers can interact directly with each other without passing through any centralized middleman. All transactions are accomplished through Ricardian contracts, a form of smart contract that is readable by computers and humans and can be cryptographically signed, which enable the buyer, the seller, and a potential third-party arbitrator to agree for the funds to be released in one of the most widely used cryptocurrencies, once a contractual condition is satisfied. Decentralized marketplaces such as OpenBazaar may challenge the dominance of online retail platforms. ModulTrade aims to replace the letter of credit used quite often in global trade, in particular for small and medium-sized enterprises ('SMEs') and, thus, provide important savings from the significant costs that banks charge for acting as an escrow between two companies.[54] The Origami Network offers a decentralized peer-to-peer marketplace. Powered by the Ethereum smart contract technology, it is combined with a decentralized escrow and payment solution developed for both e-commerce and online marketplaces, without the need to provide any personal information nor for a third party to control the cash flow, as the escrow payment management is automated, together with a decentralized customer review management, connected to the external data sources via Oracles.[55] Other decentralized marketplaces have been built on networks different to Ethereum.[56] The economic and social implications of the emergence of these global decentralized marketplaces for the organization of global e-commerce and for the position of incumbent online intermediaries and online marketplaces cannot be overstated.

---

[53] See Serguei Popov, 'The Tangle' (2018) Report, https://iotatoken.com/IOTA_Whitepaper.pdf.
[54] See ModulTrade, (*modultrade.com*) https://modultrade.com.
[55] See Origami Network, (*ori.network*) https://ori.network.
[56] For a discussion, see Christine Comben, 'Top Decentralised Marketplaces that Use Blockchain Technology' (*coincentral.com*, 9 July 2018) https://coincentral.com/decentralized-marketplace-blockchain/.

B. The blockchain profit and growth drivers: seeking strategic competitive advantage

There are two main sources of profits for the capital invested in the blockchain technologies and DApps. The first refers to the possibility of blockchain-based technologies being offered in distinct product markets as their use is expanding in various sectors of economic activity. The second refers to the possibility that the development of blockchain technology attracts funding on the expectation of future (sometimes immediate future), phenomenal returns on investment. We explore both sources of potential value capture for blockchain technology projects. Competitive strategies seek to promote both, but the two are not always interrelated to the degree that one might have expected.[57]

1. Competitive advantage in the blockchain era

To the extent that blockchain technology has not so far been implemented in a great number of product markets, one may conclude that a major driver in the profitability of the technology has not yet emerged. However, we will explore different ways in which blockchain technology may accelerate growth and lead to the establishment of strategic competitive advantage in an industry or in specific markets.

One has to conceive the blockchain as a new technology that becomes embedded in existing schema of acquiring and maintaining competitive advantage, before these schema are transformed when the full competitive potential of the technology becomes evident to economic actors, or at least a significant number of them, and there is a generalized shift to the new technology. Just being the most advanced technology in terms of technical characteristics is not sufficient to gain prominence in either a specific industry or the overall economy. The existence of significant sunk costs, path-dependencies, and network effects are some of the factors that may influence the success of a technology even vis-à-vis inferior alternatives. This illustrates the endogenous character of technological change.[58] Hence, the competitive game and the strategies developed by the players change with each shift in the dominant GPT. Resources and assets that were considered valuable may lose importance, whilst others become valuable overnight. For instance, many have referred to the significance of data in the digital economy emerging out of the third and fourth industrial revolution, these being referred to as equally valuable and essential, if not more so, than oil and electricity have been following the second industrial revolution,[59] a claim which, of course, needs to be qualified.[60]

Data will certainly constitute an essential feature of any application of blockchain technology. Blockchain puts in place an 'Internet of Value' that enables through a backbone service ensuring the security (via a distributed consensus ledger) and the immutable and uncensored history of transactions, the movement of digitized assets across the world in a few seconds. What is really transferred is not value as such but data on transactions that have

---

[57] The exuberance of some projects that still managed to have successful ICOs and attract funding may support this point.

[58] See Paul David, 'Clio and the Economics of QWERTY' (1985) 75(2) *American Economic Review*, 332–37; Paul David, 'The Hero and the Herd: Reflections on Thomas Edison and the "Battle of the Systems"' in *Favorites of Fortune: Technology, Growth, and Economic Development since the Industrial Revolution*, edited by Patrice Higonnet, David Landes, and Henry Rosovsky (Harvard University Press 1991); Paul David, 'Heroes, Herds and Hysteresis in Technological History' (1992) 1(1) *Journal of Industrial and Corporate Change*, 129; Håkan Håkansson and Anders Lundgren, 'Paths in Time and Space—Path Dependence in Industrial Networks' in *Evolutionary Economics and Path Dependence*, edited by Lars Magnusson and Jan Ottosson (Edward Elgar 1997), 119–137.

[59] See, e.g., The Economist, 'The World's Most Valuable Resource is No Longer Oil, But Data' (*economist.com*, 6 May 2017) https://www.economist.com/leaders/2017/05/06/the-worlds-most-valuable-resource-is-no-longer-oil-but-data.

[60] Data was not that valuable before the digital revolution.

value. To the extent that data is a public good, characterized by non-rivalrous consumption, that can be massively produced and/or harvested from an ever-increasing array of resources, in particular after the IoT adds billions of devices and sensors collecting data to the data production system, it may seem unlikely that it could reproduce the scarcity that makes oil such a valuable resource.[61] It is, however, possible that some actors control some key access points to data or indispensable storage facilities, which confers market power on them, or that these actors have managed to develop, on the basis of data that they have already harvested, efficient algorithms that, in tandem with network effects, may provide them with a sustainable head start and competitive advantage for a significant period of time.[62]

In the context of blockchain, the crucial issue is not the data as such, but the transaction that has been digitized and incorporated in the blockchain. From this perspective, one may consider that any scarcity generating a valuable resource would emanate from some degree of control over the digitized transactions. However, the decentralized architecture of the blockchain enables each user to maintain the resource to be exchanged in a digital wallet to which only the user has access and to use for the transaction: a private key, to which only the holder of the key has access. The transaction requires the conversion of this private key to a public key through a cryptographic transformation pursuant to the digital signature by both parties. Hence, so far, only the parties to the transaction control the resource to be exchanged in the transaction, to the exclusion of any intermediary. However, for the blockchain to operate, this private transaction needs to be communicated or broadcasted to the network, and later verified and authenticated by the miners, who, following some consensus, the form of which is specified in the specific blockchain's design rules (*lex cryptographia*), will incorporate the transaction into the blockchain. This process of verification and authentication by the miners through consensus introduces some degree of scarcity, as the assets of the blockchain value system need to be transformed from raw information about a transaction to a transaction block incorporated in a distributed and networked ledger about real valuable transactions. Scarcity may be artificially created in this case, either by specifying the amount of blocks a blockchain may have, with block space being a scarce commodity for technical reasons, or by regulating the number of native tokens that are distributed as incentive to miners to engage in their mining activity. This scarcity may be the source of value but may also give rise to strategies of exclusion and exploitation that could be of interest for competition law (see our analysis in section VI).

Competitive interactions in the digital economy are quite complex. What constitutes an established or a potential competitor becomes blurred as economic entities are actively pursuing strategies to alter the industry structure in order to alleviate competitive pressures. They seek to position the firm at the point where competition, both horizontal and vertical, is at its weakest.[63] In traditional strategy analysis, competing entities (often, corporations) seek a competitive advantage, either by imitating successful competitors while lowering their costs or by differentiating themselves from their competitors by developing idiosyncratic resources and capabilities and designing strategies to exploit these differences. The business environment in which competitive advantage strategies are integrated is formed by the relationship that the corporation has with three sets of players: customers, suppliers, and competitors.[64] Firms make profits but they must also provide value to their customers. 'Value is created when the price the customer is willing to pay for a product exceeds the costs incurred by the firm.'[65] This surplus is distributed between the customers and the producers

---

[61] See the discussion in Adam Schlosser, 'You May Have Heard Data is the New Oil. It's Not' (*weforum.org*, 10 January 2018) https://www.weforum.org/agenda/2018/01/data-is-not-the-new-oil/.

[62] Autorité de la concurrence (France) and Bundeskartellamt (Germany), 'Competition Law and Data' (2016) Report.

[63] Robert Grant, *Contemporary Strategy Analysis* (Wiley 2013), 74–76.   [64] ibid, 61.

[65] ibid, 62.

by the forces of competition. If competition is strong, consumers will receive the higher percentage of the surplus value (the so-called 'consumer surplus', which measures the difference between the price they paid and the price they were willing to pay). The rest of the surplus value will be received by producers (the so-called 'producer surplus', which measures the difference between the amount a producer receives and the minimum amount the producer is willing to accept for the product). The profitability of different industries varies; some earn high rates of profit, whilst others can barely cover their cost of capital.[66] This largely depends on the degree of competition that prevails in each industry, as intense price competition generally leads to weak margins. Profitability within a specific industry may also be quite different, with some firms earning significant profits whilst others struggle to maintain themselves on the market.[67]

The most widely used competition framework in business strategy is that put forward by Michael Porter, the 'five forces of competition framework'[68] (see Fig. 18.1). According to this framework, the profitability of an industry is determined by five sources of competitive pressure: competition from existing industry players; competition from substitutes; competition from new entrants in the industry; competition from established rivals, which can be characterized as sources of 'horizontal' competition; competition from the bargaining power of suppliers; and competition from the power of buyers, which can be characterized as sources of 'vertical competition'.[69]

Competition economics has largely focused on horizontal competition from established competitors producing substitute products or on the threat of entry of potential competitors. Rivalry between established competitors is often measured by reference to the level of market concentration, often measured by a concentration ratio, the market share of the largest producers in a specific market. However, it is still unclear how the level of market concentration impacts upon profitability and, consequently, the allocation of the surplus between consumers and producers. The likelihood of a new entry (i.e. potential competition) largely depends on barriers to entry, that is, an advantage that an established firm enjoys vis-à-vis its rivals, which may include economies of scale (to the extent that large, indivisible investments in production facilities, research and technology, or marketing may be more easily amortized over a large volume of output); absolute cost advantages (which may come from an easy access to an indispensable input); capital requirements (because of the large fixed costs required in order to kick-start economic activity in an industry); product differentiation (as it might be quite difficult to enter a market where consumers have strong loyalty ties to existing brands); access to channels of efficient distribution; strategic barriers to entry because of competitive strategies that aim to increase the potential rivals' costs if they enter the market; or legal and regulatory barriers, etc. Competition law aims to limit the effectiveness of barriers to entry in order to increase the 'contestability' of the market.[70]

In contrast, vertical competition has not been the primary focus of competition economists, even if it may play a significant role in the allocation of the total surplus value generated by a value chain. The relative bargaining power of a supplier upstream or of a customer downstream has been considered as playing a less important role than 'horizontal competition' because it is assumed that, in most cases, they have a limited impact on the overall

---

[66] ibid.

[67] The advent of the digital economy has led to the development of what has been characterized as the rise of 'superstar firms' which are able to take advantage of technology, including Big Data and artificial intelligence, in understanding better than 'standard' firms the competitive game. See David Autor, David Dorn, Lawrence Katz, Christina Patterson, and John Van Reenen, 'The Fall of the Labor Share and the Rise of Superstar Firms' (2017) NBER Working Paper No. 23396.

[68] Michael Porter, 'The Five Competitive Forces that Shape Strategy' (2008) 25 *Harvard Business Review*, 25.

[69] Grant (n 63), 65.

[70] William Baumol, John Panzar, and Robert Willig, *Contestable Markets and the Theory of Industry Structure* (Harcourt Brace Jovanovic 1982).

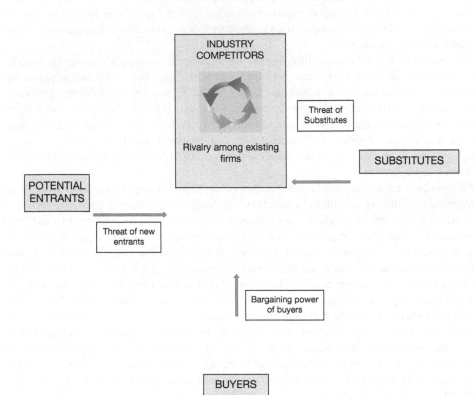

Fig. 18.1 Porter's Five Forces

Source: The graph reproduces Figure 3.2 in Grant (n 63), 65.

economic efficiency of the transactions. If public policy shifts its focus on to the productivity and ability of 'superstar' large digital platforms to pull away from competition and enjoy tremendous levels of profitability, without these accumulated profits being used for productive investments vertical competition may become an important concern.

Interactions between economic actors may focus on either the horizontal or vertical competition dimension. They can be qualified as strategic to the extent that each actor considers how rivals will react. Simply put, there are two possibilities:[71]

- Economic actors' decisions may be *strategic complements* in that they tend to reinforce each other (i.e. they move in the same direction). For instance, setting prices among horizontal rivals is such that a decision to raise (reduce) prices will incentivize (or even, force) rivals to do likewise.

---

[71] This terminology is inspired by Jeremy Bulow, John Geanakoplos, and Paul Klemperer, 'Multimarket Oligopoly: Strategic Substitutes and Strategic Complements' (1985) 93 *Journal of Political Economy*, 488–511.

- Economic actors' decisions may be *strategic substitutes* in that they tend to offset each other (i.e. they move in opposite direction). In the horizontal competition scenario, setting capacity is such that a decision to expand capacity will force rivals to reduce theirs.

There is a difference, though, between the two strategic settings. Under strategic complements, economic actors' moves reinforce each other (i.e., there is a positive feedback loop), but this competitive mode tends to produce more extreme outcomes than under strategic substitutes. However, even in the context of strategic substitutes, the intensity of the strategic response may vary and be 'tough' or 'accommodating', depending on the economic actor's decision to create more room for rivals.[72]

Although there is a plethora of blockchain-based projects with a number of hypothetical-use cases (see for a discussion our analysis in section III.A), it is still unclear how DLT can contribute to create value within economic organizations.[73] It is clear that blockchain provides some intangible resources (to the extent that blockchain consists essentially in code and, occasionally, its combination with purpose-built hardware) to economic organizations that can be employed to gain sustainable competitive advantage in product markets. However, in view of the immaturity of the technology, it is still too early to venture specific predictions. It is only possible to refer broadly to some potential sources of strategic competitive advantage.

The adoption of blockchain technology will certainly lead to an important reduction of verification costs that have typically been required for transactions in digital markets.[74] These are close to zero, in particular because the computation and energy costs may be reduced by a more systematic recourse to PoS protocols, blockchain is a technology allowing for costless verification, and because administrative costs for record keeping can be significantly reduced, to the extent that this is delegated to a distributed ledger. To the extent that blockchain technology may substitute trust in the code to trust in intermediaries (DLT has been qualified by some as the 'trust machine'),[75] it can also lead to a significant reduction of costs associated with the presence of intermediaries in the economy. A recent McKinsey report has looked to ninety use cases of blockchain technology in fourteen industries and found that 70% of the value at stake in the short term brought in by the implementation of blockchain technology was in cost reduction.[76] Such significant reductions in costs may provide important cost advantages and operational efficiencies to economic entities employing blockchain technology. It could also shift the flow of value by creating new revenue streams for blockchain as service ('BaaS') providers that offer integrated solutions of online distributed ledger technology to companies eager to develop blockchain-based solutions.

According to the same report, 'over time, the value of blockchain will shift from driving cost reduction to enabling entirely new business models and revenue streams', one of the 'most promising and transformative use cases being the establishment of a distributed, secure digital identity and the services associated with it'.[77] This is related to the know-your-customer ('KYC') process, in which firms seek to establish the identity of their customers

---

[72] Dean Fundeberg, and Jean Tirole, 'The Fat-Cat Effect, the Puppy-Dog Ploy and the Lean and Hungry Look' (1984) 74 *American Economic Review*, 361–66.
[73] There is, however, an ongoing discussion in the literature. See, e.g., Magnus Vitsö Björnstad, Joar Gunnarsjaa Harkestad, and Simen Krogh, 'A Study on Blockchain Technology as a Source for Competitive Advantage' (2017) *Norwegian University of Sicence and Technology*, https://brage.bibsys.no/vmlui/bitstream/handle/11250/2472245/ 17527_FULLTEXT.pdf?sequence=1; Brant Carson, Giulio Romanelli, Patricia Walsh, and Askhat Zhumaev, 'Blockchain Beyond the Hype: What is the Strategic Business Value?' (*mckinsey.com*, June 2018) https://www. mckinsey.com/business-functions/digital-mckinsey/our-insights/blockchain-beyond-the-hype-what-is-the-strategic-business-value?cid=other-eml-nsl-mip-mck-oth-1807&hlkid=8ca56a40fe474c7497e74038a1f43fe7&hct ky=9280917&hdpid=bb9f89f0-458b-4b4e-a1ee-ad99e602294e.
[74] Catalini and Gans (n 23).
[75] The Economist, 'The Trust Machine' (*economist.com*, 31 October 2015) https://www.economist.com/leaders/ 2015/10/31/the-trust-machine.
[76] Carson et al. (n 73).　　　[77] ibid.

both before and after entering in transactions with them. This is particularly important for implementing anti-corruption legislation and laws pertaining to terrorist financing and money laundering, and implementing economic sanctions regimes. This may lead to a more intensive use of blockchain technology in the banking and, more generally, financial industries. The application of blockchain technology on a larger scale will certainly lead to network effects, although not as pronounced as those for digital platforms, for reasons already explained in section II, and could also be a source of competitive advantage.

However, blockchain technology has some inherent limitations that may interfere with the process of transforming the competitive advantage to dominance and higher profitability. First, blockchain largely consists in combining code that is open source and could be easily replicated by competitors with purpose-built hardware, which is also available, sometimes at a relatively low cost, to competitors. Furthermore, blockchain technology does not enable the development of mechanisms isolating the incumbent from actual or potential competition. As explained in section II, the possibility of developing a blockchain fork, in the case that some blockchain actors disagree with the blockchain developers, diminishes any likelihood that direct and indirect network effects will set high barriers to entry.

In order to transform the competitive advantage provided by capabilities acquired in blockchain technology to *sustainable strategic* advantage, economic actors should adopt conduct in complementary spheres or markets that will be strategically linked with the blockchain technology with the objectives of protecting the advantage provided by these blockchain capabilities and of limiting the possibility of their rivals to copy them. Thus, in order to protect their profits, economic actors will have to develop isolating mechanisms.

Acquiring a first-mover advantage is certainly a successful strategy but for it to be maintained and eventually expanded on, the firm should make considerable investments on innovation. It also makes sense for the firm to focus on difficult problems that no one else has previously explored, seeking technical solutions that could potentially be implemented throughout the whole industry.

Another mechanism to protect the competitive advantage in the long term is technical complexity. By combining cryptographic techniques, unique computational power, cheap and extensive storage capabilities, and powerful algorithms, firms can make it more difficult for their competitors to reproduce the firm's original competitive advantage. Attracting highly specialized staff (blockchain core developers), who have been specifically trained in this complex combination of assets, may also have significant effects on competition, in view of the relative scarcity of 'blockchain experts', at least at the initial stages of the development of this technology.[78]

This may be combined with a strategy of patenting blockchain technologies, developing an IP portfolio protecting investments in these technologies, and/or proceeding with a simple protection as a trade secret. The last option may not be that attractive, as currently blockchain applications are open source (i.e. the source code is accessible and editable by everyone). This is essential in order to attract the user community. Although the original blockchain codes used for Bitcoin and Ethereum (smart contracts) are open source, patent applications may be made for algorithms improving the blockchain processing operations and/or for algorithms or hardware enabling new uses of blockchain. Patenting software is a distinct possibility in the United States, as the Patent Act (35 U.S.C. § 101) enables the grant of patents for decentralized data structure management technology software and some aspects of internet-implemented applications of blockchain technology.[79] As Singh

---

[78] See Marcin Zduniak, '6 Ways to Stay Ahead of Blockchain Competition' (*espeoblockchain.com*, 23 May 2018) https://espeoblockchain.com/blog/blockchain-competition-example/.

[79] Gumeet Singh, 'Are Internet-Implemented Applications of Blockchain Technology Patent-Eligible in the United States?' (2018) 17(2) *Chicago Kent Journal of Intellectual Property*, 357.

explains, one may apply for patent protection for several internet-implemented applications of blockchain:

- 'Applications that use the blockchain technology over the internet, such as applications for financial data, such as cryptocurrencies, public records, identification';

- 'Improvements in the architecture of one or more of the following individual technologies that collectively form the blockchain technology implemented over the internet, such as: asymmetric encryption, hash functions, Merkle trees, key-value database, peer-to-peer ("P2P") communication protocol and proof of work';

- 'Improvements in methods executed [...] such as: (a) a method of sharing transactions and blocks as executed using the P2P communication protocol, (b) a process of validating transactions and achieving distributed consensus, which use the blockchain concepts of proof of work, proof of stake, and decentralized consensus, (c) a method of efficiently packaging transactions into blocks, using the concept of Merkle trees, (d) a method of performing hashing of at least one of the blocks and transactions, and a method of obfuscating public keys, (e) a method of searching previous transactions to prevent double-spends, which uses the concept of key-value database, and (f) a method of signing transactions, which can use the technologies of digital signatures based on public and private keys, asymmetric encryption, and elliptic curve cryptography'; and

- 'Computing systems or devices, computer program products and articles of manufacture that are used by the end customer to execute the internet-implemented applications that implement the block-chain technology'.[80]

The issue of patentability of blockchain-based technologies can be set in different terms in the United States and in the European Union, due to some specific limitations to the patentability of software that exist in Europe. Section 101 of the US Patent Act, in defining the subject matter eligible for patent protection, contains an implicit exception for 'laws of nature, natural phenomena, and abstract ideas'. In applying this exception, the Supreme Court distinguishes between patents that claim the 'building blocks' of human ingenuity, which are ineligible for patent protection, from those that integrate the building blocks into something more, thereby 'transforming them into a patent-eligible invention'.[81] In *Alice v. CLS Bank International*, the Supreme Court implemented these principles to patent claims directed to a computer-implemented technique of intermediating settlements in the context of financial transactions.[82] The Court first found that the concept of intermediated settlement was an abstract idea and constituted a fundamental and long-prevalent economic practice in the system of commerce. It then held that claims that 'require generic computer implementation, fail to transform that abstract idea into a patent-eligible invention'.[83] Hence, the fact that the well-established concept of intermediation is performed by a generic computer was not sufficient for making the claims eligible for patentability. It should also have been necessary to provide evidence that the technology improved the functioning of the computer or any other technology or technical field.

Under the joint *Mayo/Alice* test, courts should first assess whether, on the whole, the claims are 'directed to' patenting an abstract idea, before, in the second step, considering whether the claims contain 'an inventive concept' that would transform the nature of the claim into a patent-eligible application. According to the Court, the claim should contain 'an element or combination of elements that is sufficient to ensure that the patent, in practice, amounts to *significantly more* than a patent upon the [ineligible concept] itself'. Such would be the case, if the claim limitations 'involve more than performance of well-understood, routine, [and] conventional activities previously known to the industry'. This requirement of 'significantly

[80] ibid., 358–59.
[81] *Mayo Collaborative Services v. Prometheus Laboratories, Inc.*, 142 S.Ct 1289 (2012).
[82] *Alice v. CLES Bank International*, 134 S. Ct 2347 (2014).   [83] ibid.

more' contribution than the use of a generic computer implementation is assessed on a case-by-case basis by the courts. To the extent that blockchain technology significantly improves the functionality of a computer because it enables immutability, a decentralized architecture and cryptographic security of data (or the way the system stores, tracks, and processes data), and the fact that it puts forward 'unconventional' solutions to technological problems, going beyond performance of 'well-understood, routine, and conventional activities previously known to the industry', makes it possible to patent some implementations of blockchain technology and, thus, exclude rivals from using the technology.

In the EU, although computer programmes 'as such' are, in principle, excluded from patentability in view of Article 52(d)(2) of the European Patent Convention, which creates an exception to their patentability, by virtue of the interpretation of Articles 52(d)(2) and 52(d)(3), software-based patents may be eligible to patentability if the claimed subject matter has a technical character. The European Patent Office ('EPO') has already granted thousands of patents related to software-based technologies and a quite complex, and not necessarily clear, jurisprudence of the Technical Boards of Appeal of the EPO has attempted to interpret the limits of patentability in this area.[84] Traditionally, improvements in CPU processing speed, a decrease in energy consumption or memory usage for a particular device, and/or progress in information encryption have been considered as providing a technical solution to a technical problem having technical effects and, thus, to be eligible for patentability. This could also be the case for some aspects of blockchain technology. It was reported that from the twenty-seven European patent procedures related to blockchain published in 2017 and 2018, only two patents were granted, which proves that blockchain is patentable in Europe.[85]

In recent years there has been some significant patent activity related to blockchain technology. It has been reported that patent applications towards blockchain technology started as early as 2007/2008 and that the number has grown substantially, in particular, since 2015.[86] From less than two dozen applications per year, during 2007–2013, the number of applications has increased to 1,237 filed worldwide in 2017, up from 594 in 2016 and 258 in 2015 (see Box 18.1).[87]

Box 18.1: Blockchain Patent Applications

USPTO: the search was conducted using the US patent application search and using the keyword 'blockchain' in the title and/or abstract of the patent application. This resulted in the finding of 226 patent applications.

EPO: the search was conducted using the European Patent Register and using the keyword 'blockchain' in the title of the patent application. This resulted in finding of 187 patent applications.

CNIPA: the search was conducted using Chinese National Intellectual Property Administration's database and using the keyword 'blockchain' in the title of the patent application. This resulted in the finding of 236 patent applications.

Espacenet: EPO contains a special database of worldwide patent applications. We searched for the keyword 'blockchain' in the title and abstract sections, which resulted in 1,237 patent applications.

US PTO	EPO	China	Worldwide (Espacenet)
226	187	236	1,237

---

[84] See European Patent Office, 'Programs for Computers', Guidelines for Examination https://www.epo.org/law-practice/legal-texts/html/guidelines/e/g_ii_3_6.htm.

[85] These are patents EP3125489 and EP3257191. See the discussion in João Cabral, 'The Patentability of Blockchain Technology in Europe' (*inventa.com*, 24 April 2018) https://inventa.com/en/news/article/300/the-patenteability-of-blockchain-technology-in-europe.

[86] Johan Ståhlberg and Isabel Fiol, 'Analysing Blockchain Patent Trends' (*managingip.com*, 24 April 2018) http://www.managingip.com/Article/3802483/Analysing-blockchain-patent-trends.html.

[87] See Bruce Berman, 'Blockchain Patent Applications Doubled in 2017 to More than 1,200' (*ipcloseup.com*, 27 March 2018) https://ipcloseup.com/2018/03/27/blockchain-patent-applications-doubled-in-2017-to-over-1200/.

Most of these filings take place in China, South Korea, Australia, the United States, and the EU (including the UK),[88] with China recently overtaking the United States for the number of patents filed. European patents have been sparsely granted to blockchain technology, with only a handful of patents (no more than ten) granted between 2011 and 2016.[89] With regard to the number of patents granted, US patents are the most prevalent, followed by those granted in China, Korea, and Australia[90] (see Box 18.2).

Box 18.2: Blockchain Granted Patents

USPTO: the search was conducted using the search of granted patents and using the keyword 'blockchain' in the title or abstract of the patent.

EPO: the search was conducted using European Patent Register and using the keyword 'blockchain' in the title of the patent/patent application and for searching only for issued patents.

China: there was no option in the CNIPA database to search for granted patents so we could not conclusively find how many patents have been granted from these 236 patent applications.

US PTO	EPO
37	2

It was reported that 'of the top nine filings for blockchain patents between 2012 and 2017, six were Chinese, led by Beijing Technology Development'.[91] Mastercard, Digital Asset Holdings, Bank of America, Intel, Coinbase, Security First Corp, Microsoft, IBM, Qualcomm, and Medici are among the leading US patent applications, while NChain, Accenture, and British Telecom are the top EU-based assignees.[92] These patents cover different areas and include both business methods and software patents (see Box 18.3).

Box 18.3: Blockchain Patenting Technological Areas (USPTO)

The most common classification of blockchain patents are in the following categories:

G06F—Electric Digital Data Processing

G06Q—Data Processing Systems or Methods

G06N—Computer Systems Based on Specific Computational Models

H04L—Transmission of Digital Information

Blockchain patents include both business method and software patents.

---

[88] Ståhlberg and Fiol (n 86).

[89] See PatentlyGerman, 'Blockchain Patent Activity Increases—but Granted Patents are Still Rare in the Field' (*patentlygerman.com*, 14 February 2018) https://patentlygerman.com/2018/02/14/blockchain-patent-activity-increases-but-granted-patents-are-still-rare-in-this-field/.

[90] Ståhlberg and Fiol (n 86).

[91] See Financial Times, 'China Leads Blockchain Patent Applications' (*ft.com*) https://www.ft.com/content/197db4c8-2e92-11e8-9b4b-bc4b9f08f381.

[92] Compilation of data reported in Henry Chiu, 'An Overview of the Blockchain Patent Landscape' (*clarivate.com*, 8 November 2017) https://clarivate.com/blog/overview-blockchain-patent-landscape/; PatentlyGerman (n 89).

Can blockchain be protected by copyright (database right)? Due to the specific decentralized nature of blockchain technology, a blockchain, in and of itself, is unlikely to be considered as a 'database' and enjoy copyright protection under the EU Directive on the Legal Protection of Databases (EU Database Directive).[93] Blockchain is a distributed ledger on which transactions are anonymously recoded and blocks are maintained simultaneously across a network of unrelated computers or servers. A new block of data will be appended to the end of the blockchain only after the computers on the network reach consensus as to the validity of the transaction.[94] After a block has been added to the blockchain, it can no longer be deleted. The transactions it contains can be accessed and verified by everyone on the network. It becomes a permanent record that all of the computers on the network can use to coordinate an action or verify an event.[95] Consequently, the principles of decentralization and participation by all users characterize blockchain technology.[96] In contrast, the EU Database Directive protects, with a copyright-like right, those databases that are centralized and created by a specific natural or legal person. Article 3 of the EU Database Directive emphasizes that the database should constitute the author's own intellectual creation. Article 4 provides that there must be a known author of the database, in particular a 'natural person or group of natural persons who created the base or, where the legislation of the Member States so permits, the legal person designated as the rightsholder by that legislation'. Blockchain does not have a sole or defined group of authors who 'created the database'. Hence, it does not seem to fit within the traditional legal boundaries of the right protecting 'databases'.

As already explained, acquiring a sustainable strategic competitive advantage may require the tailoring of strategies that leverage the market position of the economic entity, in particular strategies concerning essential infrastructure and services for maintaining the operation of the blockchain in order to acquire the ability to shape the ecosystem, for instance by establishing industry standards or by influencing regulation.[97] We will explore the second strategy in a subsequent section. With regard to the effort to develop industry standards, in the absence of a dominant position which may impose de facto standardization, a voluntary standardization process requires some degree of cooperation between multiple industry players, including between horizontal competitors. This may give rise to situations of 'co-opetition', a concept put forward by Brandeburger and Nalebuff to describe the 'future of competitive interactions in the economy, whereby businesses become more competitive by cooperating with each other and develop unique capabilities that add value and complement those of their competitors'.[98] Competitors could, thus, cooperate in setting the standards of the industry.

The presence of multiple players renders the effort of standardization more complex and may, thus, affect the possibilities of cooperation. In most cases, the industry players form consortia. For instance, a number of financial institutions collaborated in the R3 consortium with the aim of developing the financial-grade, open-source Corda blockchain platform. The establishment of common standards for the operation of the blockchain is particularly important in the context of the IoT. These standards may relate to a number of design choices, for instance the size of the blocks, the consensus protocol employed for the governance of the blockchain, the type for storage, interoperability between different blockchains,[99] and

---

[93] Directive 96/9/EC (11 March 1996) on the Legal Protection of Databases [1996] L77/20.

[94] Primavera De Filippi and Aaron Wright, 'Decentralized Blockchain Technology and the Rise of Lex Cryptographia' (20 March 2015) https://papers.ssrn.com/sol3/papers.cfm?abstract_id=2580664, 7.

[95] ibid., 8.

[96] Nolan Bauerle, 'What is the Difference Between a Blockchain and a Database?' (*Coindesk.com*) https://www.coindesk.com/information/what-is-the-difference-blockchain-and-database/.

[97] Carson et al. (n 73).

[98] Adam Brandenburger and Barry Nalebuff, *Co-opetition* (Currency Doubleday 1997).

[99] On this issue, see Chapter 1 by Tasca and Piselli in this volume.

technologies connecting the blockchain with the outside world (such as IoT and biomet-rics) in a way that can maintain the security of the blockchain ledger, even if the physical sensors or APIs of existing systems and databases are interrupted.[100] The important costs for building the blockchain infrastructure, and the presence of network effects, has led some commentators to observe that 'few start-ups have sufficient credibility and technology sta-bility' for deploying the optimal scale of these technologies. A number of large corporations are instead pursuing a BaaS approach, using a model similar to that employed for cloud-based storage in order to assist more rapid diffusion of the technology among small and medium undertakings and the deployment of new applications.[101]

2. Competitive advantage and financial markets

ICOs emerged as the main source of funding blockchain projects, in particular, outperforming venture capital ('VC') for the financing of cryptocurrency and blockchain start-ups since 2017.[102] Despite their similarities to initial public offerings ('IPOs') and crowdfunding cam-paigns, ICOs can be distinguished from the former, as they involve the pre-sale of native software-based tokens, not through regulated exchange platforms, but through a distrib-uted ledger. These tokens are purchased through fiat or digital currency, thereby creating the capital inflow needed for the financing of the specific blockchain project. ICOs can be dis-tinguished from the latter because they provide a financial stake in the company, carry self-enforcing rights on a code-is-law basis, and cannot be qualified as a 'donation'.[103] Investors are usually driven by the high returns that may follow if the token's evaluation increases, by the specific product or service they can have access to, and/or by the cause followed by the specific blockchain project.

Blockchain 2.0, especially with the creation of platforms like Ethereum, has introduced a new paradigm in fundraising that threatens to disrupt the existing one of VC. Smart con-tracts make it easy for any entity (company or individual) to release its own tokens and distribute them to potential investors around the globe. These tokens are divided into two main categories: utility tokens and security tokens. Utility tokens give future access to a company's product or service. Security tokens can be any kind of tradable asset (usually they represent equity) and they promise to deliver dividends from future company profits. The procedure is as follows. There is a certain period in which the potential investors can send cryptocurrencies to certain addresses and get back tokens according to a fixed prede-termined ratio. This is a similar tactic to crowdfunding, and companies in the space have managed to raise cryptocurrencies worth of millions of dollars in a matter of a few days, often driven by the speculation frenzy and the huge, recent appreciation in the value of cryptocurrencies.

Ethereum itself, the platform that has actually facilitated and driven the adoption of ICOs, was one of the first to take place, raising 3,700 BTC (worth around 18 million USD at that moment) in the first twelve hours of the crowdfunding, back in 2014. The 'pre-mined' coins, i.e. pre-generated coins for the crowd sale were 11.9 million, which corresponds to 13% of the current supply, which indicated the intense futurity dimension of these pro-jects. One of the most ambitious projects that proved to be a great failure was the DAO. The DAO was launched in April 2016, raising over $150 million, and setting the record for the largest crowd sale at that time. However, a 'bug' in the code implementation led to a major vulnerability that allowed a hacker to steal one-third of the funds. This led to a price

---

[100] Carson et al. (n 73).   [101] ibid.

[102] See TechCrunch, (*techcrunch.com*) https://techcrunch.com/2018/03/04/icos-delivered-at-least-3-5x-more-capital-to-blockchain-startups-than-vc-since-2017/?guccounter=1.

[103] Marco Dell'Erba, 'Initial Coin Offerings. A Primer. The First Response of Regulatory Authorities' (2017) 14 *NYU Journal of Law and Business*, 1109.

crash in both the DAO token and 'Ether' (the native currency of Ethereum). This generated discussion about whether action should be pursued against the theft or not. Advocates of the latter option contended that pursuing reversion would go against the decentralized, irreversible nature of the blockchain, ruin the reputation of and trust held in the technology, and would violate the 'code is law' attribute of smart contracts. Finally, the Ethereum developers decided to revert the hack, but the whole incident drew the attention of the Securities Exchange Commission ('SEC') which, after a long investigation, announced that the DAO crowd sale was a securities sale. It raised community awareness of the risks involved in such cases.

After the DAO, many other ICOs have raised capital, paid upfront, often in a few hours or days, something that would be otherwise impossible with a traditional fundraising model. At the time of writing the cumulative all-time ICO funding exceeds $20 billion. The most important of those are EOS, attracting $ 4.2 billion, and TaTaTu, attracting $575 million in 2018, Filecoin attracting $262 million, and Tezos $232 million in 2017.[104] Recently, non-blockchain-related companies were also attracted by the ICO hype and moved in that direction. Kodak announced that they are developing their own crypto token (KODAKCoin) and Telegram, a popular messaging service and WhatsApp competitor, attracted $1.7 billion from private investors (before the public sale was cancelled), with the project aiming to leverage their important customer base of 200 million active users and their expertise in 'encrypted data storage' in order to build a decentralized supercomputer and value transfer system that may become an alternative to VISA/Mastercard.[105]

The quite considerable valuation of some of these tokens cannot be explained by the expectation of future revenues on the basis of market sales and profitability (for instance on the basis of a discounted cash-flow method that would explore price-to-earnings rations), because often there are no revenues or costs of inputs to analyse. Usage is more important than revenues. Various methodologies have been put forward for the evaluation of crypto-assets.[106] These rely on the relative valuation of crypto-assets, on the basis of a comparison of the relative use of the network over time, or alternatively on the square of the number of connected users to different blockchain systems ('Metcalfe's Law'). However, there are also absolute valuation methods based on the cost of production or on an analysis of the total addressable market ('TAM') for which the token is going to be used (the 'INET model'). There are other methods to model the velocity of money (the 'VOLT model').

In view of the crucial role of ICOs in incentivizing blockchain developers, at the initial stages of the launch of a blockchain project, it is important to consider the process of market valuation in order to understand the competitive strategies developed by the blockchain developers. Valuation by financial markets also plays a significant role in driving competitive strategies for digital platforms. The most important driver of value creation is not based on net cash flows and expected profits short term but on pots of gold being found far into the future.[107] However, in the context of the blockchain, market valuation is even more devoid of a link with present revenues. These links do not exist: the token sales are pre-sold and short-term performance in identifiable product markets is complex as it is quite probable that the native token may not necessarily be used for a specific product.

---

[104] See CoinDesk, (*coindesk.com*) https://www.coindesk.com/ico-tracker.
[105] See Telegram Open Network, https://drive.google.com/file/d/1ucUeKg_NiR8RxNAonb8Q55jZha03WC0O/view.
[106] See Federico Caccia, 'A Review of Cryptoasset Valuation Frameworks' (*blog.coinfabrik.com*, 18 July 2018) https://blog.coinfabrik.com/a-review-on-cryptoasset-valuation-frameworks/.
[107] See The Economist, 'Are Technology Firms Madly Overrated?' (*economist.com*, 23 February 2017) https://www.economist.com/business/2017/02/23/are-technology-firms-madly-overvalued.

IV. Blockchain Competition: Architectural Advantage

Competition fights are not only won through the use of traditional strategic competitive advantage, in terms of lower costs, higher quality products, etc. Increasingly, firms engage with the overall structure—economic and legal—of the industry in which they are active, seeking opportunities to frame their architecture in a way that favours their position. Section A explains the concept of 'architectural advantage'. Section B will explore the specific strategy of building architectural advantage by influencing the regulator and shaping, through regulation, the rules of the competitive game. In Section C, a short case study on the financial services value chain, one of the first economic sectors to be affected by the implementation of DLT, provides an illustration of how this architectural advantage may operate in practice.

A. Architectural advantage: the concept

At the early years of technological transformation, when new players emerge, the industry is likely to be marked 'by relatively high price-cost margins, at least for the more competent firms'.[108] This may lead some of the actors that have acquired superior resources and developed superior capabilities to benefit from 'abnormal profits'. These erode as the industry matures; there is new entry, and industry capacity is aligned with industry demand.[109] However, the industry is still marked by firm heterogeneity. Some firms continue to benefit from high rates of return and sustainable 'abnormal' profitability, 'in spite of competition',[110] while others see their profits erode when the market, following the initial hype generated by the newness of the technology, returns to equilibrium.[111]

This heterogeneity as to the profitability of firms present in the industry may be due to the business acumen of a firm's leaders, the creativity and persistent effort of the firm's human resources, a timely purchase of key resources that establish entry barriers to potential competitors, or even to happenstance. Some authors submit the view that it may also be explained by investments made in the possession of 'idiosyncratic rent-earning resources' or by developing capabilities that cannot be imitated by competitors.[112] These resources and capabilities are acquired through a process of customization that ties them with the specific firm. One could therefore distinguish between generic resources and capabilities, which may be easily acquired through the market, and customized or specialized resources and capabilities that can only be developed within the firm, often following a long period of investment and institutional learning.[113] The acquisition of these 'idiosyncratic' resources and capabilities, often after a lengthy process of customization so that they become part of the firm's 'productive fabric', constitutes one of the possible routes for achieving a sustainable competitive advantage.[114] These resources and capabilities may be leveraged by a number of strategies put in place by the firms in order to ensure they can maintain their scale advantage, such as denying efficient scale to their competitors or raising barriers to entry, for instance through the use of exclusionary practices and aggressive intellectual property (IP) rights strategies.

In addition to these competitive strategies that engage directly with the actual and potential sources of competition, a firm may also acquire a durable competitive advantage if it holds a position that enables it to reshape the 'industry architecture' to its own advantage. The concept of 'industry architecture' follows David Teece's seminal contribution on how profits from innovation and how the various governance arrangements between

---

[108] Michael Jacobides, Sidney Winter, and Stefan Kassberger, 'The Dynamics of Wealth, Profit, and Sustainable Advantage' (2012) 33 *Strategic Management Journal*, 1386.
[109] ibid.   [110] ibid., 1388.   [111] ibid., 1385.   [112] ibid., 1404.   [113] ibid., 1386.
[114] ibid., 1406.

the innovator and other vertically related firms may influence the distribution of these innovation gains.[115] Teece suggested a theoretical framework. First, it focuses on the co-specialization of firms so that their assets are tailored to each other and the firms develop a high degree of complementarity, as the combination of assets yields a higher value. Second, it focuses on 'factor mobility', which relates to the ability of a firm to appropriate value without necessarily owning the complementary asset. Teece focused on the dyadic relation between the innovator and outside asset holders, finding that complementarity usually leads to lower factor mobility. However, more recently, Michael Jacobides et al. disentangled the two constituent components of co-specialization by finding that a firm may manage to 'obtain *both* high complementarity *and* high mobility in their vertically adjacent segments', which led them to expand Teece's analytical framework beyond 'dyadic relations' to also cover the 'industry architecture', which is 'the various templates circumscribing the division of labor among co-specialized firms at the level of an industry, or economic sector'.[116] According to Jacobides et al.,

> the concept of industry architecture ('IA') describes how labor is typically organized and structured within an industry ('who does what') and which firms capture value and profit as a result ('who takes what'). It encompasses features such as the degree of vertical integration, the division of labor between firms and the 'rules and roles' that determine how firms interact and the business models, available to them. While IA reflects the conditions under which firms operate, it is influenced, in the medium term, by firms' attempts to reshape those conditions to their own advantage.[117]

As Jacobides further explains, 'architectures provide the contours and framework within which actors interact: they are usually partly designed (e.g. by regulation or *de facto*, by standards), and partly emergent (by the creation of socially understood templates and means to coordinate economic activities)'.[118]

Industry architecture is framed by the various economic actors at the birth of a new industry, the new players defining the interfaces (technological, institutional, or social) that allow different entities to co-specialize and divide labour.[119] As the industry progressively matures, we observe the emergence of 'winners', who strive to frame the industry architecture in their own advantage by developing complex strategies. The objective of these strategies is to capture a disproportionate amount of the surplus value created by the innovation. In some situations, the most effective strategy will be to opt for an 'open architecture' that nurtures complementarity through an open ecosystem, should a system of 'open innovation' be the most effective way to generate higher value in this industry. In other situations, firms may opt for a 'walled garden approach', opting for a closed architecture with regard to firms, with competing assets and capabilities entering the value chain while keeping it open for firms with complementary assets. Finally, in other circumstances, firms may opt for vertical integration; taking full control over the rents generated by the complementarities brought by the innovation whilst maintaining the possibility to exclude or marginalize any new entrant, for instance, by denying interoperability with regard to some indispensable technological interfaces.

Industry architectures are not meant to last forever, although they tend to be relatively stable for some time once the technology has sufficiently diffused. There are various reasons

---

[115] David Teece, 'Profiting from Technological Innovation: Implications for Integration, Collaboration, Licensing and Public Policy' (1986) 15(6) *Research Policy*, 285.
[116] Michael Jacobides, Thorbjørn Knudsen, and Mie Augier, 'Benefiting from Innovation: Value Creation, Value Appropriation and the Role of Industry Architectures' (2006) 35 *Research Policy*, 1201.
[117] See Michael Jacobides, 'Industry Architecture' in *The Palgrave Encyclopaedia of Strategic Mangement*, edited by Mie Augier and David Teece (Palgrave Macmillan 2016) https://link.springer.com/referenceworkentry/10.1057/978-1-349-94848-2-390-1.
[118] Jacobides et al., 'Benefiting from Innovation' (n 116), 1203.   [119] ibid.

for this stability, such as the requirement for any new technology to be interoperable with the technical standards of the industry architect who benefits from an installed base; the quality certification barrier from which the technologies of the industry architect benefit, to the extent that consumers' expectations have been framed according to the industry architect's quality standard; the favourable legal framework from which the industry architect benefits, as it may have been framed so to respond to the risks generated by the technology of the incumbent or to accommodate the needs of the industry architect. However, as Jacobides et al. observe:

> industry architectures can ... also change whenever new ways are found to put together the various industry participants: legal innovations that alter transaction costs ..., new ways of safeguarding against loss from transactional hazards ..., and technical innovations that alter the payoff to bundling specialized production factors ... could inspire adjustment of an industry's architecture.[120]

This shift from the dyad to industry-wide networks of relationships regarding the allocation of the financial returns of innovation also explains the reason for the competitive game being more complex and wider than the usual focus of competition law on a relevant market.

Various factors may influence industry architecture. One is technological path dependence, which results from a self-reinforcing process triggered by an event, such as a first-mover advantage leading to the choice of a widely used technology standard, which leads to a 'lock-in' to a less optimal—from a quality-of-technology perspective—equilibrium, without that being the intention of the agents in the first place.[121] The legal/regulatory framework may also play a crucial role in the definition of the boundaries of an industry and of its governance. Quite often it supports the existing industry architecture. Finally, path dependence and 'lock-in' may result from intentional strategies seeking to manipulate the industry architecture so as to create a bottleneck. This is a segment of the value chain where there is limited mobility.[122] The firm controlling the bottleneck is in a position to extract all surplus value in the specific segment as well as a higher percentage of the surplus generated by innovation in vertically adjacent segments.[123] This may take different forms, such as manipulating the setting of technology standards, as often standards shape industry architecture, or influencing the regulators and/or the legislative framework shaping the architecture of the industry, either directly through lobbying activity and pressure groups or indirectly by developing a narrative that will catch the imagination of policy-makers and legislators so that the emergent regulatory framework serves the interests of industry architect.

In conclusion, being in a position to influence the way the industry is organized or structured and the value allocation between the industry (or ecosystem) actors, provides 'architectural advantage'.[124] This may be a quite important source of sustainable abnormal profits. This is probably the reason why 'architectural fights'[125] have characterized the evolution of all industries. The competition to become the industry architect plays a crucial role in periods of profound technological transformation, such as the development of new GPTs; in periods when new technologies that confer significant advantages, such as reducing costs or increasing productivity, are progressively integrated in the production process in the context of a specific industry.[126] These technologies offer a higher rate of return on investment and often attract capital from other industries. In the context of the inter-industry competition, that is one of the characteristics of financial capitalism.[127] The important role of financial markets in the development of the digital economy and the monetization of digital

---

[120] ibid., fn 3.   [121] Arthur, 'Competing Technologies' (n 24), 116.
[122] Jacobides et al., 'Benefiting from Innovation' (n 116), fn 13.   [123] ibid., 1208.
[124] ibid., 1200.   [125] ibid., fn 13.
[126] Charles Ferguson and Charles Morris, 'How Architecture Wins Technology Wars' (1993) 71(2) *Harvard Business Review*, 86.
[127] Anwar Shaikh, *Capitalism: Competition, Conflict, Crises* (Oxford University Press 2016).

inputs also shifts attention away from the traditional focus of competition law on competition within an industry, to competition between industries, capital (in the sense of value-enhancing activity, which does not constitute labour) moving from one industry to another in search of higher profits. The concept of 'ecosystem' offers an additional space where intra- and inter-industry competition occurs.

According to the architectural advantage approach, the boundaries of an industry should not be considered as a given. Firms with superior performance (due to superior resources and capabilities[128]) aim to shape 'industry architectures' in a way that provides them control of a 'bottleneck', i.e. that would enable them to leverage their position of strength over all other companies that collaborate with them in the creation of surplus value.[129] Hence, to understand this process of value extraction that motivates strategies of competition, it is important to analyse the market level and the industry and ecosystem levels. It also challenges the idea that there are cycles in the life of an industry: an industry being marked by a dominant design, with an established hierarchy and stable market shares, that slowly erodes as the industry matures, with product innovation mainly occurring through new entry. According to this view, the competition of capabilities takes place not only at market or segment level (e.g. among mobile handset manufacturers), but also at the value-chain level (e.g. among mobile handset manufacturers, network providers, content providers, etc.). Contrary to (industrial) economics, which assumes that 'firms compete only within a market, and it is their performance, within that market, relative to other firms, that determines their profitability', the architectural advantage perspective focuses on the role of vertical competition and the way this affects the relative proportion of value (i.e. the 'NPV of future profits') that each segment captures, which may lead to important value shifts from one part of the value chain to another. The firms acquiring architectural advantage (the 'kingpins') take a central role in the overall industry architecture, influencing not only the segment they belong to but also multiple segments within a single industry or ecosystem.[130]

However, acquiring a bottleneck is not the only way architectural advantage converts to abnormal profits. Focusing on the appropriation of value from other value-chain participants makes sense if one conceptualizes competition (horizontal or vertical) as essentially a process taking place on product or technology markets or ecosystems and focusing on capturing value through the protection and/or leveraging of innovation. However, value may also be created by 'investing in assets that will appreciate'[131] and will, thus, increase the market value of the firm from the perspective of financial markets. Jacobides et al. note how this 'subtle shift of mindset from profit (and isolating mechanisms) to wealth creation (and the potential for asset appreciation)', explains why an industry architect may favour imitation by competitors, even if this reduces profitability, provided this strategy of openness increases the value of the underlying assets.[132]

B. Architectural advantage through performative regulation

In view of the newness of the technology and the absence of a well-established legal framework regulating its use so as to limit the eventual social costs that may flow from its diffusion in the rest of the economy, it becomes crucial for the economic actors promoting the use of DLT to engage with the legal field, and, in particular, to influence the government in favour of adopting policies that will either promote the new technology, or will not, at least, negatively affect its development. It is a well-known fact that the economy mirrors technological

---

[128] Birger Wernerfelt, 'A Resource-Based View of the Firm' (1984) 5(2) *Strategic Management Journal*, 171; C. K. Prahalad and Gary Hamel, 'The Core Competence of the Corporation' (1990) *Harvard Business Review*, 79.

[129] Michael Jacobides and Jennifer Tae, 'Kingpins, Bottlenecks, and Value Dynamics Along a Sector' (2015) 26(3) *Organization Science*, 889.

[130] ibid.   [131] Jacobides et al., 'Benefiting from Innovation' (n 116), 1201.   [132] ibid., 1212.

change,[133] and that, sooner or later, the economic regulator will have to deal with the economic implications of this change. However, the culture of innovation, which has in recent times become the holy grail sought by governments in the various public policies they pursue and the narrative of disruption that has overtaken that of order as the dominant logic driving state intervention, has produced significant changes in the way regulators engage with new technologies and has literally shifted their approach from being re-active to being, or at least aspiring to be, pro-active. This change is perceptible in the way the economic actors that promote the use of this new technology have engaged so far with regulators and the narratives they have put forward in their interactions with them.

As mentioned in section IV.A, regulation and regulators may be used as weapons in fights for architectural advantage. These fights may divide, on the one side, economic actors that rely on the new technology to foray economic sectors and to disrupt existing industry architectures, and, on the other, industry architects who would prefer to either slow down the process of diffusion of this new technology, in order to maintain their competitive position, or to control it in their interest by emulating the successful strategies of the new players and/ or incorporating them in one way or another, into their existing ecosystems.

It is clear that to the extent that blockchain technology, and the automation and decentralization it brings forward, expands to different industries, there is need for the legal system and for the regulatory state as a whole to respond to such rapid changes and to reconceptualize the philosophy and mechanisms of its intervention. As for any GPT, regulators are confronted with difficult choices regarding the application of the existing regulatory framework if this is judged appropriate for the technology or the development of a new regulatory framework with a better 'fit' to the specific GPT. Regulators also rely on foresight to predict the possible problems that may emerge from the implementation of the GPT in its later stages, the choice being here between a strategy of incremental changes to the existing regulation or the design of a new regulatory framework upfront. The latter option may be more appropriate if the regulator feels less empowered to deal effectively with such problems in the future because of path dependency and sunk costs.

Quite often there is still uncertainty over the risks of the new technology and the lack of appropriate empirically based knowledge. In this case, regulators may appeal to first principles (or meta-principles), which will determine the broad direction of their regulatory strategy. In the absence of a solid body of knowledge or expertise in the technology and its possible implications, the choice of regulatory strategy will, most likely, not only been driven by empirical evidence or solidly established theory, but also by the struggle between competing narratives communicated to the regulators. These often represent the interests of the main stakeholders concerning the implementation of the specific technology.

With regard to the regulation of DLT, it is possible to identify two paradigms that may influence the dominant regulatory narrative: (i) a market failure paradigm that perceives the state as taking action against the possible risks that the implementation of blockchain may entail for market and non-market actors; and (ii) a 'Schumpeterian' paradigm, which may perceive the role of the state as being that of nurturing or facilitating the innovation process in industries, even if this has the potential to generate market failures, such as, for instance, the constitution of bottlenecks in some segments of the value chain. Even in the presence of some empirical evidence about the social effects of a specific regulation of such technology, the prior beliefs the specific regulator has on the regulatory paradigms discussed will very much determine his action.

The tension between these paradigms of state action is particularly intense in periods of technological change, when regulators have to make clear choices about either taking a hands-on (and possibly prophylactic) approach, addressing all the possible social costs

---

[133] Brian Arthur, *The Nature of Technology* (Penguin 2009), Ch. 10.

following the implementation of this technology, even if these have not yet materialized, thus, implementing the principle of precaution with the risk of stifling innovation, or a hands-off approach of 'permission-less innovation', thereby effectively accepting that the 'public good' may be better pursued if entrepreneurs are left undisturbed in their effort to develop new business models and to explore new ways of implementing the GPT. There is also the possibility of a compromise to continue regulating as usual but to open spaces for monitored experimentation that may later, if proved successful, be generalized and lead to structured regulatory change.

These meta-principles of regulatory action form the broader institutional context that economic actors riding the wave of new technology consider when they shape their strategies to gain architectural advantage. They often realize that the permanence of the existing industry architecture, which is dominated by the industry architect that emerged victorious out of past technology wars, largely depends on the support of the existing regulatory framework that has been shaped over time to fit the dominant business models imposed by the winners of these wars. Influencing state action so that it assists the industry architect to maintain bottlenecks and to limit the possibility of new entry is one of the key competitive strategies deployed in order to preserve abnormal profitability as the industry matures. Drawing on rent-seeking theory, one may argue that influencing the government and the broader institutions of our societies (the rules of the social game) in order to reduce competition has become a prevalent competitive strategy if one judges by the 'investments' made in lobbying in recent years.[134]

The narrative of de-centralization and disintermediation was a very important feature of the presentation of the blockchain technology to the specialized community and the general public.[135] Blockchain evangelists often referred to the disruptive innovation potential of the new technology in industries dominated by stable oligopolies or by dominant digital platforms with poor consumer satisfaction, little innovation, and rising concerns over privacy. Policy-makers were particularly receptive to this narrative. Although some have embraced it to the extent of adopting a paradigm of 'permissionless innovation', they have opted for an experimental approach that has provided blockchain-based disruptors the opportunity to influence regulators so that they are able to curtail the architectural advantage of the incumbents and, eventually, become the industry architects. This experimentalism has taken various forms; the constant is the focus on innovation as the driving principle of regulatory action.

However, in the absence of a clear body of expertise determining objective and systematic instruments to measure innovation and, consequently, to guide state action in this context, regulation loses its substantive/rule-based or economic-based approach and becomes performative. By performative I mean, first, that regulation takes the form of a 'more dispersed intangible authority built into relationships and practices'.[136] Power is deployed in a dramaturgical way through symbolic interaction between the regulators and the industry. The struggle between worldviews that are trying to prevail becomes visible in these contexts, before eventually giving rise to 'socio-technical agencements'[137] that shape the form of the

---

[134] James Bessen, 'Accounting for Rising Corporate Profits: Intangibles or Regulatory Rents?' (2016) Boston University School of Law, Law and Economics Research Paper No. 16-18.

[135] See Wessel Reijers and Mark Coeckelbergh, 'The Blockchain as a Narrative Technology: Investigating the Social Ontology and Normative Configurations of Cryptocurrencies' (2018) 31 *Philosophy & Technology*, 103–30, noting the development of blockchain as a 'narrative technology' re-configuring social reality, in particular by promising the decentralization of authority.

[136] Susie Scott, 'Revisiting the Total Institution: Performative Regulation in the Reinventive Institution' (2010) 44(2) *Sociology*, 219.

[137] I borrow this term from Michael Callon, 'What Does it Mean to Say That Economics is Performative?' in *Do Economists Make Markets? On the Performativity of Economics*, edited by Donald MacKenzie, Fabian Muniesa, and Lucia Siu (Princeton University Press 2007), 311.

industry architecture. In the absence of a clear, expert body determining the boundaries of state action, the activity of the regulators, through the focus on innovation and their objectives, meet those of the industry, the regulators transforming themselves to facilitators instead of their traditional role of prescribers.

However, by 'performative' I also mean that through these interactions the authority comes to internalize the values of the dominant narrative and, to the extent that regulation may shape industry architecture, the dominant narrative becomes a self-fulfilling prophecy. Performative regulation will naturally play a more significant role in industries 'marked by futurity'. Swartz provides a good explanation of this fundamental characteristic of blockchain:

> '(a)s soon as a proposal is offered—whether as a white paper, a slide deck, or a blog post—it is treated as though it already exists, ready to go. Indeed, blockchain projects exist in a particular temporality and have their own sense of the past and future, of change. It performatively leans into a future, always just around the corner, which might as well be here already.[138]

This reflexivity obviously influences the strategies of economic actors in their interaction with the state, in particular as regulation becomes 'performative' in the two senses I give to this term. The interaction of banks and FinTechs in the architectural fight opposing them in the financial value chain provides a useful illustration of interplay between strategies to gain architectural advantage and performative regulation.

C. Competing over industry architecture: FinTechs and banks

1. *The FinTech revolution in the financial services industry*

The financial services industry has seen some remarkable changes brought about by the application of information and communication technologies, including digitalization in recent years. Banks, since the 1960s, have been pioneers in the use of 'in-house' IT with these systems evolving over the years to enable electronic interfaces to consumers (through the use of automated teller machines (ATMs) and online banking).[139] Banks have also been active in the payment services segment of the value chain, where they have put in place a number of card networks, such as Visa and Mastercard, and have set the technical infrastructure and rules for payment processing. Finally, in the interbank area, banks have put in place multinational electronic networks, such as SWIFT and TARGET, in order to handle international transactions that require an international interface to the bank's internal systems. Banks are also present in both retail and wholesale banking, promoting themselves as a supermarket for financial services, providing a single source of financial products to their customers. Banks typically offer a broad product portfolio in retail, private, commercial, investment, and transaction banking, along with wealth and asset management and insurance (the 'universal banking model'). The universal banking model has enabled customers to have easy access to just one single source of financial products. Banks are present in both the conventional deposit and loan services and in the provision of investment advice and insurance products. This vertical integration provides banks with a stable retail funding, which ensures sufficient liquidity and facilitates risk-pooling and risk-bearing. A large capital base also serves as a buffer to absorb losses, thereby providing the bank more credibility and also an easier access to capital by issuing debt or equity in larger issue sizes. However, this industry architecture also leads to very limited customer switching and limited consumer engagement.[140]

---

[138] Swartz (n 14), 89.

[139] Rainer Alt, Roman Beck, and Martin Smits, 'FinTech and the Transformation of the Financial Industry' (2018) 28 *Electronic Markets*, 236.

[140] See, e.g., the findings in the Competition and Markets Authority, 'CMA, Retail Banking Market Investigation' (2016) Final Report, [64]–[66], noting that the level of customer engagement is quite low, with only 8% of the customers having switched to other retail banks in the last three years. According to the report, 'despite variations

The digital revolution has affected the banking sector in many different ways. Its most important implication is the opportunities this opened up for modularizing the banking sector and unbundling the various segments of it. The shift from the branch to online banking in the 1990s was followed by mobile banking in the 2000s, and the use of Big Data in the 2010s, with the current account and the interface linking banks with their customers providing a wealth of valuable data relating to various dimensions of the life of their clients, such as consumption patterns, propensity to save and invest, travel preferences, etc. During this period of digitalization, the number of banks has considerably decreased[141] and the sector has become increasingly more concentrated.[142] It is unclear whether this consolidation of the banking industry may be explained by the lack of competition or by the fact that the endogenous sunk costs resulting from the banks' investments in new technologies, communication networks, and specialized human capital lead to a 'natural banking oligopoly'.[143]

In recent years, a number of start-ups developed new business models, on the basis of big data, machine learning, and blockchain technology, with the aim of disrupting financial intermediaries and banks. FinTechs developed peer-to-peer lending platforms (e.g. Zopa in the UK) matching borrowers and lenders in the most effective way, sometimes the lenders choosing the borrowers. Their capacity for innovation is certainly larger than the traditional vertically integrated model of universal banking. Although the payment systems market is still dominated by banks, through Visa and Mastercard, big tech digital platforms and companies, such as PayPal, Apple, or Google have developed important payment innovations. One of the most interesting payment innovations is the multi-purpose social media/ messaging service/payment app 'WeChat' developed by the Chinese company, Tencent. Amazon has recently launched a lending service and social media platform taking advantage of their knowledge of the characteristics and preferences of their users to cross-sell financial services.

DLT may transform various activities in the financial services value chain[144] (see Fig. 18.2). It may bring important cost savings. It has been reported that the implementation of blockchain in clearing and settlement which records loans and securities will bring significant reduction of costs for the largest investment banks.[145] Similar cost reductions are also expected in trade finance, identity verifications of customers, and other back-office activity, as well as cross-border payments, security trading, and compliance.[146] Hence, blockchain may enable traditional banks to cut down their costs and improve their efficiency. The use of blockchain technology has the potential to considerably lower the costs of financial intermediation and to provide a more consumer-centric and personalized approach to the provision of financial services. For instance, access to data may provide a better picture of the creditworthiness of loan applicants and enable price discrimination strategies.

---

between banks in prices and quality and the gains from switching, market shares have remained broadly stable with those banks offering the lower average prices and/or higher service quality only gaining market share slowly'.

[141] See the figures reported in Alt et al. (n 139), 237, noting that in both the United States and Germany the number of institutions has almost been reduced by half.

[142] Concentration is usually measured by reference to the share of assets of the three largest banks in total banking system assets in a domestic system, which is not relevant, as such, for competition assessment, which focuses instead on the markets for deposits and for loans to small and medium enterprises: see, Organisation for Economic Cooperation and Development (OECD), 'Competition, Concentration and Stability in the Banking Sector' (2010) Report, 20.

[143] For a discussion, see Xavier Vives, 'Competition in the Changing World of Banking' (2001) 17(4) *Oxford Review of Economic Policy*, 541.

[144] See Martin Arnold, 'Five Way Banks are Using Blockchain' (*ft.com*, 16 October 2017) https://www.ft.com/content/615b3bd8-97a9-11e7-a652-cde3f882dd7b.

[145] See David Treat, 'Blockchain: Do the Numbers Add Up?' (*accenture.com*) https://www.accenture.com/gb-en/insight-perspectives-capital-markets-blockchain-numbers.

[146] See Santander, 'Fintech 2.0: Rebooting Financial Services' (2015) Paper.

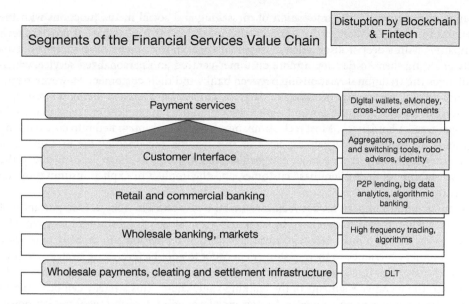

Fig. 18.2 Blockchain, FinTech, and the financial services value chain

Source: the diagram is inspired by that in Mark Carney, 'The Promise of FinTech—Something New Under the Sun?' (25 January 2017) Speech.

However, blockchain also has the potential to disrupt the traditional financial system in more fundamental ways. Take, for example, the payment system segment 'Ripple', an open-source internet software-using DLT protocol, which enables users to conduct cross-border payments in multiple currencies blockchain, competing with traditional cross-border payment system, which because of the lack of a global central settlement institution is currently relying on a highly complex system managing the interface between separate national settlement processes.[147] Ripple facilitates cross-border payments through a distributed settlement system, the ledger being distributed among the collective action of Ripple users rather than through a central settlement authority. This 'flips the correspondent-banking model on its head'.[148] The nature of its decentralized internet payment protocol is quite different from traditional payment systems, thus, creating important challenges for regulators.[149] More importantly, blockchain provides new actors, merging technology with financial expertise (the so-called 'FinTechs'), the opportunity to make an efficient entry into the financial services value chain at only one 'niche' segment without having to compete with the vertically integrated banks at all other segments of the chain. This constitutes an important threat to the universal banking model. Not all FinTechs are implementers of blockchain technology, nor do they rely heavily on blockchain technology for their business models. However, the blockchain disintermediation and decentralization narratives form an integral part of their communication strategy and explain their emphasis on disruptive innovation and the opportunities that it brings to new market players.

Fintechs test two traditional sources of competitive advantage from which traditional banks benefit. First, banks can borrow cheaply as they have access to cheap deposits and benefit from an explicit or implicit insurance by the government. Second, they enjoy a stable relationship with their customers and have a large customer base; this enables them to sell

---

[147] For a discussion, see Marcel Rosner and Andrew Kang, 'Understanding and Regulating Twenty-First Century Payment Systems: The Ripple Case Study' (2016) 114 *Michigan Law Review*, 649.
[148] ibid., 658.   [149] For an in-depth discussion, see ibid., 664–81.

a range of products.[150] The integration of messaging and social media functions with the payment functions challenges the second source of competitive advantage. It provides tech companies with a deeper knowledge of the preferences of their client base, thereby potentially enabling them to develop a more customer-centred and personalized service, which challenges the traditional relationship between banks and their customers. However, banks still hold a massive amount of customer data, the current bank account being the principal financial gateway for customers and a major social and technological interface that could be considered a bottleneck. Most tech companies have not yet integrated into core banking segments by applying for a banking license. This may be explained by the first source of competitive advantage from which retail banks benefit, access to cheap deposits due to the relative stability of their client base customer, and the implicit or explicit insurance by the government.

In envisioning competition between traditional banks and FinTechs, it is important first to analyse when the services offered by each may act as strategic substitutes for or complements to each other. Banks may take advantage of their reputation and capacity to provide omni-channel experience to their customers in order to adopt a leveraging strategy, eventually blocking or marginalizing the FinTech threat by making it quite difficult for FinTechs to enter into the lucrative segments of the banking value chain. This strategy can be achieved through bundling or tying strategies, for instance leveraging the substantial market power of the banks in the current account and mortgages market to the more competitive credit cards and insurance markets. Bundling/tying may be used either to deter or to accommodate competitors. Vives explains:

> As a deterrence strategy, it increases the aggressiveness of the incumbent and makes life for entrants more difficult, since the entrant has to succeed in both markets. Tying makes sense to foreclose entry when it is irreversible and A and B are not very complementary, since then the incumbent is more aggressive; when there are cost links between markets, or when entry in B is uncertain since then tying makes entry more costly and uncertain since the entrant has to succeed in both complementary markets. As an accommodating strategy, it may serve as a price discrimination device among heterogeneous customers. Typically, tying by the incumbent will decrease the incentives to innovate by the rival but increase those of the incumbent. It is worth noting that innovations in payments systems are primarily generated by non-banks like PayPal, Google, and Apple. Banks may prefer accommodation of entry because they gain interchange fees paid to them by new service operators and because the cut in revenues to banks for each purchase may be more than compensated by the increase in aggregate transactions performed by customers. In summary, the incumbents may partner with the new entrants, buy them up partially or totally, or decide to fight them. The details of each segment of the market will matter for the decision as well as the extent of legacy technologies in each institution. Indeed, the response of institutions is likely to be heterogeneous according to their specificity.[151]

Banks may also try to properly compete with FinTech, by adopting new technologies, such as blockchain, AI, and Big Data. There is clearly the perception that FinTech, and the disintermediation and decentralization it may bring forward, puts various aspects of the financial institutions' business at risk.[152] Banks have made considerable investments in upgrading their technology systems and have also started acquiring FinTechs, with the number of banks/ FinTechs mergers and acquisitions transactions rising considerably in 2017. However, the

---

[150] Xavier Vives, 'The Impact of FinTech on Banking, in European Economy Banks, Regulation, and the Real Sector' (2017) 2, 101.

[151] See CBInsights, 'Banks are Finally Going After Fintech Startups' (*cbsinsights.com*, 13 February 2018) https://www.cbinsights.com/research/top-us-banks-fintech-acquisitions/.

[152] PwC, 'Blurred Lines: How FinTech is Shaping Financial Services' (2016) Report.

majority of the banks have not yet acquired a FinTech, and there are important challenges to integrate FinTechs into the traditional hierarchical organizations of the banking industry.[153]

Another option for banking institutions is to partner with FinTechs, integrating them into their ecosystem. This could take place in different ways. The banks may opt to abandon the universal banking model by limiting their activity to commoditized banking services, such as deposits, for which they benefit from a large and stable installed base of customers, while using open platform capabilities in order to connect their consumers with a number of FinTech players offering superior or specialized products. The bank may even develop a multi-sided platform pricing strategy that charges both groups of users or only one side of the market, and subsidizes the other. Although, in theory, the bank will face competition in the provision of high-added-value services to its customers, the trade-off may be positive overall for the bank, if such a strategy increases its market share vis-à-vis other banking ecosystems, or if it has the effect of increasing the value of its brand and other intangible assets, which may be significant drivers of financial value.

Alternatively, banks may re-brand themselves as platform-based digital banking ecosystems offering their customers a wide range of financial services from a single source. Banks may in this case opt for a 'walled garden' strategy. While opening programming interfaces in their IT systems so as to incentivize FinTechs to join the ecosystem, banks will retain control over the software, the hardware, and the content displayed. This control enables an easier monetarization of the products and services provided.[154] A 'walled garden' approach requires interoperability and open interface policy with regard to application programming interfaces in order to tie third parties more easily to the ecosystem and enable a seamless connection between interfaces, whilst also providing incentives for innovation.[155] This will also offer banks the possibility to 'lock-in' customers and third parties, such as external retailers, for instance, by integrating a mobile payment system through proprietary technology into retail banking and integrating different technological standards to those of other banking platforms.[156] Cross-subsidization strategies may also be used in this context, the banks supplying their customers with free smartphone devices made by other manufacturers but with the bank's branding in order to monetarize financial services sold through the banking app store.[157] A 'walled garden' strategy may, however, face some constraints from a competition law perspective, in particular if this leads to the leveraging of a dominant position or a position of market power in vertically adjacent markets.

Similarly, FinTechs have the choice to join existing banking ecosystems, or to apply for a full banking license and compete with them directly, something that has already been tried by some peer-to-peer lenders.[158] They may also strive to form their own ecosystem, taking advantage of the unbundling of financial services that has been quite disruptive for banks. Traditional financial institutions may form part of this ecosystem but their role will be confined to the banking infrastructure level, thereby leaving the most lucrative consumer interface to the FinTechs, which may collaborate with technology companies to offer one-stop-shop social media/payment and financial services solutions to consumers. The unbundling and consequent re-organization of the industry towards a more decentralized

---

[153] See Yizhu Wang and Elizabeth Lim, 'Banks Face Challenges Acquiring Fintech Firms' (*forbes.com*, 5 January 2018) https://www.forbes.com/sites/mergermarket/2018/01/05/banks-face-challenges-acquiring-fintech-firms/#34ca6512428a.

[154] For a discussion of the benefits of such a strategy, see Deutsche Bank, 'Fintech Reloaded—Traditional Banks as Digital Ecosystems' (2015), 8–12.

[155] ibid., 10.   [156] ibid., 11.   [157] ibid., 11–12.

[158] See, e.g., the recent application of Zopa, 'the world's oldest P2P lender, for a baking licence': Financial Times, 'P2P Lender Zopa Raises £44m to Fund New Bank' (*ft.com*, 3 August 2018) https://www.ft.com/content/6ce5f960-96e1-11e8-b67b-b8205561c3fe. TransferWise, which has launched cross-border bank accounts: Financial Times, 'TransferWise to Offer Cross-Border Bank Accounts' (*ft.com*, 23 May 2017) https://www.ft.com/content/29adbe9a-3efd-11e7-82b6-896b95f30f58.

model may enhance consumer choice, with consumers no longer relying on a single financial institution for their needs, but being able to choose from a variety of FinTech companies, some of them exclusively offered online.

2. Regulatory interventions and the quest for architectural advantage in the financial services value chain

These architectural fights over the control and the structure of the competition game in the financial services value chain have naturally framed the regulatory intervention in this area. The regulation of the financial industry, in particular, following the emergence of FinTech, has been the first regulatory response to the challenges introduced by blockchain, as well as the decentralization and disintermediation narrative that identifies with DLT. There has been a considerable effort in recent years, in particular, following the financial crisis of 2008, to move the regulatory paradigm in the financial industry from its exclusive focus on the traditional prudential and systemic risks concerns, based on the conventional 'market failure' analysis, to a 'innovation-focused' paradigm that emphasizes the duty of regulators to promote competition and innovation.

UK regulators struggled to introduce some degree of flexibility and space for experimentation, largely relying on the important discretion provided to them for the regulation of the financial system, and, in particular, the emphasis put by the framework legislation on the values of competition and innovation.[159] The overall rationality of their intervention has been to favour the unbundling of the banking sector and the development of 'open banking standards' that would enable the FinTechs to flourish, either by developing their own ecosystem or by joining those of traditional banks. It is noteworthy that the regulators seem to have completely embraced the disruptive innovation narrative of FinTechs and seem to question the essence of the universal banking model. Parallel developments in competition regulation have also been inspired by the same principles and indicate that the architectural advantage of traditional banks is in jeopardy.

In its 2015 Productivity Plan, the UK Government required regulators to develop regulatory frameworks that support disruptive business models, innovation, emerging technologies, and the digital economy, imposing on them the duty to publish innovation plans which cover how they are creating a more supportive and agile regulatory and enforcement framework.[160] If we look to the regulators of the financial sector in the UK, each of them has the statutory duty to promote competition and innovation. The Financial Conduct Authority ('FCA') has a duty to promote effective competition insofar as that is compatible with its consumer protection or market integrity objectives. It also has an operational objective to promote effective competition in the interests of consumers in the markets it regulates.

The Payment Systems Regulator ('PSR'), an independent subsidiary of the FCA, has a specific objective to promote innovation in the UK payments sector. This complements its two other objectives to promote effective competition in the markets for payment systems and associated services, and to promote the interests of actual or likely users of services provided by payment systems. The PSR has strong powers over the main interbank and international card schemes to promote these objectives.

The Prudential Regulation Authority ('PRA') is a part of the Bank of England and has a secondary competition objective to act, as far as is reasonably possible, to facilitate effective competition in the markets it regulates when discharging its functions in a way that advances safety and soundness and insurance policy-holder protection.

---

[159] See, e.g., the discussion in Financial Conduct Authority, 'Our Approach to Competition' (*fca.org.uk*, 11 December 2017) https://www.fca.org.uk/publications/corporate-documents/our-approach-competition.

[160] HM Treasury, 'Fixing the Foundations: Creating A More Prosperous Nation' (2015) Cm 9098, Policy Paper, Section 13.6.

The aim of these regulators is to facilitate disruptive innovation—which presumably satisfies both the competition and innovation objectives.

These regulators were confronted with the emergence of a plethora of new actors and business models following the introduction of blockchain technology in the financial services sector and the development of FinTech. The regulators viewed these changes positively, as an opportunity to infuse more innovation and competition in the relatively stable oligopolistic structure of the financial industry, which has been dominated for a long time by a few large commercial banks. The financial crisis of 2008 and the risks raised by 'too-big-to-fail' banks, which has led to a process of regulatory unbundling, provided further impetus to the need for change by promoting the unbundling through the market, this time of many activities that were traditionally organized and being held under the control of banking institutions. In October 2014, the FCA launched 'Project Innovate' in order to encourage and support innovation in financial services.[161] This work is central to delivering the FCA's competition objective—it aims to encourage innovation in the interests of consumers and to promote competition through disruptive innovation that offers new services to customers and challenges existing business models. Project Innovate has embedded constructive engagement with innovative firms—from smaller start-ups to mass-market new models—its aim being to 'remove unnecessary barriers to innovation'. The purpose of the Project was to assist innovative firms to gain access to 'timely and frank feedback' on the regulatory implications of their concepts, plans, and choices, but also, more generally, to tackle the structural issues that impede the progress of innovators entering the market.

A central part of Project Innovate was the 'Innovation Hub', which aims to help new and established businesses (both regulated and non-regulated) to introduce innovative financial products and services to the market, essentially providing an end-to-end experience for new entrants. Firms that receive initial support from the Innovation Hub have their applications for authorization handled via a specialized Project Innovate authorization process. The FCA provides firms with dedicated supervisory support, usually for one year post-authorization, which gives firms a seamless regulatory experience and minimizes the risk of unnecessary delay. There are no restrictions on the areas of financial services covered by the Innovation Hub: firms innovating in mortgages, capital markets, and pensions can all access the Innovation Hub for help in introducing their products to market. The Innovation Hub also performs a horizon-scanning role by identifying new technologies and areas where the regulatory framework needs to adapt to enable further innovation in the interests of consumers.

In November 2015, the FCA published its plans to open a 'regulatory sandbox'.[162] This was defined as 'a safe space where both regulated and unregulated firms can experiment with innovative products, services, business models and delivery mechanisms without immediately incurring all the normal regulatory consequences of engaging in such activity'. This is akin to Phase III clinical trials, where new products, services, and delivery models can be safely tested with customers. Given the high demand for this service, the FCA expanded the sandbox team and the scheme beyond the initial period of its deployment.

The sandbox may be useful for unauthorized firms that need to become authorized before being able to test their innovation in a live environment. It provides for a tailored authorization process for unauthorized firms that want to join the sandbox. Successful firms are granted restricted authorization that only allows them to test their ideas. These firms will still need to apply for authorization and meet threshold conditions, but only for the limited purposes of the sandbox test. This will make it easier for firms to reduce regulatory costs and the time they need to set up. It is explicitly mentioned that the restricted authorization is not available to firms looking for a banking license. The sandbox may also be useful

---

[161] Financial Conduct Authority, 'Project Innovate: Call for Input' (2014) Feedback Statement FS14/2.
[162] Financial Conduct Authority, 'Regulatory Sandbox' (2015) Research Paper.

for authorized firms looking for clarity around applicable rules before testing an idea that does not easily fit into the existing regulatory framework. These may benefit from individual guidance from the FCA that can instruct them in how the financial regulator will interpret relevant rules. This creates a safe space because if firms act in accordance with this guidance, the FCA will proceed on the basis that the firms have complied with the aspects of the FCA rules that the guidance relates to. It also provides waivers or modifications to the FCA rules where these rules were considered unduly burdensome or not achieving their purpose, and this waiver or modification would not adversely affect the advancement of any of the FCA's objectives. Finally, firms may benefit from not receiving enforcement action letters; this should provide them some comfort because so long as they deal with the FCA openly, keep to the agreed testing parameters, and treat customers fairly, there will be no disciplinary action for any unexpected issues that may arise.

The FCA also recommended the establishment, with the support of Project Innovate, of a FinTech industry-led virtual sandbox, which would allow firms to experiment in a virtual environment without entering the real market, using their own or publicly available data and a sandbox umbrella company.[163] The virtual sandbox could allow collaboration between innovators to develop solutions quicker and in a more informed way.

As well as directly supporting firms through the Innovation Hub and the Regulatory Sandbox, the FCA has introduced broader changes to help innovators, such as using informal steers on proposed innovations to enable more direct communication with firms, or working with the government to create a bespoke regulatory regime for peer-to-peer lending. Also, in June 2016, it launched an 'Advice Unit' to provide regulatory feedback to firms developing automated advice models, with the potential to deliver lower-cost advice to unserved or underserved consumers, following the 2015 Financial Advice Market Review ('FAMR').[164] The Advice Unit focuses on models in the investments, protection, and pensions sectors. Since September 2015, the FCA has also facilitated a series of themed weeks, designed to stimulate intense engagement with stakeholders interested in a particular area of innovation. The FCA also promotes RegTech—encouraging the adoption of new technologies (and new companies) to support the delivery of regulatory requirements.[165]

The PSR has strong objectives to promote innovation and competition in the UK payments sector. The promotion of innovation in payment systems can be driven either competitively or collaboratively, or as a combination of the two.

The PRA, in order to assist innovative firms to come to the market, in January 2016, established a Bank Start-Up Unit ('NBSU') to help prospective new banks enter the market and through the early days of authorization. This Unit comprises staff from both the PRA and the FCA and provides new banks the information and materials they need to navigate the process to become a new bank.

The Bank of England has finally set up a Research Hub in order to facilitate open dialogue between the Bank and the research community to support the Bank's work. In June 2016, the Bank launched its own FinTech Accelerator to partner with new technology firms to help it harness FinTech innovations for central banking applications. By running proofs of concept, the Bank is able to explore the benefits new technology can bring, whilst mitigating some of the associated risks.

Similar developments favouring FinTechs in this architectural fight over the financial services value chain have taken place, from a competition law and policy perspective, in the

---

[163] For more details, see Industry Sandbox, 'A Blueprint for an Industry-Led Virtual Sandbox for Financial Innovation' (2016) Consultation Guide.

[164] See Financial Conduct Authority, Advice Unit (*fca.org.uk*, 22 October 2018) https://www.fca.org.uk/firms/advice-unit.

[165] See Financial Conduct Authority, RegTech (*fca.org.uk*, 5 December 2018) https://www.fca.org.uk/firms/regtech.

value chain segments relating to customer relationships. These may finish by eroding the bottleneck from which traditional banks benefit because of the central role played by current accounts in the consumer/financial service providers interaction.[166]

The UK Competition and Markets Authority ('CMA') paved the way towards 'Open Banking' by implementing a competition law remedy it had imposed in 2016, following the retail banking market investigation.[167] The Open Banking regulatory intervention requires the six largest deposit-taking financial institutions (i.e. banks) in the UK to enable personal customers and small businesses to share their data securely with other banks and third parties and to manage their accounts with multiple providers through a single 'digital app'. This also provides them with more possibilities to compare financial services and products from competing providers, including account information service providers ('AISPs') and payment initiation service providers ('PISPs'). During this same period, however, this time in the payment system segment of the financial services value chain, the EU Payment Services Directive ('PSD2')[168] was transposed into UK law. It provides a similar access to APIs for any payment account (including credit card accounts) in favour of third parties, again with the same idea to promote competition in the provision of account aggregation services aiming to help consumers manage their finances by bringing all of their bank account data together in one place.[169] Finally, following a decision, the Bank of England decided to provide its non-bank payment service providers access to its real-time, gross settlement system, thus, enabling them to not have to rely on an agent bank for accessing the UK payment system.[170] These regulatory interventions have the potential to increase competition among banks, to further unbundle the financial services value chain, and to promote competition in these unbundled segments by FinTech companies by connecting the banks' IT systems through open APIs, with the third-party apps thereby leading to further disintermediation in this sector.[171]

The financial services industry provides an interesting case study for the deployment of architectural advantage strategies and the role performative regulatory intervention may play in this. Section V takes stock of these developments and aims to explain how these different forms of competitive advantage may transform blockchain competition.

V. Preliminary Conclusions on Blockchain Competition: From 'Winner-Takes-Most' Platform Competition Dynamics to Co-Opetition in Ecosystems?

The rise of platforms and online intermediaries in the governance of the digital economy has changed the competitive game and has led to the emergence of a new industry architecture characterized by 'winner-takes-most' competition. A more concentrated market structure in the various domains of activity that became digitized and interconnected through the internet developed as a consequence. The result, after a little more than two decades of development of the internet economy, is that the top five companies in the world, in

---

[166] These developments are discussed in detail in Paolo Siciliani, 'The Disruption of Retail Banking: A Competition Analysis of the Implications for Financial Stability and Monetary Policy' (2018) CLES Research Paper Series 3/2018.

[167] Competition and Markets Authority, 'CMA' (n 140), 441–61.

[168] Directive (EU) 2015/2366 of the European Parliament and of the Council (25 November 2015) on Payment Services in the Internal Market, amending Directives 2002/65/EC, 2009/110/EC and 2013/36/EU and Regulation (EU) No. 1093/2010, and repealing Directive 2007/64/EC, [2015] OJ L 337/.

[169] Payment Services Regulations 2017, SI 2017/752.

[170] See Bank of England, 'First Non-Bank Payment Service Provider Directly Accesses UK Payment System' (*bankofengland.co.uk*, 18 April 2018) https://www.bankofengland.co.uk/news/2018/april/non-bank-psp-access-to-the-payments-system-announcement.

[171] For a discussion of the possible implications and counter-strategies that may be adopted by the banks, see Siciliani (n 166).

terms of capitalization, are tech companies and all of them are platforms. 'Network effects' has become the buzzword to explain the phenomenally rapid rise of digital platforms, as well as their impressive profitability. Economies of scale make it difficult for new entrants to challenge the position of these digital platforms once network effects have enabled it to build a strong position on a part of the digital economy. While some may have thought that these positions of power will soon erode due to innovation competition, it is increasingly clear that this process might take a considerable period of time, counted in decades, as the industry matures and a stable industry hierarchy has now emerged with a small group of industry leaders controlling the industry. This permanence of positions of power is not only due to network effects, but to the ability of these industry leaders to shape the industry architecture for their advantage and to impose their rules in the competitive game. This stems from the central role platform operators play as a certain type of intermediary in the digital economy, match-making different groups of users and enabling them to enter into transactions that would not have occurred but for the presence of the platform. The demand of different customer groups for the platform is related to the supply of other platform customer groups and vice versa. The main function of the platform operator is to internalize the indirect network externalities that are generated by the fact that the decisions of each group of users affects the outcomes of the other group of users. Platforms take advantage of these interdependencies of demand when designing their business models and choosing the level and structure of their pricing. These multi-sided market strategies focus on platform profitability, rather than on market profitability, and have considerable implications on the shaping of the boundaries of markets, as traditional one-sided market players are not able to defend their position and fight back, even if their products are of superior quality. The result is that they are forced to join the dominant industry architecture devised by the platforms, or otherwise face extinction.

This active shaping of the industry architecture may explain the durability of positions of power of a few digital platforms, even in the presence of intense innovation competition that characterizes the modern digital economy. Although a platform is not the only form of organizing economic activity in the digital economy, its success as an organizational tool has led other intermediaries, such as traditional resellers, to organize their activity in a way that emulates the multi-sided markets strategies of digital platforms. Platforms have therefore, for a considerable part, substituted the organizing role of markets as the dominant form of ordering economic activity. The emergence of industry architectures completes this process of re-ordering of the digital economy, which was, ironically, initiated by the dream of competition and decentralization at the beginning of the internet era.

The dynamic forces of innovation competition may, however, sooner or later, erode the barriers set by the current industry architecture. The development of technologies that accentuate the distributed imaginary of the internet and question the architectural advantage of digital platforms may accelerate this process. DLT plays precisely this role; it offers an opportunity to eliminate the centralized control of digital platforms and, consequently, to re-design the industry architecture in order to promote competition. As innovation competition intensifies, due to the introduction of technologies enabling a new industry architecture, the dominant digital platforms face an important strategic choice. They can, of course, stick to the competitive advantage provided by their scale and installed base in order to develop strategies that suppress any effort to question their hold on the industry, through leveraging and discriminatory practices, or by buying their potential competitors, and thus profiting directly from their innovative efforts. Imposing a 'winner-takes-most' rationality through a set of designed leveraging strategies may, of course, result in disgruntled customers and could be jeopardized by the enforcement activity of competition authorities and/ or regulatory intervention. Furthermore, in the long term it proves counter-productive as the bottlenecks controlled by the platforms become less and less relevant for competition.

Another option is to reshape the industry architecture in a way that enables the incumbents to take advantage of the dynamism and innovation brought about by the new industry players, by initiating an effort of co-specialization that requires cooperation, as well as competition between them, to the extent that a firm may be (at least, partially) vertically integrated. The 'ecosystem' forms this new space where strategies of cooperation and competition take place. The concept of 'co-opetition' (or 'war and peace'), largely explains business strategies in the digital economy—as it denotes, on the one hand, a situation where market players cooperate in order to create value (i.e. a bigger pie) with this cooperative activity involving customers and suppliers—and on the other hand, divide up the pie, thus also competing with each other.[172] In this co-opetition framework, business is not a 'winner-takes-all' or 'zero-sum' game, nor cannot it be a 'winner-takes-most' game, as the industry architecture should be judged by all economic actors as being 'fair', in order for them to maintain their incentives to participate in it and for the relations between the various firms forming the ecosystem to maintain some form of stability.[173]

Developed in the early 1990s,[174] the concept of 'ecosystem' has been defined in broad terms as 'a group of interacting firms that depend on each other's activities'.[175] Teece notes that a characteristic of ecosystems is their 'co-evolution', in the sense that the 'attributes of two or more organizations become more closely complementary, the system being typically reliant on the technological leadership of one or two firms that provide a platform around which other system members, providing inputs and complementary goods, align their investments and strategies', and 'co-creation' as two or more organizations 'combine forces to pioneer new markets'.[176] Adner observes that 'the ecosystem is defined by the alignment structure of the multilateral set of partners that need to interact in order for a focal value proposition to materialize', this alignment structure being defined as 'the extent to which there is mutual agreement among the members regarding positions and flows'.[177] The concept of 'ecosystem' has emerged as the dominant idea to depict the competitive environment in the modern digital economy. The 'ecosystem manager' will determine the elements of the value chain that need to be internalized and which of these elements will be supported externally in order to capture value. Most studies on ecosystems focus on the role of the ecosystem as a 'hub' of interfirm relations taking place within the context of a platform, often referred to as the 'lead firm' or 'ecosystem captain', which 'defines the hierarchical differentiation of members' roles and establishes standards and interfaces', a number of formal mechanisms, such as the management of standards and interfaces, platform governance, IP rights, etc. forming the 'key tools that hubs use to discipline and motivate ecosystem members'.[178] However, from a theoretical perspective, a platform ecosystem has never been the only option, even if practically the platform model has become dominant: it is possible to imagine an ecosystem where power will not be centralized in a hub and governed by a platform, but where authority will be distributed among various economic actors and stakeholders, who will take decisions by consensus.

---

[172] Barry Nalebuff, 'Co-opetition: Competitive and Cooperative Business Strategies for the Digital Economy' (1997) 26(6) *Strategy and Leadership*, 28.

[173] For the importance of fairness in order to keep stable a social equilibrium, see Ken Binmore, *Natural Justice* (Oxford University Press, 2005), 3–14, who takes an 'evolutionary approach to social contract theory', advancing that a social contract may be 'internally stable' if it combines efficiency and fairness.

[174] James Moore, 'Predators and Prey: A New Ecology of Competition' (1993) 71(3) *Harvard Business Review*, 75.

[175] Michael Jacobides, Carmelo Cennamo, and Annabelle Gawer, 'Towards a Theory of Ecosystems' (2018) 39 *Strategic Management Journal*, 2255.

[176] David Teece, 'Next-Generation Competition: New Concepts for Understanding How Innovation Shapes Competition and Policy in the Digital Economy' (2012) 9 *Journal of Law and Policy*, 105–06.

[177] Ron Adner, 'Ecosystem as Structure—an Actionable Construct for Strategy' (2017) 43(1) *Journal of Management*, 42.

[178] Jacobides et al., 'Towards a Theory of Ecosystems' (n 175), 2258–259 and the literature review provided.

The definition of 'ecosystem' by Jacobides et al. espouses this broader theoretical canvass that accepts that there are 'different *types* of ecosystems',[179] which can include a 'platform ecosystem' among other alternative governance structures, while also providing some criteria in order to distinguish 'ecosystems' from markets or supply chains managed hierarchically. The possibility of 'modular architecture' constitutes the starting point for an ecosystem to form. Its main function is to 'help coordinate interrelated organizations that have significant autonomy' from each other.[180] The fact that modularity acts as an enabler for ecosystems to form does not, however, exhaust all the necessary conditions for the emergence of an ecosystem, as this is the dominant trend in the organization of economic production in a global digital economy.[181] As Jacobides et al. rightly observe, 'modularization and the subsequent reduction of frictional transaction costs are more likely to lead to the emergence of *markets*'.[182] Thus, if the concept of 'the ecosystem' is to be useful, it will need to rely on something additional. This is the mutual dependency between the members of the ecosystem, which is driven by the nature of the multilateral complementarities that exist between them. The nature of multilateral complementarities that underpin ecosystems is indeed quite specific: these are of a 'non-generic' type; they are unique (as they lead to some degree of co-specialization) or 'supermodular', requiring 'the creation of a specific structure of relationships and alignment to create value' (i.e. 'A is more valuable to X in the presence of B').[183]

The mutual dependence resulting from these unique and supermodular complementarities requires some (formal or informal) governance structure, which will manage how the different types of complementarities between the members of the ecosystem will create value. However, there are important differences here with some other forms of organization of value-generating activity in the digital economy. In contrast to supplier-mediated arrangements, such as supply chains, 'final customers can choose among the components (the elements of the offering) that are supplied by each participant, and can also, in some cases choose how they are combined'.[184] Hence, the level and structure of prices, quantities, and product bundles are not determined hierarchically in ecosystems. In contrast to market-based arrangements, 'end customers choose from a set of producers or complementors who are bound together through some form of interdependencies—by all adhering to certain standards'.[185] Hence, to the extent that they require some degree of affiliation of the participants to the standards, conventions, and rules of the ecosystem, ecosystems appear to have more shape than markets. This does not mean that these standards and rules are set by a hierarchy. Jacobides et al. explain that 'ecosystems allow for some degree of coordination without requiring hierarchical governance precisely because of the ability to use some standards or base requirements that allow complementors to make their own decisions ... while still allowing for a complex interdependent product or service to be produced'.[186]

For some, 'the concept of ecosystem might now substitute for the industry for performing analysis'.[187] The essence of this new insight comes from the realization that competition analysis should engage with the 'value capture strategies' put in place by economic actors competing for strategic or architectural advantage.[188] That should form the starting point of competition analysis, rather than the relevant market concept which no longer constitutes the sole reference point that firms take into account when devising their strategies, and the

---

[179] ibid., 2259.   [180] ibid., 2260.

[181] See, e.g., the analysis in Richard Baldwin, *The Great Convergence: Information Technology and the New Globalization* (Harvard University Press 2017).

[182] Jacobides et al., 'Towards a Theory of Ecosystems' (n 175), 2260 (emphasis in the original).

[183] ibid., 2263.   [184] ibid., 2260.   [185] ibid., 2261.   [186] ibid.

[187] David Teece, 'Business Ecosystems' in *The Palgrave Encyclopaedia of Strategic Management*, edited by Mie Augier and David Teece (Palgrave Macmillan 2016), 1.

[188] David Teece, 'Business Models, Value Capture, and the Digital Enterprise' (2017) 6(8) *Journal of Organizational Design*.

competitive constraints to which they are subject. Abandoning the sole focus on the relevant market also stems from the relatively more limited role of price competition in the digital economy.

Firms often compete for customers in order to enlarge their customer base, to take advantage of network effects, and to be perceived by financial markets as holding a 'bottleneck', even if such trade, from a price/cost perspective, may not be profitable. This struggle for a large customer base explains why firms offer 'free goods' and may continue to do so, even if these gains in market share and, consequently, the harvesting of consumer data (personal data being the 'price' to pay for these 'free goods'), may not be immediately monetized in data markets. However, capturing a large customer base at reduced or negative profitability is not the ultimate aim of these strategies. This strategy makes sense if, by acquiring a large customer base, firms are able to develop dynamic capabilities (for instance the use of consumer data will enable them to improve their algorithms). These benefits do not only materialize in the long term but may also be enjoyed through higher market valuation by financial markets in the short term. Due to their futurity, financial markets realize that such strategies bring a sustainable architectural advantage, as other suppliers (of competing or complementary products) realize that the ecosystem leader benefits from idiosyncratic dynamic capabilities, which may not be replicated by other firms in the industry, as well as a privileged access to an important customer base. By providing a limited (the 'walled garden approach'), or more open ('the open innovation' approach) access to this customer base, while considering the appropriability regime that applies to the given innovation,[189] the firm is in a position to frame the industry architecture to its own advantage and capture most of the value that is generated by innovation.

The implementation of blockchain in larger parts of the digital economy has the potential to accelerate this shift of attention from platforms to ecosystems. Although in some settings blockchain technology may produce network effects, one of the inherent characteristics of DLT is that network effects are less pronounced as there are fewer barriers, in comparison to centralized digital platforms, for the participants to abandon a blockchain and join a fork.[190] Hence, a blockchain participant may invest in a blockchain, knowing that such investment is to a certain extent fungible and can be redeployed elsewhere. However, for an ecosystem to form, the investment should not be fully fungible, thus indicating that there may be some opportunity cost should one decide to abandon the specific ecosystem. Of course, competition between ecosystems may provide good reasons to a participant to switch. However, by its very essence, the ecosystem cannot be 'hierarchically controlled'. The lack of hierarchical controls and the fact that members retain residual control and claims over their assets distinguishes it from traditional firm groupings or captive supply networks.[191] Jacobides et al. highlight that 'ecosystems need to be run, both *de jure* and *de facto*, with decision-making processes that are to some extent distributed, and without *all* decisions (especially on both prices and quantities) being hierarchically set ...'[192] Depending on the governance protocol chosen for the specific blockchain, DLT enables each participant to contribute to the formation of a consensus over the standards, rules, and interfaces that will apply, these no longer being set by a lead firm or a platform. However, our discussion on the difficulties of decentralization and disintermediation shows that even in permissionless blockchains many of the rules of the game will be set by a hub formed by the core developers and the new blockchain intermediaries.

---

[189] See Teece, 'Profiting from Technological Innovation' (n 115), 285; David Teece, 'Profiting from Innovation in the Digital Economy: Standards, Complementary Assets, and Business Models in the Wireless World' (2018) 47 *Research Policy*, 1367.

[190] See the analysis in section II.

[191] Jacobides et al., 'Towards a Theory of Ecosystems' (n 175), 2266.   [192] ibid., 2267.

These intricacies of the classifications of the various forms of organization of economic activity, competition, and cooperation in the digital economy notwithstanding, it becomes clear that DLT fits perfectly well into this new paradigm of competition in the ecosystem and the development of new forms of acquiring strategic, but also architectural, advantage. In order to succeed, an economic actor needs a strategy for the whole ecosystem. The emergence, demise, and mutation of ecosystems[193] puts emphasis on the process of value creation and appropriation within ecosystems, but also value migration between ecosystems, that characterizes today's financialized economy, where value is negotiated day-by-day in financial markets on the basis of a reflexive system where perceptions or broader narratives about future expectations of return on investment plays a crucial role.[194] The role of industry architects and industry architectures in this process has not yet been examined in depth. It is still unclear how the different ecosystems and their interactions will affect final consumers. This impact can, of course, be determined at the level of a relevant market and that should, of course, continue. However, the changes brought, first, by platform competition, and then by ecosystem co-opetition, raise questions as to the continuing relevance of the sole relevant market framework for conducting a competition analysis. This also raises questions as to the different dimensions of ecosystem power, combining both sources of strategic and architectural advantage and appropriate metrics. Section VI examines some competition law implications.

VI. Blockchain and Competition Law: Setting the Agenda

Any discussion over the implications of blockchain on competition law will, in the absence of any decisional practice on this issue by competition authorities, be quite general and hypothetical. First, one may ask if the implementation of blockchain technology may increase the risk of anticompetitive conduct, either because it facilitates cooperation between rivals or because its implementation may facilitate exclusionary conduct, which are issues that are explored in section A. Second, it becomes important to examine whether the existing competition law doctrines and tools may still be relevant with this new technology, or whether there is a case to re-conceptualize competition law so as to make it more aware of the complexities of blockchain competition.

A. The competition risks of the implementation
of blockchain technology

The decentralized nature of the public permissionless blockchain seems, at first sight, be beneficial to competition as it enables the contestability, at least of the back-office segments of the value chain. This fares better than the current, highly concentrated structure of the digital economy dominated by digital platforms, or than the stable oligopolistic structure we may observe in the financial services sector. Blockchain technology makes possible the substitution of centralized systems, where one entity controls the information about transactions and effectively is able to monetize this asset in product or financial markets, with a

---

[193] Note that in his seminal contribution James Moore had described an ecosystem lifecycle consisting of four phases: birth, expansion, leadership, and self-renewal: Moore (n 174), 75.

[194] Indeed, to the extent that there is interaction between various agents and non-linear feedback between the actors and their environment, the system of interactions that emerges is 'reflexive' and cannot be adequately described by equilibrium systems, as agents frame their strategies observing the broader environment, assessing their position in it and determining their actions in order to alter the environment according to their aims: see George Soros, 'General Theory of Reflexivity' (*ft.com*, 26 October 2009) https://www.ft.com/content/0ca06172-bfe9-11de-aed2-00144feab49a.

decentralized distributed ledger. This is achieved by reducing the network effects barrier that usually protects the position of digital platforms.

According to Catalini and Tucker:

> in theory, blockchain technology can be used to overcome the coordination challenges that otherwise lead network effects to be a source of market power, as it allows platform architects to design digital ecosystems where the benefits from adoption and growth are shared among different stakeholders such as users, developers of complementary applications, and providers of key resources.[195]

Blockchain implementations may also promote multi-homing, with consumers using competing platforms and facing lower switching costs as they keep control over their data at all times because this has not been collected and kept by a centralized digital platform.[196] Being open source, permissionless blockchain platforms allow other applications and platforms 'to interface with their network as long as they comply with the requirements of their protocol'.[197] Furthermore, 'many platforms have a native token that not only facilitates exchanges on the platform, but also makes it extremely easy to convert assets between different ecosystems'.[198] Heavily inspired by libertarian ideals, the world of the blockchain is one of minimal friction. The technology empowers direct peer-to-peer interaction, without involving an intermediary. It is also a world where consensus, rather than power, becomes the default governance method. Forking provides a credible exit option for disgruntled developers and users, with the 'team maintaining the code or the rules through which the protocol forms consensus over time and allocates rewards to contributors', recognizing in them the possibility to start 'a separate, backwards compatible blockchain'.[199] This reduces the likelihood of hold-up strategies.

This optimistic scenario only concerns permissionless public blockchains. The situation is different for private permissioned blockchains, which may raise challenges similar to those raised by an entity controlling a database.[200] However, there is a more pessimistic scenario in which even permissionless blockchains could raise some competition concerns. I will examine the various competition law concerns different types of blockchain may raise.

1. Facilitation of collusion

The most obvious concern, raised by both permissioned and permissionless blockchains, is the possible facilitation of collusion. This may result from the public character of the blockchain and the enhanced data visibility that it offers. Indeed, a key characteristic of the most well-known blockchain technologies, those supporting cryptocurrencies, is that all transactions are visible to all users. This increasing sharing of data may accommodate broader public policy to make data more open and less proprietary (e.g. Open Banking), but data transparency may also facilitate collusion between competitors. There are two possible concerns.

One may envisage the possibility where a cartel (i.e. explicit collusion) is enforced, not through law, as this would be illegal and would constitute a restriction of competition by nature, but through code, by devising a smart contract that will enforce collusion, in particular, if this is coupled with pricing algorithms that are adjusted automatically when the conditions of the smart contract are satisfied. For instance, it is possible to envisage a smart contract between members of a cartel, which could condition the release of a 'guarantee', paid in cryptocurrency by each of the members of the cartel and kept in an 'escrow account' at one of the digital wallets, automatically if certain conditions with regard to the deviation of prices from the cartelized price are identified by one of the parties to this cartel arrangement.

---

[195] Catalini and Tucker (n 23), 6.   [196] ibid, 7.   [197] ibid.   [198] ibid.   [199] ibid, 8.
[200] ibid.

The implementation of this smart agreement could be ensured by algorithms relying on off-blockchain data harvested by oracles. Firms may also constitute a federated blockchain (a 'consortium'), where they will exchange data on their prices, output in real time, and other sensitive, or non-sensitive information. In this case, the arrangement to establish this federated blockchain will constitute an information exchange agreement/concerted practice that would first need to be assessed under Article 101(1) TFEU,[201] and, in the case that it constitutes a restriction of competition, potentially be justified under Article 101(3) TFEU.[202]

Once it is found that the information exchange results from collusive action, the next step is to examine, at least in EU competition law, if it leads to a restriction of competition, by object or by effect. The context and the nature of the information exchanged will be particularly important in this context. For instance, strategic information, which relates to prices (e.g. actual prices, discounts, increases, reductions, or rebates), customer lists, production costs, quantities, turnovers, sales, capacities, qualities, marketing plans, risks, investments, technologies, and research and development programmes and their results, is more likely to produce restrictive effects to competition and be caught by Article 101 than exchanges of other types of information.[203] Historic data is unlikely to lead to a collusive outcome as it is unlikely to be indicative of the competitors' future conduct or to provide a common understanding on the market.[204] However, there is no predetermined threshold when data becomes historic, that is to say, old enough not to pose a risk to competition. Whether data is genuinely historic depends on the data's nature, aggregation, frequency of the exchange, and the characteristics of the relevant market. Finally, exchanges of genuinely public information are unlikely to constitute an infringement of Article 101 TFEU.

If the parties form a consortium, this may be analysed as a cooperative joint venture agreement.[205] In this situation, the case law provides that the analysis under Article 101(1) TFEU requires analysis of whether there is a restriction of competition among the undertakings forming the joint venture and, in particular, to explore whether there were possibilities of competition between the parent undertakings in the absence of the joint venture agreement, thus, conducting some form of counterfactual analysis. The second step in the analysis is to examine if there is a restriction on competition vis-à-vis third parties, in particular, if third-party access to the relevant markets is likely to be impeded by the existence of a special relationship between the joint venture and its parent undertakings, thereby placing other competing operators at a disadvantage. However, even if there is a restriction of competition under Article 101(1) TFEU, it is possible to justify the joint venture arrangement under Article 101(3) provided the conditions of this provision are satisfied.[206]

A possible theory of harm is the fact that a public ledger, visible to all, on which industry data may be published in real time and which could be easily accessible, will *facilitate* collusion. Information exchange may occur at the initial steps of forming a cartel, as the cartelists will need to identify the parameters of their cooperation and the selection of the cooperative equilibrium, for instance, by determining the price or output level of the cartel or of its individual members, but may also facilitate the maintenance of the stability of a cartel by

---

[201] See, for information exchange arrangements, Case T-35/92, *John Deere Ltd v. Commission of the European Communities* [1994] ECR II-957; Case C-238/05, *Asnef-Equifax, Servicios de Información sobre Solvencia y Crédito, SL v. Asociación de Usuarios de Servicios Bancarios (Ausbanc)* [2006] ECR I-11125. This analysis will include a counterfactual test, exploring whether the information exchanged was liable to lead to a collusive outcome, a pure information exchange not necessarily leading to a finding of a restriction of competition under Article 101(1) of the Treaty on the Functioning of the European Union (TFEU).

[202] Guidelines on the Applicability of Article 101 TFEU to Horizontal Cooperation Agreements [2011] OJ C11/1, [77]–[104].

[203] ibid., [86].　　　　[204] ibid., [90].

[205] See, Joined Cases T-374/94, T-375/94, T-384/94, and T-388/94, *European Night Services Ltd (ENS) et al. v. Commission* [1998] ECR II-3141; Case T-112/99, *Métropole Télévision (M6) and Others v. Commission* [2002] ECR II-2459; Case T-328/03, *O2 (Germany) GmbH & Co. OHG v. Commission* [2006] ECR-II 1231.

[206] See Guidelines on the Applicability of Article 101 (n 202).

supporting the monitoring of any possible deviations from the cartel equilibrium reached by the parties. However, for Article 101 TFEU to apply, the information exchange should result from some form of collusive action, which can take the form of an agreement, concerted practice, or a decision of an association of undertakings. Would the fact of making data publicly available to a public blockchain constitute, in this case, an agreement or a concerted practice that could fall under Article 101 TFEU, or would it consist in a unilateral practice that may escape this provision?

The issue here would be that the transparency created by the public communication of information between actual or potential competitors in real time may soften competition because it can reduce strategic uncertainty in the market. Again, one may here distinguish between private and public blockchains, the former raising more concerns, from a competition law perspective, than the latter. However, even genuinely public unilateral communication of information between competitors may have the potential to dampen competition,[207] for instance by constituting price signaling capable of facilitating collusion.

However, note that in the United States it is possible to bring in a Section 5, Federal Trade Commission ('FTC') Act case against 'facilitating practices',[208] even in the absence of proof of conspiracy or, more generally, communication, provided the conscious parallelism produces anticompetitive effects, at least under certain specific circumstances.[209] Price signaling involving one-way public disclosures of information to third-party investors, was found anticompetitive in the United States, under Section 5 of the FTC Act, without any evidence of reciprocity from the competitors, in the case where collusion could be inferred from the overall context.[210] In the absence of a provision equivalent to Section 5 FTC Act in EU competition law, the possibility of applying Article 101 TFEU is quite remote. In *Bananas*, the General Court,[211] later confirmed by the CJEU,[212] held that price signals removing the degree of uncertainty as to the behaviour of competitors on the market in question may be seen as capable of harming competition to a sufficient degree to be considered as by object restrictions.[213] However, price signaling may fall under the scope of Article 101 TFEU if there is evidence of collusion. In *Bananas*, this was not an issue, as there was ample evidence of bilateral and private pre-pricing communications between the undertakings in question, even if these conversations were of more generic nature, and other factors influenced supply and demand. Yet, the Commission, upheld by both the General Court and the CJEU, found that there was a sufficient causal link between these practices and a possible effect, not only

---

[207] This possibility is recognized by the Guidelines on the Applicability of Article 101 (n 202), [94], noting that the fact that information is exchanged in public may decrease the likelihood of a collusive outcome on the market to the extent that non-coordinating companies, potential competitors, and also customers may be able to constrain potential restrictive effect on competition. However, the possibility cannot be entirely excluded that even genuinely public exchanges of information may facilitate a collusive outcome in the market.

[208] Section 5 of the Federal Trade Commission (FTC) Act prohibits unfair methods of competition.

[209] See, e.g., *E.I. Du Pont de Nemours & Co. v. FTC*, 729 F.2d 128 (2nd Cir. 1984) where, although the court of appeal dismissed the case, it acknowledged that Section 5 of the FTC Act can be violated by 'non-collusive, non-predatory and independent conduct of a non-artificial nature', at least when it results in a substantial lessening of competition if 'some indicial of oppressiveness' exist, such as evidence of anticompetitive intent, or the absence of an independent legitimate business reason for the conduct.

[210] See, e.g., Valassis Communications, Inc., Analysis of Agreement Containing consent Order to Aid Public Comment (20 March 2006) 71 Fed. Reg. 13976, 13978–79, where the FTC noted that 'given the obligation under the securities laws not to make false and misleading statements with regard to material facts, Valassis' invitation to collude, made in the context of a conference call with analysts, may have been viewed by News America [its competitor] as even more credible than a private communication'.

[211] Case T-588/08, *Dole Food Company, Inc. and Dole Germany OHG v. European Commission*, ECLI:EU:T:2013:130.

[212] Case C-286/13 P, *Dole Food Company Inc. and Dole Fresh Fruit Europe v. European Commission*, ECLI:EU:C:2015:184.

[213] See also the recent European Commission's proceedings against contained liner shipping companies for making regular public announcements of their (intended) future increases of prices through press releases on their websites and in the specialized trade press: Communication of Commission Published Pursuant to Article 27(4) of Council Regulation (EC) No. 1/2003 in Case AT.39850—Container Shipping, [2016] OJ C 60/7.

on prices for consumers, but more generally on the integrity of the competitive process, as 'the pre-pricing communications had the object of creating conditions of competition that do not correspond to the normal conditions on the market'.[214] Determining the 'normal conditions of the market' in the context of a blockchain may require some in-depth analysis of the characteristics of the blockchain and the possibilities it offers to identify the various parties. The use of encryption technology does not always guarantee anonymity, as it is possible to link organizational information, such as an IP address, to a real entity. This may be more achievable in the context of a private or permissioned blockchain, where the identity of the users exchanging information can be more easily identified.

2. Risks flowing from the development of oligopolistic structures

Mining constitutes an obvious illustration of the development of oligopolistic structures in the blockchain ecosystem. There are twenty major mining pools, more than two-thirds of them based in China. It is estimated that three mining pool operators, BTC.com, Antpool, and ViaBTC, currently control 52.5% of hashing power.[215] The six largest operators, the three just mentioned, and in addition, Slushpool, F2pool, and BTC.Top, control more than two-thirds of the hashing power.[216] Although mining was more consolidated a couple of years ago,[217] this is a cause for concern for policy-makers, requiring them to be vigilant so that the industry does not become more concentrated and that there is adequate monitoring for the possibility of coordination between some of the pools, for instance, by secretly partnering to gain control over new block generation.

The oligopolistic structure of mining is problematic because, depending on the governance of the specific blockchain, it may provide control levers for its overall activity to just a few players and, in particular, increase the risk of a 51% attack, thus, compromising the integrity of the blockchain. This could provide arguments for introducing a threshold automatically breaking mining pools in case their size reaches a particular limit that may increase the risk of a 51% attack in order to protect the integrity of the blockchain. Furthermore, the consolidation of industrial mining also raises competition concerns because a concentrated market structure may increase the risk of tacit collusion and lead to anticompetitive practices, such as charging excessive transaction fees. However, in the absence of clear evidence of an agreement or concerted practice restricting competition, this may not fall under Article 101 TFEU.

The concept of collective dominance may provide an alternative ground for action against practices in oligopolies, even if there is no agreement or concerted practice, when there is a 'connecting factor' between the undertakings forming part of the oligopoly and their conduct constitutes an abuse of a dominant position.[218] Although tacit collusion is covered by Article 102 TFEU, there has not been any case where tacit collusion was considered as sufficient to constitute the requisite 'connecting factor' for a finding of a collective dominance position.[219] The DG Staff Discussion Paper, published in December 2005, recognized that

---

[214] Case C-286/13 (n 212), [134], referring to the Commission's decision.

[215] See Jordan Tuwiner, 'Bitcoin Mining Pools' (*buybitcoinworldwide.com*, 30 June 2018) https://www. buybitcoinworldwide.com/mining/pools/.

[216] ibid.

[217] See the figures for 2016 in Rob Price, 'The 18 Companies that Control Bitcoin in 2016' (*ukbusinessinsider. com*, 30 June 2016) http://uk.businessinsider.com/bitcoin-pools-miners-ranked-2016-6/#18-p2poolorg-01-1.

[218] See Case C-395/96 P, *Compagnie Maritime Belge* [2000] ECR I-1365, [45], noting that 'the existence of an agreement or of other links in law is not indispensable to a finding of a collective dominant position; such a finding may be based on other connecting factors and would depend on an economic assessment and, in particular, on an assessment of the structure of the market in question'; Case T-193/02, *Laurent Piau v. Commission* [2005] ECR II-209.

[219] See, e.g., the General Court and CJEU in Case T-296/09, *European Federation of Ink and Ink Cartridge Manufacturers (EFIM) v. Commission* [2011] ECR II-425; Case C-56/12 P, *European Federation of Ink and Ink Cartridge Manufacturers (EFIM) v. Commission* ECLI:EU:C:2013:575, where both the General Court and the

'undertakings in oligopolistic markets may, sometimes, be able to raise prices substantially above the competitive level without having recourse to any explicit agreement or concerted practice', yet it confirmed the possibility of applying Article 102 TFEU only to the extent that the cumulative criteria for the application of the theory of tacit collusion are satisfied.[220] Yet, the Commission's priority Guidance briefly mentioned the concept, without providing any details as to the criteria for each use, thereby indicating that collective dominance cases are not within the priorities of the Commission, at least with regard to exclusionary practices.[221] There are considerable uncertainties as to the content of the concept of abuse in collective dominance cases. Some authors take a broad perspective, suggesting that abusive excessive prices (but one could also argue any form the exploitation of consumers takes, e.g. quality) charged by tacitly collusive oligopolists may be found an abuse.[222] Others take the more traditional, and narrower, approach of targeting facilitating practices, which can be the only 'conduct' found abusive.[223]

The possible emergence of oligopolistic structures is not only limited to mining but could also affect other blockchain intermediaries, such as exchanges, digital wallets, etc. The risks raised by oligopoly may be accentuated in the context of the important technological progress recently made in artificial intelligence, the development of algorithms, and deep machine learning in the modern digital economy.[224] Businesses become 'algorithmic' by using algorithms to automatize processes relating to their relations with their customers and suppliers, with the aim of gaining an 'algorithmic' competitive advantage against their competitors. In principle, such use of algorithms should not raise any issues, unless it leads to the exploitation of consumers through algorithmic discrimination, algorithmic pricing, or other exploitative practices, or may impose unfair conditions to their suppliers, in the event that these could be considered as a competition law problem, to the extent that these firms may reinforce their superior bargaining power. They may also be tempted to employ these algorithms in order to collude with their competitors in ways that escape the scrutiny of competition authorities.[225]

The transparency offered by the blockchain may facilitate such strategic use of algorithms. Indeed, 'algorithms make collusive outcomes easier to sustain and more likely to be observed in digital markets'.[226] This is achieved, first, by the capabilities of algorithms 'to identify any market threats very fast, for instance, through a phenomenon known as "now-casting", allowing incumbents to pre-emptively acquire any potential competitors or to react aggressively to market entry',[227] thus increasing strategic barriers to entry. Second, they increase market transparency and the frequency of interaction, making the industries 'more prone to collusion'.[228] Prices can be updated in real time, 'allowing for an immediate retaliation to deviations from collusion', as well as accurately predicting rivals' actions and anticipating any deviations before these actually take place.[229] Third, they can act as facilitators of collusion

---

CJEU refused the existence of a collective dominant position in view of the aggressive competitive strategy of some of the undertakings in question.

[220] DG Competition, 'The Application of Article 82 of the Treaty to Exclusionary Abuses' (2005) Discussion Paper, [47].

[221] Communication from the Commission—Guidance on the Commission's Enforcement Priorities in Applying Article [102 TFEU] to Abusive Exclusionary Conduct by Dominant Undertakings [2009] OJ C 45/7, [4].

[222] Richard Whish and Brenda Sufrin, 'Oligopolistic Markets and Competition Law' (1992) 12 *Yearbook of European Law*, 59.

[223] Giorgio Monti, 'The Scope of Collective Dominance under Article 82 EC' (2001) *Common Market Law Review*, 131.

[224] See, Organisation for Economic Cooperation and Development (OECD), Algorithms and Collusion: Competition Policy in the Digital Age (2017) Report (hereinafter 'OECD (2017)'); Ariel Ezrachi and Maurice Stucke, 'Two Artificial Neural Networks Meet in an Online Hub and Change the Future (of Competition, Market Dynamics and Society)' (2017) Oxford Legal Studies Research Paper No. 24/2017.

[225] See our discussion in section I. [226] OECD (2017) (n 224), 20. [227] ibid., 21.

[228] ibid. [229] ibid., 22.

in monitoring competitors' actions in order to enforce a collusive agreement, enabling a quick identification of cartel price' deviations and retaliation strategies.[230] Fourth, they may facilitate 'hub-and-spoke' strategies, for instance, the firms in an industry may outsource the creation of algorithms to the same IT companies and programmers.[231] Fifth, 'signaling algorithms' may enable companies to automatically set very fast iterative actions, such as snapshot price changes during the middle of the night, that cannot be exploited by consumers, but which can facilitate collusion with rivals possessing good analytical algorithms.[232] Finally, 'self-learning' algorithms may eliminate the need for human intermediation. With deep machine learning technologies, the algorithms may assist firms in actually reaching a collusive outcome without them being aware of it.[233] This raises some interesting issues with regard to the scope of the concept of agreement or concerted practice under Article 101 TFEU, as we have hinted above, and also highlights the need to develop a more holistic approach to the risks of algorithmic collusion, in particular, in the context of blockchains.

It is also possible to consider the concerns raised by a more concentrated oligopolistic structure in the context of merger control. It may seem reasonable to carefully scrutinize mergers between mining farms or mining pools, not only in the context of the PoW framework, where this is indispensable in order to preserve the system from the possibility of a 51% attack, but also in the context of a transfer of control taking place in the context of a PoS system, in view of the competition concerns raised by concentrated oligopolistic structures in the digital economy. Furthermore, competition authorities dispose the tools of sector enquiries, or, in the context of the UK, market or cross-market investigation references, which provide additional tools to take on industry-wide practices that may cause consumer detriment.[234]

3. Standardization issues

The implementation of blockchain technology in various economic sectors will require the development of various standards, as DLT will inevitably lead to a more fragmented IT ecosystem, also due to the 'forking' of existing DLTs, which could increase fragmentation and slow down transaction processing speeds. For example, one may cite the work undertaken in the context of the International Organization of Standardization, established following Australia's proposal in September 2016, where ten ISO DLT-related standards are in development (relating to interoperability, security, privacy, identity, interactions among cloud computing systems and DLT, smart contracts and their application)[235] or the work in the context of the International Communication Union ('ITU').[236]

Another possible standardization issue could emerge when blockchain technology is used to develop certification and labelling standards in order to promote social and environmental

---

[230] ibid., 26.   [231] ibid., 28.   [232] ibid., 29–31.   [233] ibid., 32–33.

[234] In the EU, see Article 17 of Regulation 1/2003. In the UK, the Competition and Markets Authority ('CMA') may conduct market studies under its general function in section 5 of the Enterprise Act 2002, as modified by the Enterprise and Regulatory Reform Act (ERRA) 2013, which includes the functions of obtaining information and conducting research. These market studies may lead to various outcomes, including investigation and enforcement action under the provisions of the CA 98 and/or the TFEU, and a market investigation reference: Competition and Markets Authority, 'Market Studies and Market Investigations' (2014) Annex, Supplemental Guidance on the CMA's Approach, 33. Cross-market references are possible since the passage of ERRA 2013: Sections 131(2A) and (6) of the EA02.

[235] See International Organisation for Standardisation, 'ISO/TC 307 Blockchain and Distributed Ledger Technologies' (2016) https://www.iso.org/committee/6266604.html.

[236] See, e.g., ITU-T Focus Group on Digital Financial Services, 'Distributed Ledger Technologies and Financial Inclusion' (2017) Technical Report; and many study groups including the ITU-T Study Group on the development of the blockchain of things as decentralized service platform, ITU-T Work Programme, 'Declared Patents' (2017) Recommendation [SG20]:[Q4/20]; the ITU-T Study Group on scenarios and capability requirements of blockchain in next-generation network evolution, ITU-T Work Programme, 'Declared Patents' (2017) Recommendation [SG13]:[Q2/13].

sustainability or other public interest aims.[237] Horizontal cooperation agreements between undertakings restricting competition may provide benefits, not only directly to the category of consumers affected by the anticompetitive practice as this results from the relevant market definition, but also to the economy and the 'public at large'. These benefits relate to broader public interests, linked either to existing regulations or more broadly to values and principles animating public policy at a more general level. In this case the standardization is not related, as such, to blockchain technology, but to the definition of social and environmental standards and their implementation through DLT technology. This could raise questions as to the possibility of justifying possible restrictions of competition resulting from these standardization agreements for broader public-interest-related purposes, such as the protection of the environment, a possibility that is not available under the current mainstream interpretation of Article 101(3) TFEU.[238]

Standards provide increased compatibility between different products (i.e. increased interoperability), thereby enabling the launch of a network. At the same time, standardization may impose costs; it may lock in consumers to a legacy system, enable hold up in cases where 'essential' IPRs have not been declared prior to the standard, or enable dominance by big players. The way the industry standard emerges is of particular importance for assessing its effects on competition. A cooperative standard is likely to enable multiple firms to be active in the industry, while the development of a de facto standard may lead to a single, proprietary product, controlled by a dominant undertaking.

The development of standards in the context of standard-setting organizations ('SSOs') is viewed positively in EU competition law. For instance, the Commission's Guidelines on Horizontal Cooperation note that, from an economic perspective, 'standardization agreements usually produce significant positive economic effects', by enabling, among other things, the development of new and improved products or markets and improved supply conditions.[239] The positive economic effects may not be only for the specific parties to the agreement but for 'economies as a whole', in view of the lower output and sales' costs, the maintenance and the enhancement of quality, the provision of information and interoperability or compatibility, which provide value to the consumers. However, the EU Guidelines also recognize that standardization agreements may also produce anticompetitive effects by potentially restricting price competition and limiting or controlling production, markets, innovation, or technical development.[240] The Guidelines identify the following theories of harm or anticompetitive scenarios, noting that the competition risks of standard terms becoming industry practice, in particular, and, thus, access to them may be vital for entry into the market.[241]

Standardization agreements raise particular competition concerns if they also involve intellectual property rights ('IPRs'), such as patents. One may refer to situations where there has been deceptive conduct in the context of a SSO, when a patent holder adopts the strategy to conceal a patent that he holds on a specific technology during the standard-setting process, letting the other stakeholders agree on a standard incorporating a patented technology and, upon the standard gaining widespread acceptance, later revealing the information that

---

[237] For a discussion, see Margaret Fowler, 'Linking the Public Benefit to the Corporation: Blockchain as a Solution for Certification in an Age of Do-Good Business' (2018) 20 *Vanderbilt Journal of Entertainment and Technology Law*, 881.

[238] In the *CECED* case, the European Commission took into account the 'collective environmental benefits' brought by an agreement between washing machine manufacturers to cease production and importation of less energy-efficient machines: Case COMP IV.F.1/36.718, *CECED* Commission Decision 2000/475/EC [2000] OJ L 187/47. However, the Commission's 2011 horizontal cooperation guidelines do not include a separate section on 'environmental agreements', nor did their 2000 version. Note also, that even the 2000 Guidelines were careful not to refer to the existence of 'collective benefits' arising out of these agreements and was referring instead to 'economic benefits', 'either at individual or aggregate *consumer* level'.

[239] Guidelines on the Applicability of Article 101 (n 202), [257]–[260] and 263.   [240] ibid., [264].

[241] ibid., [265]–[271].

the technology is covered by a patent at a point when the negotiating position of the other stakeholders will be weakened as they would have made standard specific investments and will be kept hostage (i.e. 'patent ambush').[242] The holder of a standard essential patent ('SEP') may also seek a court injunction to block companies from producing any products compliant with the standard and to ask for higher royalties than that which he would have asked for prior to the adoption of the standard.[243] The issue may arise if the SEP holders have made a commitment to license on (F)RAND terms.[244] The risk of hold-up is particularly important in complex technical markets in which detailed standards have been developed cooperatively by many companies.

The assessment of the restrictive effects of standard-setting should take into account their legal and economic context with regard to their actual and likely effect on competition and should, in particular, focus on the following relevant markets: (i) the product or service market(s) to which the standard or standards relates; (ii) where the standard-setting involves the selection of technology and where the rights to intellectual property are marketed separately from the products to which they relate, the relevant technology market; (iii) different standard-setting bodies or agreements; (iv) where relevant, a distinct market for testing and certification.[245] However, even if the process of standardization gives rise to possible restrictions on competition, it is possible to justify these restrictions under certain conditions, under Article 101(3) TFEU.

4. Vertical conduct and abuse of a dominant position

As analysed in section IV.A., one of the possible strategies that may be adopted by blockchain firms to maintain a strategic competitive advantage and extend the period for which they may gain abnormal profits, beyond the initial hype about the new technology, is to adopt strategies linking blockchain with complementary spheres or markets where the firm maintains some absolute strategic advantage. These will most often be markets with significant network effects, thus 'off-blockchain', but one may also envisage the possibility that an economic entity acquires such a pre-eminent position in the blockchain space.

One may, for instance, envisage that Ethereum could develop to be the dominant platform for decentralized applications ('DApps') and smart contracts in the blockchain space. It is very hard, and irresponsible, to make predictions in a nascent space like blockchain but since its launch, Ethereum has seen rapid development and mass adoption. The reasons behind this are that Ethereum benefitted from a first-mover advantage, as it was the first DApp and smart contract platform to enter the market, the flexibility and simplicity offered by the Solidity programming language in DApps are written on the Ethereum platform, and the network effects that followed because most smart contract applications are written for the Ethereum platform (more than 250,000 developers use the Ethereum platform). The fact that Ethereum enables the implementation of blockchain technology in the wider economy, captured the attention of big corporations, banks, and consulting firms (such as Intel, JP Morgan, and Deloitte), which invested in the technology. Furthermore, Ethereum is supported by a non-profit organization, the *Enterprise Ethereum Alliance*, connecting 'Fortune 500 enterprises, start-ups, academics and technology vendors' with the community of Ethereum subject matter experts, which forms a big network of collaboration and innovation promotion.[246] The openness and flexibility of Ethereum led to a number of DApp and

---

[242] See, e.g., Case COMP/38.636, *Rambus* (2009) Commission Decision.
[243] See Case C-170/13, *Huawei Technologies Co. Ltd v. ZTE Corp. and ZTE Deutschland GmbH* [2015] ECLI:EU:C:2015:477.
[244] FRAND stands for 'fair and reasonable non-discriminatory prices'.
[245] Guidelines on the Applicability of Article 101 (n 202), [261].
[246] See Enterprise Ethereum Alliance, 'Introduction and Overview' (*entethalliance.org*, 2017) https://entethalliance.org/wp-content/themes/ethereum/img/intro-eea.pdf.

smart contract applications being launched on the basis of this platform which, following the ICO explosion of the past three years, has led to the emergence of the Ethereum ecosystem with a market capitalization worth around US$45 billion in the second quarter of 2018.[247]

A number of other platform projects for DApps have also emerged since the launch of Ethereum in 2015, such as NEO (often called the 'Chinese Ethereum'), Waves (providing a scalable smart contract platform for decentralized applications), Lisk (deploying blockchain applications in JavaScript and making use of Sidechains), Microsoft-compatible Stratis, Cardano (uses the Haskell and Plutus programming languages and is split into two layers), the Cardano Settlement Layer ('CSL'), which is the value ledger, and the Cardano Computation Layer ('CCL') which handles the reasons why value transfers from one account to the other. In a decentralized ledger world, with weaker network effects, having multiple concurrent platforms interacting with each other, exchanging both data and value, is a plausible scenario. Blockstack also offers a platform for DApps that enables users to have access to the apps on the platform through a browser, and not an app store, the apps running locally on their computer with software installed from Blockstack.[248] Users create their ID to log in to Blockstack apps. Blockstack provides users a choice of where to store their encrypted data, a choice of their own server, or a storage network powered by Blockstack.

Before concluding on the possibility for a dominant DApp platform emerging, it is important to explore how a dominant position may be identified and evaluated in the context of the blockchain. This remains an open question that will be discussed in section VI.B.3.

Access to private or permissioned blockchains constitutes one form of conduct that may raise competition concerns, in particular, if this is used by incumbents in an industry in order to raise entry barriers to potential competitors. Companies operating in supply chains may collaborate through a digital supply chain managed by blockchain technology and smart contracts, with a public ledger of transactions copied to all nodes of the blockchain network. This may enable better monitoring and tracking of information, which may bring efficiency gains, but may also be used to monitor the implementation of some vertical foreclosure strategies vis-à-vis competitors. When blockchains are set by collaborations or consortia that set up blockchains, this may raise concerns over a horizontal restriction of competition, if the consortium includes actual or potential competitors. A recent Organisation for Economic Cooperation and Development (OECD) 'Issues Paper' also raises the possibility that a 'refusal to access the blockchain might be used to exclude maverick firms or new entrants' and, in general, to 'exclude or raise the costs of rivals outside of the consortium' (foreclosure).[249] The competition risks increase as access to the permissioned blockchain becomes indispensable for non-members to compete.[250] Eventual business reasons justifying the refusal to grant access to the permissioned blockchain should also be taken into account.

Other vertical exclusionary restraints may also raise concerns. These may attempt to leverage the dominant position an undertaking may hold in complementary markets. For instance, an OECD 'Issues Paper' provides the example of 'firms that sell the specialized

---

[247] See Statista, 'Market Capitalization of Ethereum from the 3rd Quarter 2015 to 2nd Quarter 2018' (*statista. com*) https://www.statista.com/statistics/807195/ethereum-market-capitalization-quarterly/.

[248] See Blockstack, 'The Easiest Way to Start Building Decentralised Blockchain Apps', https://blockstack.org.

[249] Organisation for Economic Cooperation and Development (OECD), 'Blockchain Technology and Competition Policy' (2018) Issues paper by the Secretariat, [19].

[250] A refusal to grant access may fall under the scope of the prohibition of the abuse of a dominant position (under Article 102 TFEU) in competition EU law: see Case C-7/97, *Oscar Bronner GmbH & Co. KG v. Mediaprint Zeitungs- und Zeitschriftenverlag GmbH & Co. KG* [1998] ECR I-7791, [46], on the requirement of the indispensability of access to the specific input. The possibility that a unilateral refusal to grant access be considered as an infringement of Section 2 of the Sherman Act is more remote. See, e.g., the position of the US Supreme Court in *Verizon Communications Inc. v. Law Offices of Curtis v. Trinko*, LL P, 540 US 398 (2004), where the Court noted that there are several problems with imposing a duty to deal. However, when such refusal to grant access concerns a blockchain put in place by a joint venture or consortium of industry incumbents, US antitrust law provides more possibilities to take antitrust action.

hardware that is required for mining tokens, which might find themselves with market power over inputs required by blockchain users which may seek to leverage their market power in (specialized) mining hardware into downstream markets'.[251] Another practice could consist in a vertical agreement, between a cryptocurrency and a provider of an ancillary services (e.g. digital wallet or exchange), bundling the uses of a dominant cryptocurrency to the use of a specific digital exchange or wallet. Similar bundling effects may occur if an undertaking links the use of the blockchain with ancillary services offered outside the blockchain, on which an undertaking holds a dominant position.[252] Østbye gives the example of a cryptocurrency with market power that bundles ancillary services upon its cryptocurrency, or a digital wallet provider that builds in a digital exchange into its wallet, or vice versa.[253] One may also envisage the possibility that a digital content platform controlling a dominant oracle service provider leverages its dominant position off-blockchain within the blockchain or attempts to maintain its dominant position off-blockchain, for instance, by adopting bundling practices that link the use of the specific oracle services with the data sources it controls.

Exclusive dealing agreements linking the decentralized environment of the blockchain with the centralized environment off-blockchain, or exclusionary discriminatory/preferential treatment practices, may also raise similar vertical (input or customer) foreclosure concerns. As Østbye observes, predatory pricing may also be a concern, if, for example, a large block validator or a mining pool sets transaction fees below cost so as to exclude a rival cryptocurrency, or cross-subsidizes certain key merchants and suppliers in order to prevent a competing cryptocurrency from reaching efficient scale and, thus, profitably entering the market. These practices may be successful as they will not usually require the dominant undertaking to sacrifice profits; this usually acts as a disincentive for adopting exclusionary practices. In view of the lower likelihood of successful entry, because of these exclusionary practices, investors may be discouraged from participating in the ICOs launched by potential entrants, which, in view of the significance of this upfront method of attracting investment for blockchain projects, will certainly be sufficient to deter entry. Hence, because of the specificity of the funding of blockchain technology, the dominant firm may achieve its exclusionary purposes by just a credible commitment to employ exclusionary strategies, without effectively incurring any cost.

Possible exploitative practices include excessive pricing, for instance by mining pools, with market power, that decide to raise the transaction fees charged when validating the blockchain.[254]

5. Mergers

Mergers between undertakings participating in the blockchain ecosystem may also raise horizontal and vertical competition concerns. This would be, for instance, in the case of a horizontal merger between two undertakings active at the same level of the specific value chain related to the blockchain: for example a merger between undertakings active in industrial mining, or between digital exchanges, or between undertakings operating digital wallets, which raises concerns over collusion. Østbye also describes the possibility of a horizontal merger occurring across cryptocurrencies, for instance when a person holding significant mining resources in one PoW consensus managed cryptocurrency or a significant stake in a PoS cryptocurrency buys significant mining power or a significant stake in

[251] Organisation for Economic Cooperation and Development (OECD), 'Blockchain Technology and Competition Policy' (2018) Issues paper by the Secretariat, [19].
[252] Østbye, 'The Adequacy of Competition' (n 23), 28.   [253] ibid.
[254] OECD, 'Blockchain Technology' (n 249), [19].

a competing cryptocurrency, to the extent that the merger brings the two cryptocurrencies into single control,[255] and may produce horizontal unilateral or coordinated effects.

A merger between an entity controlling high stakes in a specific cryptocurrency (in particular, if the consensus is managed by a PoS governance arrangement) and a dominant digital wallet or exchange could raise foreclosure concerns, to the extent that it may exclude or marginalize the use of competing cryptocurrencies.

One may also envisage a conglomerate merger between a digital platform which, for instance, holds a dominant position in an oracle services market, has access to indispensable (Big) data and algorithms, or controls specific smart modules or smart objects markets in the context of the IoT, with a blockchain platform, providing the new entity with the incentive and capability to bundle the use of the blockchain platform in order to launch DApps and smart contracts with the use of the off-blockchain services on which the digital platform holds a dominant position, thus leveraging its dominant position off-blockchain within the blockchain.

B. Implications for competition analysis

1. The scope of competition law: the concept of 'undertaking'

The various provisions of EU competition law apply to 'undertakings'. Article 101 TFEU applies to agreements between undertakings, decisions by associations of undertakings, or concerted practices between undertakings. Article 102 TFEU applies to the abuse of a dominant position by an undertaking. EU Merger Regulation 139/2004 applies also to a concentration between undertakings or part of undertakings; either this takes the form of a merger or through 'the acquisition, by one or more persons already controlling at least one undertaking, or by one or more undertakings, whether by purchase of securities or assets, by contract or by any other means, of direct or indirect control of the whole or parts of one or more other undertakings'.[256] In *Klaus Höfner and Fritz Elser v. Macrotron*, the CJEU explained that any entity 'engaged in an economic activity, irrespective of the legal status in which it is financed' may be qualified as an undertaking for the purposes of competition law'.[257] In *Commission v. Italy*, the CJEU explained that the concept of 'economic activity' should be interpreted as 'any activity consisting in offering goods and services on a given market', an often-repeated definition of the concept of economic activity.[258] EU competition law takes a functional approach, focusing more on the concept of 'activity', rather than that of 'entity'. Hence, the first question one needs to ask with regard to the definition of the material scope of the competition law, is not 'who' is an undertaking but 'what is economic activity'.[259] Such analysis differs, depending on the conduct examined and the facts of the specific case. It is possible that the same entity might be found to be an 'undertaking' for some activities but not qualified as such for other activities.

Hence, it is crucial to examine the various forms of anticompetitive conduct in the context of blockchain, before answering the question, each time in view of the specific facts, as to

---

[255] Østbye, 'The Adequacy of Competition' (n 23), 28.

[256] Council Regulation 139/2004 (20 January 2004) on the Control of Concentrations Between Undertakings, [2004] OJ L 24/1, Article 3(1) .

[257] See Case C-41/90, Klaus *Höfner and Fritz Elser v. Macrotron* [1991] ECR I-1979, [21]; Case C-244/94, *Fédération Française des Sociétés d'Assurance (FFSA) and Others v. Ministère de l'Agriculture et de la Pêche* [1995] ECR I-4013, para. 14; Case C-55/96, *Job Centre coop arl* [1997] ECR I-7119, [21]; Case C-138/11, *Compass Datenbank v. Republik Österreich*, [35]; Case C-440/11 P, *Commission v. Stichting Administrattiekantoor Portielje*, [36].

[258] See Case C-118/85, *Commission v. Italy* [1987] ECR 2599, [7]; Case C-82/01 P, *Aéroports de Paris v. Commission* [2002] ECR I-9297, [79]; Case C-49/07, *Motosykletistiki Omospondia Ellados NPID (MOTOE) v. Elliniko Dimosio* [2008] ECR I-4863, [22]; Case C-138/11 (n 257), [35].

[259] Okeoghene Odudu, 'The Meaning of Undertaking within 81 EC' in *Cambridge Yearbook of European Legal Studies*, edited by John Bell and Claire Kilpatrick (Cambridge University Press 2005), 212–13.

whether the activity in question could be qualified as 'economic' and, thus, the entity exercising it an 'undertaking'.

Determining whether the activity in question is an undertaking can be relatively simple. If one takes the example of collusion managed or facilitated by DLT, it will all depend on the activity of the owners of the nodes (e.g. any active electronic device connected to the internet and disposing of an IP address) supporting the network by maintaining a copy of a blockchain and eventually processing transactions. To the extent that the owners of the nodes willingly contribute their computing resources to store and validate transactions, earning a transaction fee or a reward in the native token of the specific blockchain, they exercise an economic activity. EU case law accepts that even if the activity is non-profit, it could still be considered as an economic activity if it has the potential to be 'at least, in principle' exercised by a 'private undertaking in order to make profits'.[260] The absence of a profit-motive does not mean that the entity does not exercise an economic activity. EU competition law does not make any distinction between altruistic entities and entities motivated by profits, as in both cases it is possible that the specific conduct reduces competition and/or welfare regardless of the motives and preferences of the producers. A similar conclusion may be reached if one examines the activity of other intermediaries of the blockchain, such as oracles, digital wallets, digital exchanges, DApps providers, or even blockchain as a service ('BaaS') providers. However, it is also possible that the blockchain activity may not be qualified as economic, if, for instance, it relates to 'the exercise of official authority',[261] for instance the establishment of a public land registry using blockchain technology, even if access to the public database (the registry) is provided in return for remuneration,[262] or if it is related to an exclusively social function based on the principle of 'solidarity', such as a blockchain operating in a compulsory sickness insurance scheme in order to ensure transparency and reduce the opportunity of fraud.[263]

Determining the 'entity' to be held liable for the competition law infringement presents more difficulties due to the decentralized nature of the blockchain. Although the concept of 'entity' is less important in order to determine the existence of an 'economic activity', in view of the functional approach followed by EU competition law it becomes crucial when it comes to (i) determining the liability under Article 101 TFEU of two entities because they entered into an illegal agreement or concerted practice; (ii) attributing liability for the illegal conduct, and the related issue of remedies/sanctions; and (iii) determining the market shares of the undertaking involved in the infringement of competition law, either this being in the context of merger control or in the context of an abuse of a dominant position, or in determining the existence of a single undertaking for the application of a Block Exemption Regulation. I will focus here on (i), issues; (ii) and (iii) being examined in sections VI.B.2 and VI.B.3.

The concept of 'control' plays an important role in the process of defining the scope of the competition law intervention against an 'economic entity'. It determines the tangible or intangible assets that constitute the core of the 'undertaking', defines its boundaries, and is thus presumed to be under the authority of the undertaking's agents, which may engage

---

[260] See Joined Cases C-264/01, C-306/01, C-354/01, and C-355/01, *AOK Bundesverband and Others* [2004] ECR I-2493, Opinion of AG Jacobs, [27]. For an example, see Case C-437/09, *AG2R Prévoyance v. Beaudout Père et Fils SARL* [2011] ECR I-973.

[261] See Case C-343/95, *Diego Cali & Figli SrL v. Servizi Ecologici Porto di Genova Spa* [1997] ECR I-1547; Case C-364/92, *SAT Fluggesellschaft mbH v. Eurocontrol* [1994] ECR I-43; Case C-138/11 (n 257).

[262] This was not considered by the CJEU as sufficient on its own right for the activity carried out to be classified as an economic activity, as its payment was laid down by law and not determined, directly or indirectly, by that entity: see Case C-138/11 (n 257), [39] and [42].

[263] See Joined Cases C-159/91 and C-160/91, *Poucet and Pistre v. AGF and Cancava* [1993] ECR I-637; Case C-437/09 (n 260).

through anticompetitive strategies the undertaking's liability.[264] Under the 'single entity doctrine', several legal persons may form an 'economic entity' if a control relationship exists between them, the application of the doctrine presupposing the exercise of 'control' or 'decisive influence'.[265]

Should an entity, such as a mining pool, a blockchain intermediary, or an intermediary or platform off-blockchain, take control of the blockchain, and the existence of 'control' will have to be determined according to the specific consensus protocol utilized by the blockchain (and whether this is based on PoW, PoS, or something else), then it may be considered as reasonable to hold this entity liable for anticompetitive conduct perpetrated in the context of the specific blockchain. The same deterrence reasons that have so far justified the liability of parent companies for the anticompetitive activity of their subsidiaries may also operate in this case.[266] However, this expansion of the personal scope of liability has also been criticized.[267] The discussions over the boundaries of the 'single entity' doctrine constitute a specific facet of the broader debate over 'enterprise liability' versus business participant liability, and over when the corporate veil should be pierced.[268]

This discussion is indirectly related to the debate about the boundaries of the 'firm' in economics, with a number of approaches glossing over Ronald Coase's seminal, but incomplete from a descriptive perspective, distinction between 'markets' and 'hierarchies'.[269] The discussion over the boundaries of the firm has also caught the attention of blockchain experts, who rightly observe that blockchain technology contributes to the 'hollowing out' of the firm as initiated by the digital revolution.[270] It is expected that blockchain technology will challenge the 'efficiency' justification for establishing centralized islands of authority (as this is put forward by the proponents of the TCE/contractual theory approach) whilst also enabling a wider distribution of entrepreneurial finance through its distinctive way of attracting finance, the ICO. 'Hollowing out' the firm does not, however, necessarily imply a corresponding growth of the sphere of activities organized through markets to the extent that the dominant strategy of blockchain developers and intermediaries may be to build 'walled gardens' and to architecture ecosystems that could progressively lead to some form

---

[264] Case 170/83, *Hydrotherm Gerätebau GmbH v. Compact del Dott. Ing. Mario Andreoli & C. Sas.* [1984] ECR 2999.

[265] See, inter alia, Case C-97/08 P, *Akzo Nobel and Others v. Commission* [2009] ECR I-8237; Joined Cases C-628/10 P and C-14/11 P, *Alliance One International and Standard Commercial Tobacco v. Commission* and *Commission v. Alliance One International and Others*, ECLI:EU:C:2012:479, [46]–[47], with regard to the liability of a parent company for the conduct of its wholly owned subsidiary or on which it exercises a decisive influence; Arts 3(2) and 3(3) of Council Regulation (EC) No. 139/2004 (n 256) (in the context of merger control).

[266] Carsten Koenig, 'An Economic Analysis of the Single Economic Entity Doctrine in EU Competition Law' (2017) 13(2) *Journal of Competition Law and Economics*, 281–327.

[267] For a criticism of this case law, see Andriani Kalintiri, 'Revisiting Parental Liability in EU Competition Law' (2018) 43(2) *European Law Review*, 145, noting that it may deprive undertakings of the protection afforded to them by the Charter of Fundamental Rights and the general principles of EU law.

[268] For a discussion, see Eric Orts, *Business Persons—A Legal Theory of the Firm* (Oxford University Press 2013).

[269] Ronald Coase, 'The Nature of the Firm' (1937) 4(16) *Economica*, 386. Williamson added 'hybrids': Oliver Williamson, *The Mechanisms of Governance* (Oxford University Press 1996). Some approaches explain the emergence of firms, and their boundaries, by transaction costs economics ('TCE') and more broadly contractual theories of vertical integration (see, inter alia, Oliver Williamson, *The Economic Institutions of Capitalism* (Free Press 1985); Paul Joskow, 'The New Institutional Economics: Alternative Approaches' (1995) 151(1) *Journal of Institutional and Theoretical Economics*, 248). Others focus on property rights, by identifying the allocation of residual decision rights with the ownership of the assets of the firm (tangible and intangible) Oliver Hart and John Moore, 'Property Rights and the Nature of the Firm' (1990) 98 *Journal of Political Economy*, 1119. Others take an agency perspective, defining the firm as 'a nexus of agency relationships including managerial lines of authority, employment and structures of governance': Orts (n 268), 13. A more dynamic perspective views the boundaries of a firm as related to its strategy to leverage its internal capabilities in related markets or to exploit its superior management capabilities and resources: Wernerfelt (n 128), 171.

[270] Catherine Mulligan, 'Blockchain Will Kill the Traditional Firm' (*imperial.ac.uk*, 16 October 2017) https://www.imperial.ac.uk/business-school/knowledge/finance/blockchain-will-kill-the-traditional-firm /.

of centralization. In this context, determining the entity that could be found liable for a competition law infringement might be an easier task.

Note that, in contrast to the functional approach of EU competition law in defining an undertaking, US antitrust law applies, in principle, to 'persons', the concept being broad enough to cover entities having various forms without being necessary to define *ex ante* if the specific entity exercises an economic activity. The term 'person' is defined in Section 7 of the Sherman Act as including '[. . .] corporations and associations existing under or authorized by the laws of either the United States, the laws of any of the Territories, the laws of any State, or the laws of any foreign country', hence, adopting a purely organic definition of the concept, which contrasts with the functional definition of the concept of 'undertaking' in EU law. In the absence of a centralized entity or fiduciary, to which liability for the competition law infringement may be ascribed, it may be difficult to determine the 'person' subject to the scope of the Sherman Act.

2. Blockchain and collusion: an oxymoron?

Even if the activity related to the use of blockchain is economic and it is possible to ascribe liability to a specific entity, considered for this purpose as an 'undertaking', there may be additional difficulties in applying the traditional concepts of competition law, such as, for the purposes of implementing Article 101 TFEU, the existence of an agreement or concerted practice (i.e. of collusive conduct). If one takes the example of Bitcoin, miners may be found to exercise an economic activity and, therefore, be qualified as undertakings. However, could their contribution to validate the blocks of the blockchain and maintain its operation qualify as collusion? Østbye presents the hypothetical of the currency cap used by the Bitcoin protocol, which limits the number of bitcoins to be released to 21 million.[271] Could this amount to an illegal output restriction? It certainly consists in an output restriction, but it cannot be illegal unless the restriction results from collusive, not unilateral, conduct. The Bitcoin miners contribute to the operation of the Bitcoin blockchain by validating the blocks, thus, exercising an economic activity, to the extent they may receive compensation for this activity. In performing this activity, they abide by the 'consensus' process put in place by the blockchain protocol: can their activity be qualified as unilateral, or can this be considered as coordination amounting to an antitrust agreement/concerted practice?

A second hypothetical raising similar questions would occur in the context of a decentralized blockchain-based marketplace, where data is exchanged by various industry actors, some being competitors, and where value-added services are provided, such as access to the data pool for training better algorithms. An algorithm based on machine learning may set the prices for data via the blockchain protocol, choosing from multiple pricing models.[272] Would the fact of sharing and pricing this data through this decentralized blockchain-based marketplace constitute a unilateral conduct? Or should we consider the data providers as entering into some form of collusive information exchange-related conduct?

For an antitrust agreement to be formed, it is required that there is evidence of the 'concurrence of wills between at least two parties, the form in which it is manifested being unimportant so long as it constitutes the faithful expression of the parties' intention'.[273] The case law explains that this 'concurrence of wills' materializes through the existence of an offer and

---

[271] Peder Østbye, 'The Case for a 21 Million Bitcoin Conspiracy' (8 March 2018) https://papers.ssrn.com/sol3/papers.cfm?abstract_id=3136044.

[272] Ocean provides an early example of such decentralized blockchain-based data exchange platform: see Ocean, 'A Decentralized Data Exchange Protocol to Unlock Data for AI', https://oceanprotocol.com.

[273] Case C-2 and 3/01 P, *Bundesverband der Arzneimittel-Importeure eV & Commission v. Bayer* [2004] ECR I-23, [69].

an acceptance. However, the interpretation of these conditions has been quite flexible, and even tacit acquiescence has been found sufficient.[274]

It is also possible that the conduct may fit into the category of concerted practice. In this case, it is not necessary to prove the existence of an offer and acceptance, but one should, at least, bring evidence that the concerted action is 'the result of a consensus', which equally encompasses 'tacit approval'.[275] Returning to our first hypothetical, although the miners have not explicitly acquiesced to the Bitcoin protocol that imposed this output restriction, the fact that they are continuously contributing to its operation may amount to acquiescence, to the extent that their apparently unilateral activity (e.g. validating a block) requires a mutual reliance that other miners will accept the new block, generated by the miner who has been the first to solve the mathematical puzzle (in PoW systems). By authenticating the transaction, they make sure that the proof string really solves the encryption puzzle, these being considered as equivalent to 'voting' in favour of the integration of the transaction in the blockchain. Returning to our second hypothetical, it will all depend on the consideration of the practice of sharing data in the decentralized blockchain-based platform as a form of communication between competitors that may be qualified as a concerted practice, to the extent that it is followed by price parallelism implemented through the use of a common learning algorithm.

This will not be the first time the EU case law found the existence of collusion, despite the 'unusual nature of the method of communication'.[276] In *E-turas*, the director of E-turas, a common online travel booking system, which is used by most travel agents, had sent an email to the travel agencies having an electronic account in the E-turas system asking them to 'vote' on the appropriateness of reducing the discounts offered on booking made through that system. A few days after sending this message, the administrator of E-turas sent through the internal messaging system of E-turas an additional message indicating that a capping of the discount rate will be introduced 'following the appraisal of the statements, proposals and wishes expressed by the travel agencies'. Travel agents were not prevented from granting their customers greater discounts but in order to do so they were required to take additional technical steps. The Lithuanian Competition Council considered that the travel agents using the E-turas booking system during the period in question had participated, along with E-turas, in an anticompetitive concerted practice, the E-turas system being used as a tool for coordinating the travel agents' actions and eliminating the need for meetings. In a preliminary ruling, the CJEU held that a finding of a concertation between the travel agencies was justified, as they were aware of the content of the message at issue and therefore had tacitly assented to a common anticompetitive practice.[277] However, it also noted that 'if it cannot be established that a travel agency was aware of that message, its participation in a concertation cannot be inferred from the mere existence of a technical restriction implemented in the system at issue', unless there are 'other objective and consistent indicia that it tacitly assented to an anticompetitive action'.[278]

Therefore, it becomes important to examine whether the miners (in our first hypothetical) or the service providers (in our second hypothetical) were *aware* of the anticompetitive nature of the arrangement. This may be inferred by the fact that in both cases, the blockchain protocol is well known in advance, as it is usually published when the blockchain developers release their white paper and further documentation, and its anticompetitive potential may be, more or less easily, assessed. The Bitcoin cap is explicitly mentioned in the Bitcoin protocol. The situation is not as straightforward with the second hypothetical; it will all depend on the design of the pricing algorithm and how much autonomy it is afforded, to

---

[274] Case T-208/01, *Volkswagen AG v. Commission* [2003] ECR II-5141.
[275] See the discussion in Case C-74/14, *Eturas UAB et al v. Lietuvos Respublikos konkurencijos taryba*, ECLI:EU:C:2015:493, Opinion of AG Szpunar.
[276] ibid., [61].   [277] ibid., [44].   [278] ibid., [45].

the extent that the service providers may not be able to understand how pricing decisions are made. This issue has raised important questions in recent literature focusing on algorithmic collusion.[279] If the collusive outcome is just the result of the use of the system (i.e. the 'learning algorithm'), without any other objective and consistent indicia of collusion, it is unclear how the practice may fall under the scope of Article 101 TFEU, at least as evidence of direct collusion.

EU competition law offers an additional possibility by bringing some forms of indirect collusion within the scope of Article 101(1) TFEU. The literature on cartels has noted the operation in some horizontal price-fixing conspiracies of an undertaking/agent, situated at a different relevant market than the one covered by the cartel, whose function is to serve as 'an intermediary that speaks individually to each of the competitors and then relays each competitor's agreement [...] to the other competitors in a series of one-to-one conversations'.[280] The main concern of the participants to these conspiracies is to facilitate the implementation of the cartel, even if they do not benefit from its effects directly (although they might receive some other form of compensation from the cartel members).

The presence of these intermediaries on vertically related upstream or downstream markets or on markets that are simply not related to the one the cartel operates may introduce some non-horizontal/triangular element into the collusion, making its qualification more complex, with the concerted practice being indirect rather than direct. A common characteristic of these situations of indirect concerted practice is that the undertakings in this triangular relation are all concerned with the implementation of the horizontal collusion scheme. According to well-established case law, this intermediary may be found to infringe Article 101 TFEU, which strictly precludes 'any direct *or indirect* contact' between competitors.[281] This is the case if, for instance, information on future prices is exchanged between competitors through this intermediary. In *AC-Treuhand AG v. Commission*, AC-Treuhand (a consultancy firm) did not trade on the relevant markets or on related markets, but was found to play an essential role in the infringement as it had organized meetings for the cartel participants which it attended and in which it actively participated, collecting and supplying to the participants data on sales on the relevant markets, offering to act as moderator in case of tensions between the cartel participants, and encouraging the parties to find compromises.[282] The CJEU found AC-Treuhand *directly* liable for the commission of the infringement, finding that the subjective element of the offence was satisfied in this case as its conduct was directly linked to the efforts of the cartelists.[283] This broad interpretation of the direct nature of liability leaves open the possibility of broadly interpreting the concept of 'indirect' contact. Could this be expanded to impose a fiduciary duty not to infringe competition law to all blockchain intermediaries if they are involved in, or are in contact, with a DLT system that has led to an infringement of competition? Could one compare this situation to that of the parent company vis-à-vis the conduct of its subsidiaries? This is an important issue, that does not only relate to competition law but more broadly raises the issue of the 'distributed liability' concerning the legal risks emerging from the use of blockchain systems.[284]

Returning to our first hypothetical, it is possible that, in view of their contribution to the day-to-day operation of the Bitcoin blockchain, the miners could argue that they may benefit from the 'single economic entity' doctrine and that, despite not having any employment

---

[279] See OECD (2017) (n 224); Joseph Harrington, 'Developing Competition Law for Collusion by Autonomous Price-Setting Agents' (2017) University of Pennsylvania.

[280] George Hay, 'Horizontal Agreements: Concept and Proof' (2006) 51 *Antitrust Bulletin*, 882.

[281] Joined Cases 40–48, 50, 54–56, 111, 113–114/73, *Cooperatieve Vereniging 'Suiker Unie' UA v. Commission* [1975] ECR 1663, [174] (emphasis added).

[282] Case COMP/38.589, *Heat Stabilisers* [2009].

[283] Case C-194/14 P, *AC-Treuhand AG v. Commission*, [2015], ECLI:EU:C:2015:717, notably para. 38.

[284] For a thorough discussion, see Dirk Zetzshe, Ross Buckley, and Douglas Arner, 'The Distributed Liability of Distributed Ledgers: Legal Risks of Blockchain' (2018) 4 *University of Illinois Law Review* 1361.

contract, they are, in reality, operating as employees of the blockchain. If they are qualified as employees, they cannot then be qualified as an undertaking exercising an autonomous economic activity, in the sense of offering goods or services on a market and bearing the financial risk attached to the performance of such activity.[285] Hence, their activity could not be considered as constituting collusion between undertakings under Article 101 TFEU. The CJEU focuses on the *nature* of the relation before concluding on the existence of an 'undertaking'. In its most recent case law, the CJEU has taken a more cautious approach, rejecting categorical distinctions, such as workers and self-employed. It addresses these situations as a *continuum* going from situations of complete dependence (in which case, the relation will be considered as akin to employment) to a situation of complete independence (in which case, the entity in question will be considered as an independent undertaking).[286] This is quite unlikely in this context, as industrial mining activity is concentrated in a limited number of mining pools, many of which contribute to the activity of several cryptocurrencies and other crypto-assets.

One may finally refer to the agency theory and consider that the miners constitute the agents of a principal (the blockchain), the existence of a genuine agency relation immunizing their conduct, as this could be considered as taking place within the boundaries of a 'single economic entity'.[287] This approach has already been tried in analysing the relations between digital platforms, such as Uber and the various economic operators linked to that platform (Uber drivers).[288] However, even assuming that miners would be considered as the agents of the blockchain, this cannot immunize horizontal collusion between miners, the scope of the immunity being limited to vertical relations between the principal and the agent.[289]

3. Reconceptualizing (market) power in blockchain competition

The digital economy gives rise to a variety of strategies to acquire competitive advantage and convert this to surplus value to be later collected in product and financial markets. In this fast-moving environment, innovation competition provides the main constraint to 'winner-takes-most' competition, as new economic actors rely on cost-cutting technology to break into markets, disrupt the existing competitive structure, and eventually acquire a position of economic power, before they give way to new actors making a more efficient use of the technology or relying on a better technological alternative. As explained above in section V, the boundaries of markets and industries become blurred. The financialization of the economy leads to the superposition of global financial markets, characterized by higher volatility, the operation of complex information systems, and future-driven rationalities which sit on top of the various product markets on which competitive interactions have traditionally been thought to occur. Competition does not only take place within a product or a technology

---

[285] Case C-22/98, *Criminal Proceedings against Jean Claude Becu, Annie Verweire, Smeg NV and Adia Interim NV* [1999] ECR I-5665.

[286] Case C-413/13, *FNV Kunsten Informatie en Media*, ECLI:EU:C:2014:2411.

[287] EU Vertical Restraints Guidelines [2010] OJ C 130/1, [12]–[20].

[288] See, e.g., a recent judgment of the UK Employment Appeal Tribunal ('UKEAT') regarding the employment status of Uber drivers, which although relating to employment law may provide some insights for competition law. Although the UKEAT noted that the drivers incurred commercial risks as they were responsible for all costs incidental to owning and running the vehicle, and were also able to work for or through other organizations, including direct competitors with Uber operating through digital platforms, which could hint at the existence of an agency relation, it rejected this qualification in favour of an employment relation in view of the relative bargaining power of the parties (Uber being much more powerful than the drivers, acting individually), the integration of Uber drivers into Uber's business, in particular as, among other things, they were prevented from building up a business relationship with the end user of the service, they were in practice obliged to accept all trip requests if they wanted to keep their account status, and Uber held a significant market share in London, which left them no other equally effective competitive alternative.

[289] Vertical Restraints Guidelines (n 287), [20].

market, or even an industry, but also within broader competition 'ecosystems',[290] which may include various industries, as inter-industrial investment flows focus on the lowest cost techniques that provide higher rates of return for the capital invested, capital moving from one industry to another in search of higher profits.[291]

The disruptive promise of the blockchain lays exactly in its ability to contest hard-won positions of market power, held by digital platforms, which have emerged victorious in the different 'competition-for-the-market' contests that opposed them to 'old economy' incumbents. If digital platforms have relied on the complex economics of multi-sided markets to question the dominance of incumbents on single relevant markets, the competitive strategies of blockchain participants may challenge the centralizing role of platforms. The competitive game does not only refer to neck-to neck rivalry but, as explained in section V, takes more complex dimensions, finding expression in the concept of co-opetition. Co-opetition does not only take place on relevant product markets, but also on financial and technology markets and at various segments of the value chain. The allocation of the surplus value does not result only from competition within an industry, but also from competition between industries.

These changes certainly influence the concept of economic power relevant for competition assessment. This cannot only be defined as power over price exercised on a specified relevant market, but it also needs to consider that most competitive strategies take place at the level of the ecosystem, with firms competing for architectural advantage in it.

Usually, economic concentration indexes serve as an appropriate proxy for inferring the existence of market power in its traditional dimension of power over price. In the absence of barriers to entry, a highly concentrated relevant market provides a good indicator that the entity controlling a large market share in a product or technology market has the ability to raise prices profitably or to negatively affect other parameters of competition (i.e. the entity has market power).[292] Determining the existence of a dominant position will usually require the definition of a relevant market and the computation of the market share held by the specific entity (or entities). The relevant market may be narrow or wide, depending on the availability of substitutable products and technologies. There are various ways to evaluate market power on the basis of market shares: one may refer to the users of the blockchain, the number of recorded transactions, or the position of the blockchain participants on markets off-blockchain, among other options.[293] The hashing power spent to validate the blockchain is also a relevant assessment criterion, to the extent that the community of nodes running the protocol and validating the transactions indicate the attractiveness of a specific blockchain vis-à-vis competing ones, eventually also a blockchain fork, should some of the members move to a different one. It is also possible that all competitors within the market use the same blockchain, in which case the number of participants, recorded transactions, and hashing power may prove relevant. Product differentiation, the control of IP rights, and other barriers to entry may also be relevant for the analysis.

Cryptocurrencies also raise difficult questions of market definition, in view of their volatility and the fact that they may be considered in competition with each other, with other national fiat currencies and private currencies as a means of payment,[294] or in competition

---

[290] Jacobides et al., 'Towards a Theory of Ecosystems' (n 175).   [291] Shaikh (n 127).

[292] According to the Commission's Transfer of Technology Block Exemption Regulation Guidelines '[t]he relevant technology markets consist of the licensed technology rights and its substitutes, that is to say, other technologies which are regarded by the licensees as interchangeable with or substitutable for the licensed technology rights, by reason of the technologies' characteristics, their royalties and their intended use': Guidelines on the Application of Article 101 of the Treaty on the Functioning of the European Union to Technology Transfer Agreements [2014] OJ C 89/3, [22].

[293] Schrepel (n 23).

[294] Østbye, 'The Adequacy of Competition' (n 23), 8, noting that 'all cryptocurrencies cannot necessarily be considered to be sufficiently substitutable to be considered competitors'.

with other investments, if they are perceived as providing a store of value. Network effects and product differentiation, such as emphasis on security, capacity, speed, and anonymity, may protect the position of a dominant cryptocurrency. Blockchain developers may also link additional services with a cryptocurrency. Some of them, such as Ripple, which act simultaneously as a cryptocurrency and a real-time gross settlement system, currency exchange, and remittance network, may even be considered in competition with traditional payment systems. Indeed, Ripple provides an open-source internet software enabling users to conduct international payments in multiple currencies. The emergence of the blockchain has unleashed enormous amounts of creativity, generating an ever-increasing number of idiosyncratic crypto-assets, and Dapps. Hence, competition authorities should proceed to a concrete analysis of the specific economic context and of the facts of each case, always focusing, as a starting point for the analysis, on the competitive strategies that may adopted by the various economic actors.

However, it becomes apparent that the problem with the traditional measures of market power is that, even if they do provide an accurate picture of the position of the blockchain participant on a product or technology market, they do not necessarily account for its position in the broader ecosystem (what I will call 'ecosystem power'), which is, in view of the central importance of ecosystems in the competitive interactions in the digital economy, the most important factor to consider. Ecosystem power does not only refer to the ability of the blockchain participant, or another entity, to limit horizontal competition on a product or technology market in order to increase its profitability, but also to its capacity to restrict vertical competition by constituting a bottleneck that may enable it to extract a larger percentage of the surplus value generated by the specific value chain. This capability to restrict both horizontal and vertical competition may also signal to financial markets the existence of a sustainable strategic or architectural advantage that could create expectations for abnormal profits in the medium and long term, thus attracting capital and leading to an increase of the market value of the entity or of the funds that can be raised through an ICO.

Competition law still lacks the operational and measurement tools to map competitive interactions taking place outside the relevant market, something that may lead to a rather myopic competition law enforcement that would only focus on restrictions of horizontal competition in relevant markets, to the detriment of the vertical competition dimension and co-opetition taking place at the boundaries of relevant markets or industries. Although it has focused increasingly on innovation and has started to develop specific tools to deal with the innovation effects of horizontal mergers,[295] it has yet to engage with all the dimensions of futurity, that influence, through the evaluation mechanism of financial markets, the perceived competitive promise of blockchain projects and the arrangements governing the allocation of surplus value between the various participants and stakeholders in the specific ecosystem. I have advanced elsewhere the concept of 'digital value chain' as a useful mapping tool and conceptual framework for the full canopy of competitive interactions in the digital economy.[296] There is still work to be done in order to operationalize this concept and also to develop specific tools that would measure ecosystem power. However, the lack of adequate metrics for the time being should not constitute an insurmountable barrier to widening the scope of competition assessment and to providing a real, as opposed to distorted, picture of competition, taking into account the various forms of competitive advantage.

A natural extension of this project is to also account for the various dimensions of 'power'.[297] The concept of market power is remotely linked to resource dependency theories

---

[295] See Giulio Federico, Gregor Langus, and Tommasso Valletti, 'Horizontal Mergers and Product Innovation' (2018) 59 *International Journal of Industrial Organization*, 1; Bruno Jullien and Yassine Lefouili, 'Horizontal Mergers and Innovation' (2018) Toulouse School of Economics Working Paper, 18-892.

[296] Ioannis Lianos, 'Digital Value Chains in Competition Law' (2019) CLES Research Paper 1/2019.

[297] For an in-depth discussion see, Ioannis Lianos, *The Different Dimensions of Economic Power in Competition Law: Concepts and Measurement* (Mimeo, 2017).

of power, with the entity controlling more resources, or indispensable resources, having power over entities that control fewer resources or need access to this indispensable resource.[298] Controlling access to a strategic bottleneck certainly provides the entity in question with the capability to charge supra-competitive prices and, eventually, to restrict quality and innovation competition. However, this is not the only type of power in operation in the blockchain arena, and more generally, in the digital economy. Power may also take the form of being in a position to control the agenda of what is considered for decision.[299] This dimension is particularly important when accounting for architectural advantage. The blockchain community is still quite small, and a number of actors have achieved almost totemic position with thousands of 'followers' in their twitter accounts, blogs, and social media, often exercising an important influence on the valuation of cryptocurrencies and other crypto-assets or in promoting an optimistic narrative as to the competitive prospects of the technology vis-à-vis competing ones.[300] These narratives also influence policy-makers and regulators, which, as I have previously described, constitute an important dimension of acquiring competitive advantage vis-à-vis incumbents relying on competing technologies. Developing operational theoretical frameworks and adequate metrics in order to measure architectural advantage is an area for further research.

4. The 'unregulatability' of the blockchain: remedies and sanctions

Blockchain may also curtail the ability of competition regulators to identify the entities that would be liable for competition law infringements and to adopt appropriate remedies and sanctions. At the early stages of the development of the internet, the thesis of the 'unregulatability' of the internet was refuted by authors claiming that there were clearly points of control and entities that could be held liable for the risks their activity contributed in surging.[301] Like the internet, blockchain is borderless, but crucially it is decentralized, which makes it difficult, in particular if the activity takes place in the context of public permissionless blockchains, to determine who should bear the responsibility for the social costs and the private harms generated by the blockchain-related activity. A distributed ledger may need forms of 'distributed liability': 'all entities in the system need to consider contingent liability risk'.[302] Should that extend to all the blockchain participants, irrespective of their governance roles, or only to those that exercise a significant influence on the activity that led to the specific social costs or to the specific private harm to be compensated? And if the option of collective responsibility is finally chosen, how would this be apportioned between the various nodes, to the extent that node owners in a permissionless blockchain may not even be aware of the specific conduct, or of who were the other node owners involved. Zetzsche et al. emphasize the governance structure of the DLT system, noting the existence, in most DLT projects, even permissionless blockchains, of a 'DLT hierarchy' consisting of the following groups:

(i) 'the core group that sets-up the code design and (*de facto*) governs the DLT, for instance by having the technical ability and opinion leadership to prompt a hard fork of the system (under certain conditions);

---

[298] For a discussion, Richard Emmerson, 'Power-Dependence Relations' (1962) 27(1) *American Sociological Review*, 33; Karen Cook and Richard Emerson, 'Power, Equity and Commitment in Exchange Networks' (1978) 43(5) *American Sociological Review*, 721.

[299] Mark Granovetter, *Society and Economy* (Harvard University Press 2017), 101.

[300] See, e.g., Feng Mai, Zhe Shan, Qing Bai, Xin Wang, and Roger Chiang, 'How Does Social Media Impact Bitcoin Value? A Test of the Silent Majority Hypothesis' (2018) 35(1) *Journal of Management Information Systems*, 19.

[301] See Jack Goldsmith and Tim Wu, *Who Controls the Internet? Illusions of a Borderless World* (Oxford University Press 2006), cited by De Filippi and Wright, *Blockchain and the Law* (n 22), 50.

[302] See Zetzsche et al. (n 284), 9.

(ii)   the owners of additional servers running the distributed ledger code for validation purposes [...];

(iii) qualified users of the distributed ledger, such as exchanges, lending institutions, miners etc.; and

(iv)   third parties affected by the system without directly relying on the technology, for instance, [...] simple users, clients of intermediaries [...] etc.'[303]

Some of these blockchain participants, but not all, may be qualified as undertakings, in that they offer goods and services on a market. For instance, it is clear that category (iv) will most likely comprise end users or consumers that do not offer products or services on a market and, therefore, will not be qualified as 'undertakings'. Of course, being a natural person does not exclude *ipso facto* the possibility of being qualified as an 'undertaking' if that person exercises an economic activity and does so independent of the power or influence exercised by the specific natural person in the governance of the DLT. For instance, it is likely that the members of the core group will not be qualified as undertakings in the case that they are employees, who lead their DLT activity outside their normal working hours and without supervision of their employer, on a voluntary basis. In any case, it becomes crucial to identify the entities that form part of, at least the first four groups of the DLT hierarchy, before determining the governance structure of the DLT.

The knowledge about the governance structure of the DLT may assist regulators and competition authorities in deciding to expand, or not, the scope of liability to all DLT participants, even if they have not actively contributed to the governance of the blockchain. Legal fictions, such as the concept of 'business networks' may provide the conceptual framework to expand the scope of liability beyond the confines of pure 'enterprise liability', in order to also include entities that facilitated and/or took advantage of the activities assisted by the DLT in their own economic activity, such as the owners of nodes and qualified users. These can be various forms of blockchain participants, such as code developers (for blockchain-based protocols and smart contracts), miners, oracles, digital exchanges and wallets, information intermediaries, hardware manufacturers (in particular, for the IoT), and other commercial operators interacting with the blockchain system.[304] However, one should be careful before expanding the scope of liability too far, in view of the principle of personal responsibility for infringements of competition law[305] and the requirements of the European Convention on Human Rights ('ECHR'), notably the presumption of innocence.[306]

Deciding on how wide this liability net should extend depends on a first-principles analysis of the values of the specific enforcement system: corrective justice or economic efficiency and the least cost-avoidable principle. These first principles will influence the

---

[303]   ibid., 22.

[304]   The various layers of blockchain technology that may be subject to regulation are discussed in De Filippi and Wright, *Blockchain and the Law* (n 22), 184–87.

[305]   This principle explains why some fault or negligence is usually required for holding an undertaking liable for infringing competition law. The case law of the EU courts also requires, in case the conduct to which the undertaking contributed is found to be an infringement of competition law results from some collective activity with other undertakings, that the 'undertaking in question was *aware* of the offending conduct of the other participants or that it could *reasonably have foreseen* it and that it was prepared to take the risk': Case T-410/09, *Almanet v. Commission*, ECLI:EU:T:2012:676, [153] (emphasis added). According to the General Court, what counts is the intention of the undertaking to 'help bring about the infringement as a whole': ibid. Although this case law concerns the concept of 'single overall agreement', in my view it shows the importance of the principle of personal responsibility in EU competition law.

[306]   The jurisprudence of the EU Courts is constrained by the presumption of innocence, or the principle *in dubio pro reo* (literally: 'when in doubt, in favour of the accused'), enshrined in Article 6(2) of the European Convention of Human Rights and Article 48(1) of the Charter of Fundamental Rights of the European Union, which requires that 'any doubt in the mind of the Court must operate to the advantage of the undertaking to which the decision finding an infringement was addressed', in particular for decisions imposing fines or periodic penalty payments: see Case T-44/02, *Dresdner Bank AG and Others v. Commission* [2006] II-3567, [60]–[61]; Case T-36/05, *Coats Holdings Ltd v. Commission*, [2007] ECR II-110, [69].

conceptualization of the causal link that would be required to ascribe liability to a specific entity, from the various groups listed above. One may expect the development of standards reflecting social values and concerns with regard to the allocation of risks and responsibilities, once the technology and governance structure of DLT becomes more widely understood by courts and policy-makers. This may lead to different choices. A corrective justice perspective focusing on deterrence, will insist on the liability of any entity that may have contributed with its actions or omissions to the social harm. An efficiency perspective on the basis of the least cost avoidance principle will focus on the liability of the core group of developers in view of their crucial role in the design of the governance of the system.[307] Others may focus on engineering the right incentives for key blockchain participants, for instance by extending liability to miners or owners of the nodes, in view of their crucial role in the operation of the DLT.

The type of sanctions and remedies will also be a matter for further analysis. Individual sanctions may constitute the best option, for instance imposing a fine on the core developers. However, there is no such possibility in EU competition law if these core developers cannot be qualified as undertakings. Similarly, in EU competition law, these sanctions can only be administrative; not criminal. Remedies may also raise different challenges. With regard to infringements of Articles 101 and 102 TFEU, they intervene *ex post* and, in these fast-moving technology sectors, they often come too late, although one may not exclude the possibility of prophylactic remedies in some circumstances. Behavioural remedies will require a continuous supervision by the competition authority of the operation of the blockchain, which, in view of the fact that it is public and transparent, may be more easily implemented than behavioural remedies imposed against centralized platforms, which have led to quite a cumbersome process because of the mistrust between the competition authority and the undertaking controlling the platform with regard to the accuracy of the information provided to the authority. Structural remedies may be more difficult to design in view of the lack of clear points of control on which the competition authority may act, for instance by ordering divestiture and other conventional structural remedies. It is more likely that the competition authorities will adopt a mechanism design approach, taking into account the complex system of incentives in operation in blockchains to promote competition-compatible blockchain architectures.

Competition authorities may also choose to emphasize 'compliance by design', by clarifying in some guidance document(s) the specific duties of blockchain developers and other 'fiduciaries' when they design and operate DLT. This will not necessarily require competition authorities to adoption a system of auditing blockchain projects *ex ante* in order to assess the possible competition risks, which will be quite cumbersome and will eventually require a significant revamp of the capabilities of competition authorities, in terms of technical expertise and legal tools at their disposal. The 'competition by design'[308] agenda may be promoted through competition advocacy and a more active informal engagement of competition authorities with the blockchain community so to nudge them to the right direction.

Blockchain technology does not only set challenges to competition authorities; it also provides a lot of opportunities to assist them in their work. For instance, cartel enforcement may become more effective if DLT is used for the submission of leniency applications, but also in order to handle the sheer amount of evidence usually collected in a competition law case. Access to the file will also be more easily managed, thus, more effectively protecting the rights of defence. Competition authorities and courts may also have access to a data stream kept on blockchain with all the relevant transactions. This could be valuable information in

---

[307] According to the cost-avoidance principle, responsibility should be imposed on the person best placed to avoid the loss most cheaply.

[308] On this concept, see Simonetta Vezzoso, 'Competition by Design' (2017) Presentation for 12th ASCOLA Conference, Stockholm University.

order to provide evidence of a competition law infringement, but also in the context of actions for damages. The availability of this data will also facilitate the monitoring of markets by competition authorities and the early detection of cartels, as well as other anticompetitive activity.

VII. Conclusion

The first industrial revolution offered interesting insights as to the interaction of technology with economic regulation, and more specifically the regulation of railways, the new GPT at that time. The 1844 Railways Act (the 'Parliamentary Trains' Act), which followed Gladstone's Committee of Inquiry into Railway Policy, was animated by the classical theory of economics with its fear of oligopolies, even at a time when Cournot's work on oligopoly was not known in the English-speaking world. Gladstone had cautioned, in his Committee report, on the discriminatory practices of railways monopolies that charged fares guaranteeing a substantial operating profit but which also undercut stagecoach fares. This incident built the foundations of subsequent work in the regulation of fares. The concepts of natural monopoly and market failure were later generalized in other economic sectors and built the broader rationale for state intervention in the form of regulation.

Travelling through time to the third industrial revolution and the development of platforms, regulation has been increasingly influenced by the paradigm of two-sided or multi-sided platforms that adds a new level of analysis than the 'market' and by the emphasis put on 'disruptive innovation' rather than on just maintaining the competitive 'order'. The customers also become the 'raw material' in platforms' business models, their data monetized in product or financial markets. Whether customers' single-home or multi-home becomes crucial for the competition analysis performed. The concentration of data in few digital hands, and the likely risks of exploitation of internet users, raise important concerns not only for competition law, but more generally, in view of the centrality of the internet in modern societies, for our broader constitutional, social, and economic arrangements. However, we have witnessed the building in less than two decades of a relatively solid, although still evolving, area of economic and legal 'expertise' relating to platforms, with the aim of informing collective action regulating them.

Blockchains are not similar to platforms. The most revolutionary aspect of blockchain technology is that it can run software in a secure and decentralized manner. With a blockchain, software applications no longer need to be deployed on a centralized server. They run instead on a peer-to-peer network that is not controlled by any single party. Furthermore, DLT applications can be used to coordinate the activities of a large number of individuals, who can organize themselves without the help of a third party. Ultimately, blockchain technology is a means for individuals to coordinate common activities, to interact directly with one another, and to govern themselves in a more secure and decentralized manner. This change in the governance of the digital economy towards a more competitive and decentralized model, similar in some respects to that contemplated by the original internet project, has so far constituted the main appeal of blockchain for the general public, including competition lawyers and economists. The challenge of regulating a decentralized network and the global character of the blockchain also raise broader questions about the effectiveness of competition law enforcement in the DLT era.

As important as these concerns may be, and useful as the static competition analysis offered by some studies may be from a practical perspective, this work has not yet provided a leap forward by promoting the effort to understand the full implications of blockchain competition for competition law and policy. This chapter has attempted to explore the complex dynamics of competitive advantage in blockchain competition in an effort to build the foundations of a conceptual framework for analysing how DLT may affect existing constellations of power and may lead to new ones. This bottom-up re-conceptualization of the competition game in the DLT space, by drawing on the competitive strategies of economic actors, rather than on the formal theoretical frameworks of neoclassical price theory, is crucial if one is to fully grasp the different dimensions of economic power and its potential abuse, which competition law should aim to tame and eventually curtail in the blockchain space.

The chapter also offers a broader conceptual mapping that may assist competition authorities to form an informed view of blockchain competition from a strategic and dynamic perspective, and, in particular, to reflect on new concepts, methods, and tools that may be required for competition law analysis. Blockchain competition is an illustration of what some authors have called the 'next-generation' or 'turbo-charged' competition already in operation in the digital economy.[309] This is a complex economy, with various spaces of competitive interaction (industries, platforms, value chains, ecosystems), the study of which requires a greater degree of sophistication in the analytical tools employed. The ambition of this chapter was to advocate for a more holistic view of the competitive process, as this is transformed by new GPT, such as DLT, and to share some broader insights and preliminary conclusions for competition law analysis in the digital economy.

VIII. Bibliography

Abadi Joseph and Brunnermeier Markus, 'Blockchain Economics' (1 May 2018) https://scholar.princeton.edu/sites/default/files/markus/files/blockchain_paper_v2c.pdf, accessed on 17 January 2019.

Adner Ron, 'Ecosystem as Structure—An Actionable Construct for Strategy', (2017) 43(1) *Journal of Management*, 39.

Alt Rainer, Beck Roman, and Smits Martin, 'FinTech and the Transformation of the Financial Industry' (2018) 28(3) *Electronic Markets*, 235.

Alyoshkin Roman, 'Blockchain 2.0. The Purpose of Blockchain' (3 October 2017) https://medium.com/polys-blog/blockchain-2-0-the-purpose-of-blockchain-e84e5a95cdd9, accessed on 17 January 2019.

Arnold Martin, 'Five Way Banks Are Using Blockchain' (*ft.com*, 16 October 2017) https://www.ft.com/content/615b3bd8-97a9-11e7-a652-cde3f882dd7b, accessed on 17 January 2019.

Arruñada Benito, 'Blockchain's Struggle to Deliver Impersonal Exchange' (2018) 19(1) *Minnesota Journal of Law, Science and Technology*, 55.

Arthur Brian, 'Competing Technologies, Increasing Returns, and Lock-In by Historical Events' (1989) 99(394) *The Economic Journal*, 116.

Arthur Brian, *The Nature of Technology* (Penguin 2009).

Autor David, Dorn David, Katz Lawrence, Patterson Christina, and Van Reenen John, 'The Fall of the Labor Share and the Rise of Superstar Firms' (2017) NBER Working Paper No. 23396.

Autorité de la concurrence (France) and Bundeskartellamt (Germany), 'Competition Law and Data' (2016) Report.

Bank of England, 'First Non-Bank Payment Service Provider Directly Accesses UK Payment System' (*bankofengland.co.uk*, 18 April 2018) https://www.bankofengland.co.uk/news/2018/april/non-bank-psp-access-to-the-payments-system-announcement, accessed on 17 January 2019.

Baldwin Richard, *The Great Convergence: Information Technology and the New Globalization* (Harvard University Press 2017).

Bartels Andrew, Bartoletti Dave, Rymer John, Guarini Matthew, and Valdovinos Robert, 'The Coming Consolidation of Cloud' (2017) Forrester Report.

Bauerle Nolan, 'What is the Difference Between a Blockchain and a Database?' (*coindesk.com*) https://www.coindesk.com/information/what-is-the-difference-blockchain-and-database/, accessed on 17 January 2019.

---

[309] Teece, 'Next-Generation Competition' (n 176), 98.

Baumol William, Panzar John, and Willig Robert, *Contestable Markets and the Theory of Industry Structure* (Harcourt Brace Jovanovic 1982).

Benkler Yochai, 'Degrees of Freedom, Dimensions of Power' (2016) 145(1) *Daedalus*, 18.

Berman Bruce, 'Blockchain Patent Applications Doubled in 2017 to More than 1,200' (*ipcloseup. com*, 27 March 2018) https://ipcloseup.com/2018/03/27/blockchain-patent-applications-doubled-in-2017-to-over-1200/, accessed on 17 January 2019.

Bessen James, 'Accounting for Rising Corporate Profits: Intangibles or Regulatory Rents?' (2016) Boston University School of Law, Law and Economics Research Paper No. 16-18.

Binmore Ken, *Natural Justice* (Oxford University Press, 2005).

Bjørnstad Magnus Vitsø, Harkestad Joar Gunnarsjaa, and Krogh Simen, 'A Study on Blockchain Technology as a Resource for Competitive Advantage' (2017) *Norwegian University of Science and Technology*, https://brage.no/xmlui/bitstream/handle/11250/2472245/17527_FULLTEXT. pdf?sequence=1, accessed on 16 February 2019.

Blockstack, 'The Easiest Way to Start Building Decentralised Blockchain Apps', https://blockstack. org, accessed on 17 January 2019.

Brandenburger Adam and Nalebuff Barry, *Co-opetition* (Currency Doubleday, 1997).

Bresnahan Timothy and Trajtenberg Manuel, 'General Purpose Technologies: Engines of Growth?' (1995) 65(1) *Journal of Econometrics*, 83.

Bulow Jeremy, Geanakoplos John, and Klemperer Paul, 'Multimarket Oligopoly: Strategic Substitutes and Strategic Complements' (1985) 93 *Journal of Political Economy*, 488.

Buterin Vitaliak, 'DAOs, DACs, DAs and More: An Incomplete Terminology Guide' (*blog. ethereum.org*, 6 May 2014) https://blog.ethereum.org/2014/05/06/daos-dacs-das-and-more-an-incomplete-terminology-guide/, accessed on 17 January 2019.

Buterin Vitaliak, 'The Meaning of Decentralisation' (*medium.com*, 6 February 2017) https://medium.com/@VitalikButerin/the-meaning-of-decentralization-a0c92b76a274, accessed on 17 January 2019.

Cabral João, 'The Patentability of Blockchain Technology in Europe' (*inventa.com*, 24 April 2018) https://inventa.com/en/news/article/300/the-patenteability-of-blockchain-technology-in-europe, accessed on 17 January 2019.

Caccia Federico, 'A Review of Cryptoasset Valuation Frameworks' (*blog.coinfabrik.com*, 18 July 2018) https://blog.coinfabrik.com/a-review-on-cryptoasset-valuation-frameworks/, accessed on 17 January 2019.

Callon Michael, 'What Does It Mean to Say that Economics is Performative?' in *Do Economists Make Markets? On the Performativity of Economics*, edited by Donald MacKenzie, Fabian Muniesa, and Lucia Siu (Princeton University Press 2007).

Carney Mark, 'The Promise of FinTech—Something New Under the Sun?' (25 January 2017) Speech.

Carson Brant, Romanelli Giulio, Walsh Patricia, and Zhumaev Askhat, 'Blockchain Beyond the Hype: What is the Strategic Business Value' (*mckinsey.com*, June 2018) https://www.mckinsey. com/business-functions/digital-mckinsey/our-insights/blockchain-beyond-the-hype-what-is-the-strategic-business-value?cid=other-eml-nsl-mip-mck-oth-1807&hlkid=8ca56a40fe474c74 97e74038a1f43fe7&hctky=9280917&hdpid=bb9f89f0-458b-4b4e-a1ee-ad99e602294e, accessed on 17 January 2019.

Catalini Christian and Gans Joshua, 'Some Simple Economics of the Blockchain' (2017) Rotman School of Management Working Paper No. 2874598, MIT Sloan Research Paper No. 5191-16.

Catalini Christian and Tucker Catherine, 'Antitrust and Costless Verification: An Optimistic and a Pessimistic View of the Implications of Blockchain Technology' (2018) MIT Sloan Research Paper.

CBInsights, 'Banks are Finally Going After Fintech Startups' (*cbsinsights.com*, 13 February 2018) https://www.cbinsights.com/research/top-us-banks-fintech-acquisitions/, accessed on 17 January 2019.

Chiu Henry, 'An Overview of the Blockchain Patent Landscape' (*clarivate.com*, 8 November 2017) https://clarivate.com/blog/overview-blockchain-patent-landscape/, accessed on 17 January 2019.

Coase Ronald, 'The Nature of the Firm' (1937) 4(16) *Economica*, 386.

Cohen Julie, 'Law for the Platform Economy'(2017) 51 *U.C. Davis School of Law Review*, 133.

CoinDesk, ICO Tracker (*coindesk.com*) https://www.coindesk.com/ico-tracker/, accessed on 17 January 2019.

Comben Christine, 'Top Decentralised Marketplaces that Use Blockchain Technology' (*coincentral. com*, 9 July 2018) https://coincentral.com/decentralized-marketplace-blockchain/, accessed on 17 January 2019.

Communication from the Commission—Guidance on the Commission's Enforcement Priorities in Applying Article [102 TFEU] to Abusive Exclusionary Conduct by Dominant Undertakings [2009] OJ C 45/7.

Communication of the Commission Published Pursuant to Article 27(4) of Council Regulation (EC) No. 1/2003 in Case AT.39850—Container Shipping, [2016] OJ C 60/7.

Competition and Markets Authority, 'Market Studies and Market Investigations' (2014) Annex, Supplemental Guidance on the CMA's Approach.

Competition and Markets Authority, 'CMA, Retail Banking Market Investigation' (2016) Final Report.

Competition and Markets Authority (UK) and Autorité de la Concurrence (France), 'The Economics of Open and Closed Systems' (2014) Report.

Cook Karen and Emerson Richard, 'Power, Equity and Commitment in Exchange Networks' (1978) 43(5) *American Sociological Review*, 721.

Dale Oliver, 'JUR ICO: Decentralised Dispute Resolution Platform' (*Blockonomi.com*, 11 July 2018) https://blockonomi.com/jur-ico/, accessed on 17 January 2019.

David Paul, 'Clio and the Economics of QWERTY' (1985) 75(2) *American Economic Review*, 332.

David Paul, 'The Hero and the Herd: Reflections on Thomas Edison and the "Battle of the Systems"' in *Favorites of Fortune: Technology, Growth, and Economic Development since the Industrial Revolution*, edited by Patrice Higonnet, David Landes, and Henry Rosovsky (Harvard University Press 1991).

David Paul, 'Heroes, Herds and Hysteresis in Technological History' (1992) 1(1) *Journal of Industrial and Corporate Change* 129.

Davidson Sinclair, De Filippi Primavera, and Potts Jason, 'Blockchains and the Economic Institutions of Capitalism' (2018) 14(4) *Journal of Institutional Economics* 639.

De Filippi Primavera and McCarthy Smari, 'Cloud Computing: Centralization and Data Sovereignty' (2012) 3(2) *European Journal for Law and Technology*, http://ejlt.org/article/view/101/234, accessed on 16 February 2019.

De Filippi Primavera and Wright Aaron, 'Decentralized Blockchain Technology and the Rise of Lex Cryptographia' (25 July 2017) https://papers.ssrn.com/sol3/papers.cfm?abstract_id=2580664, accessed on 17 January 2019.

De Filippi Primavera and Wright Aaron, *Blockchain and the Law* (Harvard University Press 2018).

Dell'Erba Marco, 'Initial Coin Offerings. A Primer. The First Response of Regulatory Authorities' (2018) 14 *NYU Journal of Law and Business*, 1109.

Deloitte, 'Global Survey: Breaking Blockchain Open' (2018) https://www2.deloitte.com/us/en/pages/consulting/articles/innovation-blockchain-survey.html, accessed on 17 January 2019.

Deutsche Bank, 'Fintech Reloaded—Traditional Banks as Digital Ecosystems' (2015).

Dosi Giovanni, 'Technological Paradigms and Technological Trajectories' (1982) 11 *Research Policy*, 147.

Emmerson Richard, 'Power-Dependence Relations' (1962) 27(1) *American Sociological Review*, 31.

Enterprise Ethereum Alliance, 'Introduction and Overview' (*entethalliance.org*, 2017) https://entethalliance.org/wp-content/themes/ethereum/img/intro-eea.pdf, accessed on 17 January 2019.

EtherFlip, (*etherflip.co*) http://www.etherflip.co/, accessed on 17 January 2019.

Ezrachi Ariel and Stucke Maurice, 'Two Artificial Neural Networks Meet in an Online Hub and Change the Future (of Competition, Market Dynamics and Society)' (2017) Oxford Legal Studies Research Paper No. 24/2017.

Federico Giulio, Langus Gregor, and Valletti Tommasso, 'Horizontal Mergers and Product Innovation' (2018) 59 *International Journal of Industrial Organization*, 1.

Ferguson Charles and Morris Charles, 'How Architecture Wins Technology Wars' (1993) 71(2) *Harvard Business Review*, 117.

Fernández-Villaverde Jesús and Sanches Daniel, 'Can Currency Competition Work?' (2016) National Bureau of Economic Research No. w22157.

Financial Conduct Authority, 'Regulatory Sandbox' (2015) Research Paper.

Financial Conduct Authority, 'Our Approach to Competition' (*fca.org.uk*, 11 December 2017) https://www.fca.org.uk/publications/corporate-documents/our-approach-competition, accessed on 17 January 2019.

Financial Times, 'China Leads Blockchain Patent Applications' (*ft.com*) https://www.ft.com/content/197db4c8-2e92-11e8-9b4b-bc4b9f08f381, accessed on 17 January 2019.

Financial Times, 'TransferWise to Offer Cross-Border Bank Accounts' (*ft.com*, 23 May 2017) https://www.ft.com/content/29adbe9a-3efd-11e7-82b6-896b95f30f58 , accessed on 17 January 2019.

Financial Times, 'P2P Lender Zopa Raises £44m to Fund New Bank' (*ft.com*, 3 August 2018) https://www.ft.com/content/6ce5f960-96e1-11e8-b67b-b8205561c3fe, accessed on 17 January 2019.

Finney Brad, 'Blockchain and Antitrust: New Tech Meets Old Regs' (2018) 19 *Transactions: The Tennessee Journal of Business Law*, 709.

Fowler Margaret, 'Linking the Public Benefit to the Corporation: Blockchain as a Solution for Certification in an Age of Do-Good Business' (2018) 20 (3) *Vanderbilt Journal of Entertainment and Technology Law*, 881.

Fundeberg Dean and Tirole Jean, 'The Fat-Cat Effect, the Puppy-Dog Ploy and the Lean and Hungry Look' (1984) 74 *American Economic Review*, 361.

Funfair Technologies, 'Blockchain Solutions for Gaming' (*funfair.io*) https://funfair.io/, accessed on 17 January 2019.

GitHub, Orisi White Paper (29 November 2014) https://github.com/orisi/wiki/wiki/Orisi-White-Paper, accessed on 17 January 2019.

Goldsmith Jack and Wu Tim, *Who Controls the Internet? Illusions of a Borderless World* (Oxford University Press 2006).

Grannick Jennifer, 'The End of the Internet Dream?' (*Wired.com*, 17 August 2015) https://www.wired.com/2015/08/the-end-of-the-internet-dream/, accessed on 17 January 2019.

Granovetter Mark, *Society and Economy* (Harvard University Press 2017).

Grant Robert, *Contemporary Strategy Analysis* (Wiley 2013).

Håkansson Håkan and Lundgren Anders, 'Paths in Time and Space —Path Dependence in Industrial Networks' in *Evolutionary Economics and Path Dependence*, edited by Lars Magnusson and Jan Ottosson (Edward Elgar 1997).

Harrington Joseph, 'Developing Competition Law for Collusion by Autonomous Price-Setting Agents' (2017) University of Pennsylvania.

Hay George, 'Horizontal Agreements: Concept and Proof' (2006) *Antitrust Bulletin*, 882.

Hart Oliver and Moore John, 'Property Rights and the Nature of the Firm' (1990) 98 *Journal of Political Economy*, 1119.

HM Treasury, 'Fixing the Foundations: Creating A More Prosperous Nation' (2015) Cm 9098, Policy Paper.

Industry Sandbox, 'A Blueprint for an Industry-Led Virtual Sandbox for Financial Innovation' (2016) Consultation Guide.

International Organisation for Standardisation, 'ISO/TC 307 Blockchain and Distributed Ledger Technologies' (2016) https://www.iso.org/committee/6266604.html, accessed on 17 January 2019.

ITU-T Focus Group on Digital Financial Services, 'Distributed Ledger Technologies and Financial Inclusion' (2017) Technical Report.

ITU-T Work Programme, 'Declared Patents' (2017) Recommendation [SG13]:[Q2/13].

ITU-T Work Programme, 'Declared Patents' (2017) Recommendation [SG20]:[Q4/20].

Jacobides Michael, 'Industry Architecture' in *The Palgrave Encyclopaedia of Strategic Management*, edited by Mie Augier and David Teece (Palgrave Macmillan 2016) https://link.springer.com/referenceworkentry/10.1057/978-1-349-94848-2-390-1, accessed on 16 February 2019.

Jacobides Michael and Tae Jennifer, 'Kingpins, Bottlenecks, and Value Dynamics Along a Sector' (2015) 26(3) *Organization Science*, 633.

Jacobides Michael, Knudsen Thorbjørn, and Augier Mie, 'Benefiting from Innovation: Value Creation, Value Appropriation and the Role of Industry Architectures' (2006) 35(8) *Research Policy*, 1200.

Jacobides Michael, Winter Sidney, and Kassberger Stefan, 'The Dynamics of Wealth, Profit, and Sustainable Advantage' (2012) 33 *Strategic Management Journal*, 1384.

Jacobides Michael, Cennamo Carmelo, and Gawer Annabelle, 'Towards a Theory of Ecosystems' (2018) 39 *Strategic Management Journal*, 2255.

Joskow Paul, 'The New Institutional Economics: Alternative Approaches' (1995) 151(1) *Journal of Institutional and Theoretical Economics*, 248.

Jovanovic Boyan and Rousseau Peter, 'General Purpose Technologies' in *Handbook of Economic Growth*, edited by Philippe Aghion and Steven Durlauf (Volume 1, Elsevier 2005).

Jullien Bruno and Lefouili Yassine, 'Horizontal Mergers and Innovation' (2018) Toulouse School of Economics Working Paper.

Kalintiri Andriani, 'Revisiting Parental Liability in EU Competition Law' (2018) *European Law Review*, 145.

Kane Ethan, 'Is Blockchain a General Purpose Technology?' (30 March 2017) https://ssrn.com/abstract=2932585 , accessed on 17 January 2019.

Katz Michael and Shapiro Carl, 'Systems Competition and Network Effects' (1994) 8(2) *Journal of Economic Perspectives*, 93.

Koenig Carsten, 'An Economic Analysis of the Single Economic Entity Doctrine in EU Competition Law' (2017) 13(2) *Journal of Competition Law and Economics*, 281.

Ioannis Lianos, *The Different Dimensions of Economic Power in Competition Law: Concepts and Measurement* (Mimeo 2017).

Lianos Ioannis, 'Digital Value Chains in Competition Law' (2019) CLES Research Paper 1/2019.

Lopucki Lynn, 'Algorithmic Entities' (2018) 95 *Washington University Law Review*, 887.

Ma June, Gans Joshua, and Tourky Rabee, 'Market Structure in Bitcoin Mining' (2018) Rotman School of Management Working Paper No. 3103104.

Mai Feng, Shan Zhe, Bai Qing, Wang Xin, and Chiang Roger, 'How 'Does Social Media Impact Bitcoin Value? A Test of the Silent Majority Hypothesis' (2018) 35(1) *Journal of Management Information Systems*, 19.

Mathew Ashwin, 'The Myth of the Decentralised Internet' (2016) 5(3) *Internet Policy Review*, https://policyreview.info/node/425/pdf, accessed 16 February 2019.

McKinsey&Company, 'Getting Serious about Blockchain' (*mckinsey.com*, May 2017) https://www.mckinsey.com/industries/high-tech/our-insights/getting-serious-about-blockchain, accessed on 17 January 2019.

ModulTrade, (*modultrade.com*) https://modultrade.com, accessed on 17 January 2019.

Monti Giorgio, 'The Scope of Collective Dominance under Article 82 EC' (2001) 38(1) *Common Market Law Review*, 131.

Moore James, 'Predators and Prey: A New Ecology of Competition' (1993) 71(3) *Harvard Business Review*, 75.

Mulligan Catherine, 'Blockchain Will Kill the Traditional Firm' (*imperial.ac.uk*, 16 October 2017) https://www.imperial.ac.uk/business-school/knowledge/finance/blockchain-will-kill-the-traditional-firm/, accessed on 17 January 2019.

Nakamoto Satoshi, 'Bitcoin: A Peer-to-Peer Electronic Cash System' (2008) https://bitcoin.org/bitcoin.pdf, accessed on 17 January 2019.

Nalebuff Barry, 'Co-opetition: Competitive and Cooperative Business Strategies for the Digital Economy' (1997) 26(6) *Strategy and Leadership*, 28.

Organisation for Economic Cooperation and Development (OECD), 'Blockchain Technology and Competition Policy' (2018) Issues paper by the Secretariat.

Østbye Peder, 'The Adequacy of Competition Policy for Cryptocurrency Markets' (24 August 2017) https://ssrn.com/abstract=3025732, accessed on 17 January 2019.

Østbye Peder, 'The Case for a 21 Million Bitcoin Conspiracy' (8 March 2018) https://papers.ssrn.com/sol3/papers.cfm?abstract_id=3136044, accessed on 17 January 2019.

Ocean, 'A Decentralised Data Exchange Protocol to Unlock Data for AI', https://oceanprotocol.com, accessed on 17 January 2019.

Odudu Okeoghene, 'The Meaning of Undertaking within 81 EC' in *Cambridge Yearbook of European Legal Studies*, edited by John Bell and Claire Kilpatrick (Cambridge University Press 2005).

Organisation for Economic Cooperation and Development (OECD), 'Competition, Concentration and Stability in the Banking Sector' (2010) Report.

Organisation for Economic Cooperation and Development (OECD), 'Algorithms and Collusion: Competition Policy in the Digital Age' (2017) Report.

Organisation for Economic Cooperation and Development (OECD), 'Blockchain Technology and Competition Policy' (2018) Issues Paper by the Secretariat.

Origami Network, (*ori.network*) https://ori.network, accessed on 17 January 2019.

Orts Eric, *Business Persons—A Legal Theory of the Firm* (Oxford University Press 2013).

Pasquale Frank, *The Black Box Society—The Secret Algorithms that Control Money and Information* (Harvard University Press 2015).

Popov Serguei, 'The Tangle' (2018) Report, https://iotatoken.com/IOTA_Whitepaper.pdf, accessed on 17 January 2019.

Porter Michael, 'The Five Competitive Forces that Shape Strategy' (2008) 25 *Harvard Business Review*, 25.

Prahalad C. K. and Hamel Gary, 'The Core Competence of the Corporation' (1990) *Harvard Business Review*, 79.

Price Rob, 'The 18 Companies that Control Bitcoin in 2016' (*ukbusinessinsider.com*, 30 June 2016) http://uk.businessinsider.com/bitcoin-pools-miners-ranked-2016-6/#18-p2poolorg-01-1, accessed on 17 January 2019.

PwC, 'Blurred Lines: How FinTech is Shaping Financial Services' (2016) Report.

Reijers Wessel and Coeckelbergh Mark, 'The Blockchain as a Narrative Technology: Investigating the Social Ontology and Normative Configurations of Cryptocurrencies' (2018) 31 *Philosophy & Technology*, 103.

Rosner Marcel and Kang Andrew, 'Understanding and Regulating Twenty-First Century Payment Systems: The Ripple Case Study' (2016) 114 *Michigan Law Review*, 649.

Santander, 'Fintech 2.0: Rebooting Financial Services' (2015) Paper.

Schlosser Adam, 'You May Have Heard Data is the New Oil. It's Not' (*weforum.org*, 10 January 2018) https://www.weforum.org/agenda/2018/01/data-is-not-the-new-oil/, accessed on 17 January 2019.

Schrepel Thibault, 'Is Blockchain the Death of Antitrust Law? The Blockchain Antitrust Paradox' (6 October 2018) https://ssrn.com/abstract=3193576 , accessed on 17 January 2019.

Scott Susie, 'Revisiting the Total Institution: Performative Regulation in the Reinventive Institution' (2010) 44(2) *Sociology*, 213.

Shaikh Anwar, *Capitalism: Competition, Conflict, Crises* (Oxford University Press 2016).

Siciliani Paolo, 'The Disruption of Retail Banking: A Competition Analysis of the Implications for Financial Stability and Monetary Policy' (2018) CLES Research Paper Series 3/2018.

Singh Gumeet, 'Are Internet-Implemented Applications of Blockchain Technology Patent-Eligible in the United States?' (2018) 17(2) *Chicago Kent Journal of Intellectual Property*, 356.

Soros George, 'General Theory of Reflexivity' (*ft.com*, 26 October 2009) https://www.ft.com/content/0ca06172-bfe9-11de-aed2-00144feab49a, accessed on 17 January 2019.

Ståhlberg Johan and Fiol Isabel, 'Analysing Blockchain Patent Trends' (*managingip.com*, 24 April 2018) http://www.managingip.com/Article/3802483/Analysing-blockchain-patent-trends.html, accessed on 17 January 2019.

Statista, 'Market Capitalization of Ethereum from the 3rd Quarter 2015 to 2nd Quarter 2018' (*statista.com*) https://www.statista.com/statistics/807195/ethereum-market-capitalization-quarterly/, accessed on 17 January 2019.

Steemit, (*steemit.com*) https://steemit.com/, accessed on 17 January 2019.

Swartz Lana, 'Blockchain Dreams: Imagining Techno-Economic Alternatives after Bitcoin' in *Another Economy is Possible: Culture and Economy in a Time of Crisis*, edited by Manel Castells (Polity Press 2017).

TechCrunch, (*techcrunch.com*) https://techcrunch.com/2018/03/04/icos-delivered-at-least-3-5x-more-capital-to-blockchain-startups-than-vc-since-2017/?guccounter=1, accessed on 17 January 2019.

Teece David, 'Profiting from Technological Innovation: Implications for Integration, Collaboration, Licensing and Public Policy' (1986) 15(6) *Research Policy*, 285.

Teece David, 'Next-Generation Competition: New Concepts for Understanding How Innovation Shapes Competition and Policy in the Digital Economy' (2012) 9 *Journal of Law and Policy*, 97.

Teece David, 'Business Ecosystems' in *The Palgrave Encyclopaedia of Strategic Management*, edited by Mie Augier and David Teece (Palgrave Macmillan 2016).

Teece David, 'Business Models, Value Capture, and the Digital Enterprise' (2017) 6(8) *Journal of Organizational Design*, https://link.springer.com/content/pdf/10.118%2Fs41469-017-0018-x.pdf, accessed 17 February 2019.

Teece David, 'Profiting from Innovation in the Digital Economy: Standards, Complementary Assets, and Business Models in the Wireless World' (2018) 47 *Research Policy*, 1367.

The Economist, 'The Trust Machine' (*economist.com*, 31 October 2015) https://www.economist.com/leaders/2015/10/31/the-trust-machine, accessed on 17 January 2019.

The Economist, 'Are Technology Firms Madly Overrated?' (*economist.com*, 23 February 2017) https://www.economist.com/business/2017/02/23/are-technology-firms-madly-overvalued, accessed on 17 January 2019.

The Economist, 'The World's Most Valuable Resource is No Longer Oil, But Data' (*economist.com*, 6 May 2017) https://www.economist.com/leaders/2017/05/06/the-worlds-most-valuable-resource-is-no-longer-oil-but-data, accessed on 17 January 2019.

Treat David, 'Blockchain: Do the Numbers Add Up?' (*accenture.com*) https://www.accenture.com/gb-en/insight-perspectives-capital-markets-blockchain-numbers, accessed on 17 January 2019.

Tual Stephen, 'On DAO Contractors and Curators' (*blog.slock.it*, 10 April 2016) https://blog.slock.it/on-contractors-and-curators-2fb9238b2553, accessed on 17 January 2019.

Tuwiner Jordan, 'Bitcoin Mining Pools' (*buybitcoinworldwide.com*, 30 June 2018) https://www.buybitcoinworldwide.com/mining/pools/, accessed on 17 January 2019.

Van Loo Rory, 'Making Innovation More Competitive: The Case of Fintech' (2018) 65 *UCLA Law Review*, 232.

Vives Xavier, 'Competition in the Changing World of Banking' (2001) 17(4) *Oxford Review of Economic Policy*, 541.

Vives Xavier, 'The Impact of FinTech on Banking, in European Economy Banks, Regulation, and the Real Sector' (2017) 2.

Wang Yizhu and Lim Elizabeth, 'Banks Face Challenges Acquiring Fintech Firms' (*forbes.com*, 5 January 2018) https://www.forbes.com/sites/mergermarket/2018/01/05/banks-face-challenges-acquiring-fintech-firms/#34ca6512428a, accessed on 17 January 2019.

Wernerfelt Birger, 'A Resource-Based View of the Firm' (1984) 5(2) *Strategic Management Journal*, 171.

Whish Richard and Sufrin Brenda, 'Oligopolistic Markets and Competition Law' (1992) 12 *Yearbook of European Law*, 59.

Wilhelm Alex, 'Big Tech Goes Five for Five' (*techcrunch.com*, October 2017) https://techcrunch.com/2017/11/06/big-tech-goes-five-for-five/, accessed on 17 January 2019.

Williamson Oliver, *The Economic Institutions of Capitalism* (Free Press 1985).

Williamson Oliver, *The Mechanisms of Governance* (Oxford University Press 1996).

Wu Tim, *The Master Switch: The Rise and Fall of Information Empires* (First Vintage Book 2011).

Wu Tim, T*he Attention Merchants: The Epic Scramble to Get Inside Our Heads* (Penguin, 2016).

Zduniak Marcin, '6 Ways to Stay Ahead of Blockchain Competition' (*espeoblockchain.com*, 23 May 2018) https://espeoblockchain.com/blog/blockchain-competition-example/, accessed on 17 January 2019.

Zetzsche Dirk, Buckley Ross, and Arner Douglas, 'The Distributed Liability of Distributed Ledgers: Legal Risks of Blockchain', (2018) 4 *University of Illinois Law Review*, 1361.

Index

For the benefit of digital users, indexed terms that span two pages (e.g., 52–53) may, on occasion, appear on only one of those pages.